The Unofficial Guide®

DISNEY
Cruise Line 2017

MOUNT RUSTMORE

ELEVATION 15'11"
POPULATION 552
HAT HAT 111

Len Testa with Erin Foster, Laurel Stewart, and Ritchey Halphen

All ships in the DCL fleet have classic lines reminiscent of the glory days of cruising. (Photo: Laurel Stewart)

The *Wonder* leaves Nassau in the twilight after a day in port. (Photo: Laurel Stewart)

Minnie is right at home in the Art Nouveau atrium of the *Fantasy*. (Photo: Scott Smith)

The *Disney Dream*'s three-deck atrium features this magnificent chandelier. (Photo: Laurel Stewart)

Disney's plush buses can provide round-trip service between the Orlando airport and Port Canaveral. (Photo: Laurel Stewart)

Donald's Pool on the *Fantasy*. You can see the AquaDuck waterslide and Mickey's Pool in the background. (Photo: Laurel Stewart)

The *Magic*'s Twist 'n' Spout waterslide (Photo: Len Testa)

Some of the most peaceful views on any ship can be found on the *Wonder*'s Deck 4. (Photo: Laurel Stewart)

The *Fantasy*'s AquaLab splash area (Photo: Ricky Brigante)

Guests on the *Dream* and *Fantasy* can enjoy Goofy-themed minigolf on Deck 13. (Photo: Laurel Stewart)

The Rainforest Room in Senses Spa on the *Dream* and *Fantasy* has themed showers. (Photo: Laurel Stewart)

The *Fantasy*'s adult pool at night (Photo: Laurel Stewart)

The *Magic*'s Quiet Cove Pool at night (Photo: Laurel Stewart)

Marvel Avengers Academy is found in the Oceaneer Club on the *Magic* and the *Wonder*. (Photo: Laurel Stewart)

Kids on the *Dream* can experience piloting *Star Wars'* Millennium Falcon at the Oceaneer Club. (Photo: Julia Mascardo)

Getting started with the excellent Midship Detective Agency interactive adventure game on the *Dream* (Photo: Laurel Stewart)

Little princesses get ready for their close-ups at the Bibbidi Bobbidi Boutique, now on all four DCL ships. (Photo: Laurel Stewart)

Monsters Academy, the *Monsters, Inc.*–themed play area in the Oceaneer Club on the *Dream* and the *Fantasy* (Photo: Laurel Stewart)

All four ships' Oceaneer Clubs have Andy's Room, a *Toy Story*–themed play area. (Photo: Laurel Stewart)

D Lounge is the place to find family-friendly activities all day long on board. (Photo: Laurel Stewart)

Vibe, shown here on the *Fantasy*, gives kids ages 14–17 a place of their own to hang out. (Photo: Joe Tolley)

The Race Kart Sundae at the *Dream*'s Vanellope's Sweets & Treats is a dessert to remember. (Photo: Julia Mascardo)

Cabanas buffet, found on the *Magic*, *Dream*, and *Fantasy*, is a great spot for breakfast and lunch. (Photo: Laurel Stewart)

Cruisers dance the night away at Fathoms on the *Magic*. (Photo: Laurel Stewart)

Big-city vistas unfold behind the bar at Skyline Lounge on the *Dream*. (Photo: Laurel Stewart)

The *Magic*'s Brazilian-themed restaurant, Carioca's (Photo: Len Testa)

Animator's Palate uses light and video monitors to change scenes during your meal. (Photo: Laurel Stewart)

The *Fantasy*'s Enchanted Garden restaurant has a ceiling whose lighting changes from day to night. (Photo: Laurel Stewart)

DCL's Concierge-level suites raise the bar on space and luxury. (Photos: Laurel Stewart)

Deluxe Oceanview Stateroom with Verandah on the *Dream* (Photo: Scott Sanders/disneycruiselineblog.com)

"Virtual portholes" in the inside cabins of the *Dream* and *Fantasy* give guests a view even without a window. (Photo: Laurel Stewart)

DCL guests love to decorate their cabin doors. (Photos: Laurel Stewart)

Castaway Cay's Pelican Plunge, a floating platform of fun
(Photo: Scott Smith; inset: Laurel Stewart)

Guests head out from the *Fantasy* for a day of beach fun on Castaway Cay. (Photo: Laurel Stewart)

Cruisers enjoy the still waters of Castaway Cay's protected bay with the *Dream* in the distance. (Photo: Laurel Stewart)

Cabana guests at Castaway Cay have a dedicated beach area on the island.
(Photo: Laurel Stewart)

Castaway Cay cleverly mixes the highly theme like the Conched Out bar, with the natural beauty of the Caribbean. (Photo: Laurel Stewart)

The *Magic* docked at Akershus, Norway (Photo: Erin Foster)

Guests try for the perfect shot of the glaciers at Tracy Arm, Alaska. (Photo: Laurel Stewart)

Mush! Dogsledding in Alaska (Photo: Erin Foster)

Cruisers snorkel off a "pirate ship" on an excursion in St. Thomas. (Photo: Laurel Stewart)

Taxis and tour operators at the port in St. Maarten are ready to guide Eastern Caribbean guests. (Photo: Laurel Stewart)

THE
unofficial GUIDE®
to Disney
Cruise Line

2017

COME CHECK US OUT!

Supplement your valuable guidebook with tips, news, and deals by visiting our websites:

theunofficialguides.com
touringplans.com

Also, while there, sign up for The Unofficial Guide newsletter for even more travel tips and special offers.

Join the conversation on social media:

@theUGSeries   theUnofficialGuides

theUGSeries   theUGSeries

#theUGseries

Other Unofficial Guides

Beyond Disney: The Unofficial Guide to SeaWorld, Universal Orlando, & the Best of Central Florida

The Disneyland Story: The Unofficial Guide to the Evolution of Walt Disney's Dream

Mini-Mickey: The Pocket-Sized Unofficial Guide to Walt Disney World

Universal vs. Disney: The Unofficial Guide to American Theme Parks' Greatest Rivalry

The Unofficial Guide Color Companion to Walt Disney World

The Unofficial Guide to Disneyland

The Unofficial Guide to Las Vegas

The Unofficial Guide to Mall of America

The Unofficial Guide to Universal Orlando

The Unofficial Guide to Walt Disney World

The Unofficial Guide to Washington, D.C.

THE *unofficial* GUIDE®

TO Disney Cruise Line

2017

LEN TESTA with ERIN FOSTER,
LAUREL STEWART, and RITCHEY HALPHEN

Please note that prices fluctuate in the course of time and that travel information changes under the impact of many factors that influence the travel industry. We therefore suggest that you write or call ahead for confirmation when making your travel plans. Every effort has been made to ensure the accuracy of information throughout this book, and the contents of this publication are believed to be correct at the time of printing. Nevertheless, the publishers cannot accept responsibility for errors or omissions, for changes in details given in this guide, or for the consequences of any reliance on the information provided by the same. Assessments of attractions and so forth are based upon the author's own experience; therefore, descriptions given in this guide necessarily contain an element of subjective opinion, which may not reflect the publisher's opinion or dictate a reader's own experience on another occasion. Readers are invited to write the publisher with ideas, comments, and suggestions for future editions.

The Unofficial Guides
An imprint of AdventureKEEN
2204 First Ave. S., Suite 102
Birmingham, AL 35233
theunofficialguides.com, facebook.com/theunofficialguides, twitter.com/theugseries

Managing editor: Ritchey Halphen
Editor: Lisa C. Bailey
Cover and color-insert design: Scott McGrew
Text design: Vertigo Design with updates by Annie Long
Maps and illustrations: Steve Jones
Indexer: Sylvia Coates

Graphics on pages 78, 83–84, and 90 © The Walt Disney Company. Used with permission.

For information on our other products and services or to obtain technical support, please contact us from within the United States at 888-604-4537 or by fax at 205-326-1012.

AdventureKEEN also publishes its books in a variety of electronic formats. Some content that appears in print may not be available in electronic formats.

ISBN-13: 978-1-62809-064-2; eISBN: 978-1-62809-065-9

Distributed by Publishers Group West

Manufactured in the United States of America

5   4   3   2   1

CONTENTS

LIST *of* MAPS *and* DIAGRAMS

ABOUT *the* AUTHORS

LEN TESTA is the coauthor of *The Unofficial Guide to Walt Disney World; The Unofficial Guide to Disneyland; The Unofficial Guide to Walt Disney World with Kids; The Unofficial Guide Color Companion to Walt Disney World*; and *Mini-Mickey: The Pocket-Sized Unofficial Guide to Walt Disney World*. A computer scientist, Len created both the *Unofficial Guides* touring plan software and the touringplans.com website. The father of a teenage daughter, he lives in Greensboro, North Carolina.

As a charter member of the official Disney Parks Moms Panel, **ERIN FOSTER** has researched and written answers to more than 11,000 guest questions about Disney travel. Erin has visited Walt Disney World, Disneyland, Disneyland Paris, and Hong Kong Disneyland. Her travels also include Disney Cruise Line voyages throughout the world and Adventures by Disney journeys on four continents, including AbD ocean cruise supplements and river cruising. She is a regular contributor to the touringplans.com blog and has frequently written for disneyfoodblog.com, as well as serving as a guest contributor to more than a dozen other Disney-related blogs and podcasts. Erin lives near New York City with her husband and three high school– and college-age daughters.

LAUREL STEWART has contributed to *The Unofficial Guide to Walt Disney World* and *The Unofficial Guide Color Companion to Walt Disney World* and works for touringplans.com. Despite not enjoying sand, seawater, or direct sunlight, she's always up for a cruise. Laurel was born in the Bahamas and lives in North Carolina.

RITCHEY HALPHEN is a managing editor at AdventureKEEN in Birmingham, Alabama. He is also a coauthor (with Bob Sehlinger and Len Testa) of *Mini-Mickey: The Pocket-Sized Unofficial Guide to Walt Disney World*.

ACKNOWLEDGMENTS

IT TOOK A LIFEBOAT FULL OF PEOPLE to produce this book and its companion web content. David Davies created our website for Disney Cruise Line (DCL) information, wrote the Fare Tracker tool, and lent an expert eye to the proofreading of the text. Scott Sanders from disney cruiselineblog.com keeps us updated on the latest DCL news. Also, thanks to Emily and Isabelle Sanders for testing the waterslides with us.

DCL kids' club research was carried out by Alex Duncan, "Captain" Kieran Duncan, Jacklyn Scirica, and Hannah Testa. Kelsey and Kathy Lubetich bravely navigated the waters and lumberjacks of Alaska for that coverage. Thanks also to Tammy Whiting of Storybook Destinations, Beci Mahnken and Stephanie Hudson of Mouse Fan Travel, and Sue Pisaturo and Lynne Amodeo of Small World Vacations for their help in determining cruise-pricing trends. Much respect to Matt Hochberg of royalcaribbeanblog.com for his comparison of DCL and RCL.

—*Len Testa* and *Laurel Stewart*

I WOULD LIKE TO THANK my husband, Jeff, and daughters, Josie, Louisa, and Charlie, for always reminding me to take photos of the hotel room before we settle in. Additional thanks to the team at touring plans.com for their unfailing support and kindness. And I am always grateful to the women and men of the Disney Parks Moms Panel for sharing their all-encompassing knowledge of all things Disney. Special thanks to Moms Panelists Bernie Edwards for proofreading and suggestions and Kirsten Etmanski for her detailed understanding of Disney Cruise Line and Adventures by Disney booking nuances.

—*Erin Foster*

MANY THANKS TO THE CREW at AdventureKEEN who contributed to this book: my good buddy Lisa Bailey, who edited this edition; Annie Long, our indefatigable typesetter; Steve Jones, who produced the maps and diagrams; Scott McGrew, who designed the cover and the color insert; and Sylvia Coates, who prepared the index.

—*Ritchey Halphen*

INTRODUCTION

ABOUT *This* GUIDE

WHY "UNOFFICIAL"?

THE MATERIAL HEREIN originated with the authors and has not been reviewed, edited, or approved by the Walt Disney Company, Inc., or Disney Cruise Line (DCL). To the contrary, we represent and serve you, the consumer: If a ship serves mediocre food or has subpar entertainment, we say so. Through our independence, we hope that we can make selecting a cruise efficient and economical and help make your cruise experience on-target and fun.

Toward that end, our *unofficial* guide offers the following:

- Our recommendations for which ship to choose for your first cruise
- How to find the perfect itinerary, including specific cruises and dates
- When to book your cruise to get the cheapest fares
- What to pack, including travel documents for you and your children
- Color photos from throughout the ships, plus deck and stateroom diagrams
- Unbiased reviews of onboard restaurants, live entertainment, and nightlife
- The best family activities, including children's clubs, family games, outdoor sports, and more
- Where and when to meet Disney characters on board
- Full coverage of Disney's private island, Castaway Cay, along with ports and shore excursions

DISNEY CRUISE LINE:
An Overview

IN 1998, THE WALT DISNEY COMPANY LAUNCHED—literally— its own cruise line with the 2,400-passenger *Disney Magic.* An almost identical ship, the *Disney Wonder,* entered service in 1999. Two larger ships, the *Disney Dream* and the *Disney Fantasy,* joined the fleet in 2011 and 2012, respectively.

In starting a cruise line, Disney put together a team of respected industry veterans, dozens of the world's best-known ship designers, and its own unrivaled creative talent. Together, they created the Disney ships, recognizing that every detail would be critical to the line's success.

The result? They've succeeded, starting with the ships' appearance: simultaneously classic and innovative. Exteriors are traditional, reminiscent of the great ocean liners of the past, but even here you'll find a Disney twist or two. Inside, the ships feature up-to-the-minute technology and are full of novel ideas for dining, entertainment, and cabin design. Even Disney's exclusive cruise terminal at Port Canaveral, Florida, is part of the overall strategy, aiming to make even embarking and disembarking enjoyable.

unofficial **TIP**
Because DCL ships' decor and entertainment are based almost entirely on Disney films and characters, we don't recommend a Disney cruise to anyone who isn't at least mildly fond of Mickey and the gang.

For Port Canaveral and Miami cruises, Disney's private island, **Castaway Cay,** was chosen to avoid the hassle of tendering. As for dining, Disney practically reinvented the concept for cruises when it introduced rotational dining (see Part Seven), where each evening you not only dine in a different restaurant with a different motif, but your waiters and dining companions also move with you.

The foundation of DCL's business is built on Bahamian and Caribbean cruises out of Port Canaveral, about 90 minutes from Walt Disney World, and Miami. Disney also offers Alaskan, Californian, Canadian, and European cruises, as well as repositioning cruises. Other departure ports include Barcelona, Spain; Copenhagen, Denmark; Dover, England; Galveston, Texas; New York City; San Diego, California; San Juan, Puerto Rico; and Vancouver, Canada; and.

All Bahamian cruises originating in Port Canaveral and Miami make at least one port call at Castaway Cay. DCL's Alaskan and European itineraries are well conceived and interesting; by comparison, its Bahamian and Caribbean itineraries are unimaginative and prosaic, but they're still good for first-time cruisers.

DISNEY CRUISE LINE IS EXPANDING

IN EARLY 2016, DISNEY ANNOUNCED that it will be expanding the DCL fleet. The company has placed orders for two additional ships (as yet unnamed). Before you get too excited, the anticipated launch dates will be in 2021 and 2023, so you'll have a bit of a wait before you'll be able to set sail on the new vessels.

The ships will be constructed by Meyer Werft, the same shipyard that built the *Dream* and the *Fantasy,* and are expected to be of similar size to their Meyer Werft sisters. We don't have any details yet about amenities or itineraries, but it's always fun to speculate.

Will the new ships offer more family-size staterooms that sleep five or six? Will one or more of the ships have a permanent home port other than Port Canaveral? Is a regular route to Cuba in the offing? Will DCL venture into sailing in the Asia or Australia markets? How will Castaway Cay be impacted? Will the new ships cut into the popularity of Disney's older vessels, the *Magic* and the *Wonder*? How will the ships be decorated? Will one of the ships be fitted with more-adult amenities than the other? How will the dining and entertainment offerings differ from those of the existing fleet?

While the list of questions is endless, real answers likely won't be forthcoming until 2019 at the earliest, when sales would likely begin for sailings during the first half of 2021.

IS DISNEY CRUISE LINE RIGHT FOR ME?

MANY TRAVELERS, PARTICULARLY ADULTS traveling without children, may wonder if they'll enjoy a Disney Cruise Line vacation. It's a legitimate question: Disney charges a premium for its voyages, particularly in the Caribbean, banking on brand loyalty and its reputation for high-quality family experiences.

We're fans. We (Len, Erin, and Laurel) have more than 40 Disney cruises among us, and we keep booking more. But we acknowledge that there are many fine options for cruise vacations, and that some may fit your needs and tastes better than DCL's.

- If you're looking for the *ne plus ultra* in cruise-ship technology, choose **Royal Caribbean.** Their megaships are marvels.
- If you're looking for a cruise without many children or younger families, choose **Holland America.**
- If you're looking for an all-out luxury experience, choose **Viking** or another European river-cruise company.
- If you want to rock-and-roll all night and party every day, choose **Carnival.**
- If you're looking for that sweet spot between family-friendly and true upscale, choose **Celebrity.**
- If your valet normally carries your steamer trunk for you, choose **Cunard.**
- If you're looking for Disney service in a smaller, more intimate, environment, choose an **Adventures by Disney** river cruise on an **AmaWaterways** ship. See page 358 for details.

We find that Disney offers great service, has some of the most attractive ships sailing, and goes out of its way to make sure all their guests have a good time. While other lines may be better in some areas, Disney gets among the most consistently good marks across all categories.

DCL'S TARGET MARKET

DISNEY CRUISES ARE TAILORED to families who are new to cruising. But like the theme parks, the cruise line is a Disney product for kids of all ages.

DISNEY CRUISE LINE SHIPS IN A NUTSHELL				
	Disney Magic	Disney Wonder	Disney Dream	Disney Fantasy
YEAR LAUNCHED	1998	1999	2011	2012
CAPACITY				
PASSENGERS (maximum)	2,713	2,713	4,000	4,000
CREW	950	950	1,458	1,458
TOTAL	3,663	3,663	5,458	5,458
PASSENGER DECKS	11	11	14	14
STATEROOMS				
INSIDE	256	256	150	150
OCEANVIEW	362	362	199	199
OUTSIDE VERANDAH	259	259	901	901
TOTAL	877	877	1,250	1,250
THEME	Art Deco	Art Nouveau	Art Deco	Art Nouveau

To cater to varied constituencies, some facilities, services, activities, and programs are designed specifically for adults without children, including seniors and honeymooning couples. For example, in addition to the themed restaurants, each ship has at least one alternative restaurant, swimming pool, and nightclub for adults only, as well as entertainment for the whole family. DCL continues trying to enhance the adult experience with such facilities as adults-only cafés, adult-oriented sports bars, and areas for teens.

Initially, cruise experts questioned whether Disney could fill its ships when kids are in school, but Disney determined that if 1–2% of the estimated 40 million annual visitors to its resorts and parks bought a Disney cruise vacation, the ships would sell out. Disney was right—now, after nearly 20 years of success, no one is questioning them.

Disney offers a "seamless vacation package" to those who want to combine a stay at Walt Disney World with a cruise departing from Florida. DCL passengers are met at the airport by Disney staff and transported to the terminal in easily identifiable buses. When your cruise is packaged with a stay at most Disney hotels, you check in to both the land and sea portions of your vacation at once.

COMPETITORS AND PRICES

DCL USES ITS REPUTATION for high quality, service, and entertainment to dispel novices' doubts about cruise vacations. Disney's main competitor seems to be **Royal Caribbean International,** which offers Caribbean, Mediterranean, and Alaskan cruises similar to Disney's, with most of the same departure and destination ports. The two cruise lines often have ships departing within days—sometimes hours—of each other, headed mostly to the same places.

Beyond staterooms, you'll find everything from bars and lounges to small art galleries, expansive spas, dedicated shopping areas, and specialty restaurants on both cruise lines. Here's how those offerings, plus pre- and postcruise services, compare between DCL and Royal Caribbean's newer ships, such as the *Allure of the Seas, Oasis of the Seas,* and *Quantum of the Seas.*

AREA YOUTH CLUBS

WHO'S BETTER: Disney The children and teens we've interviewed, including our own, prefer Disney's kids' clubs by a wide margin. During our observations, DCL staff ensured that every child new to the club was introduced to the existing members, and the staff actively participated in planning and keeping organized a continuous set of games, crafts, and playtime.

If your vacation includes letting your children use one of the kids' clubs for any length of time, this is all you need to know.

AREA PRE-TRIP PLANNING AND RESERVATIONS

WHO'S BETTER: Disney Both cruise lines have good phone-based customer service. Disney's website is easier to use, especially for booking activities. On Royal Caribbean's website, we were never able to link reservations between our cabins, and we had to reenter all of our credit card information each time we booked a shore excursion or specialty meal.

AREA BOARDING PROCESS

WHO'S BETTER: Royal Caribbean Its boarding is faster and more efficient, even on ships such as the *Allure,* which holds 50% more passengers than Disney's largest ships.

AREA GETTING AROUND AND GETTING ORIENTED

WHO'S BETTER: Disney DCL's daily *Personal Navigator* and free companion mobile app let you see quickly what's going on at any time of day. We do like Royal Caribbean's touchscreen maps, near the elevators.

AREA THEMING AND DETAIL OF PUBLIC SPACES

WHO'S BETTER: Tie DCL's stem-to-stern theming, based on the decor of classic ocean liners, makes its ships far prettier than Royal Caribbean's, which, as one of our dinner companions once remarked, feel "like a really nice mall."

That said, Royal Caribbean's largest ships are big enough to have scaled-down versions of New York's Central Park and Atlantic City's boardwalk, which Disney can't match. Royal's collection of onboard art, curated from contemporary artists worldwide and found in walkways and stairwells, is more interesting to many adults than Disney's collection, which comes from its animated films.

AREA DINING

WHO'S BETTER: Disney Both cruise lines provide breakfast, lunch, and dinner in standard restaurants as part of your fare. Disney's food is tastier and its restaurants more creatively themed.

On the other hand, Royal Caribbean's larger ships have more than 20 optional dining locations (where you pay extra to eat), while DCL's ships have just 1 or 2. If you think you'll tire of visiting the same restaurant several times, Royal is a better choice.

Service is excellent on both lines.

AREA LIVE ENTERTAINMENT

WHO'S BETTER: Royal Caribbean Both lines put on large, elaborate stage shows: Royal Caribbean's lineup includes Broadway hits such as *Chicago;* Disney generally rehashes its animated stories. Royal's shows are more varied and appeal more to adults; we also think its performers and musicians are better than DCL's.

AREA NIGHTCLUBS, BARS, AND LOUNGES

WHO'S BETTER: Disney Surprised? Where Royal Caribbean's bars tend to be large, open to pedestrian traffic, and barely themed, Disney's are more intimate and have appropriately atmospheric music and decor, and many sit in a dedicated adults-only area, far away from crowded public spaces. (Case in point: Disney's Champagne bars play Édith Piaf and Frank Sinatra in the background, as the good Lord intended; Royal's bars play The Eagles and Gordon Lightfoot.) Plus, service is more personal on DCL.

AREA SHOPPING

WHO'S BETTER: Royal Caribbean Its larger ships carry a wider variety of men's and women's clothing, art, housewares, and more. Both lines sell men's and women's jewelry, duty-free alcohol, and sundries.

AREA SPA

WHO'S BETTER: Disney Another area where DCL wins on theming and detail. While Senses Spa on the *Dream* and the *Fantasy* are smaller than Royal Caribbean's spas, Disney's overlook the ocean and have more heated stone loungers, more themed showers, and better steam rooms.

AREA POOLS

WHO'S BETTER: Disney for kids, Royal Caribbean for adults The children's play areas, slides, and water rides on Disney's ships are better than Royal Caribbean's. Additionally, Disney is one of the few cruise lines to staff their child and family pools with lifeguards. Currently, Royal Caribbean does not use lifeguards at their shipboard pools. For adults, Royal's newer ships have larger pools and more of them, spread across an even wider area than on Disney's largest ships.

AREA DEBARKATION

WHO'S BETTER: Royal Caribbean Both DCL and Royal Caribbean can get you off the ship in a hurry, although Royal does it a bit faster. Disney's baggage-claim area is better organized, however, making it easier to find your checked luggage.

A ROYAL CARIBBEAN FAN SPEAKS OUT

INSPIRED BY SEEING the lovely Barbi Benton on a rerun of *Fantasy Island,* we asked our good friend MATT HOCHBERG from royalcaribbeanblog.com to weigh in on the differences between Disney and Royal Caribbean. A lifelong Disney fan who has run Disney-related podcasts and websites for more than a decade, Matt has an in-depth perspective on both cruise lines.

EVEN DISNEY CRUISE LINE FANS AGREE that Royal Caribbean offers a great family vacation at a fraction of Disney's prices. But beyond that, Royal Caribbean became my family's preferred cruise choice for a few simple reasons: more ships, more destinations, more latest-and-greatest cruising innovations, and more dining choices.

Where DCL has 4 ships in its fleet (with 2 to come after 2020), Royal Caribbean has 25, with another 4 currently under construction. More ships means more destinations to visit and more embarkation ports to choose from. So while Royal and Disney both sail to the Caribbean, Alaska, Northern Europe, and the Mediterranean, only Royal goes to Australia, China, and other destinations. What's more, Royal offers many cruises to these places, not just one per year.

Royal's ships also push the envelope in terms of what guests can do onboard—surfing lessons, bumper cars, rock walls, zip lines, and ice skating—while Disney's don't.

Families often think of DCL as a no-brainer because of its programming for children, but Royal Caribbean's kids' offerings are getting steadily better. Each new ship has more space dedicated to children and more programming options than the one before. Adventure Ocean, Royal Caribbean's youth program, provides supervised games, events, and activities throughout the day and evening. Of course, there are all the fun onboard activities listed earlier for kids to enjoy, in addition to enhanced kids-only facilities and programming on select Royal Caribbean ships.

When it comes to theme parks, there's definitely a quality difference between Disney and the competition. But when it comes to cruising, I think Disney and Royal Caribbean are much more similar than they are different. If you find the idea of a Disney cruise appealing, you should also consider Royal Caribbean. I think they're equally engaging—and Royal Caribbean a far better value.

AREA GAMBLING

WHO'S BETTER: Depends on your perspective Many of Royal Caribbean's ships have full casinos with slot machines and tables dedicated to poker, blackjack, roulette, craps, and more. Admittance to the casinos is limited to guests age 18 and up on most sailings. By contrast, the only onboard gambling offered on DCL is a bingo game once or twice a day, at which kids are welcome (see page 182 for details on bingo). Which cruise line's version of gambling is best depends on your proclivities.

AREA HEALTH AND SAFETY

WHO'S BETTER: Disney DCL ships consistently receive the highest marks of any cruise line in ProPublica's overall assessment of ship health and safety, which includes data on Centers for Disease Control inspections, illness outbreaks, crime and accident/incident reports, Coast Guard inspections, and environmental-impact assessments. The *Dream* and *Fantasy* currently have ratings of 100 (on a scale of 0–100); the *Magic* and *Wonder* have ratings of 99. In contrast, Royal Caribbean's ships earned ratings of 92–100, except for *Freedom of the Seas,* which got an 86—but that's just above failing according to ProPublica's criteria. For more information on cruise-line safety, visit projects.propublica.org/cruises.

Cost Considerations

Disney's fares include unlimited fountain soda, plain coffee, tea, and water (bottled versions cost extra), while Royal Caribbean charges around $22 per person per day for fountain soda as part of a beverage package (which also includes bottled water, orange juice, premium coffee, and nonalcoholic cocktails), or more than $600 for a family of four for a seven-night cruise. We don't recommend Royal's beverage package—for one thing, their free coffee is better than Disney's, and our family was happy to drink water, tea, and lemonade throughout our cruise. We each had an occasional soda at mealtime, but we didn't spend anything close to $600 on extra drinks on our weeklong cruise.

When it comes to the bottom line, however, the fact is that Disney charges a premium for its cruise product. For example, on seven-night Eastern Caribbean cruises out of Port Canaveral during the second half of 2016 for one inside cabin, Disney's prices were more than $7,200 for holiday and specialty itineraries, and $4,500–$5,000 for standard dates, depending on the itinerary and your booking date. Royal Caribbean's prices were $2,200–$3,000, 40–50% less than Disney for a similar cruise. (All cruise prices assume two adults and two children ages 12 and 6 in one cabin.)

We initially thought Disney was charging more for these cruises because its Orlando theme parks provide a built-in audience for Port Canaveral sailing; the port is, after all, within 90 minutes of Walt Disney World. But Disney is more expensive for ports far away from its theme parks: We spot-checked Disney's seven-night Alaska cruises out of Vancouver for 2016 and 2017 and found that they run around 50% more than Royal Caribbean's—a difference of $2,100–$2,700 per cruise. That kind of money buys a lot of ice.

One area where Disney seems to be price-competitive with Royal Caribbean is on seven-night Mediterranean cruises out of Barcelona, Spain. Fares for random dates in 2016 for Disney cruises were slightly lower or the same, on average, than Royal Caribbean.

REASSURING WORDS FOR RELUCTANT CRUISERS

IF YOU'RE CONSIDERING YOUR FIRST CRUISE, or your first cruise with Disney, you may have some concerns about what is a fairly pricey vacation. We were all there once.

Here are the things we were most worried about and how things turned out:

> **unofficial TIP**
> In addition to the authors' collective wisdom, check out **Scott Says**—practical tips from Scott Sanders, webmaster of disneycruiselineblog.com—throughout this edition of the guide.

ERIN: I did absolutely nothing to prepare for my first Disney cruise. It was hastily tacked on to a Walt Disney World vacation, without much forethought. I'll be honest—that first cruise, a Bahamian three-nighter on the *Wonder,* back when there were only two ships in the fleet, was not our best vacation. I had envisioned sitting in the sun with umbrella drinks while my kids played in the clubs. Instead, my then-3-year-old daughter decided to have a severe case of separation anxiety and refused to leave my side (I had no idea there were activities for little ones other than the kids' clubs) while I battled seasickness and drank only ginger ale. *Never again,* I swore.

Well, fast-forward about eight years to when my husband decided that the easiest and most efficient way to introduce our daughters to Europe was on a cruise. With the bribe of a side trip to Disneyland Paris dangling before me, I reluctantly agreed to a Mediterranean sailing on the *Magic.* This time I did my homework: I had an arsenal of motion-sickness-remediation tools suggested by my doctor, my daughters had matured enough to enjoy the kids' clubs (and I had researched things to do with them if they chose not to use the clubs), and I found that it truly was easy to see much of southern Europe via cruise ship.

We introduced our children to Barcelona, the French Riviera, Rome, Naples, Florence, and Majorca, and I had to unpack only once. *I was hooked!* I still prefer cruises with calmer waters (typically in Europe and Alaska), but I've gotten my sea legs and am also happy to hop on the *Dream* or *Fantasy* for a jaunt through the Caribbean anytime. Cruising is a terrific way to see the world as long as you're prepared.

LAUREL: Disney was my first cruise ever, and only because a friend of mine wanted someone to travel with. My worries centered around the number of children onboard and feeling that the whole experience would be like being herded from one scheduled "fun" or "food" activity to another.

The *Dream*'s adult areas were beautiful, and Serenity Bay was fantastic. As I've cruised more, I realize that I don't have to see your children (or even the ones I'm traveling with) more than I want to. I even think your kids dressed up for formal night are pretty darn cute.

As far as sticking to a schedule—I stopped that a long time ago. Because I don't enjoy the mass of people heading to the early or late dinner seatings or to the buffet lunch on embarkation day, I tend to skip or replace those with alternatives. Room service, snacks on the pool deck, or dinner at Palo or Remy are my ways to go.

LEN: I'm a workaholic who thinks constant high-speed Internet access is an inalienable right. (True story: I once tried to charter a helicopter at midnight to extract me from a family camping trip to the Outer Banks of North Carolina, because there was no air-conditioning or web connectivity.) So I wasn't looking forward to a weeklong cruise, which I imagined as huddled masses essentially disconnected from the civilized world with Jimmy Buffett playing in the background.

But my first cruise, on the *Disney Fantasy,* couldn't have gone better. There were more than enough activities to keep me busy all day, and just enough Internet access to help me feel connected to the office. I even learned to "relax" in the *Fantasy*'s Rainforest Spa (if *relax* means "catch up on *The New York Times*'s mobile edition").

If you're like me, you'll probably appreciate the additional restaurants, lounges, and activities on the *Dream* and *Fantasy.* And while I wouldn't recommend a seven-night cruise for your first trip on the high seas, I think a three-night cruise is too short: You're either packing or unpacking every day. A four-night cruise is the bare minimum and includes a day at sea for you to explore the ship, and a five-night cruise (with two sea days) is probably the best choice.

HOW *to* CONTACT *the* AUTHORS

MANY WHO USE THE *UNOFFICIAL GUIDES* write to us with questions, comments, or their own strategies for planning and enjoying travel. We appreciate all such input, both positive and critical. Readers' comments are frequently incorporated into revised editions and have contributed immeasurably to their improvement. Please write to us at the following address:

Len, Erin, Laurel, and Ritchey
The Unofficial Guide to Disney Cruise Line
2204 1st Ave. S., Suite 102
Birmingham, AL 35233
unofficialguides@menasharidge.com

You can also find the *Unofficial* gang on social media at facebook .com/theunofficialguides, twitter.com/theugseries, instagram.com/the ugseries, and pinterest.com/theugseries.

When you write, put your address on both your letter and envelope; the two sometimes get separated. It's also a good idea to include your phone number. If you e-mail us, please tell us where you're from. Remember, as travel writers, we're often out of the office for long periods of time, so forgive us if our response is slow. *Unofficial Guide* e-mail isn't forwarded to us when we're traveling, but we'll respond as soon as possible after we return.

READER SURVEY

OUR WEBSITE HOSTS A QUESTIONNAIRE you can use to express opinions about your Disney cruise, at touringplans.com/disney-cruise-line/survey. The questionnaire lets every member of your party, regardless of age, tell us what he or she thinks about attractions, restaurants, and more.

If you'd rather print out the survey and send it to us, mail it to **Reader Survey, *The Unofficial Guides,* 2204 First Ave. S., Suite 102, Birmingham, AL 35233.**

PART ONE

DOLLARS *and* CENTS

WHAT'S INCLUDED *in* YOUR DISNEY CRUISE FARE

A DISNEY CRUISE ISN'T CHEAP. Given the cost, you might be wondering how much more you'll have to pay once you're aboard the ship. Here's a quick rundown of what is and isn't included in your cruise fare. We've included some rough estimates of the optional items to help with budgeting.

FOOD

INCLUDED: LOTS OF FOOD All meals, including snacks, are free at all of the ship's restaurants except for Remy and Palo. You can order as much food as you like.

NOT INCLUDED: FANCY RESTAURANTS Meals at Remy and Palo require an additional charge of $85 and $30, plus gratuity, respectively, for dinner; Palo also charges $30 for its brunch, while Remy's brunch is $55. Alcoholic beverages are an extra charge beyond those prices, at each meal.

INCLUDED: MOST ROOM-SERVICE ITEMS Your fare includes room-service meals, except as noted below. Room service is a great option if you're in the mood for breakfast on your verandah or you don't feel like dressing up for dinner.

NOT INCLUDED: PACKAGED SNACKS AND BOTTLED DRINKS Beverages such as bottled water ($3), soda not served as part of meal service or from the self-service dispensers on the pool deck ($3), beer ($6), and wine ($8 and up) cost extra, as do packaged snacks such as popcorn and peanuts. Tips are another additional charge.

INCLUDED: ALL-YOU-WANT SOFT DRINKS AND ICE CREAM Soda, coffee, water, cocoa, and hot and iced tea are free and unlimited at meals, as are beverages served from drink dispensers on deck. Self-serve ice cream from the onboard dispensers is free; note, however, that the specialty ice creams sold at Vanellope's Sweets and Treats on the *Dream* cost extra, as do the smoothies at Frozone Treats on the *Dream* and *Fantasy*.

NOT INCLUDED: BOTTLED WATER, ALCOHOLIC BEVERAGES, AND FANCY COFFEES Bottled water, beer, wine, and cocktails cost extra. A wine package is available. You'll also pay out-of-pocket for specialty coffees, espresso, cappuccinos, and teas from bars and cafés (such as the Cove Café). A 15% gratuity is automatically added to bar and beverage tabs. Adults age 21 and older also may bring a limited amount of beer, wine, and liquor aboard in their carry-on luggage; a $25 corking fee applies if you bring your own wine or Champagne to a full-service restaurant on board.

ENTERTAINMENT AND ACTIVITIES

INCLUDED: LOTS OF ENTERTAINMENT There's no extra charge for live performances, movies, and character greetings.

NOT INCLUDED: BINGO, SOME ONBOARD SEMINARS, AND MOVIE SNACKS A few activities, such as bingo, cost money to play. Beverage seminars, which typically offer several kinds of spirits for sampling, cost $20–$25, depending on the alcohol. Likewise, at the movie theater, candy bars and what-not cost extra.

INCLUDED: GYM FACILITIES Covered in your fare is use of the fitness center, including free weights and other fitness equipment. The center also has changing rooms with showers and sauna.

NOT INCLUDED: SPA AND SALON SERVICES Spa treatments (including massages, facials, steam rooms, and upscale showers) cost from $115 to upwards of $500 per person, per treatment. Salon services range from $50 to $70 for manicures and pedicures, and from $35 to around $75 for hairstyling, depending on hair length.

INCLUDED: POOLS, GAMES, AND MOST SPORTS These include all of the pools and waterslides and activities, such as miniature golf, basketball, table tennis, and shuffleboard. Board games are available at no charge in some lounges.

INCLUDED: CASTAWAY CAY BEACHES AND RESTAURANTS Food, lounge chairs, and beach umbrellas are free, as is Castaway Cay's 5K road run.

NOT INCLUDED: CASTAWAY CAY RECREATION AND ALCOHOL DCL charges for bike rentals ($10.75 per hour), snorkeling ($15–$31 for one

Continued on page 16

The 10 Best Bangs for Your Buck
(and One Freebie) on a Disney Caribbean Cruise

1. Rainforest at Senses Spa *(Dream* and *Fantasy)* At around $25 per day, this is a must-do. Only a limited number of passes are sold per cruise, so make a point of buying your pass soon after boarding. Because of the limits on how many passes are sold (we've heard 20 per cruise), there are many times when you'll have the entire Rainforest to yourself. This is the ultimate in quiet relaxation for adults, and a total bargain at that. The package is also available at Senses Spa on the *Magic* and Vista Spa on the *Wonder* (about $16 per day), but the smaller Rainforest area means that you're more likely to have company, and the number of showers and saunas is a little disappointing if you've ever experienced the spa on the larger ships. Try the body scrubs (extra charge) at least once.

2. Porters for your bags The $2–$5 per bag you'll tip your porter both boarding and returning home through customs is money well spent. These guys work hard and make our lives so much easier. When boarding, not having to handle your own bags is one less hassle in a hectic process. When you leave the ship, it helps you end your cruise on a high note.

3. Oceanview staterooms If three to seven nights in a cabin with no natural light is more than you can bear and the price of a verandah room cuts too much into your port-adventure budget, we happily recommend a room with a porthole. These cabins, on lower decks, offer a closer view of the ocean, and one that's really grown on us in the last year. You may have good luck finding deals on this category, as it doesn't sell as quickly as inside (least expensive) and verandah (often in the highest demand). These cabins have the best access to the main dining rooms, Guest Services, and the adult lounge areas.

4. Cabanas on Castaway Cay *Hold up! How can you possibly recommend something that costs at least $400 as a bang for your buck?* Here's the thing: The amenities that come with a cabana ($400 at Serenity Bay for 4 people, $550 at the Family Beach for 6 people, and $975 at the Family Beach for a 12-person Grand Cabana) equal more than the sum of its parts. If you have enough people to fill a cabana or can find someone to share with, the free equipment rentals, shelter from the sun, dedicated beach (Family Beach), and personalized service make this something well worth checking out. Our only qualm in including the cabanas here is the fact that they're notoriously difficult to book. See page 228 for more.

5. Palo A quiet, no-rush brunch or dinner for adults with great service and fantastic food for just $30 plus tip? *Heck yeah!* Let's face it: Your kids are probably ready to spend some time away from you, too. Come for the food, linger for the atmosphere.

6. Adult-beverage tastings For around $20–$25, you're treated to several wines, liquors, or cocktails. (*Warning:* You don't spit out the spirits, and they can sneak up on you. Eat something first so you don't get smashed.) We've been lucky enough to be the only participants on a few occasions, allowing us to interact with the guides. Our favorite is the Champagne tasting, but we haven't been let down by any of them. One author discovered a new favorite wine during a tasting at Meridian on the *Fantasy*. Another time we were asked, "How would you like to try the most expensive whiskey we sell?" Our reply: "Yes, please!"

7. Castaway Ray's Stingray Adventure This is both less expensive and better organized than stingray encounters in other ports. It's a winner with kids ($39) and adults ($48). There's no time wasted getting back and forth to your port adventure because it's on Castaway Cay—just show up at the ray area at your appointed time, and have fun.

8. It's a Small World Nursery Parents of children younger than age 3 can enjoy some downtime and let the excellent staff watch their little ones for $9 per hour for the first child and $8 per hour per additional child in the same family. Feedback from parents is consistently positive.

9. Coffee The swill at the beverage stations can best be described as a tepid, vaguely coffee-flavored substance that may make you question your will to live. Pony up for the real thing at Cove Café, Vista Café, or the coffee bar at the buffets. Sure, it's around $3–$5 plus tip, but that's less than you'd pay at Starbucks, and it doesn't make you regret your caffeine habit. Ask for a Café Fanatic rewards card and get every sixth coffee drink free. (For us, that's sometime early in day two of any cruise.)

10. Castaway Cay 5K This port adventure is free, and you get the moral superiority of knowing you've gotten in your exercise for the day while being among the first to exit the ship at the island. There are race bibs and plastic medals. Try to beat your Castaway Cay personal best every time you come to the island.

11. Gratuities DCL ships are full of energetic young men and women, many of whom are far away from home, who make your trip magical. In addition to tipping our servers and stateroom attendants generously—yes, that means more than the recommended amount—we also start our trip off right by meeting our baristas and bartenders on the first day and night of the cruise and treating them well. We don't do it because we expect anything extra (though being known as good customers never hurts); we do it because we get fantastic service. And don't forget these folks when you're filling out your comment cards at the end of the cruise. It's always good to help a deserving person's career when you can.

Continued from page 13

day, $18–$36 for two days), and use of boats ($14–$27 per half-hour) and watercraft ($95 per hour for one rider, $160 per hour for two riders). The same goes for private cabanas—which start at about $400 and go up to a whopping $1,000+ per day—and alcoholic drinks at Castaway Cay's bars.

KID STUFF

INCLUDED: KIDS' CLUBS (AGES 3 AND UP) These include the **Oceaneer Club/Oceaneer Lab** for kids ages 3–12, the **Edge** club for tweens ages 11–14, and the **Vibe** club for teens ages 14–17.

NOT INCLUDED: CHILD CARE FOR KIDS UNDER 3 The **It's a Small World Nursery** charges $9 per hour for the first child and $8 per hour for a second child in the same family.

NOT INCLUDED: CHILDREN'S MAKEOVER EXPERIENCES All ships (including the *Wonder* after fall 2016) have a **Bibbidi Bobbidi Boutique** that provides princess makeovers (plus pirate makeovers on Pirate Nights). Salon services start at $20 and can top $500 (yikes!).

NOT INCLUDED: CHILDREN'S SPECIAL DINING EXPERIENCES Some ships may offer special dining experiences for children. For example, the **Royal Court Tea** currently costs $279 for one adult and one child (additional children and adults in the same family may be added at an extra charge). The experience includes sweet and savory tea courses, a visit with Disney princesses, and elaborate gifts for the children.

MISCELLANEOUS

INCLUDED: CALLS TO ANYWHERE ON THE SHIP Use of the ships' **Wave Phones** (see below) is free. Guests may also use the **DCL Navigator app** with their own phones to text other guests for free using onboard Wi-Fi.

NOT INCLUDED: SHIP-TO-SHORE CALLS AND INTERNET Ship-to-shore calls from onboard phones cost an exorbitant $7 per minute. Each stateroom has a landline-style phone with voice mail, plus a **Wave Phone,** a mobile phone you may use free of charge on the ship and Castaway Cay for calls, voice mail, and text messaging (only from Wave Phone to Wave Phone). See page 84 for more about using the Internet while on board.

NOT INCLUDED: PHOTOS Similar to its Memory Maker packages at Walt Disney World, Disney offers packages of prints or digital images burned to CDs or loaded on flash drives. Pricing varies depending on the length of your voyage. Typically, a package of 10 prints costs about $150. An unlimited number of JPEG files will cost about $200–$400, depending on the number of sail days, with an additional $100 buying you the physical printouts of your images. Photo packages may be prepurchased, sometimes at a discount, at mycruisephotos.com. Onboard staff also will shoot pictures at free with your own camera.

SCOTT SAYS *by Scott Sanders*

SCOTT'S MONEY-SAVING STRATEGIES

IT'S COMPLETELY POSSIBLE to go on a Disney cruise and not spend a dime aside from gratuities. The ships offer essentially everything you need while you're on board. Sure, it's nice to buy drinks or souvenirs, but we had a great time without spending any additional money.

On the subject of tipping, you can prepay the base gratuities prior to sailing. Then you can just add any additional tip on at the end of the cruise.

Another money-saving strategy is to book excursions via third parties. This comes with a catch: sticking to the all-aboard time so you don't miss the ship. If that sounds too stressful, though, just explore the port on your own (where it's safe to do so).

My top money-saving tip is to book an inside stateroom. The money you save can be put toward onboard splurges. If you're only going to sleep, shower, and change in your stateroom, why spend more on a higher category?

NOT INCLUDED: SHORE EXCURSIONS Known in DCL-speak as "port adventures," these cost anywhere from $10.75 (for a 1-hour bike rental on Castaway Cay) to $1,900 (for a private catamaran tour of St. Maarten). Be aware that many shore excursions carry additional optional costs beyond the stated price. For example, many excursion operators offer souvenir photo packages for an additional fee. Additionally, meals are not included in the price of many shore excursions.

NOT INCLUDED: LAUNDRY It costs $2 to wash and $2 to dry a load of clothes in the onboard guest laundry rooms. Soap, fabric softener, and dryer sheets are available for $1 each, per load. Dry-cleaning is also available for an additional fee. Typical pricing is $4 to dry-clean a sweater, $8 to dry-clean an evening dress, and $7 to dry-clean a man's two-piece suit. Garment pressing is available at about half the price of dry-cleaning.

NOT INCLUDED: GRATUITIES Disney automatically adds gratuities of around $12 per person per day to your onboard account. A 15% gratuity is automatically added to bar and beverage tabs. See page 88 for more information.

NOT INCLUDED: TRANSPORTATION TO THE PORT Round-trip service between Walt Disney World and Port Canaveral runs $70 per person; transportation costs between any city's cruise terminal and airport may vary. See the section starting on page 65 for more details.

CRUISING *with* KIDS

WE'LL START BY SAYING that there's a good chance your kids will have a great time. (See page 185 for our advice on cruising with teens and tweens.)

As parents, we know that one of the most difficult parts of planning a vacation with kids is ensuring that they stay entertained throughout the trip. For us, this usually means making sure that every travel day has at least a couple of things specifically designed to appeal to our kids and their friends—things that we'd prefer didn't involve shopping or sitting passively in front of a screen.

It can be exhausting to plan this way (and we're *professionals*!). In fact, we think this is one of the main reasons why a trip to Disney World is so appealing to parents: Disney's theme parks provide a nearly constant and wide-ranging set of entertainment options for kids and adults. A family that hasn't planned a thing can show up and find something fun to do. Disney cruises work the same way—family activities, including trivia contests, scavenger hunts, and shuffleboard, are scheduled throughout the day, on virtually every day of every sailing.

If you think your kids would benefit from spending some time with their peers, Disney provides organized activities throughout the day for children ages 3–17. Some activities for younger children get started as early as 7 a.m., while activities for older teens can run until 2 a.m. Off the ships, Castaway Cay offers dedicated beach and recreation spots for families, teens, and tweens, plus a splash area for little ones. There are shore excursions created just for families, too. Some sailings also offer teen-only excursions and sightseeing events.

Disney is also keeping up with two recent trends in the cruise industry. The first is setting aside more space per ship for kids' clubs. On the newer *Dream* and *Fantasy,* these clubs take up substantially more space than on older DCL ships. Second, Disney frequently runs concurrent, age-appropriate activities within the same club. For example, the Oceaneer Club accepts children ages 3–12; however, Disney may group together the younger kids for a game with marshmallows in one area of the club while the older kids sing karaoke in another.

Our own children have found Disney's children's activities more fun than hanging around with us on the ship. It may be a cliché, but it's true: We saw the kids only during meals, at bedtime, or when we specifically scheduled things to do as a family. Thanks to the web, our kids are still in contact with the friends they've made on their cruises, even though some are an ocean away.

On the other hand, if your kids aren't interested in the kids' clubs, or if you're determined to make your cruise a time for family togetherness, there are also many activities that you can do together. These include structured things like family game shows and trivia contests, and unstructured things like board games and scavenger hunts. Many styles of family travel can be accommodated on the ships.

CRUISING *Without* KIDS

GIVEN DISNEY'S REPUTATION for family-friendly entertainment, it's natural for those who travel without children to wonder if DCL is a good choice for them. Happily, just as with the Disney parks, there's something for folks of all ages to enjoy on a Disney cruise. Disney ships have an adults-only pool and coffeehouse, the spa is limited to guests age 18 and up (with the exception of the Chill teen spa on the *Dream* and *Fantasy*), and some of the entertainment districts are limited to cruisers age 18 and up every night after around 9 p.m. For those wanting to dine in an adults-only atmosphere, Remy (*Dream* and *Fantasy* only) and Palo (see Part Seven) are likewise restricted to those age 18 and older. Castaway Cay has an adult beach with its own dining, bar, and cabanas (which must be reserved in advance).

unofficial TIP
DCL seems to be very popular with women because of its safe atmosphere.

We recommend traveling when school is in session if you're looking for a more adult-oriented vacation, and the good news is that these times tend to be far less expensive. Disney cast members have told us that the long ship-repositioning cruises (such as the Panama Canal itinerary) or transatlantic voyages tend to have the lowest percentage of children on board.

If your idea of a fun cruise is a party barge, then DCL probably isn't for you—there's no casino, and honestly the nightlife is more mild than wild. But we've traveled several times with just adults in our party and had a fantastic time. Spend some time at the spa, get to know the bartenders and baristas at the various bars and lounges, skip the stage shows, dine at Palo or Remy (or both!), and enjoy some downtime.

WHERE *to* FIND MORE INFORMATION

DISNEY CRUISE LINE'S official website is disneycruise.disney.go .com. Here you can see which itineraries are served by each ship; search for cruises by destination, month, and length; and see prices for various kinds of staterooms. Once you've made a reservation, you can book shore excursions, restaurants, and children's activities through the site.

DCL also will send you a free promotional and planning DVD. To order, go to disneycruise.disney.go.com/cruise-planning-tools. In addition to providing planning tips, the DVD can be a good resource to show children who are unfamiliar with cruising. The visuals will give them an idea of what to expect.

PassPorter's Disney Cruise Line and Its Ports of Call guidebook ($24.95 for the basic edition) provides a good overview of DCL. The deluxe edition ($49.95) includes paper worksheets that you can use to plan everything from a cruise budget to a daily schedule. The book's companion website, passporter.com, has user-led discussion forums, where folks from all over can ask questions and provide answers to almost any cruise-related scenario.

Scott Sanders's disneycruiselineblog.com posts almost-daily updates, including everything from new-itinerary rumors to new shopping merchandise on board. The site also has a neat feature that lets you see the current location of every ship in the Disney fleet. Also look for tips and advice from Scott in the new **Scott Says** sections throughout this book.

The **Disney Parks Moms Panel** (disneyworldforum.disney.go.com) features Disney Cruise Line specialists. These moms are veterans of many DCL voyages and have received training from DCL cast members. They're able to answer any individual Disney cruise–planning question, big or small.

Popular general Disney websites with **dedicated DCL forums** include disboards.com, forums.wdwmagic.com, micechat.com, and, for Brits, thedibb.co.uk (*DIBB* stands for "Disney Information Bulletin Board").

The **US government** offers a wealth of online resources for citizens traveling to other countries. The **Department of State** travel website, travel.state.gov, includes weather and safety advisories, advice on what to do if you've lost your passport, information on visa requirements, and more. The travel website for the **Centers for Disease Control and Prevention** (**CDC**), cdc.gov/travel, provides wellness advice specific to foreign destinations, including a section on cruise travel and the latest news about outbreaks of the Zika virus.

The CDC also offers a free e-mail-alert service with travelers' health updates (subscribe at cdc.gov/emailupdates), as well as the mobile apps **Can I Eat This?,** which offers food-safety tips for travelers, and **TravWell,** which includes customizable packing lists and emergency phone numbers for every destination. Both apps are free at the Apple App Store and the Google Play Store.

Also try searching **Facebook** for a group specific to your sailing. Many cruise-specific groups share tips on excursion booking, pricing changes, and other information, as well as organizing private mixology classes or gift exchanges. If you're a social person, this can be a nice way to meet new friends prior to the trip. For our 2016 Northern European sailing, we found that voyage's Facebook group to be a good resource for tips on airfare rates to Copenhagen.

PART TWO

PLANNING YOUR CRUISE

CHOOSING *an* ITINERARY

DISNEY CRUISE LINE OFFERS ALMOST 50 separate itineraries, ranging from 2-night weekend getaways to 15-night voyages between two oceans using the Panama Canal. The cruise you select is likely to be determined by how much vacation time you have, the ship on which you want to sail, the cost, and the ports that interest you.

ITINERARY RECOMMENDATIONS FOR FIRST-TIME CRUISERS

WE THINK THE IDEAL ITINERARY for first-time cruisers is four or five nights aboard the *Dream* or *Fantasy*. Why? They're newer ships, with better restaurants, bars, and spas; interactive areas, such as the Midship Detective Agency; more space for kids' activities; and more space on deck for pools and lounging.

unofficial **TIP**
The average Disney cruise lasts five nights, sails somewhere in the Caribbean, and stops at Disney's Castaway Cay island in the Bahamas.

GENERAL RECOMMENDATIONS

IF YOU'RE TRYING TO DECIDE among Eastern Caribbean, Western Caribbean, and Bahamian cruises, you have just two questions to answer: First, are you interested in exploring the culture of the ports you're visiting? Second, if so, are you more interested in Caribbean towns or Mayan history?

If the answer to the first question is no—if your perfect vacation involves lying on a beach, taking the kids snorkeling, scuba diving, or swimming with dolphins—you can do that in every port from Barbados to Cozumel. Pick any itinerary that includes Castaway Cay and that also fits your schedule and budget, and you're set.

If you're interested in local color, choose between the Eastern and Western Caribbean itineraries. The Eastern itineraries offer the best ports to explore. **St. John** and **St. Thomas** are great stops, but Disney gives you only 5 or 6 hours there. **St. Maarten** is fun because it's Dutch.

On Western Caribbean cruises, **Costa Maya** and **Cozumel** are notable only for their inland tours of Mayan ruins. If those interest you more than Caribbean towns, pick a Western itinerary.

Now, lest you think we're making an "all those people look the same" argument in advising you how to choose between Bahamian and Caribbean itineraries, rest assured we're not. Rather, our advice is based on the observation that the cruise industry's overbooking of the same Caribbean ports has led to a certain sameness of experience virtually everywhere. As Julia Cosgrove, editor-in-chief of *Afar* magazine, observes, "There's no sense of 'I should go to this island as opposed to that because I'm going to get this deeper cultural experience by connecting with people in one place versus another.'"

Disney's Alaskan itineraries, all served by the *Wonder,* are virtually identical. Choose whichever sailing suits your budget and schedule.

Disney's Mediterranean cruises are distinguished primarily by their length (typically 4, 5, 7, 9, or 12 nights), departure port, and, in some years, whether they visit **Venice.** (*Note:* Venice wasn't on DCL's 2017–18 schedule at press time.)

unofficial **TIP**

When you're combing through the DCL website for discounts, look for stateroom categories with the codes **IGT, OGT,** and **VGT.** These indicate heavily discounted inside, outside, and verandah staterooms.

There is more variability in Northern European itineraries than any other region. These sailings range from 7 to 11 days, with some focusing on **Norway** and **Iceland** and others visiting **Estonia** and **Russia** or sailing the **British Isles.** Be aware that the limited availability of some itineraries makes them particularly popular (some ports are only visited on one or two sailings per year). If you find that your preferred itinerary is fully booked, check back often to see if other guests have canceled, or enlist the assistance of a travel agent who can check for cancellations on your behalf.

Guests with special needs (see Part Five, pages 99–101) will want to think about the port-adventure options available with the itineraries they're considering. Because some ports have a preponderance of excursions that prohibit wheelchair access, you may not want to book a trip where your choice of off-ship activities could be limited.

SAVING MONEY

THERE ARE SEVEN PRIMARY STRATEGIES for saving money on a Disney cruise:

1. **Book as early as possible.** Most cruise fares start low and begin to rise as the ship fills up. It's possible to save 10-20% by booking a year in advance. This is the strategy to use if you're looking for the least-expensive stateroom in any category. See the charts starting on page 24 for examples.

2. **Book at the last minute.** Conversely, if your travel schedule is very flexible, savings of up to 25% off are possible when you book a cruise within two weeks of its sailing date. These deals are especially good if you live within a day's drive of the departure port because you can avoid the last-minute price hikes on airline tickets. Offers including last-minute deals can be found on DCL's website (disneycruise.disney.go.com), as well as on our favorite money-saving site, **MouseSavers** (mousesavers.com), under "Disney Cruise Line." This strategy works best when you're looking for one of the more expensive staterooms in a category, such as those on higher decks. Again, see the charts starting on the next page for examples.

3. **Book your next cruise while on board.** DCL offers discounts up to 10% off the lowest prevailing rates, occasionally along with onboard ship credits. Stop by the Future Cruise Sales Desk, usually on Deck 4 Midship, for details. Be aware that discount blackout dates may apply—when we tried to book a cruise coinciding with Easter, we were told that the standard 10% discount was unavailable. We were, however, able to get an onboard credit and a reduced deposit.

4. **Depart from a less popular port.** Disney offers aggressive discounts on cruises from ports that aren't in great demand. Your travel agent should know which ports aren't selling as quickly as others. Armed with this information, you'll find it easy to compare transportation costs to the ports you're considering. (See Part Four for more tips on choosing a port.)

5. **Take advantage of onboard credit offers.** While pricing for cruise fares is consistent from Disney to independent travel agents to larger online sites, such as Orbitz and Expedia, some agencies are able to sweeten the pot with generous onboard credits. Shop around for the best packages.

6. **Use your special status.** Members of various groups may have access to discounts that are unavailable to the general public. For example, there are often special rates available for military personnel, Canadian residents, and Florida residents. These are typically noted on the DCL website's Special Offers page: disneycruise.disney.go.com/special-offers. Additionally, AAA and Costco members may be able to book at a discount via the travel arms of these organizations. If you're traveling with a group of at least eight staterooms or 16 adults (cruising for a wedding or family reunion, for example), you may be eligible for perks like special gifts or private parties. For more information about group bookings, call ☎ 800-511-6333.

7. **Sail during an off-peak time.** Disney charges a premium for its cruises, and we think they're worth it. But the same cruise on the same ship can often cost twice as much on peak dates than during the off-season. An example follows using the Fantasy—an easy ship for comparing fares, because it sails just two itineraries: seven-night Eastern and Western Caribbean cruises out of Port Canaveral.

The chart on the next page shows the cost of the *Fantasy*'s standard seven-night cruises for all of 2017, based on two adults in a Category 4A Deluxe Family Oceanview Stateroom with Verandah.

There are few surprises here: It's cheapest to sail when the kids are in school, and most expensive over the winter holidays. Specifically,

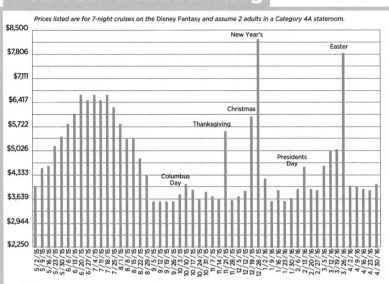

DCL Year-Round Pricing

Prices listed are for 7-night cruises on the Disney Fantasy and assume 2 adults in a Category 4A stateroom.

early fall, the beginning of December, and right after New Year's are the least expensive times to take your Disney cruise.

Other than holidays, the middle of summer is the most expensive time to cruise. If you have children and want to cruise with them, try to book a cruise that leaves as soon as school gets out for summer or right before it starts back in the fall. Your fare won't be as low when school is in session, but it's the best you're going to get.

What's truly astounding is the difference in price between December 9 and December 23. That two-week difference will cost you $2,000 per person more to celebrate Christmas aboard the *Fantasy*. Or, put another way, you could sail back-to-back from December 2 to December 16—14 nights—for only $550 more per person than the Christmas cruise. We know which option we'd choose.

That said, with fall and winter fares, you run the risk of encountering bad weather. The likelihood of hurricanes during a given year, for instance, is something to consider when picking your dates. Plus, high December winds have kept us from docking at ports including Castaway Cay and Grand Cayman.

You'll notice that "book early" and "book late" are complementary suggestions—if you can't do one, do the other. But if you can do both, what's the best strategy? And does it depend on the destination? After all, there's enough competition in the cruise industry to make a four-night Bahamas cruise almost a commodity, but less competition for extended Alaska and Mediterranean cruises.

To answer this question for Disney Cruise Line, we gathered more than 5.1 million prices from DCL's website over the past two years, for every combination of family size, stateroom category, ship, and cruise.

To simplify this discussion, we looked at the prices for two-adult, two-child families in DCL's Deluxe Family Ocean View Stateroom with Verandah staterooms for sailings in July 2016, from 15 months to 3 days in advance, as follows:

- Four-night Bahamian cruises on the *Dream*
- Seven-night Alaskan cruises on the *Wonder*
- Seven-night Western Caribbean cruises on the *Fantasy*
- Seven-night Mediterranean cruises on the *Magic*

Disney charges different prices for its Deluxe Family Ocean View Staterooms with Verandah (DFOVSV); staterooms on higher decks usually cost more than the same room on a lower deck. In the charts that follow, we show the price trends for the highest- and lowest-priced staterooms in that category, along with the average price of all DFO-VSVs on all decks. The charts use a 20-day rolling average for the prices to smooth out tiny variations over time.

Disney Dream *4-Night Bahamian Cruises: July 2016 Price Trends*

Cruise Price (2 Adults & 2 Children)

If Purchased This Many Days In Advance

High Fare
Low Fare
Average Fare

For **Bahamian** cruises, "book early" is a great strategy, as shown in the previous chart. Our typical family would save about 13%—more than $600—by booking eight months in advance or more, versus booking 90 days out. And because the price goes up consistently for the least expensive of these staterooms the closer you get to the cruise date, it's always cheaper to book them as soon as you can. That's true regardless of whether you're booking a stateroom on a high deck or a lower one.

The "book-early" strategy seems to work almost as well on seven-night **Alaskan** cruises on the *Wonder*. The price lines are a little more choppy, reflecting variations of less than 1% in the cost of the cruise, but the overall trend is for prices to increase as time passes. If you're interested in booking the cheapest of these staterooms, though, there's a minor dip in the three- to five-month booking window during which you could save $100 instead of booking five to six months out. A hundred bucks is a lot of salmon cakes.

Pricing strategies get a little more interesting when you look at the *Fantasy*'s seven-night **Western Caribbean** cruises. On these, "book early" is a great strategy if you want the least-expensive stateroom in this category—again, those are typically on Deck 2. If you're looking for something on a higher deck, however, your best bet is to book within two months of departure, with savings of up to $200. Granted,

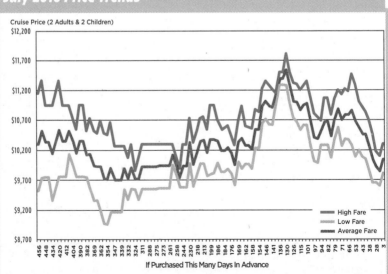

Disney Wonder *7-Night Alaskan Cruises: July 2016 Price Trends*

Cruise Price (2 Adults & 2 Children)

If Purchased This Many Days In Advance

High Fare
Low Fare
Average Fare

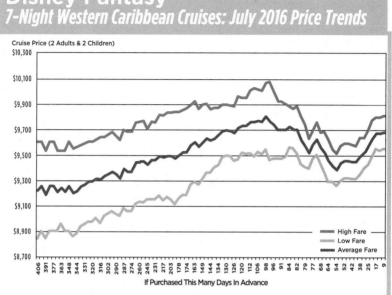

Disney Fantasy
7-Night Western Caribbean Cruises: July 2016 Price Trends

Cruise Price (2 Adults & 2 Children)

If Purchased This Many Days In Advance

High Fare
Low Fare
Average Fare

$200 isn't much on a cruise that approaches 10 grand, but it's enough for a nice meal at Palo or the wine pairing at Remy.

How often does this pricing trend appear for these cabins? Over the first 10 months of 2015, it happened four times: March, April, June, and July (all months with long school breaks, too). In three other months (January, August, and September), prices were lowest more than a year in advance, but it was still cheaper to book within 60 days of departure than to book 2–10 months ahead. The only months in which "book early" was the best choice were February and May.

The other interesting thing to note about these prices is how remarkably stable they are. The *Fantasy* is a big ship, and there's lot's of competition for Western Caribbean cruises, so that definitely contributes to predictable pricing.

The most variable pricing we found in this study is with the *Magic*'s **Mediterranean** itineraries. For these cruises, prices go up consistently from the time they're announced until around 10 months in advance. If you know you're going on a Mediterranean cruise more than a year from now, the "book early" strategy works swimmingly.

If you're thinking about a Mediterranean cruise within the next year, though, **7-10 months in advance** is the absolute worst time to book a cruise. Cruise prices seem to peak during that 90-day window. Why? Most families plan their big annual summer vacations in late

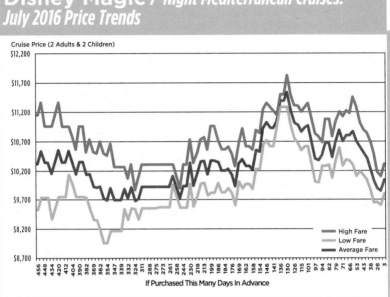

Disney Magic *7-Night Mediterranean Cruises:* July 2016 Price Trends

Cruise Price (2 Adults & 2 Children)

High Fare
Low Fare
Average Fare

If Purchased This Many Days In Advance

December and January. Our theory is that the 7- to 10-month window falls right on those dates, when families are doing their planning and demand is highest for these cruises. Prices are lower in February, March, and April, presumably when people are preparing their tax returns (and seeing how much they owe), then jump up again around 80 or 90 days out from departure (perhaps because they got refunds and decided to splurge).

If you can't book early, booking about four months in advance seems to get you the best cruise deals and allows you enough time to get a deal on airfare.

SURF *and* TURF, DISNEY-STYLE

COMBINING YOUR CRUISE WITH A WALT DISNEY WORLD VACATION

DISNEY SELLS PACKAGES THAT COMBINE A DISNEY CRUISE with a trip to Walt Disney World for cruises departing from Port Canaveral. Called **Land and Sea** packages, these itineraries include the Bahamas, the Eastern and Western Caribbean, and the *Magic*'s Eastbound Transatlantic cruise to Barcelona. Land and Sea packages include lodging

SCOTT SAYS   *by Scott Sanders*

PLAN OF ATTACK

THERE IS NO RIGHT OR WRONG WAY to pick a cruise. Ultimately, it comes down to where you want to cruise, when you want to cruise, and how much you want to spend. If you're flexible about the where and the when, then you might score a lower cruise fare.

We've discovered that our trips are more enjoyable when we include our daughter in the planning process. One way to do that is to look at *Personal Navigator*s from prior sailings with a similar itinerary and ship. The daily schedules give an idea of what may be offered, and when. Whether you prefer to plan every hour of your vacation or just go with the flow, having a general idea of what might be interesting can make it easier when it comes to packing.

Take some time to review the deck plans for the ship you'll be sailing. The better you know the layout, the easier it will be to move around the ship during your vacation.

at a Disney World resort; theme park admission, dining plans, and other extras can be added to the Disney World portion of the trip.

Because of the lack of flexibility with a Land and Sea package booked through DCL, and because you save money when you book components à la carte, we recommend making reservations for each part of a theme park–cruise vacation separately. Regardless of whether you book land and sea together or separately, you will be able to arrange bus transportation between Port Canaveral and your Walt Disney World resort for a fee.

The most frequent question we're asked about combining a theme park vacation with a cruise is whether to visit Disney World before or after the cruise. The majority of people who've done both say they were more relaxed on the cruise than at Walt Disney World, so they prefer to take the cruise after the park visit. Some

*un*official **TIP**
We recommend seeing the World first—chances are that your tired legs (and wallet) will appreciate some downtime at sea.

families don't have a preference either way. A relatively small number prefer to see Walt Disney World second because they prefer the faster pace of WDW after a cruise.

COMBINING YOUR CRUISE WITH AN ADVENTURES BY DISNEY TRIP

MANY EUROPEAN CRUISES out of Barcelona, Copenhagen, Dover, and Venice can be combined with a pre-cruise or onboard **Adventures by Disney (AbD)** guided vacation. Pre-cruise AbD trips include lodging, meals, and tours. AbD trips that are concurrent with a cruise include preselected port adventures accompanied by Disney-trained guides, as well as special onboard assistance. For more details, see adventuresby disney.com (click "Destinations," then click "Europe") or read our blog post on what the AbD cruise supplement looks like at tinyurl.com /abdsupplement.

In addition to its DCL supplements, AbD now offers **European river cruising** on the Danube and the Rhine. See page 358 for more details.

▌ BACK-*to*-BACK CRUISING

HAVE YOU EVER ENDED A CRUISE and thought, "I don't want to go home! Can't I just stay onboard?" That's almost exactly what you do when you book back-to-back cruises—cruises on the same ship where the second cruise begins the day the first cruise ends. And it's *glorious.*

Other than not wanting to leave, why might you consider a back-to-back cruise?

1. **The ship you like doesn't offer longer cruises.** Our first back-to-back cruises were three and four nights on the *Dream.* You want a week on the *Dream? Voilà!* You got it.

2. **You want to see more ports.** Want to see both the Eastern *and* Western Caribbean? Book two consecutive cruises on the *Fantasy.* The Baltics *and* the Mediterranean? The *Magic* has you covered.

3. **You want to save on transportation costs.** Combining two itineraries can be less expensive (assuming you're planning to do both in the first place). For instance, it was much less expensive for us to fly to Vancouver, British Columbia, and do a 7-night Alaskan cruise immediately followed by a 10-night cruise to Hawaii and then fly home from Oahu than to book round-trip airfare to Canada *and* round-trip airfare to Honolulu. (*Note:* At press time, no Hawaii cruises were scheduled for 2017.)

4. **You're amassing Castaway Club credits.** We're not saying that Laurel booked a back-to-back cruise just because the second cruise was the one that pushed her into Platinum Castaway Club status. But we're not saying she didn't either.

So how does it work?

First a caveat: Not every consecutive cruise can be booked back-to-back due to federal maritime law. It's a bit confusing, and it applies only to ships registered outside of the United States—including DCL's ships, which are registered in the Bahamas. If your first cruise leaves from a US port, your last cruise ends in another US port, *and* you haven't visited a "distant foreign port" along the way, you're in violation of the Merchant Marine Act of 1920.

Oddly, the Disney website will let you book back-to-back cruises that violate the law, but once DCL catches your mistake, you'll be forced to choose one cruise or the other. Countries that this affects include the United States, Italy, and Norway. Because at this time no Disney cruises depart from Norway or Italy (though they obviously visit them), you'll need to pay close attention if you're booking a back-to-back that travels either US coast.

unofficial **TIP**
If you're interested in back-to-back cruising, your best bet is to contact Disney before you book—and definitely before you've booked airfare—to be absolutely sure that you'll be allowed on the ship.

Here's a back-to-back example that's OK: an Alaskan cruise starting in Vancouver, followed by Vancouver to San Diego—this works because you're starting in Canada.

Not OK: New York to San Juan followed by San Juan to Miami, because you start in one US city and end in another. Also not OK: Honolulu to Vancouver followed by Vancouver to San Diego—again, you start in one US city and end in another; plus, Vancouver, despite being in Canada, is too close to the United States to be considered a *distant* foreign port.

Once you've booked successfully, you're going to be in one of two situations: Either you were able to book the same cabin for each cruise or you weren't. If you have the same cabin, life is beautiful—you pack a carry-off with any medications or valuables you need with you, leave everything else in your cabin (unpacked, still in the closets and drawers), and walk off with the debarking passengers. Then you check in again (in the Castaway Club platinum lounge), share a smug look with your fellow passengers who are doing the same thing, and walk back on once you're cleared. The ship is so empty when you board again that Len once did carpet angels in the atrium after reboarding.

unofficial **TIP**
If you're truly a travel-by-the-seat-of-your-swim-trunks cruiser, you can book a back-to-back onboard while you're on what would be the first cruise. You'll pay in full at booking, and technically you can't be within 24 hours of the second sail date, but the Future Cruise Sales folks tell us people do this all the time.

If you're changing cabins, you'll have to pack as if you're leaving, but DCL will move your bags to your new cabin for you. You still have to carry off only a day bag, and you won't need to go through customs between cruises. Your room attendant will know ahead of time that you're a back-to-back cruiser, and you'll be given written instructions on the last night for how things will go. Then you just enjoy your next cruise.

Note that if you've bought an onboard Internet package (see page 84), none of your unused data will roll over on a back-to-back cruise, so don't make the mistake of buying a new package on the last night of your first cruise thinking that you'll be able to keep it. Because you'll get two onboard account statements, your unspent credits won't remain valid from cruise to cruise.

On the other hand, your arcade card will work not only on your next cruise but also on any future cruise.

The BOOKING PROCESS

GETTING STARTED

ONCE YOU'VE SETTLED ON A SHIP, an itinerary, and dates, it's time to book your trip. You have three ways to do this:

1. Use the Disney Cruise Line website (**disneycruise.disney.go.com**).

2. Call DCL at ☎ 800-951-3532.

3. Use a travel agent.

There are advantages to each. The main advantage to booking yourself, either online or by phone, is that you can usually do it immediately. If you have booked a cruise before, have access to each traveler's information, don't have questions about the ship or itinerary, and want instant gratification, this may be your best option.

The advantage of using a travel agent is that he or she can save you time by doing most of the tedious legwork for you, plus the agent may also offer a discount in the form of onboard credit, money you can use to pay for items like adult beverages, port excursions, photography services, or babysitting. Many agents have booked dozens, if not hundreds, of cruises, and have a single-page form for you to fill out, where you provide your preferences for everything from what time you prefer to board the ship to when you prefer to eat. Some travel agencies will also rebook your cruise automatically if a lower fare becomes available; a travel agent might also be able to save you money because he or she might have access to group space for a particular cruise. (You're not required to participate in any group activities, but you do get the price advantage of the group booking.) Finally, a seasoned travel agent may be able to help you find rooms with special characteristics, such as an oversized verandah, a particular view, or one of the few sets of inside staterooms connected to porthole staterooms.

DEPOSIT TERMS AND CANCELLATION POLICIES

MOST CRUISE RESERVATIONS REQUIRE A DEPOSIT equal to 20% of the cruise's price (not including taxes) for each passenger age 3 and older on that reservation. Some DCL promotions, such as booking a follow-up cruise while you're already on a current cruise, require only a 10% deposit. Booking a future cruise while you're on the ship almost always includes an onboard credit for the cruise you're booking, too.

Disney Cruise Line's full cancellation policy can be found online at the DCL website; click "Terms and Conditions" at the bottom of the home page. You can cancel a reservation in writing or by phone; also, moving the date of your cruise or changing the name of someone on your reservation is considered a cancellation.

The amount of your refund depends on a variety of criteria. If you've booked a Concierge-level stateroom or suite, the following policy applies, regardless of the length of your cruise or the ports you visit:

CONCIERGE CANCELLATION POLICY	
IF YOU CANCEL THIS MANY DAYS BEFORE SAILING	DCL CHARGES THIS FOR CANCELLATION
90 days or more	Your deposit (typically 20%)
89–56 days	50% of cruise cost, per person
55–30 days	75% of cruise cost, per person
29 days or fewer	100% of cruise cost, per person
14 days or fewer	100% of cruise cost, per person

For non-Concierge staterooms, a "holiday" cancellation policy applies to cruises of one to five nights or six to nine nights if your sailing starts or ends in the United States and includes these dates: January 1, July 4, Thanksgiving (the fourth Thursday in November), or December 25:

HOLIDAY CANCELLATION POLICY: 1- to 5-Night Cruises	
IF YOU CANCEL THIS MANY DAYS BEFORE SAILING	DCL CHARGES THIS FOR CANCELLATION
90 days or more	Nothing (full refund + deposit)
89–56 days	Your deposit
64–43 days	50% of cruise cost, per person
42–15 days	75% of cruise cost, per person
14 days or fewer	100% of cruise cost, per person

HOLIDAY CANCELLATION POLICY: 6- to 9-Night Cruises	
IF YOU CANCEL THIS MANY DAYS BEFORE SAILING	DCL CHARGES THIS FOR CANCELLATION
105 days or more	Nothing
104–75 days	Your deposit

Continued on next page

| HOLIDAY CANCELLATION POLICY:
6- to 9-Night Cruises ||
IF YOU CANCEL THIS MANY DAYS BEFORE SAILING	DCL CHARGES THIS FOR CANCELLATION
74-43 days	50% of cruise cost, per person
42-15 days	75% of cruise cost, per person
14 days or fewer	100% of cruise cost, per person

The standard (nonholiday) cancellation policy is less restrictive:

| STANDARD CANCELLATION POLICY:
1- to 5-Night Cruises ||
IF YOU CANCEL THIS MANY DAYS BEFORE SAILING	DCL CHARGES THIS FOR CANCELLATION
75 days or more	Nothing
74-45 days	Your deposit
44-30 days	50% of cruise cost, per person
29-15 days	75% of cruise cost, per person
14 days or fewer	100% of cruise cost, per person

| STANDARD CANCELLATION POLICY:
6- to 9-Night Cruises ||
IF YOU CANCEL THIS MANY DAYS BEFORE SAILING	DCL CHARGES THIS FOR CANCELLATION
90 days or more	Nothing
89-56 days	Your deposit
55-30 days	50% of cruise cost, per person
29-15 days	75% of cruise cost, per person
14 days or fewer	100% of cruise cost, per person

If your cruise starts or ends outside the United States *or* lasts 10 days or more, the cancellation terms are as follows:

| SAILINGS OUTSIDE THE US OR
10+ DAYS IN LENGTH ||
IF YOU CANCEL THIS MANY DAYS BEFORE SAILING	DCL CHARGES THIS FOR CANCELLATION
120 days or more	Nothing
119-56 days	Your deposit
55-30 days	50% of cruise cost, per person
29-15 days	75% of cruise cost, per person
14 days or fewer	100% of cruise cost, per person

Cruises booked with a "restricted rate" discount code are always nonrefundable and nontransferable—you eat the cost of the entire cruise if you don't sail.

Airfare and port-hotel bookings made through Disney Cruise Line have unique cancellation policies. Check with DCL or your travel agent for specifics.

AGE REQUIREMENTS FOR BOOKING

DCL ALLOWS ADULTS age 18 and up to travel unaccompanied and book their own staterooms. However, **guests age 17 and younger must be booked into a room with an adult age 21 or older.**

DCL's age requirement is liberal compared with, say, Carnival's, which at this writing allows only adults age 21 and above to book and travel unaccompanied and requires minors to be booked in a room with an adult who's at least 25. The policy gives young newlyweds, young military personnel, and most college students the freedom to cruise unchaperoned.

Nevertheless, any group that includes minors needs to consider the implications of the age requirement when planning a Disney cruise. For example, a single parent who wants to travel with four minor kids would have to book a suite. That's often a more expensive option than booking two individual rooms, but it's the *only* option in this case because DCL doesn't allow minors to stay by themselves in a different stateroom, even if the rooms are connected by an inside door.

In the case of a couple who are traveling with just one minor child but want to book more than one room, Disney requires that one parent be booked into a room with the child. Further, if the parent who is registered in a different room wants to leave the ship with the child, that parent must first sign a waiver at the Guest Services desk.

A few situations that would either be a no-go or require altering to meet the age requirement:

- High school and college spring breakers, some of whom are 18 and some whom aren't

- Young adults ages 18–20 who want to travel with younger siblings but without their parents

- Families traveling with an under-21 child-care provider whom they wish to book in the same room as the child

- Guests wanting to travel with minors who aren't in their immediate family— for example, a child's friend or grandchild whom you're happy to have along but whom you might not want sleeping in the same room as you

In general, DCL requires that guests be 21 or older to drink alcohol. Guests ages 18–20 may drink—with restrictions—on some European cruises (see page 162 for details).

THE DCL PLANNING CENTER

A KEY PART OF YOUR Disney Cruise Line booking is the Planning Center at the DCL website: disneycruiseline.com/plan. You can access the Planning Center only with a reservation number—available after you've paid your deposit and received your confirmation e-mail. In addition to the reservation number, you'll need access to the birth date of at least one member of your party. If you've cruised with Disney previously, you may also access your reservation without your reservation number through the Castaway Club section of the DCL site.

The Planning Center includes the following:

- **Reservation Summary** Basic info such as your stateroom number; dining-time assignment; names of the guests in your party; air transportation, ground transportation, and WDW hotel information, if you've booked any of these through Disney; and trip itinerary, including ashore and onboard times for port days. Remember that if your party has booked multiple staterooms, you'll have multiple reservation numbers. To reserve excursions or onboard activities, you'll need the correct reservation number for each member of your party, and you'll need to be in the Planning Center for the correct stateroom.

- **My Cruise Activities** Descriptions of the port adventures and onboard activities available during your sailing, including excursions, spa treatments, adult dining, child care, and more. After you've paid your cruise fee in full and as your travel date nears, this becomes the booking center for these items. Note that Disney has recently added prebooking of some character greetings and onboard character-dining experiences to the My Cruise Activities section for some sailings. These options may become available days or weeks after the standard port-adventure and adult-dining options appear. If you're interested in reserving character experiences, keep checking back.

- **My Online Check-In** You may check in online up to three days before your sailing. This is where you'll give DCL specifics about your travel, authorize credit card payment for onboard purchases, and provide additional information about your party. While Online Check-In is optional, it can reduce your wait time at the port terminal. If you're using My Online Check-In, you'll be able to print a signature and payment-authorization form. Bring this with you to your embarkation port.

- **Fun Aboard the Ship** Information on amenities specific to your sailing vessel.

- **Character Calls** Arrange for a Disney character to place a recorded phone call to your home welcoming members of your party to their cruise (which is particularly fun if the cruise is a surprise for those with whom you're cruising).

- **Packing List** General recommendations for what to pack, along with some specifics based on your cruise itinerary.

- **Air & Ground Transportation** This is where you'll enter your flight/port-transfer information or add port transfers and so on to your package. If you have arranged for Disney-supplied ground transportation, they will require your flight information a few weeks in advance.

- **Passport & Travel Documentation** Notifications about specific travel documents required for your itinerary.

- **Stay Connected** Allows you to register for e-mail or text reminders about your trip.

- **In-Room Gifts & Shopping** Lets you buy presents and floral arrangements for members of your party who may be celebrating birthdays, anniversaries, or other milestones during your voyage. Gifts will be delivered to your stateroom during your sailing.

- **Driving Directions** Detailed directions to your port. Also includes the correct address to make your GPS happy.

- **Custom Pre-Arrival Guide** You can download a PDF of most of the information provided at the Planning Center. The file will include your booking information as well as your general itinerary and any excursions, spa treatments, or adult dining you may have booked.

If you're like most of us, you'll visit the Planning Center more than a few times before your trip. One of our most recent DCL voyages was a four-day quickie, with just two guests. Even with this relatively simple profile, we stopped by the Planning Center nearly a dozen times before our trip—sometimes just to feel good knowing we were headed out on a cruise.

OTHER PREP WORK

PACKING

HAVING TRAVELED WITH LOTS OF PEOPLE over many years, we realize that asking "What do I need to pack?" is like asking "What is art?" Everyone will have their own answer based on their experience and preferences. Some people assume they're going to do laundry on the ship and pack three days' worth of clothes for a seven-night cruise. Others would rather pay for an extra suitcase to carry more clean clothes. The amount you pack is up to you.

unofficial **TIP**
Check out contributor Scott Sanders's excellent DCL packing tips at tinyurl.com /cruisepackingtips.

Knowing what to pack is equally important, and the range of opinions regarding packing essentials is huge. The DCL Planning Center has a pretty good page with suggestions on appropriate clothing for the ship's restaurants and ports of call, along with a short, reasonable list of incidentals to pack (as well as stuff you can't bring aboard).

Beyond that, type "Disney Cruise Line packing list" into any search engine and you'll see thousands of lists with hundreds of items. Some of them read like an Amazon jungle-trek prep list (mosquito netting appears on more than one). It's useful to read through a couple of lists to see if they mention anything you can't live without. Our most important packing advice is this: Don't drive yourself crazy trying to pack for every scenario. You're going to lug those bags a lot farther than you might think. If you're not absolutely certain you're going to use something, *leave it at home.*

You can buy most everyday personal items on board the ship if needed. We generally don't make a special trip to the drugstore to buy motion-sickness pills, antibiotic/anti-itch creams, or over-the-counter pain relievers if we don't already have them on hand at home. The primary exception to the over-the-counter medications being available on the ship is remedies for gastric distress, which are not sold onboard. (See page 45 for more on gastric distress and motion sickness.)

Besides appropriate clothing, our short packing list includes the following essentials:

- **Prescription medication** Pack these in carry-on luggage, in their original containers.

- **Tablet computer** Load enough books, music, movies, TV shows, games, and apps for the cruise plus the trip to and from the port.

- **White-noise mobile app** This is useful for drowning out noise from hallways, next-door cabins, and ship machinery. A good one to try is **Sleepmaker Rain** (available in free and paid versions at the Apple App Store and Google Play).

- **Hats, sunglasses, and sunscreen** Sunscreen is reasonably priced on the ships, in case you don't want to pack it.

- **Water shoes or flip-flops** You'll need these for the pool and beach.

Some guests may find that they have more luggage than they can reasonably manage to transport to the ship on their own; this often happens to guests with small children sailing on longer voyages with bulky items such as diapers and wipes. In such cases, you can mail a package to yourself at Port Canaveral for delivery to the ship. Only one mailed box is allowed per stateroom. Use the following address for mailing the package:

DISNEY CRUISE LINE WAREHOUSE
[Guest name + stateroom number or
GTY if you don't know your room number]
8633 Transport Drive
Orlando, FL 32832
ATTN: Housekeeping

The package must have your name, the ship name, your sail date, and your stateroom number noted on the outside of the box. Your box should also have a packing slip (something like a FedEx window envelope) affixed to the exterior, detailing the contents of the package. Packages must arrive at least 24 hours prior to sail-away time. If you have questions about the process, contact DCL at ☎ 407-566-8196.

If you're departing from a port other than Port Canaveral, you may be able to ship a box to yourself at your pre-sail hotel. Speak to the hotel directly for address information and other instructions.

Some guests choose to economize on alcohol by bringing their own. In late 2015, Disney tightened their rules on the type and quantity of alcohol guests may bring with them onto the ship. The new rules state that each guest age 21 or older may bring a maximum of two bottles of unopened wine or Champagne (no larger than 750 milliliters) or a sixpack of beer (bottles or cans no larger than 12 ounces each) on board at the beginning of the trip *and at each port of call.* These beverages must be packed in carry-on bags—*not* your checked luggage. Alcohol packed in checked luggage will be removed and stored.

unofficial **TIP**
Food is prohibited in shipped boxes. This includes baby food and formula.

If you bring hard liquor, powdered alcohol, or an excess quantity of beer or wine, it will be stored until the end of the cruise. If you plan on purchasing the local firewater while in port, ask to have it packaged for travel (for example, in bubble wrap) because the ship will hold it for you when you board; the next time you'll see it is when you're getting ready to head home.

While you're packing, it makes sense to take a peek at the fairly extensive list of items that are prohibited aboard the ship. Not surprisingly, you can't bring weapons or fireworks, but did you know that you also can't bring pool noodles, musical instruments, inline skates, fishing gear, or kites? Even if you've cruised previously, a repeat look at the prohibited items list is prudent. Recent additions to the list include a ban on toy guns (even Disney-themed guns such as Star Wars laser blasters), remote-controlled drones, and the Samsung Galaxy Note 7. Find the complete list of banned items at tinyurl.com/dclprohibiteditems.

ELECTRICAL OUTLETS

ALL OUTLETS ON THE SHIPS conform to the North American 110V/60Hz standard. If you live in the United States or Canada, any device you have that operates normally at home should work fine on board. All staterooms have hair dryers, so if you're tight on space or not attached to your own model, you won't need to pack one.

If you're visiting from outside the United States, you may need an adapter or converter for your electric gadgets. What's the difference? An adapter ensures that the plug on your device will fit into the electrical receptacle in the wall, but it doesn't change the electrical voltage. A converter does both (and costs more). Your local version of Amazon almost certainly has an excellent selection. Our advice is to bring one converter per person, two if you're traveling alone.

Be aware that there is a real scarcity of electrical outlets in most staterooms, particularly on the *Wonder.* If you'll have more than two people over age 8 in one stateroom, you will almost certainly need to bring some mechanism to add outlet access. Power strips and extension cords are technically prohibited on board; we've never had one confiscated, although other cruisers reportedly have. To hedge your bets, bring along a plug-in USB hub: Many inexpensive models allow four or five USB devices (phones, tablets, and the like) to charge on one outlet, without any extra wires. If you're bringing a laptop with you, remember that you can use it as a charging hub for your phone/tablet, allowing you to avoid plugging those devices directly into a wall outlet.

unofficial **TIP**
When you're searching for outlets in your stateroom, be thorough: We've often found unoccupied outlets behind the TV. And feel free to leave your Wave Phone unplugged if you know you won't be using it.

Another possible workaround is to bring an international electrical converter, even if your cruising takes place in the United States. Most staterooms have a 220-volt outlet near the desk, which is intended for the 220-volt hair dryer provided on board. If you have a converter, you can use this outlet for your 120-volt US devices.

PASSPORTS AND TRAVEL DOCUMENTS

EVERYONE IN YOUR FAMILY, including children, will need to provide proof of citizenship before boarding the ship. If you're a US citizen and you have a valid passport or passport card, it's easiest if you bring that.

unofficial **TIP**
If you're a US citizen taking a cruise that begins or ends outside the States, you **must** have a passport.

If you don't have a passport but (1) you're a US citizen traveling from an American port such as Port Canaveral, Miami, or San Juan; (2) you're traveling only within the Western Hemisphere (the United States, Canada, Mexico, or the Caribbean); and (3) you're returning to the same port on the same ship, you may be able to present a valid driver's license or state-issued ID card plus proof of citizenship—an original or state-issued copy of a birth certificate, a Consular Report of Birth Abroad, or a Certificate of Naturalization. Most Disney cruises to Canada, Alaska, the Caribbean, and the Bahamas qualify. See get youhome.gov for details (click "USA" on the home page, then click the "Special Groups" link).

Other valid forms of identification include a state-issued Enhanced Driver's License (currently available only in Michigan, Minnesota, New York State, Vermont, and Washington State) or a valid Trusted Traveler Card. For the latter, see getyouhome.gov for details (click "USA" on the home page, then click "Trusted Traveler Programs"). Children under age 16 can present a birth certificate (original or copy), a Consular Report of Birth Abroad, or a Certificate of Naturalization.

Requirements for Canadian citizens are almost identical: A Canadian passport, a Canadian Enhanced Driver's License, and a Trusted Traveler Card are all valid forms of ID.

Citizens of countries other than the United States and Canada should remember that some countries may require them to present a visa or passport to enter regardless of their rules for US citizens.

Be sure to check the specifics of your sailing when choosing excursions. If you're an American citizen and your cruise starts from a non-US port, you must have a valid passport to get to your embarkation destination. In addition, some port adventures on Alaskan voyages require a valid passport because you cross into Canada during the trip. Some foreign ports, notably those in Russia, also require special visas for guests who plan to explore the port on their own versus with an approved excursion group or tour guide.

MINOR AUTHORIZATION If you're an adult age 21 or older traveling with someone else's minor child, Disney Cruise Line requires written permission from the child's parent or legal guardian in addition to proof of the child's citizenship. DCL's **Minor Authorization Form** is available as a PDF at tinyurl.com/dclminorauthorizationform. Present the form at check-in at the cruise terminal.

If you're cruising outside the United States with your minor child but without the child's other parent—whether you're a single parent or your spouse couldn't make the trip—US Customs and Border Control recommends that you also bring along a signed, notarized letter of permission in addition to proof of the child's citizenship. Adults traveling with someone else's minor child are advised to do the same in addition to filling out the Minor Authorization Form.

The permission letter isn't legally required, and many cruisers, including Erin, report that they've never been asked for it. That said, customs reserves the right to investigate situations it deems suspicious—so better safe than sorry.

The letter should include the following information:

- The child's full name and birth date
- The other parent's full name, address, and phone number
- Your full name, address, and phone number
- A description of the entire trip, including dates, countries, and cruise information, plus transportation information if available
- The purpose of the trip
- The other parent's original signature, in ink, and the date of his or her signature

Banks and post offices usually have a notary public on staff, but don't put off this task until the last minute in case you can't locate one easily. The notary will have to witness the other parent signing the form, so it's best to have the other parent present the form to the notary. DCL doesn't require that the Minor Authorization Form be notarized, but if you're already getting a permission letter notarized, it couldn't hurt to get that notarized as well.

CREDIT CARDS AND PAYMENT METHODS

DCL SHIPS ACCEPT CASH, traveler's checks, Visa, MasterCard, American Express, Discover, Diners Club, JCB, and the Disney Visa card for payment. They also accept Disney gift cards, Disney Rewards Dollars (available to Disney Chase Visa holders), and Disney Dollars.

Your stateroom key serves as a credit card. Cash is not accepted as payment for beverages, spa or salon services, photography, laundry, or retail purchases, although you'll want to keep some cash on hand to tip luggage attendants and pay for stuff while you're in port. You can cash checks and obtain change from the Guest Services desk; you also can use other credit cards while on board.

unofficial **TIP**
To prevent any sudden stops on your accounts, let your bank and credit card companies know that you're traveling abroad before you leave home.

US dollars are widely accepted throughout most of the Caribbean and in the Bahamas, and most prices are quoted in dollars. US-based credit cards are also accepted at many shops and stores, but don't expect smaller stores, bodegas, markets, and taxis to take them.

If you're traveling to Europe, Mexico, or Canada, you have a few options:

- **Ask your local bank to convert your US dollars before you leave home.** Many US banks will do this at a reasonable exchange rate; some charge a small exchange fee. Give your bank about a week to obtain the currency you need, because many branches don't keep euros, pesos, or Canadian dollars on hand. Your bank will likely convert any unspent foreign currency back to dollars when you return, too.

- **Use a local ATM that's part of your bank's network.** If you're traveling in Europe and you're not sure how much cash to bring, you can usually get a fair exchange rate by withdrawing money at a local cash machine. Visa's website has a handy worldwide ATM locator (visa.com/atmlocator), and in our experience there are usually many more ATMs available than the ones listed online. Keep in mind that your local bank will probably add a withdrawal fee and a foreign-transaction fee, so it's better to make a few large withdrawals than lots of small ones.

- **Exchange traveler's checks for local currency when you disembark.** Traveler's checks are safer than carrying cash because they can be replaced if lost or stolen. The downside: Converting them to local currency takes more time than using an ATM or obtaining local currency before you leave home.

If you want to convert your traveler's checks to cash, try to find a local bank willing to do the exchange, and verify the exchange calculations by hand. We've heard from readers who were promised one exchange rate outside a local currency-exchange stand (not a bank) and got another, lower rate when the conversion was done inside.

Finally, note that the US dollar is unofficially accepted by many markets, bodegas, and taxis throughout Mexico, but you'll rarely get a good deal that way. You'll probably be offered a simple exchange rate of 10 pesos per dollar, whereas the current exchange rate is something like 12 pesos per dollar—almost 17% more than what you're likely to be offered.

HEALTH INSURANCE

US RESIDENTS TRAVELING OUTSIDE OF THE STATES should contact their health insurance providers to check their coverage for emergencies outside the country. While Disney offers trip insurance for its cruises, it currently limits coverage to $10,000 per person for medical and dental emergencies. Ten grand at most hospitals these days is going to get you some ice, a Band-Aid, and a kiss from the doctor to make your boo-boo better . . . if you're lucky. If you're going to pay for additional insurance, make sure it's enough to be helpful in an emergency.

> **unofficial TIP**
> As you pack for your trip, plan to carry three copies of your health-insurance information: one in a wallet or purse, one in carry-on luggage, and one in checked luggage.

Residents of most European countries who are planning a Disney cruise in Europe should also investigate the use of the **European Health Insurance Card,** which covers travel through much of Europe (visit **ehic.org.uk** for details). If you need additional travel insurance, companies such as American Express offer it for around 3% of the total cost of your trip.

Finally, some websites, such as insuremytrip.com, offer a handy feature for comparing travel insurance policies from different companies. **MouseSavers** (mousesavers.com) also contains some good tips.

PHONE SERVICE

ON BOARD Wave Phones are cell phones that you can use to call and text other members of your party on the ship and at Castaway Cay. Each stateroom also has a landline-style phone with voice mail.

> **unofficial TIP**
> If you must use your phone to make calls from the ship, keep them brief and infrequent. Texting is cheaper but can still add up.

Regular cellular service is also available in your stateroom but not in public areas. Pay-as-you-go talk, text, and data roaming through your wireless carrier are expensive on board compared with a standard cellular plan; some carriers offer special cruise-ship bundles that reduce costs somewhat, but the rates are still high for what you get. Check with your carrier for details.

If you don't have a cell phone or you don't want to use your phone on the ship, you can use your stateroom phone to make and receive ship-to-shore calls in an emergency, but that's not cheap either. Rates are high—about $7 per minute—and are charged to your stateroom. The number for incoming calls is ☎ 888-322-8732 in the US or ☎ 732-335-3281 outside the US. Callers need to provide a credit card number along with your ship and stateroom number.

IN PORT Most wireless carriers in the United States now offer international talk, text, and data at rates far more reasonable than simply paying roaming charges as you go. Check with your carrier before your cruise, though, to make sure they offer coverage in the countries you plan to visit.

At this writing, **T-Mobile** includes free unlimited text and data in more than 140 countries as part of its "unlimited everything" T-Mobile One plan; free calling is also included within Canada and Mexico (calls elsewhere cost 20¢ per minute). The data is limited to slow 2G versus high-speed 4G LTE, but if all you're doing is checking e-mail, it's fine.

Sprint has coverage similar to T-Mobile's and offers free unlimited international text and 2G data as an add-on to a regular plan (calls are 20¢ per minute), plus a separate package with free unlimited talk and text and 1GB of high-speed data covering Canada, Mexico, and most of Latin America.

AT&T offers free unlimited talk, text, and (mostly) high-speed data in the US, Canada, and Mexico to wireless customers who also have a DirecTV or U-Verse TV package.

Verizon offers wireless coverage in more than 100 countries but simply tacks a daily fee for each device ($2 or $10 depending on the country) onto the cost of a standard plan, which consists of unlimited talk and text plus a "bucket" of high-speed data that's subject to over-age fees if you exceed your monthly allowance.

Sprint and T-Mobile also offer international data-only add-on pack-ages, but if you use up your high-speed allowance, you'll be bumped down to pokey 2G speeds. AT&T and Verizon offer international talk, text, and data plans, but be aware of overage fees. A **prepaid interna-tional SIM card** could be a good option; check online for the best deals.

The easiest ways to keep your wireless bill from spiraling out of control both on and off the ship are as follows:

1. **Keep your phone turned off when you're not using it.** This is the simplest option if you have a "dumb" phone.

2. **Put your phone in airplane mode.** If you have a smartphone, this shuts off your voice, text, and data connections but still lets you take pictures, listen to music, and access Wi-Fi (see below).

3. **Disable data unless you absolutely need it.** Look for an icon or button called "Settings" on your phone, and from there look for "Cellular," "Wireless and Networks," or the like. Under that, look for "Data Usage," "Cellular Data," "Data Roaming," "Mobile Data," or something similar. Make sure that's turned off. Otherwise your phone will use a foreign carrier's data network to sync e-mail, cloud storage, etc., in the background. Simply turning off data is easier than tinkering with sync settings in individual apps. Airplane mode (see above) accomplishes the same thing but also disables talk and text.

4. **Use Wi-Fi for calling and messaging in addition to web and e-mail.** The four major US wireless carriers offer free Wi-Fi calling to the US from international locations, depending on your plan. You need a phone that supports Wi-Fi

calling; check with your carrier for details. You can also use messaging apps such as iMessage and WhatsApp over Wi-Fi. The catches, of course, are finding a hotspot with a strong signal and deciding whether to pay for Wi-Fi versus scrounging for free access (try Googling "free Wi-Fi in cruise ports"). If you find a free hotspot, say, at a restaurant, keep in mind that you may be expected to buy a little something in return. (DCL's onboard Wi-Fi generally isn't reliable enough for making calls.)

In addition to watching costs, you also need to make sure your phone's wireless hardware is compatible with the wireless infrastructure of the countries you plan to visit. Almost all cell phones throughout the world use either **CDMA** or **GSM** to transmit calls.

In the US, Verizon, Sprint, and U.S. Cellular use CDMA, while AT&T and T-Mobile use GSM, which is also the standard in most of the rest of the world. Discount carriers such as MetroPCS, Straight Talk, and Tracfone piggyback on the major carriers' networks.

Note that the two technologies don't work together, so a phone that has only CDMA hardware won't work on a GSM network, and vice versa. (If your phone doesn't have a SIM card, it uses CDMA, although the latest CDMA smartphones have SIM cards as well.) The 4S and newer editions of the **iPhone,** whether sold unlocked through Apple or sold through a wireless carrier, have both CDMA and GSM hardware, as do a number of newer Android and BlackBerry devices; check with your carrier or your phone's manufacturer to be sure. *Note:* The **Samsung Galaxy Note 7** is now prohibited on board DCL ships.

unofficial **TIP**
If you use AT&T or T-Mobile, or you own a newer iPhone regardless of the carrier, your phone should work virtually anywhere DCL travels that has wireless coverage.

Each of Disney's ships has a dedicated desk for questions about Internet packages (see pages 84–85). The staff has printouts available detailing specific phone settings that will minimize your data consumption. If you're planning to use any data during your vacation, it's well worth stopping by the Internet desk for information. *Note:* Disney's onboard Wi-Fi is free to use with the **DCL Navigator** app (see page 81).

Using your phone in Alaska, Hawaii, Puerto Rico, and the US Virgin Islands (including St. Thomas) won't add to your bill, but you may experience service levels different from those you might expect on the mainland. For example, our AT&T service in Skagway, Alaska, was acceptable, but our Verizon service was spotty at best.

MOTION SICKNESS AND GASTRIC DISTRESS

THE DISNEY SHIPS ARE LARGE VESSELS with sophisticated stabilizers and other technology that keep motion to a minimum, and the navigation staff does as much as possible to minimize the impact of weather on ship motion. Most of the time you'll feel no different on the ship than you would if you were strolling across your own front yard;

nonetheless, there may be times when you feel the motion of the ocean. Depending on your level of sensitivity, the ship's route, sea conditions, and other factors, your perception of this situation might range from mild amusement to abject misery.

If you know that you're prone to motion sickness issues in other situations (long car rides, roller coasters, and so on), you may want to speak with your doctor, and possibly your child's, before you sail. He or she may suggest natural or over-the-counter remedies such as ginger supplements, Queasy Pops, or peppermint essential oil; acupressure tools such as SeaBands; electrical-stimulation tools such as ReliefBands; Bonine or Dramamine (available in children's and nondrowsy versions); or, in severe cases, prescription remedies such as the Transderm Scop (scopolamine) patch.

unofficial **TIP**
Be aware that any news of a guest's GI distress will result in a report to the onboard medical staff and a likely 24-hour quarantine.

We're not doctors, but in our experience it can be more effective to alleviate motion sickness before it starts than to try to quell a full-blown attack. Coauthor Erin has had personal success with starting a daily dose of Dramamine two days before sailing and continuing through the voyage. Other guests swear by SeaBands, wearing them throughout their trip. You may have to experiment a bit to find the best solution for you.

Regular and kids' versions of Dramamine are available for sale in the ships' gift shops, as well as in single-dose form at Guest Services and at the onboard health center, but you'll likely save a few dollars if you buy it at home.

Another component of motion sickness may be the location of your stateroom. The rule of thumb is that midship staterooms experience the least rocking, followed by aft and then forward staterooms. Lower decks are more stable than high decks. If you're prone to motion sickness, a Deck 2 midship cabin may be more comfortable than a Deck 9 forward cabin. The exception to this might be if you find that fresh air helps you, in which case a midship stateroom with a verandah on Deck 6 might be your best bet.

While motion-sickness medications are available at the onboard shops, you'll have to head to the ship's infirmary to get medicines for gastric distress, such as Imodium or Pepto-Bismol. DCL wants to reassure guests that they're on top of possible outbreaks of norovirus and the like, so if you have unexpected stomach or intestinal issues, do the safe and sane thing and head to the onboard health center. But if you know that you typically experience minor issues in any travel situation and you don't need a doctor, bring your own over-the-counter GI meds.

Again, preventing "traveler's tummy" is preferable to combating it once it's started. Tips for keeping comfortable at sea include the following:

- **Make good decisions your first day aboard.** If you traveled from home the same day you boarded the ship, chances are you got up several hours before normal, packed yourself onto a plane or into a car, maybe ate something healthy (but probably didn't), and headed to the cruise terminal. What are you going to do first? Head to the buffet, of course! It's a cruise, and you want to start off with a bang. That's great, but perhaps reconsider that second slice of prime rib or plate of crab legs—there's no shortage of food, after all. Try some fruit or peppermint tea as a light alternative to dessert.

- **Stay hydrated.** Coauthor Laurel likes to carry a water bottle and fill it every time she passes a beverage station (which is on the pool deck, and really only convenient to, well, the pools). Fill it at night and keep it in your cabin's beverage chiller for morning.

- **Take a walk.** Stretch your legs on the outside decks and enjoy the sea air. It may be just what you need.

- **Take an antacid.** Tums and Zantac are typically stocked onboard, or you can bring your own.

- **Lay off the soda.** Yes, fountain drinks are included in your cruise fees, but just because you can have all you want doesn't mean you should. Bubbly beverages put air in your stomach, and anyone who's ever fed a baby knows, that's not a good thing. Water is good. Add some lemon if needed.

- **Eat modestly.** This is super-tough for anyone who has or has had parents or grandparents who went through the Great Depression, even when you're not on a cruise. Just remember that you can always get more food if you're still hungry. You can also skip dessert, get two appetizers instead of an entrée, or order from the kids' menu. What you eat is up to you, not your tablemates or your servers.

- **Pack some loose-fitting clothing to avoid constriction.** Be sure to pack at least one dinner-appropriate outfit that you know will fit no matter what's going on in your gut. Maybe that's a caftan, a maxi-dress, or palazzo pants with a drawstring waist. Guys, you're on your own here—just try to leave a few notches to spare on your belts and you should be OK.

- **Make good choices in port.** Drinking from a water fountain in Mexico is probably playing with fire. Stick with bottled water and cooked food in ports with possible sanitation issues. Additionally, if you're prone to motion sickness or GI issues, choose port activities with minimal movement. Avoid stuff like rides on small boats or jeep trips down bumpy dirt roads.

- **Wash your hands.** The disinfecting wipes handed out every time you come within 20 feet of food are only a start. The very best way to avoid major and minor bugs is to wash your hands at every opportunity.

A WORD ABOUT THE WEATHER

AS MUCH AS WE'RE SURE THEY'D LIKE TO, Disney can't control the weather. You're probably envisioning spending your Caribbean cruise sipping piña coladas on the pool deck, but the reality is that you may encounter inclement weather during your sailing. Don't worry if it rains; there are plenty of indoor activities for children and adults. Disney also does a terrific job of providing extra indoor programming if conditions warrant. Be sure to check the mobile version of the *Personal Navigator*, which is updated more frequently than the print version, for up-to-the-minute additions to the schedule. (See page 81 for more details.)

In extreme situations, DCL will alter plans more substantially than just running a few more games of bingo. Hurricanes and tropical storms do sometimes necessitate a significant change of itinerary. On rare occasions, sailings have left their embarkation port a day or two late, omitted or changed a midtrip port stop, or ended a voyage at a port other than the one planned, all in the interest of guest safety.

While there is an official hurricane policy for Walt Disney World travel (disneyworld.disney.go.com/faq/hurricane-policy), there is no comparable codification for DCL. Disney does, however, have an admirable record of assisting guests with refunds or remediation for missed sailing days and fees at skipped ports. Bear in mind that if your itinerary changes, it may be easier to get refunds for excursions booked through Disney rather than for those booked on your own. (See page 328 for more information about booking on your own.)

If you encounter storms, rest assured that the chance of real danger due to a hurricane is virtually zero. Weather tracking is such that cruise lines typically know about impending severe weather at least three days before its impact, giving them plenty of time to change course. Captains also have great latitude to reroute ships to avoid areas of concern. Large ships such as the Disney fleet even have the ability to outpace the danger zone of a storm: Most hurricanes travel at a speed of about 10 knots, and the ships are able to sail at more than 20 knots.

If you want to delve into the minutiae of maritime weather tracking, passageweather.com is a terrific source of information about phenomena that affect ships: surface winds, wave height and direction, sea-surface temperatures, and more. The **National Weather Service** also offers detailed current information at its Ocean Prediction Center: opc.ncep.noaa.gov.

Weather issues are possible at any time of year but are more common in the Caribbean and Bahamas from mid-August until early November. But even if you avoid sailing in the Caribbean during that time, weather might affect your cruise in other ways. In August 2011, coauthor Erin sailed on the *Disney Magic* in the Mediterranean. The weather during the voyage was spectacular, with clear skies and calm seas throughout. But when she disembarked in Barcelona, she found that Hurricane Irene—the seventh-costliest hurricane in US history—was busy pummeling the eastern United States, forcing the closure of all the airports near her home. Her European vacation was unexpectedly extended by several days until the airports reopened.

Whenever possible, build in a day or two on both sides of your sailing to account for unexpected weather situations. You may also want to consider whether trip insurance makes sense for your family. Depending on the policy, it may cover flight-change fees and/or unexpected hotel stays. Be sure to read the fine print on any trip insurance contract to understand exactly what it covers before you purchase (see page 43 for more details).

On the other end of the spectrum, some guests, equating cruising with the tropics, are wary of booking a sailing to colder-weather regions such as Canada, Alaska, and Northern Europe. We've sailed itineraries to these areas and rank them among our favorites. During a Norwegian Fjords cruise on the *Magic,* we often heard the maxim, "There is no bad weather, only bad clothing." As long as you're dressed appropriately, touring in a cooler climate can be a fabulous experience, with more variety to the sights than you're likely to find on a beach-intensive voyage in the Caribbean.

The ships also feel particularly cozy on cold-weather routes. For example, on the glacier-viewing Tracy Arm day of Alaskan sailings, the DCL staff places piles of fleece blankets on deck and rolls around a cart stocked with hot cocoa, Irish coffee, and hot toddies. Cuddling up with your honey, sipping a warm beverage, and watching seals and whales swim by makes for a truly memorable day. We're with Elsa on this one: "The cold never bothered us anyway."

CASTAWAY CLUB

DCL USES THIS PROGRAM TO REWARD REPEAT CRUISERS. It works somewhat along the lines of a frequent-flyer program—the more you cruise with Disney, the better your status and the more perks you get.

Castaway Club status is determined solely by the number of DCL voyages you've completed, not by how much money you've spent. A guest who's sailed on five 3-day cruises in the smallest inside cabin belongs to a higher level than a guest who has spent more money on one 12-day voyage in the largest cabin.

The club levels are as follows:

- If you've never taken a Disney cruise before, you're a **First-Time Guest.**
- Guests who have completed 1–5 Disney cruises have **Silver** status.
- Guests who have completed 6–10 Disney cruises have **Gold** status.
- Guests who have completed more than 10 Disney cruises have **Platinum** status.

Most guests will be able to count all of their cruising toward their status level, with a few rare exceptions, such as a Disney cast member cruising on business. (Tough life, eh?)

A number of perks are available to all Castaway Club members, including "Welcome Back" stateroom gifts and priority check-in at the port terminal. As your membership level increases, so do your benefits. Gold and Platinum guests receive 10% off many onboard merchandise purchases; Platinum guests may also earn a free meal at Palo. While neither of these perks is enough incentive to book another trip, they are a nice way to acknowledge loyal customers.

For many guests, one of the chief benefits of Castaway Club membership is that the higher your status level, the earlier you can reserve many aspects of your cruise, including port excursions, onboard dining at the adults-only Palo and Remy, spa visits, and some child-care situations:

- **First-Time Guests** may make reservations 75 days prior to sailing.
- **Silver** Castaway Club members may make reservations 90 days prior to sailing.
- **Gold** members may make reservations 105 days prior to sailing.
- **Platinum** members may make reservations 120 days prior to sailing.

Castaway Club status may not make much of a difference in some situations. For example, nearly everyone will be able to rent a bike at Castaway Cay. In other circumstances, however, belonging to a higher level can be a real boon. For example, Castaway Cay has only 21 private cabanas, split between the family and adult beach areas. With several thousand guests aboard your ship, competition for these private oases can be fierce, and Castaway Club members get first crack at them. It may be impossible for a First-Time Guest traveling during peak season to reserve a cabana. Other popular experiences include dining at Palo and Remy on days at sea, massages at Castaway Cay, and Flounder's Reef babysitting during showtimes.

Sometimes not everyone in a single stateroom has the same Castaway Club status. In that case, the benefits for each guest are determined by the Castaway Club member with the highest status in that room. For example, if I (Erin) have been on a few more cruises than my husband (lucky me!) and my status is higher than his, I can make reservations for both of us at my level. However, if we're also traveling with First-Time Guests staying in another stateroom, they *can't* take advantage of my higher status level, even though they're in our party. Effectively, then, Castaway Club status on any particular cruise is applied by stateroom, not by party. Keep this in mind if you're planning activities for a large group—not everyone will have equal access to reservations if members of your party have different status levels.

One other benefit of Castaway Club status comes when Disney announces new itineraries. When new sailings are announced, Disney typically grants access to booking first to Platinum and Gold Castaway Club members, followed by general access to Silver and First-Time Guests a day or two later. While cruises seldom become fully booked in the first two days, a new cruiser could possibly be locked out of a unique stateroom type on a particularly popular voyage.

PART THREE

STATEROOMS

DISNEY CRUISE LINE'S SHIPS BOAST some of the largest cabins in the industry, which helps explain—a bit—why their fares are correspondingly high. An inside cabin, generally the least expensive on any ship, is 169–184 square feet on Disney's ships, compared with 114–165 square feet on Royal Caribbean and 160–185 on Carnival. Disney's Oceanview and Verandah (balcony) cabins are larger than Royal Caribbean's and Carnival's, too.

In addition to space, Disney's bathroom layout is an improvement over those of other cruise lines. Disney staterooms in Categories 10–4 feature a split-bath design, in which the shower and toilet are in separate compartments, each with its own door and sink. The advantage of this design is that two people can get ready at the same time. (Category 11 staterooms have the shower and toilet in the same compartment.)

DCL's clever incorporation of storage space is one of the things we were most impressed with on our first few cruises. Most cabins have two closets, each big enough for one large or two small suitcases; under-bed storage for carry-on or soft-sided luggage; and several drawers built in to the cabin's desk area. In addition, some cabins on the *Wonder* offer a steamer trunk for storage, while the *Magic* has dressers instead of trunks. (For a list of these cabins, see tinyurl.com/steamertrunklist.) As we were going to press, the *Wonder* was completing an extended dry dock for maintenance and refurbishment; we think the *Wonder*'s room fittings may be changed to conform to those on the other ships.

While Disney's staterooms are well designed and large for the cruise industry, most are smaller than the typical hotel room. A room at a Walt Disney World Value hotel, such as Pop Century Resort, is

unofficial **TIP**
On the *Dream* and *Fantasy*, some inside cabins have "virtual portholes"—video screens that combine real-time views from outside the ship with animated snippets of various Disney characters. Many children strongly prefer these to actual Verandah views, and inside cabins are usually much less expensive.

about 260 square feet—about 40% larger than a DCL inside cabin. Even a well-appointed Family Oceanview Stateroom with Verandah is 304 square feet, a little smaller than a room at a Disney Moderate hotel, such as Caribbean Beach Resort.

HOW YOUR STATEROOM CATEGORY AFFECTS *the* PRICE *of* YOUR DISNEY CRUISE

ALONG WITH YOUR DEPARTURE DATE AND HOW FAR in advance you book, the type of stateroom you choose is one of the major factors in determining your cruise's cost.

The chart below shows how much a fare increases, based on cabin category, for a typical seven-night cruise on the *Disney Fantasy* for two adults.

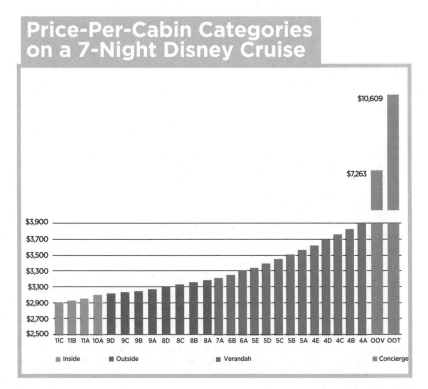

Price-Per-Cabin Categories on a 7-Night Disney Cruise

$10,609

$7,263

$3,900
$3,700
$3,500
$3,300
$3,100
$2,900
$2,700
$2,500

11C 11B 11A 10A 9D 9C 9B 9A 8D 8C 8B 8A 7A 6B 6A 5E 5D 5C 5B 5A 4E 4D 4C 4B 4A OOV OOT

■ Inside ■ Outside ■ Verandah ■ Concierge

A Category 4A stateroom—the most expensive non-Concierge category—will, on average, cost about 30% more than the least expensive cabin. For this you get another 130 square feet of space and a better view.

What's remarkable is the slow, steady slope of the line until you reach the Concierge level. This shows that Disney is very consistent in its pricing across stateroom categories. That's interesting because there aren't the same number of staterooms in each category—the vast majority are verandah staterooms, but in this case a larger supply doesn't equal a lower price. Disney seems to have just the right amount of each type of stateroom to meet guest demand.

OUR STATEROOM RECOMMENDATIONS

AT 169–184 SQUARE FEET, an **Inside Stateroom** has enough room for two adults, or two adults and one small child. (Just remember: They give you 60 square feet per person in prison.) These are Category 10 and 11 cabins, so a family of this size shouldn't have much contention for bathrooms when getting ready.

If you're a family of three or four and you have two tweens or teens, you'll appreciate the extra space of a **Deluxe Oceanview with Verandah Stateroom** (246 or 268 square feet) or **Deluxe Family Oceanview with Verandah Stateroom** (about 300 square feet). Alternatively, you could book two cabins: two inside connecting rooms or an inside and outside cabin across the hall from each other. The advantage to two rooms, besides the extra space and extra bathroom, is that the kids can sleep late if they want. Additionally, putting the kids in a different room allows the parents to access the television and verandah (both of which are located on what is typically the kids' side of the room) without fear of disturbing anyone.

CABIN APPOINTMENTS

EVERY DCL STATEROOM is outfitted with the following:

- **Bedside lamps**
- **Beverage cooler**—keeps drinks cool, not necessarily cold; no freezer
- **Closet** with two sliding doors (*Magic* and *Wonder*) or two hinged doors (*Dream* and *Fantasy*)
- **Coffee table**—the top opens for storage (*Dream* and *Fantasy* only).
- **Custom artwork**—usually depicts Disney characters and themes relevant to the cruise line, ships, islands, or travel
- **Desk with chair and dedicated lighting**—big enough to actually get work done

- **Electronic safe**—just big enough for passports, wallets, and other small valuables
- **Hair dryer**
- **Hooks** (for towels) and **hangers** (for clothes)
- **Ice bucket** and glasses
- **In-room phone** with voice mail
- **In-room thermostat** (digital on the *Dream* and *Fantasy;* older-style dial on the *Magic* and *Wonder*)
- **Life jackets**
- **Privacy curtain**—separates the sleeping area from the sofa
- **Private bath** with sink and toilet
- **Room-service menus**
- **Satellite television** with remote
- **Sleeper sofa**
- **Toiletries**—H2O Plus brand soap, shampoo, conditioner, and body lotion are available in standard guest rooms. Elemis bath products are stocked in the Concierge-level suites.
- **Wave Phone**—a mobile phone you can use aboard the ship

Cabins with exterior windows also include blackout curtains, which do an amazing job of blocking the sun. If you need light to wake up in the morning, don't shut them unless you want to sleep until noon.

WHAT YOU WON'T FIND Cabins don't have minibars, coffeemakers, microwaves, teakettles, steam irons, or ironing boards. An iron and ironing board are available in most of the ships' laundry rooms.

A NOTE ABOUT YOUR STATEROOM DOORS The door to your stateroom is made of metal and is thus magnetic. Repeat cruisers are often fond of decorating their doors with magnets related to family celebrations, the cruise destination, a holiday, or something Disney-related in general. The longer your cruise, the more likely you are to see doors decorated with magnets, sometimes quite elaborately. When cruising in the Caribbean, Erin's teenage daughters like to break out a pirate version of Magnetic Poetry's build-a-sentence kits. Other guests have used our door magnets to create some very amusing stories.

There is, of course, no obligation to decorate your door, but if you choose to do so, be aware that while magnets are acceptable, you can't tape or hook anything to your door, nor may you use sticky gel wall/window clings. Any damage to your door will result in a charge to your stateroom account.

STATEROOM CATEGORIES
CATEGORIES 11A–11C: Standard Inside Stateroom
MAXIMUM OCCUPANCY 4 people
SIZE (square feet) *Magic/Wonder,* 184; *Dream/Fantasy,* 169

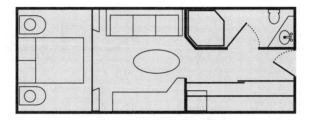

STANDARD INSIDE STATEROOM

DESCRIPTION These cabins have one queen-size bed, a sleeper sofa, and combined bath with tub and shower. Some rooms have a pull-down upper berth. These cabins are on Decks 2, 5, 6, and 7 on the *Magic* and *Wonder,* and on Decks 2, 5, 6, 7, 8, 9, and 10 on the *Dream* and *Fantasy.* They're generally available in the Forward (toward the bow/front), Midship (center), and Aft (toward the stern/rear) sections of the ships.

CATEGORY 10A (all ships), **CATEGORIES 10B** and **10C** (*Magic* and *Wonder*): **Deluxe Inside Stateroom**

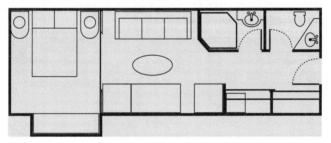

MAXIMUM OCCUPANCY 4 people

SIZE (square feet) *Magic/Wonder,* 214; *Dream/Fantasy,* 204

DESCRIPTION These cabins have one queen-size bed, one sleeper sofa, and split bath. Some rooms have a pull-down upper berth. Category 10C rooms on the *Magic* and *Wonder* are located entirely on Deck 1 Midship and Deck 2 Aft. Category 10B rooms, also found on the *Magic* and *Wonder,* are located entirely on Deck 2 Midship. Category 10A rooms are on Decks 5 and 7 on the *Magic* and *Wonder* and Decks 5, 6, 7, 8, and 9 on the *Dream* and *Fantasy,* anywhere along the ship.

CATEGORIES 9A–9D: **Deluxe Oceanview Stateroom** *(see next page)*

MAXIMUM OCCUPANCY 4 people

SIZE (square feet) *Magic/Wonder,* 214; *Dream/Fantasy,* 204

DESCRIPTION Same size and features as a Category 10 Deluxe Inside, plus a window view of the ocean. These cabins have one queen-size bed. All cabins on all ships have a sleeper sofa and split bath; some rooms have a pull-down upper berth. Categories 9B–9D are found only on Decks

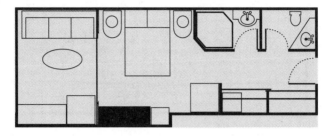

DELUXE OCEANVIEW STATEROOM

1 and 2 on the *Magic* and *Wonder* and only on Deck 2 Midship on the *Dream* and *Fantasy*. Category 9A cabins are found on the Forward section of Decks 5, 6, and 7 on the *Magic* and *Wonder,* and on Decks 5, 6, 7, and 8 of the *Dream* and *Fantasy*. The 9A cabins on Decks 6, 7, and 8 of the *Dream* and *Fantasy* are interesting because they're at the extreme Forward and Aft ends of the ships, affording them unique views at a relatively low cost.

CATEGORIES 8A–8D (exclusive to the *Dream* and *Fantasy*):
Deluxe Family Oceanview Stateroom

MAXIMUM OCCUPANCY 5 people
SIZE (square feet) 241
DESCRIPTION These cabins have one queen-size bed. Most have a one-person pull-down bed in the wall; a few also have one-person pull-down beds in the ceiling. All cabins have a one-person sleeper sofa. Some 8As have a single bathroom, others a split-bath configuration. Most bathrooms have round tubs and showers.

CATEGORY 7A: **Deluxe Oceanview Stateroom with Navigator's Verandah**
MAXIMUM OCCUPANCY 4 people
SIZE (square feet) *Magic/Wonder,* 268 (including verandah); *Dream/Fantasy,* 246 (including verandah)
DESCRIPTION Found on Decks 5, 6, and 7 on all ships (Fore and Aft on the *Dream* and *Fantasy;* Aft only on the *Magic* and *Wonder*), these cabins have one queen-size bed. All cabins have a one-person sleeper sofa

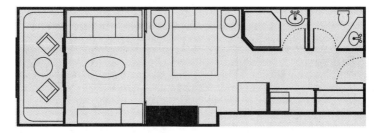

**DELUXE OCEANVIEW STATEROOM
WITH NAVIGATOR'S VERANDAH**

and split bath. The interesting feature about these cabins is the Navigator's Verandah: a small, semienclosed, teak-floored deck attached to the stateroom and featuring either a large exterior window or open railing. The window doesn't open, so in those rooms the extra space and teak deck are the difference between these cabins and the Category 9 staterooms on the *Magic* and *Wonder.* On the *Dream* and *Fantasy,* these cabins have an undersize or obstructed-view verandah.

CATEGORIES 6A (all ships) and 6B (*Dream* and *Fantasy* only): Deluxe Oceanview Stateroom with Verandah

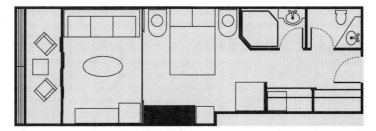

MAXIMUM OCCUPANCY 4 people

SIZE (square feet) *Magic/Wonder,* 268 (including verandah); *Dream/Fantasy,* 246 (including verandah)

DESCRIPTION These cabins have a queen-size bed, a one-person sleeper sofa, and a one-person pull-down bed, typically above the sofa. All have a split bath, most with round tubs and showers. Category 6A cabins are found Aft on Decks 5, 6, and 7 of the *Magic* and *Wonder* and Aft on Decks 8, 9, and 10 on the *Dream* and *Fantasy.* Category 6B staterooms are found only on the *Dream* and *Fantasy,* Aft on Decks 5, 6, and 7. These staterooms differ from Category 5 staterooms because they have private verandahs with a short white wall instead of a railing with plexiglass. In addition, some of the Category 5 cabins are found Midship, whereas all Category 6 cabins seem to be Aft.

CATEGORIES 5A–5C (all ships), **5D** and **5E** (*Dream* and *Fantasy* only): **Deluxe Oceanview Stateroom with Verandah**

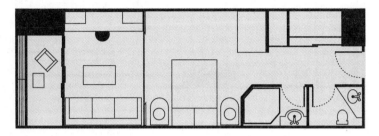

MAXIMUM OCCUPANCY 4 people

SIZE (square feet) *Magic/Wonder,* 268 (including verandah); *Dream/ Fantasy,* 246 (including verandah)

DESCRIPTION There seems to be little difference between these and the Category 6 cabins on the *Magic* and *Wonder.* All have the same square footage and amenities, and all are on Decks 5, 6, and 7. Category 5E cabins have oversize verandahs, and some have a white wall instead of a railing with plexiglass. No other Category 5 cabins have a white wall on the verandah.

CATEGORIES 4A and **4B** (all ships), **4C** and **4D** (*Dream* and *Fantasy* only), **4E** (*Magic* and *Wonder* only): **Deluxe Family Oceanview Stateroom with Verandah**

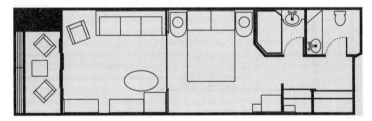

MAXIMUM OCCUPANCY 5 people

SIZE (square feet) *Magic/Wonder,* 304 (including verandah); *Dream/ Fantasy,* 299 (including verandah)

DESCRIPTION These cabins have a queen-size bed and sleeper sofa (fits one person); most have a pull-down wall bed (sleeps one). Some also have a pull-down upper-berth bed. All have a split bath, most with round tubs and showers. One issue with the pull-down wall bed in these cabins is that you'll have to move the desk chair in order to use the bed. The Category 4E cabins are found only Aft on Decks 7 and 8 of the *Magic* and *Wonder.* There are only two 4E cabins on Deck 7, and what makes them interesting is that they have an angled view directly off the ship's stern. They're also adjacent to Deck 7's "secret" sun deck. On the *Dream* and *Fantasy,* the A–D designations for this category represent the deck on which the stateroom is located: 4A staterooms are on Decks 9 and 10 Midship, 4B staterooms are on Deck 8 Midship, 4C staterooms are on Deck 7 Midship, and 4D staterooms are on Deck 6 Midship.

CATEGORY V (*Dream* and *Fantasy* only): Concierge Family Oceanview Stateroom with Verandah

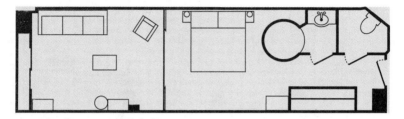

MAXIMUM OCCUPANCY 5 people
SIZE (square feet) 306 (including verandah)
DESCRIPTION These cabins have a queen-size bed, a sleeper sofa for two, and an upper-berth pull-down bed that sleeps one. These rooms have an extra half-bath, giving the shower side of the split bath a sink and vanity. Category V staterooms are on Decks 11 and 12 Forward.

CATEGORY T: Concierge 1-Bedroom Suite with Verandah

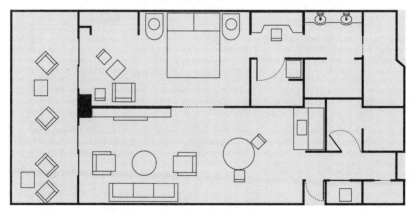

MAXIMUM OCCUPANCY 5 people
SIZE (square feet) *Magic/Wonder,* 614 (including verandah); *Dream/Fantasy,* 622 (including verandah)
DESCRIPTION These cabins feature a separate bedroom with queen-size bed and a bathroom with whirlpool tub and separate shower. The

living room has upholstered chairs and a sofa, plus a separate table and chairs. The living room also sleeps three: two on the convertible sofa and one in the pull-down bed. These staterooms are found all along Deck 8 on the *Magic* and *Wonder* and the Forward sections of Decks 11 and 12 on the *Dream* and *Fantasy.*

CATEGORY S (*Magic* and *Wonder* only): **Concierge 2-Bedroom Suite with Verandah**

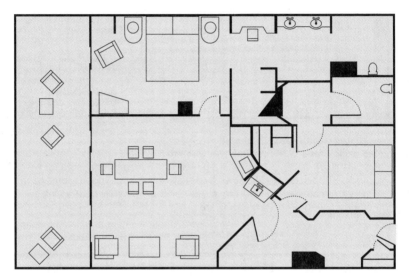

MAXIMUM OCCUPANCY 7 people
SIZE (square feet) 954 (including verandah)
DESCRIPTION The master bedroom has a queen-size bed, a walk-in closet, a vanity, two sinks, and a walk-in shower. The other bedroom has twin beds, a bathroom with tub and sink, and a walk-in closet. Two others can sleep on the convertible sofa in the living room, and a pull-down bed sleeps one more. In addition, the 2-Bedroom Suite features a large living room with seating for 10 people, a huge private verandah suitable for entertaining a few guests, and another half-bath. Category S cabins are on Deck 8 Forward.

CATEGORY R: Concierge Royal Suite *(see right)*
MAXIMUM OCCUPANCY 7 people (*Magic/Wonder*); 5 people (*Dream/ Fantasy*)
SIZE (square feet) *Magic/Wonder,* 1,029 (including verandah); *Dream/ Fantasy,* 1,781 (including verandah)
DESCRIPTION On the *Magic* and *Wonder,* the master bedroom has a queen-size bed, a walk-in closet, a vanity, two sinks, and a walk-in shower. The

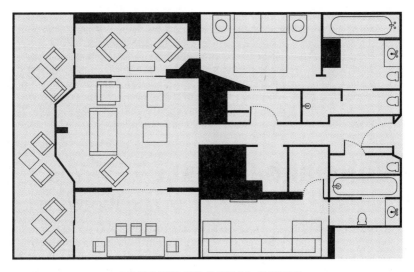

CONCIERGE ROYAL SUITE

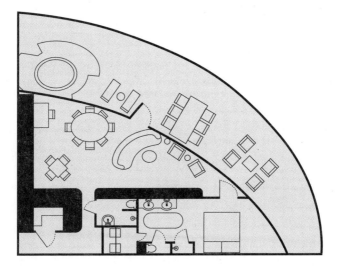

CONCIERGE ROYAL SUITE WITH VERANDAH

other bedroom has twin beds, a bathroom with tub and sink, and a walk-in closet. Two others can sleep on the convertible sofa in the living room, and a pull-down bed sleeps one more. On the *Magic* and *Wonder*, the Royal Suite includes a separate dining room, living room, and media room, plus a private verandah that you should rent out to other families for birthdays (it'll fit an elephant) and another half-bath. Royal Suites on the *Dream* and *Fantasy* have one long room separated into dining and living areas. The master bedroom features a queen-size bed and bath with two sinks, a shower, and a tub. An in-wall pull-down double bed and a single pull-down bed in the living room complete the sleeping arrangements. The most impressive feature of these suites on the *Dream* and *Fantasy* may be the verandah, which curves around the suite to follow the contour of the deck. Besides being large enough to land aircraft on, it includes a whirlpool tub.

CONCIERGE LEVEL: *What You Need to Know, and If It's Worth It*

A DISNEY CRUISE IS ALREADY A FAIRLY LUXE VACATION, but what you do you do when you want to plus it up? Booking a stateroom on the Concierge level is one option. Concierge levels are similar but not identical across the ships. In this section, we'll go over the amenities, the differences, and try to answer the question "Is it worth the money?" (*Spoiler:* It depends.)

The Concierge levels on the *Dream* and *Fantasy* are nearly identical. The cabins are on Decks 11 and 12, with an exclusive Concierge lounge on Deck 12. The lounge opens to a private outdoor-sunning area (it's right by Satellite Falls).

On the *Magic* and *Wonder,* Concierge level is on Deck 8. The Magic added a new lounge during its 2015 dry dock; we suspect the Wonder will do the same during its 2016 dry dock.

Concierge categories are as follows:

1. **Category V: Concierge Family Oceanview Stateroom with Verandah.** This is the same layout as a Category 4, but with the added bonus of Concierge service. These can connect to 1-Bedroom Suites to make a 2-Bedroom Suite. Category V is available only on the *Dream* and *Fantasy.*

2. **Category T: Concierge 1-Bedroom Suite.**

3. **Category S: Concierge 2-Bedroom Suite** (*Magic* and *Wonder* only).

4. **Category R: Concierge Royal Suite.**

See the floor plans for a Concierge 2-Bedroom Suite on page 60 and two Concierge Royal Suites on page 61. Prepare to be wowed upon walking in. These are seriously nice cabins with lots of room to spread out. We already think Disney has great staterooms, but the finishing touches in Concierge are beyond our expectations. In fact, if you're considering booking here, we think you'd do well to choose it for an itinerary and ship you've already taken so you're not torn between exploring the ship and port and just enjoying the Concierge level.

SCOTT SAYS   *by Scott Sanders*

A ROOM OF ONE'S OWN

CONSIDER HOW MUCH TIME you'll actually be spending in your stateroom. Is a porthole or balcony really going to make a thousand-dollar difference in the quality of your trip, when most of what you'll see is open ocean? There are plenty of spots on the ship to sit outside and enjoy the scenery.

If light affects your sleep, an inside stateroom may be a blessing in disguise if your itinerary takes you to a region where the sun doesn't fully set at night (on some Northern European and Alaskan cruises).

The benefits of booking this level are quantifiable—more space, lounge access, early booking opportunities for specialty dining and port excursions (notably cabanas on Castaway Cay)—but they're also intangible when it comes to the added level of service. Also quantifiable is the cost: Expect to pay for all this luxury and space. For an apples-to-apples comparison, plan to pay around 50% more for a Category V versus a Category 4, or around twice as much as a Category 4 for a Concierge 1-Bedroom Suite.

Concierge level has some perks that range from "really useful" to "we can take it or leave it." The pampering begins before boarding. The Concierge team will contact you before your booking window for port excursions and dining to ask for your requests. While making Palo or Remy reservations usually isn't a problem no matter where you're booked, getting a cabana on Castaway Cay is nearly impossible if you're not in Concierge.

On boarding day, Concierge guests check in with Platinum-level guests in a separate area (Port Canaveral only) or line (other ports). While Platinum and Concierge guests may both board at will, with no waiting for your boarding group to be announced, Concierge guests are escorted to the lounge by the staff. This helps you get around the usual wait for an elevator on embarkation day.

The lounge itself is fantastic. Snacks and beverages are served all day, and Concierge staff are available from morning to evening to assist with anything you need help with. You'll never need to stand in line at Guest Services for anything. The quiet and calm of the lounge are pretty much the opposite of the chaos of the nearby pool deck. You may never want to leave.

One of our favorite Concierge benefits is room service from the main dining room. A server will bring your entire meal—you pick from the menu as you would at the table—and serve it course by course in the privacy of your cabin. He or she waits in the hallway between courses.

So is Concierge worth it? Being logical types, we like to try to approach the question methodically. If you accept that (1) a Disney cruise is worth the surcharge that you pay over other lines and (2) a verandah-view room is worth what you pay over an inside room, then the next linear progression is that, yes, the extra space of a Concierge room (we're talking one-bedroom) is worth the price Disney charges for it, provided you can afford it. Basically, staying on Concierge level means not just upgraded accommodations but also avoiding all the little annoyances of a cruise vacation—lines, noise, masses of fellow cruisers—by waving them away with a magic wand made of money.

If a Concierge stay is in the cards for you, by all means try it out. But if it's not, don't sweat it—you'll have a great time anyway.

PART FOUR

ARRIVING, GETTING YOUR SEA LEGS, *and* DEPARTING

TRANSPORTATION *to* YOUR CRUISE

CHOOSING A DEPARTURE PORT BASED ON TIME AND MONEY

MOST DISNEY CRUISE LINE ITINERARIES depart from two or three different ports at various times of the year. While the differences in quality are relatively small, your departure port is more likely to affect your trip's transportation cost.

If you live within a few hours' drive of one of Disney's ports, your least expensive option is almost certainly going to be using that port. Otherwise, consider flying in the day before you depart to account for flight cancellations.

If you're taking a European cruise and flying in from North America, consider arriving two days before your cruise. This will protect you against most flight cancellations and also give you a bit more time to adjust to the time-zone difference.

As for quality, Disney's Port Canaveral terminal is the nicest in the United States, with easy, ample parking; good directional signage; and a comfortable waiting area. We wouldn't choose a cruise, however, based on the hour or so spent in the terminal. Instead, include the transportation cost to and from the port, plus lodging, in the total cost of the cruises you're considering to see how the overall cost shakes out.

GETTING TO AND FROM THE PORT

MOST NORTH AMERICAN DCL GUESTS have three options when arranging transportation to the cruise terminal: Book transportation through Disney, book through a third-party service, or drive themselves.

This section covers all three options in detail, including driving directions, GPS settings, and terminal parking rates for those taking their own car.

Using Disney Transportation from the Airport or a Disney-Approved Hotel

If you're flying to Orlando, you can use Disney's shuttle service to get to Port Canaveral. The cost is $70, per person, round-trip, free for kids under age 3. You can also use this service in just one direction for $35 per person. DCL recommends that your flight into Orlando arrive by 1:45 p.m. and your flight out depart after 11:30 a.m.

Disney also provides shuttle service from other city airports to its cruise terminals. Round-trip prices in Barcelona, Spain, for instance, are $60–$120 per person, depending on whether you're staying at a hotel the night before and/or the night after your cruise. It's $40–$80 in Miami; $90 in Galveston, Texas; $100 in San Diego; $40 in San Juan, Puerto Rico; $50–$66 in Vancouver, British Columbia (depending on the airport); and $150 in Dover, United Kingdom. See tinyurl .com/dclgroundtransfers for more details.

While Disney's shuttle service is certainly convenient, particularly if you're in an unfamiliar foreign country, a quick reality check is warranted to understand how much of a premium you'll be paying for that convenience. For example, in a particularly egregious example of price gouging, guests staying at the Disney-approved New York Marriott Marquis hotel before the fall 2016 Canadian sailing on the *Magic* were offered transfers to the Manhattan Cruise Terminal for $35 *per person*. For a family of four, this would total $140. The distance from the Marriott Marquis, in Times Square, to the terminal is about a mile—easily walkable for free if you don't have much luggage. (Disney charges the same $35 price for the 60-mile transfer from Walt Disney World hotels to Port Canaveral.) Taxis and ride-share services, plentiful in midtown Manhattan, typically charge less than $15, including a tip, for four people and luggage to drive from Times Square to the terminal.

If you've purchased ground transfers from Disney, you must give them your flight information; you can do this on the DCL website at disneycruiseline.com/plan. Disney provides few details about where to find your ground-transportation driver. Unless you hear otherwise, assume that a uniformed DCL greeter will be stationed near the airport baggage-claim area holding either a DCL sign or a sign with your party's name on it.

Using Disney Transportation from Walt Disney World to Port Canaveral

Disney provides round-trip transfer service between Walt Disney World hotels at a cost of $70 per person, round-trip. One-way service is also available for $35 per person.

LUGGAGE TRANSFER If you're taking a DCL cruise after staying at a Disney-owned resort at Walt Disney World and you've booked transportation from the resort to the ship through Disney, cruise representatives can transfer your luggage from your hotel room to your ship's stateroom.

Contact DCL at least three days before you leave home to take advantage of this service. They'll ask you for the number of bags and tell you when and where to meet for your drive to the ship. They'll also give you instructions on what to do with your bags; typically, you'll simply leave them in your hotel room, with your DCL luggage tags attached, and Disney will transfer them directly to your stateroom.

Surprisingly, you may not find this service as smooth as one might expect from Disney, as this reader reports:

> The staff at Pop Century Resort want nothing to do with helping you get ready for your cruise. When I stopped at the Concierge desk to ask about luggage transfer, they simply gave me a card with the DCL phone number on it and told me to call it myself. When I called the number, I got an automated message telling me what time I would be picked up, but there was no indication of the meeting spot or what to do with our bags. We finally did get printed instructions about the port transfer at 9:30 p.m. We were told to leave our luggage in the room, by the door, with the DCL tags attached no later than 8:30 a.m. and that we should meet in the Pop Century lobby at 12:30 p.m. to check in with the cruise-line staff.
>
> You really do have to be ready on time—cast members were at our door at 8:31 to collect our luggage. Also, the DCL staff was in the Pop lobby at noon; we left as soon as everyone scheduled to be on the bus was there.
>
> One thing to note: If you use Disney transportation to get to Port Canaveral, you don't have any control over what time you get to the port. They tell you where to be and when to be there. So if you want a few more minutes in the parks, you can't leave WDW a bit later, and if you want more time to explore the ship, you can't leave earlier.

Third-Party Shuttle Services

If you have more than four people, it's often less expensive to hire a third-party shuttle service to transport you to your cruise terminal.

GALVESTON SuperShuttle (☎ 800-258-3826; supershuttle.com) offers town-car, SUV, and van-shuttle service between Houston and Galveston. Round-trip costs are $302 for the town car for up to 4 people, $338 for a 10-passenger van, or $338 for a 5-passenger SUV.

PORT CANAVERAL Mears Transportation (☎ 407-423-5566; mears transportation.com) offers private town cars, SUVs, and van shuttles from Orlando to Port Canaveral. Round-trip costs are $270 for up to

3 people in a town car ($90 per person), $360 for up to 5 in an SUV ($72 per person), or $360 for up to 10 in a van ($36 per person). The big advantage to using a third-party service is that you can depart as soon as your group is ready. One-way rates are half of the round-trip figures listed; tips aren't included.

SAN DIEGO If you're flying in for a cruise out of San Diego, **SuperShuttle** (☎ 800-258-3826; supershuttle.com) offers one-way and round-trip transfers from virtually every airport in the region. Cost is about $12 per person between San Diego's airport and port. Check SuperShuttle's website for details; use "San Diego Cruise Ship Terminal" as your destination when you reserve online.

Driving Yourself

This section provides driving directions to Disney's ports in Florida, California, New York, Texas, and Canada, plus information on parking rates at the various cruise terminals.

TO PORT CANAVERAL It takes about an hour to drive from Orlando to Port Canaveral under normal conditions. Traffic and road construction on the Beachline Expressway (FL 528), a toll road, can turn that 60-minute trip into a 3-hour ordeal. And because Port Canaveral and Orlando are linked by only three main roads—with only limited connections between them—there are a couple of points along the Beachline where you have no way of taking an alternate route if traffic is delayed. Our advice is to allow at least 2 hours for this trip or, better yet, 2½ hours. If you get to the port early, Disney's cruise terminal is air-conditioned and comfortable, with enough room for restless kids to run around in while you wait to board.

*un*official **TIP**
Text the location and a photo of your parking spot to other members of your group before you leave the parking facility. This will help you remember where you parked when you return from your cruise.

If you're using a GPS, enter this address as your destination: **Port Canaveral Terminal A, 9155 Charles M. Rowland Drive, Port Canaveral, FL 32920.** Use **Cape Canaveral** if your GPS doesn't recognize Port Canaveral as a city.

If you're not using a GPS, DCL's Planning Center (disneycruiseline .com/plan) has very clear driving directions for getting to Port Canaveral. If you're driving from Walt Disney World, the most direct route uses eastbound FL 536 to the Central Florida GreeneWay (FL 417) and then to the Beachline Expressway. The GreeneWay and Beachline are toll roads, so have $10 in cash available for the round-trip.

You're on the Beachline almost the entire way to Port Canaveral. Once you arrive, the port's terminals function almost exactly like an airport's. The same kinds of signs for airline terminals are posted for cruise-line terminals at Port Canaveral. DCL ships usually depart from

Terminal A, so you'll be looking for road signs to that effect. If you want to see what the drive looks like, the Canaveral Port Authority has an excellent video (complete with catchy reggae soundtrack) that shows what the exits, terminal, and parking options look like from a car passenger's perspective: portcanaveral.com/drive.

Once you arrive at Terminal A, you'll park and walk to the security checkpoint. Parking rates at DCL's Port Canaveral terminal are $64 for three nights, $80 for four nights, and $128 for seven nights. You may also prepay for your parking at the terminal online at portcanaveral.com/cruising/parking.php. There is no discount for booking ahead of time.

TO MIAMI Driving here is a challenge because of the traffic, one-way streets, and constant construction. We recommend using a GPS, preferably one with traffic information, to guide you to the port. Use this address: **Port of Miami, 1015 North America Way, Miami, FL 33132.** DCL recommends turning off your GPS once you've reached the port's bridge, then staying in the left lane and following the signs to the parking garage closest to your terminal.

Like Port Canaveral, Miami has both parking garages and open-air lots. Parking is $20 per day. If the lots closest to your ship are full, drop off some of your family and luggage near the cruise terminal, then swing around and find a spot in one of the other garages—the nearest open garages can be half a mile from the terminal, and there's no reason to have everyone haul their luggage that far.

Miami's ports are supposed to have shuttles running between the parking garages and terminals, but we've never seen them operating. (We *have* seen giant iguanas running around, though, so keep your eyes open.)

Once inside the terminal, you'll be directed to a check-in line. Miami's terminals are older and smaller than Port Canaveral's, but DCL's section is well maintained and efficient. Once checked in, you'll go up a set of escalators and then through a long corridor to board the ship.

TO GALVESTON The port is about 71 miles from Houston's George Bush Intercontinental Airport (IAH), roughly a 90-minute drive with traffic. If you're just dropping off passengers, the address to use for your GPS for Terminal Number 1 is **2502 Harborside Drive, Galveston, TX 77550;** Terminal Number 2 is at **2702 Harborside Drive.** If you're parking, the GPS address for the parking lots is the **intersection of 33rd Street and Harborside Drive.** Valet parking is $20 per day; extended parking ranges from $45 for four days to $100 for two weeks, with a $5 discount if you prepay online at portofgalvestonparking.com.

TO NEW YORK CITY The **Manhattan Cruise Terminal** is located at 711 12th Ave., New York, NY 10019. The closest cross street is West 52nd Street. The port is located about a mile from Times Square. Standard yellow-taxi rates (exclusive of tolls and tips) from area airports are as follows: John F. Kennedy International Airport, $52 flat rate; LaGuardia Airport, $25–$35; Newark International Airport, $80–$100 (negotiate the price with the driver in advance). From the Port Authority Bus Terminal, the fare is $8–$10.

If you're driving, note that all cars enter the cruise terminal from the north at the intersection of West 55th Street and 12th Avenue (New York Route 9A, also known as the Henry Hudson Parkway and the West Side Highway).

• **FROM NEW JERSEY AND POINTS SOUTH** From the Lincoln Tunnel, follow the signs to West 42nd Street, make a left onto 42nd Street, go three blocks, and make a right onto 12th Avenue. Take 12th Avenue for a half-mile and make a left on West 55th Street, which is the entrance to the terminal. From the Holland Tunnel, take Exit 1 (NY 9A). Go through three lights and make a right onto West Street, which is also 12th Avenue (NY 9A). Take West Street/12th Avenue 1 mile and make a left onto West 55th Street, which is the entrance to the terminal.

• **FROM THE GEORGE WASHINGTON BRIDGE, WESTCHESTER COUNTY, AND POINTS NORTH** Go south on the Henry Hudson Parkway (NY 9A) and then exit to the right at West 55th Street, which is the entrance to the terminal.

• **FROM LONG ISLAND VIA THE QUEENS-MIDTOWN TUNNEL** Go west on 34th Street to 12th Avenue. Turn right onto 12th Avenue and continue north to the terminal on West 55th Street.

• **FROM MIDTOWN MANHATTAN** Take West 55th Street across 12th Avenue to the terminal.

Parking is located above each of the piers. To park at the official port lot, drive up the viaduct ramp at 55th Street to the receiving area adjacent to the cruise vessel's berth. Passengers who are parking a car must enter the terminal and park before bringing in bags to the second level for check-in. The daily rate for up to 10 hours (drop-offs and visitors) is $35; parking for 1–10 nights is $40 per night.

With hundreds of other parking lots located within walking or taxi-drop-off distance to the port, it's quite possible to find nearby parking for substantially less than the port's rates. We're fans of the **Best Parking** app (free for iOS and Android). Input your dates and desired location, and the app will direct you to the parking lot with the best pricing. Using Best Parking, we spot-checked the dates of DCL's 2016 New York sailings and were able to find several lots with rates about 20% less than the cruise terminal's parking rate.

The closest New York City–Metropolitan Transit Authority **buses** to the terminal are the **M57-57th Street Cross Town** and the **M31-57th Street/York Avenue.**

The closest subway trains to the terminal are the **A, B, C, D,** and **1** at Columbus Circle. From Columbus Circle, walk south on Eighth

Avenue and turn right onto 52nd Street. Continue down 52nd Street to 12th Avenue and the terminal.

TO SAN DIEGO You will need to park in the Economy Lot on Pacific Highway (**3302 Pacific Highway, San Diego, CA 92101**) at San Diego International Airport, then take a shuttle from the lot to the Port of San Diego. Parking is $13 per day.

TO VANCOUVER The port is about a 30-minute drive from Vancouver's airport: **Cruise Terminal, 999 Canada Place, Vancouver, BC, Canada V6C 3C1.** Traffic in the several blocks surrounding Canada Place can be quite congested on cruise-departure mornings, so budget an extra 20 minutes for the last three blocks of travel if you're planning to arrive at the port during the late morning of your sail date. The cruise terminal has 775 parking spaces, which cost $32 CDN (about $32 US) or $184 CDN ($184 US) per week. Reservations are recommended and can be made online at vinciparkcanadaplace.ca/reserve-a-space.html.

If you're a group of able-bodied adults with a reasonable amount of luggage, the easiest and cheapest way to get from the airport to the cruise terminal is Vancouver's clean and efficient **subway–light rail service.** The one-way trip costs about $9 CDN (about $7 US) and takes about half an hour, with no transfers needed. Visit translink.ca for more information. (Input **YVR** as your start point and **Canada Place** as your end point.)

Adding Air Travel to Your Package? Don't!

While you can purchase airfare through Disney, we don't recommend it—rarely do you save money by doing so, not to mention if you book through Disney, you lose all control of your flight selection—they'll do it for you.

We've been cautioned by both Disney-specialist travel agents and a travel-specialist Disney cast member that DCL air bookers will get you from point A to point B, but they generally won't pay attention to the presence or length of layovers, fine details about departure times, the size of the aircraft, local airport selection, or other particulars that can turn a good trip into a logistical headache.

You also may find that flight refunds are more difficult to obtain if you arrange your air travel through Disney. Book your flight yourself, or use a travel agent who will consider personal factors and logistics as well as pricing.

The **DAY** *Before* **YOUR CRUISE**

STAYING AT A LOCAL HOTEL THE NIGHT BEFORE

YOUR CRUISE WILL START ON TIME, even if you're not on the ship. One way to minimize the chance of that happening is to arrive at the port the day before your cruise and spend the night at a local hotel.

While it adds a night's lodging to your trip's cost and another day to your trip's length, we think the peace of mind you get from knowing you'll make your cruise is worth it.

DCL has relationships with hotels in each of its port cities. You can book your pre- or post-cruise hotel stay through Disney as part of your vacation package, no matter which port you're sailing from. The pros: Disney has vetted the property, so you're unlikely to end up with a real dud, and transportation to/from the port will be seamless if you've also purchased ground transfers. The cons include the limited range of price-point options and a lack of choices at non-mainstream properties—if, say, you've got your heart set on staying at a hip new boutique hotel in Barcelona, you'll likely have to book it on your own rather than through DCL.

If you have Disney book your hotel stay, be prepared to have the process feel somewhat different than if you booked on your own. For example, during a recent Alaskan DCL voyage, we had Disney book our pre-trip hotel stay at the convenient Fairmont Vancouver Airport Hotel. Because we booked through Disney, we got no direct information from the Fairmont, not even a confirmation number. This proved slightly problematic when we called about six weeks before our trip to inquire about the type of room we were in: We learned that Disney doesn't even tell the hotel the names of its guests or their room needs until about two weeks in advance. Rest assured that if you've booked a room through Disney, you'll have one. But for hyper-planners used to having every detail mapped out, the process may feel somewhat unsettling.

If you're driving to your cruise, most hotels near cruise ports offer their guests inexpensive parking and taxi and shuttle transportation to the port; some offer these services to the general public, too. The hotel's parking rates are often substantially less than what you'd pay at the cruise terminal. For example, parking at many Port Canaveral hotels costs less than $10 per day, compared with $18–$21 per day at the terminal.

If You're Cruising out of Port Canaveral

You have the option of spending the night at a hotel in Port Canaveral or Orlando. We've done both, and there are advantages to each. The advantage to staying in Port Canaveral is that you're only a few minutes from the cruise terminal. You can have a relaxed breakfast on the morning of your cruise, take a swim in the pool, and pick up any last-minute items at one of Port Canaveral's grocery stores. The one downside to Port Canaveral is that it doesn't offer as many entertainment options as Orlando, and you may find yourself staying at your hotel for the evening, either watching TV or swimming. While many families find this relaxing, some would prefer to maximize their vacation activities.

Our favorite hotel in Port Canaveral is the **Residence Inn Cape Canaveral Cocoa Beach** (8959 Astronaut Blvd.; ☎ 321-323-1100; tinyurl .com/residenceinncanaveral). This hotel offers studio, one-bedroom, and two-bedroom suites that sleep up to six people, plus a free breakfast buffet and Internet access at reasonable prices. There's no restaurant on-site, but you have plenty of nearby options.

The advantage to staying in Orlando is that you can visit a Disney theme park, Downtown Disney, or Universal Orlando before your trip. You'll have a wide variety of entertainment options and dozens of restaurants from which to choose. Some hotels, including the **Hyatt Regency Orlando International Airport** (9300 Jeff Fuqua Blvd.; ☎ 407-825-1234; orlandoairport.hyatt.com), offer transportation to Port Canaveral for cruise guests. The downside to staying in Orlando is that you'll still need to allow a couple of hours in the morning for the trip to the cruise terminal. See page 68 for more details.

If You're Cruising out of Miami

You'll have many hotel options. We've spent the night before our Miami departures as far away as Orlando. Because there are so many ways to get to the Port of Miami by car, traffic and construction aren't as much of a concern as for Port Canaveral, although driving in a city as large as Miami has its own challenges (see page 69). And unlike hotels in Port Canaveral, most in Miami charge about as much for parking—around $15 per day—as does the Port of Miami (around $20), so there's little benefit to parking off-site.

The **Holiday Inn Port of Miami–Downtown** (340 Biscayne Blvd.; ☎ 305-371-4400; tinyurl.com/hiportofmiami) sits within a mile of the port, with plenty of restaurants, shopping, and activities a short walk or drive away, plus an on-site fitness center and high-speed wireless Internet. Its one weakness is the small number of on-site parking spaces: If one isn't available, you'll have to find space at a nearby pay-parking lot and walk back. The **Courtyard by Marriott Miami Downtown** (200 SE Second Ave.; ☎ 305-374-3000; miamicourtyard.com) is another moderately priced hotel. Renovated at the end of 2012, the Courtyard is near restaurants, shopping, and other activities; has an on-site gym; and offers high-speed wireless Internet.

If You're Cruising out of New York

There are more than 1,500 hotels in New York City, plus many more in the surrounding area. They range from flophouses to palatial luxury accommodations and everything in between. If you're looking for moderately priced digs in Midtown Manhattan, a couple of reliable choices include **The Row NYC** (700 Eighth Ave.; ☎ 888-352-3650; rownyc .com/the-hotel), which is also home to the wonderful **City Kitchen** food court (citykitchen.rownyc.com), and the **Hampton Inn Manhattan–Times**

Square North (851 Eighth Ave.; ☎ 212-581-4100). If you have Starwood hotel points, the **Sheraton New York Times Square Hotel** (811 Seventh Ave.; ☎ 212-581-1000; sheratonnewyork.com) is typically the most economical use of your points in Midtown.

If You're Cruising out of Galveston

Wyndham offers two upscale choices, both of which we like: The **Hotel Galvez & Spa** (2024 Seawall Blvd.; ☎ 409-765-7721; hotelgalvez.com) is a century-old beachside hotel with modern rooms, a spa, heated pool, and free shuttle service to the port and Galveston's Strand Historic District, both less than 2 miles away. Rates are as low as $130 per night during the off-season. **The Tremont House,** in the Strand, is only a few blocks from the port (2300 Ship's Mechanic Row; ☎ 409-763-0300; thetremonthouse.com). Like the Galvez, the Tremont House is modern and luxurious; while it doesn't have a pool or spa, its location near downtown is better for people who want to explore the area on foot. Rates are less than $200 per night most of the year.

If You're Cruising out of San Diego

You're in luck—it's possible to stay at a Disneyland hotel before your trip! Disneyland is typically less than 3 hours (with traffic) from the San Diego port terminal. The **Disneyland Hotel** (1150 Magic Way, Anaheim; ☎ 714-778-6600; disneyland.disney.go.com/disneyland-hotel) is our favorite Disney-run hotel on-property, while **Disney's Paradise Pier Hotel** (1717 S. Disneyland Drive; ☎ 714-999-0990; disneyland.disney.go .com/paradise-pier-hotel is usually the least expensive. **Disney's Grand Californian Hotel & Spa** (1600 S. Disneyland Drive; ☎ 714-635-2300; disneyland.disney.go.com/grand-californian-hotel) has the advantage of being adjacent to Disney California Adventure, making it an easy walk if you'd like to enjoy DCA's Cars Land during the evening.

In addition to Disney's hotels, many good off-site hotels are situated around the park. One of the most popular is the **Howard Johnson Anaheim** (1380 S. Harbor Blvd.; ☎ 714-776-6120; hojoanaheim.com), across the street from Disneyland and a shorter walk to Disneyland's entrance than Disney's own Paradise Pier Hotel.

If You're Cruising out of Vancouver

The **Pan Pacific Vancouver** (999 Canada Place, Suite 300; ☎ 604-662-8111; panpacificvancouver.com) is located at Vancouver's port. It's posh and pricey, with rates between $400 and $500 US per night. Also pricey—and fabulous!—is the **Shangri-La Vancouver** (1128 W. Georgia St.; ☎ 604-689-1120; shangri-la.com/vancouver), with spectacular views of the ocean and mountains, huge marble bathrooms, and friendly staff. A more economical option is the **Metropolitan Hotel Vancouver**

SCOTT SAYS   *by Scott Sanders*

BABY, YOU'VE ARRIVED!

IF YOU'RE NOT DRIVING YOURSELF TO THE PORT, arrange your pre- and post-cruise transportation yourself in advance. Also, while it adds to the cost of your trip, arriving the day before your cruise creates a safety buffer in the event of transportation delays like a delayed flight.

When it's time to go to the port, assign a point person for your party to be in charge of the check-in documents and government-issued IDs. The check-in process is much quicker if you have all your documents signed and ready to present.

Need to change a dinner seating or you don't like your assigned rotation? Check the *Personal Navigator* and arrive at the designated location before the listed time to increase your chances of having your change request granted. This is also the time to make reservations at Palo and Remy if you didn't do so previously online, or if you want to make additional reservations.

Before the end of your first day on the ship, sign-up for the free 50MB Internet package even if you don't intend to use it. At the very least, you'll have it case you need to get online or check in at home.

(645 Howe St.; ☎ 604-687-1122; metropolitan.com/vanc), with rates around $200 US per night.

Vancouver is a worthwhile destination in its own right, combining global sophistication and Canadian charm. The city is easily accessible by foot, taxi, and transit. Cruisers in search of international cuisine should make a point to sample the city's Asian specialties, from sushi to Indian to dim sum. For upscale dining, stick close to the downtown core around **Robson Street** and the cruise terminal. For an authentic experience, head to Vancouver's **Chinatown** (vancouver-chinatown.com), one of the largest in North America. If you're looking for something unique, try a Japanese-style hot dog sold from a food cart. It's Tokyo meets New York meets your belly.

Another must-stop for foodies is the **Granville Island Market.** We've found everything from fresh mangosteens to maple-glazed walnuts here, as well as prepared foods like salmon potpie and gooseberry tarts. Disney geeks will want to keep an eye out for the Dole Whip vendor.

Fashionistas will love hitting the high-end designer shops (**Chanel, Hermès, Louis Vuitton,** and the like), while shoppers looking for a Canadian experience should head to **Roots** (1001 Robson St.; ☎ 604-683-4305; canada.roots.com) or **Hudson's Bay Company** (674 Granville St.; ☎ 604-681-6211; thebay.com), home of the eponymous blankets. Fans of food souvenirs can pick up maple treats, British sweets and biscuits, and ketchup-flavored crisps all over the city.

If you arrive in the afternoon, walk to **Stanley Park,** along the waterfront, to see the beautiful Canadian Rockies in the distance (vancouver .ca/parks-recreation-culture/stanley-park.aspx). Or check out **Gastown** (gastown.org) and its steam-powered clock. For nightlife, check ahead before your arrival for live theater, musical concerts, or any festivals that are happening during your stay. A few good websites to try are tourismvancouver.com, hellobc.com /vancouver, and timeout.com/vancouver.

unofficial **TIP**
If you're planning to return home via the Vancouver airport, be aware that you can't check in earlier than 3 hours before your flight or later than 1 hour before for international flights—you must check in *exactly* 1-3 hours before your departure. Timing is critical.

If you're a Disney-theme-park nut, you won't want to miss the **FlyOver Canada** attraction (flyovercanada.com) located at Canada Place, adjacent to the cruise terminal. The experience is nearly identical to Soarin' at Epcot and Disney California Adventure, only with footage of Canada rather than international points of interest. It ain't cheap—about $20 CND for adults (age 18+), $18 CND for seniors (age 65+) and youth (ages 13–17), and $15 CND for kids age 12 and younger for a 10-ish minute ride—but it may be worth it to see the similarity to Soarin', even in the preshow safety video.

GET *in the* BOAT, MEN
(and Women and Kids)!

CHOOSING A BOARDING TIME

YOU'LL BE ABLE TO CHECK IN at least 75 days in advance using DCL's online **Planning Center** (see page 35). This offers you a chance to verify information, ensure that you have the right credit card on file, and so on. You'll also be able to choose your boarding window—the time when you provide Disney your travel documents and board the ship.

The earliest boarding windows are usually around 10:30 a.m. We recommend choosing as early a board time as you can, or after 1:30 p.m. Here are the pros and cons to both approaches:

Early Boarding Time

PROS An uncrowded ship. You'll find smaller crowds at the pools and buffet, and you'll be among the first in line for coveted character meet-and-greet tickets, as well as last-minute spa, restaurant, or port-adventure availability.

CONS Most staterooms don't open to guests until at least 1:30 p.m. This means you'll be carrying everything you brought on board with you until you're able to enter your room. Guests with lots of camera equipment or big laptops may find this inconvenient.

Later Boarding Time

PROS The ability to sleep later on your boarding day and the ability to access your stateroom as soon as you board the ship. If you have kids who require an afternoon nap, this may be your best option.

CONS The ship is already full of people, including lines for the pools and food. Moreover, the elevators off the atrium tend to be packed with folks and their luggage trying to get to their rooms. Guests who arrive at the ship late may be locked out of some spa, restaurant, or character-greeting reservations.

CHECKING IN AT THE TERMINAL

HAVE YOUR CRUISE DOCUMENTS and government-issued ID ready as soon as you get out of the car. Many terminals, including Port Canaveral, have an initial security checkpoint outside the perimeter to ensure that only ticketed passengers enter.

Once you're past that checkpoint, you'll undergo another round of security screening just inside the terminal's entrance. You'll pass through a metal detector, and your luggage will undergo X-ray scanning. If you have bags too large to get through the security screening, use the porters at the terminal.

Disney's cruise terminals, especially those at Port Canaveral and Vancouver, are spacious, clean, and comfortable. (Miami's is a little smaller than the others, and Barcelona's offers Spain's finest folding chairs for you to sit in while you wait.) If you have to wait a few minutes for your group to be called, you'll find enough seating for your family to sit down and relax. Vending machines and bathrooms are available, and Disney provides everything from character greetings to ship models to maps on the floor to keep your kids occupied.

If you haven't already received this by e-mail, once in the terminal look for cast members handing out a mandatory (but mercifully short) health questionnaire. This questionnaire asks if anyone in your travel party is currently suffering from fever or has experienced vomiting or diarrhea in the previous three days. You'll also be asked questions about recent travel to any West African countries or contact with

Ebola patients. Answering "yes" to any of the questions means you may be denied boarding, so be sure everyone you're traveling with is in good health.

Head for the check-in desk and have your signed cruise documents, health questionnaire, and IDs ready. (All guests must check in whether they've cruised with DCL before or not.) Concierge has a dedicated check-in desk, and returning DCL guests can use a separate line for its Castaway Club (though given the number of return cruisers DCL sees, it's not always as fast as you'd think).

The check-in desk is where you'll receive your cabin number (if you don't already have one) and get issued your magnetic-stripe Key to the World stateroom cards. Disney will also take your photo, which will be used for identification purposes when you exit and enter the ship.

The check-in desk also will issue your party a boarding number, usually 1–30. Rather than have everyone try to board the ship at once, Disney organizes passengers into boarding groups of about 25–30 families at a time. Loudspeakers announce every few minutes which group numbers are currently allowed to board.

If you've not yet done so, you'll have an opportunity in the cruise terminal to sign up your children for the kids' clubs before boarding. A good time to do that is while you're waiting for your boarding group to be announced.

Your Key to the World Card Explained

This card contains helpful information about your cruise.

Your dining schedule will be printed on your card as a series of letters. One letter will be shown for each night of your cruise. In the example above, the seven-letter code **RAERAER** indicates that this is a seven-night cruise. Each letter in the series also represents the first

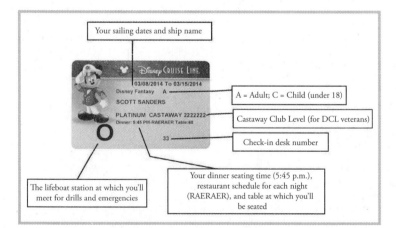

letter of the name of one of the ship's standard restaurants. In the example above, **R** is the *Fantasy*'s Royal Court, **A** is for Animator's Palate, and **E** signifies Enchanted Garden.

Finally, your Key to the World card also shows your transfer information, if you booked transportation through Disney to or from the port.

BOARDING THE SHIP

YOU CAN BOARD THE SHIP anytime after your boarding number is called. Have your room keys out, because they're scanned whenever you come on and off the ship.

Just before you enter the ship, photographers will offer to take a photo of your party. If this is important to you, a quick mirror check in the restroom and dressing in something you'd like recorded for posterity is a good idea. If you don't care to be photographed, breeze on past the people getting photos; they're certainly not mandatory, and lines can back up.

As you step on board, a cast member will ask your family name. Why they do this when so many parties traveling together don't necessarily have the same last name, we don't know. Either give your first names (Thurston and Lovey are our favorites) or make up a portmanteau combining your last names—no one is checking your ID—or just give any old name. What doesn't work is saying you'd rather not, and it's easiest to just board as the Howells if you'd rather not announce your presence. (We all know how the paparazzi are.)

YOUR FIRST AFTERNOON ABOARD

IF YOU DIDN'T GET A *Personal Navigator* handout (see page 81) in the terminal, pick one up at Guest Relations while you're still on Deck 3. This is also a good time to do any last-minute reservations or change your dining rotation or seating time. If this isn't your first Disney cruise and you're already familiar with the ship, you may choose to split up your group to do these tasks and meet up after you're done. It will save you time running around the ship.

Our first stop is usually Senses Spa to book its Rainforest Room. It has even more limited availability than adult dining or a beach cabana, and you can't book it ahead of time.

Next, check for any last-minute openings at Palo or Remy if you wish to dine there and haven't booked yet. The location for this check-in desk will be noted in your *Personal Navigator.*

Disney has been tinkering with procedures for character meeting experiences. On some sailings, a subset of character greetings have been available to book prior to sailing (see Planning Center info on page 35). Other recent cruises have offered special ticketed character-greeting appointments to meet Frozen characters Anna and Elsa (and sometimes Olaf); Marvel superheroes such as Captain America, Thor, and Spider-Man; or a cadre of Disney princesses. The greetings are free, but if you want to meet these select characters, you'll likely need a ticket to do so. Tickets are typically available for only a few hours on arrival day, so check your printed *Personal Navigator* for the distribution time and location. Please be aware that ticket distribution is not usually noted on the *Navigator* app.

If it's after 1:30 p.m., you can head to your room and drop any bags you carried on. You may also see your room attendant already sprucing up your cabin for the evening.

In the afternoon, people will start to swarm the Cabanas buffet as if they've never seen food before. A nearly identical buffet is usually served in Enchanted Garden on the *Dream* and *Fantasy,* Carioca's on the *Magic,* and Tiana's Place on the *Wonder* (you'll also find far fewer people at all three restaurants). If all you're looking for is a quick bite to eat and you're all over age 18, try the quick-service Vista Café or Cove Café. We love Cabanas, but there's no shortage of food on the ship, and you've already spent enough of your day in lines.

If you're sailing from a warm-weather location, the pool deck will be full of folks swimming and lounging. And when we say "full," we mean hectic to chaotic. If you want to relax, don't go there. But do pick up a drink at the beverage station to stay hydrated.

The chaos comes to a head with the **Sail-Away Celebration,** the kind you've seen memorialized in reruns of *The Love Boat,* with Champagne toasts, confetti, and Gavin MacLeod in short shorts. It's kind of fun and a nice way to start your cruise, but it's not a must-do for us.

THE LIFEBOAT DRILL

THIS IS USUALLY HELD around 4 p.m. before the ship leaves port. Every member of your group will need to be present, and you'll need to bring your stateroom keys to the drill; attendance is tracked by computer, which reads your room key to validate your presence.

Many years ago, guests were required to wear their life vests to the drill. This is no longer the case, but it makes sense to do a quick check of your stateroom closet to make sure that it contains the appropriate number and size flotation devices for your party. If you don't have the proper life vests, address this with your stateroom attendant as soon as possible.

The lifeboat drill is the last mandatory activity for the day. If you're down for an early dinner seating, it will soon be time to dress for dinner. If not, you may choose to attend the first evening show. And with that, your afternoon is done, things calm down, and you can finally relax and start your vacation.

▐▌ BARE NECESSITIES

THE *PERSONAL NAVIGATOR*

YOU'LL BE GIVEN THIS HANDOUT, shown on the next two pages, when you board the ship. The *Personal Navigator* is a daily guide to the ship's activities and events, including times, locations, shop and restaurant hours, and more. You'll receive a new one every night for the following day; extra copies are available at Guest Services and from your stateroom attendant by request.

The format is roughly the same each day. Page 1 usually shows the date, ship's location, and sunrise–sunset times. If the ship is in port, the *Navigator* will list the time you need to be back on the ship ("All Aboard") and the ship's departure time. Also listed are the times and locations for the evening's entertainment; important announcements; games, shows, and events, including times and locations; and the dinner-menu theme and "Drink of the Day."

Page 3 holds the ship's schedule for every hour of the day, separated into three sections: The top section holds the morning's activities, usually running from 8:30 a.m. until 1:30 p.m.; the middle section contains afternoon activities, from 1:45 p.m. until around 6:45 p.m.; and the bottom section lists the evening's events, from about 7 p.m. to midnight.

Each section is separated into approximately 10 rows of activities, and each row generally corresponds to an age group, location, or event. For example, you'll see rows for special events at the pool, character greetings, movies, family activities, and stuff for adults, plus the schedule for the Vibe, Edge, and Oceaneer Club/Lab kids' activities.

Page 4 has in-depth information about the daily activities described on page 3. Page 5 lists the ship's restaurant, store, and service-desk hours, plus mealtimes. Other services, such as onboard airline check-in, are also listed here. Finally, any open space on this page is usually filled with shopping advertisements.

DISNEY CRUISE LINE NAVIGATOR APP Yes, there's an app for that! Available free at the Apple App Store and Google Play, it works through the ships' onboard Wi-Fi, so you can keep your device in airplane mode while using it. *Note:* You will not be charged for Wi-Fi if you're using it only with the Navigator app.

There are six main categories of app function: Dining Information (including menus); Deck Plans (maps of the ship); the hours of the various ship services (shops, gym, and so on); Activity Schedules; Debarkation Information (what you need to do at the end of your vacation); and our favorite feature, Onboard Chat.

Onboard Chat allows you to text other passengers on the ship at no charge; there are even DCL-specific emojis of Disney, Marvel, and

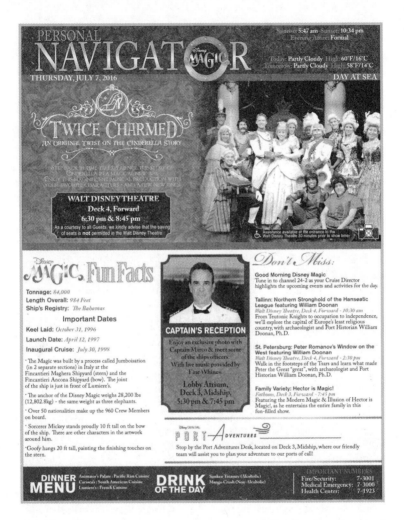

Star Wars characters to spice up your messages. Previously, guests had a version of Onboard Chat on the Wave Phones provided in the DCL cabins. But the app functionality is far superior—it makes communicating with family and friends on the ship as easy and intuitive as it is back at home. Here's why:

- It uses a device—your phone or tablet—that you're already familiar with.
- You'll likely have your phone with you for use as a camera anyway. There's no need to remember to bring a different piece of electronics like the Wave Phone.

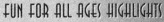

ADULT ACTIVITY HIGHLIGHTS

SENSES SPA FITNESS CLASSES & SEMINARS

Wake Up & Stretch Class - Senses Fitness Center - 7:00 am
Ship Shape Boot Camp (Nom. Fee) - Senses Fitness Center - 7:30 am
Fab Abs - Senses Fitness Center - 8:00 am
Yoga on the Beach - Serenity Bay - 10:30 am
Good Feet: Improving Posture - Senses Fitness Center - 2:00 pm
Pure Form Pilates - Senses Fitness Center - 3:00 pm
Seminar: Chinese Herbal Remedies - Senses Spa & Salon - 4:00 pm
Eat More to Weigh Less - Senses Spa & Salon - 4:30 pm

TASTING CLASSES

Beer Tasting (21+) - Pub 687 - 3:30 pm
Champagne Tasting (21+) - Pink, Wine and Champagne Bar - 4:00 pm
Please make reservations for tastings at Guest Services for a nominal fee.
Tasting Seminars are only for Guests 21 and older.

1820 SOCIETY: ISLAND BIKE RIDE
Bike Rentals, Disney Castaway Cay - 10:45 am
Join your Cruise Staff team as they take you on a bike riding adventure around the island. Meet at the Bike Rentals where the fun will begin!

1820 SOCIETY: BASKETBALL FREE THROW
In Da Shade Game Pavilion, Disney Castaway Cay - 1:00 pm
Join your Cruise Staff in this fun tournament and see how many you can sink in 30 seconds!

1820 SOCIETY: MINI GOLF
Goofy Golf, Deck 13, Aft - 3:00 pm
Can you get a hole in one? Give it a try with some mini golf.

1820 SOCIETY: FAREWELL
Evolution, Deck 4, Aft - 9:45 pm
Join your Cruise Staff and your new friends in this last gathering for some fun.

MAKING OF THE DREAM
Evolution, Deck 4, Aft - 3:00 pm
Explore the origins of Disney Cruise Line and the latest and greatest innovations conjured especially for the Disney Dream in this fascinating and entertaining behind-the-scenes program.

DREAM QUEST
Evolution, Deck 4, Aft - 10:15 pm
Enjoy the wildest and wackiest scavenger team event on the seven seas!

FUN FOR ALL AGES HIGHLIGHTS

FAMILY MOVIE FUN TIME: ZOOTOPIA - (PG)

Buena Vista Theatre, Deck 4 & 5, Midship - 8:30 am
Come join us for a special opportunity to enjoy Zootopia in the Buena Vista Theatre. We will leave some lights on and turn the volume down as audience members are welcome to talk, leave their seats, move about and (most importantly) have fun!

CASTAWAY CAY 5K (10+)
Evolution, Deck 4, Aft - 8:00 am
Runners (10+) meet together on the ship. We will depart the ship shortly thereafter, and make our way to the Bike Rentals where the run will begin. Photo ID required for Guests 18 years and older.

WAKE UP WITH DISNEY JUNIOR

D Lounge, Deck 4, Midship - 8:30 am
What happens when you experience unlimited fun with your favorite Disney Junior shows? You get an exciting dance party designed especially for preschoolers ages seven and under.

FAMILY WHALE DIG
Monstro Point, Disney Castaway Cay - 1:15 pm
Our island paleontologist leads us in the excavation of a giant whale skeleton and other fossilized treasures! Make no bones about it, this is an adventure every beachcomber is sure to dig!

DISNEY ANIMATION: CREATING A CHARACTER

D Lounge, Deck 4, Midship - 2:45 pm
Go behind the scenes at Walt Disney Animation Studios as Walt Disney himself talks about his most famous characters, then learn the basic techniques of drawing your favorite pals in this fun and interesting enrichment program.

CHIP-IT GOLF (12+)

Lobby Atrium, Deck 3, Midship - 3:00 pm
It's par for the course for our Guests 12 and older to compete on our special "greens" in this fun tournament.

DISNEY VACATION CLUB GROUP PREVIEW
D Lounge, Deck 4, Midship - 4:30 pm
Want to learn more about taking magical vacations year after year? Please see a Disney Vacation Club representative on Deck 4, Midship, or call 7-2805 from your stateroom phone for more information about our interactive group presentation.

$10,000 FINAL MEGA JACKPOT BINGO
Bingo Pre-Sales start at 4:00 pm
Evolution, Deck 4, Aft - 4:30 pm
It's Big, it's Massive, it's Supersized! It's $10,000 MEGA Jackpot Bingo! Take home $10,000 if you can cover your card in 46 numbers or less. If not, we carry on to play for the biggest cash prize of the session! Plus, the Snowball Jackpot must be won at this final game of bingo! Pre-Sales start 30 minutes prior to game.

FAMILY SUPERSTAR KARAOKE
D Lounge, Deck 4, Midship - 10:45 pm
Join your Cruise Staff in D Lounge tonight and sing along to your favorite song - fun for everyone.

- You can chat with every phone owner in your party, even if they're not together.
- You can easily share your chat information and interact with other guests you meet on the ship, if you want to.
- Parents can configure children's access to the chat function to meet their own specifications, allowing the level of access that's comfortable for each family.

The app also shows you the complete menus for every restaurant on the ship, usually several days in advance. Of course, you can always wait until they hand you the menu at the restaurant to see what your dining options are, but there may be some instances when knowing the menu in advance, or knowing what's being served in a different restaurant, can be very helpful.

- If the evening menu is particularly appealing (or unappealing), you can adjust your eating for the rest of the day accordingly.

- If you have a particularly picky child in your party, you can plan in advance whether to dine at Cabanas, try room service, or have the child eat in the kids' club.

- If you see a favorite dish on the main-dining-room menu for a night that you have a reservation at Palo, you can try to modify your Palo reservation for a different evening.

- If you see something particularly appealing on the menu of a different dining room, you can ask to have it brought to you at your meal. (Yes, you can order anything served at any of the three main dining rooms—not just the one you're assigned to.)

The onboard-activities section of the app includes information about activities the print version doesn't have room to include. For example, with the Cartoon Physics activity, the printed *Navigator* lists just "Cartoon Physics Class," but the app includes a description of the class and a listing of alternative times for the same activity at other points in the sailing. This is particularly helpful with the kids' club activities, which tend to be labeled with inscrutable names on the print *Navigator*.

Other nice features of the app are the ability to set alarms to remind you when favorite activities are starting and real-time updates to the ship's schedule.

INTERNET

FOR MANY OF US, being offline for the duration of a cruise is simply not an option. The good news is that DCL ships offer **Connect@Sea** Internet packages in a variety of sizes that will meet most people's needs. Here are the packages offered and our recommendations:

PLAN	DATA (MB)	COST	NOTES
Pay as You Go	1	25¢	Use if you have a one-off need to check or send e-mail
Small	100	$19 (19¢/MB)	For guests who need to check e-mail from time to time but don't need to web-surf during their cruise
Medium	300	$39 (13¢/MB)	For guests who wish to use social media to let their friends know how much fun they're having on board
Large	1,000	$89 (9¢/MB)	For guests who are unable to leave their work at home or who wish to stream music. (Video is another story— most movies take up more than the 1GB allowance, and an HD movie can take up to four times this much. *Our advice:* Don't waste your time.)

So how well does it work? For the most part, we've been happy enough. However, it's not perfect, and at times we've found ourselves with either no connectivity or speeds so slow that there may as well have been no connection. Still, it's probably cheaper than ordering an onboard data package through your wireless carrier.

Here's what we've learned along the way:

1. Update your apps and download any other content (movies, etc.) before you're on the ship. To do otherwise is a waste of your time and money.

2. The first day of your cruise (and only the first day), you'll be offered 50MB of free Internet. Every person in your cabin age 18 or older may sign up for this. Use this until you need more.

3. Download the latest version of the **DCL Navigator** app (see page 81) before you're on the ship. **DCL Wi-Fi is free for use with this app.**

4. Don't bother trying to stream video content—it just won't work. It's probably not enough to be usable for Wi-Fi calling either.

5. The system will throttle your usage if you use too much bandwidth at once. This affects everyone who is using your package, not just the computer with too many connections.

6. If you have a business-critical need for e-mail, put an auto-responder on your account so people will know there may be a delay in replies. (You may or may not choose to state that the reason is that you're off having a great time on a cruise.)

7. If you have multiple e-mail accounts, turn off syncing on the ones that tend to get a lot of junk mail.

8. If you use Apple's iMessage, you can also use it on the ship for quick texts back to land (to other iMessage users).

9. The more remote the ship's location, the worse your Internet connection is likely to be. Service is usually good in the Caribbean, where you're never too far from pockets of civilization. During a Northern European voyage that included a long day at sea from Iceland to Scotland, service was nonexistent.

8. If you don't want to bring your own laptop or smart device while traveling, there are a few public areas on board where you can use DCL-provided computers to access the Internet (with a package). These include **Cove Café,** an adults-only lounge on all four ships; **Vista Café,** a family café on the Dream and Fantasy, and the **Promenade Internet Café** on the Wonder.

The Connect@Sea help desk on each ship should have a printout of helpful tips to bring your extraneous data consumption down to the bare minimum. The instructions are slightly different depending on whether you have an Apple or Android device, but in general the steps you'll want to take include the following:

- Turning off location services
- Turning off background app refreshes

- Turning off music and app updates
- Turning off e-mail sync
- Turning off cloud backups of data and photos
- Disabling automatic video plays on social media

ONBOARD SERVICES

A 24-HOUR GUEST SERVICES DESK is just off the lobby on each ship to answer questions, make reservations, and provide other help. You can also contact Guest Services from your stateroom by touching the Guest Services button on your phone.

The best amenity that comes with your stateroom is likely to be your stateroom attendant, who will tidy up your cabin after you depart in the morning, deliver your *Personal Navigator,* and turn down your beds each night. You'll almost certainly see him or her more than any other crew member, and you'll be amazed at how little sleep these hardworking staff seem to need.

Given the nature of a cruise, you'll find that your stateroom attendant is in and out of your room much more often than a typical hotel housekeeper would be. This makes it particularly important to make ample use of your DO NOT DISTURB sign if you plan to sleep late, take an afternoon nap, or otherwise just don't want to be bothered for a while.

AIRLINE CHECK-IN FOR SAILINGS ENDING AT PORT CANAVERAL

EVEN BEFORE YOU BOARD THE SHIP, you can request airline check-in for your flight home by making arrangements at your terminal's check-in desk. To do this, have the airline name, flight number(s), departure time and date, names of passengers as printed on their ticket(s), and the flight confirmation number(s) for each flight segment.

While on board, you can ask Guest Services to check you in to your flight if you're flying home the day your cruise returns to port. Stop by the Guest Services desk before 10 p.m. on your second night to make this request. This service is available to anyone flying out of Orlando International Airport on domestic flights (including the US Virgin Islands and Puerto Rico) on AirTran Airways, Alaska Airlines, American Airlines, Delta Air Lines, JetBlue Airways, United Airlines, and US Airways.

No matter when you register, your first flight's departure must be after 11:30 a.m. on the day your cruise ends, to ensure the ship has enough time to make it back. There's a limit of two bags per person, and each bag must weigh less than 50 pounds. (According to Disney, a few randomly selected passengers may be required to undergo additional screening at the airport, and thus are ineligible for early check-in.)

The day before your cruise ends, you'll receive printed instructions in your stateroom, along with your boarding passes and temporary luggage tags. Affix the tags to your bags and leave them in the hallway outside your stateroom between 8:30 and 10:30 p.m. The next time you see your bags will be on the baggage carousel at your destination airport. This makes for easy maneuvering at Orlando International (the airport for most DCL guests) because you simply proceed directly to the security line and on to your gate. Your airline's baggage fee will be added to your DCL bill and will appear on your checkout statement.

LAUNDRY SERVICES

SELF-SERVICE LAUNDRY FACILITIES are available on several decks on each ship, furnished with washers, dryers, and detergent for purchase. It costs around $2 to wash a load of clothes and another $2 to dry them; detergent is another $1 per load.

You're likely to find the ships' laundry rooms sparsely used during three- and four-night sailings originating in the United States. Competition for washers and dryers can reach Hunger Games intensity on long European voyages where guests with substantial pre- and post-cruise travel use the machines on board as a way to keep their packing manageable. You'll find laundry rooms less crowded on non-sea-days, after 11:00 p.m., or before 7 a.m.

In addition to do-it-yourself laundry, each ship offers full-service laundry and dry cleaning on board, with pickup from and delivery to your stateroom. Simply drop your clothes in the dry-cleaning bag hanging inside your closet and complete the attached paper form with any cleaning instructions. The laundry service usually takes 24 hours, but we've had simple requests—laundering and ironing a couple of shirts—done on the same day.

PORT ADVENTURES

IN ADDITION TO GUEST SERVICES, a separate Port Adventures desk on Deck 3 (*Magic* and *Wonder*) or Deck 5 (*Dream* and *Fantasy*) handles booking for shore excursions. The staff are usually knowledgeable about the most popular excursions at each port. In addition to providing information about cost and time, they can typically answer questions regarding the appropriateness of a particular activity for the members of your family. They also can help you reschedule an activity if needed. (See Part Eleven for details.)

HEALTH SERVICES

EACH SHIP'S HEALTH CENTER employs a third-party doctor and nurse for medical issues. The most common reasons for visiting the Health Center are motion sickness, sunburn, and nausea, although the staff have seen their share of broken bones over the years. The Health

Center (Deck 1 Forward; open 9:30–11 a.m. and 4:30–7 p.m.) can provide doses of basic over-the-counter and some prescription medicines; anything serious, such as surgery, will probably require an airlift to the nearest hospital. Also, note that use of the Health Center isn't free, and rates are comparable to those of US hospitals—in other words, expensive—so check your insurance coverage before you leave home (see page 43 for more on that). However, just like the First Aid Centers in the Disney parks, Health Services will often provide you with a dose or two of over-the-counter medicine, such as aspirin or motion-sickness tablets, for free. The Guest Services desk also has a supply of basic over-the-counter medicines and first aid. If you just need Tylenol or a Band-Aid, that's a good first place to start.

SHIP-TO-SHORE CALLS

IF YOU DON'T HAVE A CELL PHONE or you don't want to use it on the ship, you can use your stateroom phone to make and receive off-ship calls. Friends and family can reach you by calling ☎ 888-322-8732 in the US or ☎ 732-335-3281 internationally; they'll need to know which ship you're sailing on and your stateroom number. Rates run about $7 per minute, so consider this an emergency-only option.

TRANSFERS TO WALT DISNEY WORLD HOTELS

DISNEY HAS RECENTLY BEGUN TINKERING with ship-departure procedures for guests who have purchased transfers from the ship to a Walt Disney World resort hotel. In years past, buses started running to Disney World as soon as the ship cleared customs, usually around 7 or 7:30 a.m. More recently, Disney hasn't begun running its port-transfer buses from Port Canaveral to Disney World until 9 a.m. If you're an early riser, this can feel like a lot of unnecessary waiting around.

We recently used Disney's transfer from Port Canaveral to Disney's Wilderness Lodge resort. Our bus didn't leave the port until about 9:30 a.m. and made several stops at other hotels before ours, so we didn't get to our resort until after 11:30 and didn't get to the Magic Kingdom until well after noon. Had we scheduled our own transportation, we could have been picked up at 7:30 a.m. and been driven directly to our hotel, putting us at the Magic Kingdom much closer to 10 a.m. When time is tight, 2 extra hours in the theme parks can be a major asset. Next time we'll arrange a town car.

TIPPING

YOU'LL ENCOUNTER CREW MEMBERS throughout your cruise, many of whom you'll see several times per day and who will have a direct impact on the quality of your trip. It's customary to give a small tip to these crew members in recognition of their service. The chart below indicates the suggested tip for these staff for each person in your cabin. Thus, if you have four people in your family and you're taking a seven-night cruise, budget $336 ($84 times four) for the personnel shown, plus any spa, bar, or other dining gratuities you anticipate.

STAFF MEMBER	SUGGESTED GRATUITY PER DAY	SUGGESTED GRATUITY 3 NIGHTS	SUGGESTED GRATUITY 4 NIGHTS	SUGGESTED GRATUITY 7 NIGHTS
Stateroom Attendant	$4	$12	$16	$28
Dining Room Server	$4	$12	$16	$28
Dining Room Assistant Server	$3	$9	$12	$21
Dining Room Head Server	$1	$3	$4	$7
TOTAL (Per Guest)	$12	$36	$48	$84

These suggested gratuity amounts are automatically added to your stateroom account based on the number of people in your cabin and your cruise length. Once on board, you can adjust these amounts or pay in cash by visiting the Guest Services desk (open 24 hours a day) on Deck 3. Lines at Guest Services get long on the last night of your cruise, so plan to make any adjustments sooner rather than later if you wish to avoid a wait. If it makes your budgeting process easier, you're welcome to prepay many of your gratuities weeks or months before boarding the ship. Call Disney Cruise Line or your travel agent to arrange this.

At Palo and Remy, a gratuity is automatically added only for alcohol; an additional gratuity for dining service is left to your discretion. It's also customary to add a gratuity for room service, again at your discretion. Finally, note that an automatic 15% gratuity is added to Cove Café and bar tabs, plus any alcohol ordered elsewhere on deck.

CHECKOUT *and* DEPARTURE

YOUR LAST NIGHT ON THE SHIP

YOU'LL RECEIVE DEBARKATION INFORMATION—including what to do with your luggage, where you'll be eating breakfast, and when you need to be off the ship—the night before your last night on board (for example night six of a seven-night cruise). This information is also available at Guest Services the last night of the cruise.

unofficial **TIP**
You'll need your **Key to the World** cards to exit the ship, so keep them handy until you're back on land.

Packing

If you haven't already arranged onboard airline check-in, you'll receive luggage tags in your stateroom on your last evening aboard, along with instructions for getting breakfast before departing in the morning and gratuity envelopes. Use the luggage tags if you'd like Disney to transport your bags from the ship to the port terminal upon docking. (This enables you to walk off the ship without having to carry bags; you'll pick up your luggage before you go through customs.) The luggage tags will be

in colorful shapes of Disney characters: green Tinker Bell, orange Goofy, blue Donald Duck, and so on. Write your stateroom number, name, home address, and number of bags on each tag, and attach one tag to each piece of luggage you want Disney to transport. Place your tagged bags outside your stateroom during the hours noted on the instruction form placed in your stateroom. For sailings ending at Port Canaveral, this is typically between 8:30 and 10:30 p.m., but other ports may have different instructions.

A few packing tips:

- Don't forget to lay out clothes to wear to breakfast and off the ship the last morning.
- If you're flying home, note that any alcohol you purchased on the ship must be packed in your checked bags.
- Don't pack your passports, birth certificates, Key to the World card, or any other travel documents in your checked bags. You'll need them before you can pick up your luggage, so keep them in a bag you plan to carry by hand off the ship.
- Remove any old airline or cruise tags from your luggage before you affix any new tags.
- Keep inside your stateroom any luggage you'll carry off the ship by hand. When you've gotten off the ship, you'll find a section of the terminal dedicated to checked baggage. Checked bags will be organized by color and character, with all of the green Tinker Bell–tagged luggage together, all of the orange Goofy luggage together, and so on. Overhead signs will direct you to each section.

unofficial **TIP**
Concierge guests may order room-service breakfast the last morning of the cruise.

Luggage will be sorted by stateroom number within each section, so look for yours by finding your stateroom number within your section. If you can't find one of your bags, check a few feet up and down the row, too—sometimes the stateroom order isn't exact. Ask a cast member for help if you still can't find your luggage after checking the nearby spaces.

EXPRESS WALK-OFF

FOR GUESTS WHO WISH TO BE among the very first off the ship (those who need to get straight to the airport or who have other time-dependent plans that day), DCL offers Express Walk-Off. As soon as the ship clears customs, guests may depart the ship. You must carry all of your own luggage to take advantage of this service; you may not set it out the night before. Be considerate and let your cabin attendant know if you're doing this, so he or she isn't waiting for your bags to appear in the hallway the last night of the cruise.

BREAKFAST ON THE MORNING OF YOUR DEPARTURE

YOU'LL HAVE THE CHANCE FOR ONE MORE SIT-DOWN MEAL. The table-service breakfast seatings are assigned based on your seating time for dinner. Guests with the early dinner seating are scheduled for their final breakfast on board at 6:30 a.m. Guests with the later dinner seating get a last-day breakfast assignment at 8 a.m. This effectively means that any guest with a late dinner seating and an early flight will be unable to eat a table-service breakfast on their last morning. For guests in this situation, the Cabanas buffet is open beginning at 6:30 a.m. This isn't quite the gargantuan spread offered on other mornings— expect pastries, fruit, bacon, eggs, cold cereal, and not much else. Cove Café is also open beginning at 6 a.m.

PHOTO PURCHASES

unofficial **TIP**
Guests with flights out of Orlando International Airport before 1 p.m. are required to leave the ship by 8 a.m.

IF YOU'VE PURCHASED A PHOTO CD, JPEG-loaded flash drive, photo book, or other photo product, it will be available for pickup on the morning of your departure. Pickup time usually starts at 7 a.m., and lines begin to form earlier than that. If you have an early flight and are using Express Walk-Off, plan to be in line to grab your photo products by about 6:30 a.m. Have another member of your party grab you a banana and coffee (or one last pastry) from the buffet line for you to eat while you wait.

If you've purchased a JPEG-loaded flash drive and you have a laptop with you, it makes sense to take a moment to verify that the drive is indeed loaded, that you understand the download process, that the photos are yours, and that the package is indeed the one you paid for. We've had a few instances when there were problems. We were able to be resolved them once we were home, but it took several weeks of phone calls and e-mails to get the right photos—something that would have taken just a few minutes had we noticed while we were still on the ship.

Although we certainly don't recommend this, it may be possible to purchase your shipboard photos while you're at home, up to six weeks after your sailing. Contact support.mycruisephotos.com for more information.

US CUSTOMS ALLOWANCES

EACH FAMILY WILL NEED to fill out a **Customs Declaration form** (see next two pages). Besides the usual name and address, the form asks which countries you've visited, whether you're bringing in prohibited items such as fruits or vegetables, whether you've handled livestock, and whether you're carrying more than $10,000 in cash. (Answering "yes" to all three is probably the start of the next installment in the *Hangover* series.) See tinyurl.com/customsdutyinfo for more information.

U.S. Customs and Border Protection

Customs Declaration
19 CFR 122.27, 148.12, 148.13, 148.110,148.111, 1498; 31 CFR 5316

FORM APPROVED
OMB NO. 1651-0009

Each arriving traveler or responsible family member must provide the following information (only ONE written declaration per family is required):

1. Family **Name**
   First *(Given)*   Middle

2. **Birth date**   Day   Month   Year

3. Number of **Family members** traveling with you

4. (a) U.S. Street **Address** (hotel name/destination)

   (b) City   (c) State

5. **Passport issued by** (country)

6. **Passport number**

7. Country of **Residence**

8. **Countries visited** on this trip prior to U.S. arrival

9. **Airline/Flight No.** or **Vessel Name**

10. The primary purpose of this trip is **business**:   Yes   No

11. I am (We are) bringing
    (a) fruits, vegetables, plants, seeds, food, insects: Yes   No
    (b) meats, animals, animal/wildlife products: Yes   No
    (c) disease agents, cell cultures, snails: Yes   No
    (d) soil or have been on a farm/ranch/pasture: Yes   No

12. I have (We have) been in close proximity of
    (such as touching or handling) **livestock**:   Yes   No

13. I am (We are) carrying **currency or monetary instruments** over $10,000 U.S. or foreign equivalent: Yes   No
    (see definition of monetary instruments on reverse)

14. I have (We have) **commercial merchandise**:   Yes   No
    (articles for sale, samples used for soliciting orders, or goods that are not considered personal effects)

15. **Residents** — the **total value of all goods,** including commercial merchandise I/we have purchased or acquired abroad, (including gifts for someone else, but not items mailed to the U.S.) and am/are bringing to the U.S. is: $

    Visitors — the **total value of all articles** that will remain in the U.S., including commercial merchandise is: $

Read the instructions on the back of this form. Space is provided to list all the items you must declare.

I HAVE READ THE IMPORTANT INFORMATION ON THE REVERSE SIDE OF THIS FORM AND HAVE MADE A TRUTHFUL DECLARATION.

X
(Signature)   Date (day/month/year)

For Official Use Only

CBP Form 6059B (10/07)

U.S. Customs and Border Protection Welcomes You to the United States

U.S. Customs and Border Protection is responsible for protecting the United States against the illegal importation of prohibited items. CBP officers have the authority to question you and to examine you and your personal property. If you are one of the travelers selected for an examination, you will be treated in a courteous, professional, and dignified manner. CBP Supervisors and Passenger Service Representatives are available to answer your questions. Comment cards are available to compliment or provide feedback.

Important Information

U.S. Residents — Declare all articles that you have acquired abroad and are bringing into the United States.

Visitors (Non-Residents) — Declare the value of all articles that will remain in the United States.

Declare all articles on this declaration form and show the value in U.S. dollars. For gifts, please indicate the retail value.

Duty — CBP officers will determine duty. U.S. residents are normally entitled to a duty-free exemption of $800 on items accompanying them. Visitors (non-residents) are normally entitled to an exemption of $100. Duty will be assessed at the current rate on the first $1,000 above the exemption.

Agricultural and Wildlife Products — To prevent the entry of dangerous agricultural pests and prohibited wildlife, the following are restricted: Fruits, vegetables, plants, plant products, soil, meat, meat products, birds, snails, and other live animals or animal products. Failure to declare such items to a Customs and Border Protection Officer/Customs and Border Protection Agriculture Specialist/Fish and Wildlife Inspector can result in penalties and the items may be subject to seizure.

Controlled substances, obscene articles, and toxic substances are generally prohibited entry.

Thank You, and Welcome to the United States.

The transportation of currency or **monetary instruments**, regardless of the amount, is legal. However, if you bring in to or take out of the United States more than $10,000 (U.S. or foreign equivalent, or a combination of both), you are required by law to file a report on FinCEN 105 (formerly Customs Form 4790) with U.S. Customs and Border Protection. Monetary instruments include coin, currency, travelers checks and bearer instruments such as personal or cashiers checks and stocks and bonds. If you have someone else carry the currency or monetary instrument for you, you must also file a report on FinCEN 105. Failure to file the required report or failure to report the *total* amount that you are carrying may lead to the seizure of *all* the currency or monetary instruments, and may subject you to civil penalties and/or criminal prosecution. SIGN ON THE OPPOSITE SIDE OF THIS FORM AFTER YOU HAVE READ THE IMPORTANT INFORMATION ABOVE AND MADE A TRUTHFUL DECLARATION.

Description of Articles (List may continue on another CBP Form 6059B)	Value	CBP Use Only
Total		

PART FIVE

SPECIAL TIPS *for* SPECIAL PEOPLE

DCL *for* SINGLES

BECAUSE DISNEY CRUISE LINE IS TARGETED TO FAMILIES, roughly 90% of its guests are couples or parents and kids. That's about 10 points higher than the cruise industry's average, and it means that there are around 200 solo travelers per cruise on the *Magic* and *Wonder,* and around 400 on the *Dream* and *Fantasy.*

Like the Disney parks, DCL is great for singles. It's safe, clean, and low-pressure. Safety and comfort are excellent, especially for women. If you're looking for places to relax without being hit on, Disney's ships are perfect. The bars, lounges, and nightclubs are clean, friendly, and interesting; the restaurants are welcoming; and the spas are excellent places for grabbing some solo time in public. One aspect that you do have to be vigilant about when traveling alone is shore excursions in foreign countries—more on that a bit later.

If you're interested in meeting other singles, Disney usually runs a **Singles Mingle** session on one of the first few days of each cruise. These are informal get-togethers that last about an hour and are typically held at the Cove Café in the adults-only part of the ship. Similarly, single and not-so-single guests ages 18–20 are welcome to attend an **1820 Society** gathering during one night of their cruise. It's a meetup attended by guests and crew, generally during the evening after the second dinner seating, also usually at the Cove Café.

DINING Single travelers will likely be paired with other groups for dinner at the standard restaurants. When we've cruised solo, our dinner companions are usually one or two couples, which means we're sitting at a table for four or six. If the cruise is especially popular, Disney may try to squeeze in another single person to your group, too, so that everyone has a table. Our dinners with these new friends couldn't have gone better, and we say that as pretty strong introverts. We've met interesting people from many different places, never run out of things to talk about, and even kept in touch with a few folks when we got back home.

Solo travelers are also welcome at Palo and Remy, and we've had many fine dinners and brunches there. If you're having difficulty making a reservation for one using the DCL website before your trip, try stopping by the restaurant on the afternoon you board. We've found the staff to be exceptionally accommodating for these requests, especially if you're willing to arrive either early or late.

unofficial **TIP**
US law requires Disney to disclose most claims of crimes alleged to have taken place on board. DCL voluntarily discloses all such incidents on its website.

CRUISE FARES While some cruise lines are adding stateroom cabins designed especially for solo travelers, cabins on Disney's ships are all designed to hold at least two people. To make up for the room, bar, and shore-excursion revenue lost when one person books a cabin that could hold two paying passengers, Disney adds a 100% surcharge (or "single supplement," in cruise-industry lingo) to most solo-traveler fares, making the cost equivalent to two people taking the same trip. There's a small chance that you can find last-minute deals on unsold cabins without paying the full 100% supplement. Your best bet is to check the DCL website or have a travel agent research for you.

PORT ADVENTURES As with dining, there's a good chance you'll be paired with other couples for shore excursions. But unlike dinner, it's possible for a solo traveler to simply be a quiet observer during many excursions, especially those designed for groups.

We've been single travelers on everything from cooking demonstrations to snorkeling to city tours, and they've all gone well. All of the programs we've tried can accommodate single guests, and the Port Adventures staff makes everyone feel welcome. That said, some excursions run by third-party companies will use private taxi or shuttle services to transport guests from the ship to their activity, and it's possible for a solo traveler to be the odd man out if the vehicle doesn't have enough seats to accommodate the entire group, as Len recounts:

unofficial **TIP**
If your port adventure involves boating, snorkeling, or any other water-based activity, you will almost certainly be assigned another traveler or couple as a buddy for safety reasons.

I was once the only solo traveler in a group of nine for an excursion in Mexico that involved a 30-minute bus ride. When we got to the departure point, we saw that not all of us were going to fit on the eight-person bus that the excursion company brought. The couples were placed together, and the Port Adventures staff hurriedly brought around an unmarked, nondescript "taxi" for me.

As I got in this random car on a random street in a random Mexican town, my last words to the others were, "Take a good look. This is what I was wearing the last time you saw me." Of course, I made

*it to and from the shore excursion just fine, and we all had a laugh
once we were reunited. But I wouldn't recommend that others do this,
especially women traveling alone.*

In the (unlikely) event that you're asked to travel alone to a shore
excursion, decline politely. Ask to be accompanied by a staff member
or to be escorted back to the ship. Along the same lines, if you're not
comfortable walking back to your stateroom at night, ask a member
of the crew to escort you. And use extra caution walking to and from
the parking lot at the cruise terminal.

DCL *"At Large"*

AS WITH ITS THEME PARK GUESTS, Disney realizes that its cruise
guests come in all shapes and sizes and makes many accommodations
to ensure that they're treated well.

Your stateroom's personal flotation devices (PFDs, or life jackets)
are designed to fit most bodies. With PFDs, chest size, not weight, is
the measurement that determines proper fit. Disney's PFDs include
a nylon strap that wraps around your body to keep the PFD snug
against your chest. Try on your PFD when you first get to your stateroom to ensure that the strap fits around your body. If it doesn't, mention it to your group's leader during the lifeboat drill.

The AquaDuck waterslides on the *Dream* and *Fantasy* seem able to
accommodate virtually all body shapes and sizes. We've heard success
stories from individuals weighing more than 300 pounds and couples
weighing more than 400. The AquaDunk slide on the *Magic* has a
weight limit of 300 pounds.

If an activity or port adventure has a weight limit, it will be printed
in the details describing the activity; look for phrases such as "Guests
must weigh" or "Weight must be" in the activity's listing. Some shore
excursions, including kayaking and some scuba and snorkeling trips,
have weight limits of 240 or 300 pounds per person. Segway tours
generally accommodate persons of up to 250 pounds. Many Alaskan
excursions involving helicopters or seaplanes have a weight limit of
250 pounds inclusive of all gear (clothing, cameras, and such); it may
be possible to modify this requirement by paying an excess-weight fee
for additional fuel. Other activities have weight limits of up to 350
pounds per person. Again, check the activity's details for more information, or check with the Port Adventures desk on board.

Ask for bench seating or chairs without arms at restaurants and
lounges. If you don't see them, the staff should be able to provide one.

Wear comfortable shoes. You'll be surprised at the amount of
walking you do on board the ship, not to mention the walking you'll
do from the cruise terminal to the ship.

DCL *for* EXPECTANT MOMS

DISNEY PROHIBITS MOTHERS-TO-BE FROM SAILING if they will reach their 24th week of pregnancy at any time during the cruise. For example, a woman who is 23 weeks pregnant would not be allowed by Disney to take a 12-night transatlantic cruise. In addition, note that if you're flying to or from your cruise, airlines may have their own, different policies regarding pregnant travelers.

On board, the AquaDuck and AquaDunk waterslides are off-limits to expectant mothers, as is the waterslide at Castaway Cay. Other shore excursions, such as scuba activities, off-road driving, and parasailing, also prohibit expectant mothers from participating. In addition, some tour operators have restrictions on snorkeling and dolphin encounters.

To understand the risk of disease or injury to you or your baby, talk to your doctor about any shore visits you plan to take. For example, in 2015 and 2016 US federal health officials issued warnings for pregnant women (and women hoping to become pregnant) who were visiting areas in Latin American and Caribbean countries where mosquitoes spread the Zika virus, linked to infant brain damage. If you become pregnant after booking a cruise to a Zika-affected area, speak with Disney about remediation. While nothing is guaranteed, we have heard of guests having rebooking penalties waived for postponed trips. (See page 20 for additional resources on travel health.)

Also note that some excursions require lengthy drives on pothole-strewn roads—some of them dirt, gravel, or sand—in vehicles that have seen years of use. Even if all you're planning to do is relax on a beach, the drive to get there may be bumpy enough to make you reconsider going. Remember that it's always OK to stay on the ship and take advantage of the entertainment and activities on board.

DCL *for* YOUNGER CHILDREN

DISNEY CRUISE LINE REQUIRES that infant guests be at least 6 months of age on most sailings and at least 1 year of age on some longer voyages. Depending on how early you've booked your cruise, a surprise addition to the family may influence whether you're able to sail. If you find yourself in this situation, contact Disney as soon as possible to understand your options.

Guests with young children should think about the family's sleeping arrangements when planning their cruise. Disney does provide "pack-and-play"–style cribs free of charge to guests who need them. However, given the small square footage of most staterooms, the crib's footprint will have an outsized impact on the room's usable space for other family members, particularly if the child will be napping during the day. Training your young child to sleep in a bed rather than a crib might enhance your family's enjoyment of their living quarters.

In general, the younger the child, the more you'll want to stick as closely as possible to his usual eat/sleep schedule, which for most guests with young kids means that you'll want to choose the earlier dinner seating. However, you should also consider the influence of time-zone changes if you're cruising in a locale that's distant from your home.

For sailings out of the United States, the earlier seating is often more popular, becoming fully booked more quickly. On European sailings, where late dining is more common, the late seating may be more popular. If your preferred seating is fully booked at the time you purchase your cruise, keep checking back. It's often possible to make a switch, even in the middle of a trip. To make a change before your sailing, call DCL directly at ☎ 800-951-3532, or speak to Guest Services while you're on board.

Parents of fussy young eaters should understand that while the Disney ships offer a wide variety of food, available virtually around the clock, the limited capacity of a ship's kitchens means that not every possible food will be available in every possible form. For example, the macaroni and cheese served on the ship may not be the same mac and cheese that your child is used to. ("*Orange?* I want white!") If your child is a truly limited eater, you'll need to strategize in advance.

Another potential issue for parents of younger children is separation anxiety. Many young children adore spending time in the nursery or shipboard kids' clubs. However, if your child is in a separation-anxiety phase, you may feel that this isn't the best time to leave him in the care of strangers, even if you're just a deck or two away. If you have a skittish youngster, be realistic about your expectations. Assume that most of your cruise will be family time rather than "Mom and Dad at the spa" time, and be pleasantly surprised if your preschooler ends up spending significant time in the kids' club.

unofficial **TIP**
For more on cruising with children, see "Cruising with Kids" in Part One (page 18) and "Special Considerations" in Part Nine (page 185).

Breastfeeding is allowed in all areas of the Disney ships. Your stateroom is never far away when you're on a ship, but you shouldn't feel like you have to rush back to your room every time your little one needs to eat. You're welcome to nurse in the theaters, in the dining rooms, or in other public areas of the ship; however, the same rules may not apply when you're off the ship. If you're traveling with a baby, you may want to research the customs and regulations of your specific destinations.

DCL *for* OLDER CHILDREN

SOME FAMILIES WITH 17- AND 18-YEAR-OLD kids may encounter frustration during their trip due to Disney's strict enforcement of age restrictions on teen and adult activities. We recently traveled with a teen just days away from her 18th birthday—in fact, we booked the trip to celebrate her birthday. Even though she was a high school graduate, she was still not allowed to dine at Palo (yes, we tried bribery, and no, it didn't work), exercise in the ship's fitness center, or go to some of the adults-only cooking demonstrations. We've seen 17- and 18-year-old cousins unable to do virtually anything together because the older teen wasn't allowed into the Vibe teen club and the younger one wasn't allowed into any of the adult activities. If you have an older teen, consider whether choosing a slightly different travel date would affect his or her enjoyment of the trip.

DCL *for* SENIORS

MOST SENIORS find a Disney cruise less tiring than a Walt Disney World vacation. First, most seniors find considerably less walking required on the ship versus the parks. Second, the ships' adults-only areas provide a break from children (and their families) when needed. And even the most energetic onboard attraction, the AquaDuck/AquaDunk, isn't as intense as a ride on Space Mountain or Big Thunder Mountain Railroad.

Because of their flexible schedules, retirees can often take advantage of off-peak cruise fares, especially during fall or spring, when the weather is nicest and crowds are lower because school is in session. If you're cruising to the Caribbean, the Bahamas, or Mexico, be sure to bring a jacket and sweater along with your warm-weather clothing. While temperature averages hover around 70°F in most of those locations, a cold front can drop temps into the upper 40s with little notice, and it's not uncommon to have morning temperatures in the lower 50s.

GUESTS *with* DISABILITIES

DCL STRIVES TO MAKE ITS SHIPS ACCESSIBLE TO ALL. Virtually the entire ship, from staterooms to restaurants to nightclubs and pools, is wheelchair- and ECV-friendly. More accommodations are available for other special needs, too. This section describes each of those in more detail. Call DCL's Accessibility Desk at ☎ 407-566-3500 (voice) or 407-566-7455 (TTY) for specific questions.

Stateroom Furnishings

In addition to the standard amenities offered in each stateroom, Disney offers the following special equipment for guests with disabilities:

• Close-captioned TV (most stations)	• Portable toilet	• Rubber bed pads
	• Raised toilet seat	• Shower stool
• Bed boards and rails	• Refrigerator	• Transfer benches
• A Stateroom Communication Kit, including an alarm clock, door-knock and phone alerts, phone amplifier, bed-shaker notification, strobe-light smoke detector, and text typewriter (TTY)		

WHEELCHAIR AND ECV USERS DCL suggests that guests using a wheelchair or ECV request a wheelchair-accessible stateroom or suite. Found on every Disney ship, wheelchair-accessible staterooms include the following features:

• Doorways at least 32 inches wide	• Fold-down shower seating and hand-held showerheads	• Open bed frame for easier entry and exit
• Bathroom and shower handrails	• Lowered towel and closet bars	• Ramped bathroom thresholds
• Emergency call buttons and additional phones in the bath and stateroom		

One advantage to having an accessible stateroom is that its wider door lets you store your wheelchair or ECV inside your cabin when it's not in use. This also makes it easier to recharge the equipment when needed. If you find yourself in a standard stateroom whose door won't fit your vehicle, you may be asked to park the vehicle in a designated area elsewhere on the ship, even at night. In practice, we've seen many ECVs parked in a corner of each deck's elevator-landing areas. Chances are that your vehicle will be stored within a short walk of your cabin.

Outside of your stateroom, special areas are designated at most ship activities for guests in wheelchairs. At the Walt Disney Theatre, for example, Disney cast members direct guests in wheelchairs to a reserved seating area. Shops, restaurants, bars, and nightclubs are all accessible, and accessible restrooms are available throughout the ship's public areas. A limited number of sand wheelchairs are available on Castaway Cay, too, on a first-come, first-served basis.

Note that DCL's pools require a transfer from wheelchair to use. For this reason, Disney recommends that guests in wheelchairs travel with someone who can help transfer them to and from the wheelchair.

unofficial **TIP**
Service animals are welcome on board, and each ship has a designated animal-relief area on an outside deck.

Another area to be aware of is tendering from ship to shore. Some ports, such as the one at Grand Cayman, aren't deep enough to accommodate large cruise ships such as Disney's. When DCL ships anchor at Grand Cayman, smaller boats, or tenders, pull up next to the ship, and guests board them for travel to and from Grand Cayman.

Some tenders use steps instead of ramps to get guests on board. In those cases, wheelchair passengers must use the steps. Also keep in mind that the Disney ship and tender craft both float freely in the ocean. It's not uncommon for the stairs to move 2 or 3 feet up and down during the course of a transfer. If the seas are too rough, wheelchair guests may be denied transfer.

SIGHT- AND HEARING-IMPAIRED GUESTS In addition to closed-caption TVs, assistive listening devices and printed scripts are available for shows at the ships' main theaters and show stages. Stop by the Guest Services

SCOTT SAYS   *by Scott Sanders*

SCOTT'S SUPER-SPECIAL SPECIAL-PEOPLE TIP

DISNEY IS GREAT ABOUT accommodating the various needs of its passengers. It's usually best to contact DCL before your sailing to discuss your specific needs so they can be appropriately noted on your reservation (or have your travel agent do this for you). In my case, I have a shellfish allergy that I've noted on my reservation, but I always make it a point on the first night at dinner to tell each member of my serving team.

desk to pick those up. In addition, American Sign Language interpreters are available for live performances on some cruise dates.

CHILDREN WITH DISABILITIES Disney's youth programs are open to special-needs children ages 3–17. All children must be toilet-trained and able to play well with kids who are about their same age and size.

The number of children who can participate is limited and is based on the number of available counselors, the number of other children in the programs, the number of special-needs children already enrolled, and the specific needs of the child wishing to enroll. Check with the Youth Activities team when you get on board for more details. Disney is unable to provide youth counselors for medical attention, one-on-one care, or training for a specific need.

PORT ADVENTURES Many Port Adventures have requirements concerning mobility. These are noted in the Port Adventure descriptions. You may also inquire about which activities are available to you at the Port Adventures desk while on board.

Other amenities, such as disabled parking at the cruise terminal, are also available. See DCL's Guests with Disabilities FAQ (tinyurl .com/dclguestswithdisabilities) for more information.

EQUIPMENT RENTALS Guests who need medical equipment onboard may find it convenient to rent from the service **Special Needs at Sea** (specialneedsatsea.com). They offer rentals delivered to all the Disney ships at most embarkation ports, including Barcelona, Copenhagen, Miami, New York, Port Canaveral, and Vancouver. Among the products they rent are wheelchairs, ECVs, walkers, oxygen and respiratory equipment, and audio- and visual-aid materials.

DIETARY RESTRICTIONS

WITH ENOUGH ADVANCE NOTICE, DCL's sit-down restaurants can accommodate a wide variety of special dietary needs, including low-sodium, kosher, and allergen-free requests, at no additional cost. The best way to communicate these needs to Disney is through the **Special Services Information Form,** available when you check in online (see page 36). Disney asks that the form be submitted by e-mail, fax, or snail mail at least 30 days before your cruise. Note that counter-service restaurants and room service usually can't accommodate special requests, although some allergies, such as gluten, are more easily accommodated. If you book through a travel agent, he or she can make a note of this on your reservation. You should also let your serving team (including the head server) know your requirements on the first night of your cruise.

Note that most port adventures are run by independent contractors, not Disney. Your food requests and accommodations will *not* be automatically transferred to excursion contractors, and some providers may not be able to work with certain dietary issues. What's more, due to legal and agricultural restrictions, in many ports you will not be able to bring certain types of food off the ship. Check with Guest Services for advice on how best to handle your dietary needs while in port.

SMOKING *on* BOARD

SMOKING, INCLUDING CIGARETTES, CIGARS, PIPES, and electronic cigarettes, is prohibited in your stateroom, on your stateroom's outdoor verandah (if it has one), and in any indoor space on the ship. On the *Magic* and *Wonder,* outdoor smoking areas are available on Deck 4 starboard (right side of the ship) between 6 p.m. and 6 a.m., and on Deck 9, forward, port (left) side, excluding the AquaLab area on the *Magic* and the Mickey's Pool area on the *Wonder.*

Smoking areas on the *Dream* and *Fantasy* are on the port side of Deck 4 Aft, also from 6 p.m. to 6 a.m.; the port side of Deck 12 Aft, accessed by walking through the Meridian Lounge; and near Currents Bar on Deck 13 Forward, port side.

TRAVELING *with* MEDICATION

IF YOU'RE BRINGING PRESCRIPTION MEDICINE on your cruise, your best bet is to transport it in its original containers. The problem you're trying to avoid isn't one with Disney's security staff, but the customs staffs of the countries you're visiting and US border control when you return. While it's unlikely, those folks may ask to see either the original containers (with your name on them) or a copy of a valid prescription, to ensure that you're not importing illegal or prohibited substances. We also recommend that you keep these medicines in your carry-on bag instead of checked luggage. Finally, note that Disney's onboard Health Center may not to be able to refill prescriptions (especially for controlled substances) that run out during your cruise, so get them refilled before you leave home.

FRIENDS *of* BILL W.

BEER, WINE, AND SPIRITS flow freely on cruise ships, even those run by Disney. Daily **Alcoholics Anonymous** meetings are available on each cruise. While the times and locations may vary, they're generally found here:

- 8:30 a.m. at Animator's Palate on the *Magic*
- 8:30 a.m. at the Cadillac Lounge on the *Wonder*
- 8:30 a.m. at the Outlook Lounge on the *Dream* and *Fantasy*

While the Cadillac and Outlook Lounges display and serve alcohol, the ship's bartenders lock up the entire stock every night, so nothing is out in the open during the meetings.

FRIENDS *of* DOROTHY

UNLIKE OTHER CRUISE LINES, DCL doesn't offer onboard activities specifically designed for LGBT travelers—you won't find a "Gay Mingle" event listed in your *Personal Navigator*. Nevertheless, DCL is very welcoming to the LGBT community. Many of our gay friends, both with and without children, offer extremely positive feedback about their Disney cruises. One friend notes:

After about the second day, you can start picking out who's "family." We met more gay people traveling on the Disney cruise than on any of our other nongay cruises.

We also encountered several gay couples and many gay staff on our Adventures by Disney river cruise (see page 358).

Single gay travelers may feel somewhat isolated, but couples, families, or groups of friends should have no problems.

While LGBT travelers will have no issues on board the Disney ships, experiences in port will vary depending on the itinerary. In most port locations, you'll be absolutely fine; if, however, you're an LGBT cruiser on a sailing with a stop in Jamaica or Russia, for example, use common sense.

PART SIX

THE SHIPS
at a GLANCE

OVERVIEW *and* OUR RECOMMENDATIONS

LAUNCHED IN 1998, the **Disney Magic** holds roughly 2,700 passengers and 950 crew members. The **Disney Wonder** has the same capacity and was launched in 1999. The **Disney Dream** and **Disney Fantasy,** which took their maiden voyages in 2011 and 2012, respectively, hold up to 4,000 passengers and 1,450 crew. The *Magic* and *Wonder* are the workhorses of the fleet: The *Magic* covers everything from Mexico to the Mediterranean, while the *Wonder* plies the seas from Alaska to the Caribbean.

> ✳ *unofficial* **TIP**
> When it comes to choosing a ship, you'll do well with either the *Dream* or the *Fantasy.* We recommend going with whichever has the price or itinerary to meet your needs.

All four ships share sleek lines, twin smokestacks, and nautical styling that calls to mind classic ocean liners, but with instantly recognizable Disney signatures. The colors—dark blue, white, red, and yellow—and the famous face-and-ears silhouette on the stacks are clearly those of Mickey Mouse. Look closely at the *Magic*'s stern ornamentation, for example, and you'll see a 15-foot Goofy hanging by his overalls. (It's Donald on the *Wonder*'s stern, Mickey on the *Dream*'s, and Dumbo on the *Fantasy*'s.)

The ships' interiors combine nautical themes with Art Nouveau and Art Deco inspiration. (Art Nouveau, popular at the turn of the century. incorporates natural shapes, such as from plants and animals, into its geometric designs; Art Deco has the geometry without the nature—think those sleek interiors from 1930s movies.) Disney images are everywhere, from Mickey's profile in the wrought-iron balustrades to the bronze statue of Helmsman Mickey featured prominently in the *Magic*'s atrium, Ariel on the *Wonder*, Admiral Donald on the *Dream*, and Mademoiselle

Minnie decked out in full flapper style on the *Fantasy*. Disney art is on every wall and in every stairwell and corridor. A grand staircase on each ship sweeps from the atrium lobby to shops peddling DCL-themed clothing, collectibles, jewelry, and more.

Ships have two lower decks with cabins, three decks with dining rooms and showrooms, and then three or five upper decks of cabins. Two sports and sun decks offer separate pools and facilities for families and for adults without children. Signs point toward lounges and facilities, and all elevators are clearly marked as Forward, Aft, or Midship.

Our main complaint concerning the ships' design is that outdoor public areas focus inward toward the pools instead of seaward, as if Disney wants you to forget that you're on a cruise liner. On the *Magic* and the *Wonder,* there's no public place where you can curl up in the shade and watch the ocean—at least not without a plexiglass wall between you and it. On Deck 4 of the *Dream* and the *Fantasy,* however, an open promenade, complete with comfy deck chairs, circles the ship. It's shady and fairly well protected from wind, and it offers the opportunity to sit back and enjoy the sea without your having to look through plexiglass barriers.

Speaking of plexiglass, a predictable but none- *unofficial* **TIP** theless irritating design characteristic is the extensive childproofing. There's enough plexiglass on all four ships to build a subdivision of see-through homes. On

> **unofficial TIP**
> Disney ships have no casinos or libraries.

the pool decks especially, it feels as if the ships are hermetically sealed. Plus, verandah doors have a two-part locking mechanism, with one of the two parts 6 feet off the floor—causing even adults occasional consternation in trying to operate them.

DCL CHEAT SHEET

CAN'T REMEMBER, SAY, which ship has the AquaDunk and which has the AquaDunk without looking it up? Neither can we from time to time. These handy charts summarize what's the same and what's different across the ships. An asterisk in the charts (*) indicates new features and amenities coming to the *Wonder* after its 2016 dry dock.

• WHAT'S THE SAME ACROSS THE SHIPS •
DINING
After the *Wonder*'s 2016 dry dock was completed, all ships now have a **Cabanas** buffet.
FAMILY ENTERTAINMENT
Following the *Wonder*'s dry dock, all ships now have a **D Lounge** family nightclub and a **Bibbidi Bobbidi Boutique** for princess and pirate makeovers.

Continued on next page

• WHAT'S THE SAME ACROSS THE SHIPS •

KIDS' CLUBS

All ships have **It's a Small World Nursery, Oceaneer Club/Lab** for older kids, **Edge** tween club, and **Vibe** teen club. The nursery on the *Wonder* (formerly Flounder's Reef) was rethemed to match the others during the dry dock. The Oceaneer Clubs/Labs on the *Dream* and *Fantasy* are identical but somewhat different from the version on the *Magic;* the version on the *Wonder* was unique to that ship (read: outdated) pre–dry dock and will continue to be unique (read: awesome) afterward. We think Edge on the *Wonder* is getting a makeover and a change of location, but we're not sure just yet how different it will look from Edge on the *Magic,* which looks completely different from the matching Edges on the *Dream* and *Fantasy.* Vibe will continue to be identical on the two older ships and the two newer ships but totally different between the pairs.

FITNESS AND SPAS

All ships have a fitness center, an outdoor running track, and a **Rainforest** sauna complex. Following the *Wonder's* dry dock, all ships will also have a **Senses Spa** and a **Chill Spa** for teens. We suspect that the *Wonder's* Chill Spa will be closer to the one on the *Magic*—a single treatment room—than the fully fledged space for teens on the *Dream* and the *Fantasy.*

TECHNOLOGY

All ships have pay Wi-Fi (free to use with the **DCL Navigator** app) and **Wave Phones** for calling/messaging others on board.

• WHAT'S DIFFERENT ACROSS THE SHIPS •

SHIP

Magic	Wonder	Dream	Fantasy
FEATURE (* = new on the Wonder as of fall 2016)			
DINING			
ADULT DINING			
Palo	Palo	Palo, Remy	Palo, Remy
COUNTER SERVICE			
Daisy's De-Lites, Pete's Boiler Bites, Pinocchio's Pizzeria	Daisy's De-Lites*, Pete's Boiler Bites*, Pinocchio's Pizzeria	Fillmore's Favorites, Luigi's Pizza, Tow Mater's Grill, Vanellope's Sweets & Treats	Fillmore's Favorites, Luigi's Pizza, Tow Mater's Grill
ROTATIONAL DINING			
Animator's Palate, Carioca's, Lumiere's	Animator's Palate, Tiana's Place*, Triton's	Animator's Palate, Enchanted Garden, Royal Palace	Animator's Palate, Enchanted Garden, Royal Court
FAMILY ENTERTAINMENT			
LIVE STAGE SHOWS			
All Aboard!, Disney Dreams, Remember the Magic, Tangled: The Musical, Twice Charmed, Walt Disney: The Dream Lives On	*Disney Dreams, Frozen: A Musical Spectacular*, The Golden Mickeys*	*Disney's Believe, The Golden Mickeys, Villains Tonight!*	*Disney's Aladdin, Disney's Believe, Disney Wishes*

SHIP/FEATURE	*Magic*	*Wonder*	*Dream*	*Fantasy*
NIGHTLIFE AND BARS				
ADULT-NIGHTLIFE AREA	After Hours	After Hours*	The District	Europa
CHAMPAGNE BAR	No	No	Pink	Ooh La La
COFFEE BAR	Cove Café	Cove Café, Outlook Café	Cove Café	Cove Café
DANCE CLUB	Fathoms	Azure	Evolution	The Tube
LIVE-MUSIC CLUB	Keys, Promenade Lounge	Cadillac Lounge, Promenade Lounge	District Lounge	La Piazza
MARTINI BAR	No	No	Meridian	Meridian
POOL BARS	Signals (21+)	Signals (21+)	Currents, Waves *(all ages)*	Currents, Waves *(all ages)*
PUB/SPORTS BAR	O'Gills Pub	Crown & Fin*	687	O'Gills Pub
UPSCALE "CRAFT COCKTAIL" BAR	No	No	Skyline	Skyline
POOLS				
ADULT POOLS	Quiet Cove Pool	Quiet Cove Pool	Quiet Cove Pool, Satellite Falls	Quiet Cove Pool, Satellite Falls
FAMILY POOL	Goofy's Pool	Goofy's Pool	Donald's Pool	Donald's Pool
KIDS' POOLS/ SPLASH AREAS	AquaLab, Mickey's Pool, Nephews' Pool/ Splash Zone	AquaLab*, Dory's Reef*, Mickey's Pool/ Splash Zone	Mickey's Pool, Nemo's Reef	AquaLab, Mickey's Pool, Nemo's Reef
TEEN SPLASH POOL *(ages 14–17)*	No	No	Vibe	Vibe
WATER RIDES	AquaDunk *(vertical waterslide)*, Twist 'n' Spout *(kids' waterslide)*	Mickey's Slide, Twist 'n' Spout*	AquaDuck *(water coaster)*, Mickey's Slide	AquaDuck, Mickey's Slide
SPORTS AND RECREATION				
GAMES	Basketball, shuffleboard, Foosball, table tennis	Basketball, shuffleboard, Foosball, table tennis	Basketball, shuffleboard, Foosball, minigolf, table tennis	Basketball, shuffleboard, Foosball, minigolf, table tennis
TECHNOLOGY				
"ENCHANTED" (INTERACTIVE) ART	No	No	Yes	Yes
INTERACTIVE GAME PLAYED AROUND THE SHIP	No	Midship Detective Agency*	Midship Detective Agency	Midship Detective Agency
VIRTUAL PORTHOLES	No	No	Yes	Yes

FEATURES FOUND ON EVERY DCL SHIP

ALL DISNEY SHIPS HAVE AMENITIES in common, including the following:

Adult pool and deck areas	Outdoor basketball court, shuffleboard, and other sports areas
Bars, lounges, and cafés	Outdoor LED screen for movies, concerts, and videos
Buffet restaurant	
Family pools and water-play areas	**Palo,** an upscale Italian restaurant
Fitness center	Photo gallery for purchasing onboard photos
Full-service spa and salon, with sauna	Retail shopping, including duty-free alcohol
Guest Services desk	Theater for live performances
Health Center	
Infant, child, tween, and teen clubs	
Movie theater	

Some ships offer amenities not found on others. The *Dream* and *Fantasy,* for example, have the following features not found on the *Magic* or the *Wonder:*

AquaDuck water coaster	**Remy,** an upscale French restaurant
Champagne bar (**Pink** on the *Dream,* **Ooh La La** on the *Fantasy*)	**Meridian,** a martini bar
Chill Spa for teens. (The *Magic* has a treatment room branded as Chill Spa, but it's vastly different from the version on the two newer ships. We think the version coming to the *Wonder* will be similar to the *Magic*'s.)	Miniature-golf course
	Satellite Falls, an adults-only splash pool and sun deck
	Separate decks for Concierge rooms
	Skyline bar

FEATURES UNIQUE TO SOME SHIPS

IT SEEMS WITH EVERY DRY DOCK, each DCL ship loses a little more of its unique character. Still, each of the following ships has something that sets it apart:

UNIQUE TO THE *MAGIC* AquaDunk, a vertical waterslide. (The **AquaDuck** on the *Dream* and *Fantasy* sounds similar—the name is off by just one letter—but it's a horizontal water coaster.)

UNIQUE TO THE *WONDER* Outlook Café, upstairs from Cove Café, is an adults-only lounge with 270-degree views of the sea.

UNIQUE TO THE *DREAM* Vanellope's Sweets & Treats, a premium-ice-cream shop. (The other ships merely have stations that dispense free soft-serve.)

That leaves the *Fantasy* as the odd ship out despite its also being the newest. Many of the innovations that came to the other ships later had their genesis on the *Fantasy,* such as the Bibbidi Bobbidi Boutique and the Satellite Falls adult splash pool and sunbathing area. And though it wasn't technically a first, the *Fantasy*'s enhanced version of the Midship Detective Agency interactive game is superior to the one that originated on the *Dream.* But all of the "first and onlys" on the *Fantasy* have made their way to the *Dream* and many even to the *Magic* and *Wonder.* We hope that the *Fantasy,* next in line for a dry dock, will get some new and awesome features in the future.

> *unofficial* **TIP**
> We rank the *Fantasy* highest because of its **Skyline** bar, **The Tube** lounge, and the onboard **Midship Detective Agency** game, which we feel outshines the version on the *Dream.*

RANKING THE SHIPS

IF YOUR CRUISE DESTINATION is the Bahamas or the Caribbean, one decision you'll need to make is whether to sail on either the *Magic* and *Wonder* or on the *Dream* and *Fantasy.* Ignoring the different itineraries each ship serves, here's how we rank the Disney ships:

1. *Fantasy*   **2.** *Dream*   **3.** *Magic*   **4.** *Wonder (pre-refurbishment)*

The *Fantasy* and *Dream* have better restaurants, bars, and pools than the older ships, plus more on-deck activities, more space for children's activities, more deck space for tanning, better spas, and more interactive games. These advantages make up for the slightly smaller cabin sizes on the *Dream* and *Fantasy,* whose non-Concierge staterooms are 2–9% (5–22 square feet) smaller than corresponding cabins on the *Magic* and *Wonder.* Another minor downside: Because the newer ships carry more passengers, Castaway Cay is more crowded when they're in port.

As we were going to press, the *Wonder* was undergoing a substantial dry-dock refurbishment in Cádiz, Spain. Reimagined elements of the ship will include the following:

- A retheming of the tired Parrot Cay dining room to **Tiana's Place,** a Southern-style restaurant inspired by Princess Tiana in *The Princess and the Frog*
- The addition of **Marvel Super Hero Academy** and **Frozen Adventures** themed areas to the **Oceaneer Club**
- A change in location and makeover for the **Edge** tween club
- The addition of **Crown & Fin,** a brass-and-leather-appointed British-style tavern serving specialty beers
- The addition of the **Midship Detective Agency** interactive game, currently only on the *Dream* and *Fantasy,* along with a **Bibbidi Bobbidi Boutique** children's-makeover salon

Continued on page 116

Disney Magic / Disney Wonder
DECK PLANS

DECK 1

Health Center

Tender Lobby — Forward Elevator Lobby — Tender Lobby

1030, 1032, 1034, 1036, 1037, 1038, 1039, 1040, 1041, 1042, 1043, 1044, 1045, 1046, 1047, 1048, 1049, 1050, 1051, 1052, 1053, 1054, 1055, 1056

Midship Elevator Lobby

1058, 1060, 1062, 1064, 1065, 1066, 1067, 1068, 1069, 1070, 1071, 1072, 1073, 1074, 1075, 1076, 1077, 1078, 1079

Tender Lobby — Aft Elevator Lobby — Tender Lobby

DECK 2

2000, 2002, 2004, 2006, 2008, 2009, 2010, 2011, 2012, 2013, 2014, 2015, 2016, 2017, 2018, 2019, 2020, 2021, 2022, 2024, 2026, 2028

2500, 2502, 2504, 2506, 2508, 2509, 2510, 2511, 2512, 2513, 2514, 2515, 2516, 2517, 2518, 2519, 2520, 2522, 2524, 2526, 2528

Forward Elevator Lobby

2030, 2032, 2034, 2035, 2036, 2037, 2038, 2039, 2040, 2041, 2042, 2043, 2044, 2045, 2046, 2047, 2048, 2050, 2052, 2054, 2056

2529, 2530, 2532, 2534, 2535, 2536, 2537, 2538, 2539, 2540, 2541, 2542, 2543, 2544, 2545, 2546, 2547, 2548, 2550, 2552, 2554, 2556

Midship Elevator Lobby

2058, 2060, 2062, 2063, 2064, 2065, 2066, 2067, 2068, 2070, 2071, 2072, 2073, 2074, 2075, 2076, 2077, 2078, 2080, 2082, 2083, 2084, 2085, 2086

2558, 2560, 2562, 2563, 2564, 2565, 2566, 2567, 2568, 2570, 2571, 2572, 2573, 2574, 2575, 2576, 2578, 2579, 2580, 2581, 2582, 2583, 2584, 2585, 2586

2088, 2090, 2092, 2094, 2096, 2098, 2100, 2101, 2102, 2103, 2104, 2105, 2106, 2107, 2108, 2109, 2110, 2111, 2112, 2114, 2116, 2118, 2120

2588, 2590, 2592, 2594, 2596, 2598, 2600, 2601, 2602, 2603, 2604, 2605, 2606, 2607, 2608, 2609, 2610, 2611, 2612, 2614, 2616, 2618, 2620

Aft Elevator Lobby

2122, 2124, 2126, 2128, 2129, 2130, 2131, 2132, 2133, 2134, 2135, 2136, 2137, 2138, 2139, 2140, 2141, 2142, 2143, 2144, 2145, 2146, 2147

2622, 2624, 2626, 2628, 2629, 2630, 2631, 2632, 2633, 2635, 2637, 2638, 2639, 2640, 2641, 2642, 2643, 2644, 2645, 2646, 2647

DECK 3

After Hours

Keys (Magic)/ Iliac Lounge (Wonder)

O'Gills (Magic)/ Diversions (Wonder)

Forward Elevator Lobby

Fathoms (Magic)/ Azure (Wonder)

Guest Services

Port Adventures Desk

Lobby Atrium

Lumiere's (Magic)/ Triton's (Wonder)

Promenade Lounge

Aft Elevator Lobby

Restrooms

Carioca's (Magic)/ Tiana's Place (Wonder)

DECK 4

Walt Disney Theatre

Restrooms — Forward Elevator Lobby — Restrooms

Preludes Bar

Mickey's Mainsail

White Caps

Restrooms — Midship Elevator Lobby — Restrooms

Atrium

Promenade

Shutters Photo Studio

D Lounge

Theatre Exit

Aft Elevator Lobby

Animator's Palate

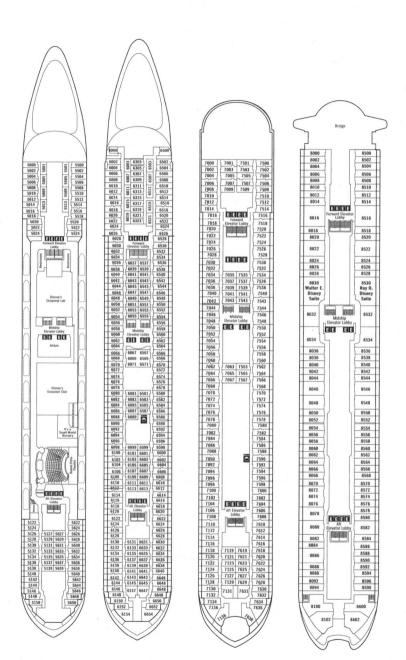

Continued on next page

Disney Magic / Disney Wonder
DECK PLANS

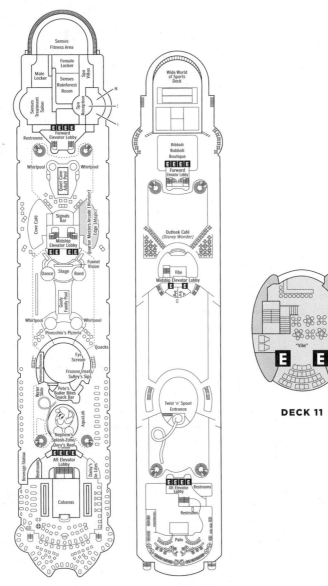

DECK 9

DECK 10

DECK 11

Disney Dream / Disney Fantasy
DECK PLANS

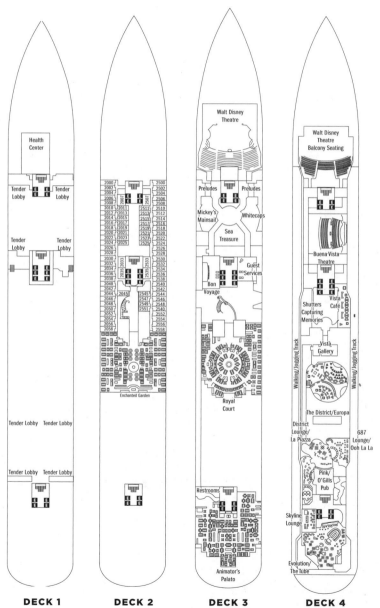

DECK 1 **DECK 2** **DECK 3** **DECK 4**

Continued on next page

Disney Dream / Disney Fantasy
DECK PLANS

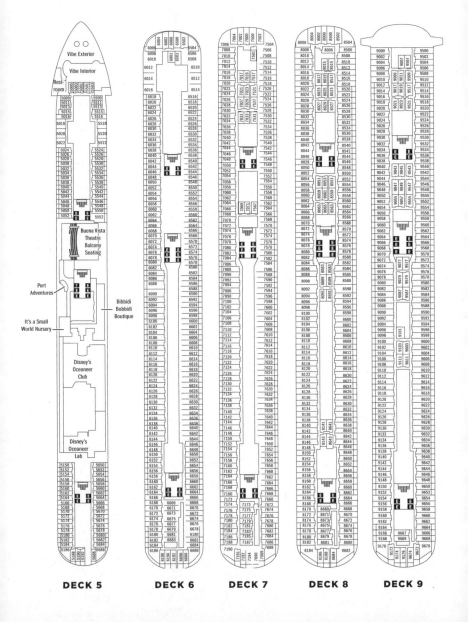

DECK 5 **DECK 6** **DECK 7** **DECK 8** **DECK 9**

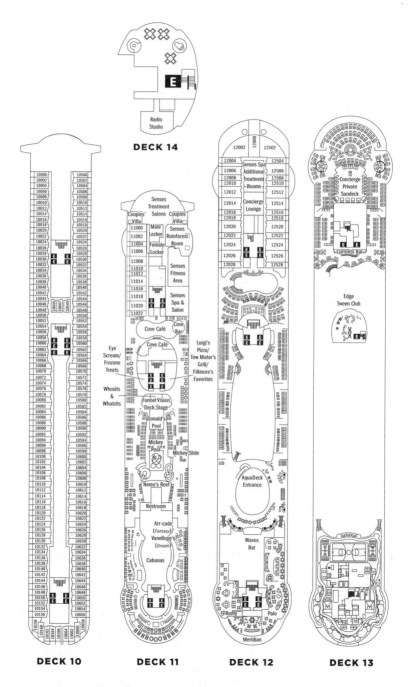

DECK 14

DECK 10

DECK 11

DECK 12

DECK 13

Continued from page 109

- A retheming of Vista Spa to **Senses Spa** and the addition of a **Chill Spa** for teens

- Updates to the ships' water-play areas, buffet restaurant, **Animator's Palate** dining room, and many more public spaces

THE *Disney Magic*

THE FIRST DCL SHIP, the *Magic* was launched in 1998 and underwent an extensive renovation—or reimagining, in Disney-speak—during a two-month dry dock in Cádiz, Spain, during the summer of 2013. Major changes included the following:

- **After Hours,** a retheming of the *Magic*'s nightlife area, formerly known as Beat Street and one of the ship's weakest areas

- The **AquaDunk** vertical-start waterslide. You begin by standing on top of a trapdoor, then plunge down almost vertically before spinning through a couple of turns and sliding to a stop on the main deck.

- A rethemed buffet, **Cabanas,** on Deck 9

- **Carioca's,** a new Brazilian-themed restaurant—a big improvement over the dire Parrot Cay

- A rethemed **Nephews' Pool,** the **Twist 'n' Spout** waterslide, the **AquaLab** water-play area for older kids, and the **Nephews' Splash Zone** water-play area for toddlers

- Rethemed **Oceaneer Club** and **Oceaneer Lab** kids' clubs, including the Marvel Avengers Academy in the Oceaneer Lab

- An Irish-themed sports bar, **O'Gills Pub,** which replaced the generic Diversions sports bar

- Refurbished retail shops

- A new stage show, ***Walt Disney: The Dream Goes On***

The 2013 makeover also included cosmetic updates to the *Magic*'s lobby atrium; **Keys** (formerly Sessions), the piano bar; **Palo,** the adults-only, fine-dining Italian restaurant; and **Fathoms** (formerly Rockin' Bar D), the dance club. In addition, Vista Spa became **Senses Spa.**

The *Magic* underwent additional dry-dock tweaking in late 2015. Changes at that time included the addition of a **Bibbidi Bobbidi Boutique** children's makeover salon and a location update for the **Edge** tween club.

THE *Disney Wonder*

LAUNCHED IN 1999 as the second of DCL's four current ships, the *Wonder* was beginning to show her age by 2016, with visible wear and tear and dated decor in many guest areas. At press time, the *Wonder* was undergoing a major dry-dock refurbishment that's expected to bring its amenities, entertainment, and finishings in line with those on the *Dream, Fantasy,* and *Magic.*

The *Wonder* continues to have the most in common with its sister the *Magic,* but with slightly different theming. When you board the ship at Deck 3, you're greeted by Ariel instead of Mickey and an Art Nouveau–style atrium rather than Art Deco. In keeping with the *Little Mermaid* theme, one of the standard rotational-dining restaurants on the *Wonder* is **Triton's,** named for Ariel's dad (its counterpart on the *Magic* is the *Beauty and the Beast*–themed **Lumiere's**).

Before the 2016 dry dock, the *Wonder* was home to our two least favorite dining spots in the Disney fleet: **Beach Blanket Buffet** and **Parrot Cay.** The refurbishment is replacing these outmoded venues with the more modern **Cabanas** buffet and a unique restaurant, **Tiana's Place,** inspired by the film *The Princess and the Frog* and serving New Orleans–style cuisine accompanied by live jazz. Additionally, the *Wonder*'s antiquated version of **Animator's Palate** is being retrofitted with an interactive show to match its counterparts on the other ships. We're hopeful that these changes will bring the *Wonder*'s dining up to par with the rest of the DCL fleet's.

The kids' clubs were also reimagined. The **Oceaneer Club** now features **Marvel Super Hero Academy,** in which young guests train to become superheroes (with help from Spider-Man during live character appearances), and **Frozen Adventures,** where a digital Olaf leads kids in games and songs. We're pretty sure that a version of the **Midship Detective Agency** interactive game is coming as well.

From a technological standpoint, the *Wonder* continues to lag a bit behind the newer ships. There is no headliner waterslide like the AquaDuck (*Dream* and *Fantasy*) or AquaDunk (*Magic*) on the pool deck, and inside staterooms on the *Wonder* lack the virtual portholes found on the *Dream* and *Fantasy.* Nevertheless, the *Wonder* is Erin's sentimental favorite of the DCL fleet:

> *I prefer the smaller size of the* Magic *and* Wonder. *The smaller capacity of the older ships means there are fewer people jockeying for space on Castaway Cay; I also think the older ships have a more cozy, homey atmosphere. By the end of a long sailing on a small ship, the cast members feel like family—something I haven't experienced as often on the* Dream *and* Fantasy.

The *Wonder* splits its time among Alaska, the California coast, the Caribbean, and sometimes Hawaii. Repositioning cruises also take it through the Panama Canal. She sets sail from Galveston, Miami, San Diego, and Vancouver.

Our favorite spot on the *Wonder* is the **Outlook Café,** just upstairs from the **Cove Café.**

THE *Disney Dream*

FOLLOWING THE SUCCESSES OF THE *MAGIC* AND *WONDER,* DCL ordered two new ships that would more than double the number of guests they could serve, allow them to expand the number of itineraries offered, and bring several first-evers to a cruise ship. The new *Dream*-class vessels were built by Meyer Werft in Germany rather than Italy's Fincantieri, which created the *Magic* and *Wonder.*

The *Disney Dream,* the first of these new ships, set sail in 2011. It's 151 feet longer, 35 feet taller, and 15 feet wider than the *Magic* or *Wonder.* With three additional passenger decks, the ship can hold 50% more passengers and crew than its predecessors, yet it still has the classic lines of the smaller ships.

Disney Imagineering had great fun designing the second-generation ships. Inside cabins were given virtual portholes, which show the view from the bridge on a round screen. This feature proved so popular with kids that on many cruises, interior cabins had fares higher than those of ocean-view cabins. On the top deck, the **AquaDuck,** a waterslide that circles the ship, was added to the usual pools. Between the pool deck and your cabin, you'll find interactive art that reacts when you pass by it, along with the **Midship Detective Agency,** a scavenger hunt–type game that sends families all over the ship collecting clues.

unofficial **TIP**
We recommend the *Dream* or *Fantasy* over the *Magic* and *Wonder* to travelers who care more about the ships and their amenities than where they cruise.

Restaurants were given a huge makeover as well. The terrible Topsiders (formerly on the *Magic*) and Beach Blanket Buffet (formerly on the *Wonder*) were replaced with **Cabanas,** a buffet that improved on both traffic flow and food quality. **Animator's Palate** remained on board but was plussed up with new technology as part of the dinner show. The mediocre Parrot Cay became **Enchanted Garden,** the prettiest of the main dining rooms on board. Finally, Lumiere's (*Magic*) and Triton's (*Wonder*) were reimagined as **Royal Palace,** a tribute to all things Disney princess, but mostly Cinderella.

Both adults and kids scored big with improvements to the new ship. In addition to the adults-only Palo, **Remy** was added as another upscale-dining option for the 18-and-up crowd. With a subtle *Ratatouille* theme, and not one but two celebrated chefs creating the menus, Remy initially shocked cruisers with its surcharge—now $85 plus alcohol per dinner, the highest in the industry—but diners were pleased nonetheless. The adult lounges, in the area called **The District** on Deck 4, provide more-intimate, better-themed spaces to take the edge off than the old Beat Street on the *Magic* and Route 66 on the *Wonder*. **Skyline,** one of The District's bars, showcases a great use of technology, with a cityscape behind the bar that changes every 15 minutes. It's mesmerizing.

Senses Spa replaced the Vista Spa and outdid it in every way.

Kids got greatly expanded club areas with a Pixar theme. The teen area got a makeover that left it one of the most stylish spaces on board and gave it its own pool (the cast-member pool area from the older ships). Teens also got their own pampering spot, **Chill Spa.**

Though the *Dream* still feels very new, Disney continues to improve the ship. A 2015 dry-dock refresh added the following:

- A **Bibbidi Bobbidi Boutique** makeover salon for children, on Deck 5

- **Vanellope's Sweets & Treats,** a premium-ice-cream shop, on Deck 11. (Think of it as Palo for kids.)

- A new **Star Wars**–themed area of the Oceaneer Club. Children "pilot" a faux *Millennium Falcon* and participate in a shipboard version of the *Jedi Training Academy* show currently running at Walt Disney World.

- A new *Disney Infinity*–themed area of the Oceaneer Club. Kids can have fun in an immersive virtual world while on board.

The *Dream* is more glossy and high-tech than her DCL predecessors. Despite this, guests coming to it from the *Magic* or *Wonder* will have a strong sense of familiarity—kind of like seeing Walt Disney World after going to Disneyland. The theme is still Art Deco. The Cove Café still serves great coffee. And most of the stage shows are still not worth your time.

▌█ THE *Disney Fantasy*

THE *FANTASY* SAILED ITS MAIDEN VOYAGE in 2012, one year after the *Dream* came into service. The ship is nearly identical to its sister but got some tweaks as a result of guest and cast-member feedback. Both the *Dream* and the *Fantasy* are based out of Port Canaveral and sail the Caribbean. While the *Dream* has mostly three- and four-night itineraries, the *Fantasy* is almost exclusively seven-night sailings.

Walking into the atrium of the *Fantasy,* you see a bronze statue of Minnie Mouse and a striking peacock-inspired carpet—an indication of the Art Nouveau style of the *Fantasy* as opposed to the *Dream*'s Deco look.

The *Dream*'s technology package got some enhancements on the *Fantasy*. The **Midship Detective Agency** has three different storylines (including the Muppets) for guests to experience, surpassing the version on the *Dream*, and the show at **Animator's Palate** got a very cool audience-interaction element that we won't spoil here. Other than this addition, the restaurants are identical to the *Dream*'s, with one subtle name change: Royal Palace is **Royal Court** and includes even more princess-y goodness. **Cabanas, Enchanted Garden, Palo,** and **Remy** are the same.

On the pool deck, the **AquaDuck** adds the **AquaLab** splash area.

The *Fantasy*'s nightlife area is **Europa. Skyline** is the one constant between the two bar–nightclub areas on the ships, though it displays different cityscapes in this rendition. **The Tube**'s *Austin Powers*–style decor makes it a very fun place to hang out, but **Ooh La La** is either too high-concept or low-concept for our tastes; we prefer the whimsical look of the *Dream*'s **Pink** for our Champagne needs. **O'Gills Pub** doesn't feel particularly Irish, though it has the same big-screen TVs as **687,** the sports bar on the *Dream*.

On Deck: **NEW SHIPS**

IN THE SPRING OF 2016, Disney Cruise Line announced that it had ordered two new ships to join its fleet. These unnamed vessels will be built by Meyer Werft in Germany, the same company responsible for the *Dream* and *Fantasy.* Each ship will be slightly larger than the *Dream* and the *Fantasy*—a disappointment for those hoping for a megaship that would compete with Royal Caribbean's largest ships.

The ships are scheduled for completion in 2021 and 2023. Increasing the size of the fleet by 50% will open up more itinerary possibilities for DCL. Many analysts believe at least one of these ships will have a permanent home in Asia.

PART SEVEN

DINING

NOSHES, NOSHES *Everywhere*

THE FIRST THING MANY FOLKS DISCOVER when exploring the ships on embarkation day is the buffet. In the way that some people remember the birth of their first child, we remember our first look at the spread at Cabanas. (Sorry, Hannah. Love, Dad.) On one table sat a pile of crab legs that almost reached eye level. Next to this sat a trawler's worth of peel-and-eat shrimp. Surrounding these were tubs of melted butter and enough cocktail sauce to float the ship itself. On the other side of the aisle, a chef was flash-cooking a steak, the spices, sizzle, and flame making the air smell savory. It was glorious.

You'll never go hungry on a Disney cruise. The variety of dining options is staggering, including everything from coffee shops and pizza stands to Vegas-size buffets to ritzy French and Italian restaurants. That said, we've learned a few ways to increase your chances of enjoying memorable meals on board. This section describes your dining options in detail and includes our advice on how to make the most of them.

ROTATIONAL DINING

ONE OF THE INNOVATIONS that DCL brought to the cruise industry is the concept of rotational dining, in which you visit one of three standard restaurants on each different night of your cruise. As you change from restaurant to restaurant, your server team—your waiter, beverage person, head waiter, and maî-tre d'—all move with you. Your team will quickly learn your dining proclivities, including preferred drinks and favorite desserts, and make menu suggestions. Along with your stateroom attendant, you'll almost certainly rely on your dining team more than any other members of the crew during your trip.

*un*official **TIP**
DCL restaurants (except Palo and Remy, naturally) offer kids' menus for breakfast, lunch, and dinner. Kids (except for infants in the nursery) may also dine in their designated clubs free of charge.

The rotational restaurants have two dinner seatings, typically 5:45 p.m. and 8:15 p.m. Because Disney sets the schedule, there's no need to make reservations each night. You can request either the earlier or later seating when booking your trip or once aboard the ship. You also can request changes to your rotation, specifying which restaurants you visit each night.

Unlike other cruise lines, which may seat several families or groups together, Disney generally keeps families at their own tables. The exception to this would be singles or couples, who are routinely seated with other groups. If you're traveling alone or in a group of two or three and you prefer not to be seated with others during your rotational dining, call DCL in advance to make this request, which is not guaranteed but almost always honored.

On cruises of four nights or longer, you'll repeat at least one of the three standard restaurants. The menus will change each night, but the decor remains the same. Rather than visit the same restaurant twice on a four-night cruise, we recommend using one of those nights to visit Palo (on any ship) or Remy (on the *Dream* and *Fantasy*). You must pay an additional charge to dine at these restaurants, but the food is stellar, the crowds are small, and the service is impeccable.

You may request a particular dining rotation by calling DCL directly at ☎ 800-951-3532. This way, for example, you can pick which restaurant you're assigned to visit twice on a four-night cruise, or three times on a seven-night cruise. You may want to do this if you vastly prefer the decor of one restaurant over the others. Requests are not guaranteed, but they are often honored.

A less formal (and less expensive) option than rotational dining is having dinner in the buffet restaurant on each ship. At dinner, these restaurants serve from a menu rather than offering a full buffet, but you can arrive when you want and receive generally faster service than in the main dining rooms. This may be a good option if you have an early dinner seating but you get back to the ship in a rush after a port adventure, or if your kids are too famished to wait until the later seating.

Another alternative to rotational dining is ordering room service. Finally, note that at least one of the rotational restaurants is open for breakfast and lunch each day. Check your *Personal Navigator* for details.

DCL RESTAURANT CATEGORIES

IN GENERAL, FOOD OFFERINGS on Disney Cruise Line are differentiated by freshness, quality, and service:

COUNTER SERVICE Available on each ship's pool deck, fast food includes staples such as burgers, chicken strips, pizza, and sandwiches. In *The Unofficial Guide to Walt Disney World,* we equate the quality of the counter-service restaurants in the theme parks with that of McDonald's and Taco Bell. With a few exceptions, the food quality at DCL's counter-service restaurants is more like what you'd find in your local supermarket's frozen-food aisle: edible but not as good as something made from scratch (or even at McDonald's). The best items on board are the fresh sandwiches and wraps and, if your timing is right, pizza straight from the oven. Counter-service restaurants for each ship are listed starting with the *Magic*'s, on page 131.

CAFÉS AND LOUNGES   Each ship has a dedicated coffee bar called **Cove Café** that serves espresso, cappuccino, teas, and smoothies, plus wine, mixed drinks, and spirits. A good alternative to a big dinner is Cove Café's small selection of complimentary cold appetizers, available each evening.

Besides Cove Café, a few of the ships' bars and lounges serve appetizers, too. These are described in detail in Part Eight, Entertainment and Nightlife.

BUFFETS   Each ship has one large buffet venue, usually open for breakfast and lunch. Buffets tend to serve a bit of everything at each meal and are the easiest way to satisfy disparate appetites. As large and diverse as those at many Las Vegas hotels, the buffets let picky kids (and adults) see exactly what kind of food they're getting. The buffets also offer plenty of seating with ocean views, indoors and out.

FULL-SERVICE RESTAURANTS   Each Disney Cruise Line ship has four or five dedicated full-service restaurants. Three of these are part of the standard rotational dinner schedule available to every guest on the ship, with the remaining venues available to adult guests for an additional fee. Additionally, the restaurant on each ship that serves buffet breakfast and lunch also will serve a menu-based dinner that's free and open to all guests.

Along with dinner, one sit-down restaurant is usually open for breakfast and lunch each day, even when the ship is in port. Breakfast and lunch may include both buffet components (an appetizer salad bar, for example) and the option to order from a menu.

Virtually all of the food served at the rotational restaurants will be familiar to American palates. Most dishes, especially at dinner, feature cuts of steak, pork, chicken, and fish similar to those you'd find at a chain eatery. DCL's chefs will add some sort of flavor twist to these such as soy and sesame if it's an Asian-themed menu, but the basic ingredients will be recognizable to almost everyone. If you want your entrée largely unadorned, look for the "Lighter Note" section of the menu. You'll see here that you can always get plain steak or chicken served with plain rice or a baked potato. Those in the mood for mild need not worry.

Although fresher and of higher quality than the counter-service restaurants, most of the food served at the full-service restaurants is prepared well ahead of time. You get your order faster this way, but it's also well-nigh impossible to customize that order. We've been told, for instance, that we couldn't order a roast-beef-and-mayo sandwich without the mayo. If you're a moderately finicky eater, you can do the customizing yourself, provided your dish consists of discrete ingredients that you can subtract easily. A BLT without lettuce is probably doable; tomato-and-basil soup sans the basil probably isn't.

While the quality of food in the main rotational dining rooms is generally fine, it's not unheard of to get a poorly prepared meal. Unfortunately, such missteps seem to be more common on DCL now than they used to be. A reader tells us:

> The food quality in the main dining rooms has been in a steady decline over the past several years. On our most recent trip, the fish was always overcooked and my steak was tough. We found ourselves getting on the waitlist for extra reservations at Palo and Remy to avoid being let down. It also got old dealing with the multiple levels of staff in the main dining rooms once they realize you are not enjoying your food. It's true that the staff will do everything possible to make it right, but at 9 p.m. I am too tired and grumpy to want to wait for the issue to be resolved. The issue is never with the staff but the quality of food and the preparation in the kitchen.

ADULT DINING The upscale Italian restaurant **Palo,** found on each ship and for which Disney charges an additional fee of $30, serves dinner to cruisers 18 and older. The *Dream* and *Fantasy* have a fifth restaurant, **Remy,** which serves high-end French cuisine and levies an $85 surcharge. Both Palo and Remy serve brunch on selected sea days (still adults-only). Both are also difficult to get into, so book a table at disneycruise.com at least 75 days before you sail. See page 130 for more information.

In addition to serving food that's superior to the main dining rooms', the adult dining restaurants also have a higher level of service. Another reader reports:

> We went to Palo for dinner on our first night. I asked if the chef could make me chicken parmigiana, which wasn't on the menu. One minute later, the chef himself came out and apologized—he didn't have the ingredients on hand to make it. The next day, I got a call in my stateroom. It was my server from Palo. He said he had something special for me and came down to our stateroom with an entire tray of chicken parm—the chef had made it for brunch that day and wanted me to try his take on it. Truly amazing!

Disney often tinkers with its adult-dining offerings, testing special events for specific sailings or individual ships. For example, some voyages have had a Palo option of a five-course tasting menu and Italian wine pairing called **Esperienza del Vino.** The cost was $59 above the standard Palo charge. In late 2016, some sailings of the Fantasy began offering a $279 experience at Palo, **Be Our Chef,** providing guests with the opportunity to learn how to prepare four of the Northern Italian Palo dishes, plus a special keepsake. If you're interested in enhanced adult-dining experiences, check your online Planning Center (see page 35) or call DCL at ☎ 800-951-3532.

ROOM SERVICE

OTHER THAN THE LAST MORNING OF YOUR CRUISE, room service is available on the Disney ships 24 hours a day. With the exception of a few packaged snacks and bottled beverages, there is no charge for room service other than a small tip for the porter who brings your meal ($1 or $2 per person or item ordered is appropriate). Typical lunch and dinner offerings include hamburgers, pizza, sandwiches, chicken fingers, salads, soups, and fresh fruit. The cheese-and-crackers plate is a particularly popular early-evening snack for guests assigned to the later dinner seating. Continental breakfast items are offered in the morning.

Room service can be a great option if you want to eat breakfast quickly before heading out on a port excursion, if you want to dine on your verandah, if you want to eat while enjoying a movie on your stateroom TV, or if you just don't feel like getting dressed for dinner.

The room-service menus always include a selection of warm giant cookies, usually chocolate chip or oatmeal raisin. If you want to be a hero to your kids (or your spouse), have room service bring them surprise cookies and milk as a bedtime snack. Or, even better, dive into the unadvertised room-service menu and order a round of Mickey ice-cream bars or Mickey-shaped marshmallow crispy treats for the room. All you have to do is ask!

THEME NIGHTS

ON CRUISES OF LONGER THAN THREE NIGHTS, DCL adds themed dinners. These include a **Pirates' menu** (somewhat Caribbean-influenced on Pirate Night), **Till We Meet Again** (the last night of your cruise), the **Captain's Gala,** and **Prince and Princess menus.** The menus available on your cruise will depend on your itinerary—for example, Alaskan voyages typically add a seafood-focused night featuring local salmon and king crab.

> *un*official **TIP**
> On theme nights, each main dining area serves the same menu, so no one misses out on the fun.

In 2015, DCL added **Frozen-themed days** to some Alaskan and Northern European sailings. The movie-themed menu we were served on the *Magic* in Iceland included items like Sven's Carrot Soup, The Duke of Weselton's Favorite Assorted Meats, Oaken Warm Apple Pudding Cake, and Olaf's White Chocolate Floro Dome. In 2016, **Star Wars–themed days** were added to some sailings on the *Fantasy.* The themed menu items included Sand People Salad, Bantha Steak Empanadas, Opee Sea Killer Shrimp Cocktail, and Qui-Gon's Crisp Chicken. Dessert offerings included Calrissian Velvet Cake, Cloud City Macaroons, and a Frozen Carbonite Sundae.

DINING WITH KIDS

ON DISNEY CRUISE LINE, kids are people, too, when it comes to dining. While there are kids' menus featuring standard fare like chicken nuggets and mac and cheese, kids of all ages are welcome to eat from any part of the upper-deck buffet and order any item in the main dining rooms. If *you* want chicken nuggets for dinner and your 6-year-old wants escargot and prime rib, those are both equally fine.

Your serving team should be your partner in planning a strategy on how to best meet your family's dining needs. Do you want your kids' food brought to the table first so they're not ravenous? Do you want the bread basket left off the table so your kids fill up on more protein and veggies than carbs? Do you want only milk and water offered to your kids, not soda? Tell your serving team those things on the first night and they'll make notes about your preferences.

If you've been assigned to the second dinner seating, you can even arrange to have staff from the onboard child-care centers pick your kids up in the dining room so that you can linger over dessert while they're off playing. Speak to the kids' club staff if you'd like to do this. However, you should be aware that there are some special experiences that occur toward the end of the usual dinner hour, some of which your children might not want to miss. For example, at the end of dinner on one night at Animator's Palate on the *Fantasy* and the *Magic*, guests are treated to a short animated film created from diners' drawings. Most kids get a real kick out of seeing their artwork on screen.

In the realm of healthy eating, Disney has taken positive steps toward offering healthful options at its theme parks and on its ships. **Mickey Check** meals are available on all the rotational-dining restaurant kids' menus and on the menus posted on the DCL Navigator app. The Mickey Check symbol indicates that the meal falls within specific dietary guidelines for calorie count; percentage of sugar, sodium, and fat; and recommended amounts of vitamins and other nutrients. You can see details on the program at tinyurl.com/dclmickeycheck.

Parents of infants should know that there is a small selection of commercially packaged baby food available on the Disney ships; look for it in the gift shop near the over-the-counter medications. You'll typically find two to four different flavors of jarred baby food and one brand of single-serve baby formula sold in the shops.

unofficial **TIP**
If you want your baby to have warm food, you have only two options: Ask the kitchen staff to puree food that they've prepared, or improvise by getting a bowl of very hot water and placing a jar of baby food in the water for a few minutes. (A buffet cereal bowl and hot water from the coffee/tea dispenser should do the trick.)

You're also welcome to bring your own packaged baby food aboard the ship. This must be sealed, commercially prepared baby food—homemade foods and open containers of any type are prohibited. You must bring this baby food with you in your carry-on luggage, not in your checked bags. DCL chefs will also puree any food available on the ship for you. For instance, they can whip up something like pureed peas, carrots, or chicken quite easily. Also keep in mind that many of the soft foods already available on the ship may be fine for older babies and toddlers: mashed potatoes, oatmeal, soups, scrambled eggs, and so on.

If you're planning to bring your own baby food on board, be aware that your child will likely have to eat it cold. (At Walt Disney World, by contrast, guests have free use of microwave ovens in the food courts.) Additionally, you may not bring any cooking appliances on board with you: no electric kettles, rice cookers, hot plates, Sterno cans, or anything else that could be a fire hazard. Further complicating matters, DCL kitchens won't heat any food you've brought with you onto the ship, nor will they heat baby food that you've purchased in the onboard gift shop.

Children are welcome to eat in the main dining rooms on their own or with young siblings, cousins, or friends in their party. If, for example, the grown-ups are having dinner at the adults-only Palo restaurant, the kids can still have a nice meal of their own in their regular rotational restaurant. Parents will have to assess at what age their kids are ready for this, but we've seen many 8- and 9-year-olds dining together in the main dining rooms while their parents were having a romantic meal elsewhere. Let your server know that you're planning to do this, and they'll be sure to take special care of your child's dining needs.

On longer sailings, Disney often offers a character breakfast in one of the main rotational dining rooms. Mickey, Goofy, Pluto, and sometimes other Disney favorites will stop by each guest table to sign autographs and pose for photos. While kids are the main fans of these meals, parties with adults only are also welcome to partake. There is no additional charge for character meals, but they do typically need to be reserved in advance. On some sailings, reservations will be made available through DCL's online Planning Center (see page 35), while on others tickets will be distributed on a first-come, first-serve basis on embarkation day (see page 79).

DRESS CODE

SHORTS AND T-SHIRTS are acceptable at all meals at the standard restaurants, even for adults. We think most adults will feel more appropriately dressed in pants or dresses at dinner; Bermuda shorts paired with a nice button-down shirt and shoes would probably also work.

unofficial **TIP**
Remy's dress code requires a tuxedo or jacket for men, along with dress pants. Ties are optional. Acceptable women's attire includes evening gowns, cocktail dresses, blouses and skirts, and pantsuits.

A mother of four from Midland, Texas, praises this shorts-tolerant policy:

> There was no way I was going to pack 8–10 pairs of pants—minimum!—for my kids and my husband for our seven-night cruise. Shorts take up less luggage space and can be worn all day. It's less laundry for me to do when we get home, too.

Swimwear and tank tops are prohibited at any time, and frankly you'd be freezing for most of your meal.

Many cruises of four nights or longer will have a designated **Formal Night.** The food served in the rotational dining rooms is essentially the same as any other night. And while dress-up clothing is not absolutely required (Disney wouldn't kick you out of a rotational restaurant for being slightly underdressed), you will find that many people up their dinnerwear game for the occasion. The definition of *formal* is fluid: If you own a tux or evening gown that fits, go ahead and bring it. We typically opt for a suit and cocktail attire, but you'll also see khakis and a pressed golf shirt on some. Kids should wear whatever nice clothes seem comfortable and appropriate. For girls, a cute sundress is fine; boys may wear a button-down shirt or a tie to look dapper.

The dress code at Palo is more upscale. As of April 2016, the restaurant's official dress code reads, "Guests are asked to preserve the ambience of this fine-dining venue. Dress pants, slacks, and collared shirts are recommended for men, and a dress, skirt, or pants and a blouse are recommended for women. Jeans may also be worn if in good condition (no holes). Please, no tank tops, swimsuits, swimsuit cover-ups, shorts, hats, cutoffs, torn clothing, T-shirts with offensive language and/or graphics, flip-flops, or tennis shoes."

SPECIAL DIETS

TRAVELING WHEN YOU EAT A SPECIAL DIET—gluten-free, vegan/ vegetarian, allergen-free, kosher, and so on—can be a challenge. Disney as a company has a pretty good reputation for handling special diets, but guests should be prepared (by investigating options ahead of time and noting dietary requests when booking) and be proactive (by making their needs known while on the ship) to ensure the best experience with the dining staff.

In addition to noting any food allergies or dietary requests at booking, you should consult DCL's official guidelines for guests with special diets. You can find this information online at disneycruise.disney.go .com/guest-services/special-dietary-requests. We also recommend that you follow up with a phone call at ☎ 407-566-3602. Other aspects of guest care also may be addressed by consulting Disney's guidelines for guests with disabilities: disneycruise.disney.go.com/guest-services /guests-with-disabilities; complete the **Special Services Information Form** on that page if any member of your party requires unique care or attention. If you've booked your cruise through a travel agent, he or she may also be able to assist you in your communication with Disney.

Once you're on the ship, your servers also will ask you at the beginning of your cruise about any allergies or special diets. Be sure to confirm your needs with them. There are no separate kitchen facilities on board for guests with allergies, nor are there separate dining areas for allergen-free items. Also be aware that you will need to restate your dining needs to any excursion company or restaurant serving you food while you're not onboard. Use particular caution when dining in unfamiliar areas or when communicating in a language other than your own.

If you have a specific brand preference, for instance a type of soy milk or gluten-free waffle, you will most likely be disappointed to find there isn't much in the way of choice, and there's not a lot that can be done about this when you're at sea. If your child will eat only one brand of something, your best bet is to bring it with you.

Coauthor Laurel sticks to a vegan diet at home. Here's her experience with DCL:

I have a strong preference for a diet that is entirely plant-based. That said, as a travel writer, I often find myself reviewing foods for the sake of research that I wouldn't normally eat. The last thing I want to do is make a big deal over what I eat, mostly because I don't want to be a bother. For vegetarians who eat eggs and/or dairy, DCL is easy: There are multiple options available to you at each meal, and there's no need to involve the servers. For vegans, however, it's a little more difficult. Here are my meal-by-meal tips:

- **BREAKFAST:** *Your easiest and best bet is the buffet, where you can see exactly what you're getting. Ask a server for nondairy milk.*
- **LUNCH:** *There's the buffet again. Also, you can request cheeseless pizza from the pool deck. I've gotten yummy wraps here, along with veggie burgers (vegans should skip the buns) and fries.*
- **DINNER:** *The main dining rooms are OK, but return cruisers who are vegan or vegetarian are going to get tired of the same choices quickly. Vegetarian entrées (a separate section of the menu) tend to be vegan, too, but good luck finding an appetizer or dessert that's egg- and dairy-free. Skip the appetizer and choose fresh fruit or sorbet for dessert. You may also be offered a nondairy ice cream like Tofutti or Rice Dream (which is great if you like those—I don't).*
- **SPECIALTY DINING (Palo or Remy):** *If your whole table is vegan, skip these. They're not worth it, and Remy in particular seems not to understand the difference between gluten-free and vegan. (I get it—vegan is not a French thing.) If you're traveling with an omnivore who wants to dine at either place, go ahead, but be prepared to feel you're missing out. If you do dine at either location, be sure you've noted on your reservation that you have dietary restrictions. Ovo-lacto vegetarians will do fine at either location.*
- **CASTAWAY CAY:** *You can ask ahead for veggie burgers. Many, but not all, of the sides are vegan. There is plenty of fresh fruit.*
- **MISCELLANEOUS:** *Room service doesn't offer great options right off the menu, but ask when you call if there's anything that can be modified. The antipasti at Cove Café and Vista Café in the evenings are a good choice if you skip the cheeses.*

MAKING RESERVATIONS

NO RESERVATIONS ARE REQUIRED for any night at any of the three standard rotational-dining restaurants. Reservations are required for Palo and Remy and can be made up to 120 days in advance in some circumstances. Reserve online at the DCL Planning Center (see page 35).

CATEGORY	DAYS IN ADVANCE RESERVATIONS CAN BE MADE
Guests in suites or Concierge staterooms	**120 DAYS**
Platinum Castaway Club members	**120 DAYS**
Gold Castaway Club members	**105 DAYS**
Silver Castaway Club members	**90 DAYS**
All other guests	**75 DAYS**

FULL-SERVICE RESTAURANTS: RATED AND RANKED

TO HELP YOU MAKE YOUR DINING CHOICES, we've developed profiles of DCL's sit-down restaurants, listed alphabetically by restaurant following each ship's counter-service dining coverage. The profiles allow you to quickly check a given restaurant's cuisine, star rating, quality rating, and specialties.

DCL Rotational Restaurants by Cuisine

RESTAURANT	SHIP	OVERALL RATING	QUALITY RATING
AMERICAN/ASIAN			
Animator's Palate	All	★★★	★★★
AMERICAN/BRAZILIAN			
Carioca's	*Magic*	★★★	★★★
AMERICAN/SOUTHERN			
Tiana's Place	*Wonder*	★★★	★★★
AMERICAN/CONTINENTAL			
Enchanted Garden	*Dream, Fantasy*	★★★	★★★
AMERICAN/FRENCH			
Lumiere's	*Magic*	★★★	★★★
Royal Court	*Fantasy*	★★★	★★★
Royal Palace	*Dream*	★★★	★★★
Triton's	*Wonder*	★★★	★★★
BUFFET			
Cabanas	All	★★★	★★★

STAR RATING The star rating represents the entire dining experience: style, service, and ambience, in addition to the taste, presentation, and quality of the food. Five stars is the highest rating and indicates that the restaurant offers the best of everything. Four-star restaurants are above average; three-star restaurants offer good, though not necessarily memorable, meals. Two-star restaurants serve mediocre fare. (No DCL restaurants merit one star.) Our star ratings don't correspond to ratings awarded by AAA, Mobil, Zagat, or other restaurant reviewers.

DCL Adult-Only Restaurants by Cuisine

CUISINE / SHIP	OVERALL RATING	QUALITY RATING	VALUE RATING
FRENCH / REMY			
Dream, Fantasy	★★★★½	★★★★½	★★★★½
ITALIAN / PALO			
All ships	★★★½* /	★★★½* /	★★★½* /
*Magic, Wonder **Dream, Fantasy*	★★★★**	★★★★**	★★★★**

QUALITY RATING The food quality is rated on a scale of one to five stars, five being the best rating attainable. The quality rating is based on the taste, freshness of ingredients, preparation, presentation, and creativity of the food served. Price is not a consideration. If you want the best food available and cost is not an issue, you need look no further than the quality ratings.

Disney Magic DINING

COUNTER-SERVICE RESTAURANTS

Daisy's De-Lites

QUALITY B   **PORTION** Small-Medium   **LOCATION** Deck 9 Aft

WHEN TO GO Typical hours: breakfast, 6:30 a.m.–9 a.m.; lunch, 11 a.m.–6:30 p.m. Check your *Personal Navigator* for exact schedule.

SELECTIONS Breakfast includes pastries, croissants, muffins, and yogurt; lunch offerings include sandwiches, wraps, salads, fruit, and cookies.

COMMENTS A good alternative to the breakfast buffet if all you're looking for is a few croissants and some coffee. The wraps are small and tasty, and they make an excellent snack between lunch and dinner.

Pete's Boiler Bites

QUALITY B   **PORTION** Medium   **LOCATION** Deck 9 Aft

WHEN TO GO Typical hours: 11 a.m.–6 p.m. Check your *Personal Navigator* for exact schedule.

SELECTIONS Grilled hot dogs and sausages; hamburgers and veggie burgers; chicken strips; chicken sandwiches; tacos; fries.

COMMENTS The tacos are a surprise find here. A nearby fixin's bar provides toppings for your order.

Pinocchio's Pizzeria

QUALITY C   **PORTION** Medium   **LOCATION** Deck 9 Aft

WHEN TO GO Typical hours: 11 a.m.–6 p.m. Check your *Personal Navigator* for exact schedule.

SELECTIONS Cheese, pepperoni, and specialty pizzas (including veggie). Cheeseless pizza on request. DCL recently has added freshly baked pretzels, both salty and cheese-stuffed sweet, here. We think this is the best thing since warm, twisty bread.

COMMENTS About the same quality as frozen pizza . . . but there are plenty of times when that's exactly what you want.

FULL-SERVICE RESTAURANTS
Animator's Palate ★ ★ ★   Deck 4 Aft

AMERICAN/ASIAN   QUALITY ★ ★ ★   SERVICE ★ ★ ★ ★   FRIENDLINESS ★ ★ ★ ★

Reservations Not accepted. **When to go** Dinner. **Bar** Yes. **Alcohol** Red, white, and sparkling wines, plus mixed drinks and spirits. All alcohol costs extra. **Dress** Casual; no tank tops or swimwear. **Hours** Nightly dinner seatings usually at 5:45 and 8:15 p.m.; check your *Personal Navigator* for the exact schedule.

SETTING AND ATMOSPHERE The idea behind Animator's Palate is that you begin dining inside an old-fashioned black-and-white animated film that is slowly colorized as dinner goes along. The entrance's walls are decorated with black charcoal sketches of various Disney characters. Inside, the entire color scheme starts out in black, white, and gray from floor to ceiling, including checkerboard-tile floor, black chairs, white tablecloths with black napkins, and black-and-white uniforms for the waitstaff. Even the ship's support columns are dressed up, in this case as white artist's brushes pointed to the ceiling.

Along the outside wall are video monitors that display images and "how-to-draw" sketches from Disney films. As the evening progresses, you'll notice bits of color being added to the walls and artwork, eventually becoming fully saturated by the end of your meal.

Animator's Palate on the *Magic* received an upgrade during summer 2014, adding the *Animation Magic* dinner show that debuted on the *Fantasy*.

At the beginning of *Animation Magic* night (typically your second evening at Animator's Palate on a seven-night cruise or your third evening at Animator's Palate on a longer sailing), you're given a sheet of paper and a marker and told to draw a self-portrait. (There are guidelines on how to do this.) At the end of the evening, all of the diners' self-portraits are shown in an animated cartoon similar to Disney's 1929 short cartoon *The Skeleton Dance.*

HOUSE SPECIALTIES Vegetable stir-fry; roasted-garlic or red-pepper dip with bread.

COMMENTS Disney characterizes the cuisine at Animator's Palate as Pacific Rim/American, but it's really just standard chain-restaurant fare. There are probably as many Italian selections—pasta, risotto, focaccia—as Asian. A handful of dishes, such as the vegetable stir-fry, have origins in the East; others are American dishes enrobed in a culinary kimono of sesame, ginger, or teriyaki sauce to make them "Pacific Rim." The food isn't *bad* . . . but it's not Asian either.

Cabanas   ★★★   Deck 9 Aft

AMERICAN/BUFFET   QUALITY ★★★   SERVICE ★★★★   FRIENDLINESS ★★★★

Reservations Not accepted. **When to go** Breakfast, lunch, and dinner. **Bar** Yes. **Alcohol** Red, white, and sparkling wines, plus mixed drinks and spirits. All alcohol costs extra. **Dress** Casual; no tank tops or swimwear at dinner. **Hours** Daily breakfast buffet, 7–10:45 a.m.; daily lunch buffet, noon–1:30 p.m.; nightly sit-down dinner, 6:30–8:30 p.m. Hours are subject to change, so check your *Personal Navigator* for the exact schedule.

SETTING AND ATMOSPHERE Cabanas is entered from either side of Deck 9 Aft. On either side is a line of buffet tables that run the length of the restaurant. Indoor and outdoor seating are arranged around the buffet. The indoor seating is air-conditioned and features floor-to-ceiling windows, affording excellent ocean views. Outdoor seating is great on mornings when the ship is docking because you're sometimes able to watch the port come into view. Large murals lining the walls display pirate and fish imagery. Coffee, soft drinks, juices, and water are served from dispensers placed at regular intervals throughout the restaurant.

HOUSE SPECIALTIES Made-to-order omelets for breakfast; lunch seafood bar including oysters, clams, crab legs, and peel-and-eat shrimp. Look for special regional breakfast items on Northern European sailings.

COMMENTS The breakfast and lunch buffets would be competitive with those at many Las Vegas resorts and serve about as wide a variety of items as you'll find anywhere. Breakfast includes everything from fruit, yogurt, and oatmeal to doughnuts, lox, and custom-made omelets. Even cold cereal has options: Besides the usual cornflakes and granola, there's a "build-your-own" muesli bar where you can add ingredients ranging from brown sugar to exotic dried fruits. Don't worry if you skipped dessert last night—you can get several at breakfast here. We haven't asked, but we'd bet hard cash that the staff would make you filet mignon if you requested nicely.

Lunch is a similarly lavish spread, with everything from chicken tenders, sandwiches, and burgers to salmon steaks and pasta. A big draw at lunch is the peel-and-eat shrimp, usually complemented by clams, oysters, and crab legs.

Cabanas switches from buffet to sit-down service for dinner. The menu changes frequently, usually along with the menus at the other main restaurants. Appetizers typically include soups and salads, along with meat- and fish-based dishes. Entrées usually include chicken, fish, steak, and vegetarian options. We recommend Cabanas for dinner at sunset on longer cruises, as an alternative to dining a second time at one of the main restaurants, especially Lumiere's.

Carioca's ★★★   Deck 3 Aft

AMERICAN/BRAZILIAN QUALITY ★★★ SERVICE ★★★★ FRIENDLINESS ★★★★

Reservations Not accepted. **When to go** Dinner. **Bar** Yes. **Alcohol** A decent selection of reds, whites, and sparkling wines. If you're in the mood for a cocktail, try the berry-flavored Caipirosa. All alcohol costs extra. **Dress** Casual; no tank tops or swimwear at dinner. **Hours** Breakfast buffet on select days, 8:30–10:45 a.m.; lunch buffet on select days (hours vary); nightly dinner seatings usually at 5:30 and 8 p.m. Hours are subject to change, so check your *Personal Navigator* for the exact schedule.

SETTING AND ATMOSPHERE The *Magic's* newest restaurant, Carioca's is named for José Carioca, one of the three birds in Disney's animated 1944 film *The Three Caballeros.* The word *carioca* is slang for a native of Rio de Janeiro, and so Carioca's theme is Brazilian festival. The restaurant uses lighting effects to transform the setting: When the lighting effects are off at breakfast and lunch, Carioca's interior has a cool white-and-gray floor, white walls, and white tablecloths. Round white lanterns hang from the ceiling, accented by a handful of colorful red, orange, and yellow lights. For dinner, rich yellow and brown lighting transforms the restaurant into a cinnamon-and-gold nightspot. It's a little darker than you'd expect at night, but still way nicer than when it was Parrot Cay.

HOUSE SPECIALTIES The menu also got an overhaul, and it's much improved. Lunch and breakfast are unremarkable American fare—dinner is when Carioca's really shines. The signature dish is the José Carioca's: three grilled skewers of Brazilian sausage, chili-crusted lamb, and beef tenderloin, with a side of tomato-flavored rice and a delicious *chimichurri* sauce (think South American pesto). The tenderloin and lamb can be a bit dry, but the chimichurri sauce balances it out. At least one person at your table should try this.

The other entrée we really liked—in small bites—was the slow-roasted pork belly, with sides of mashed sweet potato, grits, and collard greens. The pork's skin was incredibly crispy, almost to the point where you'd think it was fried, yet the meat underneath was tender and juicy. Combined with the grits and sweet potatoes, it's almost *too* rich, which is why we suggest ordering this as an entrée for the table to share, with each person also ordering another entrée.

Vegetarian options include corn tortillas with Veracruzan refried-bean dip and a relish of green tomatillo, chile, and shredded white cabbage and carrot. It's not as spicy as the black-bean soup appetizer, which has a touch of habanero pepper, but the tortillas are a filling dish.

Beyond the vegetarian black-bean soup, the other appetizers we like are salads: the tiger shrimp ceviche, with cucumber, cilantro, and tomato-citrus dressing; and the cuban salad, with avocado, pineapple, toasted Cuban bread, and a tangy cider-vinegar dressing. We would avoid the ahi-tuna-and-avocado tower—the tuna at Palo is much better.

OTHER RECOMMENDATIONS If you subscribe to the "everything tastes better on a stick" philosophy and you're also in the mood for seafood, try the lobster, shrimp, and mahimahi skewers. These are served on a salad of quinoa (the grain of the moment, judging from how many recipes in which Disney uses it) with dried-mango, pineapple, and toasted-coconut salsa.

COMMENTS We're glad to see the menu improve, and we'd be happy to dine at Carioca's twice on longer sailings.

Lumiere's ★ ★ ★   Deck 3 Midship

AMERICAN/FRENCH   QUALITY ★ ★ ★   SERVICE ★ ★ ★ ★   FRIENDLINESS ★ ★ ★ ★

Reservations Not accepted. **When to go** Breakfast. **Bar** Yes. **Alcohol** Limited selection of red, white, and sparkling wines, plus mixed drinks and spirits. All alcohol costs extra. **Dress** Casual; no tank tops or swimwear at dinner. **Hours** À la carte breakfast on select days, 8–9:30 a.m.; à la carte lunch on select days, 11:45 a.m.–1:30 p.m.; nightly dinner seatings usually at 5:45 and 8:15 p.m. Hours are subject to change, so check your *Personal Navigator* for the exact schedule.

SETTING AND ATMOSPHERE Despite the name, there are only a few references to *Beauty and the Beast* inside the restaurant. The most notable are the light fixtures, which contain a single red rose. There's also a mural on the back wall that depicts characters from the movie. Besides these, most of Lumiere's decor is Art Deco, which makes sense given the restaurant's location, just off the ship's atrium.

HOUSE SPECIALTIES Lobster mac and cheese; crispy roasted duck breast.

COMMENTS Disney puts escargot and French onion soup on the menu of each French-themed standard dining room in the cruise line. Besides these, however, most of the rest of the menu is decidedly un-French and would be equally at home at your neighborhood TGI Friday's: grilled meats and chicken, a vegetarian tofu selection, and pasta. A couple of entrées, such as the lamb shank and crispy duck breast, stand out. The Grand Marnier soufflé is the most popular dessert, but the brioche bread pudding with toffee sauce is better.

Palo ★ ★ ★ ½   Deck 10 Aft

ITALIAN   QUALITY ★ ★ ★ ½   VALUE ★ ★ ★ ½   SERVICE ★ ★ ★ ★ ½   FRIENDLINESS ★ ★ ★ ★

Reservations Required. **When to go** Brunch on sea days; dinner nightly. **Bar** Yes. **Alcohol** Large list of Italian wines, listed by region, plus select wines from around the world; mixed drinks and spirits; *limoncello*; grappa; ice wine. All alcohol costs extra. **Dress** Dress pants, slacks, and collared shirts are recommended for men; a dress, skirt, or pants and a blouse are recommended for women. Jeans may be worn if in good condition (no holes). No tank tops, swimsuits, swimsuit cover-ups, shorts, hats, cutoffs, torn clothing, T-shirts with offensive language and/or graphics, flip-flops, or tennis shoes. **Hours** Brunch on sea days on cruises of 4 nights or longer, 10 a.m.–12:30 p.m.; nightly dinner, 6–8:30 p.m. Hours are subject to change, so check your *Personal Navigator* for the exact schedule. **Special comments** An additional $30/person charge will be added to your cruise bill for each meal at Palo (charge may be waived for Platinum Castaway Club members). If you need to cancel a reservation, you must do so 24 hours in advance or the full per-person charge may be applied to your bill. Guests must be 18 or older to dine.

SETTING AND ATMOSPHERE Palo sits across the entire Aft section of Deck 10, which means that almost every seat has a spectacular view of the ocean sunset during dinner. On the *Magic,* Palo has contemporary decor, with tan-wood panels, round leather benches, and deep-purple fabric on the wood chairs. A small bar is available for guests waiting for their tables to become available; part of the kitchen is open to the view of guests sitting in the middle of the restaurant. Red-and-white-striped poles near the bar, evocative of those used to steer gondolas, call to mind Palo's roots in Venice (*palo* means "pole").

Because Palo has an adults-only policy, the restaurant is much quieter than DCL's main dining rooms. The quietest tables are those on the port side, aft (left and forward), tucked away behind the curve of the restaurant. If you're looking to do some people-watching with dinner, request a table on the starboard (left) side of the ship, near Palo's entrance. Brunch offers open seating, so sit wherever the view is best. Background music is mostly Italian and ranges from Vivaldi to Sinatra, as God intended.

HOUSE SPECIALTIES For a first course at dinner, try the fish-and-seafood soup, laden with mussels, clams, and lobster. The *antipasto freddo,* which comprises a selection of familiar cheeses and cured meats, could be a little more adventurous. Our favorite entrées are the lobster ravioli in truffle-butter sauce; the spicy penne *arrabbiata;* and the rack of lamb, roasted with garlic and shallots. The chocolate soufflé, by far the most popular dessert, is served with both dark- and white-chocolate sauces.

Palo's brunch menu is the best on board. One large table is dedicated to breads, muffins, and pastries, along with sliced fruits and fresh vegetables (the roasted asparagus is tasty). An entire aquarium's worth of fish is available in another section, including shrimp cocktail, cured salmon, smoked-trout mousse, seared tuna, scallops, crab legs, crawfish, and mussels. Eggs cooked in every conceivable way, including Benedict, Florentine, Julia, and customized omelets, are on the menu, too. Not enough? Try the selection of made-to-order pizzas.

COMMENTS Palo, the *Magic*'s one upscale restaurant, is its own little island of adult serenity and food. Service is very good, and don't be surprised if the maître d' and your server are from Italy.

Dinners at Palo are tasty and relaxing, especially with a glass or two of wine. That being said, we think Palo is better for brunch—besides the best selection of midday food anywhere on the ship, the view out of Palo's windows is much better during the day; once the sun sets at dinner, Palo's spectacular windows just reflect the inside of the restaurant. If we could improve one thing at Palo, it would be the coffee served, which is Joffrey's. A restaurant this good should offer better.

Finally, note that we rate Palo on the *Dream* and *Fantasy* higher overall, as well as for quality and value. It's undeniably very good on both the *Magic* and the *Wonder,* but the decor on the *Dream*-class ships is more sophisticated, and the kitchens are larger, allowing for better food preparation.

Disney sometimes adds special adult-dining experiences to specific sailings; see page 143 for more information.

Disney Wonder DINING

COUNTER-SERVICE RESTAURANTS

Daisy's De-Lites

QUALITY B   **PORTION** Small–Medium   **LOCATION** Deck 9 Aft

COMMENTS See profile of Daisy's De-Lites on the *Magic* (page 131) for details.

Pete's Boiler Bites

QUALITY B   **PORTION** Medium   **LOCATION** Deck 9 Aft

COMMENTS See profile of Pete's Boiler Bites on the *Magic* (page 131) for details.

Pinocchio's Pizzeria

QUALITY C   **PORTION** Medium   **LOCATION** Deck 9 Aft

COMMENTS See profile of Pinocchio's Pizzeria on the *Magic* (page 131) for details.

FULL-SERVICE RESTAURANTS

Animator's Palate ★★★   Deck 4 Aft

AMERICAN/ASIAN   QUALITY ★★★   SERVICE ★★★★   FRIENDLINESS ★★★★

COMMENTS See profile of Animator's Palate on the *Magic* (page 132) for details. Technological enhancements to the restaurant in late 2016 have brought the *Wonder*'s Animator's Palate up to par with the ones on the other ships, at least when it comes to setting, atmosphere, and entertainment—the food, like that at the other Animator's Palates, is nothing special.

Cabanas ★★★   Deck 9 Aft

AMERICAN/BUFFET   QUALITY ★★½   SERVICE ★★★★   FRIENDLINESS ★★★★

COMMENTS See profile of Cabanas on the Magic (page 133) for details.

Palo ★★★½   Deck 10 Aft

ITALIAN   QUALITY ★★★½   VALUE ★★★½   SERVICE ★★★★½   FRIENDLINESS ★★★★

COMMENTS See profile of Palo on the *Magic* (page 135) for details.

Tiana's Place ★★★   Deck 3 Aft

AMERICAN/NEW ORLEANS   QUALITY ★★   SERVICE ★★★★   FRIENDLINESS ★★★★

Reservations Not accepted. **When to go** Breakfast, lunch, and dinner. **Bar** Yes. **Alcohol** Limited selection of red, white, and sparkling wines, plus mixed drinks and spirits. All alcohol costs extra. **Dress** Casual; no tank tops or swimwear at dinner. **Hours** Breakfast buffet on select days, 7:30–10:45 a.m.; lunch buffet on select days, noon–1:30 p.m.; nightly dinner seatings at 5:45 p.m. and 8:15 p.m. Hours are subject to change, so check your *Personal Navigator* for exact times.

SETTING AND ATMOSPHERE Tiana's Place is a complete overhaul of this restaurant's previous incarnation, the dismal Parrot Cay. An homage to the dining venue in *The Princess and the Frog* film, Tiana's Place resembles a New Orleans supper club, with rustic elements interspersed with purple-and-green fabrics and fixtures of polished gold (think Mardi Gras, only classy). Live music—a first for a DCL rotational-dining room—is performed on the main stage and features the jazz, swing, and blues sounds of Louisiana.

HOUSE SPECIALTIES Tiana's gumbo was part of the storyline in The Princess and the Frog, so expect to see that on the menu. We're fairly certain diners will see beignets for dessert as well.

COMMENTS Parrot Cay had long been the weakest spot in the Disney Cruise Line restaurant family. We're excited to see attention paid to this long-neglected venue.

Triton's ★ ★ ★   Deck 3 Midship

AMERICAN/FRENCH QUALITY ★ ★ ★   SERVICE ★ ★ ★ ★   FRIENDLINESS ★ ★ ★ ★

Reservations Not accepted. **When to go** Lunch. **Bar** Yes. **Alcohol** Limited selection of red, white, and sparkling wines, plus mixed drinks and spirits. All alcohol costs extra. **Dress** Casual; no tank tops or swimwear at dinner. **Hours** Daily breakfast, 8–9:30 a.m.; daily lunch, noon–1:30 p.m.; nightly dinner seatings at 5:45 and 8:15 p.m. Hours are subject to change, so check your *Personal Navigator* for details.

SETTING AND ATMOSPHERE In case you've forgotten that King Triton is Ariel's father in *The Little Mermaid,* a large tile mosaic of Triton and Ariel sits at the back of this restaurant as a reminder. Besides the art, Triton's blue, beige, and gray colors lend a vague sea theme to the inside, but if you've visited any of the other restaurants, you'll be inclined to think that any of them could be switched out just by changing the paint and light fixtures.

HOUSE SPECIALTIES Breakfast features the usual suspects: fruit, cereal, eggs, waffles, bacon, sausage, and pastries. Lunch includes soups, salads, sandwiches, and burgers, plus a couple of alternative offerings such as pasta or fish. Dinner appetizers include escargots and French onion soup; order one of the crispy duck breasts for the table if no one is adventurous enough to try it themselves. The Grand Marnier soufflé is probably the most popular dessert.

COMMENTS You know Disney is serious about the French theme when they put snails on the appetizer menu. *C'est si bon!* There are other Gallic influences on the menu—many of the entrées have sauces made with butter, wine, or spirits—plus enough standard vegetarian, chicken, beef, and pork dishes to make anyone happy.

Disney Dream DINING

COUNTER-SERVICE RESTAURANTS

Fillmore's Favorites

QUALITY C   **PORTION** Small-Medium   **LOCATION** Deck 11 Midship

WHEN TO GO Typical hours: 10:30 a.m.–6 p.m. Check your *Personal Navigator* for the exact schedule.

SELECTIONS Sandwiches, wraps, salads, fruit, cookies.

COMMENTS While the lineup can change, it usually includes a roast-beef-and-Cheddar sandwich, a "Greek salad" veggie wrap, and a chicken Caesar wrap. Fresh fruit, such as whole bananas, grapes, and oranges, is also available.

Luigi's Pizza

QUALITY C **PORTION** Medium **LOCATION** Deck 11 Midship

WHEN TO GO Typical hours: 10:30 a.m.–6:30 p.m. Check your *Personal Navigator* for the exact schedule.

SELECTIONS Cheese, pepperoni, barbecue-chicken, freshly baked pretzels, and veggie pizza slices.

COMMENTS As with the pizza joints on the *Magic* and *Wonder,* no one will mistake Luigi's for authentic pizza, but it's fine in a pinch. Occasionally open after dinner, when ordering a whole pie is a convenient alternative to room service or restaurant dining.

Tow Mater's Grill

QUALITY C **PORTION** Large **LOCATION** Deck 11 Midship

WHEN TO GO Typical hours: 10:30 a.m.–11 p.m. most days. Check your *Personal Navigator* for the exact schedule.

SELECTIONS Grilled hot dogs, sausages, burgers, and chicken sandwiches; fried-chicken strips; fries.

COMMENTS The fries and burgers aren't anything special—they serve primarily as sustenance for chlorine-addled kids (that is, if they can be pried out of the nearby pool long enough to eat). The chicken strips and hot dogs are the best things on the menu. A nearby fixin's bar provides toppings for burgers and sandwiches.

Vanellope's Sweets & Treats ★ ★ ★

QUALITY B **PORTION** Large **LOCATION** Deck 11 Midship

WHEN TO GO Typical hours: 11:30 a.m.– 10:30 p.m., with a 1-hour closure during the late afternoon. Hours are subject to change; check your *Personal Navigator* for updates.

SELECTIONS Named for the video-game heroine Vanellope Von Schweetz from *Wreck-It Ralph,* Vanellope's Sweets & Treats serves ice cream, house-made gelato, an extensive lineup of dessert toppings, cupcakes, cookies, candy apples, chocolate truffles, and bulk and packaged candies. Ice cream and gelato flavors vary seasonally. Espresso-based drinks are also available if you need some caffeine to kick your sugar buzz into high gear.

COMMENTS You can get free soft-serve at the **Eye Scream** machine and smoothies at an extra charge at **Frozone Treats,** both around the corner. The more upscale treats at Vanellope's start at $2.50 for a single scoop of ice cream or $2.95 for a scoop of gelato. Toppings are 50¢ each; a waffle cone costs an extra 75¢. Sundae selections are imaginative, and serving sizes are generous—even the smallest sundaes, starting at $4.95, can likely serve two. If you have a larger group, indulge in Ralph's (as in Wreck-It) Family Challenge: an eight-scoop, eight-topping sundae served in a souvenir trophy cup.

FULL-SERVICE RESTAURANTS

Animator's Palate ★★★ Deck 3 Aft

AMERICAN/ASIAN QUALITY ★★★ SERVICE ★★★★ FRIENDLINESS ★★★★

Reservations Not accepted. **When to go** Dinner. **Bar** Yes. **Alcohol** Red, white, and sparkling wines, plus mixed drinks and spirits. All alcohol costs extra. **Dress** Casual; no tank tops or swimwear. **Hours** Nightly dinner seatings usually at 5:45 and 8:15 p.m.; check your *Personal Navigator* for the exact schedule.

SETTING AND ATMOSPHERE Each DCL ship has a restaurant called Animator's Palate, and all four pay tribute to Disney's (and Pixar's) animation processes, though each ship has a slightly unique execution of the theme. Animator's Palate on the *Dream* (and the *Fantasy*) features vivid colors throughout. The floor has red carpet with stars of silver, gold, and blue, and the walls are the color of caramel. The backs of the dining-room chairs are patterned after Mickey Mouse's pants, with red backs, yellow buttons, and a black "belt" at the top.

Shelves along the walls hold small toy versions of Disney and Pixar icons, in between video screens displaying animation sketches from popular Disney movies. The more interesting ones will show on one screen how one complete animated cell is drawn, starting from sketches of the main characters to how key background elements are drawn, color samples for walls and floors, and the finished art. The art changes throughout the evening, keeping the view fresh for everyone.

At certain points during your dinner, some of the screens will switch from sketches to an interactive video featuring the surfer-dude turtle Crush from *Finding Nemo.* When we say "interactive," we mean it—Crush will ask you questions and react to your responses, allowing you to have an actual conversation with the animated turtle. Based on the same real-time computer graphics found in Epcot's *Turtle Talk with Crush* attraction (also found at other Disney parks), the technology behind this minishow allows Crush's mouth to move in the appropriate way as his words are spoken. Parents may be more amazed than children.

HOUSE SPECIALTIES Vegetable stir-fry; roasted-garlic or red-pepper dip with bread.

COMMENTS The "wow" factor doesn't extend to the food—as is the case at the other Animator's Palates, the cuisine isn't much different from what you might get at Applebee's, despite the Pacific Rim/American designation.

Cabanas ★★★ Deck 11 Aft

AMERICAN/BUFFET QUALITY ★★★ SERVICE ★★★★ FRIENDLINESS ★★★★

COMMENTS See profile of Cabanas on the *Magic* (page 133) for details.

Enchanted Garden ★★★ Deck 2 Midship

AMERICAN/CONTINENTAL QUALITY ★★★ SERVICE ★★★★ FRIENDLINESS ★★★★

Reservations Not accepted. **When to go** Lunch, especially on your embarkation day, when the crowds are headed to Cabanas. **Bar** Yes. **Alcohol** Limited selection of red, white, and sparkling wines, plus mixed drinks and spirits. All alcohol costs extra. **Hours** Breakfast buffet on select days, 8–10 a.m.; lunch on select days, noon–1:30 p.m.; nightly dinner seatings at 5:45 and 8:15 p.m. Hours are subject to change, so check your *Personal Navigator* for the exact schedule.

SETTING AND ATMOSPHERE Designed to evoke a 19th-century French greenhouse, with patinaed cast-iron arches supporting a spectacular ceiling display of plants, sun, and sky, Enchanted Garden is surely the prettiest of the *Dream*'s three main rotational restaurants.

During lunch, lights in the ceiling simulate the midday sun, and diners see what appears to be ivy climbing up the side of the ironworks; as the sun sets, the "sky" turns to dusk and eventually to dark. Lights, in the shape of flowers and hung from the ceiling, open their "petals" as night falls.

The centerpiece of Enchanted Garden is a burbling concrete fountain, 7 feet tall, topped by Mickey Mouse. The best seats are the round, raised, highbacked booths along the center walk, which allow you to see all the action in one half of the restaurant. Look for framed Hermès scarves outside the restaurant—a nice (and expensive) touch of France. Disney says Enchanted Garden is inspired by the gardens at Versailles, but we think it looks more like the hothouse at Paris's Les Jardin des Plantes. We could be wrong.

HOUSE SPECIALTIES Roast pork tenderloin seasoned with smoked salt; scallops with roasted asparagus; seared-tuna salad on field greens; and seaweed with squid.

COMMENTS The menu is more American bistro than Paris brasserie, despite the French setting. Besides substituting brioche for bread, the most French thing on the menu is usually the use of the words *julienne* to describe how the vegetables are cut and *consommé* to describe the soup.

There's usually at least one pork dish, such as roast pork tenderloin, one chicken dish (baked or roasted), and a steak or prime rib available, along with several seafood and vegetarian options. Honestly, you could serve these dishes at Animator's Palate or Royal Court without anyone noticing, but maybe the scenery here makes the food taste a little bit better.

Palo ★★★★ Deck 12 Aft and Starboard

ITALIAN QUALITY ★★★★ VALUE ★★★★ SERVICE ★★★★½ FRIENDLINESS ★★★★

Reservations Required. **When to go** Brunch on sea days; dinner nightly. **Bar** Yes. **Alcohol** Large list of Italian wines, listed by region, plus select wines from around the world; mixed drinks and spirits; *limoncello*; grappa; ice wine. All alcohol costs extra. **Dress** Dress pants, slacks, and collared shirts are recommended for men; a dress, skirt, or pants and a blouse are recommended for women. Jeans may be worn if in good condition (no holes). No tank tops, swimsuits, swimsuit cover-ups, shorts, hats, cutoffs, torn clothing, T-shirts with offensive language and/or graphics, flip-flops, or tennis shoes. **Hours** Brunch, 10 a.m.–12:30 p.m. on sea days on cruises of 4 nights or longer; nightly dinner, 6–8:30 p.m. Hours are subject to change, so check your *Personal Navigator* for the exact schedule. **Special comments** An additional $30/person charge will be added to your cruise bill for each meal at Palo (charge may be waived for Platinum Castaway Club members). If you need to cancel a reservation, you must do so 24 hours in advance or the full per-person charge may be applied to your bill. Guests must be 18 or older to dine.

SETTING AND ATMOSPHERE Palo is on the starboard side at the back of Deck 12, opposite the adults-only French restaurant Remy (see next profile) and adjacent to the Meridian bar. Although all four Disney ships have a restaurant named Palo, the restaurants on the *Dream* and *Fantasy* have the nicest furnishings.

The entrance to Palo on the *Dream* has a pretty gold-and-ruby-colored glass chandelier, surely one of the most photographed parts of the restaurant. Guests entering Palo walk past a glass-enclosed wine closet and see the main dining room, decorated with deep mahogany wood–paneled walls and columns and rich burgundy carpet. One half of the room features deep-green patterned fabric on the booths and chairs, with paintings of the Italian countryside and seashore along the walls. The other half of Palo uses a saturated red fabric for its seating; illustrations of Italian villas hang on the walls. Also within the *Dream*'s Palo, and unique to Disney's larger ships, are small private dining rooms with custom fabrics, wallpaper, and lighting. Stick your head inside if one is empty, and you'll see how the wealthy merchants of Venice might have lived.

Naturally, tables next to Palo's floor-to-ceiling windows afford the best views, but tables near the back wall sit on an elevated platform, allowing diners there to see over the tables nearest the windows. Our favorite table is to the left of the entrance, tucked by itself in a rounded corner along the inside wall and surrounded by a mural depicting Venice from the water. It's a bit high profile, though; quieter seats are available at the far ends of either side of the restaurant. Brunch offers open seating, so sit wherever the view is best.

HOUSE SPECIALTIES Start your dinner with the cioppino, a tomato-based fish stew with squid, clams, and shrimp, or the white-bean soup, with prosciutto and perfectly al dente beans. A complete selection of pasta is available, either as a separate course or as an entrée. One of these, the vegetarian mushroom risotto, is so rich you'd swear it had beef in it. Our favorite meat entrée is the rack of lamb, which comes in a crispy crust of Parmesan cheese and oregano. For seafood, we like the grilled tuna with potato risotto a bit more than the grilled scallops. The chocolate soufflé, by far the most popular dessert, comes with both dark- and white-chocolate sauces.

As on the other ships, Palo's brunch menu is very good. One large table is dedicated to breads, muffins, and pastries, along with sliced fruits and fresh vegetables (the roasted asparagus is tasty). An entire aquarium's worth of fish is available in another section, including shrimp cocktail, cured salmon, smoked-trout mousse, seared tuna, scallops, crab legs, crawfish, and mussels. Eggs cooked in every conceivable way, including Benedict, Florentine, Julia, and customized omelets, are on the menu, too. Not enough? Try the selection of made-to-order pizzas. If there's any room left for dessert, small cups of tiramisu will take care of your sweet tooth.

COMMENTS Given what you've already spent on the cruise, dropping another $30 to dine at Palo requires no thought whatsoever. Because the food is cooked to order, it tastes substantially better than anything coming from the main dining rooms. The menu offers a wide selection, and many dishes—especially the soups—are done very well. It's no wonder that DCL allows guests to make only one reservation before boarding.

Remy ★★★★½ Deck 12 Aft

FRENCH QUALITY ★★★★½ VALUE ★★★★½ SERVICE ★★★★½ FRIENDLINESS ★★★★

Reservations Required. **When to go** Dinner. **Bar** Yes. **Alcohol** An extensive selection of French wines and Champagnes. **Dress** Jackets and dress shirts for men; dresses, blouses, and skirts, or pantsuits for women. **Hours** Brunch on sea days on cruises of 4 nights or longer, 10 a.m.–12:30 p.m.; nightly dinner, 6–9 p.m. Hours are subject to change, so check your *Personal Navigator* for the exact schedule. **Special comments** An additional $55/person charge will be added to your cruise bill for each brunch at Remy, $85/person for each dinner. The wine pairing for dinner is $99/person. A Remy dessert-tasting experience is $50/person, with a Champagne pairing available for an additional $25/person. If you need to cancel a reservation, you must do so by 2 p.m. on the day of your reservation or the full per-person charge will be applied to your bill. Guests must be age 18 and older to dine.

SETTING AND ATMOSPHERE Remarkably understated for a Disney restaurant, and one named after a cartoon rat at that. The most prominent features at Remy are the floor-to-ceiling windows, which look out over the ocean on the port side of the ship from high on Deck 12; and the Art Nouveau lights, which seem to spring from the floor as thick vines, branching out into yellow lights as they reach the ceiling. Besides those touches, and perhaps the oval mirrors along the wall opposite the windows, the rest is simple and elegant: oval, round, and square tables, all with white-linen tablecloths, and round-backed wood chairs with white upholstery. The olive-green carpet pattern matches the Art Nouveau decor without being distracting. A small teak deck wraps around Remy, allowing you to walk out for a quick breath of fresh air between courses.

HOUSE SPECIALTIES The tasting menu may be one of the best 3-hour dining experiences you'll ever have. Splurge on the wine pairing. If the tasting menu sounds like too much food, Remy's meat entrées usually include Australian Wagyu beef and pork from central France.

Remy also offers an extensive brunch on days when the ship is at sea. Like the brunch at Palo, Remy's has an extensive selection, including fruit, pastries, seafood, beef, pork, pasta, and fish. A Champagne pairing is available for an additional $25 per person. We prefer the dinner experience, but spending the morning at Remy is a lovely way to start a day at sea.

Remy sometimes offers special dining experiences. Recent ones have included the **Pompidou's Patisseries Dessert Experience** (sometimes called the **Remy Dessert Experience**), which includes a sampling of six premium desserts for $50 per person, or $75 per person with a supplementary Champagne tasting, and **Petites Assiettes de Remy (Small Plates of Remy)**, a six-course savory tasting at a similar price point. During these special offerings, chefs typically describe the history of each item and explain the sourcing of the ingredients. If you're interested in these experiences, check the DCL Planning Center (see page 35) or call DCL at ☎ 800-951-3532 to see if they'll be offered during your sailing.

COMMENTS What makes a great restaurant such as Remy different from restaurants that are simply very good is that, while the latter usually have a few signature dishes that they do very well, virtually *everything* at Remy is nothing short of exceptional. An appetizer of carrots—yes, the root vegetable—will be the most extraordinary carrots you've ever had, probably in varieties and colors you didn't know existed, and with a flavor that is the pure essence of carrot-ness. Now imagine a meal of three to eight courses, all equally as good, ranging from soups, seafood, and beef, to sides, cheese courses, and desserts. That's your average evening at Remy.

Remy offers both a standard dinner menu and a chef's tasting menu. If you have the time or the inclination, order the latter—it allows you to savor every bit of creativity and technical mastery the kitchen can muster.

A couple of examples from our meals: One course early in the tasting menu was billed as the chef's interpretation of a grilled-cheese sandwich with tomato soup. The entire serving consisted of one small, golden-brown cube, about the size of a postage stamp on each side, designed to be eaten in one bite. The outside of the cube was a cheddar cheese, coated with seasoned breadcrumbs and fried lightly. Inside was a tomato sauce, barely seasoned and reduced to concentrate the flavor. The first bite—it took maybe two to finish the entire thing—tasted of crispy, butter-fried bread and melted cheese. The second was all tomato: bright, slightly acidic, and sweet at the same time, balancing out the butter and cheese from the outside coating. Remy's chefs had both amplified the flavors to their essence and reduced the size of the dish to its bare minimum.

Another appetizer was the chef's take on cheese pizza. Its base was a small, crispy wafer of baked bread, barely thicker than a sheet of paper. On top of that was a half-inch layer of white foam, about the consistency of whipped cream but made from Parmesan cheese. And on top of that were three small basil leaves.

The pizza's tomato "sauce" was presented in a Champagne flute as a clear, intensely flavored liquid. The kitchen had achieved this transparency by repeatedly filtering juice from ripe tomatoes through layers of fine cheesecloth, trapping the red bits and letting the clear juice through. We were instructed to follow a bit of the crust and cheese foam with a sip from the flute, and the flavors combined beautifully.

One last tip on the tasting menu: Remy offers a wine pairing for most courses. The selections are very good, but it's a *lot* of wine that could easily be split between two people. Len's first evening at Remy began with a martini at Meridian and continued with the wine pairing for dinner. The first few courses were memorable, but by the time he realized how much alcohol was involved, it was too late. The last quarter of the meal is a hazy memory that apparently involved Len applauding someone else's cheese cart as it rolled by for dessert. That called for another, alcohol-free, dinner at Remy. Pity his suffering.

Royal Palace ★★★ Deck 3 Midship

AMERICAN/FRENCH QUALITY ★★★ SERVICE ★★★★ FRIENDLINESS ★★★★

Reservations Not accepted. **When to go** Lunch. **Bar** Yes. **Alcohol** Limited selection of red, white, and sparkling wines, plus mixed drinks and spirits. **Dress** Casual; no tank tops or swimwear at dinner. **Hours** Daily breakfast, 8–9:30 a.m.; daily lunch, noon–1:30 p.m.; nightly dinner seatings at 5:45 and 8:15 p.m. Hours are subject to change, so check your *Personal Navigator* for the exact schedule.

SETTING AND ATMOSPHERE The most attractive part of Royal Palace may be its entrance, done in gold-and-white-marble tile below a pretty flower-shaped chandelier accented with blue-glass "diamonds" and red "rubies." Inside the doors, gold-and-white faux-marble columns form a circle just inside one ring of tables; royal-blue carpet with gold trim lines the inner part of the restaurant. Drapes cover the windows lining one side of the room, and mosaic-tile pictures of Disney princesses line another.

HOUSE SPECIALTIES Breakfast is standard buffet fare: fruit, cereal, eggs, waffles, bacon, sausage, and pastries. Lunch includes soups, salads, sandwiches, and burgers, plus a couple of alternative offerings such as pasta or fish. Dinner appetizers include escargots and French onion soup; the wildboar tenderloin entrée is tasty. The Grand Marnier soufflé is probably the most popular dessert.

COMMENTS You know Disney is serious about the French theme when they put snails on the appetizer menu. There are other Gallic influences on the menu—many of the entrées have sauces made with butter, wine, or spirits—plus enough standard vegetarian, chicken, beef, and pork dishes to make anyone happy.

Disney Fantasy DINING

COUNTER-SERVICE RESTAURANTS

Fillmore's Favorites

QUALITY C   **PORTION** Small–Medium   **LOCATION** Deck 11 Midship

COMMENTS See profile of Fillmore's Favorites on the *Dream* (page 138) for details.

Luigi's Pizza

QUALITY C   **PORTION** Medium   **LOCATION** Deck 11 Midship

COMMENTS See profile of Luigi's Pizza on the *Dream* (page 139) for details.

Tow Mater's Grill

QUALITY C   **PORTION** Large   **LOCATION** Deck 11 Midship

COMMENTS See profile of Tow Mater's Grill on the *Dream* (page 139) for details.

FULL-SERVICE RESTAURANTS

Animator's Palate ★ ★ ★   Deck 3 Aft

AMERICAN/ASIAN   QUALITY ★ ★ ★   **SERVICE** ★ ★ ★ ★   **FRIENDLINESS** ★ ★ ★ ★

Reservations Not accepted. **When to go** Dinner. **Bar** Yes. **Alcohol** Red, white, and sparkling wines, plus mixed drinks and spirits. All alcohol costs extra. **Dress** Casual; no tank tops or swimwear. **Hours** Nightly dinner seatings usually at 5:45 and 8:15 p.m.; check your *Personal Navigator* for the exact schedule.

SETTING AND ATMOSPHERE Each DCL ship has a restaurant called Animator's Palate, and all four pay tribute to Disney's (and Pixar's) animation processes, though each ship has a slightly unique execution of the theme. Animator's Palate on the Fantasy (and the Dream) features vivid colors throughout. The floor has red carpet with stars of silver, gold, and blue, and the walls are the color of caramel. The backs of the dining-room chairs are patterned after Mickey Mouse's pants, with red backs, yellow buttons, and a black "belt" at the top.

Shelves along the walls hold small toy versions of Disney and Pixar icons, in between video screens displaying animation sketches from popular Disney movies. The more interesting ones will show on one screen how one complete animated cell is drawn, starting from sketches of the main characters to how key background elements are drawn, color samples for walls and floors, and the finished art. The art changes throughout the evening, keeping the view fresh for everyone.

The version of Animator's Palate on the *Fantasy* includes *Animation Magic,* an impressive special effect. At the beginning of the second night you dine there, you're given a sheet of paper and crayon and told to draw a self-portrait. At the end of the evening, all of the diners' self-portraits are shown in an animated cartoon similar to Disney's 1929 short cartoon *The Skeleton Dance.*

At your first scheduled dinner at Animator's Palate, you get a different show. At certain points during your second dinner, some of the screens will switch from sketches to an interactive video featuring the surfer-dude turtle Crush from *Finding Nemo.* When we say *interactive,* we mean it—Crush will ask you questions and react to your responses, allowing you to have an actual conversation with the animated turtle. Based on the same real-time computer graphics found in Epcot's *Turtle Talk with Crush* attraction (also at other Disney parks), the technology behind this minishow allows Crush's mouth to move in the appropriate way as his words are spoken. Parents may be more amazed than children.

HOUSE SPECIALTIES Vegetable stir-fry; roasted-garlic or red-pepper dip with bread.

COMMENTS When it comes to the food, it's the same old story—as is the case at the other three Animator's Palates. The dishes are pedestrian chain-restaurant fare, despite the Pacific Rim/American designation. On the *Fantasy,* anyway, the entertainment makes up for whatever the food lacks.

Cabanas ★ ★ ★   Deck 11 Aft

AMERICAN/BUFFET QUALITY ★ ★ ★ ★ SERVICE ★ ★ ★ ★ FRIENDLINESS ★ ★ ★ ★

COMMENTS See profile of Cabanas on the *Magic* (page 133) for details.

Enchanted Garden ★ ★ ★   Deck 2 Midship

AMERICAN/CONTINENTAL QUALITY ★ ★ ★ SERVICE ★ ★ ★ ★ FRIENDLINESS ★ ★ ★ ★

COMMENTS See profile of Enchanted Garden on the *Dream* (page 140) for details.

Palo ★ ★ ★ ★   Deck 12 Aft and Starboard

ITALIAN QUALITY ★ ★ ★ ★ VALUE ★ ★ ★ ★ SERVICE ★ ★ ★ ★ ½ FRIENDLINESS ★ ★ ★ ★

COMMENTS See profile of Palo on the *Dream* (page 141) for details.

Remy ★★★★½ **Deck 12 Aft**

FRENCH QUALITY ★★★★½ VALUE ★★★★½ SERVICE ★★★★½ FRIENDLINESS ★★★★

COMMENTS See profile of Remy on the *Dream* (page 142) for details.

Royal Court ★★★ **Deck 3 Midship**

AMERICAN/FRENCH QUALITY ★★★ SERVICE ★★★★ FRIENDLINESS ★★★★

Reservations Not accepted. **When to go** Lunch. **Bar** Yes. **Alcohol** Limited selection of red, white, and sparkling wines, plus mixed drinks and spirits. **Dress** Casual; no tank tops or swimwear at dinner. **Hours** Breakfast, 8–9:30 a.m.; lunch, noon–1:30 p.m.; nightly dinner seatings at 5:45 and 8:15 p.m. Hours are subject to change, so check your *Personal Navigator* for the exact schedule.

SETTING AND ATMOSPHERE The most distinctive design elements of Royal Court are the gold-colored wood columns on the floor, which rise to attach to the ceiling through flared white glass decorated with plant stems and shaped like flower petals. Along with these, white-marble columns and carpet patterned to look like fancy rugs give Royal Court a formal feel, even when it's half-full of kids. Small, round lamps placed around the room are designed to look like Cinderella's pumpkin coach, and some of the walls feature tile murals depicting scenes from *Cinderella* and other Disney princess films. Tables near the starboard wall sit under portholes that offer ocean views, although these are partially blocked by a privacy wall running along the inside perimeter of the restaurant.

HOUSE SPECIALTIES Breakfast is standard buffet fare: fruit, cereal, eggs, waffles, bacon, sausage, and pastries. Lunch includes soups, salads, sandwiches, and burgers, plus a couple of alternative offerings such as pasta or fish. Dinner appetizers include escargots and French onion soup; the wild-boar tenderloin entrée is tasty. The Grand Marnier soufflé is probably the most popular dessert.

COMMENTS Only differences in decor distinguish Royal Court from Royal Palace on the *Dream* (see page 144).

PART EIGHT

ENTERTAINMENT *and* NIGHTLIFE

LIVE THEATER *on the* SHIPS

LIVE ENTERTAINMENT IS PRESENTED at the **Walt Disney Theatre** most nights, on most itineraries. Shows are typically either Disney-themed theatrical productions (typically musicals) or variety acts, including comedians, magicians, or ventriloquists. The theatrical shows are usually of two types: retellings of familiar stories, and "jukebox" musicals.

Disney's Aladdin: A Musical Spectacular, on the *Fantasy,* is an example of the retelling genre. This is DCL's unique interpretation of the *Aladdin* film—it's not the same *Aladdin* musical that's playing on Broadway, nor is it the same *Aladdin* show that's performed at Disney California Adventure theme park at Disneyland. The cruise version features live actors and multiple Arabian-themed sets reprising key scenes from the animated film, including the most popular songs, in about half the time of the original movie.

The *Magic's* **Twice Charmed: An Original Twist on the Cinderella Story** is probably the best show in the retelling category, mostly because the unique story provides more surprises than the standard film reinterpretations. We also like the *Magic's* new production **Tangled: The Musical,** which features new songs from beloved Disney composer Alan Menken. As we were going to press, the *Wonder* is debuting a new retelling-style show, **Frozen: A Musical Spectacular.** While we haven't seen it yet, we're confident that this tale of sisterly love will receive a blizzard of accolades from every 8-year-old girl in the room.

Examples of jukebox musicals include **Disney Dreams, Disney Wishes, Disney's Believe, The Golden Mickeys,** and **Villains Tonight!** Each features songs and characters from many different Disney films, the numbers linked by an original story. We're generally not fans of these shows, especially *Villains Tonight!* The storylines are threadbare, serving to string together the musical numbers rather than provide

GETTING THE MOST FROM A DCL SHOW (OR NOT)

THE BEST SHOWS ON EACH SHIP are those based on a single Disney franchise, such as *Tangled, Cinderella, Aladdin,* and (soon) *Frozen.*

Unfortunately, the shows on the *Dream* are all of the jukebox variety, each with a weak central storyline that exists only to link songs from a variety of Disney classics. But take that as an opportunity to skip the show and experience other areas of the ship while they're uncrowded. We've often been the only guests in the lounges and have had the stores all to ourselves. Alternatively, if you want to see the show but would rather stay in your room, you can just watch it on your stateroom TV.

interesting narrative. Lack of plot, however, isn't our primary objection to these shows—we realize it's a Disney cruise. Rather, they recycle the same handful of characters and songs played in every entertainment venue throughout the ship. If you haven't heard "Be Our Guest" from *Beauty and the Beast* performed a dozen times on board, have your hearing checked when you get home.

Finally, the *Magic* puts on a welcome-aboard show on the first night of its seven-nights-and-up itineraries and a farewell show on the last night. The welcome show commingles a few musical numbers with a review of the ship's major features and schedule. The farewell show is a recap of the same, with guest photos from throughout the cruise thrown in. These are good times to go to the spa.

A BIT OF ADVICE You'll probably see at least one musical if you're taking small children on your cruise. Along with reading the show profiles that follow, we recommend watching a few minutes of each show on YouTube before you leave for the cruise. This will not only help you decide which show is worth your time, but it will also let you know what you're missing in case another entertainment option is available.

Disney often uses the term "Broadway-style" to describe its theater offerings. This should not be taken to mean that you will see the national-touring-company equivalent of a Broadway hit (like the versions of *Cats, Mamma Mia!,* and *Grease* staged on some Royal Caribbean sailings), nor should you expect to see as much nuance or complexity in the storylines of DCL shows as you might in legitimate theater. Frankly, as devoted and frequent patrons of actual New York City theater, we had long bristled at the "Broadway-style" descriptor, thinking it laughable to compare the simplified storytelling onboard with recent New York productions marketed to families, such as *Matilda,* or even with Disney's own Broadway version of *The Lion King.*

After speaking with cast members about our concerns, we learned that from a technical standpoint, DCL performances do have much more in common with Times Square than Topeka: The stage mechanics, costuming, special effects, and lighting are all as close to state-of-the-art as is practicable at sea. If you find your eyes glazing over when you take your children to the show, try paying attention to the technological aspects of the programming—they'd be top-notch in most locales and are nothing less than remarkable given the constraints of an ocean liner.

And if that fails, consider that the DCL theaters, like most Broadway theaters, let you bring a glass of wine with you to your seat.

THE *MAGIC'S* SHOWS

All Aboard: Let the Magic Begin ★★
Walt Disney Theatre, Deck 4 Forward

WELCOME-ABOARD SHOW WITH A FEW SONGS AND A LOT OF TALK ABOUT THE CRUISE

When to go Typical showtimes are 6:15 and 8:30 p.m. on your embarkation day. Presented on cruises of 7 nights and longer. **Duration** 50 minutes. **Our rating** Skip it and tour the ship instead; ★★.

DESCRIPTION AND COMMENTS More than half of *All Aboard*'s 50-minute showtime consists of the *Magic*'s cruise director explaining the ship's dining, entertainment, and shopping options, plus port logistics. The rest is a handful of song-and-dance numbers featuring Disney characters and involving a young boy who dreams of becoming the ship's captain. Featuring a couple of original songs, the show serves as an introduction to the Walt Disney Theatre. It's a shame they can't put all the songs at the beginning of the show, because we'd skip the rest of it.

Disney Dreams: An Enchanted Classic ★★★½
Walt Disney Theatre, Deck 4 Forward

PETER PAN SAVES THE DAY

When to go Typical showtimes are 6:15 and 8:30 p.m. Check your *Personal Navigator* for specific dates. **Duration** 55 minutes. **Our rating** Not to be missed; ★★★½.

DESCRIPTION AND COMMENTS *Disney Dreams* is one of the better stage shows on any Disney ship. Peter Pan must help a young girl named Anne Marie "find her own magic" before sunrise. Peter does this by whisking her through settings from *Aladdin, Beauty and the Beast, Cinderella, The Little Mermaid, The Lion King,* and, as of mid-2015, *Frozen.* Each story's main characters appear in key scenes from their respective movies and sing their signature songs. The sets are attractive, the special effects are good (expect Elsa to unleash a minor blizzard in the Walt Disney Theatre), and the script is fast-paced and entertaining. The cast seems to enjoy it, too, and it shows. We rate *Disney Dreams* as not to be missed.

Remember the Magic: A Final Farewell ★★
Walt Disney Theatre, Deck 4 Forward

RECAP OF YOUR *MAGIC* CRUISE

When to go Typical showtimes are 6:15 and 8:30 p.m. on the night before your cruise concludes. Presented on cruises of 7 nights and longer. **Duration** 25 minutes. **Our rating** Not worth seeing; ★★.

DESCRIPTION AND COMMENTS *Remember the Magic* uses sets and characters from the ship's other shows, including *All Aboard* and *Disney Dreams,* to recap the cruise's highlights. Photographs and video clips of families at play, taken by Disney photographers during the itinerary, are shown on video screens during the songs. Expect songs and dances by Disney princesses and jokes about eating too much at the buffet. We recommend skipping this show and spending your last night revisiting your favorite activities on board.

Tangled: The Musical ★★★½
Walt Disney Theatre, Deck 4 Forward

GIRL WITH MOMMY ISSUES USES HER TRESSES TO GET OUT OF SOME HAIRY SITUATIONS

When to go Typical showtimes are 6:15 and 8:30 p.m. Check your *Personal Navigator* for specific dates. **Duration** 50 minutes. **Our rating** A fresh take on a classic fairy tale; ★★★½.

DESCRIPTION AND COMMENTS This faithful retelling of the *Tangled* film features songs by decorated Broadway and film composer Alan Menken (composer of *Little Shop of Horrors, The Little Mermaid, Beauty and the Beast, Aladdin, Hercules, Pocahontas, Newsies,* and many more; seriously, this guy is a national hero). Actors, singers, and dancers—and miles and miles of synthetic hair—wend their way through intricate sets. The Snuggly Duckling tavern is particularly charming. The puppetry on the larger-than-life sidekick horse Maximus is good enough to have you believing the operator is actually equine.

We found the ending lantern scene to be among the most charming segments of any DCL production. We sat in the second row of the theater the first time we saw this show and learned that the lighting is more moving and affecting if you sit more to the middle of the theater than right up front.

Twice Charmed: An Original Twist on the Cinderella Story
★★★½ **Walt Disney Theatre, Deck 4 Forward**

A FRESH TAKE ON A CLASSIC TALE

When to go Typical showtimes are 6:15 and 8:30 p.m. Check your *Personal Navigator* for specific days. **Duration** 55 minutes. **Our rating** A new narrative for a familiar story; ★★★½.

DESCRIPTION AND COMMENTS If you recall from the original *Cinderella* movie, the stepmother breaks the first glass slipper just as it's about to be fit on Cinderella's foot. Cinderella, however, produces the second glass slipper, shows that it fits, and goes on to marry the prince.

Twice Charmed begins where that story ends. As the show opens, Cinderella's evil stepmother and stepsisters are lamenting the fact that they didn't know Cinderella had the second slipper. A wicked fairy godfather appears to send the evil stepfamily back in time and destroy Cindy's slipper before the prince's foot-fitting team ever arrives. Cinderella must then find a new way to convince the prince that they're meant to be together. As is the case with any Disney film, you can guess in the first 5 minutes how it's all going to end, but *Twice Charmed* is interesting anyway because it has a new narrative. The sets are pretty, the songs aren't bad, and it's an enjoyable way to spend an evening.

Walt Disney: The Dream Goes On   ★★★
Walt Disney Theatre, Deck 4 Forward
RETROSPECTIVE OF WALT'S LIFE AND ART

When to go Typical showtimes are 6:15 and 8:30 p.m. Check your *Personal Navigator* for specific days. **Duration** 45 minutes. **Our rating** An improvement over *All Aboard*, it has potential; ★★★.

DESCRIPTION AND COMMENTS *The Dream Goes On* uses film clips, audio, and stage reenactments to trace Walt's life from the creation of Mickey Mouse through the theme parks. The show's highlights include songs from Disney-theme-park attractions, such as Main Street, U.S.A.; The Haunted Mansion; and *Country Bear Jamboree*. The show also benefits from not drawing heavily from *Beauty and the Beast, The Little Mermaid,* or *The Lion King.* The pacing is a little uneven—it could be improved with better dialogue to link the segments—but overall the show is a nice tribute to the guy who started it all.

THE *WONDER*'S SHOWS

THE WONDER IS GETTING A BRAND-NEW musical stage show version of the film *Frozen* to replace the somewhat threadbare *Toy Story: The Musical.* *Frozen: A Musical Spectacular* was debuting as we were going to press, so we haven't had a chance to review it yet, but we always look forward to seeing new shows added to the DCL repertoire. Disney's publicity for the show mentions an "innovative combination of traditional theatrical techniques, modern technology and classic Disney whimsy . . . costumes and sets, remarkable special effects, and spectacular production numbers that expand upon the most imaginative elements of the film." Also mentioned is that "dynamic puppetry by Michael Curry, whose designs are featured in Disney's Tony Award–winning Broadway musical *The Lion King*, will bring exciting physicality to characters like Sven and Olaf." The 2015 *Frozen* segment of the *Magic*'s *Disney Dreams* show was elegant and immersive; we're hopeful that this show will blow us all away.

Disney Dreams: An Enchanted Classic ★★★½
Walt Disney Theatre, Deck 4 Forward

PETER PAN SAVES THE DAY

COMMENTS See profile of this show on the *Magic* (page 150) for details.

The Golden Mickeys ★★ Walt Disney Theatre, Deck 4 Forward

DISNEY SPIN ON AN AWARDS SHOW

When to go Typical showtimes are 6:15 and 8:30 p.m. Check your *Personal Navigator* for specific days. **Duration** 45 minutes. **Our rating** There are better uses of your time; ★★.

DESCRIPTION AND COMMENTS One of the least coherent live shows on any Disney cruise ship, *The Golden Mickeys* starts out as an Oscar-style awards show, except it's the Disney gang giving themselves awards for their own movies in different, made-up categories. As each award winner is announced, live performers reenact the movie's key scenes on stage, including songs, as clips from the movies play on the stage's screen backdrop.

There are many problems with the show. For one, the "awards" stop making sense almost as soon as they're presented: The "Best Heroes" award is simply a montage of main characters from Disney films, and one of the last awards, "A Salute to Friendship," is apparently the only way the show's writers could think of getting Woody, Buzz, and Jesse together on stage. Unless you have a pressing need to see yet another rehash of songs from *The Lion King* and *Beauty and the Beast,* this show isn't worth your time.

THE *DREAM*'S SHOWS
Disney's Believe ★★★ Walt Disney Theatre, Deck 3 Forward

MAGIC TRIUMPHS OVER CYNICISM

When to go Typical showtimes are 6:15 and 8:30 p.m. Check your *Personal Navigator* for specific days. **Duration** 50 minutes. **Our rating** Nice change of pace; ★★★.

DESCRIPTION AND COMMENTS A botanist father who doesn't believe in magic must learn to believe in order to reconnect with his daughter on her birthday. The father's guide is *Aladdin*'s wisecracking Genie, who takes Dad through time, space, and Disney music on his journey to acceptance.

Believe has one of the most sophisticated sets of any Disney stage show at sea, and there are enough visual elements to entertain almost any kid. Although it's not a holiday show, the plot seems like a loose adaptation of Charles Dickens's *A Christmas Carol,* with a committee of ghosts, including Mary Poppins, Peter Pan, Baloo from *The Jungle Book,* Rafiki from *The Lion King,* and Pocahontas from Scarsdale, judging by her accent. (Erin begs to differ: "No princess from Scarsdale would be caught dead in that *shmata.*")

Many other Disney stars appear throughout the show, but, thankfully, *Believe* includes some less-familiar characters and songs. The final stretch has a hit parade of other princesses and ends with performances by Mickey and Minnie.

The Golden Mickeys ★★ Walt Disney Theatre, Deck 3 Forward

DISNEY SPIN ON AN AWARDS SHOW

COMMENTS See profile of this show on the *Wonder* (page 153) for details.

Villains Tonight! ★★ Walt Disney Theatre, Deck 4 Forward

DISNEY HEELS DO COMEDY

When to go Typical showtimes are 6:15 and 8:30 p.m. Check your *Personal Navigator* for specific days. **Duration** 55 minutes. **Our rating** The villain here is the show itself; ★★.

DESCRIPTION AND COMMENTS In *Villains Tonight!*, Hades, ruler of the under-world, has lost his edge after being defeated by Hercules. He's visited by the Fates, who tell Hades he must prove he's still truly evil or give up his throne. Hades dispatches his two sidekicks, Pain and Panic, to bring every Disney villain they can find back to the underworld. Musical num-bers pop up every time Pain and Panic make contact with a villain, includ-ing *The Little Mermaid*'s Ursula the Sea Witch in a burlesque number, the evil queen from *Snow White*, Maleficent from *Sleeping Beauty*, and *The Lion King*'s Scar, in what, judging by the costumes, is a *Mad Max Beyond Africa* musical number.

Disney villains *should* be comedy gold. They don't have to follow the same rules as Disney's good guys—they can hurl insults and petty criticisms and express self-centered opinions. There's some of that in this script, but it's done at such a glacial pace that you wonder whether the long pauses are intended solely to extend the show's run time. A tighter, more up-tempo script would make better use of the performer's talents.

Every *Villains* show includes a cringe-worthy effort to make the show hip and contemporary. On one sailing a couple of years ago, there were three separate references to the Kardashians, including making fun of Kim's baby. And on each occasion the joke fell flat and the character responded with "Too soon?" *Ugh.*

THE *FANTASY'S* SHOWS

Disney's Aladdin: A Musical Spectacular ★★★
Walt Disney Theatre, Deck 3 Forward

SONG-FILLED EXTRAVAGANZA

When to go Typical showtimes are 6:15 and 8:30 p.m. Check your *Personal Navigator* for specific days. **Duration** 45 minutes. **Our rating** Needs more Genie; ★★★.

DESCRIPTION AND COMMENTS A song-filled retelling of Disney's *Aladdin,* this live show features stage sets of Agrabah, the Cave of Wonders, and the Sultan's palace, along with the film's main characters: Aladdin, Princess Jasmine, Jafar, Iago, and the Genie. All of the major numbers are per-formed, including "Friend Like Me" and "A Whole New World." Because it's an adaptation of an existing film, *Aladdin* has less saccharine Disney sweetness than, say, *Believe*.

Having seen *Aladdin* on Broadway, the film in theaters, and an abbrevi-ated live stage-show version at Disney California Adventure (which will be replaced with a *Frozen*-themed show in 2016), we were disappointed in the *Fantasy*'s production. The actor's performances and singing were fine, but the set design and script weren't quite as good as we'd expected. For example, in the movie and the theme-park show, Genie has the most important role in the production: Besides providing narrative and background, he tells jokes to keep the script moving. In live performances at DCA, Genie often ad-libs topical humor into the act, and so many one-liners come so fast that he's virtually guaranteed the biggest ovation at the end.

For some reason, though, Genie's onboard humor has been diluted so much that it doesn't provide the spark the rest of the script needs. He tells fewer jokes, and with less bite, than in either the DCA show or the film. (Perhaps the ship's flaky onboard Wi-Fi keeps the Genie from regular access to TMZ.com.) Also, we're surprised that the stage sets on a $900 million cruise ship aren't as detailed as those made for a theme park more than 10 years ago.

Disney's Believe ★★★ Walt Disney Theatre, Deck 3 Forward

MAGIC TRIUMPHS OVER CYNICISM

COMMENTS See profile of this show on the *Dream* (page 153) for details.

Disney Wishes ★★★½ Walt Disney Theatre, Deck 3 Forward

TEEN-FOCUSED SONG AND DANCE

When to go Typical showtimes are 6:15 and 8:30 p.m. Check your *Personal Navigator* for specific days. **Duration** 50 minutes. **Our rating** Entertaining; ★★★½.

DESCRIPTION AND COMMENTS In *Disney Wishes,* graduating high-schoolers Kayla, Nicole, and Brandon are visiting Disneyland Park in search of the ride of their lives. This search is complicated by the trio's imminent split for college, as well as Brandon's hush-hush crush on Kayla. Nicole, Brandon's sister, has her own dark secret: She wants to be an artist.

Wishes has young actors, fast-moving dance numbers, and lots of visual razzle-dazzle, so it's entertaining for tweens and teens. It's not bad for parents, either, especially if they can recognize the bits of Magic Kingdom park trivia interspersed in the dialogue. According to maritime law, which requires that Disney stage shows must include at least one song from *Aladdin, Beauty and the Beast, The Lion King,* or *The Little Mermaid,* there's also a rendition of "Under the Sea." But most of the show's songs come from less-familiar Disney films, such as *Hercules, The Jungle Book, Mulan, Pinocchio,* and *Tangled,* making it easier to sit through than most other shows of this type.

OTHER LIVE PERFORMANCES

BESIDES LIVE STAGE SHOWS, the Walt Disney Theatre hosts variety acts, including everything from magicians and comedians to ventriloquists, jugglers, hypnotists, and musicians. Repositioning cruises, with their many sea days, may have guest Broadway artists or other niche celebrities. Many of these acts will do preview shows or short sets at various venues throughout the ship before their major engagement at the theater. We've seen some incredible onboard acts, but also a few for whom *mediocre* would be a kind description. If there are previews, we suggest catching a few minutes (or asking other guests who've seen them) to decide whether the act is worth your time.

In our experience, the best live acts tend to be the magicians and comedians, who can adapt their material to the audience as the show is happening, and revamp parts of their act between shows.

MOVIES

RECENT DISNEY MOVIES, including films released during the cruise, are shown at the **Buena Vista Theatre** on each Disney ship. Each theater is equipped with digital film projectors, state-of-the-art sound systems, and the capability to show 3-D films (complete with 3-D glasses for guests). Padded, upholstered seats are arranged stairlike behind the screen, allowing good views from almost anywhere in the theater. About half a dozen films are shown on any cruise, typically two or three per day beginning around 9:30 a.m. and running through midnight. Admission is free. Popcorn and drinks are sold outside the theater before and during each presentation; you can also bring your own snacks and drinks.

In the case of real blockbusters, films may be shown in the larger **Walt Disney Theatre** in addition to, or sometimes in place of, live stage shows. We were on board the *Dream* for opening week of 2015's *Star Wars: The Force Awakens;* the entire Walt Disney Theatre was packed more than once, and the concession stand outside was doing a brisk business in Darth-helmet drink holders and Han Solo in Carbonite–shaped popcorn buckets.

Classic Disney films are also shown on a giant 24-by-14-foot LED screen perched high above each ship's family pool (**Goofy's Pool** on Deck 9 of the *Magic* and *Wonder,* **Donald's Pool** on Deck 11 of the *Dream* and *Fantasy*).

Deeper cuts from the Disney film catalogue are also shown on the in-room televisions on all the Disney ships. The *Dream* and *Fantasy* have "on-demand" capability to view dozens of animated and live-action films, including some rarely seen films and documentaries. This can be a nice option if you just want to chill in your room after a long day in the sun.

LIVE SPORTS

ON THE *WONDER,* the main sports bar is **Crown & Fin;** it's **687** on the *Dream* and **O'Gills Pub** on the *Magic* and *Fantasy.* These are your primary venues for viewing baseball, basketball, and soccer. NFL football games are usually shown here, too, and some games are also shown on the ships' **Funnel Vision** big screen on the pool deck. Keep in mind that the ship gets its TV broadcasts from satellite transmissions, which can be affected by weather. If you want to watch a specific game, show up at least 30 minutes beforehand and ask a crew member to find the right station—there are hundreds of channels, and it sometimes takes a while to find your game.

If you happen to be sailing during a sporting event of national or worldwide interest, expect that it will be available for viewing in nearly every public space with seating, even if it's not immediately apparent that screens are present. We sailed on the *Wonder* during the 2014 World Cup soccer finals; the *Personal Navigator* listed only two viewing venues, but we found screens pulled down from the ceiling in every bar, lounge, and café to show the big game. In addition, the opening ceremonies for the 2016 Summer Olympics were shown on the Funnel Vision screens as well as on many televisions throughout the public areas of the ships.

And if you're interested in major live events other than sports, rest assured that Disney has you covered. For example, the 2016 Oscars show was playing on the *Fantasy* at O'Gills, in the Buena Vista Theatre, and in other lounges as well.

THEMED EVENTS *and* HOLIDAY ENTERTAINMENT

PIRATE NIGHT

THIS IS HELD ON ONE NIGHT on virtually every cruise. The crew, restaurants, and entertainment take on a pirate theme. The ship's transformation begins early in the day, when the usual background music is replaced by songs and audio from the theme parks' Pirates of the Caribbean ride and the spinoff film series. Afternoon craft sessions and family activities are pirate-themed as well. Sometime in the afternoon, your stateroom attendant will drop off in your cabin a pirate bandana for each member of your group to wear, as well as booty, such as chocolate "coins" covered in gold foil.

On cruises of four-plus nights, each ship's main restaurant will have a special menu for the evening, designed to look like a treasure map. Virtually all of the crew, as well as the ship's officers, will wear special pirate outfits, and families have an opportunity to pose for photos with them before dinner. Many guests pack special outfits just for Pirate Night, including black knee-high boots, capri pants, white puffy shirts, and eyeliner. (The women dress up, too.)

Pirate Night concludes with a stage show and video on the family pool's Funnel Vision screen, accompanied by a short fireworks display. The fireworks are usually shot from the starboard side, so you'll have a better view from there. The best viewing spots are as follows:

- *Magic* and *Wonder:* Deck 10 Starboard, looking over Goofy's Pool
- *Dream* and *Fantasy:* Deck 12 Forward, near Currents bar

FROZEN DAYS

ADDING TO THE AVALANCHE OF FROZEN TIE-INS, DCL introduced yet another one to its lineup of themed onboard activities in 2015. Frozen Days are held on sailings headed to Alaska on the *Wonder* and to Northern European countries on the *Magic*. The lobby atrium is bedecked with paper icicles; a special themed menu is served at dinner (including an Olaf-inspired carrot cake—ha!); a traditional Scandinavian dance lesson is held in the lobby; a gonna-stuff-some-chocolate-in-my-face-themed scavenger hunt takes place; and a stage show and dance party called *Freezing the Night Away* is held on the upper deck, with appearances by Anna, Elsa, Kristoff, and an animated Olaf and Sven.

We were on hand for a *Freezing the Night Away* deck party in Iceland; the wind speed and chilly outdoor temperature made us question the conviction behind Elsa's "the cold never bothered me anyway" signature statement. Costumes are by no means required, but many children, particularly girls, wore princess gowns. Erin was reminded of her Halloweens growing up in Maine, with parents urging kids to "just put on a jacket already!"

STAR WARS DAYS

IN 2016, DCL DEBUTED Star Wars Days on several seven-night cruises on the *Fantasy*. These sailings included onboard 3-D showings of *Star Wars Episode VII: The Force Awakens,* guest Star Wars costume celebrations, Star Wars–related crafts and youth activities (Padawan Mind Challenge, anyone?), a guest-participation show called *Star Wars Saga,* and a fireworks-filled stage show called *Summon the Force*. Additionally, Star Wars characters appeared for scheduled and surprise meet and greets. The ship's horn played the "Imperial March." Even much of the onboard food and drink was Star Wars–themed. The beverages of the day were Galaxy in a Glass and a Planetoid Punch; dinner selections included Sand People Salad (Cobb salad in disguise), Bantha Steak Empanadas (chopped beef in a pastry crust), and a Frozen Carbonite Sundae.

As we were going to press, DCL announced **Marvel Days at Sea** for select cruises on the *Magic* that sail from New York City.

FORMAL NIGHT

MOST CRUISES OF SEVEN NIGHTS OR LONGER will have a designated Formal Night. This is a chance for families to put on the ritz. The crew and officers also get into the act by wearing their dress whites. While there are no special meals or activities, you'll see many families getting their photos taken in the ship's atrium before or after dinner.

unofficial **TIP**
Formal Night is very popular for reservations at **Palo** and **Remy**.

If you're the kind of person for whom the words "Formal Night" cause a near-allergic reaction, not to worry: You can always eat at the upper-deck buffet or get room service to avoid the whole business altogether.

As for what *formal* or *dress-up* means, you're likely to see a wide range of interpretations. Many men, if not most, will wear a long-sleeved dress shirt, usually with a jacket; ties are optional. Most women will wear dresses or skirts, or pants with dressy tops. A nice shirt and pants are appropriate for teen boys, and teen girls usually dress as if they're going to a high school dance. Small children are not expected to dress up, but young girls frequently take this opportunity to don the outfit of their favorite Disney princess. Frequently, you'll see a family decked to the nines, with the gentlemen in tuxes and the ladies in gowns.

If you don't have any fancy duds handy, you can rent them before you leave home by visiting **Cruiseline Formalwear** (cruiselineformal .com). Your garments will be delivered directly to your stateroom, and you'll return them to your stateroom attendant at the end of your cruise.

If you're wondering whether your particular sailing will have a Formal Night or any other theme night, give DCL a call at ☎ 800-951-3532.

EASTER

EASTER IS CELEBRATED ON THE DISNEY SHIPS, but in a much more low-key fashion than many of the other holidays. There are no Easter decorations on the ship, and the festivities last for only one day rather than throughout the sailing. Religious services will be offered, typically including a sunrise service, a Catholic mass, and an interdenominational Protestant service. When we sailed on the Fantasy during one recent Easter, secular observations of the holiday included appearances by the White Rabbit from *Alice in Wonderland* (as a stand-in for the Easter Bunny), and Mickey and Minnie wearing what was supposed to be their pastel Easter finery but looked to us like what they'd be sporting on the golf course. Other Easter events include themed craft activities, face painting for children, and the distribution of candy and cookies in the lobby atrium.

INDEPENDENCE DAY

DEPENDING ON YOUR SHIP'S ITINERARY, you will likely see some special onboard activities on July 4. We recently spent Independence Day on the *Magic*. Crew members distributed small American flags to any guest who wanted one. There was a lobby party that started with a truly inspiring rendition of "The Star-Spangled Banner" sung by a Walt Disney Theatre performer, and ended with a dance party featuring Mickey in an Uncle Sam hat, Minnie dressed like Betsy Ross, and Chip 'n' Dale in tricorne caps, bopping along to patriotically themed songs like "Party in the

USA," "Born in the USA," and "American Pie," as well as "Sweet Caroline" . . . because nothing says America like Neil Diamond.

Other activities included themed crafts, American-history trivia contests, and face painting. The breakfast and lunch buffets at Cabanas were heavy on red, white, and blue desserts.

Canada Day also occurred during this same cruise. It got a one-sentence acknowledgment in the *Personal Navigator.* Sorry, Canada.

HALLOWEEN

ONE OF THE BEST PLACES TO CELEBRATE HALLOWEEN is on a Disney cruise. The crew and officers dress up, and many families bring special costumes to wear for this one night on board. Even the Disney characters dress up—one of our favorite memories is being "attacked" by Zombie Goofy one Halloween on board the *Magic* while his guide murmured "Brains!" as they shuffled along.

Most of the family activities have a Halloween theme: Animation classes feature scary characters, the crafts sessions may be villain-themed, and even the karaoke is spooky. As darkness falls, photographers are stationed in each ship's atrium before and after dinner, so families can get photos of themselves dressed up. Kids can visit various areas of the ship to trick-or-treat.

DCL ships begin celebrating Halloween in September, just as at the theme parks. Expect to see pumpkins, black cats, and other decor starting around the last week of September and running through October 31. Every ship offers Halloween-themed movies, deck parties, craft-making, and more.

Introduce your kids to the audience-participation legacy of *The Rocky Horror Picture Show* at the **Nightmare Before Christmas Sing and Scream.** Sing along with the movie, then meet Jack and Sally after the show. There's also a new Halloween-themed deck party, **Mickey's Calling All the Monsters Mouse-Querade,** along with storytelling sessions for kids. For the grown-ups, the ship's dance club hosts a costume party.

THANKSGIVING

IF YOUR CRUISE DATES INCLUDE THE FOURTH THURSDAY in November, you'll be celebrating Thanksgiving aboard your ship. Expect to see Mickey, Minnie, Goofy, and Donald in their Pilgrim costumes, plus many other Disney characters in seasonal outfits. Don't be surprised, however, to see the rest of the ship already decked out for Christmas. The main dining rooms on each ship will serve a traditional Thanksgiving menu. And it wouldn't be Turkey Day without (American) football, even on DCL. Games are broadcast on each ship's big Funnel Vision LED screen near the family pool, as well as at the sports bars.

CHRISTMAS, HANUKKAH, AND KWANZAA

DISNEY BEGINS DECORATING ITS SHIPS for the winter holidays in early to mid-November. Dates vary each year, but in 2016 **Very MerryTime Cruises** commenced on November 5 on the *Magic,* November 6 on the *Dream,* November 10 on the *Wonder,* and November 19 on the *Fantasy.* Among the many decor elements on board, expect to see the ship's atrium decked out with a massive Christmas tree, a Hanukkah menorah, and a Kwanzaa kinara. A tree-lighting ceremony typically takes place on the first night of each Very MerryTime cruise.

Family activities include making holiday greeting cards, drawing Disney characters in holiday outfits, building gingerbread houses, and so on. As at Epcot theme park, each ship will have storytellers scheduled throughout the day, along with special holiday-themed merchandise. Expect to see Mickey, Minnie, Goofy, and other characters dressed in winter finery, plus lots of holiday movies on your stateroom TV.

The most interesting decorations, however, have palm trees decorated with garland, lights, and bulbs, and plastic snowmen sitting on the sand. Disney characters wear holiday-themed island outfits, and even the shuttle bus from the dock is decorated with reindeer antlers.

Religious services are typically offered during each night of Hanukkah. A Catholic Mass is held at midnight on December 24, and a Mass and interdenominational service are held on December 25. Santa Claus distributes small gifts to children in the atrium on Christmas morning, along with milk and cookies. Should you need a little gift-wrapping help, that service is available on board at no extra charge; check your *Personal Navigator* for the location, or ask at Guest Services.

Finally, the ship's onboard music, piped into the hallways and public areas, switches from standard Disney tunes to Christmas-themed tracks. Some people enjoy it; others prefer the standard Disney music.

NEW YEAR'S EVE

DURING THE DAY, video screens on each ship's pool deck display a clock counting down the hours, minutes, and seconds until midnight. The pool deck is also the site for a big family-themed party in the evening, with DJs and live entertainment continuing through midnight. Each ship's dance club also hosts a party, complete with DJ, hats, noisemakers, confetti, and bubbly drinks at midnight. Families will want to see the special fireworks display and the atrium's balloon drop at midnight. The ships' kids' clubs host parties early in the evening, allowing the little ones to get to bed at a reasonable hour.

NIGHTCLUBS, BARS, CAFÉS, *and* LOUNGES

unofficial **TIP**
The drinking age on all DCL itineraries is 21. The exception to this is round-trip sailings from a European port, during which guests ages 18–20 traveling with a parent or guardian may, with written parental consent, purchase and drink alcohol on board while in their parent's presence.

EACH DISNEY CRUISE LINE SHIP has a collection of nightclubs and lounges for adults. Nightclubs typically offer dancing and live acts; lounges are oriented to conversation, with smaller spaces and comfortable seating.

The following section lists the clubs, bars, and lounges found across all four ships; we've included the **Cove Café** coffee bar as well, since it also serves alcoholic drinks. Check your *Personal Navigator* for exact hours.

ON THE *MAGIC*

Cove Café   LOCATION: Deck 9 Midship

SETTING AND ATMOSPHERE Cove Café is the *Magic*'s adults-only coffee bar and one of our favorite places on the ship. The walls are covered in a combination of light-cherry-colored wood paneling and upholstered fabric, while the floor is a mixture of honey-tinted hardwoods. What we like best is the way Disney has arranged seating along the curved, L-shaped bar: At one end is a private rounded corner cutout with a couple of comfortable stuffed chairs. At the opposite end is an open area with satellite TV, couches, and armchairs. Depending on how social you're feeling, you can sit by yourself at one end or be among a group at the other.

SELECTIONS Cove Café serves just about every java you can think of: espresso, cappuccino, latte, Americano, cold drip, and both regular and sugar-free flavored variations. Cove also serves hot teas and has a good selection of wines, Champagnes, spirits, and mixed drinks. Prices for these are the same as throughout the rest of the ship. Service is excellent.

unofficial **TIP**
If you're one of those people who need a coffee or six every day, ask your server for a **Café Fanatic** rewards card; you'll get every sixth specialty coffee free.

Besides beverages, the Cove Café has a self-serve refrigerated case stocked with small bites to eat throughout the day. Breakfast items usually include plain and chocolate croissants, Danish, and fruit. Afternoon and evening service usually consists of cookies, brownies, cakes, crackers, and fruit. Dinner, though, is our favorite because, for a couple of hours, Cove Café brings out a selection of prosciutto, dried sausages, marinated olives, cheeses, and bread. You can make a light supper out of these and a drink; because most families are either at dinner or preparing for it, there's a chance you'll have the café all to yourself.

COMMENTS The Wi-Fi signal here is fairly strong, making it a good spot to catch up on e-mail or the latest news. You'll also find here a small selection of current magazines and periodicals, and this is part of the real attraction at the Cove: the ability to sit in a comfy chair, sip coffee, and flip through the pages of *The New Yorker* in blessed silence, surrounded by $350 million of luxury cruise ship.

The Cove Café and other specialty coffee bars on Disney Cruise Line usually have a "frequent buyer" program. They'll stamp a card each time you buy a fancy coffee drink; buy five and the sixth is free. The cards and stamps are valid for multiple voyages and across all four ships. Hang on to a partially complete card for use on your next cruise.

ACROSS THE SHIPS All four DCL ships have a Cove Café. Those on the *Magic* and *Wonder* are more or less identical, and they're a little larger than the Cove Cafés on the *Dream* and *Fantasy.* The Cove on the *Wonder,* however, connects to the **Outlook Café** (see page 168), which is unique to that ship. The Coves on the *Dream* and *Fantasy* are likewise almost identical twins, but they don't have the televisions found in the cafés on the *Magic* and *Wonder.* Guests at all Cove Cafés must be at least age 18 to enter and at least 21 to drink alcohol.

Promenade Lounge   LOCATION: Deck 3 Aft

SETTING AND ATMOSPHERE The Promenade Lounge hosts family activities during the day and live music at night. It's done in the same Art Deco style as the rest of the *Magic,* with cherry-wood finishes, creamy lighting, and brass accents. Sixteen computers line one wall, providing 24-hour Internet access . . . because nothing goes together like booze and the web.

SELECTIONS Beer and wine by the glass, spirits, mixed drinks, and coffee. Free snacks are served, starting in the afternoon—mostly chips, salsa, and such.

COMMENTS Though one of the most attractive nightspots on the ship, the Promenade Lounge sits adjacent and open to pedestrian traffic from one of the *Magic*'s main inside walkways, making it louder and less relaxing than it could be. Nighttime entertainment is usually provided by a singing duo, such as a pianist and vocalist, making for an enjoyable way to spend half an hour after a meal. (For the performers, though, it's got to be like singing in a bus station due to the outside noise. Some glass and wood partitions would work wonders here.) We recommend using the Promenade as a meeting place for groups to get a drink before dinner at Carioca's or Lumiere's (see Part Seven, Dining) or to listen to the live music with a nightcap.

ACROSS THE SHIPS There's also a Promenade Lounge on the *Wonder.* Like the Promenade on the *Magic,* it's a nice place to have a before- or after-dinner cocktail, as long as you can deal with all the people promenading past on their way to other parts of the ship. The comparable bar on the *Dream* and *Fantasy* is **Bon Voyage** (see page 169).

Signals   LOCATION: Deck 9 Midship

SETTING AND ATMOSPHERE Signals is an adults-only outdoor bar next to the adult pool. It has a few seats for those looking to get some shade, but most patrons take their drinks back to their deck chairs to sip in the sun.

SELECTIONS Much of Signals' menu is devoted to popular beers and frozen drinks, but they can whip up almost anything you can think of. Signals also serves coffee, juices, and bottled water. Soda machines are nearby.

COMMENTS It doesn't have much atmosphere to speak of, but due to its location near the Quiet Cove Pool, it is a little quieter than most bars.

ACROSS THE SHIPS Only the *Magic* and *Wonder* have Signals bars. The *Dream* and *Fantasy* have a total of four outdoor bars: one on each ship called **Currents** and another on each ship called **Waves** (see pages 169 and 171, respectively). Drinks and service are comparable at all of these, but we think Currents has the best views and the nicest decor. Also, Signals serves guests age 21 and older only, while Currents and Waves welcome kids.

After Hours

This is Disney's name for the collection of bars on the *Magic*'s Deck 3 Forward. It includes **Fathoms,** a venue for live entertainment and dancing; **Keys,** a piano bar; and **O'Gills Pub,** a sports bar. After Hours has a contemporary urban nightclub theme, pulled together by a white-and-silver color scheme and accented by chrome light fixtures. It's a welcome improvement over the pre-2013 club space, Beat Street, which consisted of 2-D plywood shapes painted to look like a cityscape at night.

Some After Hours lounges, such as Fathoms, are home to family-oriented entertainment during the day, but all usually have an adults-only policy (age 18 and up to enter, 21 and up to drink) after 9 p.m.

After Hours' bars generally carry the same wines and beers, although each serves its own unique line of cocktails. O'Gills Pub, the sports bar, also has a collection of Irish beers not found elsewhere.

Fathoms LOCATION: Deck 3 Forward

SETTING AND ATMOSPHERE Formerly Rockin' Bar D, Fathoms has an undersea theme: fiber-optic light fixtures shaped like jellyfish, sand-art murals along the bar, and silver-and-black bench seating that undulates like ocean waves. Six sets of couches are built into Fathoms's back wall, providing an excellent semiprivate view of the entertainment stage.

The middle of the club holds a dance floor and a raised stage with a professional sound system and lighting. Armchairs upholstered in silver fabric are arranged in groups of two or three around circular cocktail tables. These help control the echo in Fathoms's large, open floor plan.

SELECTIONS Sea-themed cocktails make up most of Fathoms's bar menu, although beer, wine, and spirits are also available. Drinks range in price from $10.25 for a **Black Pearl** (Crown Royal, Drambuie, and Coke) to $11.25 for a **Blue Tang** (Grey Goose citrus vodka, peach schnapps, blue curaçao, pineapple juice, and sugared rum). Our favorite is the **Anemone** ($11.25), with gin, mango puree, and muddled lemon, orange, and lime, topped with Champagne.

COMMENTS Like other DCL nightclubs, Fathoms does double-duty during the day by hosting family-oriented activities, such as scavenger hunts, bingo, and talent shows. At night the stage hosts everything from game shows to live music, dancing, DJs, karaoke, comedians, magicians, and other performers. The game shows' setups follow well-known television models: There's one similar to *The Newlywed Game,* for example, where contestants try to guess how their partner will answer some random set of questions. This being Disney, though, you probably won't hear any questions about "making whoopee."

ACROSS THE SHIPS Fathoms doesn't have an identical sibling on the other ships, but it's most similar to **Azure** on the *Wonder* (see page 167), **Evolution** on the *Dream* (see page 173), and **The Tube** on the *Fantasy* (see page 181).

Keys LOCATION: Deck 3 Forward

SETTING AND ATMOSPHERE Keys features live piano music nightly. Six large porthole windows run along one of the rectangular room's long walls. The bar is in the middle of the opposite wall, and the piano player is between the two, at the far end of the room from the entrance doors.

Keys's theming got an overhaul during the *Magic*'s 2013 dry dock, and it's now supposed to evoke a Chicago-style lounge from the 1960s. The new furnishings include modern sofas and chairs whose curved, radius-style arms and backs are in marked contrast to the formless oversize chairs of the previous decor. Gone also is the pastel carpet, in favor of a crisp silver with geometric sunbursts. The live entertainment's audio levels tend to be a bit loud for such a small space, but it's a pleasant enough experience.

SELECTIONS The bar menu includes specialty drinks with musically themed names, such as the **Moji-Do,** a mojito; **Bloody Mi-Re,** a Bloody Mary with vodka, yellow-tomato juice, lime, and whiskey-flavored Worcestershire sauce; and **Rob Roy,** made the typical way (Scotch, vermouth, and bitters), only *Rob* is spelled with the musical symbol for a flat note. Most of these cocktails cost about $11, about $5 more per drink than at O'Gills Pub (see next profile). The most expensive drink is a $16 Manhattan, made with Jack Daniel's Sinatra Select whiskey, Antica Formula vermouth, and Cointreau. Coffee, cappuccino, and espresso are available, too, but we recommend the Cove Café if you're looking for those.

COMMENTS Live entertainment usually begins with a show around 7:30 p.m.; a typical night's schedule will have more performances around 9:30, 10:30, and 11:30 p.m. The pianists are acceptable, if nondescript, and play medleys of well-known songs by familiar artists. Some nights have themes, such as 1950s and '60s hits, Elvis, or Simon and Garfunkel, and you can always make requests.

During the day, Keys is often used for group seminars on everything from wine and spirits to acupuncture, Chinese herbs, and back-pain treatments. (We sense a "feel better one way or another" theme here.) Check your *Personal Navigator* for details. The bar typically opens anywhere from 5:30 to 6:30 p.m. Children are admitted to Keys until 9 p.m., when it becomes an adults-only venue until its midnight closing.

ACROSS THE SHIPS The *Magic*'s Keys is most similar to the *Wonder*'s **Cadillac Lounge** (see page 167). The entertainment is interchangeable between the two, and the retro decor is a toss-up.

O'Gills Pub LOCATION: Deck 3 Forward

SETTING AND ATMOSPHERE The former Diversions is now an Irish bar—the name is a nod to the Disney classic/Sean Connery vehicle *Darby O'Gill and* the *Little People*—although it's an Irish bar in the same way that Lucky Charms is an Irish breakfast, which is to say not very. Sure, there's a clover pattern woven into the green carpet and background music that features a lot of fiddle-and-flute and U2, but if you've come expecting Raglan Road at Walt Disney World, you're in for a disappointment.

Nine wall-mounted televisions provide live satellite coverage of whatever sports are being played around the world. Comfortable burgundy-leather banquettes are built into the wall, and padded leather armchairs surround the tables set within the banquettes. In the middle of the room, about a dozen bar-height tables and stools provide the best views of the most TVs.

SELECTIONS The bar menu includes a beer flight of five (5-ounce) Irish brews ($9.75). There's also a selection of Irish whiskeys: Tullamore Dew ($9.50), Kilbeggan ($9.50), Middleton ($11.75), and Connemara ($12.50). Beyond these are standard drinks you'll find throughout the ships, including cocktails; red, white, and sparkling wines; and Scotch and other whiskeys. The cocktails are reasonably priced at $5.75 each. Try the **Royal Velvet,** a mix of Guinness stout and sparkling wine.

COMMENTS A comfy spot to sit, sip, and watch the game.

ACROSS THE SHIPS O'Gills Pub on the *Magic* joins the *Fantasy*'s bar of the same name (see page 178). Along with the *Dream*'s **687** (page 174) and the *Wonder*'s new **Crown & Fin** (page 168), these are the DCL fleet's upscale sports bars. The larger televisions at the *Magic*'s O'Gills make it easier to watch events from across the room.

PALO Adults on the *Magic* and *Wonder* also have the option of grabbing a before- or after-dinner drink at Palo (see page 128 for information on the dress code and page 130 for booking information). When Palo is open for dinner, guests may sit at the bar, which is full-service and offers a view of the open kitchen. Because many people don't realize they can do this, you could find yourself with the counter to yourself. We love it because it's quiet and you can talk to the bartender and servers while they bring in drink orders for their tables. Because of the brunch setup, bar service is available only during dinner.

ON THE *WONDER*

After Hours

Following the *Wonder*'s late-2016 dry dock, the old Deck 3 Forward bar area, Route 66, was renamed After Hours, matching the nomenclature on the *Magic*. Like its counterpart on that ship, After Hours has a contemporary-urban-nightclub theme, pulled together by a uniform color scheme and similar light fixtures.

After Hours is a much appreciated update from Route 66, which boasted fake-antique road signs affixed to the walls and Rascal Flatts' cover of "Life Is a Highway" on endless loop in the corridors. Some After Hours lounges are home to family-oriented entertainment during the day, but all usually have an adults-only policy (age 18 to enter, age 21 to drink) after 9 p.m. After Hours' bars generally carry the same wines and beers, although each serves a unique line of cocktails. **Crown & Fin,** the *Wonder*'s new English pub, will feature British and specialty beers and even serve a brew made especially for the venue.

Azure   LOCATION: Deck 3 Forward

SETTING AND ATMOSPHERE Formerly WaveBands, this is the *Wonder*'s dance club. As part of the ship's dry dock, it got a renovation and a change in theming. At press time, we didn't know much more than what was available from DCL online—which is that the name and the theming are supposed to evoke the ocean, versus WaveBands' old-timey-radio theme.

SELECTIONS We expect that Azure will serve the usual wine, beer, spirits, and mixed drinks, along with free hors d'oeuvres and snacks.

COMMENTS At WaveBands, the ship's crew sometimes donned costumes and led dances. We expect a similarly festive ambience at Azure.

ACROSS THE SHIPS Azure doesn't have an identical sibling on the other ships, but it's most similar to **Fathoms** on the *Magic* (see page 164), **Evolution** on the *Dream* (see page 173), and **The Tube** on the *Fantasy* (see page 181).

Cadillac Lounge   LOCATION: Deck 3 Forward

SETTING AND ATMOSPHERE This is the *Wonder*'s piano bar. The decor pays tribute to 1950s-era Cadillac cars by way of leather-upholstered barstools and chairs, couches made to look like automobile rear seats, and a bar built into a replica of the front of a 1959 Cadillac Coupe de Ville, complete with working headlights.

"Designed by General Motors" isn't something we normally listen for when discussing bar theming, but it works here. The furnishings—with dark woods; carpets in burgundy, gold, and fuchsia; leather-covered walls; chrome accents; and those butter-and-chocolate-colored leather barstools—clearly indicate that this is a bar meant to evoke a very specific time and place.

The best seats in the house are in the far corner, opposite the main entrance and to the right of the piano player. These include a comfortable leather couch and two leather armchairs, plus a side table to hold drinks. From here you can listen to the music and watch some of the action at the bar, tucked away in your own discreet corner of the lounge.

SELECTIONS The Cadillac Lounge serves beer, wine, spirits, and cocktails, and it's the only bar in After Hours that serves Champagne by the glass (outside After Hours, the **Outlook Café** also serves Champagne; see next page). Coffee, cappuccino, and espresso are available as well, but we'd recommend the Cove Café if you're looking for those. Free snacks and appetizers, including caviar, are available all evening.

COMMENTS Live entertainment usually begins with a show around 7:30 p.m.; a typical night's schedule will have more performances around 9:30, 10:30, and 11:30 p.m. The pianists are acceptable, if nondescript, and play medleys of well-known songs by familiar artists. Some nights have themes, such as 1950s and '60s hits, Elvis, or Simon and Garfunkel, and you can always make requests.

During the day, the Cadillac Lounge is often used for group seminars on everything from wine and spirits to homeopathic treatments like acupuncture. Check your *Personal Navigator* for details. The bar typically opens anywhere from 5:30 to 6:30 p.m. Children are admitted to the Cadillac Lounge until 9 p.m., when it becomes an adults-only venue until its midnight closing.

ACROSS THE SHIPS The Cadillac Lounge is most similar to the *Magic*'s **Keys** (see page 165). The entertainment is interchangeable between the two, and the retro decor is a toss-up.

Cove Café   LOCATION: Deck 9 Forward

COMMENTS See profile of Cove Café on the *Magic* (page 162) for details.

Crown & Fin   LOCATION: Deck 3 Forward

SETTING AND ATMOSPHERE Formerly Diversions, Crown & Fin is the Wonder's new sports bar. In late 2016, it was rethemed from a generic bar into an authentic English tavern. The space is adorned with dark woods, plush leather furniture, and brass accents, and subtle nods to classic Disney films set in London can be found in artwork and props.

SELECTIONS Cocktails and British and craft beers on tap. We think a menu of pub grub will be available as well, so you can snack while you sip.

COMMENTS Given the size of the ship, the odds are good that you'll be able to find other fans of your favorite teams at Crown & Fin. Besides televised sports, Crown & Fin will host family-oriented and adult activities throughout the day, ranging from Disney-character-drawing classes for kids to trivia contests and afternoon beer tastings. Check your *Personal Navigator* for the schedule.

ACROSS THE SHIPS The Crown & Fin refurbishment brings this bar in line with the other clubby sports-viewing venues on Disney Cruise Line. We're pretty sure we'd be happy to watch the big game here, or just while away a sea day nursing a pint and playing checkers.

PALO Adults on the *Magic* and *Wonder* also have the option of grabbing a before- or after-dinner drink at Palo (see page 128 for information on the dress code and page 130 for booking information). When Palo is open for dinner, guests may sit at the bar, which is full-service and offers a view of the open kitchen. Because many people don't realize they can do this, you could find yourself with the counter to yourself. We love it because it's quiet and you can talk to the bartender and servers while they bring in drink orders for their tables. Because of the brunch setup, bar service is available only during dinner.

Outlook Café   LOCATION: Deck 10 Forward

SETTING AND ATMOSPHERE What makes the Outlook Café special is that its seating area is surrounded by large glass windows, making it the perfect venue in which to get some sun in a climate-controlled environment. This means air-conditioning when the *Wonder* is in the Caribbean and heat when it's plying the waters off Alaska.

SELECTIONS Coffees, teas, wine, beer, mixed drinks, and Champagne by the glass. Complimentary snacks are also offered.

COMMENTS An extension of the Cove Café, the Outlook Café, found upstairs via a spiral staircase, is a lovely place to while away some time. There's nothing like it on any other DCL ship.

ACROSS THE SHIPS The Outlook Café is unique to the *Wonder.* As at the Cove Cafés, guests must be age 18 to enter and 21 to drink alcohol.

Promenade Lounge   LOCATION: Deck 3 Aft

COMMENTS See profile of Promenade Lounge on the *Magic* (page 163) for details.

Signals   LOCATION: Deck 9 Midship

COMMENTS See profile of Signals on the *Magic* (page 163) for details.

ON THE *DREAM*

Bon Voyage   LOCATION: Deck 3 Midship

SETTING AND ATMOSPHERE Sitting just off the atrium, Bon Voyage is one of the prettiest, if not smallest, of the *Dream*'s bars, with just 10 seats at the counter plus 4 covered armchairs a few feet away. The two highlights here are the gorgeous Art Deco mural behind the bar—which shows well-heeled passengers in 1920s formal wear departing their touring cars to board the *Dream*—and the swirled, maize-yellow illuminated bar face, which reflects gold light off the beige-marble floors.

SELECTIONS Bon Voyage's bar menu is similar to that in The District (see page 172) and includes draft and bottled beer, wines by the glass and bottle, spirits, and mixed drinks, including a few special fruit-flavored martinis. Service is excellent.

COMMENTS Open from around noon to 11 p.m. daily, Bon Voyage is a good spot for groups to meet before dinner or to have a nightcap before departing for the elevators. Because it's in a heavily trafficked area, there's no live entertainment, and it isn't our first choice for a quiet drink or conversation, but it is a good place to fortify yourself while standing in those character-greeting lines. Sometimes you need a little liquid courage to face Chip 'n' Dale.

ACROSS THE SHIPS The *Fantasy* also has a Bon Voyage just off the Deck 3 atrium; the *Dream*'s Bon Voyage is more appealing, even without live entertainment. The **Promenade Lounge** is the comparable bar on the *Magic* and *Wonder* (see page 163).

Cove Café   LOCATION: Deck 11 Forward

COMMENTS See profile of Cove Café on the *Magic* (page 162) for details.

Currents   LOCATION: Deck 13 Forward

SETTING AND ATMOSPHERE This outdoor area has the best views of any bar on the *Dream.* Built behind and into the structure supporting the forward stairs and elevators, the curved, glossy white face of the bar mirrors the curve along the opposite deck rail and provides some shade during the day. Currents is beautiful at night, when a royal-blue neon sign (which calls to mind the nameplate on a 1950s car) lights up the bar and bar shelves, accented with matching blue tile.

Ten stationary barstools are spaced far enough apart for easy access to walk-up traffic. Most guests take drinks back to their lounge chairs, but there's also plenty of (unshaded) armchair seating around Currents.

SELECTIONS Currents serves bottled and draft beer, cocktails, and frozen drinks.

COMMENTS The one downside to Currents is that it's next to a smoking section. Depending on the prevailing winds, this is either not an issue at all or a mild annoyance.

ACROSS THE SHIPS Currents is the same on the *Dream* and the *Fantasy*. **Signals** on the *Magic* and *Wonder* is similar (see page 163), but Currents's layout is much more open, with much better views and nicer decor. Also, where Signals is adults-only, Currents welcomes kids and serves nonalcoholic concoctions just for them.

Meridian   LOCATION: Deck 12 Aft

SETTING AND ATMOSPHERE Situated between the restaurants Palo and Remy, Meridian is the *Dream*'s martini bar. It's also one of our favorite bars on the ship.

Sitting high up on Deck 12 Aft, Meridian has windows on three sides of its relatively small, square room. Panoramic views of the sunset await early diners who stop in around dusk. Antique ship-navigation maps and instruments adorn the walls and shelves. Meridian's furnishings include rich brown-leather couches and armchairs, as well as cocoa-colored teak floors with brass inlays. Meridian also has outdoor seating on a teak deck that runs along one wall of Remy. It's lovely on warm summer evenings—and in demand around dusk—so don't be surprised if it's standing-room only.

SELECTIONS Meridian's bar menu emphasizes mixed drinks and spirits over beer and wine, although those are also available, as are coffees. The best thing about Meridian is the bartending staff, who will often offer to make a custom martini for you on the spot. This usually starts with the bartender inquiring whether you like fruit- or herb-based drinks and what kinds of liquors you usually prefer. A couple of minutes of muddling, shaking, and stirring, and you have the first draft of your new drink. And if it's not quite what you expected, they'll be happy to start over.

Meridian on the *Dream* also offers an antipasti tray with wine for guests who want to snack while they drink. Prices: signature wines, $20 per person or $89 per bottle; premium wines, $28 per person or $99 per bottle; you can also omit the wine for $30 per person. We're not sure, though, why guests wouldn't simply choose the free evening antipasti at Cove Café or Vista Café.

COMMENTS We recommend stopping by Meridian for its martini experience alone, even if you don't have reservations for Remy or Palo (see Part Seven). If you're dining at Remy, though, beware of the combined effect of

Meridian's martinis and Remy's wine pairings—as Len found out, it may be more than you bargained for.

Meridian usually opens around 5 p.m. and stays open until midnight. It's one of the few DCL nightspots with a dress code: Inside the lounge, men should wear dress shirts and pants, and women should wear dresses, skirts and blouses, or pantsuits. If you're just visiting the outdoor area, jeans and shorts are allowed, but swimwear, T-shirts, or tank tops are verboten.

ACROSS THE SHIPS Both the *Dream* and the *Fantasy* have nearly identical Meridian lounges; the *Magic* and *Wonder* do not.

Vista Café LOCATION: Deck 4 Midship

SETTING AND ATMOSPHERE A small, Art Deco–themed nook in a corner of Deck 4.

SELECTIONS Vista Café serves everything from coffee and complimentary pastries in the morning to beer, wine, cocktails, and light snacks at night.

COMMENTS With only four seats at the bar, this isn't the place for large groups. It's most useful as a place for a family to get a drink and a bite to eat on their way to one of the day's activities on Decks 3 or 4.

ACROSS THE SHIPS Vista Cafés can be found on both the *Dream* and the *Fantasy* but not the *Magic* or *Wonder*. Both cafés offer the same food and drink and are about the same size; the only significant difference is the decor—the Vista on the *Fantasy* has that ship's Art Nouveau theme rather than the Art Deco styling of the *Dream*. The marble floor of the *Fantasy*'s version is a bit bigger than the *Dream*'s, making the former Vista Café seem more of an intentionally designed space versus one carved out of an underutilized corner.

Waves LOCATION: Deck 12 Aft

SETTING AND ATMOSPHERE Tucked behind the rear smokestack, Waves is an outdoor bar catering primarily to sunbathers on Deck 12. Waves's eight fixed barstools are arranged around an attractive white tile face, and the back of the bar is decorated with small tiles in varying shades of blue. An overhang above the bar provides shade for guests seated or standing at the bar, but most of the seating—upholstered blue cushions on glossy, curved-back teak booths, plus various sets of tables and chairs—is directly in the sun.

SELECTIONS The most popular drinks at Waves are bottled beers, frozen cocktails, and mixed drinks. Nonalcoholic smoothies and fruit juices are available for children and teetotalers.

COMMENTS Waves's hours vary, but it's usually open from late morning to late evening. Most visitors are coming from the lounge chairs or sports activities on Deck 13; some are just looking for a quiet spot away from the crowds.

ACROSS THE SHIPS Both the *Dream* and the *Fantasy* have Waves bars, and they're essentially identical. **Signals** is the outdoor bar on the *Magic* and *Wonder* (see page 163); Waves, however, is quieter, has nicer decor, and welcomes kids (Signals is 21-and-up only).

The District

This is the designation for the five bars and lounges on the *Dream*'s Deck 4 Aft: **District Lounge,** in a hallway connecting the different venues; **Evolution,** a dance club; **Pink,** a Champagne bar; **687,** an upscale sports bar; and **Skyline,** a cosmopolitan watering hole.

The theming is meant to evoke images of exclusive urban nightlife. Along the faux-brick walls and behind velvet ropes are black-plastic silhouettes of couples "waiting" to get in. Other walls have black-plastic images of paparazzi or simply the logos of the clubs illuminated in a repeating pattern.

Most of The District's bars open between 5 and 5:30 p.m. and stay open until midnight. District Lounge usually opens a little earlier; Evolution operates from around 10 p.m. to 2 a.m. Hot snacks are usually provided throughout the evening in one of The District's circular pedestrian walkways.

Evolution, Pink, and Skyline admit guests age 18 and up only. Families are welcome at District Lounge and 687 until 9 p.m., when the bars become adults-only.

District Lounge   LOCATION: Deck 4 Aft

SETTING AND ATMOSPHERE An attractive, contemporary bar and seating area are bisected by a walkway connecting The District's bars. The bar seats six along its curving, white-stone front. Lights hidden beneath the black-marble top point down, creating smoky gray shadows in the stone. Behind the bar is a bronze-colored wall; orange lighting illuminates the bottles and provides this side of District Lounge with its most prominent color.

A lounge with couches and armchairs sits across the walkway opposite the bar; although it's not perfect, it's one of the more stylish places on the *Dream*. While the lounge is completely open to (and exposed to noise from) guests going from club to club, off-white leather couches, Champagne-colored metal poles, and cocoa-colored carpeting provide a visual boundary marking its border. Deeper inside are U-shaped armchairs, covered outside in the same white leather and inside in deep-brown leather, arranged in groups of four around small tables. A curving, chocolate-colored, illuminated wall provides a backdrop.

SELECTIONS The bar menu has a bit of everything: draft and bottled beer, cocktails, frozen drinks, whiskeys and tequilas, and wine and Champagne by the glass and bottle. There's also a special martini menu ($8.75–$9.75) not found at other clubs in The District. A few nonalcoholic drinks and coffees are available as well.

COMMENTS The best seats are along the lounge's inside wall, where you can relax in those deep armchairs while watching everyone else shuttle between clubs. This is also the best vantage point from which to watch the District Lounge's entertainment, which includes live singers and pianists later at night. The lounge is also a good meeting place to start out the evening, especially for groups who haven't decided which of The District's bars to visit.

ACROSS THE SHIPS The District Lounge roughly corresponds to the Venice-themed **La Piazza** lounge on the *Fantasy* (see page 179) but has no relative on the *Magic* or *Wonder.* We like the District Lounge more than La Piazza: Its recessed seating allows you to enjoy a drink away from the bustle of clubgoers walking to their next destination.

Evolution LOCATION: Deck 4 Aft

SETTING AND ATMOSPHERE The *Dream*'s dance club, Evolution is, according to Disney, designed as "an artistic interpretation of the transformation of a butterfly . . . emerging from a chrysalis." What this entails is a lot of yellow, orange, and red lights arranged in the shape of butterfly wings and hung around the club. Pairs of wings hang above the dance floor, and we'll forgive you for comparing the slightly tipsy, dancing tourists to wriggling pupae. A couple of the walls are wing-patterned, too, bathing guests seated at the leather couches alongside in hues of ginger and crimson.

Fortunately, most of the butterfly theming is concentrated around the dance floor and along a couple of back walls. Between the two, it's not as noticeable; plastic-shell chairs sit in the dimly lit sections, occasionally alongside high-backed couches. Short barstools line the outside edge of the room, surrounding small, round tables. The circular bar has gold-leather seats on one side, allowing guests a view of the dance floor while they drink; the other half of the bar is for walk-up traffic.

SELECTIONS Evolution's drink menu is similar to District Lounge's, offering draft and bottled beer, cocktails, spirits, and wine and Champagne by the glass and bottle.

COMMENTS Because it's one of the largest venues on the *Dream,* Evolution is the site of family activities throughout the day, holding everything from hands-on craft-making seminars to tequila tastings to time-share presentations. Evolution's adults-only entertainment usually starts later than at other bars in The District, around 10 or 10:30 p.m.; check your *Personal Navigator* for details.

Live entertainment includes magicians, comics, singers, and more. In addition to live acts, Evolution's DJs sometimes dedicate an entire night's music to a specific genre. Common themes include classic rock, disco, and something called urban country.

ACROSS THE SHIPS Evolution is most similar to **The Tube** dance club on the *Fantasy* (see page 181), **Fathoms** on the *Magic* (see page 164), and **Azure** on the *Wonder* (see page 167). We rate Evolution as the second-best dance club on Disney Cruise Line, behind The Tube. Theming, lighting, and seating are nicer than at Fathoms and Azure, while The Tube's London Underground ambience is better executed than Evolution's more-conceptual "caterpillar to butterfly" idea.

Pink LOCATION: Deck 4 Aft

SETTING AND ATMOSPHERE Pink, the *Dream*'s Champagne bar, is our favorite nightspot on the ship. Decorated in silvers, whites, and golds, the space is intended to make you think you're sitting inside a glass of Champagne. In the walls are embedded round lights of white and pink, tiny near the floor and larger near the ceiling, imitating the carbon dioxide fizz inside a flute of bubbly. The silver carpet's starburst pattern calls to mind bubbles rising from below, and the rounded, glossy white ceiling is meant to represent the top of the glass. The light fixtures are upside-down Champagne flutes. Behind the bar are a multitude of glass "bubbles," expanding as they rise from the bar shelf to the ceiling.

Around the bar are half a dozen stools, with silver legs and clear, oval plastic backs that continue the bubble theme. Beyond the bar, a couple of burgundy chairs sit among their silver-velvet sisters. After a few drinks, we're pretty sure these are supposed to represent rosé Champagne, of which several are served at the bar. The best seats in the house, though, are on the padded couch inside a dome-shaped cubby in the wall at one end of the lounge. Move a couple of those big chairs in front and you have a private little cocoon, or slide them away for a view of the entire room.

> **unofficial TIP**
> Look carefully inside a few of the bubble lights on the wall and you'll see a tiny pink elephant from Disney's *Dumbo*. It's a little odd because Dumbo is the mascot of the *Fantasy*, which has its own Champagne bar, the French-themed **Ooh La La** (no elephants).

SELECTIONS Pink's Champagne menu includes many recognizable names: Cristal, Moët et Chandon, Taittinger, Veuve Clicquot, and the requisite Dom Pérignon. Champagne-based cocktails are also available; most include fruit juices, such as mango, pomegranate, and peach, while a few include other liquors—the **Elderbubble** ($10.75), for example, contains raspberry vodka along with Champagne and elderflower syrup. A small selection of white, red, and dessert wines is available by the glass (more by the bottle), along with a dozen or so whiskeys and Cognacs.

COMMENTS If you love Champagne, Pink is a relative bargain. Its markup is generally less than twice the average retail price—usually considerably less than what Disney charges at its theme park resorts. For example, a bottle of Taittinger La Française sells for about $35 plus tax at your local wine store. The same bottle costs $72 at Pink: a fairly standard double bar markup, but not as much the $80 charged at a Walt Disney World Signature restaurant. Similarly, Pink's Dom Pérignon, at $239 per bottle, is marked up a little more than one-and-a-half times over retail—at Walt Disney World's Grand Floridian Resort, it's nearly $300 a bottle.

ACROSS THE SHIPS Only the *Dream* and the *Fantasy* have Champagne bars, and this is one of the main reasons we prefer these ships over the *Magic* and the *Wonder*. However, we like Pink's relatively understated theming better than the *très feminine* French-boudoir decor of **Ooh La La** on the *Fantasy* (see page 178).

687 LOCATION: Deck 4 Aft

SETTING AND ATMOSPHERE Anytime you see a venue with a dozen flat-panel TVs, there's a good chance that it's a sports bar. On the *Dream* it's called 687, and the screens are set in rows above the bar, in a cluster at a far end of the room, and individually in some seating areas.

The bar is set in the middle of 687's rectangular floor. Four porthole windows across from the bar provide light during the day, and moss-colored couches beneath them work to separate the wall into group-size partitions. The scarlet, green, and gold carpet and burgundy-painted, wood-paneled walls give 687 a more masculine feel than the sports bars on the *Fantasy, Magic,* and *Wonder.*

Besides the couches, barstools and tables are arranged around the room to provide good views of either set of televisions. A few leather-covered armchairs are also arranged around the screens and across from the couches. There's plenty of room to stand between these, too, in case you want to just catch up on some scores. Couches arranged in some of the corners provide quieter spots to unwind.

SELECTIONS Bar and table service are excellent. The menu is similar to District Lounge's and includes both draft and bottled beer, cocktails, spirits, and wine and Champagne by the glass, plus coffees and nonalcoholic drinks. Unique to 687 is a selection of "Beercktails" (a word that no self-respecting adult would ever use): cocktails of beer, spirits, and fruit juice. The most popular of these is the **Baha Fog** ($5.75), which adds a shot of tequila to a glass of Corona with lime. Hot, cooked-to-order appetizers, available for an upcharge, range from chips with guac and salsa ($8) to tempura shrimp ($18).

COMMENTS We've spent a few evenings watching games at 687. The seating is comfortable, and it's easy to see and hear the action on the screens. Because of the way the seating is arranged, however, we've found it difficult to start conversations with other patrons. Try sitting at the bar if conviviality is important to you.

Besides sporting events, 687 hosts family activities during the day, including movie, music, and sports trivia. A selection of board games is available in case you want to play rather than watch. Finally, this is usually where runners meet before debarking for the start of the Castaway Cay 5K run when the *Dream* is docked there.

ACROSS THE SHIPS We find 687 more upscale than **Crown & Fin** on the *Wonder* (see page 168) or **O'Gills Pub** on the *Magic* and *Fantasy* (see pages 165 and 178, respectively). While its seating isn't as open, it's a posh place to catch up on the day's highlights in relative quiet.

Skyline LOCATION: Deck 4 Aft

SETTING AND ATMOSPHERE Along with Pink, Skyline is one of our two favorite bars on the *Dream.* The concept is that you're in a lounge high on the edge of some of the world's most famous cities. Behind the bar are seven "windows"—large HDTV screens—affording panoramic views of New York City, Chicago, Rio de Janeiro, Paris, and Hong Kong.

Each city is shown for about 15 minutes across all seven screens; then the scene changes to another locale. The foreground of each view includes close-up views of apartments and offices, while the middle and background show each city's iconic architecture and landscape.

That would be mildly interesting scenery on its own, but Disney has added special effects that make Skyline beautiful. Each view shows the city in motion: Cars move along streets, neon signs blink to illuminate sidewalks, and apartment lights go on and off as their residents come and go. (Look closely and you can even see Mickey Mouse waving to you from inside a tiny apartment in Paris.) A second effect is that the scenery changes depending on the time of day you're inside. If you get here in late afternoon, you'll see the sun setting on these towns. Stay long enough—and we have—and dusk turns to evening, then evening to night.

Last, Skyline has mirrors on the walls perpendicular to the video screens. Because the mirrors are set at right angles to the screens, they reflect the videos and make the bar look longer than it is. It's a well-known decorating trick for making a small room seem larger, but it's still nice to see it included here.

The rest of the decor is natural surfaces: wood panels, ceiling, and floors, in colors ranging from honey to mahogany; dark marble countertops; and leather chairs.

SELECTIONS The specialty is "around the world" cocktails themed to the featured cities. For example, the **1914** ($8.75), representing Chicago, pairs Absolut Vanilla and Absolut Kurant vodkas with fresh blackberries and raspberries; the **Zen-Chanted** ($10.75), representing Hong Kong, is made with 3Vodka (distilled from soybeans), Zen green-tea liqueur, Cointreau, and guava and lime juices.

COMMENTS Adding movement to the scenery means the view at Skyline doesn't get boring. It also means that the club doesn't need a television to hold its patrons' attention. And the cityscapes are a great way to break the ice with fellow cruisers.

ACROSS THE SHIPS Although there are Skylines on both the *Dream* and the *Fantasy,* their drink menus are mostly different. Drinks at the *Dream*'s Skyline tend toward the fruity, whereas drinks at the *Fantasy*'s Skyline make more use of herbs and spices, such as basil, thyme, coriander, cilantro, and paprika.

ON THE *FANTASY*

Bon Voyage   LOCATION: Deck 3 Midship

SETTING AND ATMOSPHERE Just off the atrium and done in the same Art Nouveau style as the rest of the ship, Bon Voyage is one of the prettiest bars on the *Fantasy.* Behind the bar are two gold-and-white peacocks etched in glass, while the bar's face is a translucent gold marble. Cinnamon-colored wood accents complete the look. Bon Voyage has just 10 seats at the counter, plus 2 fabric-covered couches and 6 armchairs a few feet away.

SELECTIONS The bar menu is similar to that at La Piazza (see page 179) and includes draft and bottled beer, wines by the glass and bottle, spirits, and mixed drinks, including a few special fruit-flavored martinis.

COMMENTS Near the atrium and open from around noon to 11 p.m. daily, Bon Voyage is a good spot for groups to meet before dinner or have a nightcap before departing for the elevators. Because it's in a heavily trafficked area, there's no live entertainment at the bar, and it's not our first choice for a quiet drink or conversation.

ACROSS THE SHIPS The *Dream*'s Bon Voyage is done in Art Deco rather than the *Fantasy*'s Art Nouveau version and is more appealing, even without live entertainment. The **Promenade Lounge** is the comparable bar on the *Magic* and *Wonder* (see page 163).

Cove Café   LOCATION: Deck 11 Forward

COMMENTS See profile of Cove Café on the *Magic* (page 162) for details.

Currents   LOCATION: Deck 13 Forward

COMMENTS See profile of Currents on the *Dream* (page 169) for details.

Meridian   LOCATION: Deck 12 Aft

COMMENTS See profile of Meridian on the *Dream* (page 170) for details.

Vista Café   LOCATION: Deck 4 Midship

COMMENTS See profile of Vista Café on the *Dream* (page 171) for details.

Waves   LOCATION: Deck 12 Aft

COMMENTS See profile of Waves on the *Dream* (page 171) for details.

Europa

This is the designation for the five nightspots on the *Fantasy*'s Deck 4 Aft: **O'Gills Pub,** a sports bar; **Ooh La La,** a Champagne bar; **La Piazza,** an Italian-inspired lounge; **Skyline,** a cosmopolitan watering hole; and **The Tube,** a London subway–themed dance club.

While the nightlife districts on the other three ships have distinctive theming, Europa has next to none. The ostensible theme is Europe, but the decor consists mostly of just shiny gold walls, with each club's name illuminated and repeated in a pattern. That said, one nice touch found only at Europa lies in the round black-and-white photos on the walls: The images, which feature European icons, including the Eiffel Tower, London's Big Ben, and the Leaning Tower of Pisa, turn into short animated videos. Also, for what it's worth, the bathrooms here are decorated fabulously and worth a special trip.

Most of Europa's bars open between 5 and 5:30 p.m. and stay open until midnight. La Piazza usually opens a little earlier than that; The Tube operates from around 10 p.m. to 2 a.m. Hot appetizers are usually provided throughout the evening in one of La Piazza's circular pedestrian walkways.

Ooh La La, Skyline, and The Tube admit guests age 18 and up only. Families are welcome at La Piazza and O'Gills Pub until 9 p.m., when they become adults-only.

O'Gills Pub   LOCATION: Deck 4 Aft

SETTING AND ATMOSPHERE   The *Fantasy*'s sports bar, O'Gills lies just off one side of La Piazza (see next page). It's ostensibly an Irish pub, but it's the least visually interesting bar in Europa. The attempts at theming—Irish music and liberal use of four-leaf clovers—are halfhearted at best; with some paint, antiques-store scavenging, and the right "beer of the month" subscription, O'Gills could pass as a Chicago-, Dallas-, or Green Bay–themed bar.

The centerpiece is a huge high-def video screen in the back corner, which shows sporting events and sports news all day long. Several other smaller screens are distributed throughout the room, and there's plenty of seating and standing room.

SELECTIONS   The bar menu includes bottled and draft beer, including a house draft lager and several Irish brews. Wine is available by the glass and bottle, and the friendly bartenders can mix up any cocktail you want. The specialty is Irish whiskey and Scotch; a private-label Irish cream liqueur is on the menu, too. The mixed drinks are reasonably priced at $5.75 each. Try the **Royal Velvet,** a mix of Guinness stout and sparkling wine.

COMMENTS   You wouldn't come here for the Irish ambience, but as a generic sports bar, O'Gills isn't bad.

ACROSS THE SHIPS   There's another O'Gills on the *Magic* (see page 165). As a sports bar, however, it's similar to **687** on the *Dream* (see page 174) and **Crown & Fin** on the *Wonder* (see page 168). We prefer 687, O'Gills on the *Magic,* and Crown and Fin because they have better sight lines to the TV screens from the seats.

Ooh La La   LOCATION: Deck 4 Aft

SETTING AND ATMOSPHERE   This is the *Fantasy*'s Champagne bar. The French-boudoir theme is enough to make you break out in "Lady Marmalade" from *Moulin Rouge:* rose-colored upholstery on the walls, purple carpet, and chairs lined with gold fabric. Along one wall are a series of padded couches in ivory and green. Gold-edged mirrors and fleurs-de-lis line the walls. A single red chair and a couple of small, red-topped side tables provide a touch of bold color.

The bar, at the far end of the lounge, seats six around its black marble top. In keeping with the boudoir theme, the mirror behind the bar looks like an oversize version of one you'd find on the dressing table of a fashionable Frenchwoman at the *fin de siècle.* And because it's a Champagne bar, hundreds of small glass bubbles fill the mirrors.

SELECTIONS   Ooh La La serves reasonably priced Champagnes by the glass and bottle. A couple of these, such as Pommery Rosé Brut and Bollinger La Grande Année, aren't found at Pink, the Champagne bar on the *Dream.* Available along with these are such familiar names as Taittinger and Dom Pérignon. A glass of bubbly starts at around $6 and goes up to $18; bottles cost anywhere from around $50 to $500.

Champagne cocktails, with fruit juices and other liquors, cost around $11, but remember the Second Law of Champagne: If it needs another ingredient, you're drinking the wrong Champagne. (The First Law: Champagne goes with everything!) Sparkling wines, along with reds and whites, are available by the glass and bottle, and the fully stocked bar can furnish virtually any cocktail you like.

COMMENTS The best seats in Ooh La La are on the L-shaped silver couch near the main entrance. It's the perfect private place to do some people-watching. Another nice touch is the use of area rugs to mark off sections of seats—it's possible to mingle within that small area, having individual conversations while still being part of the group. The club has three porthole windows—which we didn't expect—with ocean views and seating below. If you visit during the late afternoon, the light from outside provides a gentle transition from day to dusk. One of our favorite bartenders, Lindsay, can be found pouring bubbly and mixing cocktails at Ooh La La.

ACROSS THE SHIPS Only the *Dream* and the *Fantasy* have Champagne bars, and this is one of the main reasons we prefer these ships over the *Magic* and the *Wonder.* However, we like the relatively understated theming of **Pink** on the *Dream* (see page 173) better than the frilly decor of Ooh La La.

La Piazza LOCATION: Deck 4 Aft

SETTING AND ATMOSPHERE This Venetian-themed lounge sits near the front of Europa. Appropriately, La Piazza ("The Plaza") serves as the walkway to O'Gills and Ooh La La, whose entrances sit just off this venue; farther beyond are Skyline and The Tube, so you'll walk by La Piazza on the way.

The bar sits in the middle of a bright circular room. It's themed to look like an Italian carousel, its ceiling decorated with hundreds of carousel lights. Around the bar are rose-colored barstools; lining the wall are golden, high-backed, upholstered couches with small tables for drinks. The couches are separated, elevated, and set into niches in the walls, making them good vantages from which to watch people walk between the clubs.

SELECTIONS La Piazza's bar menu features Peroni and Moretti, two Italian beers, as well as Prosecco (Italian sparkling wine) and *limoncello* (an Italian lemon-flavored liqueur). These ingredients also make their way into La Piazza's five signature cocktails—the **Mercutio** ($5.95), for example, features Absolut Pears vodka, limoncello, grappa, and fresh lemon juice, with the sweetness of the pear and grappa balancing out the tartness of the citrus.

COMMENTS The couches are good spots for watching La Piazza's live entertainment, which has been an up-tempo jazz trio on each of our cruises. If you're not into music, our favorite pastime at La Piazza takes place starting at 11 p.m., when we start to wager a round of drinks on the number of couples who will stop to take photos on La Piazza's Vespa motorcycle-and-sidecar prop in the next 10 minutes. The over–under on that bet is usually 2.5, and the rules prohibit shouting encouragement to the *ubriachi.*

ACROSS THE SHIPS Somewhat similar to **District Lounge** on the *Dream* (see page 172), La Piazza has a better drink menu, while District Lounge has a better layout. Neither the *Magic* nor the *Wonder* has a comparable bar.

Skyline LOCATION: Deck 4 Aft

SETTING AND ATMOSPHERE Skyline is our favorite bar on the *Fantasy.* The concept is that you're in a lounge high on the edge of some of the world's most famous cities. Behind the bar are seven "windows"—large HDTV screens—affording panoramic views of seven cities: Athens, Barcelona, Budapest, Florence, London, Paris, and St. Petersburg.

Each city is shown for about 15 minutes across all seven screens; then the scene changes to another locale. The foreground of each view includes close-up views of apartments and offices, while the middle and background show each city's iconic architecture and landscape.

That would be mildly interesting scenery on its own, but Disney has added special effects that make Skyline beautiful. Each view shows the city in motion: Cars move along streets, neon signs blink to illuminate sidewalks, and apartment lights go on and off as their residents come and go. (Look closely and you can even see Mickey Mouse waving to you from inside a tiny apartment in Paris.) A second effect is that the scenery changes depending on the time of day you're inside. If you get here in late afternoon, you'll see the sun setting on these towns. Stay long enough—and we have—and dusk turns to evening, then evening to night.

Last, Skyline has mirrors on the walls perpendicular to the video screens. Because the mirrors are set at right angles to the screens, they reflect the videos and make the bar look longer than it is. It's a well-known decorating trick for making a small room seem larger, but it's still nice to see it included here.

The rest of the decor is natural surfaces: wood panels, ceiling, and floors, in colors ranging from honey to mahogany; dark marble countertops; and leather chairs.

SELECTIONS The specialty is "around the world" cocktails themed to the featured cities. For example, **El Conquistador** ($9.75), representing Barcelona, pairs Tanqueray gin and Absolut Peppar vodka with fresh muddled strawberries, basil, and cracked black pepper; the **Aquincum** ($10.75), representing Budapest, is made with 901 Tequila, Grand Marnier, paprika, and freshly squeezed lime juice.

COMMENTS Adding movement to the scenery means the view at Skyline doesn't get boring. It also means that the club doesn't need a television to hold its patrons' attention. And the cityscapes are a great way to break the ice with fellow cruisers.

ACROSS THE SHIPS Although there are Skylines on both the *Dream* and the *Fantasy,* the latter one features two more cities in its "windows" than the one on the *Dream.* Also, their drink menus are mostly different. Drinks at the *Dream*'s Skyline tend to be flavored with fruits and fruit juices, such as cranberry, pomegranate, lemon, and lime; drinks on the *Fantasy*'s Skyline are made with fruits, too, but also with herbs and spices, such as basil, thyme, coriander, cilantro, and paprika. We find that these extra ingredients add another layer of flavor and cut some of the fruits' sweetness. If you're unsure about ordering one of these cocktails, ask the bartender to make the drink without the herbs or spices, and take a sip. Then have the remaining ingredients added and sip again.

The Tube LOCATION: Deck 4 Aft

SETTING AND ATMOSPHERE With its London subway–meets–*Austin Powers* theme, The Tube is the *Fantasy*'s dance club. Its decor includes leather couches with prints that look like Underground tickets, 1960s-mod egg-shaped chairs, and a floor painted like a London subway map. We especially like the upholstered leather couch set deep inside the lounge because it's under a set of lights in the shape of a crown and across from two shiny silver armchairs designed to look like thrones. A couple of red phone booths are set on either side of the dance floor. *Yeah, baby!*

SELECTIONS The Tube's circular bar, set under Big Ben's clock face, serves a typical menu of bottled beer, mixed drinks, spirits, and wine and Champagne by the glass. The Tube also serves six signature drinks, several of which are made with sodas or sparkling wines. Our favorite is **Mind the Gap** ($8.75), a mix of whiskey, Drambuie, and Coke.

COMMENTS The Tube usually opens around 10 p.m. and sometimes gets things going with a quick game of Match Your Mate (think *The Newlywed Game,* only groovier). Dancing usually gets started around 10:30 or 11 p.m. Most of the music is contemporary dance, but there are themed nights with disco and, of course, British hits.

ACROSS THE SHIPS The club's closest counterparts are **Fathoms** on the *Magic* (see page 164), **Azure** on the *Wonder* (see page 167), and **Evolution** on the *Dream* (see page 173). The Tube, though, is our favorite dance club on any of the ships.

PART NINE

ACTIVITIES, RECREATION, *and* SHOPPING

BESIDES EAT, DRINK, BE ENTERTAINED, and explore ports, there's lots to do on every Disney Cruise Line itinerary:

- **Family activities** are held throughout the day and include trivia contests, bingo, deck parties, and more.
- **Children's programs**, the strength of Disney Cruise Line, begin as early as 7 a.m.
- It wouldn't be a Disney cruise without **character greetings,** including Mickey, Minnie, and the Disney princesses.
- Each ship's **pools and water-play areas** are the center of activity during the day on most cruises.
- **Onboard seminars** are inexpensive (some are free) and cover everything from cooking demonstrations to wine tastings.
- Runners and sports fans will find a **measured track** on each ship, plus **basketball, volleyball, miniature golf,** and more.
- After a tough day on shore, you can relax at the **spa.**
- **Shopping opportunities** are available on board and in port.

FAMILY ACTIVITIES

BINGO

DCL IS ONE OF THE FEW CRUISE LINES that have no casino gambling on board. What it does have is bingo, played most days on most ships, one or two hour-long sessions per day. The cost to play is about $20 per paper card per game, with four games played per hour. Prizes range from duffel bags filled with DCL swag to actual cash jackpots of several thousand dollars. On a recent sailing, we watched a young guy win nearly $9,000 at bingo—enough to pay for his entire vacation and then some.

With that much money at stake, it's no surprise that many people take these games seriously. Games are fast-paced, and players are expected to keep up. Additionally, DCL interjects sound effects, music, dance, and random chatter into the number calling. This makes it fun for the kiddos, but it can be somewhat overwhelming if you were expecting a level of cacophony more suited to old folks at the Elks Lodge. (*Pro-tip:* The reason the bingo crew members do a crazy dance every time the B-11 ball is called is that when the machine is in Spanish-language mode, *B-11* is *B once,* pronounced more or less like "Beyoncé.")

Children are allowed to play bingo, keeping track of the numbers and enjoying the merriment, but they must be accompanied at all times by a guest age 18 or older, who will officially be the winner of any cash prizes.

The cost to play varies, even within the same voyage. Pricing is typically higher at the end of each sailing, when the payouts are larger. Buy-in starts at about $20 for one set of traditional paper bingo cards per session. However, most guests opt to rent electronic bingo machines, often priced at $40 or $50 for 24 cards per session. The electronic machines receive signals from the bingo console, telling them which numbers have been called. Because the machines keep track of the state of the game, you don't have to be hypervigilant every second.

If you think you're going to be playing frequently, be sure to stick around at the end of each session. The caller will often give out a special one-day-only password that's good for free bingo cards if you mention it at the next session. On longer sailings, the caller will sometimes offer personal touches by asking you to bring in something original, such as a child's drawing of the ship or a phone photo of a specific thing in port, in order to get a free bingo card during the next session. On our 2016 Baltic cruise on the *Magic*, Skipper Steve—our all-time favorite DCL bingo caller—asked guests to bring him jokes related to the sailing to get an extra card. Coauthor Erin's daughter Josie brought him, "I'm **TALLIN** you that I'm so sad that my journey **RUSSIAN** around the Baltic is over! It was super **SWEDE,** but now it's **FINNISHED.**" (We visited Tallin, Estonia; St. Petersburg, Russia; and ports in Sweden and Finland. Get it?) For her effort, Josie not only got a free bingo card for Mom but also a free bingo ball–shaped lip balm emblazoned with her favorite B-11 call number for herself. *Creativity counts, people!*

There may also be frequent-player discounts for reduced fees on cards if you play several times during the same cruise—be sure to ask.

DECK PARTIES

FEATURING DISNEY CHARACTERS, deck parties are usually held several times per cruise, typically near the family pool or in the ship's

SCOTT SAYS *by Scott Sanders*

"ARE WE HAVING FUN YET?"

I OFTEN HEAR PEOPLE SAY they're concerned about being bored on a cruise. But if you look over your *Personal Navigator*, you'll see that there's almost always something interesting to do. The trick is to not try to do it all—don't overplan. This is a cruise, after all, not a theme park; relax a bit and let the day unfold.

main lobby. The first party, known as the **Sail-Away Celebration,** happens as you leave port on embarkation day. Expect to hear every Black Eyed Peas song ever recorded over the rest of your cruise.

All outdoor parties are high-energy affairs, with loud music, dancing, games, and other activities, plus videos displayed on the ship's giant LED screen. The indoor versions omit only the giant video screens. Check your *Personal Navigator* for dates and times.

FAMILY NIGHTCLUBS

IN ADDITION TO ITS MYRIAD adult-entertainment offerings (see Part Eight), DCL has what would be an oxymoron in any other context: the family nightclub. Set up like grown-up nightspots, with snazzy decor and their own bars, tables and chairs, and dance floors, these lounges offer daytime and nighttime entertainment, including comedy shows, trivia contests, cooking demos, karaoke, line dancing, and more. (Many of the same activities are also offered during the day at some adult lounges.) Refreshments are served, including cocktails for Mom and Dad and smoothies and sodas for the kids, all at an extra charge.

unofficial **TIP**
DCL prohibits guests from bringing their own musical instruments on board, However, Disney can provide a full-size electronic keyboard for performers, and the ships typically keep an acoustic guitar on hand for use in the teen clubs; ask if you can borrow it for the talent show.

Most of the family-nightclub activities take place in each ship's **D Lounge,** on Deck 4 Midship. Hours vary, so check your *Personal Navigator* for details.

On some cruises of seven nights or longer, a **guest-participation talent show** will be on the activity list. We've seen some amazingly talented child gymnasts, dancers, and magicians on board. If you're interested in performing, be sure to sign up at Guest Services early in your trip, and pack whatever shoes, costumes, karaoke tracks, or sheet music you might need to perform.

SPORTS AND FITNESS

THE DISNEY SHIPS have several sports options available for families, covered later in this chapter, beginning on page 212.

CHILDREN'S PROGRAMS
and ACTIVITIES

WHEN IT COMES TO ENTERTAINING CHILDREN, Disney Cruise Line has no equal. Youth clubs, designed for infants to 17-year-olds, open as early as 7:30 a.m. for babies and close as late as 2 a.m. for teens. Kids can participate in organized activities, ranging from craft-making to trivia contests and dance parties, or they can play individually with computer games, board games, books, and craft materials. Most of the organized activities last 60–90 minutes, so a new event will likely start soon after your child arrives; this means kids become part of the group quickly. Based on reader feedback, it's far more likely that your child will not want to leave his or her kids' club than not want to go to it in the first place.

Reservations are required for the babysitting at the nurseries, but they're not needed for the kids' clubs for children ages 3 and up. Once you've registered your kids at the club, you can drop them off there as little or as often as you like, with no need to let anyone know in advance. It's an incredibly flexible system that allows for a great deal of vacation spontaneity.

Outside of the kids' clubs, there's plenty more for children and families to do. Much like the Disney theme parks, the DCL cruise ships offer a contained environment that gives tweens and teens some autonomy to roam on their own. Wave Phones (see page 43) and the texting function of the DCL Navigator app mean that you'll always be able to reach your children, and the free food on the pool deck and at the buffet means there's no worrying about finding something to eat, or how to pay for it.

Younger children (and older ones who aren't yet pretending they don't know you) and their families have activities scheduled through-out the day, from karaoke to character greetings; check your *Personal Navigator* for times and locations. Even the not-yet-walking crew can get in on the fun, with "diaper derbies" that happen in the ships' atri-ums—these are lots of fun to watch, even if you don't have a child participating.

Other activities include minigolf (*Dream* and *Fantasy*), the arcade (**Arr-cade** on the *Fantasy*), and the sports decks, all topside.

SPECIAL CONSIDERATIONS

INFANTS In 2014, DCL increased to 6 months the minimum age for infants to sail on most Alaskan, Bahamian, Caribbean, and other

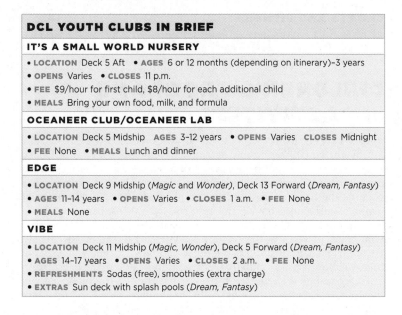

DCL YOUTH CLUBS IN BRIEF

IT'S A SMALL WORLD NURSERY

- **LOCATION** Deck 5 Aft • **AGES** 6 or 12 months (depending on itinerary)–3 years
- **OPENS** Varies • **CLOSES** 11 p.m.
- **FEE** $9/hour for first child, $8/hour for each additional child
- **MEALS** Bring your own food, milk, and formula

OCEANEER CLUB/OCEANEER LAB

- **LOCATION** Deck 5 Midship **AGES** 3–12 years • **OPENS** Varies **CLOSES** Midnight
- **FEE** None • **MEALS** Lunch and dinner

EDGE

- **LOCATION** Deck 9 Midship (*Magic* and *Wonder*), Deck 13 Forward (*Dream, Fantasy*)
- **AGES** 11–14 years • **OPENS** Varies • **CLOSES** 1 a.m. • **FEE** None
- **MEALS** None

VIBE

- **LOCATION** Deck 11 Midship (*Magic, Wonder*), Deck 5 Forward (*Dream, Fantasy*)
- **AGES** 14–17 years • **OPENS** Varies • **CLOSES** 2 a.m. • **FEE** None
- **REFRESHMENTS** Sodas (free), smoothies (extra charge)
- **EXTRAS** Sun deck with splash pools (*Dream, Fantasy*)

cruises of seven nights or fewer. For longer cruises, such as transatlantic and other repositioning cruises or Hawaiian cruises, infants must be at least 1 year old.

TWEENS AND TEENS Don't worry that your preteen or teenager is "too cool" for a Disney cruise. Based on both our own experiences and those of other parents, teens will practically forget you exist once they get a feel for the clubs and activities. In fact, before you even set foot on the ship, you should set some ground rules for how often your teen needs to check in with you. Our rule was that everyone had to eat two meals per day together during sea days and stay together during shore excursions. On Castaway Cay, we reserved morning activities for family time, and the teens were allowed to explore the island on their own after lunch.

ONLY-CHILD SITUATIONS The middle- and high-school kids' clubs are seamless for kids who are traveling with similarly aged siblings, cousins, or friends. They have a built-in companion for activities and can sample the club offerings at will, with no fear of being the odd man out. Our (multiple) children were able to pop in and out of the teen clubs whenever an activity seemed interesting, never feeling alone or out of place.

For a middle-schooler or teen traveling as the only one of his/her age group in the family, the youth clubs can be more challenging, as was the case with one of our teens on a recent trip. She was completely fine joining in the introductory games during the Sail-Away

Celebration, where the fun was orchestrated by a counselor. Several other times, however, she dropped in at Vibe and found just a few kids obviously paired off into subgroups. Because of this, our normally social and extroverted daughter had trouble slotting herself in.

Our teen's observation was that the "single" kids who did best at Vibe were the ones who participated in absolutely every activity there, including the teen activities on Castaway Cay, thus giving them the opportunity to pair off with someone. Because she was doing so much stuff with us, she found it harder to participate at Vibe on an ad hoc basis. For solo teens and tweens, then, the youth clubs might best be thought of as an all-or-nothing proposition: Those who just want to sample the clubs, as opposed to immersing themselves in the activities, should expect the social scene to be harder to break into.

ACTIVE KIDS As a parent, you're the best judge of how much physical activity your child needs. We've rarely seen truly bad behavior on the Disney ships, but when we have, it's usually been an active child running in circles around other guests after sitting in passive activities all day.

To make sure that your kids burn off their excess energy in a positive way, keep an eye out for ways to add physical activity to their day, particularly if you're spending several consecutive days at sea. The pool and sports deck are obvious solutions, but these may sometimes be unavailable due to weather or temporary maintenance issues. The many onboard dance parties can be a good way for an active child to let off steam; also carefully check your *Personal Navigator* for movement opportunities.

The activities at the kids' clubs are marked with a color-coded Mickey-head symbol. For example, the yellow "In the Spotlight" activities focus on stage presence and performance, while the black "Solve It" activities focus on problem solving and puzzles. If you have a child who needs to move a lot, steer him or her toward the green "Jump Up" activities, which include group games and movement.

YOUTH CLUBS

THE BULK OF DCL'S CHILDREN'S ACTIVITIES take place at the youth clubs on the ships. They're organized by age group, as follows:

• **Oceaneer Club** and **Oceaneer Lab,** for children ages 3–12
• **Edge,** for ages 11–14   • **Vibe,** for ages 14–17

We provide profiles of the clubs starting on page 189, organized by ship and ordered from the youngest to oldest age groups.

Children in the following age groups may choose which club they wish to participate in: 3-year-olds can choose the nursery or (as long as they're potty-trained) Oceaneer Club/Lab, 11- and 12-year-olds can choose between Oceaneer Club/Lab and Edge, and 14-year-olds can choose Edge or Vibe. This flexibility is helpful when siblings who are close in age want to be in the same club. Once a choice is made, however, it may not be changed. Disney is also strict about making sure that kids stick to the club for their age group—that is, no sneaking into Vibe if they're not old enough, or if they're even slightly too old.

Children in the nurseries, Oceaneer Club, and Oceaneer Lab will be asked to wear a wristband while they're on the premises, and parents will be given an electronic pager. The wristbands look somewhat similar to the MagicBands now in use at Walt Disney World, but they work differently. Parents will see a $12.95 charge per band on their bill if the bands are not returned at the end of the sailing.

Sensors at each club's doors will trigger an alarm if your child tries to leave without a parent to deactivate the wristband. In the event that Disney or your child needs to contact you, club staff will call you on your Wave Phone.

Youth registered at the Edge and Vibe clubs (ages 11–17) are free to come and go as they please—there's no check-in or checkout. If your kids get bored, they may leave to visit a character greeting, go to the pool, grab a snack, go back to the room, or just roam around. (Rest assured that they won't be allowed to leave the ship without adult accompaniment, unless you've specifically completed a special form allowing them to do so.) Parents enjoying some alone time while their kids are at Vibe or the Edge may run into them before they expect it.

For some kids this is an unprecedented amount of freedom, which may cause discomfort for the parent or child. Be sure to set ground rules for your kids about notifying you where they are; these might include periodic checking in via Wave Phone, sending texts using the DCL Navigator app, or leaving notes on a whiteboard posted on your stateroom door.

All kids must be registered to use the clubs. Parents can sign up their children either before boarding through online check-in (see page 36) or on embarkation day in the clubs' open houses. Signing up online has the advantage of giving busy cruisers one less thing to worry about after boarding the ship. Open houses are a great way to check out the various clubs. (*Warning:* The spaces are so well themed that adults will be sad when they have to leave.) Once a child is registered for a club, he or she may use its facilities for the entire cruise.

Some activities, such as board games, computer games, and crafts, are generally available on an ad hoc basis; kids can do them whenever they're in the club. Throughout each day there are also planned themed activities, which will be noted in your *Personal Navigator.* Some of the listed activities are self-explanatory: You can easily figure out what "Magic Show" or "Dance Party" means. Other activities may be more cryptic, such as "Nemo's Coral Reef Adventure" or

"4th Pigs Pasta Palace" (we're still not sure what that one was about). If you're not sure whether a particular planned activity will appeal to your child, or if your child has emotional or sensory-processing issues that might be exacerbated by certain stimuli, check with the club counselors for more details.

Nurseries

These operate under a reservation system and charge an hourly rate for services; parents will need to book specific times. The charge is $9 an hour for the first child and $8 an hour for each additional child in the same family. You should bring milk, formula, and baby food, along with diapers and wipes, a change of clothes, and a blanket and pacifier if your child needs these to nap.

Space is limited at each nursery; reservations are required and are first-come, first-served:

- **Concierge guests and Platinum Castaway Club members** (see page 49) can make reservations **120 days** in advance.

- **Gold Castaway Club members** can make reservations **105 days** in advance.

- **Silver Castaway Club members** can make reservations **90 days** in advance.

- **All other guests** can make reservations **75 days** out.

If you haven't made your nursery reservations by the time you board the ship, either stop by before dinner or call from your stateroom or Wave Phone: Dial ☎ **7-5864** on the *Magic, Dream,* and *Fantasy* or ☎ **7-18500** on the *Wonder*.

Hours vary, especially when the ship is in port, but on most sea days the nurseries are open 9 a.m.–11 p.m., with open-house tours 8–9 a.m.; check your *Personal Navigator* for details. The nurseries are sometimes open noon–3 p.m., and usually 5:30–11 p.m. on the first afternoon of your cruise.

The *Magic*'s Youth Clubs

It's a Small World Nursery   LOCATION: Deck 5 Aft

OVERVIEW This is the *Magic*'s onboard nursery for infants and toddlers ages 6 months–3 years (some longer sailings may require children to be 12 months or older). Trained staff play with the children throughout the day. Unlike the activities at the clubs for older kids and teens, activities at the nursery are unstructured but may include movies, story time, crafts, and occasional visits from Disney characters.

DESCRIPTION AND COMMENTS Too cute. Decorated with brilliantly colored murals inspired by the art of Mary Blair, the Disney animator who designed

It's a Small World at Disneyland and Walt Disney World, the nursery is cleverly divided into three sections. Up front is the "acclimation zone," a welcome area where kids can get used to their surroundings; this leads to a long, narrow, rectangular, brightly lit play area, off of which is a darkened, quiet room for naps. The play area is stocked with pint-size activities, including a 2-foot-tall playground slide on a padded floor, a small basketball hoop, plenty of leg-powered riding vehicles, play mats with large toys, and adorable miniature craft tables that you'd swear came from the Lilliput IKEA. A one-way mirror lets parents check up on their tots discreetly.

Around the corner, at the far end of the nursery, is the resting room, with six cribs and three glider chairs (sort of like rocking chairs, except they move linearly). Murals in soothing blues and golds adorn the walls. This room is kept dark most of the day, and the staff ensures that activities in the main room happen far enough away that noise isn't a problem. Just outside are a sink and changing area.

ACROSS THE SHIPS All DCL ships have It's a Small World Nurseries. The version on the Magic has a larger nap room than the nurseries on the other ships.

Oceaneer Club and Oceaneer Lab   LOCATION: Deck 5 Midship

OVERVIEW The Oceaneer Club and Oceaneer Lab are connected spaces that host the 3- to 12-year-old set. Activities for older kids usually take place in the Lab and are often educational or participatory in nature (such as cooking demonstrations or science experiments). Younger children's programs are generally held in the Club and include story time, character greetings, and movement activities. Disney designates 7 as the border age for the Club and Lab and provides details in your *Personal Navigator* about each area's different activity tracks. During open houses, one side remains open for activities while the other side is open to the public. Lunch and dinner are provided.

Parents must check kids up to age 7 years in and out of the club. With parental permission, 8- to 12-year-olds may check themselves in and out—just designate your preference when you register your kids.

DESCRIPTION AND COMMENTS The Oceaneer Club and Lab are separate areas connected by a short private hallway, allowing children to go from Lab to Club and back. Besides providing kids twice as much space, this arrangement separates younger and older children while giving siblings of different ages the chance to stay in contact.

The Oceaneer Club consists of four distinct sections branching off from a central "library" decorated with oversize children's books and outfitted with a huge plasma TV for movie screenings. **Andy's Room** is *Toy Story*–themed and is for smaller children. Its main feature is a tall, circular, gentle playground slide in the shape of Slinky Dog. There's also a large pink Hamm (the piggy bank) sitting in the middle of the play floor, and a giant Mr. Potato Head with equally large plug-in pieces, all scattered about.

The **Mickey Mouse Club,** the second themed room, serves as the Oceaneer Club's primary activity center. Done in black-and-white square tiles, with red tables and accents and pictures of Mickey and friends on the walls, the room has a large video screen on one wall and game consoles lining another.

The Mickey Mouse Club connects to both Andy's Room and **Marvel Avengers Academy.** In the academy you'll find Thor's hammer, Captain America's shield, and a life-size Iron Man suit, as well as another video screen and computer collection.

Disney is using the *Magic* to try out a new concept, also called Marvel Avengers Academy. The activities follow a multiday story in which kids embark on a recruitment experience that has them team up with various Avengers, hang out with Captain America, and suit up like Iron Man to battle the evil Red Skull. (No word yet on whether you can rent out Captain America's costume for private parties.)

Opposite Marvel Avengers Academy is **Pixie Hollow,** a Tinker Bell–themed dress-up and play area with costumes, an activity table, and a few computer terminals with themed games.

The Oceaneer Lab is done in a 19th-century nautical theme, with lots of exposed woods, red-leather chairs, navigation maps, and sailors' tools. More than a third of the space consists of one long room, filled with kid-size tables and stools, which serves as the primary area for arts and crafts. At the far end of this space is a set of computer terminals.

Next to the craft space, in the middle of the Lab, is a large screen for watching movies. Facing the screen is a collection of comfortable beanbags. Finally, the left side of the Lab is a set of small rooms. A couple have computer terminals or video-game consoles; one is a smaller arts-and-crafts room, and another is an animation studio where kids can learn to draw Disney characters and create their own computer animations.

ACROSS THE SHIPS All DCL ships have an Oceaneer Club/Lab. On the *Dream* and the *Fantasy,* the Club is also subdivided into themed areas, but they differ somewhat from those on the *Magic.* The Lab has a similar nautical theme and layout but is distinguished by a central "interactive floor," composed of individual video screens surrounded by foot-operated touch pads and used to play different interactive games.

Following the *Wonder*'s 2016 refurbishment, its Oceaneer Club and Lab are now on par with those on the *Magic.* Recent additions to the *Wonder*'s play areas are the **Marvel Super Hero Academy** (which is slightly different from the *Magic*'s Marvel Avengers Academy), Andy's Room, **Club Disney Junior** (an area for storytelling and games), and **Frozen Adventures** (for play related to everyone's favorite fake Scandinavian country, Arendelle).

Edge   LOCATION: Deck 9 Midship

OVERVIEW Tweens and early teens rule at Edge. Unlike at the Oceaneer Club/Lab, kids can come and go as they please. Activities range from drawing and cooking classes to scavenger hunts and computer games. Parents may be surprised to see that things are scheduled past midnight on some nights.

DESCRIPTION AND COMMENTS The Edge is the rec room your kids dream of. There are sections for electronic gaming, active play, and lounging. You'll see both a high-tech zone and comfy couches. Kids can move freely between both.

Edge is likely to be the first of the youth clubs in which the staff will treat your kids as peers to interact with rather than as children to be supervised.

The staff generally does a great job of getting to know each child and will even compete in games alongside the kids. If you ever want to feel old and slow, watch the cup-stacking competition, where the object is to stack and unstack a pyramid of 15 plastic cups as quickly as possible. Some kids can do both in less than 10 seconds total.

ACROSS THE SHIPS All DCL ships have an Edge. The amenities are more or less the same on the *Wonder,* although we hear it's getting a makeover as part of that ship's dry dock. On the *Dream* and the *Fantasy,* Edge is inside the ships' forward (nonfunctioning) smokestack. The decor and atmosphere are ultramodern and high-tech, versus the homier feel of Edge on the *Magic.*

Vibe   LOCATION: Deck 11 Midship

OVERVIEW Vibe is one of the coolest spots on the *Magic.* Even if you don't have a kid traveling with you, it's worth checking out during an open house. Counselors lead the activities (dance parties, karaoke, group games, and the like), but teens are given plenty of autonomy in their struc-ture. Parents should note that the only curfew for teens on board is what-ever one they impose themselves. One rule of note that's strictly enforced: no public displays of affection.

DESCRIPTION AND COMMENTS Vibe sits up a flight of stairs in the ship's forward smokestack, but your teens probably won't mind the climb. Inside is a two-story-tall lounge with brick walls; overstuffed leather furniture; a smoothie bar; tons of quirky decorations; and board games, video consoles, and a small room off to the side for activities. It looks more like a well-appointed summer-camp lodge than anything nautical or tropical. We think there should be a Vibe for adults.

ACROSS THE SHIPS All DCL ships have a Vibe. The layout and amenities are more or less identical on the *Wonder.* On the *Dream* and the *Fantasy,* Vibe is dramatically different but just as cool. The theming and decor are urban ultralounge rather than funky rumpus room, and teens get an indoor/out-door space, complete with a grown-up sun deck and splash pool.

The *Wonder*'s Youth Clubs

It's a Small World Nursery   LOCATION: Deck 5 Aft

OVERVIEW Formerly Flounder's Reef Nursery, this is the *Wonder*'s onboard nursery for infants and toddlers ages 6 months–3 years (some longer sail-ings may require children to be 12 months or older). Trained staff play with the children throughout the day. Unlike the activities at the clubs for older kids and teens, activities at the nursery are unstructured but may include movies, story time, crafts, and occasional visits from Disney characters.

DESCRIPTION AND COMMENTS The *Wonder*'s Small World—the cruise industry's first nursery at sea—is divided into two sections. One is a brightly lit play area, the other is a darkened quiet area for naps. The play area is stocked with play mats, toys, books, large motor play equipment, baby swings, and a TV/DVD player. The color scheme and decor reflect the design of the It's a Small World attraction at the Disney theme parks. A one-way mirror out-side lets parents check up on their tots discreetly.

At the back of the nursery is the resting area, furnished with cribs. This room is kept dark most of the day, and the staff ensures that activities in the main room happen far enough away that noise isn't a problem. A sink and changing station are adjacent.

ACROSS THE SHIPS The *Wonder*'s nursery theming now matches that on the other ships in the Disney fleet. Of course, little ones won't be too concerned with aesthetics, but the colorful and creatively themed space does provide a welcoming environment for both small children and their parents.

Oceaneer Club and Oceaneer Lab   LOCATION: Deck 5 Midship

OVERVIEW The Oceaneer Club and Oceaneer Lab are connected spaces that host the 3- to 12-year-old set. Activities for older kids usually take place in the Lab and are often educational or participatory in nature (such as cooking demonstrations or science experiments). Younger children's programs are generally held in the Club and include story time, character greetings, and movement activities. Disney designates 7 as the border age for the Club and Lab and provides details in your *Personal Navigator* about each area's different activity tracks. During open houses, one side remains open for activities while the other side is open to the public. Lunch and dinner are provided.

Parents must check kids up to age 7 years in and out of the club. With parental permission, 8- to 12-year-olds may check themselves in and out—just designate your preference when you register your kids.

DESCRIPTION AND COMMENTS The *Wonder*'s Oceaneer Club and Lab got a major refurbishment in late 2016, giving it amenities similar to those of the Clubs and Labs on the other Disney ships. The refurb added **Marvel Super Hero Academy,** an interactive play area where children can train to be super heroes and interact with current heroes in the Marvel family; Spider-Man makes regular appearances. Artifacts on display in this area include Captain America's World War II shield, Iron Man's helmet, Spider-Man's web shooters, and Black Widow's gauntlets.

Other Oceaneer spaces include the **Frozen Adventures** area for creative and interactive play. A key feature of the Frozen zone is a digital screen when an animated Olaf leads games and songs; character experiences include the requisite visits by Anna and Elsa. **Club Disney Junior** offers storytelling and games featuring *Disney Junior* characters, including Doc McStuffins. **Andy's Room** is a *Toy Story*–themed play zone with larger-than-life toys to play on.

ACROSS THE SHIPS All DCL ships have an Oceaneer Club/Lab. On the *Dream* and the *Fantasy,* the Club is also subdivided into themed areas, but they differ somewhat from those on the *Magic* and *Wonder.* In addition, the Lab on the two newer ships has a central "interactive floor," composed of individual video screens surrounded by foot-operated touch pads and used to play different interactive games.

Edge   LOCATION: Deck 9 Midship

COMMENTS See profile of Edge on the *Magic* (see page 191) for details.

Vibe LOCATION: Deck 11 Midship

COMMENTS See profile of Vibe on the *Magic* (see page 192) for details.

The *Dream*'s and *Fantasy*'s Youth Clubs

It's a Small World Nursery LOCATION: Deck 5 Aft

COMMENTS See profiles of It's a Small World Nursery on the *Magic* (see page 189) and Wonder (see page 192) for details.

Oceaneer Club and Oceaneer Lab LOCATION: Deck 5 Midship

OVERVIEW On the *Dream* and *Fantasy,* the Oceaneer Club and Oceaneer Lab are connected spaces that host the 3- to 12-year-old set. Activities for older kids usually take place in the Lab and are often educational or participatory in nature (such as cooking demonstrations or science experiments). Younger children's programs are generally held in the Club and include story time, character greetings, and movement activities. Disney designates 7 as the border age for the Club and Lab and provides details in your *Personal Navigator* about each area's different activity tracks. During open houses, one side remains open for activities while the other side is open to the public. Lunch and dinner are provided.

Parents must check kids up to age 7 years in and out of the club. With parental permission, 8- to 12-year-olds may check themselves in and out—just designate your preference when you register your kids.

DESCRIPTION AND COMMENTS The Oceaneer Lab and Club are separate areas connected by a short private hallway, allowing children to go from Lab to Club and back. Besides providing kids twice as much space, this arrangement separates younger and older children while giving siblings of different ages the chance to stay in contact.

The Oceaneer Club consists of four distinct sections branching off from a central rotunda painted royal blue; on the ceiling are "constellations" of Disney characters made up of small, twinkling electric lights. **Andy's Room** is *Toy Story*–themed and is for smaller children. There's a crawl-through tube—think a Habitrail for humans—in the shape of Slinky Dog, along with a giant pink Hamm (the piggy bank) sitting in the middle of the play floor, and a large Mr. Potato Head with equally large plug-in pieces, all invariably scattered about.

The next area is **Monsters Academy,** a brightly colored, *Monsters, Inc.*–themed space filled with all manner of interactive games, along with a climbing structure. Then there's **Pixie Hollow,** a Tinker Bell–themed dress-up and play area with costumes, an activity table, and a few computer terminals with themed games. Finally, **Disney's Explorer Pod** is a scaled-down submarine inspired by *Finding Nemo.* Inside are 16 interactive-game stations.

The Oceaneer Lab is done in a 19th-century nautical theme, with lots of exposed woods, red-leather chairs, navigation maps, sailors' tools, and inlaid images of sea horses and compasses on the floor. The main hall features a celestial map on the ceiling and a huge "Magic Play Floor," composed of 16 high-definition video screens surrounded by foot-powered touch pads and used to play interactive games. (If you remember the giant piano from the movie *Big,* you get the idea.)

Surrounding the main hall are the **Media Lounge,** for relaxing and watching movies; the **Animator's Studio,** where kids can learn to draw Disney characters and create digital animations; **The Wheelhouse,** with computer stations and interactive games; the **Sound Studio,** where kids can record their own music; and the **Craft Studio.**

The *Dream*'s Oceaneer Club has been updated with a new Star Wars–themed area where children can "pilot" a faux Millennium Falcon using a remarkably well-done simulator—yep, it goes into hyperspeed—and participate in a shipboard version of the Jedi Training activity at Walt Disney World's Hollywood Studios. Adult guests can take a turn in the captain's seat of the Falcon during regular club open-house times (check your *Personal Navigator*). Wearing a black vest and knee-high boots is completely optional.

ACROSS THE SHIPS All DCL ships have an Oceaneer Club/Lab. On the *Magic* and *Wonder,* the Club is subdivided into themed areas, but they differ somewhat from those on the *Dream* and *Fantasy;* also, the Lab on the two older ships is missing the nifty interactive floor.

Edge   LOCATION: Deck 13 Forward

OVERVIEW Tweens rule at Edge. Unlike at the Oceaneer Club/Lab, kids at the Edge can come and go as they please. Activities range from drawing and cooking classes to improv-comedy sessions and ghost-hunting and role-playing games. Parents may be surprised to see that things are scheduled past midnight on some nights.

DESCRIPTION AND COMMENTS Built into the *Dream*'s and *Fantasy*'s forward (nonfunctioning) smokestack, Edge has an open layout and a clean 21st-century feel. The walls are papered in a geometric Mickey-head design. The centerpiece of the space is a huge video wall, more than 18 feet wide and nearly 5 feet tall. Across from it are tables with built-in screens for playing interactive games, surrounded by bright-red seating that looks like something out of *The Jetsons;* behind those are cubbyholes outfitted with flat-panel TVs and Wii consoles. Recessed shelves between the game nooks are stocked with books and board games. Next to the game tables are an illuminated dance floor (think *Saturday Night Fever*) and a lounge area with beanbags arranged next to floor-to-ceiling windows. On the other side of the video wall are laptop stations loaded with video games and an onboard social-media app.

Edge is likely to be the first of the youth clubs in which the staff will treat your kids as peers to interact with rather than as children to be supervised. The staff generally does a great job of getting to know each child and getting in on the fun.

ACROSS THE SHIPS All DCL ships have an Edge. On the *Magic* and *Wonder,* it has a totally different layout and atmosphere—more like a family rec room than a high-tech hangout.

Vibe   LOCATION: Deck 5 Forward

OVERVIEW Up a flight of stairs from Deck 4 to Deck 5 Forward, Vibe is one of the coolest spots on the *Dream* and *Fantasy.* Even if you don't have a kid traveling with you, it's worth checking out during an open house.

Counselors lead the activities (dance parties, karaoke, role-playing games, and the like), but teens are given plenty of autonomy in their structure. Parents should note that the only curfew for teens on board is whatever one they impose themselves. One rule of note that's strictly enforced: no public displays of affection.

DESCRIPTION AND COMMENTS Accessed through a neon-lit hallway, Vibe has a decidedly adult look and feel—if you didn't know better, you'd think you were in a trendy urban nightspot. The central indoor gathering spot is the theater–cum–TV lounge, accented with soft pink neon lighting and featuring a 103-inch flat-panel television. Two rows of couches are arranged in a semicircle in front of the screen; giant throw pillows scattered on the floor make for additional places to lounge. Behind the couches and built into the rear wall are a row of podlike, porthole-shaped nooks for playing video games, watching videos, or hooking up an electronic device. Just off the row of pods is a smoothie bar with a multicolored floor in Day-Glo hues; ultramodern stools with low, curved backs; and white banquette seating.

Off the TV lounge is another sleek space for socializing. The walls are covered in alternating black and silver horizontal bars. Black leather-look benches line the walls; next to those are retro-mod tables and chairs arranged nightclub-style. Video-game booths stand nearby. Across from the seating area are a dance floor and DJ booth, a karaoke stage, and another large video screen.

The main attraction, though, lies outside: the **Vibe Splash Zone,** a private deck with two splash pools, chaise lounges, sets of tables and chairs, and recessed seating. Furnishings and decor share the same ultramod style as the indoor spaces.

ACROSS THE SHIPS All DCL ships have a Vibe. On the *Magic* and the *Wonder,* Vibe is dramatically different but just as cool. Built into the ships' forward smokestack, the two-story-tall lounge features brick walls, overstuffed leather furniture, and quirky decor. It looks more like a well-appointed summer-camp lodge than anything you'd find on a cruise ship.

WHAT GOES ON IN A KIDS' CLUB?

IN ADDITION TO FREE PLAY AND OPEN HOURS, all levels of kids' clubs offer a range of physical, quiet, creative, collaborative, and competitive age-appropriate activities. If your kids prefer directed activity to self-initiated play, be sure to keep a careful eye on the DCL Navigator app and the print *Personal Navigator,* both of which list the times of planned activities at the Oceaneer Club/Lab, Edge, and Vibe. Additionally, the app provides a sentence or two of description about the activity, plus alternate times during the cruise when that activity will be offered again. Activities vary, but some sample activities from recent cruises, along with their Navigator app descriptions, include the following:

OCEANEER CLUB AND LAB

- **Anyone Can Cook:** Anyone can cook as we work together to create some of our favorite treats.

- **Big Top Fun Fest:** Come rediscover the circus Disney-style, with clowns, jugglers, and classic Disney cartoons.

- **Craft Corner:** Imagination is the key. It's time to get creative and put your crafty skills to use!

- **Cruisin' With Crush:** Be sure to check out Disney's Oceaneer Club to see Crush when he stops by!

- **Gaga Ball:** Come take part in this great game as your try to outlast your opponents. [*Note:* According to coauthor Ritchey's research, this is the Israeli version of dodgeball, not a sport with a Lady Gaga theme.]

- **Once Upon a Time:** Join Bartleby the Bookmaker for a magical, musical story time featuring a Disney Princess.

- **Parachute Games:** Have a blast playing fun games with our colorful parachutes.

- **Piston Cup Challenge:** Design your own race car and see if you've got what it takes to end up in the winner's circle.

- **Super Sloppy Science:** Join Professor Make-O-Mess in some the most extreme experiments you'll ever see.

- **Wacky Relays:** Show off your wacky skills in some the wackiest races at sea.

- **Wii Challenge:** Take on the challenge in this fun active computer game.

EDGE

- **Animation Cells:** Learn what it takes to be a Disney Animator, then put your skills to the test as you create your very own animation cell.

- **Cards Tournament:** Join your friends for a friendly game of cards.

- **Crowning of the Couch Potato:** Do you think you know your movies, TV, and commercials? Well, it's time to test your knowledge.

- **Foosball Tournament:** Come show us your Foosball skills and see who's the best of the best.

- **Gaga Ball:** Come take part in this great game as you try to outlast your opponents.

- **Gender Wars:** Join us as we find out who really are the kings or queens of the castle.

- **Goofy's World Records:** Goofy and his pals have created a variety of games and contests for a wild time.

- **Pathfinders:** A path has been chosen for you. Can you find it?

- **Pelican Plunge:** Enjoy some sliding with your Edge team.

- **Profiles:** Show off who you really are and make some new friends while you do it.

Continued on next page

EDGE

- **Scattergories:** See who can think of the most creative answers.
- **That's Hilarious:** Ever wanted to show off your comedy skills? Then be a part of the cast for this crazy improv show.
- **Volleyball.**

VIBE

- **Dream Now! Sea How! Animal, Science, and Environment:** Ever wonder how man and animal can connect and live in harmony? In an interactive session, you will dive into the background, education, mentors, and dreams that sent animal-care workers into their profession.
- **Gotcha!:** Compete in a sophisticated game of hide-and-seek.
- **Homecoming:** Come and join your fellow teens in our very own version of Homecoming, and dance the night away.
- **Ice Cream Social:** Make Your Own Frosty treat with your counselors.
- **Ninja:** How fast and stealthy can you be?
- **Ping Pong Tournament.**
- **Smoothie Hour:** Create your own custom smoothie.
- **Sports Deck Fun:** The topside sports deck is reserved for teen use.
- **Teen Choice Movie Viewing.**
- **Trivia Time:** Test your gray matter with fun trivia.
- **Zombified:** Work to create an actual zombie movie that will premiere on board.

Additionally, Edge and Vibe may take kids in groups to some of the all-ages performances, game shows, or other events on board.

OTHER KIDS' ACTIVITIES ON BOARD

On the *Magic* and *Wonder*

Many activities take place in the **Promenade Lounge** on Deck 3 Aft, including the following:

• *Playhouse Disney* Dance Party	• Pirate Scavenger Maps
• Pirate Trivia Quest • Pop Decades Dance	• Wildcat Bingo

On the *Dream* and the *Fantasy*

Midship Detective Agency is an interactive, self-guided game in which kids help Disney characters solve a mystery. Similar to Sorcerers of the Magic Kingdom at Walt Disney World, this is one of the most fun onboard activities in the fleet. You begin by signing up on a computer inside a small desk on Deck 5 Midship. There you'll obtain a small, numbered cardboard game piece. One side of the game piece holds a 2-D bar code and your agent number; the other side displays a detective's badge icon.

Along with your badge card, you'll receive a pamphlet describing each of the agency's suspects behind the mystery. The pamphlet also includes a map of the ship that shows where to find clues to solve the mystery. Once you've signed up and obtained your game material, you'll watch a short video that explains the mystery you're solving. You'll also be told where to go to find your first clue.

Each clue is presented on an "Enchanted Art" video screen somewhere on the ship. The amazing thing about the video screens is that they look like ordinary wall art to anyone not playing the game—it's only when you hold up your badge that the screen comes alive with video and sound. (The technology embedded behind the screens' frames includes a bar-code reader for your badge, speakers, and a network of computers to keep track of your accomplishments.) To obtain the clue, you'll first have to solve a simple puzzle or win a simple game. You do this by using your badge as a sort of game controller while you're playing, tilting and moving the badge to guide the action on the screen. It takes a little practice to get used to, so tell your kids before they start that their first try at each screen is just a dry run. You can repeat the action as often as needed.

Once you've obtained the clue, you can eliminate one of the suspects from the mystery; then it's off to another section of the ship to get another clue. Make no mistake: Playing this game involves climbing a lot of stairs. However, you get to see a lot of the ship, and it's good exercise for the kids. You'll see them playing at all times of the day and night, and lines often form in front of each video screen, especially on sea days.

There are three different games: **The Case of the Plundered Paintings** and **The Case of the Missing Puppies,** both featuring Mickey and friends, and **The Case of the Stolen Show,** starring the Muppets. We think the last one is the most fun—the game's designers expertly incorporate the Muppets' humor into the scenes.

Bibbidi Bobbidi Boutique

All DCL ships have varying incarnations of this wildly popular Disney-theme-park makeover spot for kids ages 3–12. Bibbidi Bobbidi Boutique sessions take about 45 minutes; makeover variations for girls have included Disney Diva, Pop Princess, and Fairy Tale Princess. Pricing currently starts at about $65 for the **Crown Package,** which includes hairstyling (but not washing or cutting), nail polish, shimmering makeup, and a face gem. The **Castle Package,** currently about $200, includes all of the above plus a princess sash, a tiara, a wand, and choice of princess costume. There's also a special Frozen version of the make-over for about $165, which includes your choice of Anna or Elsa hair-styling and costume, plus shimmering makeup, a face gem, nail polish, a princess sash, a princess tote, and a plush Olaf doll.

Young princes may sign up for the **Royal Knight** package (about $19), which includes hairstyling plus a sword and shield.

On Pirate Night (see page 157), the boutique becomes **The Pirates League** and gives buccaneer-themed makeovers to any guest age 3 and up (guests 17 and younger must be accompanied by an adult). Varia-tions on the pirate makeover are priced between $45 and $100 and include items such as swords, earrings, and costume elements, depend-ing on the package chosen.

For the princess who has everything, there's the **Royal Sea Pack-age,** which gets her three nights of makeovers plus a gift delivered to her bedchamber, um, stateroom. It can be hers for $595 and must be booked by e-mail; go to tinyurl.com/royalseareservations and click "download the Royal Sea Package reservation form" (a Microsoft Word file), or ask your travel agent for details.

CHILDREN'S PERFORMANCE OPPORTUNITIES

DURING MOST SAILINGS OF SEVEN DAYS OR MORE, the Ocea-neer Club and Lab invite kids ages 3–12 to participate in a show per-formed on stage in the Walt Disney Theater. The show, often called *Friendship Rocks!,* mostly involves having the little ones sit on stage and sing along with a few Disney classics. Mickey will make an appearance. Many younger kids (and their parents) think that being on stage with Mickey makes them rock stars, while others will be completely over-whelmed by the experience—use your best judgment.

Kids with a real yen to perform can check out **karaoke** opportuni-ties on most sailings or **talent show** opportunities on many longer sailings (see "Family Nightclubs," page 184).

CHILDREN'S ACTIVITIES IN PORT

WHEN BOOKING PORT EXCURSIONS, look for activities that are specified for families. Some tours will be specially designated for those traveling with kids. All excursion descriptions (see Part Twelve) include a recommendation for ages (or a requirement, depending on the type of activity) and an indication of the amount of stamina needed to partici-pate. Another option for days when you're in port is to stay aboard and enjoy the lower crowds at the pools and waterslides.

CHILDREN'S ACTIVITIES AT CASTAWAY CAY

DCL'S PRIVATE ISLAND (see Part Ten) has designated areas just for children and families. The teen area, **The Hide Out,** is tucked away, though not on the beach, and offers sports, such as volleyball and table tennis, and scheduled activities. **Scuttle's Cove,** a play area for young children, has youth-club counselors on hand to direct activities. Both The Hide Out and Scuttle's Cove are monitored by Disney cast members to ensure that only children and their parents enter.

CHILL SPA FOR TEENS

EACH DCL SHIP HAS A **Chill Spa,** a dedicated area inside Senses Spa & Salon that's just for guests ages 13–17. Chill Spa on the *Dream* and Fantasy is spacious and plush, less so on the *Magic* and *Wonder* (where it's a single treatment room).

Spa services for teens must be booked on board; you can't reserve them in advance via the online Planning Center (see page 35) as you would for adult spa services. If you have a stressed-out teen who needs a massage, you're going to incur a bit of stress yourself high-tailing it up to the spa on embarkation day to score a reservation before they fill up.

Officially, a parent or guardian must be present during all Chill Spa treatments; in practice, however, this varies depending on the ship. When coauthor Erin's teen daughter was getting a massage on the *Dream*, Erin was asked to stay in the actual treatment room with her. When the same daughter got a massage on the *Magic* a few months later, Erin was required to wait in the spa lounge because the *Magic*'s treatment room was too small. (Bring a book if you're the designated waiting parent.) If you have a strong preference about whether you stay in the same room with your child at all times, be sure to inquire about the ship's practices when you book the appointment.

If you don't want your teen to be offered any additional spa services or ancillary lotions and potions, note that when you make your reservation. Read more about the DCL spas on page 214.

WHERE TO MEET CHARACTERS

DISNEY CHARACTERS ARE AVAILABLE for photos and autographs several times per day at various locations on the ships; they also make occasional visits to the nurseries and kids' clubs. A complete schedule is usually available at the Character Information Board in your ship's atrium. The schedule is printed in the Character Appearances section of each day's *Personal Navigator* and in the DCL Navigator app; it's also available by calling ☎ 7-PALS (7257) from your stateroom phone.

unofficial **TIP**
If you're trying to meet the Disney princesses without a timed ticket, arrive at least a half-hour ahead of the scheduled greeting. We've arrived 45 minutes ahead to get a spot for our kids to meet Belle—and we weren't the first people in line.

Disney has begun offering free timed tickets for meeting the hugely popular Frozen characters Anna, Elsa, and Olaf, a selection of Marvel superheroes, and what coauthor Laurel calls the "princess bomb," where four or five of the Disney princesses appear in the atrium at once. Previously, lines for these coveted characters would begin forming more than an hour in advance, resulting in crowded walkways and cranky families. Thankfully, the timed tickets have cut down on much of the chaos.

There are two possible modes of ticket distribution: in advance online or in person on embarkation day. We haven't yet figured out a rhyme or reason for why particular sailings use one method or the other. If your sailing offers advance character greetings (and onboard character dining experiences), this option will appear in the Planning Center for your sailing under My Cruise Activities on the Disney Cruise Line website. This option may become available days or weeks after your standard port-adventure and adult-dining selections appear. If you're interested in reserving character experiences, keep checking back. If your specific cruise doesn't offer prebooking, then be sure to check your *Personal Navigator* for a note about whether character-greeting ticket distribution is in effect for your specific sailing.

Tickets for these most popular greetings are generally available for just a few hours on embarkation day and not at any point after that, but be aware that **you absolutely will need them** if they're being used on your voyage. Some princesses may greet guests individually during your cruise, but Anna, Elsa, Olaf, and the Marvel characters are unlikely to make any general public appearances.

There may also be nonticketed character greetings, for which guests will begin queuing up far in advance of the posted start time. (Captain Jack Sparrow is always a big draw on Pirate Night, for example.) Unique characters will have long lines; we had quite a wait to see the White Rabbit from *Alice in Wonderland*, who was serving as the de facto Easter Bunny on Easter Day on the *Fantasy*. You can also expect longer waits for common characters appearing in unusual costumes. For example, Mickey Mouse wearing red, white, and blue on the Fourth of July or Goofy wearing a parka during an Alaskan voyage will be more popular than those characters wearing their standard theme-park gear.

Most onboard character greetings are limited to 15 minutes or half an hour. The line will be closed once it's been determined that no more guests can be accommodated in the character's remaining time. If your child is intent on meeting a specific character, your best bet is to get in line 15–30 minutes before that character is scheduled to appear.

On longer cruises, characters such as Mickey, Minnie, Donald, Goofy, and Pluto may make onboard appearances many times throughout the voyage (albeit usually in different attire). The lines for these Disney classics are typically shorter later in the trip, when most folks have already had their fill of photos with the Big Cheese and company.

Character photo ops, including classic Disney characters in beach attire, take place on Castaway Cay near the ship dock, weather permitting.

A Note About Autographs

A significant subset of Disney-theme-park and Disney Cruise Line guests collect character autographs as souvenirs. Some of the autographs are quite fanciful and can provide a decorative element to objects. The medium for collection is not required to be an autograph book; guests often have characters sign items such as photo mats, pillowcases, T-shirts, and the like. (One of Erin's favorite signature-collection devices was a pair of canvas shoes: See tinyurl.com/autographshoes.) In the theme parks, guests wait in line to meet the characters, present them with an item to be signed, pose for a photo, and then head on their way.

In recent years, DCL had an unofficial autograph program known as "Mickey Mail," in which guests could drop off an item with Guest Services and have the item signed backstage. Initially a nice little-known extra, Mickey Mail became a staple topic on Pinterest and Disney Cruise chat groups, which resulted in sometimes thousands of elaborate items being left for signatures at Guest Services on a single cruise. (We've heard of more than one guest asking for signatures on a full-size replica ship's anchor!) Unable to keep up with demand, DCL discontinued Mickey Mail in August 2015. Now if you'd like an item signed on your cruise, you have to stand in line at the character-greeting points, just as you would in the theme parks.

What's more, DCL now imposes limits on the specific types of items that may be signed. Characters will sign the following:

- Any autograph book
- Disney-branded items that are appropriate to the character doing the signing. For example, Cinderella would be unable to sign a Buzz Lightyear item.
- A Disney-approved photo. Only characters in the photo can sign the photo.
- Disney notecards
- Disney Dollars. Once signed, a Disney Dollar becomes a souvenir and can no longer be used as currency. Note that distribution of new Disney Dollars was discontinued in May 2016; existing Disney Dollars may still be used, however.
- Clothing. Must not be worn while being signed.

Characters will *not* sign the following items:

- Flags of any nation
- Money other than Disney Dollars
- Non-Disney merchandise
- Receipts or banking slips
- Skin
- Non-family-friendly or sexually explicit items

POOLS *and*
WATER-PLAY AREAS

EACH SHIP HAS SEPARATE FRESHWATER POOLS designed for small children, families, and adults. All are heated to a minimum temperature of 75°F. Health regulations require that children be toilet-trained to use the pools, while swim diapers are mandatory in the water-play areas. You may bring water wings and other Coast Guard–approved flotation devices into the pools, but not rafts, floats, or those foam noodles you see every summer. Snorkels and masks covering the nose/mouth are also prohibited on the ships.

THE *MAGIC*'S AND *WONDER*'S POOLS

AFTER THE *WONDER* WAS REFURBISHED IN FALL 2016, its pool deck became very much like that of the *Magic,* with one major exception: The *Wonder* does not have an AquaDunk. The AquaDunk waterslide, a variation on the AquaDuck slide found on the *Dream* and *Fantasy, is* short and mildly fast, with a vertical start. It starts with your entering a vertical tube. You lean against one side of the tube while a clear plexiglass door closes opposite you to seal the tube. Suddenly, the floor drops away and you plunge nearly vertically down the tube, through a quick 270-degree turn and into a braking pool of water. The entire experience takes perhaps 7 or 8 seconds, but the initial sensation of falling is fun enough to make it worth repeating. The AquaDunk usually opens at 9 a.m. and closes around 11 p.m.

Because the AquaDunk has an hourly capacity of only around 120 riders, long lines will develop quickly; we've seen 80-minute waits posted. If you're not there first thing in the morning, try during lunchtime or the first dinner seating around 6:15 p.m.

Parents of children with sensitive eyes should be aware that while swim goggles may be worn in the ships' pools and on the smaller slides, goggles and face masks are prohibited on the AquaDunk. The force of the drop all but guarantees that the goggles would be pulled off the face.

AquaLab, the *Magic*'s and *Wonder*'s water-play area for small children (age 3 and up), is on Deck 9 Aft. It consists of four areas: AquaLab, the Twist 'n' Spout waterslide (age 4 and up and over 38 inches tall), the Nephews' Pool, and the Nephews' Splash Zone.

Every inch of AquaLab is covered in water, which comes out from both vertical and horizontal surfaces. Overhead buckets, slowly filling with water, will dump their contents periodically on anyone standing below, while sprays from faux ship-plumbing will drench anyone walking within

*un*official **TIP**
Swim masks that cover the nose and/or mouth are not allowed in any of DCL's onboard pools or water-play areas, or on water rides.

10 feet. Your kids will probably spend hours here, so it's a good thing that both covered seating and refreshments are available nearby.

Next to the main AquaLab area is the **Nephews' Splash Zone,** a water-play area for kids up to 3 years old. This plexiglass-enclosed area has water spouting from pint-size Huey, Dewey, and Louie figures. Padding on the ground allows kids to jump and run around safely, and you'll find parents sitting and relaxing nearby while the little ones get soaked.

A three-story spiral waterslide, **Twist 'n' Spout** is a lot longer and slower than AquaDunk, making it perfect for kids not quite tall enough for the big slide. Twist 'n' Spout starts above Deck 11 and ends on Deck 9 next to AquaLab. The top part of the slide isn't usually staffed, but a camera system there allows the attendant at the bottom of the slide to monitor both the start and the end simultaneously. Kids must be 4–14 years old and 38–64 inches tall to ride. There's plenty of nearby seating for parents to get some sun while watching the little ones splash around.

The **Nephews' Pool** is a shallow, circular pool in the middle of the deck, touching both AquaLab and the Nephews' Splash Zone. Small children can splash around to their hearts' content while parents sit on ledge seating. Just past the forward end of AquaLab is **Pete's Boiler Bites** snack bar, and on the aft end is **Daisy's De-Lites.**

Goofy's Pool, the *Magic*'s and *Wonder*'s family pool, is on Deck 9 Midship. It's the focal point of outdoor activity on the ship. The pool is 4 feet deep at every point, and deck chairs and lounges are arranged on both sides along its length. At the forward end of the pool is the **Funnel Vision** LED screen, which plays movies, TV shows, and videos almost constantly. At the aft end are **Pinocchio's Pizzeria** and two covered whirlpools. Both Goofy's and the Nephews' Pools are typically open 8 a.m.–10 p.m. every day; check your *Personal Navigator* for specific hours.

*un*official **TIP**

The ships' pools are relatively small. On the *Magic,* Goofy's Pool measures 16 x 34 feet, about the size of a typical suburban home's pool. It can accommodate around 13 of the ship's 2,700 passengers at one time.

The adults-only **Quiet Cove Pool** is on Deck 9 Forward. Like Goofy's Pool, it's 4 feet deep throughout, and two adults-only whirlpools are nearby. Teak lounge chairs are provided for relaxing. Just past the aft end of the pool are **Signals** bar and **Cove Café.**

The *Wonder*'s pool deck got a refurbishment as part of the ship's 2016 dry dock. While the *Wonder* still lacks a thrill-style feature slide, the ship now has a spiral Twist 'n' Spout waterslide. As on the *Magic,* the slide starts above Deck 1; it ends next to a new **AquaLab** children's play area on Deck 9.

On both the *Wonder* and the *Magic* you'll find **Mickey's Pool,** for children age 3 and up, toward Deck 9 Aft. Divided into three smaller pools corresponding to Mickey's face and ears, the pool has a maximum depth of 2 feet, and the bright-yellow spiral **Mickey's Slide** rises about one deck high (about the same level as Deck 10). Kids must be 4–14 years old and 38–64 inches tall to use the waterslide. There's plenty of nearby seating for parents to get some sun while watching the little ones splash around. Just past the forward end of Mickey's Pool is **Pete's Boiler Bites** snack bar, and on the aft end is **Daisy's De-Lites.**

Children who don't meet the requirements for Mickey's Pool on the *Wonder* can play in the nearby **Dory's Reef,** on the port side of the pool. Surrounded by short walls and themed to *Finding Nemo,* this water-play area for kids age 3 and under features gurgling sprays, jets, and sprinkles of water bubbling up from fountains in the floor. Best of all, there's plenty of covered seating nearby. Kids playing in Dory's Reef must be supervised.

Goofy's Pool, the family pool, is on Deck 9 Midship. It's the focal point of outdoor activity on the ship. The pool is 4 feet deep at every point, and deck chairs and lounges are arranged on both sides along its length. At the forward end of the pool is the **Funnel Vision** LED screen, which plays movies, TV shows, and videos almost constantly. At the aft end are **Pinocchio's Pizzeria** and two covered whirlpools. Both Goofy's and Mickey's Pools are typically open 8 a.m.–10 p.m. every day; check your *Personal Navigator* for specific hours.

unofficial **TIP**
While the adult pools of the Dream and Fantasy are more attractive than those on the Magic and Wonder, the pools on these smaller ships are actually far more conducive to actual swimming.

The adults-only **Quiet Cove Pool** is on Deck 9 Forward. Like the corresponding pool on the *Magic,* it's 4 feet deep throughout, and two adults-only whirlpools are nearby. Teak lounge chairs are provided for relaxing. Just past the aft end of the pool are **Signals** bar and **Cove Café.**

THE *DREAM'S* POOLS

LIKE THE *FANTASY* AND *WONDER,* the *Dream* has **Mickey's Pool** for children age 3 and up, roughly midship on Deck 11. Divided into three smaller pools corresponding to Mickey's face and ears, the pool has a maximum depth of 2 feet, and the bright-yellow spiral **Mickey's Slide** rises about one deck high (about the same level as Deck 12). Kids must be 4–14 years old and 38–64 inches tall to use the waterslide. There's plenty of nearby seating for parents to get some sun while watching the little ones splash around.

Children who don't meet the requirements for Mickey's Pool can play in the nearby **Nemo's Reef,** toward the aft end of the pool. Larger and wetter than the Nephews' Splash Zone on the *Magic* and Mickey's Splash Zone on the *Wonder*, this *Finding Nemo*–themed water-play area for kids age 3 and under features gurgling sprays, jets, and sprinkles of water bubbling up from fountains in the floor and from kid-size replicas of some of the movie's characters. A set of restrooms is just behind Nemo's Reef.

Found on Deck 11 Midship is the *Dream*'s family pool, **Donald's Pool**. Like Goofy's Pool on the *Magic* and *Wonder*, it's the center of outdoor activity on the ship. The rectangular pool is about a foot deep close to its edges; in the middle is a roughly circular section that drops to a maximum depth of around 5 feet. The different depths allow younger swimmers to relax in the shallows without having to get out of the pool.

Deck chairs and lounges line both sides of Donald's Pool. At the forward end of the pool is the **Funnel Vision** LED screen, which plays movies, TV shows, and videos almost constantly. At the aft end is the Mickey Pool. Just beyond the Funnel Vision stage are the counter-service restaurants: **Fillmore's Favorites, Luigi's Pizza**, and **Tow Mater's Grill** on the starboard side, and the **Eye Scream** ice-cream station and **Frozone Treats** smoothie station on the port side. Both Donald's and Mickey's Pools are typically open 8 a.m.–10 p.m. every day; check your *Personal Navigator* for specific hours.

The adults-only **Quiet Cove Pool** is on Deck 11 Forward on both the *Dream* and the *Fantasy*. This pool is 4 feet deep throughout. Rather than wasting space on whirlpools, the *Dream*'s designers wisely placed an outdoor bar, **Cove Bar**, at one end of the Quiet Cove Pool. The area around the bar is a splash-friendly, nonslip surface, with white bench seating and a round otto-man-like seat in the middle; there are also a few seats directly at the bar. Behind the pool is the lovely **Cove Café**; on either side is covered seating with lounges and chairs.

unofficial **TIP**

The best time to visit the AquaDuck is between 5 and 7 p.m., when most families are either at dinner or getting ready to go. You'll also find smaller crowds on days when the ship is in port.

Both the *Dream* and the *Fantasy* have an **AquaDuck** waterslide, a 765-foot-long clear-plastic tube that's almost as popular as the Disney princesses. Riders board an inflatable plastic raft at the aft end of Deck 12. The raft is shot forward through the plastic tube by high-pressure water faucets below and to the sides, making the AquaDuck a water-powered miniature roller coaster. There's enough water pressure here to propel your raft up two full decks' worth of height, followed by a descent of four decks into a landing pool. Guests must be at least 42 inches tall to ride, and children under age 7 must ride with someone age 14 or older who also meets the height requirement.

The AquaDuck's track sits at the outside edge of Deck 12 and goes as high as one of the ship's smokestacks. If you can keep your eyes open (and your wits about you), it offers some awesome views of the surrounding ocean and any nearby islands.

In late 2015, the *Dream* saw the addition of the **Satellite Falls** pool, which had previously been only on the *Fantasy*. Satellite Falls is an adults-only splash pool and sun deck that's a terrific place to relax with a drink in the evening.

THE *FANTASY'S* POOLS

LIKE THE *DREAM* AND *WONDER*, the *Fantasy* has **Mickey's Pool** for children age 3 and up, roughly midship on Deck 11. Divided into three smaller pools corresponding to Mickey's face and ears, the pool has a maximum depth of 2 feet, and the bright-yellow spiral of **Mickey's Slide** rises about one deck high (about the same level as Deck 12). Kids must be 4–14 years old and 38–64 inches tall to use the waterslide. There's plenty of nearby seating for parents to get some sun while watching the little ones splash around.

Children who don't meet the requirements for Mickey's Pool can play in the nearby **Nemo's Reef,** toward the aft end of the pool. Larger and wetter than the Nephews' Splash Zone on the *Magic* and Dory's Reef on the *Wonder,* this *Finding Nemo*–themed water-play area for kids age 3 and under features gurgling sprays, jets, and sprinkles of water bubbling up from fountains in the floor and from kid-size replicas of some of the movie's characters. A set of restrooms is just behind Nemo's Reef.

Found on Deck 11 Midship is the *Fantasy*'s family pool, **Donald's Pool.** Like Goofy's Pool on the *Magic* and *Wonder,* it's the center of outdoor activity on the ship. The rectangular pool is about a foot deep close to its edges; in the middle is a roughly circular section that drops to a maximum depth of around 5 feet. The different depths allow younger swimmers to relax in the shallows without having to get out of the pool.

Deck and lounge chairs line both sides of Donald's Pool. At the forward end of the pool is the **Funnel Vision** LED screen, which plays movies, TV shows, and videos almost constantly. At the aft end is the Mickey Pool. Just beyond the Funnel Vision stage are the counter-service restaurants: **Fillmore's Favorites, Luigi's Pizza,** and **Tow Mater's Grill** on the starboard side, and the **Eye Scream** ice-cream station and **Frozone Treats** smoothie station on the port side. Both Donald's and Mickey's Pools are typically open 8 a.m.–10 p.m. every day; check your *Personal Navigator* for specific hours.

Like the *Magic*, the *Fantasy* has an **AquaLab** water-play area. On Deck 12 Aft, it's similar to Nemo's Reef in that its entertainment is provided by water splashing out at you, but where the water comes up from the floor at Nemo's Reef, it comes from the sky at AquaLab. High above your head are water pipes filling buckets and buckets of

water, which are counterbalanced so that they spill down on unsus-
pecting (and suspecting) kids below. In fact, water comes at you from
every angle in AquaLab, and that's exactly the appeal. AquaLab is for
kids too old or too large to play in Nemo's Reef.

The adults-only **Quiet Cove Pool** is on Deck 11 Forward on both
the *Dream* and the *Fantasy*. This pool is 4 feet deep throughout.
Rather than wasting space on whirlpools, the *Fantasy*'s designers
wisely placed an outdoor bar, **Cove Bar,** at one end of the Quiet
Cove Pool. The area around the bar is a splash-friendly, nonslip surface, with white bench seating and a round ottoman-like seat in the
middle; there are also a few seats directly at the bar. Behind the pool
is the lovely **Cove Café;** on either side is covered seating with lounges
and chairs.

Both the *Fantasy* and the *Dream* have an **AquaDuck** waterslide, a
765-foot-long clear-plastic tube that's almost as popular as the Disney
princesses. Riders board an inflatable plastic raft at the aft end of
Deck 12. The raft is shot forward through the plastic tube by high-
pressure water faucets below and to the sides, making the AquaDuck
a water-powered miniature roller coaster. There's enough water pressure here to propel your raft up two full decks' worth of height, followed by a descent of four decks into a landing pool. Guests must be
at least 42 inches tall to ride, and children under age 7 must ride with
someone age 14 or older who also meets the height requirement.

The AquaDuck's track sits at the outside edge of Deck 12 and
goes as high as one of the ship's smokestacks. If you can keep your
eyes open (and your wits about you), it offers some awesome views
of the surrounding ocean and any nearby islands. The best time to
visit is between 5 and 7 p.m., when most families are either at dinner
or getting ready to go. You'll also find smaller crowds on days when
the ship is in port.

Like the *Dream,* the *Fantasy* has **Satellite Falls,** an adults-only
splash pool and sun deck on Deck 13 Forward. Covered with long,
vertical tiles in different shades of blue and green, the pool looks great
at night. In the center, a structure that looks like a giant Doppler radar
receiver (and mimics a pair of actual satellite receivers on either side of
the pool) pours a gentle stream of water into the pool below.

ONBOARD SEMINARS

LED BY CREW MEMBERS and attended by a limited number of passengers, onboard seminars are 30- to 60-minute interactive talks. Topics
vary, but most involve food, wine, shopping, fitness activities, or how
the ship is run. The shopping seminars and tours of the ship are usually
free of charge; some of the cooking demonstrations are also free. A small

fee—usually $15 to $25—is charged for seminars involving alcohol, and for some of the fitness activities.

Cooking demonstrations where wine is served, along with fitness activities, are restricted to guests age 18 and up. Wine and spirit tastings are only for guests age 21 and up, except during cruises that sail solely in Europe, where participants may be 18 if a parent or guardian is traveling with them and has provided written permission for them to drink.

The crew members who lead these seminars generally also have duties related to the subject. Wine presentations, for example, are usually run by either a restaurant sommelier or an experienced bartender; cooking demonstrations are run by one of the ship's chefs. Not surprisingly, the crew members' presentation and speaking skills are the most important factor in determining the quality of the seminar. On one cruise, a well-versed chef butterflied three dozen shrimp in slow motion so we could all take notes on proper knife technique. On another cruise, a bartender apparently not used to public speaking ran us through seven tequila shots and margaritas in 35 minutes, rendering us useless for the rest of the afternoon (not that we minded).

Several **wine-tasting sessions** are usually held on most cruises, especially those of more than four nights. The first session is typically an introduction to wine and covers the basics: grape varietals, flavor characteristics, vocabulary, and such. Subsequent sessions may concentrate on a particular style of wine, or those from a particular region. Most tastings serve 2- or 3-ounce pours from four or five varieties. The Champagne bars on the *Dream* and *Fantasy* hold tastings, too. In addition to wine, Champagne, and tequila, cruises may offer Cognac, whiskey, martini, mojito, and beer tastings as well as general classes on mixology.

The **cooking demonstrations** are some of the best presentations on board. Like the wine sessions, cooking demos often follow a theme: The first day, for example, may show how to prepare an appetizer; the second involves an entrée; and the third will be dessert. Each of these is led by a member of the kitchen staff, usually a chef. These presentations are typically held in one of the ship's nightclubs so more people can attend. To make it easy for everyone to see what the chef is doing, several video cameras are often mounted above the chef's work table, providing a view of the preparations.

We've attended many cooking demonstrations on the Disney ships, and they've all been presented better and had more interesting foods than comparable classes elsewhere. We're always amazed at the number of ingredients used in some of these dishes, too. One shrimp-and-lobster appetizer we prepared involved 31 separate ingredients! You won't be making these for a church potluck.

If you're looking for exercise instead of food or shopping, the **walk-ing tours** of the ships are a great way to keep moving and see the inner workings of the ship. Most tours begin somewhere on the pool deck and wind their way down and back up the ship. Areas covered may include the bridge, engine room, kitchens and restaurants, and entertainment areas. One great thing about these tours is that you get to ask questions of the crew members staffing each section. If you want to know what it takes to prepare 800 appetizers at the same time, you'll find the person to ask on this tour.

Shopping seminars are usually held on sea days when the ship will be docked at a port the following day. (The seminars are also video-taped and available on your stateroom's television 24 hours a day.) Most seminars last 60–90 minutes, with multiple sessions held per day. Each session usually covers one kind of item, such as watches, or a particular kind of gemstone available at the next port. The seminar on diamonds, for example, explains how cut, color, carat, and clarity combine to form the basis of each stone's price.

Along with statements of fact, bear in mind that you may also hear specious information. During one shopping seminar on the *Wonder,* we heard the presenter say, "You don't really need to pay attention to things like clarity or gem imperfections if you love a stone, because no one will know about it except you." Of course, she didn't mention that it really *does* matter if you're buying the piece as an investment, or if you ever want to sell it or insure it. You also won't hear any negative statements about the products being shilled—while your presenter may extol the virtues of the bright-blue tanzanite, what she won't say is that this gemstone is too soft and scratch-prone to be worn regularly.

We don't understand why anyone would attend a shopping seminar. If you're considering a major purchase such as diamonds, jewelry, or an expensive watch, you're almost certainly better off postponing it until you're back at home and can do your own research. Further, with the vast array of goods available on the Internet (usually with better consumer protections), it's unlikely that you'll find many things with prices low enough to justify the risk. (See our Shopping section later in this chapter for more information.)

The spa and fitness center host **wellness seminars** most mornings. Topics include everything from stretching exercises and acupuncture to group cycling and Pilates. Many of the sessions, such as stretching and cycling, are free, although space is limited and you're strongly encouraged to sign up well in advance to guarantee a spot. Personal-training sessions, available in 30- or 60-minute increments, cost roughly $45–$80, respectively, before tip.

Finally, the **Disney Vacation Club** (**DVC**) hosts presentations on its Walt Disney World time-shares during the cruise; check your *Personal*

Navigator for the schedule. A DVC representative is often stationed at a desk somewhere just off the lobby. On sea days, you'll probably find the rep roaming the halls of the ship to get the word out on an upcoming seminar. And while you may or may not want to sit through a time-share presentation on vacation, the DVC reps are very generous in giving out free stuff, as this reader found:

> *We didn't want to sit through the DVC sales pitch, but we're suckers for swag. We stopped by the DVC desk and they practically threw goodies at us. Despite me saying that there were just two of us on board, the rep insisted on giving me four DVC baseball caps and four sturdy drawstring backpacks.*

SPORTS *and* FITNESS

EACH SHIP OFFERS AN ARRAY of outdoor and indoor sports and fitness options. While it's no substitute for your local megagym, there's enough equipment and variety on board for almost everyone to maintain muscle tone and cardio conditioning during the cruise.

Use of the fitness center is generally limited to guests age 18 and up. While the Vibe teen club may bring a group of 14- to 17-year-olds to the gym for a group activity, a high school varsity athlete shouldn't expect to be able to use the equipment at a training level, even with parental permission or supervision.

unofficial **TIP**
The Fitness Center is on Deck 9 Forward on the *Magic* and *Wonder,* and on Deck 11 Forward on the *Dream* and *Fantasy.*

Each DCL ship has a comprehensive **Fitness Center** with modern, well-maintained weight machines, free weights, treadmills, stairclimbers, elliptical machines, stationary bikes, and more.

These gyms provide yoga mats, large plastic step-aerobics benches, exercise balls, and elastic bands for stretching. Also provided are a water fountain, a basket of fresh fruit, cloth towels, paper towels, and spray bottles of sanitizer to clean the equipment when you're done. Male and female locker rooms have showers, a sauna, sinks, robes, towels, personal-grooming items, and lockers with electric locks. There is no charge to use these facilities.

unofficial **TIP**
The locker rooms at the Fitness Center can be helpful even if you're not working out. During one cruise where we had four adults in one stateroom, we ended up sending some folks up to the Fitness Center to shower, speeding our daily prep time considerably.

We've spent a lot of time in the gyms on every ship, and we've been happy with the variety of equipment available. Nautilus-style weight machines are available for working every major and minor muscle group. Virtually all of the electric cardio machines have video monitors so you can watch the ship's television while working out, along with plugs for your headphones.

The Fitness Centers are usually open from around 6 a.m. until 11 p.m.; check your *Personal Navigator* for the exact schedule. They tend to be most crowded in the morning between 8 and 11 a.m., and least crowded between 5 and 11 p.m. Group- and personal-training sessions are available, including weight training, Pilates, and other courses, for an additional fee. Group sessions start at around $12 per workout, typically about 45 minutes each. Individual training sessions cost around $40 per half-hour session.

The only thing we've found disconcerting in the gyms is that the treadmills on the *Dream* and *Fantasy* face the port (left) side of the ship, not the bow. If the ship is moving while you're running on one of these tread-mills, the scenery in front of you will be passing from left to right, but your brain expects to see the scenery moving toward you. Some people—including Len—instinctively twist their bodies left in an attempt to line up the scenery with the way their minds think they should be going. This makes for awkward running (walking doesn't seem to be much of an issue). If you find yourself unable to run correctly on the treadmill, try the outdoor course described next.

unofficial **TIP**
If your itinerary includes a trip to Castaway Cay, Disney usually hosts a 5K run around the island starting at 9 a.m. There's no cost to run. Water is provided at several points throughout the course, and Disney usually hands out Mickey-shaped plastic "med-als" to finishers. Check your *Personal Navigator* the night before your stop for where to meet on board.

Runners and walkers will appreciate the **0.3-mile track** circling Deck 4 of the *Magic* and *Wonder* and the **0.4-mile track** on Deck 4 of the *Dream* and *Fantasy*. One of the great things about running laps on the ship is the amazing scenery, which (almost) makes you forget that you're exercising while you're seeing it. We've run a few laps on both ships, and the track is certainly good enough to get in a few miles to start your day. Some sections take you through some relatively narrow corridors, and there's a good chance that you'll be running past groups of other tourists who are out enjoying the deck, too. Finally, keep an eye open for water on the deck, which can make the track slick.

If running isn't your thing, every DCL ship has **outdoor basketball courts** surrounded by woven rope fencing to keep errant balls from leaving the ship. These are popular with kids and parents looking to shoot around a bit—we've never seen a competitive game played at one. The basketball courts can be converted to a miniature soccer field or volleyball court, too, if you can find enough people to play.

Each ship also has **shuffleboard courts** near midship on Deck 4; if you're up for a challenge, outdoor **tennis tables** are available, too (Deck 9 Forward on the *Magic* and *Wonder;* Deck 13 Aft on the *Dream* and *Fantasy*). Readers report that the windy conditions on deck make it difficult to play, but perhaps your game will benefit from a bit of unpredictability.

The *Dream* and *Fantasy* both have Disney-themed **miniature-golf courses** outdoors on Deck 13 Aft, and these are a lot of fun for the entire family. The *Dream* and *Fantasy* also have **Foosball tables** outdoors. As with the table tennis, we find it helpful to have the following list available when our game fails us:

HANDY EXCUSES FOR RECREATIONAL INEPTITUDE
• Gust of wind changed ball trajectory
• Rough seas caused ship to list suddenly
• Sunglasses aren't made for the UV rays at this latitude (*note:* must be wearing sunglasses when saying this)
• Concentration broken by sound of pirate-ship cannon in distance
• Giant-squid tentacle was seen reaching up behind opponent

If you're looking to get in some individual practice time on the *Dream* and *Fantasy,* **virtual sports simulators** are available on Deck 13 Aft for golf, basketball, soccer, football, hockey, and baseball. These indoor facilities have a large movie screen set up in a dedicated room; a computer projects a simulated soccer field, basketball court, or other appropriate venue on the screen. You're given actual sports equipment to kick, throw, or swing. Your movements, and the movements of the ball, are tracked by computers and displayed on screen—there's a slight lag in the display, but it's not enough to be distracting. Half-hour sessions cost $25 for golf and $12 for other sports; hour-long sessions are $45 for golf and $20 for other sports.

SPAS

SOME OF THE MOST RELAXING TIMES we've spent on DCL's ships have been in their spas. Whether you're looking for a massage, manicure, new hairstyle, or just some time to unwind in a hot sauna, you'll find it at the spa.

This section summarizes the major spa and salon services offered on each ship, but note that many more are available. We recommend visiting the spa on your first afternoon aboard to sign up for any last-minute treatments and check for specials. *Note:* Prices listed are approximate and do not include a tip, typically 15–20% of the cost of your treatment. There's a 50% cancellation charge if you cancel within 24 hours of your appointment.

unofficial **TIP**
The best time to visit the spa is during dinner or when the ship is in port.

Salon services must be booked after 1 p.m. on your first day aboard—you can't book them online. If you're trying to book spa services before your cruise, Disney's website may not let you book some services, such as facials, for two people at the same time of day. (We think the website assumes that only one person per ship is qualified to do these tasks, and that this person is unavailable once the first service is booked.) If you run into this problem, try booking the services online one after the other, and then visit the spa in person when you board to explain what you want done.

Along the same lines, one thing that's different about spa treatments on the Disney ships versus on land is that the same person is likely to be your masseuse, facialist, and manicurist—there's simply not enough room on the ship for a whole squadron of beauty experts, so roles have to be combined. Some readers like the continuity of having one person to talk with throughout their treatments; others think that one person can't provide the same level of service as multiple dedicated professionals.

ON THE *MAGIC AND WONDER*

ON DECK 9 FORWARD is **Senses Spa & Salon.** The reception area and check-in desk are just behind the forward elevator lobby, past the adult Quiet Cove Pool. Senses has a hair salon, treatment rooms for individuals and couples, and a complex of steam baths and showers. Men's and women's locker rooms, shared with the Fitness Center, provide storage lockers with electric locks, showers, robes, slippers, and towels.

Formerly known as Vista Spa and Salon, the spa became Senses on the *Magic* in 2013 and on the *Wonder* in 2016. The *Dream*'s and *Fantasy*'s spas are also named Senses (which, incidentally, is also the name of the spas at the Grand Floridian and Saratoga Springs Resorts at Walt Disney World).

The changes to the *Magic*'s and *Wonder*'s spas were mainly cosmetic. The two major updates are a redesigned lobby and the addition of **Chill Spa** for guests ages 13–17. However, the Chill Spas on the *Magic* and *Wonder* are nothing like the versions on the *Dream* and *Fantasy*—they're single treatment rooms off the beauty salon. To call them spas is a stretch.

Senses's hair salon has services for men and women. Options for men include haircuts (around $35); the **Elemis Express Shave** with hot-towel wrap (around $45); and the wordy **Elemis Pro-Collagen Grooming Treatment with Shave** (around $95), billed as "the shave of all shaves"—an almost hour-long treatment including the towel wrap, a shave, a minifacial, and massages for your face, scalp, and hands. Men who use electric shavers for their daily toilette should be aware that a hand-held razor shaves much closer than an electric blade and can cause razor burn, even on men who aren't normally susceptible. Your face will be as smooth as a baby's bottom, though.

Women can get a literal head-to-toe makeover, starting with hair-styling. A simple shampoo and blow-dry runs about $32–$48 depending on hair length; adding a haircut is about $56–$75. Separate conditioning treatments are available: The **Frangipani Hair and Scalp Ritual,** which sounds like it's part of a tribal initiation, starts at around $30; most other standard conditioning treatments cost around $50 each. Senses also offers a treatment for color-treated hair for around $30; hair coloring starts at about $55.

Waxing for eyebrows ($25), legs ($89), arms ($39), upper lip ($19), chin ($19), and bikini line ($29) is available, too. If you're headed to Palo for dinner, you can get your makeup done for your big night out, starting at $75.

Manicures (around $50) and pedicures (around $70) come with a heated stone massage of your various digits. There seems to be no discount for a combined mani–pedi. Additional services include adding polish ($25), removing polish ($20), paraffin baths ($15), and acrylic nails ($82).

Facials and massages are administered in private, individual treatment rooms or in one of the dedicated Spa Villas for singles and couples. Five different facials are offered, including ones with microdermabrasion, fruits and herbs, enzymes, and something that involves "amazing micro-currents applied at a high frequency" to your skin . . . voluntarily. Treatments cost $115–$170 for a 50-minute session.

Massages include the traditional deep-tissue kind; a variation accompanied by heated, scented stones placed on various parts of your body; and another where warmed bamboo sticks are rolled over you in addition to the massage. Prices range from $129 for a basic 50-minute rubdown to $244 for 100 minutes. Besides these are massages combining hands-on therapy with slatherings of spices, minerals, and herbs designed to make you feel like a Thanksgiving turkey with a healthy glow. Among the offerings are the **Aroma Ocean Wrap with Half-Body Massage** ($188), the **Thai Herbal Poultice Massage ($195),** and the **Exotic Lime and Ginger Salt Glow with Half-Body Massage** (part of two $400-plus treatment packages for couples).

*un*official **TIP**
Some treatment rooms at Senses on the *Magic* and *Wonder* sit directly under the basketball courts. If someone is playing, you'll hear through the ceiling every time someone bounces a ball or lands after jumping. You may not care if you're screaming through your own waxing treatment, but if you're getting a relaxing massage, you may want to inquire about the location of your treatment room.

Services in the Chill Spa room for teens range from the **Magical Manicure** at the low end ($29) to the **Hot Chocolate Wrap** at the high end ($141).

Besides these spa services, 30-minute teeth-whitening treatments are available for individuals (around $150) and couples (around $260). They're not especially popular, though, probably because you're told to abstain from drinking coffee and wine after the whitening.

Our favorite spa experience is the **Rainforest,** which costs around $16 per person, per day. This gets you access to three separate steam rooms, arranged around a quiet tiled room with heated stone lounge chairs. Each steam room has its own scent, temperature, and steam setting. Outside the steam rooms are Rainforest showers, with push-button settings that allow you to vary the intensity, pattern, and temperature of the water flow.

Unfortunately, the Rainforests at Senses on the *Magic* and *Wonder* are not as nice as the versions on the *Dream* and *Fantasy:* they're considerably smaller and less spacious, with fewer showers and lounge chairs, and unlike their larger siblings, they don't have outdoor hot tubs or ocean view. That said, it's still the most relaxing thing you can do, and because DCL sells a limited number of passes per cruise— we've heard estimates of as few as 20 on the entire ship—you're unlikely to share the Rainforest with more than a handful of other people on any day. Also, a day pass at the Rainforest on the *Magic* and *Wonder* is less expensive than on the *Dream* and *Fantasy:* $16 versus $25 on the larger ships.

unofficial **TIP**
We don't recommend the length-of-cruise Rainforest pass on the *Magic* and *Wonder.* Get the cheaper one-day pass instead.

ON THE *DREAM* AND THE *FANTASY*

DISNEY'S TWO NEWEST SHIPS each have a **Senses Spa & Salon** on Deck 11 Forward. Both are gorgeous, incorporating dark woods and intricate tile and stonework, with comfortable leather chairs and soft bed linens. Senses on the *Dream* and *Fantasy* is much larger than Vista Spa & Salon on the *Wonder* and slightly larger than the *Magic*'s Senses. Some of the treatment rooms and spa areas afford sweeping views out over the sides of each ship; also, Senses on the *Dream* and *Fantasy* has two covered outdoor whirlpools available to those with a Rainforest pass. On the *Magic* and *Wonder,* ocean views and outdoor features are available only to those who book a pricey treatment in one of the private Spa Villas.

unofficial **TIP**
Bring a towel to sit on in the saunas, and wear sandals—the seats and floors are very hot.

Salon services, facials, and massages are about the same as those offered at the spas on the *Magic* and *Wonder.* Here are the major differences:

More luxurious than its counterparts on the two smaller ships, the **Rainforest** (about $25 per person, per day) gives you access to three saunas with varying levels of heat and humidity: the Laconium, a dry sauna with mild heat and low humidity; the Caldarium, with medium heat and humidity; and the Hamam, a full-on steam bath, with the hottest temperatures and lots and lots of steam. In addition to different levels of steam, each sauna has its own scent and music.

While most guests find the Rainforest peaceful, indulgent, and relaxing, one reader had a different experience:

> *Some guests enter the Rainforest thinking it's Blizzard Beach [at Walt Disney World], screeching and laughing like they're in a theme park. I wish Disney would spend 45 seconds educating them on what to expect and explaining that this is a relaxation/quiet area for adults.*

We haven't experienced this ourselves, but please speak to cast members if you encounter rowdy behavior in the spa.

We enjoy hopping between these saunas and the nearby Rainforest showers—tiled circular cutouts hidden behind the walls along the path leading to the saunas. Each shower has different options for water temperature, pressure, and spray pattern, each of which you select by pushing a button. For example, one option might be a light, cool mist, perfect for when you've just jumped out of the sauna. Another is like a warm, steady downpour in a tropical jungle.

Had enough of the steam rooms and showers? Then repair to one of the two covered outdoor whirlpool tubs or one of the stone lounge chairs in an adjacent room. The ocean views here are perhaps the biggest selling point over the Rainforests on the *Magic* and *Wonder*.

The best thing about the Rainforest package is that Disney sells only a limited number of them per cruise. We hear that number can be as low as 40 people on the *Dream* and *Fantasy*. Not 40 at a time, not 40 per day—40 people *on the entire ship*. While we haven't actually fact-checked that number ourselves, we can tell you that we've never seen more than two other people in this part of the spa on any cruise. It's the single most relaxing thing you can do on board.

Senses on the *Dream* has a new juice bar offering freshly blended juices and smoothies for $4.50–$5. We're amused that Disney has gone with the Anglophile spellings of *soya* and *yoghurt* on the menus (because they're classy that way). Exercisers and spa fans can refuel with choices like a spinach, carrot, avocado, ginger-basil, and manuka honey beverage or concoctions including everything from kale to chia seeds, spirulina, macha, and turmeric powder. We don't know if they really "restore harmony and balance" . . . but they are pretty tasty.

Finally, exclusive to the *Dream* and *Fantasy* is the teens-only **Chill Spa,** a spa-within-a-spa entirely inside Senses. (The *Magic* and *Wonder* also have areas that they call Chill Spa—but they're single treatment rooms.) Designed for guests ages 13–17, Chill has its own array of facial, massage, exfoliating, and mani–pedi packages. Prices start at around $90 for a massage, $95 for a facial, and $45 and $65 for manicures and pedicures, respectively. Hairstyling and fitness sessions in the gym are also available.

Parent–child massages are offered as well ($99 for half-body, $195 for full-body). Let us know if you've tried these with your teens, please: When we told ours about them, one replied, "Gross!" and the other gave us a look like she'd prefer being rubbed with angry ferrets.

SHOPPING

WHETHER YOU'RE AT SEA OR IN PORT, your daily *Personal Navigator* handout highlights your shopping opportunities for the day.

ONBOARD SHOPPING

ONBOARD SHOPS GENERALLY AREN'T OPEN when the ship is in port. If there's any possibility that you're going to run out of something critical during the day, be sure to stock up on it while the shops are open.

As Disney-theme-park fans, we were surprised at the relatively modest amount of space dedicated to retail stores on the Disney ships. Each ship has dedicated shopping spaces for children, women, and men. Look for them on Deck 4 Forward on the *Magic* and *Wonder* and Deck 3 Forward on the *Dream* and *Fantasy*, on either side of the walkway to the Walt Disney Theatre.

The shops sell a little bit of everything, from T-shirts and stuffed animals to snacks, bathing suits, and towels. You'll also find sunscreen, aspirin, toothpaste, diapers (in limited sizes),

> **unofficial TIP**
> A note about the "Shopping Consultants" on board: You'll note that their name tags look different from other crew members'. This is because they don't work for Disney. Both DCL and the consultants receive money back from shops that have been recommended in the *Personal Navigator* when guests buy something there. This is not to say you shouldn't buy from these shops, but remember that the shopping recommendations aren't entirely unbiased.

and other travel supplies. The onboard shops may also stock location-specific items; for example, during our Alaskan cruise, the shops stocked mittens, knit caps, binoculars, and books about local wildlife. In addition, an onboard store sells duty-free alcohol by the bottle, including wines and spirits served on board, though you won't be able to take possession of your purchase until the last night of your cruise.

In case you neglected to pack your eye patch for Pirate Night (see page 157), the shops can outfit the entire family head to toe, buccaneer-style. You'll find a variety of the same merchandise found in Disney theme parks, as well as DCL-specific souvenirs. Some of our favorites are china and brush-shaped butter knives from Animator's Palate—the

IS IT REAL?

YOU PROBABLY REALIZE that "Louis Vuitton" bag on sale for $25 at Nassau's Straw Market is a fake. Also remember that perfume and sunglasses are among the most counterfeited items out there. Many luxury brands, such as Gucci and the aforementioned LV, do have actual stores in the Caribbean and European ports, so you can buy with confidence there (though to one author's despair, Hermès doesn't have an outpost in the Bahamas). Another thing to look out for is out-of-season merchandise being sold at full price: On one trip to Nassau, we found an authentic Kate Spade bag being sold at MSRP, but it could be found 30–50% off stateside because it was from the previous season. With all purchases, do your due diligence ahead of time to know what a fair price is for anything you're considering buying.

We find that the amount of time spent bargaining in port isn't worth any potential savings, and so we don't spend a lot of time shopping on our cruises. That said, our Ports section (see Part Eleven) highlights any especially good deals we've been able to find along the way.

cynics among us wonder if this wasn't in response to these items walking off the ships on their own—and T-shirts with mash-up images of Star Wars characters in ocean-cruise situations (surfing Stormtroopers, anyone?).

Besides the retail spaces, each ship has an art gallery with limited-edition Disney-character and theme-park art, along with **Shutters** photo gallery, where you can purchase snaps from your cruise.

The most commonly heard advantage to buying on board or in port is that you don't pay US or local sales taxes, which can be significant on large purchases. US residents are still required to declare these purchases when they return to the States, and they may be subject to import duties. See page 91 for more details.

CASTAWAY CAY

THE SHOPS HERE SELL SOME ITEMS that are exclusive to the island, such as T-shirts and beach towels. We've purchased last-minute cords for our sunglasses, water-resistant pouches for our phones, and other beach supplies on Castaway Cay. Note that no sales tax is charged on the island or on board, which makes purchases cheaper than if you bought them at a Disney park.

IN PORT

MANY TRAVELERS FIND SHOPPING IN PORT as essential to the cruising experience as gambling is to the Las Vegas experience. If you approach buying things with this attitude, you won't be disappointed. You'll be surrounded by retail opportunities at each port from the moment you step off the ship; bargaining is expected, so assume that the price you're quoted the first time you ask isn't the final one. If you need T-shirts, handmade woodcrafts, or other *tchotchkes* to bring back as inexpensive souvenirs, you'll have no trouble finding them within a few hundreds yards of the ship.

The Northern European ports are the exception to the schlock-shopping onslaught. For instance, while Diamonds International shops are virtually everywhere in Alaska and the Caribbean, we were thrilled not to see a single solitary one during our recent Scandinavian and Baltic cruises on DCL. But here, as in every port, the real trick is to ask pointed questions about what you're about to purchase. If you're buying mittens in Norway, ask if they're made from local wool. Are they hand- or machine-knit? Were they knit in Norway or in a factory in China? It's up to you to understand what you're paying for.

JEWELRY Buying jewelry in port is popular with many cruisers. The problem we have with doing this is that fair prices vary greatly with the quality of the gems purchased, and you really need to be an informed shopper to know what's a good price for an item. Our recommendation is to pre-shop online (**Amazon** and **Blue Nile** [bluenile.com] are great places to start) to know the going prices for gems of the weight and quality you're interested in. One brand in particular, **Effy,** is already sold on Amazon and through its own website (effyjewelry.com), so check it out before you leave.

ALCOHOL Duty-free alcohol is available on board the ship as well as at many ports. If you're thinking about purchasing bottled spirits during your cruise, be sure to do a little pricing research before you travel. Depending on your place of residence and its tax situation, the duty-free pricing may not be much different than what you'd pay at home. Look at the per-ounce price and make sure you're comparing apples to apples, or rather tequila to tequila.

For example, a silver tequila and a *reposado* will be priced differently; be sure you know which you're buying. On the other hand, price may not be as much of an issue if you're making a sentimental purchase (the bottle of wine you learned about during a port-adventure vineyard tour) or if you're buying a noncommodity item like a liqueur made from a local flower and sold only in a particular region.

If you do decide to buy alcohol during your trip, remember to review DCL's rules for bringing alcohol on board (see page 39). In many cases, you won't have access to your purchase until the last night of the cruise.

SHOPPING DCL FROM HOME You can do some shopping for your Disney cruise before you leave home. The DCL website has a section (disneycruise.disney.go.com/gifts-and-amenities) where you can order items in advance to be delivered to your stateroom. Items can be pricey, but this may be helpful if you want to mark a celebration without carrying a lot of stuff on board with you.

If you discover that you forgot to get something once you're back home, know that a limited section of DCL-logo items is available online at disneystore.com and through the official Disney shopping app, **Shop Disney Parks** (for Apple and Android). We've found DCL-branded clothing, pins, pillows, towels, jewelry, and toys in both locations. Be aware that the online site and the app often carry different items, so check both if you're looking for something specific.

RELIGIOUS SERVICES

CRUISES OF SEVEN NIGHTS or longer hold a nondenominational Christian service on Sunday mornings and a Shabbat service on Friday evenings. Worship times depend on when the ship is in port or, in the case of Jewish services, when sunset occurs. There are no dedicated chapels on the ships—services are typically held in a lounge or theater, depending on the number of guests on board and the ship's other offerings. Guest Services can recommend houses of worship in port.

In addition to regular weekly services, there will be additional services added during religious holiday seasons. For example, during Easter week, you'll typically find a Catholic Mass offered on Good Friday morning, as well as sunrise, Catholic, and interdenominational services offered on Easter morning. Similar events will happen during the Christmas season. Check your *Personal Navigator* for details.

Many DCL ports have houses of worship as key points of interest. If you'd like to attend services while in port, check the institution's website in advance to view hours of operation or specific dress code rules (common in many European churches). Guest Services on board may also be able to offer some advice.

PART TEN

CASTAWAY CAY

CASTAWAY CAY IS LIKELY TO BE YOUR FAVORITE ISLAND on your Bahamian or Caribbean cruise. The weather is almost always gorgeous; the shore excursions are reasonably priced (mostly); and, as is the case with Walt Disney World, there's little of the "real world" to get in the way of a relaxing day. And that's before the free food and (nonalcoholic) drinks. We provide additional coverage of Castaway Cay in Part Eleven, Ports, and Part Twelve, Port Adventures.

WHAT *to* **BRING**

THE SUN AND HEAT ARE INTENSE, so bring plenty of high-SPF sunscreen and water. Insulated sports bottles are a great idea. Other solar protection you may need includes light-colored, long-sleeved, lightweight shirts; sweatpants; swimsuit cover-ups; hats; lip balm; and sunglasses.

Disney will provide you with medium-size towels for use while on Castaway Cay—as many as you can carry. If you'd prefer a full-size beach towel, bring one of your own or purchase one while you're on the island.

Disney also provides life jackets (free) for use while on the island. Strollers, wagons, and sand-capable wheelchairs are available for rent on a first-come, first-serve basis.

OTHER ITEMS YOU MAY FIND USEFUL TO BRING TO CASTAWAY CAY
• **A watch or cell phone** for checking how long everyone has been in the sun and when it's time to reapply sunscreen. Also useful for knowing whether the island's restaurants are open (usually 11 a.m.–2 p.m.).
• **An underwater or waterproof camera** for taking photos while swimming, snorkeling, or participating in other activities.

Continued on page 226

Castaway Cay

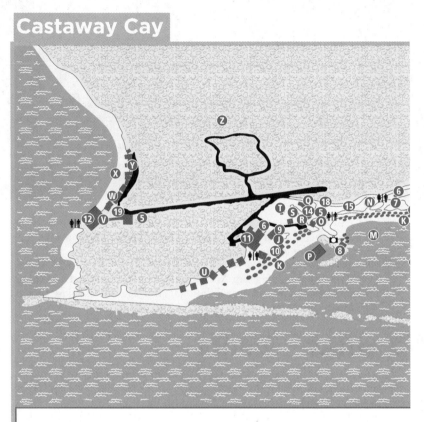

ATTRACTIONS

A. Arrival Plaza
B. Post Office
C. Marge's Barges and
     Sea Charters Dock
D. Boating Harbor
E. Scuttle's Cove
F. Boat Beach
G. Monstro Point
H. Castaway Ray's
     Stingray Adventure
I. Gil's Fins and Boats
J. Gazebos
K. Castaway Family Beaches
L. Snorkeling Lagoon
M. Swimming Lagoon
N. In-Da-Shade Games
O. Flippers and Floats
P. Pelican Plunge

ATTRACTIONS

Q. The Hide Out (teens only)
R. Bike Rentals
S. Beach Sports
T. Spring-a-Leak
U. Family Cabanas 1–21
V. The Windsock Hut
W. Massage Cabanas
X. Serenity Bay Adult Beach
Y. Adult Cabanas 22–25
Z. Observation Tower

FOOD AND DRINK

1. Pop's Props and Boat Repair
     (Covered Seating)
2. Dig In (Covered Seating)
3. Cookie's BBQ
4. Conched Out Bar

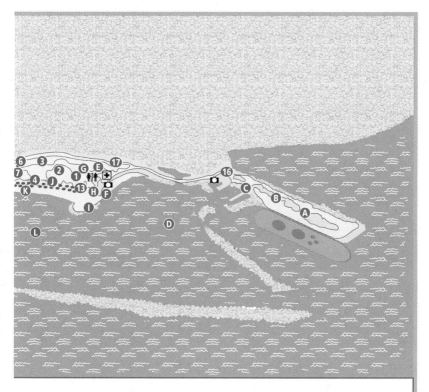

FOOD AND DRINK

5. Summertime Freeze
6. Covered Seating
7. Gumbo Limbo (Covered Seating)
8. Heads Up Bar
9. Grouper (Covered Seating)
10. Sand Bar
11. Cookie's Too BBQ
12. Castaway Air Bar

SHOPPING

13. She Sells Sea Shells . . .
    and Everything Else
14. Buy the Seashore
15. Bahamian Retail

MISCELLANEOUS

16. Kargo Handling Tram Stop
17. Scuttle's Cove Tram Stop
18. Pelican Point Tram Stop
19. Serenity Bay Tram Stop

✚ First Aid
∮∮ Restrooms and
    Outdoor Showers
◘ Photo Opportunities
■ Bike/Nature Trail

Continued from page 223

OTHER ITEMS YOU MAY FIND USEFUL TO BRING TO CASTAWAY CAY

- **A small cooler** to keep medicine, baby formula, and other perishables cool. Fill it with ice before you leave the ship, and refill it from the restaurants' ice machines on the island. The cooler must be soft-sided and no larger than 12 by 12 by 12 inches; larger coolers are not allowed to be brought on the ship when boarding.

- **Water shoes** will protect your feet from sharp rocks and coral and provide some insulation from hot sand and pavement.

- **Small beach toys,** such as a shovel and pail, though pails might present some packing issues. Toys are also available for purchase on the island.

- **Your own snorkeling gear** if you already have it, or if the idea of sharing a snorkel tube just grosses you out. DCL provides flotation vests for free.

- **Swim diapers,** if you have little ones who like the water.

- **A hairbrush or comb.** It's windy on the island, and you'll want to look good in your vacation photos.

- **Insect repellent.** Disney keeps the bug population under control, and we've never been bothered by anything. In case your family is especially sensitive to bites, however, it's a good idea to bring something like Off or Repel. With heightened concerns about the Zika virus, it's a good precaution in any case.

- **Something to read—a book or e-reader.** Be careful, however, about leaving expensive electronics alone on the island.

- **A portable music player.** Especially useful if you're going for a jog around the island's 5K course.

- **Athletic shoes and socks.** If you want to play basketball on the island, you'll also want proper footwear.

- **A change of clothes.** While Castaway Cay's sun will dry your swimsuit in a hurry, you may want dry clothes to wear while you're walking around the island, sitting down for meals, or riding bikes. You can also return to the ship to change, but going through security takes time.

- **A small amount of cash.** Castaway Cay has its own official Bahamian post office from which you can mail home postcards and letters. The post office takes cash only (no room charges), so bring a few dollars for postage. (This is the only place on the island for which you'll need cash.)

WHAT *to* DO

THERE ARE MORE THINGS TO DO than you'll have time for in a single day or even two. A list of our favorite Castaway Cay shore activities follows; see Part Twelve for details.

- **Castaway Ray's Stingray Adventure** affords you the opportunity to pet and feed small and medium-size stingrays in a dedicated lagoon.

- The **snorkeling lagoon** features underwater sights, such as a replica of the *Nautilus* submarine from *20,000 Leagues Under the Sea,* other shipwrecks and shipping artifacts, plus statues of Minnie and Mickey. Common marine life seen in the snorkeling lagoon includes stingrays, blue tang, and yellowtail snapper (plus the occasional barracuda).

- Rent **sailboats or paddleboats, personal watercraft,** or **inflatable floats and tubes.**

- Runners may want to start their day with the **Castaway Cay 5K,** a free (as in no-cost) jog through the developed parts of the island.

- Single-speed **bicycle rentals** allow you to fully explore the island, including the island's observation tower and trails, which can be accessed only on foot or bike.

Castaway Cay's lagoons are shallow, with small, gentle waves. Anchored within a short swim from shore is **Pelican Plunge,** a floating platform with two waterslides and a water-play area. The waterslides begin on the platform's second story (accessed by stairs) and end with a splash back into the lagoon. Each slide offers a different experience: One is a long, open slide with moderate turns, while the other is a shorter, enclosed slide with plenty of tight turns and twists.

Along with the slides, Pelican Plunge's water-play area includes pipes, nozzles, and plumes of water spraying out from every direction. The main feature is a giant overhead bucket, which is constantly being filled with water from the lagoon. The bucket is counterbalanced so that when the water reaches a certain level, the bucket tilts over suddenly, pouring gallons of water on anything nearby.

If you have small children who enjoy water but you're concerned about ocean currents, consider letting the little ones run around at the inland **Spring-a-Leak** water-play area, just beyond the Pelican Point tram stop, near the middle of the family beaches. Like Pelican Plunge, Spring-a-Leak has plenty of burbling, spraying, misting water to keep kids wet and happy all day long.

Scuttle's Cove, an additional area for the little ones, offers supervised activities, yet another water-play area, and a giant-whale-bone excavation site. Teens have their own dedicated area inland: **The Hide Out,** with volleyball, tetherball, and other activities. Some teens, however, may not like the fact that The Hide Out is away from the beach and has no water features or water-play areas.

Note that kids and teens must be registered at their respective youth clubs on board (see page 187) to play at Scuttle's Cove and hang out at The Hide Out.

HEIGHT AND AGE REQUIREMENTS AT CASTAWAY CAY
• **Pelican Plunge waterslide:** No official height or age requirement listed; life jackets encouraged. Tweens (ages 11–13) have scheduled time to hang out (supervised by youth counselors) at both Pelican Plunge and the **In-Da-Shade Games** pavilion.
• **The Hide Out:** Ages 14–17; must be registered for Vibe on board
• **Scuttle's Cove:** Ages 3–12; must be registered for the Oceaneer Club/Oceaneer Lab on board

WHERE *to* RELAX

CASTAWAY CAY IS ALSO A GREAT PLACE TO SIT BACK, listen to the ocean, feel the sea breeze on your face, and smell the salt air. Two family beaches are available, while adults ages 18 and up have **Serenity Bay,** a private beach with its own outdoor barbecue, bar, rental cabanas, and more.

FAMILY BEACHES Most of Castaway Cay's developed beachfront is reserved for families. If you're taking the tram from the dock, get off at the first stop, **Pelican Point,** and you'll find yourself in the middle of both family beaches.

A small, hook-shaped peninsula juts into the lagoon and effectively separates the family beaches. If you're going to rent floats or boats or do some snorkeling, you'll want to head to the left of the peninsula once you're off the tram. If you're going to play in the water, especially at the Pelican Plunge waterslide, bear right.

Both family beaches offer free lounge chairs and towels, with restrooms, food, and drink dispensers a short walk away.

CABANAS The Pelican Plunge side of the beach has 21 private cabanas for rent. The typical price is $549 per day for up to six guests. In 2016, Disney added a seasonal supplement to the base price, making the cost $599 from late April until late September. The Serenity Bay side of the beach has five cabanas available at a cost of $399 per day for up to four guests. There is also one Grand Cabana that can accommodate up to 16 guests ($966 for the first 10 guests, $54 for each additional guest).

The cabanas are covered and furnished with cushioned chairs, chaise longues, a hammock, and a bar area. Cabanas are also supplied with fresh towels, water and soft drinks, some snacks, a selection of sunscreens, a refrigerator, a private safe, an outdoor shower, and a shaded deck.

While the financial bite of a cabana is substantial, consider that a cabana rental also includes complimentary use of snorkeling equipment, floats, and bikes. Those three things total $49 a person. If you have six people in your cabana, that's a $294 value. If you'd normally spring for that equipment and several soft drinks, the price of some private shade and comfort seems a lot more reasonable. (*Note:* Snorkeling equipment is currently not included with the Serenity Bay cabanas.)

The cabanas are so popular that they're often fully booked in advance by Concierge and Platinum Castaway Club members before the general public gets a crack at them. However, cancellations do happen. If you're interested, ask at the Port Adventures desk as soon as you board the ship, and periodically check back a few times before the ship docks at Castaway Cay.

SCOTT SAYS   *by Scott Sanders*

CASTAWAY CAY DONE RIGHT

DISNEY'S PRIVATE ISLAND is an extension of the cruise-ship experience, because the ship's crew works in various roles on Castaway Cay. You may, for instance, see your serving team barbecuing at one of the lunch locations.

On the island, there are plenty of loungers and beach chairs for everyone, even if you sleep in and get a late start on the island. Hammocks are more scarce, so arrive early (or look for one around 3 p.m.) if that's part of your island dream.

My favorite time to explore the snorkeling lagoon is in the morning before it gets crowded. As for seeing the rest of the island, the bike rental is a relatively inexpensive way to cover the trails and quickly get to the observation tower.

Not interested in going ashore? No problem. There are plenty of activities onboard, and the lines for the waterslides are much shorter—sometimes nonexistent!

As far as renting a cabana goes, I'm not going to lie—the experience is amazing, but it comes at a steep price. Unless you plan to have a couple of people spending most of their time in and around the cabana, I wouldn't recommend renting one.

PART ELEVEN

PORTS

THE FOLLOWING SECTION outlines the ports visited by Disney Cruise Line. Grouped geographically, each profile summarizes the port's history, weather, port information, tourist highlights, food, and shopping opportunities.

Just for the record, some ports as classified by DCL aren't technically part of the geographic area in which they're listed; rather, they're part of an itinerary with a significant part or a majority of its route within that area. For example, Dover, England, United Kingdom, is listed in the "Mediterranean" section because it's on an itinerary that begins there; heads south along the Atlantic coast, visiting Lisbon, Portugal; and then travels north and east along the Mediterranean coast to Barcelona, Spain. Also, note that a few ports are listed in multiple areas—Dover, for instance, also appears in the "Northern Europe, British Isles, and Norway" section.

Our Itineraries Index (page 376) lists the specific itineraries that visit the ports described here and also includes maps of each area.

ALASKA

CRUISES SAIL FROM Vancouver

SHIP *Wonder*

CRUISE LENGTHS Mostly 7 nights, occasionally 9

DATES Summer

SPECIAL TOUCHES A naturalist on board who talks about the glaciers and wildlife you'll see, mulled wine on the bar menu, blankets to keep warm on the upper decks, hot soup at the counter-service food venues. A "Taste of Alaska" menu with Alaskan seafood is a big hit.

WHAT TO PACK Warm clothing, including gloves, hats, and scarves; waterproof shoes (that you can hike in); binoculars; sunscreen

SIGNATURE PORT ADVENTURE Dogsledding. It's pricey, but you'll LOVE it.

COMMENTS We realize that Caribbean-cruise fatigue is the ultimate in first-world problems, so if you're rolling your eyes at us when we say that an Alaskan cruise is the cure for too many trips to Nassau, we're there with you. That said, for the opposite of the Caribbean experience without leaving the United States—sorry, Canada, you know what we mean—we heartily recommend seeing the 49th state by ship. *Heads-up:* Marijuana (except for medical use) is illegal in British Columbia, but its use is rarely prosecuted. You may find your kids asking "What's that smell?" as you walk the streets.

PROS	CONS
■ **Vancouver,** one of the most beautiful cities in North America, is well worth visiting for a few days before or after your cruise.	■ Waters may still be iced over early in the season, so you may not be able to enter Tracy Arm.
■ Breathtaking scenery.	■ The weather can range from chilly to downright cold—and it *will* rain at some point during your cruise.
■ Ports are fairly low-key, though you can still buy that tanzanite ring you've been eyeing.	■ If shopping is a big part of your cruise experience, you'll be disappointed.
■ If you've ever wanted to see a glacier from a hot tub, here's your chance!	■ The length of the cruise plus travel time to and from Vancouver may be more than you can schedule (at least 9 days).
■ Very relaxing vibe on board.	
■ West Coasters, this is an easy trip for you.	■ Just one DCL ship, the *Wonder,* cruises Alaska, and then only during the summer.

Hubbard Glacier, Alaska

HISTORY Hubbard Glacier—the largest tidewater glacier in North America and one of eight Alaskan glaciers—is located on Disenchantment Bay, at the head of Yakutat Bay. Defying the global trend of glacial shrinkage, it is actually *increasing* in total mass and is advancing at a rate of about 85 feet per year. In 2002, the glacier advanced across the entrance to the 35-mile-long Russell Fjord, temporarily turning it into a lake. The nearest land settlement is a sport and commercial fishery in the town of Yakutat, Alaska.

WEATHER Disney Cruise Line visits Hubbard Glacier in July. Average daytime highs at this time are the mid-50s, with nighttime lows averaging in the high 40s. (*Note:* All temperatures listed in this chapter are in degrees Fahrenheit.) Typical rainfall is about 8 inches per month.

THE PORT Ships do not dock at Hubbard Glacier—there is no port. The experience is the view from aboard your ship.

TOURIST HIGHLIGHTS Hubbard Glacier is a behemoth: nearly 76 miles long, 6 miles wide, and 300 feet tall. The glacier frequently calves icebergs that are often 3–4 stories tall, sometimes as many as 10 stories. Ships must keep a safe distance—the calved icebergs sometimes splash into and shoot out of the water dramatically.

Icy Strait Point, Alaska

LANGUAGES English and Tlingit

HISTORY Icy Strait Point is located on Chichagof Island, near the town of Hoonah, Alaska. Native tribes have inhabited the area for thousands of years, primarily as fishers and hunters. In 1912, the Hoonah Packing Company built a salmon cannery nearby, becoming the major employer. The area foundered when the cannery closed in the 1950s; later, as part of the Alaska Native Claims Settlement Act of 1971, the Huna Totem Corporation was founded to stimulate job creation in the area. Huna Totem, owned by some 1,400 Alaskans with ties to native peoples (primarily the Tlingit), operates Icy Strait Point, the only privately owned tourist-cruise destination in Alaska. Cruise-ship visitors provide about half the income to the local economy.

WEATHER Disney Cruise Line visits Icy Strait Point in July. Average daytime highs during the month are in the low 60s, with average nighttime lows in the high 40s. Average precipitation for the month is about 3 inches.

THE PORT Icy Strait Point accommodates just one cruise ship at a time, so there is little chance of overcrowding on excursions or at area sights. Passengers are tendered into port at the Icy Strait Point dock, where you'll find basic services. The town of **Hoonah,** a mile away, is accessible on foot.

TOURIST HIGHLIGHTS Wilderness adventures are the focus in Icy Strait. It's located near **Point Adolphus,** one of the world's best locations for whale-watching—whales favor this area as their summer habitat so frequently, in fact, that sightings here are guaranteed by excursion operators. Icy Strait also boasts the highest density of brown grizzly bears anywhere in Alaska. Thrill seekers will enjoy the **ZipRider,** the longest zip-line experience in the United States. July is prime season for fishing, with silver, pink, and keta salmon in abundance. Kayaking and other water sports are also available, as well as a small museum and a beach area..

WHAT TO EAT The waterfront restaurants all buy their seafood from local fishermen. A specialty is Dungeness crab, often butchered and cooked while you watch.

WHAT TO BUY The historic cannery building houses 12 locally owned shops that sell such items as wood carvings, jewelry, and leatherwork. Expect to find true local crafts and few imported items. Halibut fishers may pay to have their catch processed and shipped home to them, making this a particularly personal souvenir. Other foodie take-homes include jams and candies made from local berries.

Juneau, Alaska

LANGUAGES English and Tlingit

HISTORY Juneau began as a mining camp. Gold mining was the major industry from the 1880s until the 1940s, when the last official gold mine was closed. Juneau has been the capital of Alaska since 1906, first as a district and then remaining as the government seat when Alaska became a state in 1959. Growth accelerated in the 1970s with the building of the Trans-Alaska Pipeline. Central Juneau is close to sea level and is surrounded by natural elements, including mountains, glaciers, and the Gastineau Channel. No roads lead into or out of town—travel to other areas is accomplished almost exclusively by boat or plane.

WEATHER Disney cruises dock in Juneau May–August. Average daytime highs during this period range from the mid-50s to the low 60s; nighttime lows during these months are in the low to mid-40s. Precipitation is fairly steady throughout the year. Typical rainfall ranges 4–5 inches per month during the summer.

THE PORT All ships dock within walking distance of downtown Juneau. Within a mile, you'll find the **Federal Building,** the **Governor's House,** the **State Capitol,** the **Alaska State Museum,** the **Visitor Center,** and other attractions. Shuttles and taxis service key attractions beyond downtown.

TOURIST HIGHLIGHTS Mendenhall Glacier is a primary attraction. Check at the visitor center for a guide to **walking trails** maintained by the US Forest Service. In addition to natural features, you may see **bears** fishing for salmon in glacial streams. The **Mt. Roberts Tramway** ferries guests 1,800 feet up the peak for scenic views and hiking. Points of historic interest include **St. Nicholas Russian Orthodox Church,** the oldest operating church in Alaska. Also stop by the **Red Dog Saloon,** a remnant of the mining era with an Old West atmosphere. For a walking tour that covers many of these points of interest, see page 344.

WHAT TO EAT Fresh fish is a key part of menus throughout the area. Salmon and halibut are most common, but shellfish is also easy to find. Our favorite restaurant in Alaska is **Tracy's King Crab Shack,** just steps from the dock. A moderately covered outdoor venue with a view of the harbor, Tracy's serves Alaskan king crab significantly bigger than your head. We opted for the sampler platter of crab chowder, crab cakes, and a monster crab leg, washed down with an Alaskan Brewing Company ale. A little pricey, but delish. If you ask the cook nicely, he may let you hold a crab for a fun photo op. (*Note:* We hear that Tracy's may be moving to a new location in mid-2017, so double-check their website, kingcrabshack .com, before you head over.)

WHAT TO BUY Carved Alaskan jade is abundant in souvenir shops. Also look for native arts and crafts that use natural elements such as stone, wood, and fur.

Ketchikan, Alaska

LANGUAGE English

HISTORY Ketchikan was first settled by native tribes lured by the seaside location. The area has one of the world's largest collections of standing totem poles, found both in town and scattered throughout the region, most created by the town's native founders. In the late 1800s and early 1900s, fishing and fish processing, along with lumber and lumber processing, began to attract settlers from other parts of the world. The town embodied a freewheeling, frontier spirit, with saloons and brothels aplenty. Today, Ketchikan is known in Alaska as the Salmon Capital of the World and caters to a booming tourist trade.

WEATHER Disney cruises dock in Ketchikan May–August, when average daytime highs range from the mid-50s to the mid-60s and nighttime lows from the low 40s to the low 50s. While precipitation is lowest during the summer months, Ketchikan is in a maritime-rainforest area, with abundant rainfall and cloud cover. Expect it to be wet: Typical rainfall is 6–9 inches per month during May, June, July, and August.

THE PORT Ships dock adjacent to the center of town. The town itself is just three blocks wide, and most points of interest are easily accessible from the port.

TOURIST HIGHLIGHTS An in-town highlight is the seasonal lumberjack show, where professional lumberjacks demonstrate ax throws, log rolling, and pole climbing. Those wishing to stay near port can enjoy several small museums, including the **Totem Heritage Center,** the **Tongass Historical Museum,** and the **Southeast Alaska Discovery Center.** (For a walking tour that covers these and other points of interest, see page 345.) Take a ride on the **Cape Fox Lodge** funicular, which affords spectacular views of the port and surrounding areas. Outdoor activities include kayaking, hiking, and wildlife observation.

WHAT TO EAT The local fresh fish is a must-try. Fishermen bring in frequent hauls of salmon, shrimp, crab, octopus, and more.

WHAT TO BUY Alaskan crafts such as miniature carved totems, silver and bronze sculptures, wool clothing, and regional foods are typical Ketchikan souvenirs. Our favorite souvenir purchased on any vacation is the beaver pelt we got at **Tall Tale Taxidermy,** run by the Szurley family, longtime Ketchikan residents. A stop at Tall Tale convinced Erin, a squeamish New Yorker, that taxidermy is a true art form.

Skagway, Alaska

LANGUAGE English

HISTORY Skagway was originally settled by the native Chilkoot and Chilkat peoples. Beginning in the late 1800s, Skagway became a center for gold exploration. In 1896 gold was found in the region, leading to an influx of prospectors, miners, and associated service providers. Competition among prospectors was fierce, leading to a lawless Wild West atmosphere. The gold rush was over by 1900, but the spectacular wilderness inspired many to stay and maintain the new town.

WEATHER Disney cruises dock in Skagway May–August. Average daytime highs during these months range from the mid-50s to the mid-60s, with nighttime lows averaging from the low 40s to the low 50s. Typical rainfall is 1–2 inches during the summer.

THE PORT There is no dedicated passenger terminal—cruise ships dock alongside industrial sea vessels. On the upside, the dock is an easy walk from town; there are also inexpensive buses. The entire town is accessible from one main street, **Broadway.** For a walking tour that covers the area, see page 347.

TOURIST HIGHLIGHTS At the **Klondike Gold Rush National Historical Park,** the visitor center has educational materials about the area's mining hey-day. For more-hands-on learning, try panning for gold yourself at the **Liar-sville Gold Rush Trail Camp** (see page 343 for details). **White Pass and Yukon Route Railroad,** a narrow-gauge train line, offers scenic views of mountains, waterfalls, and gorges; in **Haines,** a ferry ride away, you can enjoy watching the whales and American bald eagles. Other outdoor adventures include horseback riding, hiking, rock climbing, and dogsledding.

WHAT TO EAT Fresh fish appears on menus throughout the area. Also try the local Alaskan king crab and elk meat. *Note:* Due to the cost of shipping nonlocal food to this remote location, you may find prices here higher than you'd expect in other parts of the country.

WHAT TO BUY Skagway is a small town, catering mostly to the tourist trade, with abundant small souvenirs on offer. Typical finds include mining and railroad artifacts, hand-knit woolen garments, ceramics, carved wood, and jewelry made by local artisans. Most shops in Skagway don't open until 9 a.m. at the earliest, and there are few notable breakfast spots in town. Unless you have an early excursion, feel free to sleep a little late without feeling you're missing something.

Tracy Arm, Alaska

HISTORY Tracy Arm is a fjord—a long, narrow inlet with steep cliffs on both sides, created by glacial movement. Part of Tongass National Forest, Tracy Arm is more than 30 miles long, and ice covers about one-fifth of it. In the summer, the fjord may have significant icebergs floating in its waters.

WEATHER The weather is similar to Juneau's: Average daytime highs May–August range from the mid-50s to the low 60s, nighttime lows during these months are in the low to mid-40s, and typical rainfall is 4–5 inches per month.

THE PORT Ships do not dock at Tracy Arm—there is no port or town. The experience is the view from aboard your ship.

TOURIST HIGHLIGHTS Tracy Arm is all about the scenery of the **Sawyer Gla-ciers.** Take in the granite cliffs, icebergs, and forested mountains. You may spot wildlife such as bears, whales, bald eagles, mountain goats, and more.

About once per hour, the glaciers calve, sending massive ice sheets into the waters below. The impact of the glaciers is vastly different on different decks. Soaring vistas are best viewed from Decks 9 and 10; to spot animals, try the outdoor areas of Deck 4. If your stateroom is on a lower deck, look out your porthole from time to time. Periodically vary your location on the ship for a fuller experience.

Vancouver, British Columbia, Canada

LANGUAGE English

HISTORY Europeans first visited Vancouver in the late 1700s. The gold rush in the late 1800s brought the initial long-term settlers. Early industry focused on logging, mining, and transportation, due to the natural port. Immigrants came from England, Scotland, Ireland, and Germany, followed by an influx from China and other areas of Asia. Vancouver is now a major industrial center and cosmopolitan city bustling with high-rises, shopping, restaurants, and entertainment.

WEATHER Cruises depart from Vancouver during the summer and early fall. The average daytime highs May–September range from the low 60s to the low 70s. Average nighttime lows during those months range from the mid-40s to the mid-50s. This moderate climate makes Vancouver one of the warmest cities in Canada. Vancouver's rainfall is lowest in the summer, averaging fewer than 3 inches per month May–September.

THE PORT Disney cruises embark at the **Canada Place Cruise Terminal,** adjacent to downtown Vancouver. Within walking distance you'll find the **Pan Pacific Hotel,** along with many restaurants and bars.

TOURIST HIGHLIGHTS The **Vancouver Lookout,** near Harbour Centre, affords a panoramic overview of the city. For additional visual stimulation, check out the **Vancouver Art Gallery,** which displays more than 10,000 pieces of art. Other local attractions include **Science World,** with interactive exhibits and an Omnimax theater, and the **Vancouver Aquarium,** home to 70,000 sea creatures where whale, dolphin, and sea otter shows happen daily. The **Dr. Sun Yat-Sen Classical Chinese Garden** is the first authentic Chinese garden built outside of China. A 15-minute SkyTrain ride from Vancouver will take you to **Metropolis at Metrotown,** British Columbia's largest shopping center.

John Lee's *Walking Vancouver* (Wilderness Press) can show you other great places to explore in the city. For additional suggestions in this guide, see page 74.

WHAT TO EAT You can find nearly every world cuisine represented in the restaurants of Vancouver. Local seafood is a must. For authentic Asian dishes, visit the **Chinatown** district. **Granville Island** is a public market with fresh local seafood and produce; walk among the dozens of stalls to taste the best from local vendors.

WHAT TO BUY No trip to Canada would be complete without the purchase of something maple—syrup, candy, even mustard. Find silk robes in Chinatown, local crafts at Granville Island, and gear representing the Vancouver Canucks hockey team everywhere.

ATLANTIC CANADA

(Note: *This itinerary is not offered every year.*)

CRUISES SAIL FROM New York City

SHIP *Magic*

CRUISE LENGTHS 4–7 nights

DATES Early fall

WHAT TO PACK Rain jacket, umbrella

SIGNATURE PORT ADVENTURE Boat trip plus a lobster dinner

COMMENTS Cruises to Canada's eastern coast are a great option for anyone who can easily get to New York City—which is most of us. (DCL unhelpfully designates this region as "Canadian Coastline"—as if Canada had just one coast.) Because these stops aren't primarily tourist destinations, you get a special experience that isn't focused first and foremost on selling you stuff. Your ship will often be the only one in port, which makes for a relaxing day ashore. This cruise is a perfect fall-break vacation if you just want to get away for less than a week and be pampered while someone else does the cooking and makes your bed.

PROS	CONS
■ Nice change from beach-based cruises.	■ Not much in the way of shopping.
■ Canada residents: no need for currency exchange. US residents: Remember to pick up some loonies (Canadian dollar coins) before you embark.	■ Just a couple of ports.
	■ Your kids may not be keen on a cruise where a highlight is looking at lighthouses.
■ Lots of competition for transportation to New York City, whether by air, train, or car. Good deals can be found.	■ Itinerary is offered only on the *Magic,* and then not every year.

Bar Harbor, Maine

LANGUAGE English

HISTORY Bar Harbor is located on Mount Desert Island, named in 1604 by French explorer Samuel du Champlain when he looked at the mountains that rise up from the sea. He called this place *Île des Monts Deserts,* or "Island of Barren Mountains"—a misleading appellation considering that the island is actually covered in forest. A few years later, French Jesuits set up a mission on the island, which was contested by the British. The French and British regularly swapped control of the area until France's defeat in the Seven Years' War, which ended in 1763. In the 1840s, American landscape artists Thomas Cole and Frederic Church visited the region. Their paintings kindled the imaginations of the American public and spurred interest in the natural beauty of the island. The mid-1800s saw an influx of tourists, including Gilded Age millionaires, and the construction of numerous hotels and mansions to accommodate them. To prevent the area from becoming an overbuilt playground, locals petitioned the federal government for protection, and in 1916 much of the island was declared a national park. Bar Harbor, however, reinvented itself during the last half of the 20th century as a mecca for travelers in search of pristine wilderness.

WEATHER   Disney Cruise Line visits Bar Harbor in late September. During this time, daytime highs average in the mid-60s, with nighttime lows averaging in the high 40s. Average rainfall is 5 inches per month.

THE PORT   Bar Harbor is a tender port. Ships anchor in the harbor and passengers are transported to land on smaller boats, or tenders, which dock at **Town Pier,** adjacent to downtown Bar Harbor. The shopping district, which has cafés, banks, and other services, is within a 10-minute walk from the dock. A small number of taxis may be available at the pier, but there are no rental-car agencies in town—the closest place to rent a car is at the Bar Harbor airport, about 30 minutes away from town via taxi or shuttle. A free shuttle bus called **Island Explorer** links Bar Harbor with Acadia National Park and other communities on the island; see exploreacadia.com for schedules.

TOURIST HIGHLIGHTS   The area's primary draw is the great outdoors. Explore the coastline by kayak, or embark on a whale-watching tour. **Acadia National Park** is Bar Harbor's island neighbor. Use the hiking and biking trails to see the park's attractions, including **Cadillac Mountain,** the highest peak on the East Coast; **Sand Beach,** covered with pulverized shells; and **Thunder Hole,** where the surf races into a naturally carved inlet and explodes high into the air. On an autumn port stop, your visit may occur during prime leaf-peeping season—don't forget your camera. If you'd rather stay close to town, nearby **Agamont Park** has a shore path that follows the sea wall for more than a mile and from which you can see mansions of a bygone era, as well as the rocky coast. Bar Harbor is also home to a few small museums. The **Abbe Museum** is dedicated to the history of the native Wabanaki people. The **George B. Dorr Museum of Natural History** includes exhibits on Maine's natural ecosystems. The **Mount Desert Oceanarium & Lobster Hatchery** is a working museum offering tours of a lobster farm and salt-marsh tours.

WHAT TO EAT   When in Maine, one pronounces its ubiquitous crustacean "lobstah." Get your lobster steamed with butter, broiled with breadcrumbs, baked into a pie, spun into a creamy bisque, or mixed with mayo and piled on a toasted hot dog bun. Order a side of corn on the cob and finish off your with a hefty slab of blueberry pie, and you've consumed the quintessential Maine seashore meal. Not in the mood for seafood? Several spots offer wood-fired pizzas. Wash it all down with beer from the local **Atlantic Brewing Company.**

WHAT TO BUY   The classic Maine souvenir shop is **Cool as a Moose,** which sells everything from boxer shorts to sweatshirts emblazoned with cartoon bears and moose. Kids will find plush bears, moose, and, yes, lobsters to cuddle. More-substantial items include kitchenware, such as coasters and cutting boards made from the wood of nearby forests. if you venture into the Bangor area, look for wearables from the **University of Maine** emblazoned with its black bear mascot. If you're in the mood for edible souvenirs, try one of the many jams, sauces, syrups, or baked goods produced by Maine's **Stonewall Kitchen.**

Charlottetown, Prince Edward Island, Canada

LANGUAGES English, French

HISTORY The French explorer Jacques Cartier was looking for a route to China when he stumbled onto what is now called Prince Edward Island in 1534. French settlers followed him to the island, which they christened Île Saint-Jean; their small settlement, called Port-La-Joye, was located near present-day Charlottetown. During King George's War in the mid-1700s, the British captured the island, followed by a French retaliation and a British reclamation. At the end of the French and Indian War in 1763, the French ceded their Canadian possessions, including Île Saint-Jean, to Britain. A new harbor was named for Queen Charlotte (hence "Charlottetown"), the wife of the reigning monarch at the time, King George III. The island's population again looked to the family of King George III for a name in the late 1700s. They successfully petitioned the sovereign for permission to change the name of the island to Prince Edward Island after Prince Edward Augustus, George's fifth child and the father of Queen Victoria.

In the mid-19th century, representatives from Prince Edward Island, Nova Scotia, New Brunswick, and the then-combined colony of Ontario and Quebec met in Charlottetown to discuss creating a confederation that would be a dominion under the British crown. The talks eventually led to the formation of Canada on July 1, 1867. During World War II, Charlottetown served as a Royal Canadian Air Force location; Charlottetown's shipyards also saw extensive use during World War II for refits and upgrades to numerous Royal Canadian Navy warships. Postwar development saw the expansion of residential communities. In 1997, the Confederation Bridge was completed; the world's longest bridge spanning ice-covered water, it links Prince Edward Island to the rest of Canada via New Brunswick. As a result, a substantial tourist industry has developed, with vacationers crossing the bridge to enjoy Prince Edward Island's attractions.

WEATHER Disney Cruise Line visits Charlottetown in October, when daytime highs average in the low 50s and nighttime lows average in the high 30s. Expect average rainfall of 4 inches per month. There is a slight possibility of snow near the end of October.

THE PORT Ships dock near the town center. Shops, cafés, and other services are found within a 10-minute walk. **Founder's Hall,** across from the terminal, offers free Wi-Fi. Shuttles and taxis are available, as are rental cars. Other popular forms of transportation in the area include tours via double-decker bus and horse-drawn trolley.

TOURIST HIGHLIGHTS The **Confederation Centre of the Arts** includes a museum and two galleries. **Province House National Historic Site** is considered the birthplace of Canada, having hosted the Charlottetown Conference, where the concept of Canada was established. Fans of the *Anne of Green Gables* book series will want to visit locations dedicated to the Canadian author L. M. Montgomery and her work, including **Green Gables Heritage Place,** the **Bideford Parsonage Museum,** and **Avonlea Village,** a simulation of the hamlet depicted in the novels. While the weather will be too cold for swimming during your visit, the area beaches are a lovely place for nature hikes. Discover wonderful photo opportunities at one of the island's many historic lighthouses. **Prince Edward Island National Park** is another prime spot for outdoor exploring.

WHAT TO EAT The food industry is the largest contributor to the provincial economy, with farming and fishing as primary industries. Area restaurants feature fresh oysters, mussels, and lobster. Potatoes—the island's largest agricultural commodity—are a cherished local side dish, whether mashed, baked, or in salads, *galettes* (pancakes), and even stir-fries and scones. **Myriad View Distillery** produces a moonshine that's sure to put you in a happy mood, as will a craft beer from **Upstreet Craft Brewing.** The preferred place for dessert is **Cow's Ice Cream,** which has a number of humorously named flavors, including Wowie Cowie, Gooey Mooey, Cowberry, Calfe Latte, and Fluff 'n Udder. Also try their "Cow Chips"—chocolate-covered potato chips; Prince Edward Island residents can't get enough of them.

WHAT TO BUY Charlottetown is a village of crafters and artisans. Look for woven goods including throws and apparel, as well as yarn made from local wool. Pottery, earthenware, and ironwork are fashioned into decorative and practical items. The **Charlottetown Farmers Market** sells a wide variety of fresh, prepared, and packaged foods. Handmade soaps are another area specialty. Many Prince Edward Island visitors purchase souvenirs related to the *Anne of Green Gables* stories.

Halifax, Nova Scotia, Canada

LANGUAGE English

HISTORY The first known settlers of the Halifax area were the Acadians and the Mi'kmaq people. European settlement began in earnest when the British staked claim in the mid-1700s, leading to "Father LeLoutre's War," a dispute between the native peoples and the British. The French and Indian War spurred the establishment of the Halifax Naval Yard in 1759. The late 1700s saw a modest immigration boom comprising Germans, Dutch, New Englanders, and residents of Martinique and many other areas. During the American Revolution, Halifax became a staging area for British invasions of the colonies. The British naval stronghold remained throughout the Napoleonic wars and the War of 1812. Throughout the 1800s, Halifax was a key point for trade between Canada and Europe. In 1912, recovery efforts for the *Titanic* disaster were based in Halifax. During both World Wars, Halifax was a launch point for British efforts against their enemies. Current industries include tourism, shipping, and fishing.

WEATHER Disney Cruise Line visits Halifax in late September and early October, when daytime highs average in the high 50s and nighttime lows average in the high 40s. Typical rainfall in autumn averages fewer than 1.5 inches per month.

THE PORT The dock has minimal services. The waterfront area is easily accessible on foot. Shops, restaurants, and banking services are all within a 10-minute walk. Taxis are available near the pier, as are bicycle rentals. Car-rental desks can be found near the **Westin Nova Scotian** hotel, a 5-minute walk from the ship.

TOURIST HIGHLIGHTS **Halifax Citadel National Historic Site** is a star-shaped naval station in the center of the city. Costumed guides lead tours of musket galleries, earthen ramparts, garrison cells, and guard rooms. The **Canadian Museum of Immigration at Pier 21** is a National Historic Site focused on the experiences of immigrants as they arrived in Canada. The **Maritime Museum of the Atlantic** includes an extensive exhibit on the *Titanic.* Beer loves will want to sample the wares at **Alexander Keith's Brewery,** a local brewhouse since 1820; the **Garrison Brewery Tour** offers another view of beer-making. Also look for a pop-up farmers market near the pier that sells fresh and prepared food for purchase. For a look at classic maritime scenery, take a drive to nearby **Peggy's Cove,** a fishing village known for its picturesque lighthouse. Animal lovers will want to book a whale-watching excursion during their time in Halifax.

WHAT TO EAT Seafood reigns in Halifax. Look for lobster prepared in many styles, including lobster rolls, boiled, and broiled. Other favorites include scallops, haddock, crab, mussels, smoked eel, and jarred pickled fish. Lunenburg pork sausage is often used as the base of hearty stews or fresh fried. Many main dishes are served with cabbage or root vegetables including potatoes, carrots, and onions. "Rappie pie" isn't a pie at all; rather, it's a casserole of potatoes and chicken broth, often served with butter or molasses. Tasty local blueberries are baked into muffins, pancakes, and other goodies. A locally legendary sweet treat is the "Fat Archie": a big cookie made with molasses, cinnamon, and (usually) raisins. There are several artisanal breweries near Halifax; look for local ales to accompany your meal, particularly those from Alexander Keith.

WHAT TO BUY Halifax is known for its fine-crystal production; look for hand-blown pieces. Pewter items are also popular, as are kitchen items embellished with images of lobsters or nautical symbols. A jar of blueberry jam makes a nice take-home gift.

New York, New York   *(See page 321 for full profile.)*

Saint John, New Brunswick, Canada

Note: *Not to be confused with **St. John's, Newfoundland and Labrador,** which is a stop on DCL's Transatlantic itineraries (see page 325).*

LANGUAGE English

HISTORY The original inhabitants of New Brunswick were the Passamaquoddy and Maliseet peoples. Among the first Europeans to visit in the area was Frenchman Samuel de Champlain, in 1604. French fortifications were in place by the 1630s. Various French, British, and New England factions scuffled about during the 17th and 18th centuries. In 1785, by royal charter, the City of Saint John became the first incorporated city in Canada. In the mid-1800s, Saint John served as a quarantine station for European immigrants, particularly Irish, to receive medical screening before being admitted to North America. Shipbuilding became a major industry in the later 1800s and remained so into the early 21st century.

WEATHER Disney Cruise Line visits Saint John in September and October. Daytime highs during these months average in the high 50s to low 60s, with nighttime lows in the low to high 40s and average rainfall of about 4 inches per month.

THE PORT The ship docks near the city center. The port area has basic services. Many tourist attractions lie within a 15-minute walk of the terminal; taxis are readily available. For a romantic twist, let a horse-drawn trolley take you around town.

TOURIST HIGHLIGHTS **Saint John City Market** is a large structure housing independent vendors who sell everything from baked goods, cheese, and chocolate to jewelry, sculptures, and scenic photography—bring cash, because many vendors don't take credit cards. **The New Brunswick Museum** has exhibits devoted to logging, shipbuilding, and whaling; special kids' experiences may be available depending on when you visit. If you can time it right, the **Reversing Falls** are a unique natural phenomenon in which high tides in the Bay of Fundy cause the Saint John River to reverse its flow. You can watch the river run backwards from one of several lookouts. Another outdoor possibility is **Irving Nature Park,** which has walking trails and lovely views. **Moosehead Brewery,** Canada's oldest independent beer producer, offers tours and samples. **Stonehammer Geopark,** in southern New Brunswick, is the only North American member of the UNESCO-supported Global Geoparks Network. To experience it, take a guided tour at **Rockwood Park.**

WHAT TO EAT The seafood is wonderful here: baked oysters, fish chowder, bacon-wrapped scallops, lobster rolls. A local variation on Quebeçois *poutine* (fries, cheese curds, and gravy) is *poutines râpées*—dumplings made with raw grated potato, cooked potato, and salt pork, formed into balls, simmered, and served with brown sugar or molasses. Other traditional dishes of the region include *fricot à la poule,* chicken cooked with summer savory, potato, and dumplings; *fricot aux coques,* or clam stew; and *tourtière,* a savory pie of ground pork seasoned with cinnamon and cloves. (Nobody makes *tourtière* as good as Erin's grandma's Christmas-morning version, but you can find good facsimiles in Saint John.) Many desserts are flavored with locally harvested apples or maple. If you want a truly Canadian edible experience, stop by the local **Tim Horton's** for coffee and doughnuts.

WHAT TO BUY **Moosehead** beer rules in Saint John. Bring home a T-shirt, cap, or stein emblazoned with the brewery's logo. Other popular items include books about the area, depictions of the Canadian flag, and maple products such as candies and syrups.

Sydney, Nova Scotia, Canada

LANGUAGE English

HISTORY The indigenous residents of the area were ancestors of the Mi'kmaq people. In the 1700s, the colonial town of Old Sydney was founded by British loyalists fleeing the American Revolution. It served as the English capital of Cape Breton from its founding until 1820, when the island colony and its rich coal fields became part of Nova Scotia. Coal mining brought industry to the region, and in the early 1900s Sydney become a major steel-manufacturing center. But the prosperity brought by coal and steel diminished as plants closed in the second half of the 20th century. Today, Sydney's primary industries are tourism and call centers.

WEATHER Disney Cruise Line visits Sydney in October, when daytime highs average in the low 50s and nighttime lows average in the low 40s. October typically sees about 5 inches of rain over the course of the month; there's also a small possibility of snow in late October.

THE PORT The dock is adjacent to town. Expect a 5-minute walk to **Charlotte Street** and the city center. Services are all within walking distance, but taxis may be available. One quirk of the port is that it is home to the world's largest fiddle: Fidheal Mhor A' Ceilidh—the Big Fiddle of the Ceilidh. (You can't miss it.) The cruise pavilion itself is home to a market that houses craft vendors, along with a small museum dedicated to Cape Breton Island history.

TOURIST HIGHLIGHTS A highlight of the Sydney area is the **Alexander Graham Bell National Historic Site,** which focuses on Bell's life and work. The **Fortress of Louisbourg National Historic Site** is the largest historical reconstruction in North America; see soldiers' living quarters, cannons, and additional exhibits related to the fishing industry. At the **Underground Cape Breton Miners Museum,** you can follow a retired coal miner below ground to observe what his average workday was like. For outdoor fun, sail the **Bras D'Or Lakes** for bird-watching, or drive the **Cabot Trail** for stunning vistas.

WHAT TO EAT Fresh seafood is plentiful in Sydney. Boiled lobster is common, as are many variations of fish chowder. Blueberries are plentiful in the summer; eat them as is or find them prepared in muffins, cobblers, and pies. Maple syrup and maple candies make a nice take-home treat. Oat cakes are a traditional sweet treat.

WHAT TO BUY Nova Scotia is known for its fine woolen goods: hats, scarves, and mittens as well as woolen home goods such as tablecloths. Pewter mugs and plates are common. Also find the work of local artists sold in shops near the port.

CALIFORNIA COAST

CRUISES SAIL FROM San Diego or Vancouver

SHIP *Wonder*

CRUISE LENGTHS 7 days or fewer

DATES Before and after the Alaskan runs

WHAT TO PACK Walking shoes, sunscreen

SIGNATURE PORT ADVENTURE City tour—but you're better off exploring on your own.

CLASSIC ADD-ON Disneyland

PROS	CONS
▪ Can be very affordable, particularly if you live on the West Coast.	▪ We don't think this is the best way to see California.
▪ Short cruises are easy on your schedule.	

Cabo San Lucas, Mexico   *(See page 317 for full profile.)*

Ensenada, Mexico

LANGUAGE Spanish

HISTORY The Yuma Indians were the first known inhabitants of the region. Portugal's João Rodrigues Cabrilho conducted the first European exploration of the area in the mid-1500s. Ensenada was founded September 17, 1542, as San Mateo. In 1602 it was renamed Ensenada de Todos Santos ("Bay of All Saints") by Sebastián Vizcaíno, a Spanish explorer and diplomat. The Jesuits were the city's first permanent settlers, in the 17th century. Following a Jesuit ouster in 1768, Dominican brothers took control of the region. Ensenada became the capital of Baja California in 1882; its growth was interrupted by the Mexican Revolution. In the 1920s, prohibition of alcohol in the United States played a role in the eventual rebound of the area, as thirsty Americans began to look south for a source of booze. Today, tourism and fishing are prominent industries.

WEATHER Disney Cruise Line visits Ensenada in May and October. Average daytime highs during both these months are in the mid-70s, with variable precipitation and average nighttime lows in the mid- to high 50s. Rainfall averages fewer than 2 inches a month throughout the year.

THE PORT Cruise ships dock in the same area as commercial and fishing vessels. Near the dock, numerous pop-up vendors sell typical tourist items; there is also a drugstore along with a few cafés. From here it's a 15-minute walk to the **Avenida Lopez Mateos** tourist area. Taxis and shuttles are also available.

TOURIST HIGHLIGHTS **La Bufadora** is a natural marine blowhole about 20 miles south of town. The best beaches are 5 miles south of Ensenada, in the small town of **Chapultepec.** Activities there include horseback riding, surf fishing, and Jet Skiing. **Riviera del Pacifico,** formerly an exclusive and glamorous hotel (and, according to local lore, the birthplace of the margarita), is now a civic center. If you're in the mood for some culture, try the **Museo de Historia** or the **Estero Beach Museum** for a look at local art and artifacts.

WHAT TO EAT In two words, fresh fish. Look for halibut, clams, oysters, abalone, tuna, and more. The area's signature dish is the fish taco, typically prepared with battered, fried white fish; shredded cabbage; avocado; and a spicy mayonnaise. (If you order from a stand or a street cart, exercise caution—if there's a crowd, indicating rapid turnover, then the food is generally safe to eat.) When it comes to tipples, you'll find a large selection of beers in most restaurants, as well as the ubiquitous margarita in all manner of incarnations. Or pick up a bottle of *vino* at one of the area wineries.

WHAT TO BUY Tacky-T-shirt stands abound near the dock—make a game of trying to find the most entertaining examples. You'll also find the usual piñatas, painted maracas, and straw hats. Blankets, leather goods, and logoed shot glasses are everywhere. Note that many items advertised as silver are really tin or other soft metal. Numerous stores sell Cuban cigars—which you can bring back to the US as of October 2016. Many cruisers use a stop in Ensenada to stock up on medications for which you need a prescription in the United States but not in Mexico—use your best judgment.

San Diego, California

LANGUAGE English

HISTORY San Diego is the site of the first European settlement in what is now California, a result of exploration conducted in 1542 by João Rodrigues Cabrilho of Portugal. Subsequent European visitors were primarily from Spain. The first permanent mission in the area was established in 1769, with a population of Spanish settlers arriving in 1774. In 1821 Mexico claimed the area in the Mexican War for Independence. In 1850 California became part of the United States. A significant naval presence began in 1901, solidifying San Diego as a major West Coast port. Today, San Diego is a center of high-tech industry.

WEATHER Disney cruises visit San Diego in May, September, and October. The average daytime high temperature in May is in the high 60s, with average nighttime lows in the high 50s. Average daytime highs in September and October are in the mid-70s, while average nighttime lows are in the mid- to low 60s. Precipitation during all three months is minimal, with an average of less than an inch of rainfall per month.

THE PORT Cruise ships dock at the **B Street Cruise Terminal,** directly adjacent to downtown. An upscale mall, **Horton Plaza,** featuring a flagship Nordstrom store, is a 10-minute walk away. Public transportation and taxis are readily available for more-distant jaunts.

TOURIST HIGHLIGHTS **Balboa Park** is home to gorgeous gardens and 15 different museums, including the **San Diego Museum of Art** and the **San Diego Natural History Museum.** The **San Diego Zoo** is one of the few places in the United States where you can see giant pandas. Theme-park fans will want to visit **SeaWorld** and **Legoland.** The **Gaslamp Quarter** and the **San Diego missions** provide insight into the history of the area. **Tijuana, Mexico,** is 17 miles south of San Diego; check on legal restrictions if you plan to drive there.

WHAT TO EAT San Diego is a major metropolitan area whose restaurants serve all major cuisines. The offerings at many local restaurants are influenced by nearby Mexico: quesadillas, tacos, burritos, enchiladas, and such. Because of the city's seaside location, fresh fish is another local menu staple. A regional favorite is cioppino, a stew with fish, clams, shrimp, squid, and mussels, often served with toast.

WHAT TO BUY Sports fans will want to purchase jerseys of the local *Padres* baseball, **Chargers** football, or **San Diego State Aztecs** sports teams. Pick up clothing or shell-based jewelry, or choose some art reflecting the surf culture. Local tequila is a popular food gift.

San Francisco, California

LANGUAGE English

HISTORY The first European settlers in the area were Spaniards, who arrived in 1769 and established the Presidio of San Francisco in 1776. By the early 1800s, the Bay Area had become part of Mexico. In 1846 the United States claimed California in the Mexican-American War, and two years later, the gold rush brought an influx of miners and prospectors to the West, resulting in massive and rapid growth of the area. In 1906 a major earthquake and fire destroyed much of the city. Many edifices were rebuilt in a grand Beaux Arts style. The Golden Gate and Oakland Bay Bridges were built in 1936–37, allowing farther expansion to outlying areas. In the 1950s and '60s, San Francisco's North Beach and Haight-Ashbury neighborhoods became the Meccas of America's counterculture.

WEATHER DCL visits San Francisco in May. The weather is mild to moderate year-round. When you visit, you can expect average daytime highs in the 60s and average nighttime lows in the upper 40s to mid-50s. Rainfall in May is light, with slightly more than half an inch for the month. The (in) famous San Francisco fog doesn't hit until summer.

THE PORT Disney cruises dock at **Pier 35,** which has minimal services. Steps away, however, you'll find the **Fisherman's Wharf** shopping and dining area. Also nearby, taxis, buses, and the **Bay Area Rapid Transit** system can take you into the heart of the city, just 10 minutes away.

TOURIST HIGHLIGHTS Watch the ships, eat the snacks, and gaze at the Golden Gate from Fisherman's Wharf. For a somber look into American penal history, take the nearby ferry over to the infamous **Alcatraz** penitentiary. Wander into **Chinatown** to dine and shop. Take in a museum, such as the **San Francisco Museum of Modern Art,** the **Fine Arts Museum of San Francisco,** or the **Walt Disney Family Museum.** For an outdoor experience, take a hike among the giant redwoods of **Muir Woods National Monument.** Or drive out of town for a visit to the Napa and Sonoma wine country. To immerse yourself in the city's famed gay culture, visit the **Castro District.** Of course, no trip to San Francisco would be complete without a ride on a cable car past **Lombard Street,** said to be the crookedest street in the world.

For more jumping-off points, we suggest Tom Downs's *Walking San Francisco* (Wilderness Press).

WHAT TO EAT Virtually all major cuisines are represented in San Francisco. Along Fisherman's Wharf, look for seafood in all forms, particularly chowder. Sourdough bread is an area specialty, often serving as a chowder bowl as well as a side dish. The vineyards north of the city make San Francisco a wine lover's paradise. Authentic Chinese dishes abound in Chinatown. The **Ghirardelli** chocolate factory no longer offers tours, but the ice-cream shop is still out of this world.

WHAT TO BUY For children, a toy cable car is a fun gift. Pick up some silks or carved stone in Chinatown. Sports fans will want jerseys representing the local teams, and foodies will want to pick up some Ghirardelli chocolate, a sourdough starter, or a fabulous bottle of wine.

Vancouver, British Columbia, Canada   *(See page 236 for full profile.)*

Victoria, British Columbia, Canada

LANGUAGE English

HISTORY British settlement in Victoria began in the mid-1840s as a Hudson Bay trading post. Not long after this, the Fraser Canyon Gold Rush brought an influx of prospectors. The port then became a naval base and the commercial center of British Columbia. Victoria was designated the capital of British Columbia after the territory became a Canadian province in 1871. Today, the city is home to thriving fishing and shipbuilding industries and is a nascent technological hub. The scenic harbor is also a major tourist destination.

WEATHER DCL cruises visit Victoria in September, when daytime highs average in the high 60s and nighttime lows in the high 40s. September rainfall averages slightly more than an inch.

THE PORT The Victoria ship terminal is about 1 mile from downtown but has no facilities. Take a scenic walk through **Beacon Hill Park,** or take a shuttle or taxi.

TOURIST HIGHLIGHTS For lovers of flora, the sunken garden at **Butchart Gardens** is just one of the popular beauty spots in Victoria, known as the City of Gardens. Many remnants of Victoria's British heritage—including double-decker buses and horse-drawn carriages—remain, and the **Empress Hotel** serves a proper English tea. **Craigdarroch Castle,** a 19th-century edifice, affords panoramic city vistas and displays an impressive collection of antique furnishings. For a dose of history, visit the **Royal British Columbia Museum,** which owns more than 7 million artifacts, including an intact woolly mammoth. Outdoors enthusiasts will enjoy walking trails along the Pacific Ocean, as well as scuba diving, kayaking, and marine-life observation. Victoria is also home to a vibrant **Chinatown.**

WHAT TO EAT Victoria is a modern city, with restaurants featuring most major cuisines. Pacific cod, salmon, and halibut are on menus throughout Victoria. For Asian favorites such as noodles and broth, venture into Chinatown.

WHAT TO BUY Look for native crafts such as jewelry and carvings. You can find tea and tea-service items in the Anglophile shops. **Fort Street** is known as Antique Row due to the many older trinkets for sale in the shops along this thoroughfare. Visit Chinatown for silks, fans, and Asian ornaments.

CARIBBEAN *and* BAHAMAS

CRUISES SAIL FROM Port Canaveral, Miami, Galveston, New York

SHIPS *Dream* and *Fantasy* (year-round), *Magic* and *Wonder* (fall, winter, and spring)

CRUISE LENGTHS 3–7 nights, occasionally 8, 10, and 11

DATES Year-round

WHAT TO PACK Sunscreen, shorts, swimsuits, shoes that you don't mind getting sandy

SIGNATURE PORT ADVENTURE Castaway Cay

CLASSIC DISNEY ADD-ON Walt Disney World, Disney's Vero Beach Resort

COMMENTS Chances are if you're cruising Disney, you're on a Caribbean or Bahamian cruise. Given that two of DCL's ships sail the Caribbean and Bahamas exclusively and the other two spend half the year there, the

CARIBBEAN AND BAHAMAS

PROS	CONS
■ Nearly all major cruise lines operate in the Caribbean, which means Disney has to keep its pricing somewhat in line with other companies'.	■ The port experience (except at Castaway Cay) is *very* commercial.
■ Ports are easy to get to.	■ Your ship will most likely be on one of many in port.
■ The US dollar is accepted in all ports, and English is spoken everywhere.	■ If you're not at least a little creative, DCL's Caribbean port stops can blend into one big duty-free-jewelry/hair-braiding/frozen-cocktail blur.
■ Castaway Cay is on nearly every Caribbean itinerary.	
■ Cruises can be combined with Walt Disney World vacations.	■ The summer heat can be oppressive.
■ You have your choice of ships and cruise lengths.	

numbers are in your favor if you're looking for sun and fun. You may ask yourself, why is Bahamas singled out from the rest of the Caribbean? Because the *Dream* cruises only to Nassau and Castaway Cay, which are both Bahamian ports.

HEALTH CONSIDERATIONS In 2016, the US Centers for Disease Control and Prevention issued health warnings for many Caribbean destinations visited by DCL, stating, "Because Zika infection in a pregnant woman causes severe birth defects, pregnant women should consult with their health-care provider and, if they decide to travel, strictly follow steps to prevent mosquito bites." For more information, including the latest list of affected locations, consult cdc.gov/travel/page/zika-travel-information.

Basseterre, St. Kitts and Nevis

LANGUAGE English

HISTORY Early native inhabitants of St. Kitts were the Saladoid people, followed by the Igneri, Arawak, and Carib. The first European claim, in 1493, was by a Spanish expedition led by Christopher Columbus. About 50 years later, a French settlement ruled the area. This was replaced in 1623 by an English colony, which was almost immediately usurped by the French again. During the 17th and 18th centuries, island rule repeatedly flipped between the English and French. In 1783, the British finally wrested control. In 1883, St. Kitts joined with Nevis and Anguilla under one independent government. Anguilla left this arrangement in 1971.

WEATHER In 2017, DCL will make port stops in Basseterre throughout the year. Temperatures are consistent year-round, with daytime highs averaging in the 80s and nighttime lows averaging in the 70s year-round. Rainfall varies from an average low of 2–3 inches per month during the winter to a high of about 5 inches during the fall.

THE PORT Built in 2005, the St. Kitts cruise terminal is home to several restaurants and shops. The town of Basseterre is a 15-minute walk from the pier. Taxis are readily available.

TOURIST HIGHLIGHTS **Brimstone Hill Fortress** is a well-preserved 17th-century military fortification. During clear weather, you can see six neighboring islands from this point. **Romney Manor** is a colonial estate from the same era. The Carib petroglyphs at **Wingfield Manor Estate** show artwork and communication by the island's native inhabitants. The center of Basseterre, called the **Circus,** is home to art galleries, bookstores, and craft shops. Sun worshippers will find several local beaches on which to loll.

WHAT TO EAT Fresh fish, often served with rice and beans, is a staple in this island nation. Jerk and Creole seasonings are prevalent on most menus. The national dish is stewed saltfish with plantains and coconut dumplings. Other typical foods include roast pig or goat, goat stew, *rikkita* beef (marinated with curry and hot pepper), and mango-glazed chicken. Popular side dishes are sweet potatoes, breadfruit, and cassava. Sweets include jam cake, pineapple cake, and tropical fruit. Rum is the adult beverage of choice.

WHAT TO BUY St. Kitts is home to the **Caribelle Batik Factory,** offering colorfully dyed fabric and clothing. Also look for woven hats and bags, pottery, paintings, and carved statuary. Foodies will want to take home packaged sugar cakes and bottles of local rum.

Bridgetown, Barbados

LANGUAGE English

HISTORY The first Europeans in Barbados were Spanish explorers in the late 1400s, but neither they nor a Portuguese expedition in the early 1500s established permanent outposts. A British ship, the *Olive Blossom,* arrived on the island in 1624, claiming it for King James; Barbados then became a British colony. This is one of the few Caribbean islands that was under constant control by one nation for several hundred contiguous years. As such, the British influence is particularly pronounced here: Cars drive on the left side of the road, and most churches are Anglican. Barbados became independent in 1966.

WEATHER In 2017, Disney cruises visit Barbados during the spring, when average daytime highs are in the low to mid–80s and average nighttime lows are in the low to mid–70s. Rainfall during this time is typically light to moderate, at 2–4 inches per month.

THE PORT Basic services, including a duty-free shop and a tourist-information desk, are located at the terminal. The village of Bridgetown is about 1 mile away from the pier. Grab a taxi if you don't feel like walking.

TOURIST HIGHLIGHTS Nature enthusiasts should visit **Harrison's Cave,** with natural stalactite formations and waterfalls. **Orchid World** inspires gardeners. History lovers will enjoy the **Barbados Museum,** home to artifacts related to Barbadian heritage. For a taste of agricultural history, visit the **Morgan Lewis windmill,** one of only two remaining functional sugar windmills in the world. The **Mount Gay Distilleries,** renowned for its rum, conducts factory tours. There are also many nearby beaches for sunning and snorkeling.

WHAT TO EAT The food of Barbados shows influences from England, Portugal, Spain, and West Africa. Fish is in ample supply here. Look for it in flying fish (with a mustard-and-onion sauce) and fish cakes. Other popular dishes include pepper pot (a spicy stew made with beef, chicken, or seafood, enriched with coconut and hot pepper), peas and rice, candied sweet potatoes, and pudding and souse (pig intestines stuffed with sweet potatoes). Side dishes may include macaroni and cheese or locally grown asparagus and okra. Local sweets include tamarind balls, guava cheese, chocolate fudge, coconut bread, and peanut brittle. The adult beverage of choice is Mount Gay rum.

WHAT TO BUY Popular Barbadian take-home items include replica monkey jars, which were traditionally used to keep water cool. Other desired souvenirs include carved wood, leather goods, jewelry in the shape of fish or dolphins, and handmade soaps and lotions. Epicureans will bring home local rum, bottled local hot-pepper sauce, or packaged rum cake.

Castaway Cay, Bahamas *(also see Parts Ten and Twelve)*

LANGUAGE English

HISTORY Disney Cruise Line entered into a 99-year lease agreement with the Bahamian government in 1999, giving the cruise line the rights to develop what was then called Gorda Cay. Renamed Castaway Cay by Disney, the island measures about 1.5 square miles and sits in the Atlantic Ocean, roughly 80 miles north-northeast of Nassau, at about the same latitude as Fort Lauderdale, Florida (100 miles west).

WEATHER Castaway Cay is a year-round destination, but no matter when you visit, it's gonna be either warm or hot. Average high temperatures gradually increase from around 76 in late December–January to a peak of 89 in August before they drop again. Low temperatures are also moderate, from 62 in late January to 76 throughout the summer. Rain patterns follow the Atlantic hurricane season, with peak rainfall occurring late August–early November. Precipitation is lightest December–May.

TOURIST HIGHLIGHTS Less than 10% of Castaway Cay has been developed for cruise guests, but Disney packs plenty of activities into that relatively small space, including two family beaches; one adults-only beach; separate lagoons for boating and snorkeling; a teens-only hangout; basketball, soccer, and volleyball areas; and bike trails. Two open-air trams connect the dock with these areas.

WHAT TO EAT Castaway Cay has three all-you-care-to-eat outdoor restaurants: **Cookie's BBQ, Cookie's Too,** and **Serenity Bay BBQ.** Each restaurant serves the same menu of grilled hot dogs, hamburgers, veggie burgers, chicken, fish, and ribs. Sides include corn on the cob, coleslaw, various salads, and similar picnic food, plus cookies and soft-serve ice cream for dessert. They're generally open 11 a.m.–2 p.m. Serenity Bay BBQ is at the adults-only Serenity Bay beach—no guests under age 18.

All of Castaway Cay's bars serve similar drinks. **Conched Out Bar,** near the gazebo, is the largest bar but has only outdoor seating.

Sand Bar, near the Castaway Cay family beach, is a small shack with a couple of serving windows, specializing in beer and frozen drinks. A limited amount of shaded bench seating is available. **Castaway Air Bar,** near the Serenity Bay adult beach, is the quietest of Castaway Cay's bars, and the view is pretty good, too. **Heads Up Bar,** near Castaway Ray's Stingray Adventures, sits at the far end of the pier. The one downside to Heads Up is the lack of shade—it can get very hot here very quickly, so lingering with a drink isn't always enjoyable. The views are great, though.

WHAT TO BUY Castaway Cay offers minimal opportunities for shopping. Two Disney-operated souvenir stands offer merchandise similar to what you'll find in the onboard shops, such as T-shirts, flip-flops, and baseball caps, as well as fun-in-the-sun basics, including plastic buckets, sunscreen, and goggles. If you're looking for something that specifically says CASTAWAY CAY on it, buy it on the island. In addition to the Disney shops, one building houses a few stalls run by Bahamian merchants. You'll find items here much like you'd find at the Straw Market at Nassau: bags, sun hats, and figurines. The one item that many guests find to be a true must is a postage stamp. The island's teeny post office will imprint your letters with a special Castaway Cay postmark. The post office accepts cash only (US currency is fine), not your Key to the World Card, so be sure to carry a few bills onto the island.

Castries, St. Lucia

LANGUAGES English, Creole French

HISTORY The first known setters in St. Lucia were the Arawak Indians, circa AD 200. The first Europeans in the area were the French, who visited in about 1650, and who remained in place until a massive hurricane 130 years later. British settlers acquired the land in the late 1700s and used the island for sugarcane plantations, worked by enslaved natives and imported Africans. Slavery was finally abolished in the mid-1800s. In 1958, St. Lucia joined the West Indies Federation as a self-governing nation. It is also part of the worldwide British Commonwealth of Nations.

WEATHER Disney cruises visit St. Lucia in April during 2017. Average daytime highs during that period are in the mid-80s. Average nighttime lows are in the high 70s to low 80s. Average precipitation is about 2.5 inches of rain for the month.

THE PORT DCL ships usually dock at **Pointe Séraphine,** which is within walking distance of the center of town; occasionally, cruise ships must dock farther out, at **Port Carénage,** if the main port is too crowded. The big draw as you debark is the **Pointe Séraphine Shopping Centre,** a slice of duty-free heaven right on the pier, with an emphasis on high-end watches and jewelry. Plenty of taxis stand at the ready.

TOURIST HIGHLIGHTS The 18th-century city of **Soufrière** features both charming gingerbread architecture and naturally colorful sulfur pools. Near Soufrière is the **Diamond Botanical Gardens and Waterfall,** which allows swimming in mineral baths in a lush setting. **Pigeon Island,** a former pirate lair, has a museum, beaches, a restaurant, and panoramic views. Snorkelers will love **Jalousie Beach** and **Anse Chastanet Beach.**

WHAT TO EAT West Indian, Creole, African, British, and French cultures influence the cuisine of Saint Lucia. Popular dishes include pepper pot, callaloo (a souplike stew of leafy greens), and fried cod. Fresh seafood is on most menus. Vegetable accompaniments may include cassava, taro, or sweet potatoes. Local fruits include banana, coconut, guava, mango, passion fruit, and pineapple. Common beverages are fruit juices as well as local beer (Piton) and rum.

WHAT TO BUY The **Castries Market** features stalls with many local vendors. Look for screen-printed clothing, leather goods, carved wood, rag dolls, and handmade jewelry. Gourmands may want to purchase local spices, a jar of the regional banana ketchup, or, of course, rum.

Costa Maya, Mexico

LANGUAGE Spanish

HISTORY Mayans resided in the area beginning in about 200 BC. The Mayans first had contact with Spanish explorers in the early 1500s, battling them for control of the area. This was followed by a period of invasion by English pirates. The British claimed the region until the end of the 19th century, when the Mexican Navy came to rule. The Mexicans developed a port system, improving trade and communications. Today the primary industry is tourism.

WEATHER The temperature in Costa Maya is fairly constant throughout the year. Average daytime highs year-round fall in the mid-70s to mid-80s. Average nighttime lows year-round are in the mid-60s to low 70s. Precipitation is heaviest during the summer months. Average monthly rainfall in December, when Disney Cruise Line will visit in 2017, is less than 1.5 inches.

THE PORT Costa Maya first became a tourist cruise destination in 2001. The port area was built from scratch at that time and was significantly rebuilt in 2007 following Hurricane Dean. Though the facility is thoroughly modern, it was designed to look like an ancient Mayan city. Steps away from the terminal, you'll find restaurants, bars, shops, and saltwater pools catering to tourists.

TOURIST HIGHLIGHTS History buffs will want to visit the fourth-century Mayan ruins at **Chacchoben.** Sun lovers should venture to **Uvero Beach** to lounge on the white sands. Animal watchers will enjoy **Uyumil Che,** also known as the Monkey Farm, a rehabilitation facility for injured wild animals. More-adventurous types may want to try diving in the nearby coral reefs.

WHAT TO EAT Seafood prevails on most menus. Try it raw in seviche, prepared in dishes such as fish tacos or fish quesadillas, or simply grilled. Many dishes are served with rice or with corn tortillas and guacamole. *Remember:* Peel all fresh fruits, and drink only beverages in sealed bottles. Sweets include ices and ice creams based on local fruits.

WHAT TO BUY Much of what is sold in Costa Maya near the port is tourist-grade. You'll find jewelry and metalwork, but expect it to be silver plate. You will also see fabric, rugs, fragrances, and liquor for sale here. Vendors may be open to bargaining.

Cozumel, Mexico

LANGUAGE Spanish

HISTORY Cozumel was a Mayan outpost from the first century. Mayan legend describes Cozumel as the home of Ixchel, a love and fertility goddess. The story says that when temples were dedicated to her, she released her favorite birds, swallows, as a symbol of her gratitude. (*Cozumel* is derived from *Cuzamil,* Mayan for "Land of the Swallows.") The Spanish arrived in the early 1500s, unfortunately bringing with them diseases that decimated the Mayan population. For years after this, the region was besieged by pirates. In the late 1800s, Abraham Lincoln briefly explored the possibility of making Cozumel a relocation point for freed American slaves. Popularity as a tourist region exploded in the 1960s after explorer Jacques Cousteau mentioned it in a documentary as one of the most beautiful areas in the world for scuba diving.

WEATHER Temperatures remain consistent throughout the year. Average daytime highs are in the 80s in every season; average nighttime lows range from the high 60s to the mid-70s. Precipitation, on the other hand, varies widely: The driest season is October–March, with an average of fewer than 5 inches of rainfall during each of those months. Rainfall increases to an average of 8 inches per month in the spring and up to 10 inches per month in the summer.

THE PORT Disney ships generally dock at the **Punta Langosta Pier,** at the southern end of the downtown area. A skybridge leads to **Punta Langosta Mall,** across the street from the dock; here you'll find basic services, including shops, restaurants, and a Starbucks. Taxis travel to all outlying points.

TOURIST HIGHLIGHTS It's all about the water in Cozumel. Snorkeling and diving in the coral reefs are a popular draw, particularly at **Cozumel Reefs National Marine Park.** For history buffs, the pre-Columbian ruins at **Xelha, Chichén Itzá,** and **Tulum** offer a look into Mayan culture. **Chankanaab National Park** offers opportunities to interact with marine animals, as well as walking trails that wind among a large iguana population. Cozumel is also the perfect place to enjoy the sun as you lounge at one of its many beaches.

WHAT TO EAT Fish is plentiful here, as is familiar Mexican fare such as fajitas, tacos, and enchiladas. Many restaurants offer barbecued pork. Margaritas are found in most watering holes, and you may find that some spots have their own house-made tequila. Also try the local *michelada,* beer mixed with lime juice.

WHAT TO BUY Jewelry, Mexican handicrafts, and tourist T-shirts are all sold close to the cruise terminal. You may also find good-quality leather sandals, bags, and hammocks. For a food-related gift, look for Mexican vanilla. Tequila and Xtabentun, a honey-based liqueur, are popular purchases. If you decide to buy spirits, have them wrapped for shipping. You can bring them onto the ship, but they'll be held for you until debarkation.

Falmouth, Jamaica

LANGUAGES English and Patois

HISTORY Falmouth was founded in 1769. During the late 18th century, it served as a major distribution point for rum, sugar, coffee, and molasses. In trade for crops, Falmouth received many Africans. The port's business declined with the end of slavery in the 1800s, but tourism brought a resurgence of visitors in the late 1900s.

WEATHER Temperatures in Falmouth are consistent year-round. In all months, the average daytime high is in the 80s, and the average nighttime low is in the 70s. Falmouth averages fewer than 3 inches of rain per month January–April, but rainfall picks up later in the year, with an average of about 6 inches per month May–November. Rainfall decreases again in December, to about 4 inches.

THE PORT Falmouth's cruise port opened in 2011 to much fanfare. When ships are docked, local vendors set up stalls nearby to sell their wares. The terminal also has several permanent shops and duty-free vendors. Walking about 5 minutes past the port brings you to Falmouth proper and access to restaurants and more shops.

TOURIST HIGHLIGHTS The **Good Hope Great House** is a former sugar plantation; estate tours are a highlight of a Falmouth visit. The property also offers horse-and-buggy rides, dune-buggy excursions, river tubing, and zip lining. Many of these activities are also available at **Mystic Mountain** adventure park. **Dunn's River Falls** is a spectacular natural phenomenon. As you walk through town, stop to see the **Water Square Fountain,** the **Anglican Parish Church,** and the **Falmouth Court House.** A few beaches lie within a 10-minute taxi ride; **Montego Bay**'s famed party beaches are about a 30-minute taxi ride away.

WHAT TO EAT Jerk-style preparations are a staple of Jamaican cuisine. Meat, chicken, or fish is rubbed with spices and sugars and then grilled over a wood fire. Rice and peas is a typical side dish. To cool off, try fresh local mango, guava, and the national fruit, ackee. Also look for Jamaican patties, turnover-like pastries stuffed with meat. With many yam farms nearby, you'll also find yams on many restaurant menus. Rum and rum punch are a potent way to jump-start your relaxation. The national beer, Red Stripe, is served throughout the area.

WHAT TO BUY Many visitors bring home jarred spices, jerk seasoning, or coffee. Local artwork, jewelry, woodcarvings, and woven goods are also popular. Many guests consider Jamaican rum to be a must-purchase item. If you decide to buy spirits, have them wrapped for shipping.

Fort-de-France, Martinique

LANGUAGE French

HISTORY The earliest known settlers in Martinique were the Arawak people. Early control of the area alternated between the Arawaks and the Caribs. The Caribs called the island Madiana, or Island of Flowers. Christopher Columbus charted the island in 1493 and visited it in 1502; however, the island was deemed uninteresting by the Spanish, who decided not to colonize there. During the mid-17th century, French settlers arrived, creating fortifications and sugar mills, enslaving many natives, and establishing trade with Europe. In the 18th and 19th centuries, control of the island changed hands between Britain and France as the power of these nations fluctuated. Concurrently, several hurricanes and other natural disasters caused agricultural difficulties. The island became an official *département d'outre-mer* (overseas territory) of France in 1946; as such, Martinique is part of the European Union (read: bring your euros).

WEATHER In 2017, Disney visits Fort-de-France in June, when daytime highs average in the mid-80s and nighttime lows average in the mid-70s. Precipitation is moderate in June, with average rainfall of about 6 inches per month.

THE PORT **Pointe Simon Terminal** lies within a 10-minute walk to town; follow the signs to Centre de Ville. The terminal has basic facilities including restrooms, ATMs, and Wi-Fi, as well as duty-free shopping. Expect to find numerous tourist stalls nearby, as well as cafés and restaurants. Taxis at the port often accept US currency rather than the euros used on the island.

TOURIST HIGHLIGHTS History buffs will want to visit the **Musée de la Pagerie,** the birthplace of Marie Joseph Rose Tascher de la Pagerie, who would later become Napoleon's Empress Josephine. Architectural attractions include **Fort Royal, the Palais de Justice,** and the **Cathédrale Saint-Louis,** with its distinctive spire. The **Musée Départemental d'Archéologie** in Fort-de-France displays the island's pre-Columbian history, while the **Musée Regional d'Histoire et d'Ethnographie** features Creole furnishings, clothing, jewelry, and musical instruments. Nature lovers will enjoy hiking on **Mount Pelée,** an active volcano, or relaxing on one of the area's many beaches. Be aware that topless sunbathing is common. Shoppers should head to the **Place Monseigneur Romero** to find outposts of French boutiques or visit **Rue Blénac at Rue Antoine Siger** for the covered market featuring island-produced goods.

WHAT TO EAT The food of Martinique blends French and Creole cooking. Breakfast may be typically French, with baguettes and croissants. Crêperies and brasseries are common throughout the island. Open-air markets sell locally grown fruits (bananas, coconuts, guava, pineapples, mangoes) and vegetables (breadfruit, Chinese cabbage, yams). Much Martinican cuisine is prepared from seafood and shellfish, including salted cod, *lambi* (conch), octopus, *blaff* (boiled fish with chives), and the national dish, *court-bouillon* (fish in a spicy tomato sauce). Martinique has seven active distilleries, which primarily make rum. *Ti'* punch (rum, sugarcane juice, and lime) and planter's punch (rum, fruit juice, and lime) are two popular beverages made with the local spirits. French wines are also readily available.

WHAT TO BUY **Rue Victor Hugo** is home to purveyors of French luxury goods such as clothing, perfumes, and housewares. For island mementos, look for madras fabric, local artwork, and ceramics. The most popular souvenirs here may be food items including rums, fruit candies, and jams made from locally grown bananas.

Galveston, Texas

LANGUAGE English

HISTORY Galveston Island was first inhabited by the Karankawa and Akokisa Indians. The Spanish first explored the area in the early 1500s, and the French held force there for much of the 1600s. In 1816, the first permanent European settlement was founded by pirates, who used Galveston as a base of support for the Mexicans against the Spanish in the region. By 1860, Galveston was part of the Republic of Texas and a major port in the slave trade. Later, it became the first city in Texas to provide a secondary school for African Americans. Galveston has been subjected to several major hurricanes, including a catastrophic 1900 storm that remains the deadliest natural disaster in US history.

WEATHER Disney cruises depart from Galveston October–January. The average daytime high in October hovers around 80, with average nighttime lows in the high 60s. Daytime highs in November–January average in the 60s, with nighttime lows in the high 40s to low 50s. Precipitation is fairly constant in the winter: Expect average rainfall of 2–4 inches per month.

THE PORT The cruise terminal has basic services. About two blocks from the terminal, you'll find several hotels with shops and restaurants.

TOURIST HIGHLIGHTS Pleasure Pier, on the Galveston Seawall, is a low-key carnival area. For bigger thrills, head to **Schlitterbahn** water park. **Moody Gardens** is a botanical preserve and theme park with 3-D and 4-D theaters. Small museums in the area include the **Railroad Museum,** the **Texas Seaport Museum,** and the **Offshore Drilling Rig Museum.** If you're spending time in **Houston** before cruising, check out the **Houston Zoo,** the **Houston Museum of Natural Science,** the **Downtown Aquarium,** and of course the **Johnson Space Center.**

WHAT TO EAT Look for seafood in Galveston, particularly crab and shrimp. For a Texas-style meal, keep an eye out for barbecue brisket and chicken. The area has several Cajun restaurants, with jambalaya and New Orleans-influenced po'boys on the menu. Plus, more than a dozen steakhouses call the region home, so you'll have no problem finding beef prepared just the way you like it.

WHAT TO BUY Along the beach, you'll find shops selling the requisite T-shirts and sunglasses, along with jewelry made from shells or coral, beachwear, wind chimes, and beach toys. If you're visiting Houston before your cruise, look for NASA-related items and clothing emblazoned with the logos of the city's sports teams.

Grand Cayman, Cayman Islands

LANGUAGE English

HISTORY Christopher Columbus accidentally discovered these islands during a voyage in 1503. The Caymans came under British control following the 1670 Treaty of Madrid; during this time, they also saw an influx of settlers from Jamaica, and slaves were brought to the island beginning in the 1730s until slavery was abolished in 1834. The region was besieged by periodic attacks from pirates into the late 18th century. Jamaica (a British colony at the time) governed the islands until 1962, when Jamaica became independent and the Caymans elected to stay under British rule.

WEATHER Temperatures stay consistent throughout the year. Daytime highs average in the 80s and nighttime lows in the 70s. Precipitation, however, varies considerably: During December–April, you can expect an average of fewer than 3 inches of rainfall per month, while May–August experiences an average of about 6 inches of rainfall per month. September–November may see up to 9 inches of rainfall per month.

THE PORT Grand Cayman is a tender port—you have to take a smaller vessel to get from the ship to land. The tender brings you to the edge of downtown **George Town.** Shops and restaurants are within walking distance of the dock.

TOURIST HIGHLIGHTS **Stingray City** offers opportunities to swim with rays. The **Cayman Turtle Farm** is a research facility that studies green sea turtles; here, you'll be able to observe the 16,000 inhabitants and watch turtle hatchlings feed. Water lovers will find abundant scuba and snorkeling opportunities, including excursions to swim near the wreck of a sunken 1940s schooner. History buffs will enjoy the **Pedro St. James Historic Site** and the **Cayman Islands National Museum.** A nearby seaside village named **Hell** lures many visitors who just want to say they've been there. Numerous beaches afford opportunities for sunning and relaxation.

WHAT TO EAT Seafood—including the traditional national dish, turtle—is plentiful here. Look for rock shrimp and conch in many dishes. Jerked meats are popular on the island, as are many grilled meats. Many of the desserts, such as sticky pudding and rum cakes, have a British influence. Other sweets may include fruit, honey, and coconut.

WHAT TO BUY Decorative conch shells make a nice reminder of the area. If you've interacted with the stingrays or turtles, a carved replica of these creatures makes a good souvenir. Also look for local artwork and woven hats and bags. Gourmets will want to bring home some Tortuga rum cake.

Key West, Florida

LANGUAGE English

HISTORY The original inhabitants of the area were the Tequesta and Calusa peoples. Juan Ponce de León was the first recorded European visitor, arriving in 1521. Cubans and British used the island as a fishing spot before it was claimed by Spain; however, Spain exerted little control over the area. In 1822, Matthew C. Perry claimed the Keys for the United States. The islands became more prosperous when they were connected to mainland Florida by an overseas railway bridge in 1912.

WEATHER Daytime temperatures average in the 80s April–November, with nighttime lows during that time in the 70s. December–March, daytime temperatures average in the 70s, with nighttime lows in the 60s. Precipitation is lowest in the winter and spring, with average rainfall of fewer than 3 inches per month November–May. The summer gets wetter, with average rainfall of 3–5 inches per month in June and July. August, September, and October average 5–7 inches of rain per month.

THE PORT The entire island measures just 2 miles by 4 miles, so many services lie within a brisk walk from the port. **Mallory Square,** on the waterfront near the docks, offers bars, restaurants, and basic shopping. To get around without walking, rent golf carts, bicycles, or a pedicab near the port. The **Conch Tour Train** allows visitors to hop on and off for personalized island touring. For less kitsch and more charm, explore a bit beyond the immediate port area.

TOURIST HIGHLIGHTS The must-do for literary types is a stop at the **Ernest Hemingway Home and Museum.** See Hemingway's studio and visit with the colony of cats descended from the author's many feline companions. For excellent views of the Keys, visit the nearby **Lighthouse and Keepers Quarters Museum.** Nature experiences are available at the **Key West Aquarium** and the **Key West Butterfly Conservancy.** And no trip to Key West would be complete without some relaxation time on the beach.

WHAT TO EAT Fresh seafood is abundant here, with oysters, clams, lobster, grouper, and shrimp appearing on many menus. Conch fritters are a specialty. There is a large Cuban influence in the food culture here: Look for sandwiches of Cuban bread stuffed with meats and cheeses. Beef stews, plantains, and yellow rice are all served with a Cuban flair. The signature dessert, of course, is Key lime pie, made with the juice of local citrus. In addition to pie, you're likely to find dozens of other lime-accented foods during your visit, including cookies, candy, salsa, and barbecue sauce. Rumrunners, mojitos, and margaritas can help you ease into the island lifestyle.

WHAT TO BUY Most of the shopping is casual and beachy: T-shirts, sunglasses, swimsuits, and surf- and sun-related trinkets. Epicures can take home a bottle of Key lime juice to use in their own cooking. If you want a permanent souvenir, you could get a tattoo at one of the many shops on the island.

Miami, Florida

LANGUAGES English and Spanish

HISTORY The Tequesta Indians inhabited the area until Spain claimed it in 1566. Spain ceded Florida to the United States in 1819. Named after the Miami River, the city became a force to be reckoned with following the 1896 southward expansion of Henry Flagler's Florida East Coast Railroad. The population boomed until the Great Depression, and after a pause, the area saw another surge in population from Cuban exiles during the 1960s and '70s.

WEATHER Average daytime highs are in the 80s May–October, with nighttime lows in the 70s. Average daytime highs are in the 70s December–April, with average nighttime lows in the 60s. Precipitation is greatest during the summer. November–April, expect an average monthly rainfall of about 3 inches or less. May, July, and October average 4–5 inches of rainfall per month, while June, August, and September see average rainfall of 6–9 inches per month.

THE PORT The Port of Miami is 9 miles from Miami International Airport and about five minutes from downtown. **Bayside Market,** a shopping and dining center, is a 15-minute walk from the port. A park with a small sand beach is also nearby. Major hotels and restaurants are within walking distance.

TOURIST HIGHLIGHTS **South Beach** is where the beautiful people go. Take a stroll there to see the Art Deco architecture, and stop in a bar or club for a drink. Another interesting neighborhood is **Little Havana,** imbued with old-world charm. Learn about Miami's immigrant history at the **Cuban Museum of the Americas.** Gardeners will like the **Fruit and Spice Park,** which grows more than 500 species of edibles, while kids will love exploring the **Miami Children's Museum** and the **Seaquarium.** And, of course, you can soak in the sun at the area's many beaches.

WHAT TO EAT Many local establishments serve food with a Cuban flair. Look for stewed chicken or lamb and grilled fish or pork accompanied by tomatoes, vegetables, and rice. Seafood gumbo with rice is also popular, as are stuffed Cuban sandwiches. For a pick-me-up, try strong Cuban-style coffee. For a slow-me-down, try sangria, mojitos, and other fruity cocktails.

WHAT TO BUY Miami is a cosmopolitan city with luxury chains and chic boutiques in abundance; there are also the requisite beachside T-shirt and trinket shops. For off-the-beaten-path ideas, try the **Tropicana Flea Market,** open on weekends. Sports fans may want to pick up jerseys and other gear celebrating the **Miami Dolphins, the Miami Heat,** or the **University of Miami Hurricanes.** Hand-rolled cigars are sold around the city. A classic, and classy, choice for gentlemen would be a *guayabera,* the loose-fitting Cuban-style shirt. Ladies can start their cruise with some new swimwear.

Nassau, Bahamas   *(Please see our travel advisory on page 338.)*

LANGUAGE English

HISTORY Originally called Charles Town, Nassau was destroyed by fire in 1684 during an attack by the Spanish. It was rebuilt and renamed 10 years later by the Dutch and English. Over the next few decades, the Bahamas became a pirate stronghold. In 1718 the Brits ousted the pirates and reclaimed the area. During the American Revolutionary War, there was a brief occupation by Americans and then another Spanish occupation in 1782. Spain surrendered the land back to England a year later. In 1807 the slave trade was outlawed, and thousands of freed slaves eventually made the island their home. Today, Nassau is a major tourist destination.

WEATHER Daytime highs average in the 80s March–November. Temperatures drop slightly in winter, with daytime highs averaging in the 70s December–February. Nighttime lows average in the 70s June–October and in the 60s November–May. Precipitation is lowest in the winter, with average monthly rainfall of fewer than 3 inches November–April. A moderate rise occurs in May with average monthly rainfall of fewer than 5 inches. Precipitation increases substantially in the summer and fall, with up to 9 inches of rainfall per month June–October.

THE PORT Ships dock at **Prince George Wharf,** on which is located the **Festival Welcome Center,** with basic tourist services. Downtown Nassau is a 10-minute walk away.

TOURIST HIGHLIGHTS Our walking tour (see page 348) takes in such points of interest as the **Queen's Staircase,** the **Government House,** and **John Watling's Distillery.** Museum and history lovers will enjoy the **National Art Gallery of the Bahamas,** the **Pirate Museum,** and **Fort Charlotte.** Numerous beach, water-sports, and animal-encounter excursions are available. Casinos offer the full complement of opportunities to lose your shirt.

WHAT TO EAT For a taste of typical Bahamian food, try conch, fish stew, or crawfish. These are often served with a side of grits, rice, macaroni and cheese, or potato salad. Desserts may include pastries flavored with pine-apple, guava, or coconut.

WHAT TO BUY There is no shortage of trinket vendors aimed at the tourist trade. You'll find inexpensive T-shirts on every corner. If you visit the **Straw Market,** keep a sharp eye out for handmade straw pieces rather than ones imported from China. Other popular items include decorated conch shells or carved wood. Foodies may desire rum cakes or guava jams and jellies.

Oranjestad, Aruba

LANGUAGES Dutch, Papiamento

HISTORY The Arawak Indians were the first inhabitants of Aruba. The Spanish explorer Alonso de Ojeda, the first known European visitor, reached the island in 1499. With the arrival of the Spanish, many Indians were enslaved and relocated to Hispaniola (present-day Haiti and the Dominican Republic). In the mid-1600s, an 80-year war between Spain and Holland ended with the Dutch assuming possession of Aruba. Dutch military personnel were sent to maintain the island, but contrary to their living conditions under their previous masters, the Indians were allowed to remain free. In the early 1800s, the British and Dutch wrestled for control of the island, with the Dutch ultimately retaining control. Gold mining was a key industry throughout the 1800s. Gold, along with aloe (at one time, Aruba produced 70% of the world's crop), created a stable economy. Following the discovery of offshore oil deposits in 1928, the Royal Dutch Shell and Lago Oil companies built major refineries. These were a resource for the Allies in WWII, but they temporarily ceased operations in the 1980s due to a worldwide petroleum surplus.

Aruba became part of the island nation of the Netherlands Antilles in 1954 and then became a constituent country of the Kingdom of the Netherlands in 1986. (The four current constituent countries—Aruba, Curaçao, the Netherlands, and Sint Maarten—are roughly analogous to the United Kingdom. The three island constituencies are self-governing, but they defer to the Netherlands on matters of foreign policy and national defense.) Today, tourism is Aruba's major industry.

WEATHER Temperatures are constant throughout the year. Daytime highs in Curaçao average in the high-80s. Nighttime lows average in low 80s. Disney Cruise Line visits Aruba in the summer; expect moderate rainfall averaging 1–2 inches per month.

THE PORT The port of Oranjestad has three air-conditioned terminals with ATMs and several small shops. Taxis and shuttles are available, and **Royal Car Rental** and **Smart Rent A Car** have desks at the port, but the town of Oranjestad—less than 10 minutes away—is easily reachable by foot.

TOURIST HIGHLIGHTS The beaches are a key draw in Aruba for relaxing, marine-animal encounters, and water sports, particularly diving and snorkeling in one of many shipwreck ruins. For those who want a richer form of gambling than DCL bingo, you'll find full casinos in several of the island's hotels. Children will love the **Donkey Sanctuary,** where you can spend an hour feeding carrots and apples to these gentle creatures. **Alto Vista Chapel,** dating to 1750, offers a chance for visitors to follow a winding road marking stations of the cross. **Fort Zoutman** comprises the earliest remains of the Dutch settlement and Aruba's oldest building, now a historical museum which showcases artifacts from throughout Aruba's history. The island's many cacti, along with its free-roaming iguanas, make for some excellent photo opportunities.

WHAT TO EAT As at most tourist destinations in the Caribbean, you'll be able to find burgers and pizza at many locations, but to get a true taste of the island, you'll want to try some traditional Aruban cuisine. Typical dishes include goat meat, often prepared with curry; *stoba,* a stew of vegetables and fish; and *keshi yena,* a sort of Aruban take on a stuffed pepper: The rind from an Edam cheese is filled with meat, onions, celery, raisins, peppers, tomatoes, and spices. A favorite snack is *pastechi,* an empanada-like fried pie filled with beef or cheese. Also try *ayaca,* a dish of dough-covered banana or plantain leaves filled with chicken and pork and seasoned with curry and soy. Simpler foods include fresh grilled or broiled sea bass or other fish. Finish your meal with locally grown fruit.

WHAT TO BUY **Aruba Aloe** skin-care products are of excellent quality; look for lotions, lip balms, and other beautifiers. There are several Aruba Aloe retail stores on the island, as well as the factory itself. Items of Dutch origin are plentiful here, including Delft Blue pottery, *stroopwafel* cookies, and Edam cheese. Also look for carvings, housewares, and jewelry made by local artisans. Out-of-circulation Aruban license plates are another popular take-home item—they're inscribed with the cheery motto ONE HAPPY ISLAND. Cuban cigars are available in many shops; as noted earlier, US law now lets you take them home with you.

Philipsburg, Sint Maarten

LANGUAGES Dutch, French, and English

HISTORY The island was originally occupied by the Carib Indians. Christopher Columbus later found and named it for the medieval bishop St. Martin of Tours, which is now aptly fitting. In the early 1600s, Dutch colonists used the island as a source of salt for export. The Dutch were then ousted by the Spanish, who were subsequently removed by the French. In 1648 a treaty divided the area in half, with shared control and occupancy. Parts of the territory changed hands between the Spanish and the Dutch 16 times in about 200 years. At several points in the early 1800s, British pirates attacked and brought the area under English rule. The slave trade was a large part of the island's economy in the 17th and 18th centuries; when slavery was abolished, plantation owners imported low-wage earners from China and the East Indies. The island is currently divided and called by two names: **Saint-Martin,** controlled by the French, and **Sint Maarten,** controlled by the Dutch. It is one of the smallest landmasses overseen by more than one country. English is widely spoken on both sides of the island.

WEATHER The climate in Saint-Martin/Sint Maarten is mild, with average year-round temperatures between 82 and 89. August–November is typically the wettest time, with 4–5.5 inches of rain per month. The water temperature just off the island rarely dips below 80.

THE PORT DCL ships dock near Philipsburg, on the Dutch side of the island (Sint Maarten). A 5-minute walk from the port is a small marina called **Dock Maarten** (LOL), with a few shops and a restaurant. One mile away, accessible on foot and by taxi, is downtown Philipsburg, which is a major duty-free-shopping destination.

TOURIST HIGHLIGHTS Gamblers will enjoy the many casinos in Saint-Martin/Sint Maarten. Be sure to brush up on the rules of roulette, baccarat, craps, blackjack, and poker before you arrive. Guests looking to get their gamble on will find casinos on the Dutch side of the island near the airport and Simpson Bay, and around downtown Philipsburg. The Boardwalk area on **Great Bay,** on the Dutch side, offers beachside lounging and a long string of bars and restaurants. From **Maho Beach,** also on the Dutch side, watch planes fly incredibly low to land at the nearby airport. (The signage letting you know that getting too close to the aircraft could kill you just adds to the fun.) Water sports available here include snorkeling, scuba diving, and fishing. **Lucky Stables** offers horseback-riding opportunities.

For a quieter and more European experience, catch a cab right off the dock (as opposed to the nonlicensed "tour operators" in downtown Philipsburg) to **Marigot,** on the French side. At **Orient Beach,** women can go topless, and some sections allow you to bare it all, but the posteriors *en promenade* tend more toward Joe the Plumber than Jennifer Lopez.

See page 351 for our Saint-Martin/Sint Maarten walking tour.

WHAT TO EAT Seafood, particularly conch fritters, is plentiful here. Other dishes may have West Indian, French, and Dutch influences. More than 40 Chinese restaurants are also on the island. You may encounter the regional favorites callaloo (beef- and crab-based), crab cakes, and johnny-cake biscuits. Dessert often includes coconut pies and guava tarts.

WHAT TO BUY Saint-Martin/Sint Maarten is known for its shopping, particularly electronics, cameras, liquor, fragrances, and cigarettes. These will likely be big-name European brands. If you're looking for local flavor, typical tourist souvenirs include artwork, carvings, and woven goods.

Port Canaveral, Florida

LANGUAGE English

HISTORY In 1929 Congress approved construction of a deepwater port at Port Canaveral, completed and dedicated in 1953. Initially this was a cargo center, with a primary mission of taking orange juice to the North. Concurrent with the rise of shipping in the area was the building of the nearby space center. The first passenger ships arrived in the 1970s to see the area's newly developed theme parks on their ports of call. The first home-ported cruise ship sailed from Port Canaveral in 1982.

WEATHER It's hot here during the summer. (*Surprise!*) May–October, average daytime highs range from the mid-80s to the low 90s; nighttime lows range from the upper 60s to the low 70s. November–April, expect average daytime highs in the low 70s to low 80s, with nighttime lows in the low 50s to low 60s. Precipitation varies considerably throughout the year. The dry season is November–May, with average monthly rainfall of about 3 inches or less. June–October, monthly rainfall averages 5–8 inches. Summer storms are common.

THE PORT Disney cruises dock at **Berth 8,** at a comfortable dedicated terminal with basic facilities. **Jetty Park,** just east of the port, has a lifeguard-patrolled beach, a snack bar, and a playground. The **Cove** area at Port Canaveral is home to several restaurants and shops.

TOURIST HIGHLIGHTS The main attraction here is **Kennedy Space Center.** Visitors can tour the facilities, ride in a space simulator, and participate in special programs with astronauts. Beach lovers will want to head over to **Cocoa Beach** and relax in the sun. Twenty minutes away, in Titusville, you'll find the **Brevard Museum of Natural History and Science,** the **Great Florida Birding Trail,** and the **US Space Walk of Fame.** Of course, the Orlando theme parks are about an hour west of Port Canaveral. Many cruisers make a pre- or postvoyage visit to **Walt Disney World, Universal Orlando,** or **SeaWorld.**

WHAT TO EAT Seafood is served at most restaurants. Look for oysters, conch, and grouper. Many other cuisines, including Italian, Cuban, Asian, and German, are represented in the waterfront area. Fast food such as burgers and pizza is readily available, too.

WHAT TO BUY Look for souvenirs related to the American space program: model rockets, patches depicting moon missions, and pieces of meteorites. For a unique food experience, buy a package of dehydrated astronaut ice cream. Near the beach, stock up on swimsuits, sunglasses, sunscreen, flip-flops, and other last-minute cruising essentials. You'll find that prices on land are significantly lower than in the shops on board. And if you're visiting the theme parks before or after your trip, you'll find a nearly limitless supply of souvenirs.

San Juan, Puerto Rico

LANGUAGES Spanish and English

HISTORY Juan Ponce de León was the first European explorer to mention visiting the island of Puerto Rico. The city of San Juan was founded in 1521 by Spanish colonists who used it as a stopover on their way to the Americas. Throughout the 17th and 18th centuries, the island withstood various attacks by the English, including Sir Francis Drake, and the Dutch. In 1815, the island was opened to immigration as part of the Royal Decree of Graces. In 1898, United States warships attacked San Juan, eventually resulting in Spanish cession of Puerto Rico to the United States in the Treaty of Paris. In 1917, Puerto Ricans were granted American citizenship. Not quite a state—although 61% of its residents favored statehood in a 2012 referendum—the island sends a nonvoting representative to Congress and maintains a local legislature.

WEATHER As is the case elsewhere in the Caribbean, weather here stays consistent year-round. Average daytime highs are in the 80s throughout the year, with average nighttime lows in the 70s. Precipitation is lowest in the winter, with an average of fewer than 4 inches of rainfall per month January–March. During the rest of the year, rainfall averages 4–6 inches per month.

THE PORT The DCL dock is in **Old San Juan,** across the street from a Sheraton hotel and just steps away from the main city.

TOURIST HIGHLIGHTS History buffs will want to explore **El Morro,** a fortress built to protect the island from attack by sea, and **El Castillo de San Cristobal,** designed to protect San Juan from overland attacks. Musicians may want to stop by the **Museo de Pablo Casals,** which houses the Spanish cellist's manuscripts and personal documents. The **Museum of Contemporary Art** showcases modern artists from Latin America and the Caribbean. For fun in the sun, explore the beaches in the nearby towns of **Condado** and **Isla Verde.** Many visitors will want to stop by the **Casa Bacardí** distillery (also known as the Cathedral of Rum) for a tour and a taste (or two).

WHAT TO EAT Puerto Rican cuisine is a melting pot of Spanish, Cuban, Mexican, African, and American flavors. To start your meal, try conch fritters or *empanadillas* (pastries filled with meat or seafood). Entrées include meat or seafood stews, steak or veal, barbecued pig, broiled chicken, or grilled seafood. Beans, rice, and plantains are typical sides. Dessert will likely include coconut or caramel flan (custard). Sweets may also be flavored with guava, papaya, or mango. Coffee and local rum are the beverages of choice.

WHAT TO BUY Dominoes is a popular game here,; a domino set makes a nice souvenir. Also look for hand-tooled leather, scented soaps, and woven hats and bags. Also take home some rum or coffee. Outlet shops for American brands include **Ralph Lauren** and **Coach.**

St. George's, Grenada

LANGUAGE English

HISTORY The native settlers were the Caribs. The island of Grenada was sighted by Columbus during his third voyage, but this did not result in a European settlement at the time. The first permanent European occupation began in 1649 by French explorers from Martinique. French rule continued until Grenada was captured by the British in 1762, during the Seven Years' War. The Brits fended off intermittent attacks but maintained control until 1974, when independence was granted. In 1983, Grenada faced a US invasion related to the island's political ties to Cuba and the USSR. Today, Grenada is under democratic self-rule.

WEATHER In 2017, Disney cruises visit Grenada in April. Average daytime highs during this time are in the high 80s. Nighttime feels similar to the day, with average April evening lows in the low 80s. Rainfall can be heavy, averaging about 8 inches per month.

THE PORT Services at the terminal are minimal. The town of St. George's, which has many shops and restaurants, is less than a 10-minute walk away.

TOURIST HIGHLIGHTS Grenada is a leading exporter of such spices as allspice, cinnamon, cloves, ginger, mace, and nutmeg. Although the spice trade took a hit from Hurricane Ivan in 2004, spice-plantation tours are a popular diversion. The **River Antoine Estate** offers tours of local rum production. History lovers will enjoy tours of **Fort Frederick** or **Fort George. Grand Etang National Park** is home to rainforest hiking trails for many levels of fitness.

WHAT TO EAT The food of Grenada shows the influence of the island's French, Spanish, West Indian, and African history. Local favorites include crab and callaloo, pepper pot, conch, fresh fish, and *roti* (rolled beef or chicken with curry and potatoes). Those with truly adventurous palates will want to try *manicou* (wait for it . . . opossum). Side dishes may include rice, vegetables, plantains, peas, and macaroni. Expect to find fresh fruit and fruit juices widely available. Tipplers will enjoy the local rum.

WHAT TO BUY Not for nothing is Grenada nicknamed the Island of Spice. Spices are sold in packets, in baskets, and even in decorative necklaces. Hand-printed fabrics, local carvings, and jewelry are all easy to find. Local chocolates and rums are popular with gastronomes.

St. John's, Antigua and Barbuda

LANGUAGE English and Spanish

HISTORY This Caribbean nation comprises the inhabited islands of Antigua and Barbuda, along with several uninhabited ones. The first residents were the Ciboney Indians; later settlers included the Arawaks and Caribs. Christopher Columbus "discovered" Antigua during his second voyage in 1493. The first real European settlement took place in 1632 by an English party vacating St. Christopher Island (St. Kitts). In subsequent decades, the island became home to massive sugar plantations, farmed by enslaved native peoples. By the mid-1700s, slaves outnumbered their European masters. The American War of Independence in the late 1700s disrupted the sugar trade. Britain abolished the slave trade in 1807, and all Antiguan slaves were emancipated by 1834. In 1981 Antigua and Barbuda cut ties with Britain and are now an independent entity.

WEATHER In 2017, Disney cruises visit Antigua and Barbuda in April and May. Average daytime highs during this time are in the low to mid-80s, with average spring nighttime lows in the low to mid-70s. Precipitation is moderate, with monthly rainfall averages for this time of 4–6 inches per month.

THE PORT Ships dock at **Heritage Quay.** The town of St. John's, which has all basic services, shopping, and dining, lies within a 5-minute walk.

TOURIST HIGHLIGHTS If you're in the mood to gamble, St. John's is home to several casinos, notably the **King's Casino** near Heritage Quay. History buffs will like **Nelson's Dockyard,** which once housed 17 Royal Navy warships. **Betty's Hope** is a refurbished sugar plantation, showing life as it was during the 17th century. Several beaches offer surfing, swimming, and snorkeling.

WHAT TO EAT Antiguan food is typically Caribbean. The national dish is pepper pot (a stew of meats, vegetables, greens, and hot peppers) with *fungi* (not mushrooms, but a cornmeal mush similar to polenta). Other frequent menu items are *ducana* (sweet-potato dumplings), seasoned rice, and fresh seafood. Grilled meats, often served with side dishes of macaroni pie or plantains, are popular. Dessert may include fudge, tamarind stew, or peanut brittle. Locals drink tamarind juice, mango juice, and coconut water. For adult beverages, try local beers and rum.

WHAT TO BUY Many goods for sale in St. John's are imported from elsewhere. Look for duty-free perfumes, linen, watches, and electronics. For local flavor, consider hand-carved wood objects, natural soaps, artwork, and pottery. Those with an interest in food may purchase locally produced jams and jellies, as well as local rums.

St. Thomas and St. John, US Virgin Islands

LANGUAGE English

HISTORY The original occupants of the Virgin Islands were the Ciboney people. Christopher Columbus first sighted the islands in the late 1400s, and the Dutch West India Company founded a settlement here in 1657. This was shortly followed by occupation by the Danish West India and Guinea Company. Sugarcane, harvested by slaves on St. Thomas and the nearby islands of St. John and St. Croix, became the primary export. In 1848 slavery was abolished and the sugar trade declined. In 1917 the United States purchased St. Thomas, St. John, and St. Croix from Denmark as a means of controlling the Panama Canal during World War I, and the islands remain a US territory today (the other Virgin Islands are now under British control).

WEATHER Temperatures are constant year-round. Daytime highs average in the high 80s year-round, with nighttime lows in the 70s. Precipitation is lowest in the winter, with an average monthly rainfall of fewer than 3 inches December–April. A moderate rise occurs May–August, with an average monthly rainfall of fewer than 4 inches. Precipitation increases to about 6 inches per month September–November.

THE PORT From the cruise docks, it's a 10-minute taxi ride to **Charlotte Amalie,** the main city on St. Thomas. If you'd rather walk rather than take a cab, just follow the waterfront path for around 20 minutes to downtown. Pedestrians should note that although this is a US territory, drivers observe British road rules and use the *left* side of the road—so watch carefully when crossing streets.

Directly at the dock, you'll find outposts of many local shops, as well as some American chain stores. Some cafés, a bank, and a pharmacy are also in the immediate dock area.

TOURIST HIGHLIGHTS The **Paradise Point Skyride** offers views of the harbor. At the top, enjoy lunch and walk along trails inhabited by local wildlife. For another beautiful scene, beachgoers will want to visit beautiful **Magens Bay. Coral World** is a nearby attraction with an underwater observatory, animal interaction with sharks and stingrays, and water sports such as parasailing. For history lovers, **Fort Christian** is a great spot. This museum houses local artifacts in a 17th-century Danish fortress. Another historic site is **Blackbeard's Castle,** which was used as a lookout by Danes to protect the harbor from early pirates. (For a walking tour that takes in these two historic sites and other points of interest, see page 353.)

WHAT TO EAT Local dishes include fresh seafood such as conch and lobster. Stewed beef, goat, and chicken are also popular. For a portable bite, try a meat *pate* (a pastry filled with ground pork and beef). Side dishes may feature plantains, yams, rice, beans, and lentils. Fruit and fruit juices are available in abundance. If you're drinking alcohol here, it's likely rum made from sugar and molasses grown in the Caribbean.

WHAT TO BUY St. Thomas is the largest shopping port in the Caribbean. Most goods, including electronics, fragrances, jewelry, tobacco, crystal, and china are widely available in the States. If you're planning to shop for these, you should be familiar with discount pricing from vendors at home. Shop in the open-air markets for local artwork, carved wood, and hand-pieced leather. Foodies will want to take home Caribbean rum-ball candy.

Tortola, British Virgin Islands

LANGUAGE English

HISTORY Christopher Columbus was the first European to chart the area. Local lore holds that Columbus himself gave the island its name, which means "land of the turtle dove." Pirates Edward "Blackbeard" Teach and Captain William Kidd were among the first Europeans to actually settle in the region. The Dutch ruled the island for a time; then, in the 16th century, the English took power and established a permanent plantation colony on Tortola and the surrounding islands. The sugarcane industry, dependent on the slave labor of Africans transported from the continent, dominated Tortola's history over the next 180 years but diminished in the mid-19th century with the abolition of slavery. Today, tourism is the dominant industry.

WEATHER Temperatures in Tortola remain consistent throughout the year, with daytime highs averaging in the mid-80s and nighttime lows averaging in the low to mid-70s in all seasons. Precipitation varies seasonally: Expect monthly average rainfall of 2-4 inches during the winter and early spring. Rainfall averages 4-5 inches during late spring into early summer, increasing to an average of 6-8 inches per month during late summer and fall.

THE PORT Ships dock at **Road Town Harbor**, a 5-minute walk into town. Basic shopping and ATMs are within this walking distance; taxis and rental cars are available at the port. Be aware that residents of Tortola and the British Virgin Islands drive on the left side of the road, as per UK custom.

TOURIST HIGHLIGHTS In town, look for the **Sugar Works Museum,** once part of a cotton plantation. The **Botanic Gardens** in the center of town showcases local flora. For active recreation, visit **Sage Mountain National Park;** wear sturdy shoes if you want to do some hiking. Beaches abound, with some of the best including **Cane Garden Bay, Smuggler's Cove,** and **Apple Bay.** Many excursions feature water sports such as sailing, surfing, and scuba diving. Ferry rides to smaller nearby islands are a popular choice for day trips.

Note: Locals in the British Virgin Islands can be conservative when it comes to social mores and etiquette, and some (particularly the older generation) consider it impolite for tourists to wear beach attire away from the beach. A few establishments might even turn you away if you show up in a swimsuit and flip-flops, so bring an appropriate change of clothes if you want to eat or explore in town. Think neat and presentable rather than formal—say, a polo shirt and pressed Bermuda shorts for men and a nice sundress for women.

WHAT TO EAT Seafood is on most menus. Look for conch fritters or mahimahi served in many forms, along with crab, shrimp, and lobster. Jerk spices season many meat preparations. Several area restaurants serve *roti,* an Indian-style curry wrap. Vegetable sides include yam, sweet potato, and okra. Fresh fruit abounds. Pusser's rum is the local firewater—drink it straight or in one of the many fruity punches offered.

WHAT TO BUY The beachwear, batiks, and baskets found on Tortola are typical of those sold throughout the Caribbean. Local crafts, recordings of local musicians, and bottles of Pusser's rum make for truly authentic souvenirs.

Willemstad, Curaçao

LANGUAGE Dutch, Papiamento

HISTORY Curaçao's first inhabitants were the Arawak and Taino peoples. The Spanish colonized in 1499 and retained their claim until 1634, when the Netherlands declared independence from Spain and the Dutch East India Company usurped control. Curaçao attracted both Dutch and Jewish merchants, each of whom brought their architectural influences to the island. During the early 18th century, the island's deep port and strategic position attracted the British and French. In the early 1800s, the British and Dutch exchanged control of the area several times. The 1815 Treaty of Paris gave Curaçao back to the Dutch West India Company. Soon after the Dutch retook the island, it languished for a century. Slavery disappeared, and social and economic conditions were harsh. In 1920, oil was discovered off the nearby Venezuelan coast. This signaled a new era for Curaçao and its sister island, Aruba. They became centers for distilling crude oil imported from Venezuela, and Curaçao's Royal Dutch Shell Refinery became the island's biggest business and employer. During WWII, the Allies established an American military base at Waterfort Arches, near Willemstad.

In 1954, Curaçao, along with Bonaire, Saba, Sint Eustatius, and Sint Maarten, became the nation of the Netherlands Antilles, with Willemstad as its capital. In 1986, Aruba became a constituent country of the Kingdom of the Netherlands; in 2010, Curaçao and Sint Maarten followed suit, and the islands of Bonaire, Saba, and Sint Eustatius became special municipalities within the smaller nation of the Netherlands. (The four constituent countries of the Kingdom of the Netherlands—Aruba, Curaçao, the Netherlands, and Sint Maarten—are roughly analogous to the United Kingdom. The three island constituencies are self-governing, but they defer to the Netherlands on matters of foreign policy and national defense.)

WEATHER Disney Cruise Line visits Curaçao in the summer, but temperatures in Curaçao stay consistent all year long: Daytime highs average in the low to mid–80s, and nighttime lows average in the mid- to high 70s. Expect moderate rainfall, averaging 1–2 inches per month.

THE PORT Ships dock at a pier directly adjacent to town. Taxis and shuttles are readily available. Basic services such as ATMs, shops, cafés, and several attractions lie within a 10-minute walk of the port.

TOURIST HIGHLIGHTS Downtown **Willemstad,** designated a UNESCO World Heritage Site in 1997, features charming Dutch architecture that reminds us a lot of the Nyhavn waterfront in Copenhagen, Denmark. The city is split into two districts on either side of a narrow channel, connected by a landmark floating pedestrian bridge. Historical sites include **Landhuis Brievengat,** a museum and replica of an island plantation. **Mikve Israel-Emanuel Synagogue** is a Jewish cultural museum that's also an active house of worship. **The Curaçao Museum** displays exhibits that touch on the geological history of the island, pre-Columbian artifacts, details about the time after the abolition of slavery, antiques, paintings, and a replica of a traditional plantation kitchen. If you're interested in the distillery process, you might enjoy a visit to the **Curaçao Liqueur Factory** at Landhuis Chobolobo. If you're a gaming buff, several of the area hotels have full casinos. Children will enjoy the **Curaçao Ostrich Farm** and the **Curaçao Sea Aquarium.** And of course, the island offers an array of lovely beaches for sunning and water sports.

WHAT TO EAT The food of Curaçao is a blend of Dutch and Indonesian, with hints of other international cuisines in the mix. Traditional fare includes *funchi,* or half-and-half, which is a polenta-like side dish of half cornmeal pudding and half rice; *pika hasa,* or red snapper; and a Dutch dish called *keshi yena,* which is a Gouda or Edam cheese rind stuffed with meat or fish. A local favorite is iguana stew, which is said to taste like chicken if you're brave enough to try it. Also look for *ayaka* (meat tamales wrapped in banana leaves) and *kabritu* (stewed goat). But never fear—if you're not an adventurous eater, there are plenty of places to get pizza and burgers. The most popular alcoholic beverage is Curaçao liqueur, made from the peel of the bitter Lahara orange mixed with a variety of spices. For something without a kick, try the local fruit juices.

WHAT TO BUY Dutch Delft Blue ceramics and figurines of Curaçao's historic buildings are some of the more substantial collectibles for sale in local shops. Look also for locally made artwork and musical instruments crafted from driftwood, calabash, and coconut. Other popular items include books of local lore and photographs of the island. The most traditional consumable purchase is Curaçao liqueur. You can also find Cuban cigars for sale here.

WHAT ABOUT CUBA?

SOMETHING AMAZING HAPPENED as we were updating the 2016 edition of the book: For the first time in 50 years, the United States and Cuba normalized relations. It's telling that our first thought was, "We're going on the first Disney cruise to Havana!" Cuba has been a cruise destination for years (and let's not forget that it was a favorite US vacation destination before the embargo). Carnival Cruises has started "cultural exchange" cruises from Miami to Cuba with its **Fathom** line (fathom.org). Disney hasn't yet announced any plans for itineraries with stops in Cuba through 2016, but we have to believe they're looking closely at it. We still plan to be on the first one.

unofficial **TIP**
As of October 2016, the US government allows cruise tourists to bring home Cuban cigars, but they may not resell them.

HAWAII

(Note: *DCL doesn't visit Hawaii in 2017 but likely will in the future.*)

CRUISES SAIL FROM Vancouver or Honolulu

SHIP *Wonder*

DATES Late summer, after the Alaskan cruises

CRUISE LENGTH 10 nights in past years

SPECIAL TOUCHES Cultural ambassadors on board give seminars on lei-making, hula, ukulele, and Hawaiian entertainment with music and dance. Hawaiian menu.

SIGNATURE PORT ADVENTURE Renting a car and seeing the islands for yourself, on your own time

DEFINITELY VISIT Volcanoes National Park, on the Big Island of Hawaii

CLASSIC DISNEY ADD-ON Disney's Aulani Resort & Spa on Oahu

WHAT TO PACK A variety of clothing for warm to chilly weather; suitable shoes for hiking if you plan to venture beyond the beaches

COMMENTS The 50th state is more than just sand and surf. If you have time, stay a few days before or after your cruise to experience the islands beyond the port adventures. Though no Disney cruises are scheduled for Hawaii in 2017, we prefer to keep the port information in the book, assuming that the itineraries will return in the future. (Can you tell we love Hawaii?)

PROS

- Stops at 4 islands.
- You can see everything from blue oceans to mountains, rainforests, and volcanoes.
- Weather is mild (but can be rainy).
- Sailing from **Vancouver** eases you into the 5-hour time difference.
- You can add a stay at **Disney's Aulani Resort** if you want to keep the magic going. This is a very popular option, so don't expect reduced rates.
- **Honolulu** has world-class shopping.
- US residents: no currency exchange; you may even be able to use your own bank's ATM in port. Another bonus for US residents: no cellular roaming in port.
- Ten nights helps you really get to know your cruise staff.

CONS

- If you're sailing from Hawaii, be prepared for jet lag that ranges from heavy-duty (if you're traveling from the West Coast) to crushing (if you're traveling from the East Coast).
- Airfare to or from Honolulu can cost an arm and a leg.
- To really experience Hawaii, you're better off flying to one island and staying there.
- Disney cruises tend to hit Hawaii during the rainy season.
- Because everything has to be shipped into the islands, food and other necessities are very expensive. ("Fun" fact: Hawaii has the highest cost of living of any state.)
- A 10-night cruise is a major time commitment when you factor in transportation before and after the cruise.
- Your only choice is the *Wonder*, and only during limited dates throughout the year (if DCL offers Hawaiian itineraries at all).
- What's more, 10 nights means at least $240 in gratuities, plus more Internet to purchase if you need it while you're away, multiple opportunities for dinners or brunches at Palo, before- and/or after-dinner drinks, trips to the gift shop and spa . . . you get the idea.

Hilo, Hawaii

LANGUAGES English, Hawaiian, and Pidgin

HISTORY Hilo is the largest city on the island of Hawaii, a.k.a. the "Big Island." Archeological evidence indicates settlement by Polynesian peoples from the Marquesas Islands as early as AD 300. Centuries-old local chiefdoms were consolidated under the Hawaiian Islands' first monarch, King Kamehameha the Great, in 1782. The late 18th century also saw the arrival of British Captain James Cook as well as explorers and traders from China. In the 1820s, US missionaries arrived in Hilo, further complicating the cultural influences. During the mid-1800s, sugar plantations thrived, and sugar became a key export. In 1893, a coalition of American and European business and political leaders forced Hawaii's last monarch, Queen Lili'uokalani, to step down, and in 1898 the islands were annexed by the United States. The early 1900s saw a major influx of Japanese immigrants, followed by the arrival of many Korean immigrants. The mid-20th century saw several natural upheavals, including earthquakes, volcanic eruptions, and tsunamis. Hawaii became the 50th state in 1959. The closure of area sugar plantations during the 1990s led to a downturn in the local economy, but tourism has been fueling the rebound.

WEATHER DCL typically visits Hilo in September. Average daytime highs during this period are in the low to mid–80s, with average nighttime lows in the high 60s to low 70s. Precipitation on the Big Island is heavy throughout the year, with September rainfall averaging about 10 inches for the month.

THE PORT Cruise ships dock at piers on **Kuhio Street,** about 2 miles east of downtown Hilo. There is very little in the way of services near the dock, but taxis can take you into town; there's also a public bus system. Shuttles take guests to the local farmers market or to **Hilo Hattie,** a retailer of Hawaiian-themed clothing.

TOURIST HIGHLIGHTS The **Pacific Tsunami Museum** chronicles the 1946 and 1960 tsunamis that destroyed much of the town. A wave machine lets you experience the feel of rushing water. The **Lyman Museum** features exhibits about Hawaiian geography and history. Nature enthusiasts will want to visit **Hawai'i Volcanoes National Park,** home of Kilauea—the most active volcano on the planet—and Mauna Loa. If you're looking for natural beauty with little exertion, **Rainbow Falls** is small but close to downtown, and it requires no hiking. The **Mauna Loa Macadamia Nut Factory** offers tours and tastings.

WHAT TO EAT If you visit the large farmers market, look for unfamiliar fruits such as mangosteen, durian (*warning:* an acquired taste!), and rambutan; many vendors will allow you a small bite before buying. Some stalls sell prepared foods such as taro pastries and *musubi,* a sushilike snack made with Spam (a Hawaiian delicacy), chicken, or hot dogs. Most menus will have local fish served grilled, broiled, or in tacos. Tropical fruits abound: pineapple, bananas, guava, papaya, mango, and coconut. A great beachside refresher is a shave ice, a tropical take on a snow cone that's topped with a variety of sweet, fruity sauces and sometimes ice cream or sweetened condensed milk. Kona coffee is especially rich and delicious. Macadamia nuts are sold all over the island—try some dipped in chocolate.

WHAT TO BUY Typical Hawaiian souvenirs include floral shirts (match the whole family!), art prints of the local scenery, carved wooden objects, ukuleles, and hula accessories such as skirts and leis. Food finds are everywhere: macadamias in every form, jams and jellies, and packaged Kona coffee beans.

Honolulu, Hawaii

LANGUAGES English, Hawaiian, and Pidgin

HISTORY The capital of Hawaii and both the southernmost *and* westernmost major city in the United States, Honolulu is located on the island of Oahu. Archaeological evidence indicates settlement of the Hawaiian Islands by Polynesian peoples from the Marquesas Islands as early as AD 300. The first known foreigner to enter Honolulu Harbor was William Brown, captain of the English ship *Butterworth,* in 1794. King Kamehameha I (The Great), who conquered the islands in 1782, moved his court from the "Big Island" of Hawaii to Waikiki in 1804; he relocated to what is now downtown Honolulu five years later. In 1820, a group of New England missionaries arrived, bringing with them their religion, education, and economics. Later, immigrants from Asia, Portugal, and Puerto Rico helped make Hawaii a true cultural melting pot. King Kamehameha III proclaimed Honolulu the capital city of his kingdom in 1850. In 1893, the US overthrew the monarchy and in 1898 annexed the islands, creating the Territory of Hawaii. In 1941, the Empire of Japan bombed the Pearl Harbor military base just west of Honolulu, hastening America into World War II. Hawaii became the 50th state in 1959.

WEATHER DCL typically visits Honolulu in September. Average daytime highs during this period are in the high 80s, with average nighttime lows in the low 70s. Precipitation on Oahu is minimal at this time of year, with September rainfall averaging less than an inch for the month.

THE PORT Cruise ships dock adjacent to **Aloha Tower Marketplace,** which has shops, restaurants, and all basic services. The top floor of this 10-story building houses an observation deck (free admission) offering panoramic views of the harbor. Taxis and rental cars are readily available, and a reliable public bus system covers much of Oahu. The **Waikiki Trolley** is similar to the San Francisco cable-car system.

TOURIST HIGHLIGHTS The main draw in Oahu for many guests is the **World War II Valor in the Pacific National Monument** at Pearl Harbor, encompassing the **USS *Arizona* Memorial** and a museum complex. Tours are a must, and tickets may be purchased in advance (call ☎ 877-444-6777 or visit recreation.gov). A vibrant **Chinatown** is chockablock with unique shops and restaurants. In the Capitol District, visit historic **Iolani Palace,** the only royal residence in the United States. Culture mavens will enjoy the **Hawaii State Art Museum,** which features Hawaiian art across all media. Nature lovers will enjoy the **Lyon Arboretum,** with walking paths that border more than 600 plant species, more than 80 of which are rare or endangered. If you'd like to learn about pineapple production, the **Dole Plantation** is a worthwhile excursion nearby. **Waikiki Beach** is abuzz with hotels, shops, and restaurants, flanked by the distinctive **Diamond Head** crater. Disney fans may want to check out the company's **Aulani Resort & Spa,** part of the larger Ko Olina resort complex about 45 minutes west of Honolulu.

WHAT TO EAT Hawaiian cuisine reflects the state's natural bounty as well as its wildly diverse cultural heritage. Most menus will have local fish served grilled, broiled, or in tacos. Tropical fruits abound: pineapple, bananas, guava, papaya, mango, and coconut. Sticky rice serves as the base for everything from a *loco moco* (a burger and fried egg over rice) to the ubiquitous Spam *musubi* (think sushi, only with Spam). If you visit a luau, you're sure to encounter *kalua* pig served with a side dish of *poi* (mashed taro root). Signature sweets include *malassadas* (Portuguese-style doughnuts) and desserts and candies based on the locally grown macadamia nut. A great beachside refresher is shave ice, a tropical take on a snow cone that's topped with a variety of sweet, fruity sauces and sometimes ice cream or sweetened condensed milk. Kona coffee is rich and delicious. Kids will love POG (passion fruit, orange, and guava) juice. Bars and restaurants serve the requisite fruity cocktails, often accompanied by a paper umbrella. Hey, when in Honolulu . . .

WHAT TO BUY There's no more iconic souvenir than the classic Hawaiian shirt. If you're looking for something other than the typical floral print, the gift shop at the USS *Arizona* Memorial often sells Hawaiian-style shirts with military-themed prints. Foodies will want to bring home macadamia-nut candies, Hawaiian sea salt, tropical fruit jams, or a package of local coffee beans. Other popular items include carvings or housewares made from koa wood, leis made from shells, and recordings by Hawaiian musicians.

Kahului, Hawaii

LANGUAGES English, Hawaiian, and Pidgin

HISTORY Kahului is located on the island of Maui. Polynesian and Tahitian settlers were among the first known inhabitants. Until the late 1400s, the island was ruled by tribal chiefdoms, which were united in the mid-1550s under the rule of a single royal family. Europeans began to visit in the mid-1500s, but they did not become a significant presence until the early 1800s. In the 1820s, Christian missionaries began teaching and preaching, altering the island's traditional religious and educational systems. The 1800s saw massive deaths among the indigenous peoples due to the introduction of Western illnesses. Crops such as sugar and pineapple became mainstays of the local economy in the mid-to-late 19th century. Maui served as a recreation and training base during WWII, and the first tourist hotel was built here in 1946. Hawaii became the 50th state in 1959.

WEATHER DCL typically visits Kahului in September. Average daytime highs during the month are in the high 80s, with average nighttime lows in the low 70s. Precipitation on Maui is minimal at this time of year, with September rainfall averaging less than an inch for the month.

THE PORT Kahului is an industrial port. Within a 15-minute walk you'll find the **Maui Mall**, which houses a grocery store, a movie theater, and shops. A public beach is also within walking distance. Taxis service the harbor, but there is little public transportation—renting a car may be more efficient and less expensive than taking a cab. Shuttles can take you to the Kahului Airport, which has desks for most major auto-rental agencies.

TOURIST HIGHLIGHTS The **Road to Hana** is an internationally famous leisure drive. The narrow, twisting road requires skilled driving, and perhaps some Dramamine. Along the way you'll see tropical vegetation, waterfalls, sea caves, and swimming holes. Many guests will want to explore **Lahaina,** a historic town with numerous art galleries, shops, restaurants, and bars. For shopping and snorkeling, venture to **Kaʻanapali,** which features an upscale outdoor mall called **Whalers Village** and the **Puʻu Kekaʻa (Black Rock)** ocean-diving area. The 112-acre **Maui Tropical Plantation** offers tram tours. For panoramic views, take a **helicopter tour** of the region's volcanoes and waterfalls.

WHAT TO EAT Fresh fish abounds on most menus. Look for coconut shrimp, fish tacos, ahi tartare, ahi *poke* (a raw-tuna salad), and sushi of every sort. The Road to Hana is populated by fresh-fruit stands and vendor shacks that sell delicious banana bread. Pork is often prepared shredded with a sweet sauce on the side. Typical side dishes include pounded taro, rice, or macaroni salad. The locally made potato chips have a cult following (the **Kitch'n Cook'd** brand is particularly addictive). For a refreshing treat, try shave ice topped with fruit-flavored sauces. Favorite beverages include coffee-based drinks and cocktails made with rum and fruit.

WHAT TO BUY Typical Hawaiian souvenirs include wearables such as Aloha shirts, sarongs, and swimwear, along with recordings by local musicians and prints by local artists. Look for crafts made from koa wood such as carvings, bowls, or hair ornaments. Gourmands will want to buy unusual flavors of Spam (a beloved regional delicacy), coffee beans, macadamia-nut candies, and jams made from local fruits.

Nawiliwili, Hawaii

LANGUAGES English, Hawaiian, and Pidgin

HISTORY Nawiliwili is located on the island of Kauai. Indigenous peoples have inhabited the island since at least AD 1000. Continuous European visitation began following Captain James Cook's landing in 1778. The mid-1800s saw an expansion of agricultural trade. Nawiliwili Harbor officially opened in 1930. Hawaii officially joined the United States in 1959. Kauai's beautiful scenery has served as a backdrop for numerous Hollywood films, including *South Pacific* (1958), *Raiders of the Lost Ark* (1981), *Jurassic Park* (1993), and *The Descendants* (2011).

WEATHER Disney Cruise Line typically visits Nawiliwili in September. Average daytime highs during this period are in the mid-80s, with average nighttime lows in the mid-70s. Precipitation is moderate at this time of year, with September rainfall averaging about 2 inches for the month.

THE PORT The port itself has little in the way of services, but the shops and restaurants of the **Harbor Mall** and **Anchor Cove Shopping Center** are within walking distance. Free shuttles are also provided. **Kalapaki Beach,** adjacent to the malls, provides an area for sunning and water play. Taxis service the port, but a rental car may be the most efficient way to see the area.

TOURIST HIGHLIGHTS **Nawiliwili Beach Park** provides beaches for sunning and swimming. The natural wonders of Kauai are also evident at **Waimea Canyon** and **Kokeʻe State Park**. **Kilohana Plantation** provides a look into the lavish lifestyles of Hawaii's sugar magnates; a train trip around the plantation functions as a guided tour. Lovely **Wailua Falls** was featured in the opening shots of the 1970s TV staple *Fantasy Island*. The **Kilauea Point Lighthouse** offers sweeping ocean views, and the **Kilauea Point National Wildlife Refuge** offers prime bird-watching.

WHAT TO EAT In a word, fish. Look for *poke,* a raw-seafood salad made with *tako* (octopus) or ahi tuna; *lomi-lomi* salmon, a raw-salmon-and-tomato salad; fish tacos; and *poi,* or mashed taro root. Locals favor *musubi* (Spam or other meat served over sushi rice) and *saimin* (a noodle soup similar to ramen or lo mein). Many meat dishes show an Asian influence. Typical sides include rice, potato salad, and macaroni salad. Fresh fruit, particularly local guava, pineapple, and coconut, is found in abundance. Regional sweets include *lilikoi* (passion fruit) pie, shave ice (like a snow cone), and *haupia* (a luscious coconut pudding that's often used as a pie filling). Coffee and fruit-based drinks are excellent here.

WHAT TO BUY A prized—and pricey—local purchase is a **Niʻihau shell lei,** handcrafted from shells found on a lightly inhabited nearby island. Musicians may be interested in buying a handcrafted ukulele or CD of local songs. Aloha shirts and hula skirts are great for guests who want to wear a bit of the islands at home. Look also for candies, cookies, and jams made from locally grown fruits and nuts.

Vancouver, British Columbia, Canada   *(See page 236 for full profile.)*

MEDITERRANEAN

CRUISES SAIL FROM Barcelona

SHIP *Magic*

CRUISE LENGTHS 5, 7, or 10 nights

DATES Summer

WHAT TO PACK Good walking shoes, lots of euros

SIGNATURE PORT ADVENTURE City tour

CLASSIC DISNEY ADD-ON Adventures by Disney tour, side trip to Disneyland Paris

COMMENTS Mediterranean cruises are very popular with families who want to see a lot of southern Europe with minimal hassle. Dining has an international flair.

ADDITIONAL PORTS Disney Cruise Line is not visiting the ports of **Valletta, Malta; Vigo, Spain; Kusadasi, Turkey; Mykonos, Greece;** or **Piraeus, Greece** in 2017, but they will likely return to the schedule in the future. Also, DCL is currently using **Livorno, Italy,** for its Florence/Pisa stop rather than **La Spezia, Italy.**

MEDITERRANEAN	
PROS	**CONS**
■ Good way to sample many ports without having to move your luggage.	■ If you're coming from North America, round-trip airfare may put a serious dent in your budget.
■ Shopping opportunities abound.	■ You're only scratching the surface of all there is to see in this part of Europe.
■ Lots of family-friendly port adventures from which to choose.	■ Your budget will likely be affected by currency exchange rates.

For more information on these ports, consult *The Unofficial Guide to Disney Cruise Line 2016* or visit touringplans.com/disney-cruise-line/ports (requires a TouringPlans.com subscription).

Barcelona, Spain

LANGUAGES Catalan and Spanish

HISTORY Barcelona was founded as a Roman city. Subsequently, Visigoths and then Moors controlled the area until the early 800s. Franks held the region through the 10th and 11th centuries. From the 12th century, Barcelona and Catalonia became allied with the Kingdom of Aragón, and the Port of Barcelona became a trading thoroughfare. A period of decline ensued with the arrival of the Black Death in the 14th century, followed by the expansion of the Hapsburg monarchy as well as the rise of Turks in the region. The early 1700s brought a rejuvenation of the Barcelona dock system and then the arrival of the industrial age in the 1800s. By the mid-1800s, Barcelona was again a flourishing European port. Periods of unrest and rebuilding took place throughout the early 1900s, with stability constant since 1977, when the Catalan government was restored. Barcelona hosted the 1992 Summer Olympics, a boon for the entire region.

WEATHER Disney cruises visit Barcelona in the summer and early fall. Daytime highs average in the mid-70s to low 80s, with nighttime lows in the low to mid–60s. Even when temperatures peak, coastal breezes typically keep things comfortable. Precipitation is usually minimal during this period, with an average of fewer than 6 inches per month.

THE PORT There is little here to entice tourists, but a 5-minute taxi ride or brisk 20-minute walk from the port brings you to **La Rambla,** a pedestrian mall bustling with restaurants and smart shops. Taxis are plentiful.

TOURIST HIGHLIGHTS The premier attractions are La Rambla and **La Boqueria,** an open-air market with dozens of food stalls. The influence of artist Antoni Gaudí is in evidence throughout the area, principally in the can't-miss **Sagrada Família** cathedral and the **Park Güell** garden complex. (Our walking tour of Barcelona, page 357, includes a stop at the church.) Gothic architecture abounds in the old section of town. Art aficionados will enjoy the **Salvador Dalí Theatre and Museum,** the world's largest Surrealist object (*trippy* doesn't begin to describe it). Foodies will relish the **Museu de la Xocolata**

(Museum of Chocolate). The **Poble Espanyol,** a walled city within the city, showcases architecture, artisans, and food from each of Spain's 15 regions. Sun worshippers will appreciate the city's public beaches.

WHAT TO EAT In a word: *¡Tapas!* Most restaurants offer some version of these small plates. Look for seafood, olives, artichokes, egg dishes, breads, and local hams and sausages. La Boqueria's many sweets vendors peddle intricately shaped chocolates and marzipans.

WHAT TO BUY You can find virtually anything in Barcelona, from high-end leather goods and shoes to hand-blown glassware. Great choices are packaged foodstuffs, such as candy, olives, olive oil, and wine, or sportswear featuring the local *futbol* (soccer) teams and Antonio Gaudí–inspired artwork.

Cádiz, Spain

LANGUAGE Spanish

HISTORY Founded by the Phoenicians, Cádiz is the oldest continuously inhabited city in Spain. In its early years, it was variously controlled by the Romans, the Visigoths, and the Moors. Christopher Columbus used Cádiz as a starting point for two of his voyages. The 16th century saw minor raids by Barbary corsairs and the Englishman Sir Francis Drake. More-serious attacks came at the end of the 16th century, when Cádiz was captured by the English. The city changed hands between the Spanish and the English several times over the next two centuries. The Spanish maintained dominance in the 18th century, whereupon Cádiz gained prominence as a trading port. In the early 19th century, Cádiz became the seat of Spain's military high command. In recent years, the city has undergone much reconstruction—many monuments, cathedrals, and landmarks have been cleaned and restored, adding to the charm of this ancient city.

WEATHER During 2017, DCL visits Cádiz in the summer and early fall. Daytime highs during this period average in the low 80s, with nighttime lows averaging in the low 70s. Rainfall is minimal during the warm season, with typically less than 2 inches per month.

THE PORT Ships dock near the center of town. Across the street from the dock, you'll find the **Plaza San Juan de Dios** shopping area, with restaurants, ATMs, and other services. Many shopping and tourist sites are accessible on foot, and taxis are available. Many guests use Cádiz as a jumping-off point for a visit to **Seville,** which is about 2 hours away by train (the train station is across the street from the port).

TOURIST HIGHLIGHTS If you're staying in Cádiz, visit the **Catedral de Cádiz,** which has a glittering gold dome and striking Baroque facade. The **Museo de Cádiz** includes an archaeological section with Phoenician artifacts. Or explore the four quarters of the city: the **City Center,** which features colorful plazas and gardens; **La Viña,** dotted with bars and nightclubs; **El Populo,** replete with monuments; and **Santa María,** epicenter of the art of flamenco dancing.

If you're heading to Seville, the main draw is the **Alcazar,** an ornate Moorish palace. The **Catedral de Sevilla** is the largest cathedral in Spain as well as the largest Gothic building in the world. The **Museo de Bellas Artes** includes holdings by Velázquez and El Greco. And Seville's **Jewish Quarter** is home to many antiques shops, outdoor cafés, and traditional whitewashed homes.

WHAT TO EAT Cold tomato gazpacho is a typical meal-starter. Seafood is plentiful: shrimp, anchovies, squid, and whitefish fried in olive oil. Restaurants in Cádiz also serve dishes made of beef, pork, goat, lamb, or game birds. Cured ham is a specialty. Meat and fish dishes may be accompanied by bread, potatoes, rice, olives, and roasted vegetables. Any savory dish may be served as tapas, small plates meant for tasting or sharing. Desserts may include *pestiños* (deep-fried pastries with honey), *amarguillos* (almond cookies), wine doughnuts, or *pan de Cádiz,* a marzipan treat stuffed with fruit. Sherry and sweet wines are typical of the area.

WHAT TO BUY Intricately embroidered silk shawls are prized in the area. Other popular local craftwork can be found in the form of pottery, worked silver, or leather goods. Painted fans are displayed in many shops. Examine the work and the origin of the fan before paying top dollar; some are lovely hand-painted items, while others are imported from China. Young girls will likely want a colorful flamenco dress or flamenco-style apron.

Cannes, France

*Note: DCL typically docks along the French Riviera at **Villefranche, France,** but during a few sailings the Magic docks directly at Cannes, about 20 miles away. See Villefranche, page 287, for an in-depth profile.*

THE PORT While Cannes has few services directly at port, its tender dock lies within a 10-minute walk of town and most points of interest are within a several-block radius. A tourist-information office is located about five blocks from the dock, on the ground floor of **Palais des Festivals** (1 boulevard de la Croisette; ☎ +33 4 92 99 84 22; cannes-destination.com). In addition to walking, you can explore Cannes via a trolley service, **Le Petit Train du Cinéma,** which departs regularly from **La Croisette,** across from the Majestic hotel. It offers three tours: La Croisette (35 minutes), **Le Suquet** (35 minutes), and a combination hour-long ride. Tours are available in English; visit cannes-petit-train.com for more information. Taxis are easy to find but can be pricey. **Thrifty** and **Hertz** rental-car desks are both located at 147 rue d'Antibes, about a 15-minute walk from the dock, but be aware that they close for several midday hours for lunch.

Civitavecchia, Italy

LANGUAGE Italian

HISTORY Rome is a major metropolis with a lengthy past. According to myth, the city was founded by the twins Romulus and Remus, who were abandoned as infants and suckled by a wolf until a shepherd found them and raised them as his own. From 290 BC to AD 235, Rome was the dominant force in the Western world, controlling most of Europe and the Mediterranean. Later the Bishop of Rome (the Pope) established the city as the center of the Catholic Church. During the Renaissance, Rome became a hub for art and invention.

WEATHER Summers in Rome are hot. Average daytime highs in August, when most Disney cruises visit, are in the low to upper 80s; temperatures in the high 90s aren't unusual. Nighttime summer lows average in the low 60s. Summer is the dry season in Rome, with rainfall in August averaging fewer than 2 inches for the month.

THE PORT The pier offers nothing of note. It's a 10-minute walk from here to the train station, from which it's a 90-minute journey to Rome by bus or train.

TOURIST HIGHLIGHTS It's impossible to take in all Rome has to offer in a day—choose one or two highlights and plan to come back. Among the main attractions are **Vatican City,** with the **Sistine Chapel** and **St. Peter's Basilica;** the **Colosseum;** the **Spanish Steps;** the **Pantheon;** the **Trevi Fountain;** the **Catacombs;** the **Arch of Constantine;** and the numerous museums.

If you choose not to visit Rome or the countryside, you'll find smaller sights in Civitavecchia itself. The most popular local attraction is **Fort Michelangelo,** built in 1503 to protect the village from invaders. Another spot in town is the ancient baths, or **Terme Taurine,** which were built around natural hot sulfur springs. A seafront market—offering souvenirs, food, and, of course, gelato—is open during the summer. A public beach is near the Civitavecchia promenade.

WHAT TO EAT Pizza is available almost everywhere, as is pasta in almost every conceivable shape and size. Roasted or fried artichokes are a popular side dish. Salt cod, zucchini blossoms, and fresh and aged cheeses may be served as an appetizer. For dessert, gelato is a specialty—look for unique flavors such as licorice, melon, apple, or hazelnut.

WHAT TO BUY With every major fashion designer represented in Rome, haute couture and leather goods abound. In and around the Vatican, you'll find religious artifacts, books, and artwork for sale. Sports enthusiasts will want to purchase jerseys of the local soccer teams.

Dover, England, United Kingdom

LANGUAGE English

HISTORY Renowned for its stark white seaside cliffs, Dover has an enviable location in the south of England: It's about a 2-hour drive from London and a Chunnel trip of less than an hour to Calais, France. The city's proximity to France has made it a strategic stronghold for centuries, with evidence of occupation by various tribes and sects dating back to medieval times. During the Tudor years, Dover was fortified to withstand Continental invasion. The Napoleonic Wars saw the development of further defenses against the French. In the mid-1800s, Dover endeavored to become a tourist center with seaside amenities. During the 20th century, the city saw extensive fighting during both World Wars as it defended the English Channel, with the aforementioned white cliffs inspiring a hit song by Vera Lynn during World War II.

WEATHER Disney cruises visit Dover during the summer. In May, average daytime highs are brisk, in the high 50s, with nighttime lows in the mid-40s. June, July, and August bring warmer temperatures during the day, averaging in the low 70s, with nighttime lows remaining in the 50s. Pack a jacket for the evening. Precipitation is low throughout the year, with typically fewer than 2 inches of rain per month during the summer.

THE PORT The town center is about a mile from the docks, which offer basic services. Taxis and a shuttle bus are readily available. Stop at the **Visitor Information Centre,** inside the **Dover Museum** on Old Town Gaol Street, for directions. Buses and trains, available within a mile of the town center, provide access to London, 2 hours away.

TOURIST HIGHLIGHTS If you're staying in town, a visit to **Dover Castle,** atop those famed white cliffs, is a must. Explore secret wartime tunnels, or interact with costumed docents who reenact aspects of King Henry II's court. **Canterbury Cathedral**—the mother church of the worldwide Anglican Communion and the site of religious pilgrimages since the days of Chaucer—is about a half-hour away by car.

Many guests make their stay in Dover brief and focus instead on the sights of **London.** Must-sees there include the bustling **West End** theater district, **Buckingham Palace** and the changing of the guard, **Westminster Abbey,** the **British Museum,** the **Tower of London,** the giant **London Eye** Ferris wheel, and much, much more.

WHAT TO EAT British food isn't limited to fish-and-chips and meat pies—to the contrary, it's quite cosmopolitan. Restaurants serve most global cuisines: French, Indian, Italian, Spanish, and more.

WHAT TO BUY In Dover, look for mugs, T-shirts, and books related to the castle and the cliffs. London, of course, has shops offering nearly everything imaginable. Woolens such as sweaters and caps are popular items, as are depictions of the royal family and the city's famed red double-decker buses. And no trip to London would be complete without a stop at **Harrods,** where you can buy everything from gourmet meats and cheeses in the downstairs food halls to haute couture and pet puppies upstairs.

Livorno, Italy

Note: *DCL is currently using Livorno as its port of call for the Florence/Pisa area; in previous years, the DCL's port for this region was **La Spezia.***

LANGUAGE Italian

HISTORY Florence and Tuscany are considered the birthplace of the Italian Renaissance. From approximately 1300 to 1500, it was the most important city in Europe. Its factious history includes several changes of government, including a period of rule by the storied Medici family. For part of the 1700s, Tuscany was an Austrian territory and then later a prefecture of the French department of Arno; in the 1800s, Italian rule returned. In modern times, Tuscany has been a center of tourism, trade, and financial services.

WEATHER Disney Cruise Line visits Livorno in August and early September. Daytime highs for that period average in the low 80s; nighttime lows average in the low 60s. Precipitation is moderate, seeing an average of about 2 inches of rainfall per month in late summer.

THE PORT Large ships like the *Magic* dock in the container terminal. There are few nearby services, and pedestrian access is limited. Shuttle buses are provided for the 5-minute trip to **Piazza Grande** or the 10-minute trip to the bus or train station. Trains to **Pisa** depart about every half-hour, with the trip taking about an hour each way. Travel to **Florence** takes about 1.5–2 hours each way.

TOURIST HIGHLIGHTS Museums abound in Florence, the most famous being the **Uffizi Gallery.** Other museums include the **Bargello,** the **Pitti Palace,** the **Museo dell'Opera del Duomo,** and (for all you fashionistas) the **Gucci Museum.** The city's iconic building is its cathedral, the **Duomo di Firenze,** where for a fee you can climb to the top for a bird's-eye view of the city. A stroll along the **Ponte Vecchio** is achingly romantic. The **Boboli Gardens** feature lush plantings and an interesting sculpture garden. In Pisa, you must see the **Leaning Tower.** The cathedral there, constructed of colorful hand-carved marble, is worth a visit as well.

WHAT TO EAT Try antipasto, which often consists of thinly sliced salami, pickled vegetables, and crostini. Most menus include pasta or risotto, salads, grilled meats, and olives. Florentine desserts may include gelatos, *schiacciata con l'uva* (a sweet grape bread), and *castagnaccio* (chestnut cake).

WHAT TO BUY Florence is a city of high fashion, with most major luxury retailers in evidence. Leather goods are ubiquitous; look for jackets, gloves, wallets, briefcases, and handbags in traditional and boldly colored dyes. Gold jewelry can be a lovely buy, but watch for extreme pricing. Crafty types may enjoy hand-marbled papers or wax letter seals. Murano glassware and jewelry are popular purchases. Marionettes are wonderful takeaway items for kids.

Lisbon, Portugal

LANGUAGE Portuguese

HISTORY Lisbon has long been a major trading port between Europe and North Africa. Its first inhabitants were pre-Celtic peoples, during the Neolithic Era; successive centuries brought occupations by the Iberians, Phoenicians, Greeks, Carthaginians, Romans, and Visigoths. During the eighth century AD, Islamic Moors gained control of the region and ruled until Christian Crusaders arrived about 400 years later. Maritime exploration was a primary focus until the early 1700s.

In 1755, a major earthquake, attended by fires and tsunamis, destroyed most of the city's buildings; for this reason, much of Lisbon's architecture is newer than that of other large European cities. The area was rebuilt under the leadership of then–Secretary of State Sebastião José de Carvalho e Melo. Napoleon occupied Lisbon from 1807 until 1814, after which a new constitution was developed and the territory of Brazil was granted independence.

The early 20th century was a time of unrest, beginning with the assassination of King Carlos in 1908. In 1910, a coup d'état overthrew the constitutional monarchy and established the Portuguese Republic. The next 20 years saw more than 40 separate changes of government. The dictatorial Estado Novo regime ruled from 1926 to 1974, when it was deposed in a military coup known as the Carnation Revolution. In 1986, Portugal joined the European Community, a decision that spurred major redevelopment.

WEATHER Disney Cruise Line visits Lisbon in summer, when daytime highs average in the low 80s and nighttime lows average in the low to mid-60s. Summers are dry, with average rainfall of less than an inch per month. Expect sunny skies.

THE PORT The terminal, which has basic shops, ATMs, and a few cafés and restaurants, lies on the Tagus River, a 20-minute walk from tourist sites. Shuttles and taxis are readily available, as are light-rail and bus service.

TOURIST HIGHLIGHTS The **Alfama** neighborhood is a hilly enclave composed of tiny shops, restaurants, and clubs where traditional *fado* music (think Portuguese blues) is played and sung. While you're in the area, visit the **Castelo de São Jorge,** a Moorish church on Lisbon's highest hill—the views are spectacular. Reach it using **Tram 28,** Lisbon's version of a San Francisco cable car.

The **Belem** district is home to several notable attractions, including the **Monastery of Jerónimos,** the **Monument to the Discoveries,** and the **Museu Nacional dos Coches,** home to the world's largest collection of royal vehicles. The **National Tile Museum** displays painted works as well as intricate mosaics. The **Oceanarium,** Europe's largest indoor aquarium, features birds as well as fish and is popular with kids. **Casa das Histórias,** in the seaside suburb of Cascais, showcases the work of Surrealist artist Paula Rego.

WHAT TO EAT Contrary to what you might expect, Portuguese food isn't particularly spicy, but it is delicious. Fish and shellfish dominate many menus. The national dish is *bacalhau,* or salt cod. You can find it prepared with vegetables or fried with rice, eggs, onions, and olives. *Porco alentejana* is pork loin cooked with clams and potatoes. Warm up with *caldo verde* ("green soup"), made with cabbage, onions, potatoes, and *chouriço* sausage. Snack on *presunto,* a dry, cured ham that's somewhat like Italian prosciutto, along with local cheese made from cow, sheep, or goat milk. For a sweet treat, try *pasteis de nata*—egg-custard tarts that are typically topped with cinnamon and powdered sugar; try to get some fresh from the oven. Adult beverages include *ginjinha,* a strong sour-cherry liqueur that's sometimes served from a chocolate shot glass. And no trip to Lisbon would be complete without sampling some port or the many other varieties of fortified wine.

WHAT TO BUY Ceramic tiles are a typical Portuguese souvenir; look for hand-painted tiles in shops throughout Lisbon. Variations may include framed ceramic artwork or coasters. Portugal is a major exporter of cork; take-home treasures made with it include housewares and handbags. Fragrant **Claus Porto** soaps are a thoughtful gift to bring back for a friend or a housesitter—not only do they smell wonderful, but the ornate wrapping paper is beautiful in itself. Foodies will want to take home local olive oils or bottles of port.

Naples, Italy

LANGUAGE Italian

HISTORY Naples has been continuously inhabited since at least the second millennium BC. During the first century BC, Naples played a role in the merging of Greek and Roman cultures. Following the fall of the Western

Roman Empire, Naples became the capital city of the Kingdom of Naples and remained so from the late 1200s to the early 1800s. During World War II, Naples was the most bombed Italian city. Many of the outer buildings in the area were constructed as part of the restoration.

WEATHER Daytime highs during August and September, when DCL visits, range from the mid-70s to the mid-80s. Nighttime lows during that period fall into the low 60s. Rainfall averages less than 2 inches for the month.

THE PORT There are few services directly at the port, but from here it's a 15- to 20-minute walk into town.

TOURIST HIGHLIGHTS In the city of Naples, see the **Museo Archeologico Nazionale.** Other historic sites include the **Castel Nuovo,** the **Museo di Capodimonte,** and the **Duomo di Napoli.** Fifteen miles southeast of Naples are the ruins of **Pompeii,** where you can wander the streets of an ancient town preserved in time by the volcanic eruption of Mt. Vesuvius. If you're in the mood for a beach day, take a hydrofoil boat to the island of **Capri.**

WHAT TO EAT Naples is the birthplace of pizza, and **Antica Pizzeria Port'Alba** (founded in 1738) is the first establishment to serve it, though certainly not the only one you should consider. The classic version is the *pizza margherita,* a simple pie of tomato, basil, and fresh mozzarella. Neapolitan cuisine is also rich in seafood, often sauced with tomatoes, garlic, and olive oil. You will find house-made mozzarella available in many shops. *Limoncello* (lemon liqueur) is the adult beverage of the region; sip it alone or mixed into juices for a refreshing cocktail. Regional desserts include *baba* (a cake, perhaps soaked in liqueur), *zeppole* (like a doughnut, often filled with custard), and *sfogliatelle* (shell-shaped pastry). The local chocolatier, **Odin-Gay,** is a city favorite.

WHAT TO BUY Bring home some of the local limoncello if you want to taste Naples at home. If you're looking for jewelry, artisans here work in 18-karat gold and carved coral. Many visitors bring home replicas of the historical artifacts they see in Pompeii. Various shops sell locally carved wooden Christmas ornaments. In Capri, handmade sandals are a popular find.

Olbia, Sardinia, Italy

LANGUAGES Italian, Sardinian, Corsican, Catalan

HISTORY Olbia is located in northeastern Sardinia (Sardegna), the second largest island in the Mediterranean. The first settlers were the Nurag people, named for the beehivelike structures called *nuraghe* that they built as residences, military fortifications/lookouts, and houses of worship; many of these still stand throughout the island. The Carthaginians annexed coastal enclaves in 537 BC. After the Punic Wars, Rome took over Sardinia and left its mark before invading Vandals and Byzantines attempted to rule the island. Later, the Moors, Genoese, and Pisans attempted or gained control for varying periods of time. In 1297, Pope Boniface VIII created the Kingdom of Sardinia and Corsica, which led to more than one hundred years of war before Sardinia eventually relented and became part of the new Kingdom of Spain in 1493. Spanish rule of Sardinia ended after the War for the Spanish Succession, with a new Kingdom of Sicily and Sardinia given to the house of Savoy as part of the Congress of London in 1718. This new kingdom was part of the central holding of the House of Savoy, later to become part of the new Kingdom of Italy in 1861. In 1948, Sardinia became an autonomous region of Italy. The past 50 years have seen Sardinia become a hotspot for tourism, with the Costa Smeralda ("Emerald Coast") in the northern area becoming a favorite retreat of Italian celebrities.

WEATHER Disney Cruise Line visits Olbia in August. Daytime highs for the month average in the mid to high–80s. Nighttime lows average in the mid-60s. Precipitation is light during the summer, with about an inch of rain expected during August.

THE PORT There are minimal services directly at the port; the cruise dock is a bit over a mile from the city. Shuttles are available, or you may walk into town; all major sights in the city are walkable. Taxis and city buses are also available for transportation to nearby beaches. Expect that many shops will be closed for several hours in the afternoon for lunch.

TOURIST HIGHLIGHTS The area's primary museum is the **Museo Archeologico,** which specializes in Greek and Roman artifacts. The **Basilica of San Simplicio,** a worthy example of a Romanesque-style space, is rendered entirely in granite. **Chiesa di San Paolo** is a more colorful religious building, with a brightly hued dome and modern frescoes. Beach options include **Porto Istana Beach,** with pristine white sand and light-blue water, and **Spiaggia Pittulongu,** known for its gentle waves and warm water. The nearby town of **Porto Rotondo** is a pleasant village for strolling and people-watching, as well as gawking at the many luxury yachts in its harbor.

WHAT TO EAT Nearly all Olbia restaurants serve fine seafood, but their reputations are built on specific meats such as suckling pig. The island also produces a fine, lean lamb as well as rustic sheep and goat cheeses that can be served new or aged. Fresh pastas should be sampled widely; compare the homemade *ragùs* (meat sauces) in several spots. Lobster Catalan-style is a famous dish that you can order at one of the restaurants located right on the water. Spicy fish stews called *burrida* and *cassola,* along with lobster, crab, anchovies, squid, clams, and fresh sardines, are popular dishes. Local wines are bountiful and excellent, and no meal should end without a final glass of *limoncello.*

WHAT TO BUY Sardinian ceramics are popular, with the best coming from Costa Smeralda, Alghero, and Santa Teresa di Gallura. Other local artisans specialize in making intricately designed baskets. Wool carpets in geometric patterns are another specialty. Gourmands will want to take home at least a few edible treats such as local honey or *torrone* nougat. Legend holds that **Cannonau,** a Sardinian red wine, is the key to a long life; bottles make a great gift for the folks at home.

Palermo, Sicily, Italy

LANGUAGES Italian, Sicilian

HISTORY The island of Sicily was inhabited by a race of people known as the Sicani, resident from about 800–734 BC, when they were invaded by the Phoenicians. The Phoenicians encountered incursions from the Greeks and

Carthaginians. Following the Punic Wars, Palermo became a Roman colony. The Romans used the island as a prime trading post, equipping it well with roads, temples, and baths, many of which still exist today. Germanic invaders took control in the fifth century. The Saracens, a North African people, were the next inhabitants, seizing Palermo in 831 AD. Conquered again in 1072 by the Normans, Palermo entered a golden age architecturally as mosques were converted to churches and new castles were built. The next chapter in the history of Palermo saw the rise of the Kingdom of Sicily and Naples. In 1194, the Holy Roman Empire conquered the island, and the Palazzo dei Normanni became the regional palace. Traded between English, Spanish, and Germanic kings, Palermo became one of the wealthiest states in Europe. Baroque architecture dominated the development, and these buildings have been well maintained for modern visitors to explore. United with the Kingdom of Naples in 1734, Palermo lost a bit of its former importance. Further conquests and challenges peaked in 1848, with a major revolutionary upheaval. Things didn't settle again until 1860, when the Kingdom of Italy annexed the island and reinvested in development. In 1943, Palermo was invaded and bombed heavily by the Allied Forces; the ensuing unrest led to the growth of an underground economy, and legends about La Cosa Nostra and local smugglers have permeated popular culture ever since.

WEATHER Disney Cruise Line visits Palermo in August. Average daytime highs for the month are in the mid-80s, with average nighttime lows in the mid-70s. Precipitation is quite light during the summer, with less than an inch of rainfall expected per month.

THE PORT The port terminal is new, with an in-house café and shop. Taxis and horse-drawn carriages are available within a 5-minute walk. The town of Palermo is easily accessible on foot, with all major services within walking distance—be aware, though, that pickpockets are common, particularly after dark. Buses serve the city. If you plan to rent a car, know how to drive a stick shift.

TOURIST HIGHLIGHTS The **Palermo Cathedral** dates to the 11th century and displays Gothic, Renaissance, Baroque, and Arab architectural influences. The **Cathedral of Monreale,** on a hill above the city, is primarily Norman in style. The **Museo Archeological Regionale** displays the "Rosetta Stone of Sicily," as well as Greek and Roman antiquities. If you're interested in more-niche art, visit **Stanze al Genio,** a private home exhibiting an extensive collection of handmade painted tiles from the region. A highlight for kids is the **International Marionette Museum,** which displays thousands of antique puppets and dolls; puppet shows are performed frequently. If you're looking for some sun, try **Modello Beach,** known for its striking blue water, or take the ferry to nearby **Ustica Island** for cave snorkeling. Film geeks will want to head straight for **Teatro Massimo**—it's the largest theatre in Italy, but more importantly, it's the setting for the final moments of the Godfather trilogy.

WHAT TO EAT You're in Sicily, so *eat, eat, eat!* Try ricotta cheese in all its forms: stuffed in ravioli, salted as a snack, or sweetened as a dessert filling. (Cannoli, anyone?) Markets and street corners are filled with vendors bearing wicker baskets; from any of these vendors you can buy a *frittola,* a sandwich made with bits of meat that the vendor retrieves from the basket and places in a bun or wax-paper cone. *Stigghiole* are charcoal-grilled lamb or calf intestines; if you can stomach the idea of eating organ meat, they're said to be delicious. Of course, you'll also find lots of fish, grilled or served over pasta; a real treat is sea urchin or raw mussels directly from the fishing pier. To revive your palate, choose a *cremolose,* an icy sorbetlike treat. Almond and pistachio are favorite flavors.

WHAT TO BUY Sicily is known for its wonderful wines, particularly sweet white Zibibbo. (This is probably a good time to remind you that DCL guests age 21 and over may bring two unopened bottles of wine on board at each port.) **Caltagirone** ceramics can be expensive, but they're also the apex of Sicilian craftsmanship. Other good choices are items handmade using the lava from Mt. Etna. If you're looking for something to wear, the flat cap known as the *coppola* is one of the most well-known symbols of Sicily; you'll see it worn everywhere during your stay. The marzipan in Sicily is prized; look for elaborately decorated fruit-shaped candies. If you want to browse the local foodstuffs, the **Capo** and **Ballaro farmers markets** house vendors selling produce, meat, and fish. For children, look for hand-crafted marionettes.

Palma de Mallorca, Balearic Islands, Spain

LANGUAGES Catalan, English, German, Spanish

HISTORY Along with Formentera, Ibiza, and Minorca, Mallorca (also spelled *Mallorca*) is one of the Balearic Islands, an autonomous region of Spain; Palma de Mallorca is the capital of both the island of Mallorca and the autonomous region as a whole. Mallorcan rule has changed hands numerous times over the centuries. The island's first inhabitants were peoples of the prehistoric Talaiotic Period. Palma was found in 123 BC as a Roman camp on the remains of a Talaiotic settlement; it later came under the rule of the Byzantines and the Moors. In 1229, James I of Aragón renamed the city Palma de Mallorca. Over the centuries it has weathered attacks from the Vandals and from Turkish and Berber pirates. In the 18th century, commercial activities and trade with the Spanish colonies and the Americas blossomed, which eventually lead to the expansion of maritime tourism. Since the 1950s, Palma has been a popular tourist destination, particularly with Britons and Germans. In fact, so many of the latter vacation here or live here during the winter that it's picked up the nickname "The 17th German State."

WEATHER Mid-June–mid-September is the warm season, with daytime highs typically in the low 80s and nighttime lows typically in the low 60s. This is also the driest time of the year, with just a 16% chance of precipitation during the summer.

THE PORT The port itself is located in a remote industrial area with little to do or see. You'll want to make the 15-minute trip into town.

TOURIST HIGHLIGHTS The town of Palma is about 3 miles away from the port, easily accessible by taxi or shuttle. The **Cathedral Sa Seu** is a great place to start your touring. Located in the oldest area of town, the cathedral has views of the seaside **Parc de la Mar,** a wonderful picnic venue. Also nearby is the Avinguda d'Antoni Maura, a street lined with cafés and snack shops, and **Passeig des Borns,** a major shopping thoroughfare. Keep an eye out for Gothic, Moorish, and Renaissance architectural influences. To see the countryside, take the breathtaking 1-hour train ride through the mountains to the **Port of Sóller.**

WHAT TO EAT Mediterranean staples abound. For a sit-down meal or snack, go with tapas, the traditional Spanish small plates. Cured meats, ham, fresh fish, figs, almonds, and olives are often prominently featured on the menus. The Mallorcan countryside is known for its orange and lemon groves, so many dishes will have a citrus element.

WHAT TO BUY Palma is acclaimed for its cultured pearls and leather goods—jewelry and bags should be the focus of your shopping. Also look for carved wooden bowls and decorative objects made from felled agricultural trees.

Villefranche, France

LANGUAGES French and Italian

HISTORY The Greeks were the first organized human presence on what is now known as the French Riviera. They were followed by the Romans in the eighth century BC. Before the Dark Ages, the region saw invasions from Visigoths, Burgundians, and Ostrogoths, which were later followed by threats from the Saracens and Normans. Stability came in the 13th century with the House of Grimaldi, which took power in what is now Nice, Antibes, and Monaco. Tourism became a major influence in the area beginning in the late 1700s, when wealthy Brits began arriving to take advantage of the climate and fine air quality.

WEATHER Disney cruises visit the French Riviera in August, when it's warm and dry. Daytime highs average in the low 70s to low 80s; nighttime lows average in the mid-60s. Precipitation is low, with fewer than 2 inches of rainfall for the month.

THE PORT Disney cruises anchor in the harbor and tender to the terminal in central Villefranche. Several small shops and cafés, along with train and bus stations, are within walking distance. A soap factory in town, **La Savonnerie de Villefranche,** lets visitors watch its work. If you're staying in port and looking for relaxation, the public beach is about a 10-minute walk away from the old town.

TOURIST HIGHLIGHTS Most major and minor points on the French Riviera are accessible with less than an hour of travel away from the port. In **Nice,** stroll along the **Promenade des Anglais** or visit the **Cours Saleya** market for sweet and savory treats. In **Cannes,** look for art galleries on the **Rue d'Antibes. Monte Carlo** is famous for luxury shopping, royalty, and the **Grand Casino,** where you can try your hand if you're in a gambling mood. **Èze** is a medieval-era hilltop village from which you can see into France, Monaco, and Italy. **Grasse,** known as the fragrance capital of the world, offers tours of various perfume factories where visitors can concoct their own signature scents.

WHAT TO EAT You'll find less butter and cream in food along the French Riviera than you would in other parts of France. Look here for *bouillabaisse* (fish stew), *salade niçoise* (a salad composed of tuna, tomato, eggs, and olives), the pizzalike *pissaladière*, crêpes, and, of course, plenty of pastry.

WHAT TO BUY In Monte Carlo, look for souvenirs associated with Princess Grace and other Grimaldis, as well as trinkets representing the Grand Prix auto race. In Cannes, you'll find many items emblazoned with the logo of the city's world-renowned film festival. Throughout the area, look for wines, linens, and fragrances.

MEXICO

CRUISES SAIL FROM San Diego

SHIP *Wonder*

CRUISE LENGTH 3, 5, and 7 nights

DATES September and October

WHAT TO PACK These DCL cruises have a "Halloween on the High Seas" theme, so bring along your costumes of choice in addition to sunscreen and such if you want to join the fun on board.

SIGNATURE PORT ADVENTURES The usual: sightseeing, dolphin excursions, beach pursuits, shopping, partying

CLASSIC DISNEY ADD-ON Disneyland

COMMENTS With the exception of Mazatlán, these ports are also stops on DCL's California Coast and Panama Canal cruises—the novelty of cruising during Halloween season is the selling point.

PROS

- Can be very affordable, particularly if you live on the West Coast.
- Short cruises are easy on your schedule.

CONS

- These cruises are marketed to families, but the fact that they take place while school is in session could make scheduling a problem.

- There's really nothing that sets these itineraries apart from comparable ones on any other cruise line.
- The Mexican holiday that corresponds to Halloween in the US—**Día de Los Muertos,** or Day of the Dead (November 1), doesn't have our holiday's months-long commercialized buildup. Don't expect to find any preliminary festivities going on while you're in port, even on sailings in mid-October.

Cabo San Lucas, Mexico   (See page 317 for full profile.)

Mazatlán, Mexico

LANGUAGE Spanish

HISTORY The original occupants of Mazatlán were the native Totorames. The first European settlers were the Spaniards, who arrived in 1531. During the early 1600s, English and French pirates used the area's sheltered coastline to ambush passing merchant ships. In 1821, Mexico gained its independence from Spain, and Mazatlán began to prosper as a port city as well as the capital of the state of Sinaloa. In the second half of the 1800s, Mazatlán changed hands multiple times, moving from US occupation during the Mexican–American War in 1847 to French domination a few years later, culminating with Mexican independence in the 1860s. Port growth continued in the later 1800s with the construction of a series of lighthouses and a link with railway systems. The Mexican Revolution, which lasted from 1910 to 1917, put a hold on growth in the early 1900s. While a slight rebound occurred after the revolution, the Great Depression and WWII dampened Mexico's economy. The economy stabilized with an influx of tourism beginning in the 1960s, followed by the growth of the area fishing industry.

WEATHER Disney Cruise Line visits Mazatlán in September and October. Daytime temperatures during these months average in the high 80s, with nighttime lows dipping only into the high 70s. Rainfall peaks in Mazatlán in September, with an average of 10 inches of precipitation per month. October is slightly drier, with an average of 6 inches of rain per month.

THE PORT Ships typically dock at a commercial port, with guests transported to the cruise terminal via tram. The terminal has shops, liquor stores, and (depending on when you go) some rather aggressive pitchmen trying to entice you to buy into time-share condos. **Old Town Mazatlán** is a 1-mile walk from the cruise terminal; taxis are plentiful and can provide a 5-minute ride to the center of the city. The **Zona Dorada** ("Golden Zone"), where the beaches and touristy stuff are centered, is a 20-minute cab ride away. There are rental-car desks at the pier.

Note: A federal travel advisory is currently in effect for the area, so read and heed these recommendations from the US State Department:

Defer nonessential travel to the state of Sinaloa except the city of Mazatlán, where you should exercise caution, particularly late at night and in the early morning. One of Mexico's most powerful criminal organizations is based in the state of Sinaloa, and violent-crime rates remain high in many parts of the state. Travel off the toll roads in remote areas of Sinaloa is especially dangerous and should be avoided. We recommend that any travel in Mazatlán be limited to Zona Dorada and the historic town center, as well as direct routes to/from these locations and the airport.

TOURIST HIGHLIGHTS The beaches in Mazatlán are top-notch. **Las Gaviotas Beach** and **Sabolo Beach** are popular and, as a result, crowded—**Olas Altas Beach** is a more relaxing choice. **Stone Island** offers horseback riding and snorkeling expeditions. Architecture enthusiasts will want to visit **Immaculate Conception Basilica,** with its ornate domed ceilings. The **Teatro Ángela Peralta,** a theater from the late 1800s named for a beloved Mexican opera singer, has elaborate wrought-iron balconies and an ornate period interior; today, it shows movies and presents concerts and dance performances. The **Archeological Museum of Mazatlán** offers a look into the pre-European history and culture of the area. Kids will like the **Acuario Mazatlán,** an aquarium housing more than 250 species of sea life. **El Faro Lighthouse,** at 500 feet above sea level, is the second highest natural lighthouse in the world and makes for a nice hike.

WHAT TO EAT Mazatlán is a fishing town; you'll find all manner of seafood in its restaurants and cafés. Shrimp is a specialty: shrimp cocktail marinated in green chiles and lime, shrimp quesadillas, fried shrimp, shrimp ceviche, bacon-wrapped shrimp stuffed with cheese . . . shades of Bubba Gump! Also try *posole,* a soup made with hominy and sometimes pork; *birria,* a stew of goat or lamb; or *chorreadas,* thick corn tortillas covered with meat, onions, and cheese (think a rustic quesadilla). Your side dish may include prickly pear cactus. You'll find many varieties of beer here; if you want something sans booze, look for *agua de jamaica,* a berry-colored, tealike drink made from boiled hibiscus flowers mixed with sugar and lime, or creamy, rice-based *horchata,* flavored with sugar, vanilla, and cinnamon.

WHAT TO BUY The **Mazatlán Arts and Crafts Center,** in the Zona Dorada, sells a wide array of artisanal products from all over Mexico. Popular items include textiles, such as beach wraps, embroidered shirts, and sera-pes. Leather sandals and handbags are popular purchases as well, along with handmade housewares and decorative items in wood or pottery. Silver jewelry is everywhere, but weigh the quality against the price. *Heads-up:* Diamonds are tax-free in Mexico! In addition to crafts, the Mercado del Centro has food vendors who sell spices and local liquors; bargaining is customary.

Puerto Vallarta, Mexico *(See page 320 for full profile.)*

San Diego, California *(See page 245 for full profile.)*

NORTHERN EUROPE, BRITISH ISLES, *and* NORWAY

CRUISES SAIL FROM Dover, Copenhagen

SHIP *Magic*

CRUISE LENGTHS 7–12 nights

DATES Summer

WHAT TO PACK Binoculars, warm clothing

SIGNATURE PORT ADVENTURE It's all about the fjords.

CLASSIC DISNEY ADD-ON If you have any money left after your cruise, **Adventures by Disney** will gladly snap it up.

COMMENTS There was this movie called *Frozen* that was mildly popular a few years ago. We're not saying that Disney decided the best way for DCL to take advantage of this was to sail to Arendelle—sorry, *Norway*—but there are definitely a lot of tie-ins on the cruise. But there's also scenery that can be appreciated only from a cruise ship.

ADDITIONAL PORTS Disney Cruise Line is not visiting the Norwegian ports of **Kristiansand** and **Oslo** in 2017, but we think they'll return to the schedule

PROS	CONS
▪ Spectacular scenery.	▪ We really hope you enjoyed *Frozen*.
▪ Family-friendly way to see Northern Europe.	▪ Food in port can be quite expensive.
▪ Most of your meals are included in what are some very expensive places to visit.	▪ These are among the most expensive cruises Disney offers—and that's not including airfare to the port.

in the future. For more information on these ports, including a custom walking tour of Oslo, consult *The Unofficial Guide to Disney Cruise Line 2016* or visit touringplans.com/disney-cruise-line/ports (requires a Touring Plans.com subscription).

Akureyri, Iceland

LANGUAGE Icelandic

HISTORY The first known Viking settlement in Iceland occurred in the ninth century AD. Transient fishing camps formed and dissipated for many hundreds of years, with the first permanent settlement established in 1778; even so, the population numbered less than 100 for many more years. Growth in earnest began in the mid-1800s, when Icelanders began to appreciate the sound natural port and fine agricultural conditions. During World War II, the island served as an air base for British and Norwegian troops, and the US Air Force maintained a presence there until 2006. (Iceland, however, has no armed forces of its own and is considered the most peaceful country in the world.) Today, fishing and fish processing are the main industries, with tourism an area of growth. Perhaps its best-known export is Björk, the aggressively quirky singer-songwriter.

    With a population of just under 20,000, Akureyri is a small town by US standards, but it's the second-largest urban area in Iceland.

WEATHER They don't call it "Iceland" for nothing, but Disney cruises visit in May and June, when the average daytime highs are surprisingly mild—in the mid-40s to mid-50s. Nighttime lows in early summer average in the mid-30s to mid-40s. Precipitation is typically minimal during this time of year, with monthly rainfall estimated at fewer than 2 inches per month.

THE PORT Services at the port are few, but much of Akureyri is accessible by foot or bicycle. Taxis and free buses will take you on the short ride to town, where bike rentals and bike tours are available.

TOURIST HIGHLIGHTS Akureyri is home to several small but notable museums, including the **Safnasafið New Folk and Outsider Art Museum,** the **Aviation Museum,** and the **Industry Museum.** For an outdoor experience, try whale-watching, fishing, horseback riding, or taking a dip in a geothermal pool.

WHAT TO EAT Not surprisingly, seafood is a specialty of many restaurants in this fishing nation. Salmon, char, and mussels are particularly popular. Fish is prepared sushi-style or in traditional smoked, salted, and cured forms.

(*Hákarl*, or fermented shark, is best left to Andrew Zimmern wannabes.) Beef and dairy are also popular. *Skýr* is a tangy dairy product native to Iceland; similar in flavor and consistency to Greek yogurt, it's technically a cheese. Burgers are easy to find; locals like them topped with béarnaise sauce and French fries. You can also try exotic game such as puffin, reindeer, and whale. Several local bakeries sell a variety of breads, pastries, and doughnuts. The only microbrewery in Iceland, **Kaldi,** is a 20-minute drive from Akureyri.

WHAT TO BUY A popular stop is the **Christmas Garden** shop, which offers a wide array of candles, ornaments, decorations, and ginger-scented snacks. Viking and troll memorabilia can be found almost everywhere. Knit textiles such as sweaters and mittens make for cozy mementos of your trip. You can even buy a reindeer hide to serve as a rug or blanket back home.

Ålesund, Norway

LANGUAGE Norwegian

HISTORY Ålesund has existed as a fishing village since Viking times. According to local lore, the Viking chief Rollo hailed from the area. In 1904, a major fire destroyed much of the town, leaving nearly 10,000 residents homeless. Germany's Kaiser Wilhelm assisted in the rebuilding effort by sending ships full of construction materials. Many of the structures that stand today were built circa 1904–07 in the Art Nouveau style. But despite Germany's influence, Ålesund sided with the Allies during World War II. Today, fishing is its primary industry.

WEATHER DCL visits Ålesund in June. Average daytime highs during this period are in the mid- to upper 50s, with average nighttime lows in the mid- to upper 40s. Precipitation is minimal at this time of year, with less than an inch of rain during June.

THE PORT Ålesund's port is small, but within an easy 10-minute stroll, you'll find shops, cafés, and local points of interest.

TOURIST HIGHLIGHTS Trek up the stairs from the town park to **Fjellstua,** a mountaintop lodge and café, for panoramic views of the harbor. **Vasset Outdoor and Sports Park** offers fishing and horseback riding. The **Sunnmøre Museum** displays numerous styles of fishing boats as well as 40 historic structures. The municipal **Aalesunds Museum** provides information and exhibits about the city and about the Arctic in general.

WHAT TO EAT This is Scandinavia, so seafood is a given. Try the local delicacy *klipfish*—split, salted, and dried cod. Salted smoked herring is also popular. Adventurous types can buy prawns directly from the fishing boats and eat them raw on the docks. Cheeses and game meats are readily available as well. If you're not in the mood for Norwegian food, several local places serve pizza.

WHAT TO BUY Hand-knit woolen hats, mittens, and sweaters are easy to find in Ålesund. Blown glass and pottery stock the shelves in shops and galleries. Depictions of trolls and moose adorn all manner of objects. Foodies will want to take home some local jam or honey.

Amsterdam, The Netherlands

LANGUAGE Dutch

HISTORY Amsterdam was founded as a fishing village in the 13th century. Rapid growth occurred during the 14th and 15th centuries, with extensive building of timber-frame dwellings (most later destroyed by fire) and the development of the trading port. The 16th century brought a rebellion by the Dutch against the Habsburg King Philip II of Spain and the religious intolerance of the Spanish. The rebellion led to the Eighty Years' War and Dutch independence; subsequently, people were substantially free to believe what they wanted. In years when religious wars raged throughout Europe, many people sought refuge in the Dutch Republic and Amsterdam, making the area a haven for immigrants of many persuasions. By the mid-1600s, trade and commerce converged in Amsterdam, making it a major hub for art and agriculture. The negative by-product of this cultural melting pot was an outbreak of the bubonic plague in the 1660s, with more than 10% of the city's residents falling to the disease.

Prosperity declined in the 1700s and 1800s, with Amsterdam's fortunes reaching a low during the Napoleonic wars. Reinvigoration came in the form of the Industrial Revolution. The 19th century also saw the construction of many public buildings and a series of 42 protective forts. The Netherlands was a neutral territory during WWII, when German troops invaded. More than 100,000 Jews were deported, devastating the area's Jewish community and ruining the region's diamond trade.

Today, Amsterdam is renowned for its relaxed social attitudes, most famously demonstrated by its red-light districts and "coffee" culture. *Pro-tip:* **Coffeeshops** (English word) sell cannabis, **koffiehuizen** (Dutch word) sell the hot caffeinated beverage. Don't take Aunt Fern to a coffeeshop if all she wants is a cappuccino with light foam.

WEATHER Disney Cruise Line visits Amsterdam in May and June. Average daytime highs during this period are in the low to mid-60s. Nighttime lows average in the high 40s to low 50s. Rainfall during this time averages 2–3 inches per month.

THE PORT Cruise ships dock at **Passenger Terminal Amsterdam.** Shuttles and taxis are plentiful at the port. There is also a tram stop just outside the terminal; it's a 15-minute walk to **Central Station,** the city's main transportation hub. Biking is a major form of transport in Amsterdam; bike rentals are plentiful throughout the city. Cafés and shops are within an easy walk of the port. The public library opposite the railroad tracks from Passenger Terminal Amsterdam offers free Wi-Fi.

TOURIST HIGHLIGHTS The **Rijksmuseum** is one of the world's premier art museums, featuring works by masters such as Rembrandt and Vermeer. The nearby **Van Gogh Museum** is another must-see for art lovers. Literature and history buffs will want to see the **Anne Frank House,** the Frank family's hiding place during WWII; advance ticket purchase is recommended. The **Resistance Museum** covers WWII history from other perspectives. The **Homomonument,** a memorial in the center of the city comprising three pink-granite triangles set in the ground, honors LGBT people from around the world who have suffered persecution, including those who perished in the Nazi concentration camps. Canal tours are a must for many, as are strolls or bike excursions through the well-manicured parks and tulip gardens. A windmill tour is another iconic experience. **The Heineken Experience** is a brewery tour and tasting for those in the mood to relax.

WHAT TO EAT *Krokets* (croquettes) are meat-filled dumplings, covered with breadcrumbs and then deep-fried; find them in chicken, shrimp, and ragout (meat stew) variations. A somewhat similar fried bite is the *bitterbal,* typically filled with beef and butter. Other savory dishes include sausages and fried fish. *Patat* is the Dutch version of French fries, served in a paper cone and offered with toppings such as chopped onions, spicy mayonnaise (*fritesaus*), or peanut sauce (*pindasaus*). *Stroopwafels,* thin waffle-like wafers stuck together with caramel *syrup*, are the Dutch signature sweet; buy them from street vendors or at any café or bakery. Another area favorite is licorice, available in many varieties from soft and sweet to chewy and intensely salty. Pastry offerings include *pannenkoeken,* somewhat like crêpes, and *poffertjes,* puffy miniature pancakes served with powdered sugar or fruit.

WHAT TO BUY **Albert Cuyp Market** is the busiest outdoor market in Europe. Delft pottery in classic in blue and white can be found in simple tiles, decorative objects, home decor, and kitchenware. Knockoff pieces will set you back just a few euros, but large, authentic pieces may cost thousands. Depictions of tulips or tulip bulbs are reminders of the familiar Dutch flower. Books about the life of Anne Frank or reproductions of Van Gogh's artwork are fitting remembrances of some of the area's most famous residents. Wooden clogs may be a bit cliché, but some folks consider them a must-buy in the Netherlands—look for high-quality handcrafted pieces if you actually plan to wear them. Hard cheeses, flavored with herbs and spices, are ubiquitous; buy them vacuum-packed for easy transport and storage.

Bergen, Norway

LANGUAGE Norwegian

HISTORY Bergen, the second-largest city in Norway with about a quarter-million people, was founded circa AD 1030 as a Viking settlement and served as the national capital during the 13th century. It was only superseded in population by the current capital of Oslo in the mid-1800s. Over the centuries, Bergen has withstood a number of challenges: In the 1300s, it was decimated by the Black Plague; English and Dutch forces battled in its harbor in the 17th century; a series of fires spanning hundreds of years devastated it; and Germany occupied it for several years during World War II. Bergen has long been a Scandinavian center of trade, in particular the seafood industry.

WEATHER Disney cruises visit Bergen in June, when average daytime highs are in the mid- to upper 60s and average nighttime lows are in the mid- to upper 50s. Precipitation is typically minimal, with less than an inch of rainfall in June.

THE PORT The port is within a 10-minute walk of town. Restaurants, cafés, and shops are all nearby, as are many of Bergen's tourist attractions. Taxis are plentiful, but many people choose to walk. The wharf area is particularly photogenic.

TOURIST HIGHLIGHTS Many visitors enjoy browsing in the local fish market. Others take the funicular to **Mt. Floyen** for breathtaking views of the surrounding islands. **Bergenhus Festning,** at the entrance to Bergen's harbor, is one of the oldest, best-preserved castles in Norway, with dungeons on the ground floor. **Bryggens Museum** displays archaeological finds from the 12th century. **Bergen Aquarium** houses one of Europe's largest collections of fish and invertebrates from the North Sea. The **Fantoft Stavkirke,** about 3 miles from town, is a painstakingly reconstructed 12th-century stave church: It was built around 1150 in the town of Fortun, moved to Bergen and reassembled in 1883, burned by arsonists in 1992, and finally reopened in 1997 after an extensive restoration. Classical-music enthusiasts will want to visit **Troldhaugen,** the home of composer Edvard Grieg, which is preserved in its 1907 state, complete with Grieg's own Steinway piano.

WHAT TO EAT As a seaport, Bergen specializes in many forms of seafood, including prawns, octopus, salmon, and even smoked whale. Cod plays a starring role in fish cakes, fish balls, and fish pudding (tastes better than it sounds). Root vegetables such as carrots, potatoes, turnips, and onions are a common accompaniment. Pork and game meats are served in the form of chops, meatballs, or in stews. Berries are popular for breakfast or dessert. Several British-style pubs serve beer and ale in a cozy atmosphere—they'll also have a bottle or three of aquavit behind the bar. For the homesick, there's even a TGI Friday's in town.

WHAT TO BUY Knit woolens abound in every form: sweaters, caps, mittens, and socks. Trolls are depicted on every possible item, including clothing, kitchenware, and knickknacks. Also look for unique cheese knives and pewter serving pieces.

Copenhagen, Denmark

LANGUAGE Danish

HISTORY Copenhagen was founded as a Viking fishing village in the 11th century. The first fortresses in the area were built circa 1160. In the mid-1400s, the city was designated as the capital of Denmark, the country's first king (Christian I) was crowned, and the University of Copenhagen was founded. The mid-1600s and early 1700s were a period of turmoil and destruction, with a siege by Sweden and a series of devastating fires. In the early 1800s, Copenhagen withstood an attack by Britain. Most of the 1800s and early 1900s were a period of growth, with art and public beautification as a focus; the Tivoli Gardens amusement park and the writings of the beloved Danish author Hans Christian Andersen also came about during this time. The Nazis occupied the city during World War II, following which came another period of artistic growth and development of infrastructure.

Copenhagen is simply lovely. The beautiful scenery, the gorgeous, friendly people, the terrific, reasonably priced food, and the fact that nearly everyone speaks perfect English have prompted Erin's 15-year-old daughter to muse about moving here.

WEATHER DCL visits Copenhagen in May–July. Average daytime highs in May are typically in the mid-50s, with nighttime lows in the mid-40s. In June and July, daytime highs are in the mid- to high 60s, with nighttime lows in the low 50s. (Copenhagen's highest recorded temperatures have reached only the mid-80s.) Precipitation is minimal in the summer, averaging less than an inch of rain per month.

THE PORT The **Frihavnen (Freeport) Terminal,** about 2 miles from town, offers little in the way of services. Taxi stands are nearby, or you can take a 15-minute walk to the nearest train station to get to local sights. Copenhagen Airport is less than 10 miles from the port, making for an easy transfer.

TOURIST HIGHLIGHTS Children will enjoy a visit to **Tivoli Gardens,** an intricately landscaped amusement park that provided inspiration to Walt Disney during a 1950s visit. The park offers charming, gentle rides as well as thrills for braver souls. Speaking of Disney inspirations, a visit to Copenhagen wouldn't be complete without a stop at Edvard Eriksen's iconic *Little Mermaid* statue, near the harbor. **Rosenborg Castle** houses artifacts of Danish royalty, including many of the crown jewels. The **Latin Quarter** makes for a nice walk; you'll pass the oldest church and synagogue in the city, as well as the university. The **Staten Museum for Kunst** is the country's premier fine-art repository, and the **Nationalmuseet** is Denmark's largest museum of cultural history. Fans of **Hans Christian Andersen**'s fairy tales will want to visit one of the many places he called home in Copenhagen or pay their respects at his grave.

WHAT TO EAT Not surprisingly, Danish pastries are the thing to get for breakfast. Look for local breads and jams as well as *snegl* (snail), a type of buttery cinnamon roll. Seafood, including scallops, cod, salmon, whiting, and oysters, is served fresh, smoked, salted, and pickled. Sausages, cheeses, and deli-style meats are popular, too, particularly as part of a *smørrebrød,* or open-faced sandwich. Pork or veal meatballs, accompanied by boiled or roasted potatoes, are classic Danish comfort food. Side dishes are often cabbage- or onion-based. The local beer is **Carlsberg;** the brewery holds daily tours and tastings during the summer.

WHAT TO BUY Legos were invented in Denmark; look for unique sets that aren't available back home. Danish fashion is gaining a reputation as worldclass, thanks to hot designers like **Baum und Pfergarten, Bruuns Bazaar, Henrik Vibskov,** and **Stine Goya.** Clean lines and eco-friendly materials have long been the hallmark of Danish furniture and housewares. **Royal Copenhagen** porcelain is a perennial favorite of collectors. Viking-themed toys, statuary, and books are popular souvenirs.

Dover, England, United Kingdom *(See page 279 for full profile.)*

Dublin, Ireland

LANGUAGES English, Irish (Gaeilge)

HISTORY Documented history in Dublin begins with Viking raids in the eighth and ninth centuries, leading to the establishment of a settlement on the south side of the River Liffey. Despite fortifications, the town was sacked many times over the next two centuries. By the 11th century, trading relationships with the English towns of Chester and Bristol brought prosperity to Dublin. Seven hundred years of Norman rule began in the late 12th century. Then, from the 14th to 18th centuries, Dublin was incorporated into the English Crown and became the "second city" of the British Empire for a time. In 1650, a plague killed nearly half of Dublin's citizens, causing a major setback in civic development. The early 1700s saw a rebound as the wool and linen trades with England grew. A period of rapid expansion in the 1700s was followed by overpopulation, checked by disease and poverty in the 1800s. The break from England came with the 1916 Easter Rising, the War for Independence, and the subsequent Civil War, eventually leading to the establishment of the Republic of Ireland. Since the mid-1990s, an economic boom christened the "Celtic Tiger" has brought massive expansion and development to Dublin; it also brought many new ethnic groups into the city and created a more international feel, particularly in the north inner city.

WEATHER Disney Cruise Line visits Dublin in July. Daytime highs for the month average in the mid-60s, with nighttime lows averaging in the low 50s. Expect precipitation of about 3 inches per month.

TOURIST HIGHLIGHTS The **Guinness Storehouse** offers lessons on the history of the brew and provides a free pint at the end of the tour. Children will enjoy the **Dublin Zoo** and its elephants, tigers, and gorillas, along with the **National Aquatic Center,** home to one of the best water parks in Europe. Art lovers will want to make a stop at the **National Gallery of Ireland,** with holdings that include works by Monet, Picasso, Van Gogh, and Vermeer. The **National Botanic Gardens** is a nice spot for a relaxing stroll. History buffs will want to see the **Book of Kells at Trinity College Dublin,** as well as **St. Patrick's Cathedral** and the **National Museum of Ireland.**

WHAT TO EAT Dublin is a metropolitan city, with most major cuisines represented in its restaurants. For traditional Irish fare, look for fried fish or seafood pie, always served with some form of potatoes. Irish cheeses from goat, sheep, or cow milk are in abundant supply. Meat eaters will want to try a classic Irish stew, made with mutton, lamb, or beef, or tuck in to some corned beef and cabbage for a hearty repast. If you're looking for sweets, have some lemon-and-vanilla-curd cake, a sort of Irish cheesecake. No trip to Ireland would be complete without raising a pint of Guinness Stout or sipping some Irish whiskey. If you're looking for some warm fortification, order a mug of Irish coffee.

WHAT TO BUY Textiles are the main retail draw in Dublin. Irish linens are a nice choice, as are hand-knitted sweaters, caps, mittens, and scarves. The traditional Irish fisherman's sweater is bulky, warm, and expensive—make sure you're buying the genuine article and not a machine-knit knockoff. If you want branded items, look for jerseys and tees sporting the logo of a local pub or football (soccer) team, or buy a mug with the Guinness name on it. If you want to take some libations on board, a bottle of **Jameson's** whiskey will set you right.

Geiranger, Norway

LANGUAGE Norwegian

HISTORY Geiranger was quite isolated, inhabited by only a handful of native people, until the mid-1800s, when the first steamships and tourist boats stopped to take in views of the fjords, which are now listed as a UNESCO World Heritage Site. During the late 1800s, construction began on several hotels so that visitors could stay to enjoy the natural wonders for longer periods. Since then, Geiranger has functioned as a tourist destination from May to October each year, but it reverts to a typical Norwegian small town in the winter, with fewer than 500 permanent residents.

WEATHER Disney cruises visit Geiranger in June. Average daytime highs during this period are in the high 50s to mid-60s, with nighttime lows averaging in the high 40s to low 50s. Precipitation is typically minimal at this time of year, with less than an inch of rain for the month.

THE PORT Ships anchor in the harbor and tender into port. Geiranger is tiny—you can walk from one end of town to the other in less than 20 minutes, or you can take a taxi. Several shops and cafés are steps away from the docking area.

TOURIST HIGHLIGHTS The natural beauty of the fjords is the main attraction of the area; explore it by biking or hiking. **Brudesløret (The Bridal Veil)** is one of the most scenic waterfalls in Norway. Take in the views from the **Dalsnibba** mountain plateau or from **Flydalsjuvet,** a jutting rock formation. History buffs may enjoy **Herdalssetra,** a 300-year-old goat farm that provides a modern view into an ancient agrarian lifestyle; the goats are adorable, too. **Geiranger Church** is a lovely example of traditional architecture. Geiranger is also home to the **Norwegian Fjord Center** as well as a small local art gallery.

WHAT TO EAT Local markets sell cloudberries, strawberries, fruit juices, *sylte* (head cheese), cheeses, goat meat, *mør* (a form of preserved meat), and preserved sausages. Restaurants and cafés serve traditional Norwegian dishes, including fish prepared in many styles, smoked whale, venison, and elk. Pastry lovers will enjoy the local sweet waffle served with berries and cream.

WHAT TO BUY Geiranger shops sell the ubiquitous Norwegian knit goods and troll souvenirs. Also look for carved rock jewelry, painted wood, and tin kitchenware.

Greenock, Scotland, United Kingdom

LANGUAGES English, Scottish Gaelic (Gàidhlig)

HISTORY The area was known as a safe fishing port as early as the 12th century. Organized ownership began in 1296, when Hugh de Grenock was created a Scottish baron. Greenock became a fishing village in the early

1600s; harbor access was also important to the growing tobacco trade. In the early 1700s, shipbuilding became a prominent industry. In 1812, Europe's first steamboat service included Greenock as a stopping point, making it an attractive area for expansion of the paper, cotton, and sugar refining trades. The mid-1800s saw the expansion of rail lines to Glasgow and other points within Scotland. Greenock was the site of major torpedo manufacturing during the World Wars. Several of the area industries saw closures in the mid-1900s, and unemployment was rampant in the latter part of the last century. In the last several years, tourism has provided a boost to the community.

WEATHER Disney Cruise Line visits Greenock/Glasgow in July. Average daytime highs in July are in the high 60s. Average nighttime lows are in the high 40s to low 50s. Rainfall during July is typically 3 inches per month.

THE PORT The **Greenock Terminal** includes basic services such as snacks, currency exchange, ATMs, and car-rental desks. If you decide to rent a car, remember that driving here takes place on the left-hand side of the road. Taxis and shuttles are readily available. You can find fast-food restaurants and a few banks within a 10-minute walk of the port. The train station is a 10- to 15-minute walk away, with regular service to **Glasgow,** just under an hour away. **Edinburgh** is 2–3 hours away by train, depending on the number of stops.

TOURIST HIGHLIGHTS Most visitors to Greenock will decide to tour in Glasgow. **Glasgow Cathedral** is one of the most complete old churches in Scotland, unique for its double church structure. If you're looking to add a touch of Haunted Mansion to your visit, stop at the **Necropolis,** an atmospheric Victorian cemetery. Museum lovers will enjoy the **Burrell Collection,** an eclectic museum housing everything from ancient tapestries to Impressionist paintings. The **Kelvingrove Art Gallery and Museum** is home to works by many major artists, but it's perhaps best known for its room dedicated to the work of Scottish architect and designer Charles Rennie Mackintosh, the leading exponent of the Art Nouveau movement in Great Britain. To learn about the local spirits, try a tour of the **Glengoyne Distillery** or the **Tennents Wellpark Brewery.**

WHAT TO EAT Traditional Glaswegian dishes include cullen skink, a stew made from smoked haddock, potatoes, and onions. Haddock also can be found deep-fried or broiled and served with "tatties and neeps" (mashed potatoes and turnips). Many main dishes are based on venison, lamb, or beef. These may be accompanied by colcannon, a mashed-potato-and-cabbage mixture, or by Yorkshire pudding, a bready side dish made with a batter of eggs, flour, and milk. To truly experience Scottish cuisine, you'll want to go into *Fear Factor* mode and partake of some black pudding (blood sausage) or haggis, a boiled mix of onions, oatmeal, and organ meats. (This is probably a good place to emphasize that *pudding* in the UK refers to something savory as often as it does sweet.) Scones and oat cakes are popular snacks. Be sure to follow any meal with a good Scotch whisky or a local beer.

WHAT TO BUY Scotland is known for its quality knitwear and textiles. Try a tartan for a traditional look. A jersey from a local football (soccer) team is another popular fabric souvenir. Celtic-themed jewelry is sold throughout the region. And of course, you can't go wrong with a bottle of the local whiskey.

Hebrides Islands, Scotland, United Kingdom

LANGUAGES English, Scottish Gaelic (Gàidhlig)

HISTORY The Isles of Lewis and Harris are at the northwest corner of the group of Scottish islands known as the Hebrides, or Western Isles. The earliest known structures in the Hebrides date to 3000 BC, exemplified by the Standing Stones at Callanish. Little is known of the people who first settled on the islands, but they are presumed to be of similar Celtic background to other Scots. The Hebrides were under Norse control from AD 1079 to 1266, after which time the Scots claimed the area. Clan chiefs traded regional rule for the next 400 years, during which time the economy was primarily agrarian. Kelp farming became a key industry in the 1700 and early 1800s. After the 1815 Battle of Waterloo, the kelp market collapsed and many clans became bankrupt. The 1840 potato blight further impoverished Scotland as well as Ireland. Emigration from the area was steady through the 1920s. Following the World Wars, the Hebrides were explored by the petroleum industry; offshore oil finds brought recovery to the economy. Tourism is now a major source of income.

WEATHER Disney Cruise Line visits northern Scotland in July, when daytime highs average in the low 60s and nighttime lows average in the high 40s. Expect moderate precipitation, with an average of about 4 inches per month during the summer.

THE PORT Stornoway is a tender port—the *Magic* docks off the coast, and guests wishing to disembark the ship board a smaller vessel to take them to shore. The town of Stornoway is a 10-minute walk from the dock, which has basic services including restaurants and shops. Taxis are available.

TOURIST HIGHLIGHTS The scenic outdoors, particularly the rugged rock formations, are a key draw for tourists; the **Standing Stones of Callanish** and the **Broch at Carloway** are among Europe's most famous ancient monuments. While it will likely be too cold to swim there on your cruise, **Luskentyre Beach** has pristine turquoise waters and white sand, perfect for walking. Other guests prefer to explore the countryside by bike or watch the wildlife from small boats along the shore. History buffs will enjoy **St. Clement's Church,** a Clan Macleod place of worship since the 1500s, now a popular scenic wedding spot. The Isle of Lewis is home to the **lighthouses at Tiumpan Head,** where you can view seabird colonies and migrating birds. If you want to stay in town, find a pub and listen to local musicians play Gaelic folk songs.

WHAT TO EAT Not surprisingly, seafood is on most menus on the island, with prawns, scallops, and salmon as the most popular choices, often served smoked. Abundant local produce includes greens, root vegetables, and strawberries. If you're feeling adventurous, have some *marag dhubh,* or Stornoway black pudding, made from oatmeal and blood. This local delicacy has a Protected Geographic Indication (like Champagne in France) to protect it from impostor sausages. A regional sweet is *tablet,* similar to a dairy-based fudge. Adult-beverage connoisseurs will want to try the beers and ales of the **Hebridean Brewing Company,** gin from the **Isle of Harris Distillery,** or whisky from the **Abhainn Dearg Distillery,** made from a 400-year-old recipe.

WHAT TO BUY Woolens such as tweed or cashmere shawls and hand-knit sweaters are treasured items for many visitors. Golfers will enjoy taking home mementos, such as club covers or imprinted balls, from the area's renowned courses. An ambitious musician might enjoy a starter-size bagpipe to learn on at home. Home cooks may be interested in the offerings of Scotland's only sea-salt producer, **Hebridean Sea Salt,** which sells specialty items such as peat-smoked and seaweed-infused salt.

Helsinki, Finland

LANGUAGES Finnish and Swedish

HISTORY Helsinki was founded in 1550 by King Gustav I of Sweden as a trading port. During its early years, the city was plagued by war, poverty, fires, and the plague. More-prosperous times began with the construction of a naval fortress during the 18th century. In 1809, Russia annexed Finland after defeating Sweden in the Finnish War. Czar Alexander I of Russia named Helsinki the capital to reduce Swedish influence and bring the seat of Finnish government closer to St. Petersburg. Finland declared its independence in 1917, which was followed by a brief period of unrest and a longer period of growth and renewal. A highlight of the modern era was Helsinki's hosting of the 1952 Summer Olympics.

WEATHER Disney cruises visit Helsinki in May, June, and July. Temperatures during this period range from an average daytime high near 60 in late May to average daytime highs in the low to mid-70s throughout July. Average nighttime lows in the summer range from the low 40s to the low 50s. Precipitation is typically minimal at this time of year, with average rainfall of less than an inch per month.

THE PORT Services at the port are basic—a few souvenir shops, an ATM, and a currency exchange. Taxis and shuttles are available to take you to **Kauppatori (Market Square),** about 2 miles away. Once you're in town, you'll find many attractions within walking distance.

TOURIST HIGHLIGHTS Market Square contains many open-air stalls featuring food and flowers. Also note the architecture, which shows both Swedish and Russian influences. To get a feel for the native culture, visit a public sauna, where you can wear your birthday suit and sweat with the locals. Museum lovers have plenty of options here. The **Designmuseo** spotlights Finnish design; the **Kiasma Museum of Contemporary Art** showcases art, design, and technology; and the **National Museum of Finland** focuses on the nation's history. Area churches of note include the **Lutheran Cathedral of Finland,** a palatial white Neoclassical structure topped with green copper domes, and the **Uspenski Cathedral,** an Eastern Orthodox house of worship with a traditional golden onion-shaped dome. **Suomenlinna (Finland's Fortress),** a UNESCO World Heritage Site, is a 15-minute ferry trip from town; dating from 1748 and built on six islands, it comprises not only a fortress, museums, and gardens but also a residential community where about 800 people live year-round. Children will like **Linnanmäki,** an amusement park, or the **Helsinki Zoo.**

WHAT TO EAT Smoked and salted fish of every sort is available on menus throughout Helsinki. Look for herring, salmon, perch, and whitefish. Cheese is a staple. *Leipäjuusto* ("bread cheese"), a Finnish specialty, is a rich cow's milk cheese that's baked or grilled as part of the manufacturing process; the browning makes it resemble a pizza or flatbread. Typical meats include lamb, elk, reindeer, duck, and goose. Potatoes, carrots, turnips, and mushrooms are frequently served side dishes. Summer fruits include strawberries, blueberries, lingonberries, and cloudberries.

WHAT TO BUY Among the most recognizable souvenirs are bags, clothing, and housewares from the internationally famous Finnish design house **Marimekko.** The bold colors and patterns are unmistakable. All manner of reindeer-related products can be found in Helsinki—blankets and rugs, as well as practical and decorative objects made from bone and horn. Canned reindeer meat is a unique takeaway. Finnish sweet-and-salty black licorice is another popular purchase.

Invergordon, Scotland, United Kingdom

LANGUAGES English, Scottish Gaelic (Gàidhlig)

HISTORY The first mention of the town of Invergordon appears in the 13th century, noting the building of a castle. The region became officially organized in the early 1700s when Sir William Gordon laid out plans for a town and began the area's transformation from small agricultural community to deep-water port and industrial center. During the 20th century, Invergordon was a naval base and fueling port. In September 1931, it was the site of the Invergordon Mutiny, one of the few military strikes in British history, caused by the threat of a cut in pay. Invergordon Distillery, the largest grain distillery in Europe, was constructed in 1961 as part of an initiative to bring new industry into the area following the closure of the naval dockyard. The North Sea oil boom of the 1970s created a large influx of people now dedicated to working on deep-sea oil rigs.

WEATHER Disney Cruise Line visits Invergordon in June and July. Daytime highs for June average in the high 50s to low 60s. June nighttime lows average in the mid-40s. Rainfall averages about 3 inches in June. There is some precipitation on more then 20 days per month; expect mist and drizzle, though, rather than heavy downpours. In July, daytime highs average in the mid 60s, with nighttime lows in the high 40s, with a steady drizzle of rain on most days.

THE PORT Invergordon proper is a small town, easily accessible on foot. A 5-minute walk straight from the pier ends on **High Street,** the town's, well, high street. Basic facilities including an ATM, Wi-Fi cafés, and a post office are within a few minutes' walk. The **Invergordon train station** is about a 15-minute walk from the pier. By train, Inverness is about an hour away, **Dunrobin Castle** about an hour and a half away. Inverness is also accessible by bus, as is **Loch Ness.** Taxis are readily available near the pier. Rental cars are available, too, but remember that you'll be driving on the left side of the street—if you're inexperienced with this, you may be better off using cabs or hiring a driver.

TOURIST HIGHLIGHTS Invergordon itself is a pleasant town with a famous mural trail including 11 large wall paintings representing life in the Highlands past and present. The big draw of the area is Loch Ness, home (or not) to the storied sea monster. Even if you don't spot Nessie herself, the **Exhibition Center** is still entertaining, and the nearby landscape is spectacular. **Cawdor Castle,** home of the noble Cawdor family (as in the Thane of Cawdor from *Macbeth*) since the 15th century, is open to the public for tours of its elegant public rooms. Other nearby castles include **Dunrobin Castle, Urquhart Castle,** and **Brodie Castle.** The **Glenmorangie Distillery** is popular with adult visitors. If you're looking to get outdoors, try golfing, cycling, or hiking.

WHAT TO EAT When in Scotland . . . have the drink of the region, Scotch whisky. (Attention, word nerds: The Scots spell it without the *e.*) Skip the familiar brands and try some that you can't find in the States. If you want food to accompany your drink, look for seafood of all sorts, including traditional fish-and-chips or smoked salmon. The lamb in the area is known for its freshness, and venison and pork are in ample supply. A standard side dish is tatties and neeps (mashed potatoes and turnips). And just to say you've tried it, be brave and take a bite of haggis, a mixture of organ meats combined with oatmeal, onions, and spices, all boiled in a sheep's stomach lining. Yes, we've tried it, and no, it's not nearly as bad as it sounds.

WHAT TO BUY Cashmere and wool are of lovely quality in Scotland. Look for sweaters and scarves, or if you're feeling brave, purchase a kilt. A uniquely Scottish souvenir is a *quaich,* a shallow drinking vessel made from wood, silver, or pewter. Or you may want a spurtle—a traditional oatmeal-stirring rod—for your kitchen. Decorative shortbread molds are another interesting kitchen-related item. If you're in the mood for whimsy, you certainly can't go wrong with a purchase of canned haggis (plus some whisky to wash it down).

Kirkwall, Orkney Islands, United Kingdom

LANGUAGE English

HISTORY Kirkwall, which has about 9,200 people, is the capital of the Orkney Islands, a chain of more than 70 islands just to the north of Scotland. Archaeological evidence dates human habitation of the Orkneys to about 3500 BC. Residents during the Iron and Medieval Periods included the Picts, the Norse, and the Scots. The area was under Norwegian rule from the 9th to 13th centuries AD. In 1468, Orkney was promised by Christian I, king of Denmark, Norway, and Sweden, as collateral against a dowry to be paid to James III of Scotland, who was betrothed to Christian's daughter, Margaret. Scotland has largely retained rule (the dowry was never paid). In the late 1600s, Oliver Cromwell's troops were stationed in Orkney and taught the locals various industrial arts and methods of agriculture. The Orkneys held naval bases in both World Wars.

Though the Orkneys are part of Scotland, Norway is only about 300 miles away, and the culture and landscape feel distinctly Nordic rather than Celtic: Many place-names have Scandinavian origins, Gaelic has never been spoken here, clans and tartans aren't a thing, and *udal law*—a centuries-old Norse legal code pertaining to property ownership—is still in effect.

WEATHER Disney Cruise Line visits Kirkwall in July, when daytime highs average in the high 50s to low 60s and nighttime lows in the mid-40s. Summer is the dry season, with an average of about 2.5 inches of rain during July.

THE PORT Basic services and cafés can be found within walking distance of the dock. Free shuttle service is available from the terminal into town, about 2 miles away. There's also an auto-rental service near the dock, but availability is limited, so book early. Most of the town can be easily explored on foot.

TOURIST HIGHLIGHTS St. Magnus Cathedral is a stone masterpiece dating from 1137. The **Orkney Museum** features historical artifacts from the region. **Highland Park Distillery,** the northernmost distillery in the UK, offers samples at the end of its tour. **Skara Brae,** a UNESCO World Heritage Site, is a well-preserved Stone Age village. The **Orkney Wireless Museum** focuses on the history of radio and recorded sound. The **Ring of Brodgar** is a Stonehenge-like assemblage of 36 gigantic stones. Ferry service is available to other nearby islands.

WHAT TO EAT Fresh seafood is on many Kirkwall menus. Look for oysters, clams, lobster, and scallops, as well as less-familiar local favorites such as torsk, sea witch, and megrim. Meats include local beef, pork, and lamb; in particular, the meat from North Ronaldsay sheep, which feed mainly on seaweed, is a popular treat for visitors. Typical sides include root vegetables and potatoes. Many meals are accompanied by cheese and oat cakes (like crackers or flatbread). Orkney fudge is a prized treat, as are scones with rhubarb jam. Beer, ale, and spirits are easy to find; try the output from the two local breweries or the nearby Highland Park Distillery. The **Orkney Wine Company** produces naturally fermented wine from fruit such as raspberries and elderberries.

WHAT TO BUY Typical Kirkwall souvenirs include hand-knitted woolen goods such as sweaters and mittens. Carved wooden objects and handcrafted jewelry are also popular. Take home a taste of the islands with some Orkney fudge or oat cakes.

Le Havre, France

LANGUAGE French

HISTORY The first mention of **Graville Abbey,** the oldest building in Le Havre, is from the 9th century. Over the next several centuries, the area served as a minor port and shelter for ships, with the official city charter signed in 1517. During the mid-1500s, ships departing from Le Havre played a role in explorers setting off for the New World, as well as in development of trade from the Americas. During the religious wars of the 1500s, several fortifications were built and subsequently destroyed. The port itself regained importance in the 17th century, with the trading firm Company of the Orient making Le Havre a base and attracting other traders as well. During the French Revolution, the region saw unrest and a decrease in population. While trade recovered, epidemics of cholera and typhoid fever again checked a spurt of population growth. During the late 19th century, infrastructure and health improved, with prosperity continuing through the early 20th century. Le Havre then saw thousands of casualties during the World War I, though the city itself was largely spared. During World War II, German forces occupied Le Havre from 1940 to 1944. Many residents evacuated in secret. Nazis destroyed major areas of the city and sank many ships. Le Havre received the Legion d'Honneur in 1949 due to the "heroism with which it has faced its destruction." Postwar reconstruction continued until the mid-1960s. The reconstructed city center has been named a UNESCO World Heritage site, one of few contemporary sites in Europe so designated.

WEATHER Disney Cruise Line visits Le Havre/Paris in July. Average daytime highs in Paris in July are in the low to mid-70s; nighttime lows average in the mid-50s. Rainfall is typically minimal at this time of year, with July seeing about an inch on average.

THE PORT The port terminal at Le Havre includes basic services such as Wi-Fi, small shops, and ATMs. The town of Le Havre is about 20 minutes away on foot, but a shuttle is recommended. Taxis are readily available at the pier.

Many guests visit **Paris** from Le Havre. If you're headed to Paris on your own, the train station at Le Havre is about a mile from port, accessible via shuttle or cab. Be aware that it's at least 2 and a half hours each way between Paris and the port. If you've already experienced Paris, the beaches of **Normandy** are about 2 hours from Le Havre.

TOURIST HIGHLIGHTS If you want to stay somewhat close to port, the village of **Bayeux,** about 6 miles away, is home to a charming cathedral, while **Honfleur** is a charming village 15 miles in the other direction.

But you're probably going to Paris . . . right? There is no shortage of wonders in the City of Lights. With just a few hours to visit, you're going to have to choose to experience just one or two major sites. Some obvious choices are the **Louvre,** with its panoply of artistic masterpieces; the **Cathedral of Notre-Dame;** or the **Eiffel Tower.** Take a stroll down the **Champs-Élysées** for people-watching and shopping, or park yourself at a *pâtisserie* and don't leave until you've tried everything. If you're visiting Normandy, the must-see is **Omaha Beach,** site of the Allies' WWII incursion, and its associated war memorials. The afternoon flag lowering is particularly moving.

WHAT TO EAT What to eat in Paris? *Everything,* of course! Seriously—you're in the gourmet capital of the world, so eat whatever's good that you can get your hands on: bread, cheese, pastries, sweet and savory crepes, and chocolate, all washed down with some lovely French wine. If you absolutely need protein, a simple *steak-frites* (steak and fries) is the epitome of French comfort food. The last time we were in Paris, we decided to focus our food exploration on the classic French treat, the *macaron.* (We mean the meringue confection, by the way, not the coconut cookie called the macaroon.) We purchased the same basic flavors—lemon, chocolate, raspberry, and pistachio—from half a dozen vendors including the masters at **Ladurée, Pierre Hermé,** and **Fauchon,** as well as several smaller shops. We never did decide on a group favorite (we each had our own). I think that means we'll have to repeat the test.

WHAT TO BUY Paris is ground zero for designer fashion—think **Cartier, Chanel, Dior, Louis Vuitton.** If you've got the dough to plunk down on luxury goods, you've come to the right place. Be sure, though, that your purchase(s) isn't something you could get at a similar price point in the States without possible tax implications. For a modest shopping spree, visit **Printemps** or **Galeries Lafayette,** both of which offer a range of French fashions. France is also known for its fine fragrances and beauty products, with lotions and potions to solve any skin-care dilemma. Candy or bottled condiments are great treats for foodies.

Liverpool, England, United Kingdom

LANGUAGE English

HISTORY The first known settlement on the banks of the Mersey dates to the 1st century AD. (Theories abound regarding the meaning of the place-name, one of the most common being that it comes from the Old English *liuer pul,* or "pool of dark water.") In about 1200, King John of England advertised the establishment of a new borough at Liverpool, inviting settlers to take holdings there. For centuries, Liverpool was relatively unimportant, regarded as only a minor port and seeing only modest skirmishes. In 1699, an act of Parliament made Liverpool its own parish, beginning a period of growth and development. As trade from the West Indies increased in the in the 1700s, Liverpool's seaside location became advantageous, and by the beginning of the 19th century, 40% of the world's trade was passing through the docks at Liverpool. During World War II, the Liverpool area was hit with dozens of air raids, with almost half the homes in the metropolitan area sustaining some damage and thousands more destroyed outright. (Beatle John Lennon was born in Liverpool during an air raid on October 9, 1940.) After the war, a decline in industry in the area precipitated an economic decline, which is now reversing with an influx of tourism.

WEATHER Disney Cruise Line visits Liverpool in July, when daytime highs average in the low 60s and nighttime lows average in the low 50s. Liverpool typically sees an average of 2 inches of rainfall during the month.

THE PORT Ships dock at the **Port of Liverpool Building,** directly adjacent to the city proper. Major services are available within a 10-minute walk, including shops, cafés, and local attractions. Taxis are readily available. Buses, including the hop-on-and-off sightseeing services, are a 5-minute walk from the port. Additionally, ferry and rail stations are accessible on foot.

TOURIST HIGHLIGHTS Liverpool's favorite sons are The Beatles. Follow their footsteps in **The Beatles Story,** where you can watch scenes from their lives and see personal artifacts, including the iconic glasses John Lennon wore when he composed "Imagine." Art lovers will enjoy the Liverpool outpost of the **Tate Gallery** or the **Walker Art Gallery,** whose holdings include works by Rembrandt and Rubens. **Liverpool Cathedral** is the largest church in northern Britain; climb the 331-foot tower for impressive views of the Mersey River and surrounding areas. If it won't upset your sensibilities while sailing, pay a visit to the **Titanic Memorial** in the Pier Head area. Exhibits featuring the *Titanic* and the *Lusitania* are also on display at the **Merseyside Maritime Museum.**

WHAT TO EAT Liverpool is a meat-eating town. Main dishes are traditionally made with chicken, pork, lamb, fish, and beef. A classic meal is bubble and squeak, a sort of hash brown made with potatoes, cabbage, carrots, green beans, Brussels sprouts, or other vegetables left over from a roast dinner; "bubble and squeak" describes the sound of the veggies frying in the pan. Another popular dish is scouse, a hearty lamb stew.

(Liverpudlians are nicknamed Scousers, and the Scouse dialect is distinctive among variants of British English. *Example:* "I left me coat at home and it was proper baltic. Musta been abar minus 40." *Translation:* "I left my coat at home and it was freezing cold. It must have been about minus 40.")

Also look for cottage pie, made with ground veal and mashed potatoes, and toad in the hole, sausages coated in Yorkshire pudding. If you're in the mood for something sweet, try the black-and-white-striped hard candies called **Everton mints,** created by an enterprising 19th-century soccer devotee so that fellow fans of the Everton Football Club would have a snack to enjoy whilst watching the matches. If you need fortification, stop in a pub and ask for a pint of whatever's on tap.

WHAT TO BUY Beatles memorabilia is the key must-purchase item in Liverpool. If you're looking to add some fun to your shopping, make a game of finding the oddest item embellished with a Beatles-related image. T-shirts and hats are easy; you get bonus points for edible items or Beatles gear for your dog.

Newcastle-upon-Tyne, England, United Kingdom

LANGUAGE English

HISTORY One of the earliest mentions of Newcastle occurred in 1080, when the Normans built a bridge and fort at the lowest point of the River Tyne; the "new castle" was rebuilt in stone in the 12th century. During the Middle Ages, the region became a shipping port for wool, hides, and, most famously, coal. Shipbuilding and weaving were other early industries. During the mid-1500s, Henry VIII closed many of the religious institutions that had formed in the area. During the 16th and 17th centuries, coal exports continued to grow. The 18th century saw more organization, with roads improved and hospitals and banks built, as well as the first running water. During the 19th century, Newcastle faced a series of epidemics that killed more than 2,000 people. Further improvements in infrastructure saw better sanitation and transportation, including the development of rail lines. Coal trade and shipbuilding declined in the mid-20th century, resulting in massive unemployment. In the postwar period, an influx of service industries spurred an economic turnaround.

WEATHER Disney Cruise Line visits Newcastle in July. Daytime highs for July average in the low 60s; nighttime lows average in the mid-40s. Precipitation is typically 2 inches per month at this time of year.

THE PORT Services are sparse at the cruise terminal itself. For basic amenities, take a 5-minute walk to the **Royal Quays** shopping area, which has ATMs, food stores, and Wi-Fi access. Taxis and shuttles can take you into town, which is easily accessible on foot.

TOURIST HIGHLIGHTS The **Quayside** area covers both sides of the Tyne River, with shops, bars, and views of several lovely bridges. While you're in the area, stop by the **Baltic Center for Contemporary Art,** the largest such museum in England outside of London, or the **Sage Music Center,** which often presents daytime concerts in the summer. The **Discovery Museum** has cool interactive exhibits for kids. The **Hancock Great North Museum** has a planetarium, along with natural-history and archaeological holdings. *The Angel of the North* is a gigantic outdoor sculpture that functions as an icon for the region. If the weather is good, take a stroll in the **Alnwick Gardens,** with charming cobblestone paths and beautifully restored formal gardens. The **Tynemouth Priory** was once one of the most massively fortified castles in the UK.

WHAT TO EAT Traditional food in Newcastle is similar to other British favorites such as fish-and-chips and bangers and mash. There are, however, a few specialities from the north of England that you'll want to keep watch for: Pease pudding has the texture of hummus but is made from split peas; it's often served as a topping for a saveloy (a hot dog–like sausage). Pan haggerty is a variant on potatoes au gratin, with thinly sliced potatoes, onions, and Cheddar cheese. Most bakeries sell stotties, a dense, heavy bread with a small indentation in the middle. The local brew, Newcastle Brown Ale, is now made by Heineken, but it's still a favorite.

WHAT TO BUY Many visitors will be interested in purchased jerseys from the local sports teams, particularly Newcastle United football (soccer). Also look for gear from the Newcastle University shops. Many boutiques in the Quayside area sell cards and plaques written in the local Geordie dialect, a hodgepodge of English, Irish, and Scottish influences.

Reykjavík, Iceland

LANGUAGE Icelandic

HISTORY The year AD 871 brought the first recorded settler to Iceland: Ingólfur Arnarson, a fugitive from Norway. Almost no development beyond basic farming happened for the next 900 years. Industry and infrastructure picked up steam in the mid-1700s with the development of a textile industry based on tanning, wool harvesting, dyeing, and weaving; other early industries included fishing and shipbuilding. The first Icelandic constitution was adopted in 1874, and the island achieved independent statehood in 1904 under the crown of Denmark. Iceland asserts neutrality in global conflicts but did house Allied forces during World War II. Full independence was reached in 1944 when the first president of Iceland was elected. In more recent times, finance and technology have become key industries. A city of about 120,000 people, Reykjavík is the world's northernmost capital of a sovereign state.

WEATHER Disney cruises visit Iceland in May and June. Average daytime highs during this period are in the mid-40s to mid-50s; nighttime lows average in the mid-30s to mid-40s. (The highest recorded temperature is 78). Precipitation is typically minimal at this time of year, with an average rainfall of less than an inch per month. The sun barely sets during the summer, so expect to see folks out and about well into the night.

THE PORT The **Skarfabakki** cruise dock is about 2 miles from the center of town. There is little of interest near the dock itself, but taxis and a free shuttle will take you to the commercial district. The **Cruise Welcome Center** can direct you as well as provide information about local attractions. Once you're in Reykjavík proper, most attractions are accessible on foot.

TOURIST HIGHLIGHTS Reykjavík has a wonderful mix of urban sophistication and outdoor adventure. Because the island is nearly treeless, many Icelandic buildings are constructed from materials such as driftwood, corrugated iron, volcanic rock, and sod, making for an eclectic and innovative architectural mix. In town, visit the **Menningarmiðstoð Kópavogs,** a cultural complex with a natural-history museum; the **Hafnarborg,** a modern-art museum; or the **Hallgrimskirkja,** a Lutheran cathedral built in the Expressionist style (meaning it looks like something out of *Star Trek*). About 30 miles from the city, the **Blue Lagoon** mineral spa has interesting geothermal features. An active volcano, **Hengill,** is within a 20-minute drive and features natural hot springs. Wildlife excursions afford opportunities to see whales, birds of prey, and thousands of the island's adorable puffins.

WHAT TO EAT Seafood stews, chowders, and kabobs are local specialties. Lobster, crayfish, salmon, trout, and scallops are abundant. Sushi-style restaurants are popular. Whale meat is a treat for the adventurous. Meats may include duck, horse, and eel, as well as pork and veal served in thin slices or as cold cuts. For those in need of something familiar, pizza and burgers are easy to find. Icelanders are also proud of their hot dogs. Icelandic hot dogs have a slightly different, but nonetheless delicious, flavor than their American equivalents because they're made mostly from Icelandic lamb, along with supplements of pork and beef. Find them topped with raw or crispy fried onions, ketchup, brown mustard, or a caper-herb remoulade. Pastries, bread, and eggs are morning staples. Cheese and yogurt made from both cow and sheep milk are popular. Vegetarianism is relatively rare in Iceland, with the most prevalent plant foods being potatoes, cabbage, turnips, rutabagas, and other root vegetables. Hot chocolate and coffee are ubiquitous.

The local firewater is *brennivín,* a powerful unsweetened schnapps distilled from potatoes and flavored with caraway, cumin, and other botanicals. It packs a wallop, and thank goodness for that—*brennivín* is the traditional beverage to accompany the Icelandic specialty *hákarl,* or fermented shark.

"Fermented" doesn't really tell the whole story, though. A Greenland shark is cleaned, buried in sand and weighted with stones, and then left to cure (read: decompose) for 6–12 weeks. Then the flesh is cut into strips and hung up to dry for several months. The reason for all this advance, um, preparation? The meat is poisonous when it's fresh.

If you still think you might like to sample *hákarl* after reading this far, we'd be remiss if we didn't apprise you of the following: (1) Wikipedia advises, "Those new to it will usually gag involuntarily on the first attempt to eat it because of the high ammonia content." (2) A food blogger who was brave enough to try it likened the taste to "a tramp's sock soaked in urine." (3) It made Gordon Ramsay retch.

WHAT TO BUY Puffins, trolls, and elves are depicted on everything from clothing to housewares. Fine-quality Icelandic wool sweaters are a prized souvenir. Look for hand-knitted items as well as jewelry and carvings made from area driftwood, lava, and found items. Note that shopping in Iceland can be expensive due to high sales taxes, so be sure to ask the *full* price of something before buying.

St. Peter Port, Guernsey, United Kingdom

LANGUAGES English, Guernsey Norman French (Guernésiais)

HISTORY Evidence of human occupation on Guernsey—one of Britain's Channel Islands—dates to Neolithic times. The first known settled community dates from the 10th century, with the establishment of a Benedictine monastery. During the Middle Ages, the island was repeatedly attacked by Continental pirates and naval forces. The unrest intensified during the Hundred Years War, when, starting in 1339, the island was occupied by the Capetians on several occasions. In the mid-16th century, the island's spiritual life was influenced by Calvinist reformers from Normandy; unfortunately, anti-Protestant sentiment in England was running high, and during the so-called Marian Persecutions, which took place during the reigns of the Catholic Henry VIII and Mary I, three local women, the Guernsey Martyrs, were burned at the stake for their beliefs. Wars against France and Spain during the 17th and 18th centuries gave Guernsey ship owners and sea captains the opportunity to exploit the island's proximity to mainland Europe by applying for Letters of Marque and turning their merchantmen into privateers. The 19th century saw a dramatic increase in prosperity of the island, due to its success in the global maritime trade and the rise of the stone industry. During World War I, some 3,000 island men served in the British Expeditionary Force. For most of World War II, the area was occupied by German troops. Before the occupation, many Guernsey children had been evacuated to England to live with relatives or strangers during the war.

WEATHER Disney Cruise Line visits St. Peter Port in July. Daytime highs for July average in the low 60s; nighttime lows average in the low 50s. The area typically sees about 2 inches of rain per month during early summer.

THE PORT This is a tender port, meaning you'll be required to board a smaller vessel that will take you from the Disney ship to land. There are few services in the immediate dock area, but St. Peter Port's main streets are a 5-minute walk away. The town is largely accessible on foot, but the streets are often steep and narrow, so take a taxi if you need to.

TOURIST HIGHLIGHTS Castle Cornet is a 13th-century fortification that now holds a museum of historical artifacts. **Hauteville House** is the onetime home of writer Victor Hugo, who lived here while in exile from his native France; this is where he wrote *Les Misérables.* The **Guernsey Museum & Art Gallery** includes an entire section devoted to the adorable Guernsey dairy cow, a veritable icon of the island. If you're interested in hiking, take a quick boat ride to nearby **Herm Island,** which offers both coastal and inland walking paths.

WHAT TO EAT You'll find fresh seafood on many menus; look for prawns (shrimp) or Dover sole. Bean jar is a cassoulet (stew) not unlike American pork and beans. For a uniquely Guernsey treat, try ormer, a rare mollusk similar to but smaller than the Australian abalone. *Gâche* (a fruit loaf) and apple cake are typical desserts. If you're in the mood for something simple, scones with fresh butter or clotted cream and jam will hit the spot. You'll also find a **Marks & Spencer Food Hall** in town if you want to do some general food-shopping.

WHAT TO BUY Castle Cornet offers a selection of historically themed toys. Fine knitwear is a popular item. Also look for items depicting the adorable Guernsey cow or the Guernsey flag.

St. Petersburg, Russian Federation

LANGUAGE Russian

HISTORY The area that is now St. Petersburg has been occupied since at least the 9th century AD by a series of Slavs, Finns, Swedes, and other ethnic groups. Real turbulence in the area began during the 16th century with a series of border disputes between Russia and Sweden. Russia gained control of the region, and the city proper was founded in 1703 by Tsar Peter the Great. After Peter died in 1725, several rulers jostled for position. Eventually Peter's daughter, Elizabeth, took the crown and a period of growth and prosperity occurred in what was now the Russian capital. Catherine the Great assumed power following a 1762 coup d'état. Her reign saw the growth of trade and a flourishing of the arts. Subsequent rulers Paul I and Alexander I made the government more bureaucratic. Bureaucracy further increased under Nicholas I in the early to mid-1800s. The next ruler, Alexander II, was assassinated in 1881, and the country entered a period of capitalism. Uprisings in the early 1890s were followed by revolution and destruction during the first World War. Communism prevailed post–World War I, and the city's name was changed to Leningrad in 1924. After a German siege in 1941, food was scarce and famine common. The Soviets resumed control in 1944, but the effects of World War II lasted until well into the 1960s. With the fall of Communism in Russia in 1991, the city's original name was restored.

WEATHER DCL visits St. Petersburg in May and June. Average daytime highs during this period are in the 60s, with nighttime lows averaging in the high 40s to low 50s. Precipitation is typically minimal during the spring and summer, with less than 2 inches of rainfall per month. During the "white nights" of summer, the sun barely sets.

THE PORT A port terminal finished in 2011 houses passport control, a café, several shops, an ATM, and other basic services. Taxis are at the ready to take you on the 15-minute drive into town or to the transportation arranged by your port-adventure escort.

Note: If you'd like to explore St. Petersburg on your own, you **must** have a valid Russian tourist visa, obtained before your trip. Guests visiting on organized excursions (such as DCL's port adventures) don't need a visa.

TOURIST HIGHLIGHTS Many visitors consider the **State Hermitage Museum** their highest priority. The scope and quality of the collections are easily comparable to those of the Louvre or the Metropolitan Museum of Art. The **Peter and Paul Fortress** houses a museum of Russian history. **St. Isaac's** is the largest domed cathedral in the world. The **Church of the Savior on Spilled Blood,** in contrast to its grim name, houses a gorgeous display of mosaics.

WHAT TO EAT You'll find many cuisines represented in the restaurants of St. Petersburg. For Russian fare, try one of the many soups, either cold ones such as beet-based borscht or warm ones made with meat and cabbage. You'll often find meat boiled, served cold, or minced in a pastry or pie. Carp, salmon, pike, and trout are typical seafood offerings. Blinis and pancakes are used as a base for fillings ranging from eggs, chopped meat, and onions, to cottage cheese and jam. Most Russians drink tea on a daily basis. A popular beverage is *kvass,* which is made from fermented bread; it has an extremely low alcohol content and is sometimes flavored with fruit or spices. Vodka is plentiful, natch.

WHAT TO BUY Russian nesting dolls, or *matryoshka,* are a near-mandatory purchase. Bargaining is common in outdoor stalls. Lacquered papier-mâché boxes, painted with scenes from Russian folk tales, are a popular purchase. Look for jewelry made with amber or detailed silver filigree. Those knowledgeable about rugs or antiques may encounter some unique finds, but always ask about shipping before you buy. Pick up a book or two on local art and architecture. Of course, you'll want to take home a bottle of vodka. If you decide to buy spirits, have them wrapped for shipping. You can bring them onto the ship, but they'll be held for you until debarkation.

During our 2016 Baltic DCL cruise, the items we most often saw being purchased after nesting dolls were those featuring images of Russian President Vladimir Putin. We ourselves bought two different Putin coffee mugs (ours just had his scowling face; we skipped the ones where he was bare-chested on horseback flanked by bikini-clad beauties), an array of Putin chocolates, and yes, even a Putin nesting doll.

Stavanger, Norway

LANGUAGE Norwegian

HISTORY Stavanger has been a fishing port since the time of the Vikings. The town's official founding date is AD 1125, which coincides with the building of the local cathedral. Fishing and small-village life continued for centuries until the development of the petroleum industry, which today is a key employer in the region. The mainland base for several offshore-drilling operations, Stavanger has one of the lowest unemployment rates in all of Europe.

WEATHER Disney cruises visit Stavanger in June, when daytime highs average in the high 50s to mid-60s and nighttime lows in the 40s. Rainfall is minimal, with less than an inch of rain during June.

THE PORT Ships dock at the edge of town. Many services and points of interest are within a 10-minute walk. Taxis, buses, and bike rentals are all nearby.

TOURIST HIGHLIGHTS Stavanger's **Old Town** is home to charming whitewashed cottages, perfect for photo opportunities. For those interested in the local fishing industry, a visit to the **Norwegian Canning Museum** is in order. Other area educational sites include the **Maritime Museum, Printing Museum,** and **Petroleum Museum.** Visitors interested in religious history may want to visit **Utstein Abbey,** Norway's only preserved medieval monastery.

WHAT TO EAT Fish, shellfish, lamb, beef, and cheese figure prominently in local menus, as do moose, reindeer, and duck. Locally grown vegetables include tomatoes, cucumber, potatoes, and parsley. Look for lamb ragout and fish stew at the scenic **Flor & Fjœre** restaurant, on the nearby island of Sør-Hidle. Popular cafés in town include **Ostehuset (Cheese House)**, where the raclette is locally sourced, and **Sjokoladepiken (Chocolate Girl)**, which serves chocolate in nearly every form imaginable. A number of pubs in town serve beers from around the world.

WHAT TO BUY Textiles, knitwear, and hand-woven items are popular purchases. Pewter goods are readily available; the work of area glassblowers and potters is also popular.

Stockholm, Sweden

LANGUAGE Swedish

HISTORY The area was first settled by Vikings in about AD 1000. In the 13th century, nearby mines made Stockholm a center of the iron trade, and it subsequently served as a prominent cultural and economic center for northern Europe. During the early 1500s, Sweden and Denmark battled for control of Stockholm, resulting in much loss of life. In 1634, Stockholm became the official capital of Sweden. A period of prosperity was dampened by a great plague in 1710. By the mid-18th century, Stockholm was again a center of trade. Throughout the 19th and 20th centuries, art, design, and technology gained footholds.

WEATHER DCL visits Stockholm in June. Average daytime highs for the month are in the mid-60s to low-70s, with nighttime lows averaging in the high 40s to mid-50s. Precipitation is typically light in the summer, averaging less than an inch of rainfall per month.

THE PORT The **Frihamnen** docks include a modern passenger terminal with some basic shops and an ATM. The port is a 15-minute taxi, bus, or shuttle ride away from town.

TOURIST HIGHLIGHTS Stockholm is a city of museums. Some notable ones include **Fotografiska,** showcasing contemporary photography; the **Nationalmuseum,** with prominent Rembrandt and Nordic-art collections; and **Moderna Museet**, which houses works by Dalí, Picasso, Kandinsky, and others. **Kungliga Slottet,** the royal palace, has exhibits on weaponry and the crown jewels, as well as a charming changing of the guard. Our favorite spot is the **Vasa Museum,** home to a fully preserved 17th-century warship. Coauthor Erin's daughter Louisa proclaimed that seeing the ship was the closest thing to actually being in a *Pirates of the Caribbean* film. For a taste of the outdoors, visit **Rosendal's Garden,** where you can pick your own flowers from lush beds, paying by weight, as well as enjoy a light meal at the café. Children will enjoy **Junibacken,** an indoor park celebrating the life and work of Astrid Lindgren, the author of the *Pippi Longstocking* books, or **Tivoli Gröna Lund,** a small amusement park.

WHAT TO EAT Seafood, beef, and pork are on many menus in Stockholm. Red meat is often found in the form of meatballs, typically served with a brown cream sauce. The traditional accompaniment is a lingonberry tart and boiled or mashed potatoes. Open-faced sandwiches made with cheese, cold cuts, or hard-boiled eggs are a typical Swedish lunch. Smoked salmon and pickled herring are other usual offerings. Dark, crisp breads are served throughout the day, while sweeter rolls and pastries are served in the morning. For celebrations, Swedes like to spread out a buffet-style *smörgåsbord.* Aquavit, *punsch* (a sweet liqueur made with sugarcane, rum, and spices), and beer are typical adult libations.

WHAT TO BUY If you're in the mood for wearables, Swedish clogs are a hot item; look for game-animal leathers and hand-painted designs. Swedish glass and crystal are of particularly high quality. Other typical souvenirs are trays embellished with a repeating-triangle pattern based on the one in the pavement of Sergels Torg (Stockholm's main public square) or brightly painted Dalahäst horses carved from wood. For a relatively small country, Sweden has had an outsized influence on global pop music (not just ABBA); look for CDs from local rising performers. Foodies will want to take home tinned herring, ginger cookies, pots of berry jam, or salty licorice. Finally, if you love **IKEA** back home, you'll want to fit in a visit to Stockholm's flagship store.

Tallinn, Estonia

LANGUAGE Estonian

HISTORY The first known large-scale building in Tallinn was a fortress constructed in 1050. Danes ruled this trade port, then known as Reval, during the 1200s. During the Protestant Reformation in the 1500s, Swedes controlled the region. In the early 1700s, Russians took control. Following World War I, Estonia declared independence in 1918, but this ended during World War II, when the Soviet Union annexed the region. Estonia regained its independence in 1991, with the collapse of the USSR. In 2004, the Baltic nation joined the European Union.

WEATHER Disney Cruise Line visits Tallinn in May and June. Average daytime highs throughout the summer range from the low 60s to the low 70s, with average nighttime lows ranging from the mid-40s to low 50s. Precipitation is typically light during summer, with less than an inch of rain per month.

THE PORT Completed in 2012, the cruise terminal houses ATMs, a currency exchange, several small shops, and a tourist-information desk; free Wi-Fi is provided. The center of town is about 15 minutes away on foot. Once you get there, most attractions are easily walkable within a 0.6-square-mile area.

TOURIST HIGHLIGHTS **Raekoja Plats** is Tallinn's town square. The weather-vane atop the Town Hall has been in place since 1530. **Kiek-in-de-Kök** ("Peep in the Kitchen") is a grand six-story structure housing historical displays and an art museum; built as an artillery tower in 1475, it gained its name because soldiers on duty could see into neighboring houses from its upper floors. **Toompea Castle** is a lovely example of medieval architecture. The top floor of the **Sokos Hotel Viru** was once a secret lair where the KGB eavesdropped on guests; today it houses a small spy museum. If you'd like to get away from the city, coastal **Pirita** offers boat excursions.

WHAT TO EAT Estonian cuisine is heavy on meat (particularly pork) and pota-toes, and on seafood in coastal areas. Soups, both broth- and cream-based, are popular as starters and main courses alike. Cabbage and dark rye bread are typical accompaniments. Local delicacies include marinated eel, *sült* (jellied pork), sliced tongue, and blood sausage served with berry jam. *Kali* is a lightly carbonated nonalcoholic beverage similar to unfermented beer. *Kama,* a dairy drink made with kefir (like liquid yogurt) and ground grain, has a milkshake-like texture. The local adult beverage is **Vana Tallinn,** a rum-based, heavily spiced liqueur with an alcohol content of up to 50%.

WHAT TO BUY Handcrafted woolens are a popular take-home item. Look for sweaters, caps, mittens, and scarves adorned with geometrics or reindeer-related designs. Simple linen shirts and tunics are typical of the area. Area craftspeople expertly carve wooden items, particularly from juniper. Also look for local pottery and blown glass. **Kalev** is the biggest candy manufac-turer in Estonia; pick up a box of chocolate to bring home. You also may find Soviet-era artwork and antiques, and you may see Cuban cigars for sale.

Warnemünde, Germany

LANGUAGE German

HISTORY A town of about 8,400 people on the Baltic coast, Warnemünde has been an established village since about AD 1200 and remained a small fishing village for centuries. In 1323, it was annexed by nearby Rostock to safeguard the latter town's access to the Baltic Sea. Once completely dependent on the fishing industry, Warnemünde's economy is now driven by shipbuilding and tourism (the town first became popular as a seaside resort in the mid-1800s). Since its cruise terminal was built in 2005, War-nemünde has become the most important cruise port in Germany. The capital city of **Berlin** is about 153 miles to the south.

WEATHER Disney cruises visit Warnemünde in June, when average daytime highs are in the mid-60s and average nighttime lows are in the mid-50s. Rainfall is typically low in June, averaging about 2 inches of precipitation per month.

THE PORT The Warnemünde cruise terminal has only limited services. How-ever, the train station is about 5 minutes away on foot. The train to the town of **Rostock** takes about 20 minutes. A train trip to Berlin takes about 2 hours and 45 minutes. You could also rent a car, but you'll want to reserve in advance and make sure that you have the proper driving certification.

TOURIST HIGHLIGHTS If you're staying close to port, the **Monastery of the Holy Cross,** in Rostock, displays medieval art and functions as the local history museum. Also in Rostock, see **St. Mary's Church,** with a Baroque organ and an astronomical clock dating back to 1472.

In Berlin, the imposing **Brandenburg Gate** is a must-see for many visitors. The **Reichstag** is likewise a potent symbol of German history. The **Unter den Linden** area has lovely gardens as well as Germany's largest history museum. Visit the **Berlin Wall Memorial** on Bernauer Strasse; when Berlin was a divided city, the Wall ran along this street. **Potsdamer Platz** is a major shopping and restaurant district. Sports fans will want to check out the **Olympic Stadium.** Children will enjoy the **Berlin Zoo.**

WHAT TO EAT German cuisine is typically meat-and-potatoes comfort food: *schnitzels* (pork, veal, or chicken cutlets), roasts, and dumplings served with boiled or mashed spuds and a side dish of mushrooms or onions. You'll also find *wursts* (sausages) of all sorts, often served with pastalike *spaetzle*. Large, soft pretzels are a popular snack. A famous pastry is the Berliner, which is much like a jelly doughnut. Other desserts are apple- or caramel-based. Beer, not surprisingly, is the beverage of choice. In addition, global cuisines such as Chilean, French, Indian, and Turkish are well represented in Berlin's thriving restaurant scene.

WHAT TO BUY Bring home a beer stein, a purchase that's both practical and decorative. Cuckoo clocks and pewter serving items are popular purchases as well. Teddy bears and Haribo gummy candies are good choices for children. The cook in the family will appreciate a jar of spicy German mustard.

Here's a treat that you and your kids can enjoy only while overseas: the **Kinder Surprise,** a chocolate egg molded around a plastic capsule containing a small toy, such as a car or a miniature Disney character. Unfortunately, many Americans are unaware that they can't bring Kinder Surprises home: They're *verboten* in the United States due to a longstanding FDA regulation banning "embedded non-nutritive objects"—that is, choking hazards—in foods. At best, US Customs will seize the eggs if you get caught smuggling them in; at worst, you could be detained and slapped with a fine of $2,500 . . . *per egg.*

PANAMA CANAL

CRUISES SAIL FROM Miami, San Diego

SHIP *Wonder*

CRUISE LENGTH 14 nights

DATES Spring and fall as the ship heads to Alaska from Florida; westward in the spring and eastbound in the fall

WHAT TO PACK Your formalwear—14-night cruises give you lots of chances to dress up.

SIGNATURE PORT ADVENTURE It's all about going through the canal.

CLASSIC DISNEY ADD-ON Disneyland

PROS	CONS
▪ On a per-night basis, longer cruises are less expensive than shorter ones.	▪ With just one trip each way per year, this itinerary can be hard to schedule.
▪ Two weeks gives you lots of time to get to know the crew.	▪ Other than the canal itself and **Cartagena, Colombia,** the ports are kind of a snooze,
▪ This is a great way to see the Panama Canal.	

COMMENTS Going through the Panama Canal is a classic itinerary for cruising, and you can let your friends and family know when they can see the ship in one of the great engineering achievements of the world by sending them to pancanal.com/eng/photo/camera-java.html. Be sure to wave to the camera!

Cabo San Lucas, Mexico

LANGUAGE Spanish

HISTORY Native inhabitants of the Cabo San Lucas region include the Pericu peoples. European influence was minimal until the early 1800s. Industry and trade took hold in the early 1900s, when commercial fishing companies began to capitalize on the local tuna. The 1970s saw a surge in tourism, due in part to the completion of Mexican Federal Highway 1, linking Cabo to other parts of Mexico.

WEATHER Disney cruises visit Cabo San Lucas in spring and fall. Average daytime highs during May and October are in the mid-80s to low 90s, with average nighttime lows in the low to mid-70s. Rainfall is typically low in the spring, with about 1–2 inches per month. Precipitation is moderate in the autumn, with 5–6 inches on average.

THE PORT Cruise ships anchor in the harbor and tender guests into the marina. Once at the marina, the downtown area is a 10- to 15-minute walk away. Taxis are also readily available. A large mall near the marina offers basic services, as well as an array of luxury-brand outposts such as **Tiffany** and **Cartier.** For those looking to stock up on necessities, there's a **Walmart** at Plaza San Lucas.

TOURIST HIGHLIGHTS The cruise ship anchors in the harbor and tenders guests into the marina, where nearby lie a large mall and luxury brand outposts. White-sand beaches are the major attraction—relax on the sand or take part in active water pursuits such as snorkeling, sailing, parasailing, or sport fishing. For those wishing to be active and dry, Cabo is a golf paradise, boasting numerous world-class courses. Zip-lining is a wonderful excursion for guests with a daredevil streak. Whale-watching and interactive dolphin experiences are popular activities. Those looking to enjoy art and culture will want to visit the **Vitro-fusion Glass Blowing Factory** to watch artisans create recycled glassworks, or stay in town to explore the **Iglesia de San Lucas,** a Spanish mission with many original features still intact.

WHAT TO EAT While you can find food from many nationalities, the local Cabo cuisine is, of course, Mexican. Try the street-vendor versions of tacos, quesadillas, and tortas. Rocker Sammy Hagar's **Cabo Wabo Cantina** is a must-stop spot for many visitors. The menu features a dozen different shrimp dishes, as well as catch-of-the-day specials, served with a heaping earful of rock and roll on the side.

WHAT TO BUY Along with typical seaside tourist trinkets, shirts, caps, and shot glasses emblazoned with the Cabo Wabo logo are an obligatory purchase for many visitors. Foodies will want to take home the local hot sauce; or look for soaps and lotions made with imitation turtle oil or scented with local spices. Mexican tequila and Damiana, a liqueur made with an herb that supposedly has aphrodisiac qualities, are must-buy items for some.

Cartagena, Colombia

LANGUAGE Spanish

HISTORY Cartagena has been inhabited since 4000 BC. Spanish explorers founded the city proper during the early 1500s. This was followed by periodic plundering by pirates and privateers from France and England, and later by a major invasion from Englishman Sir Francis Drake. During the 17th century, the Spanish constructed a series of fortresses to protect the city. Throughout the 17th and 18th centuries, Cartagena was a major trading outpost. In 1811 the region declared its independence from Spain, resulting in nearly a century of crisis. Today Cartagena is a prosperous tourist destination.

WEATHER DCL visits Cartagena in April and October, but it's hot here year-round. Expect daytime highs in the upper 80s, and average nighttime lows in the 70s. Average precipitation is a moderate 3–4 inches during April, but up to 8 inches during October, which is part of the rainy season.

THE PORT The cruise terminal has basic services but not much else. A landscaped park near the dock gates has a café and small shops. Buses and taxis are available to take you to the main part of town.

TOURIST HIGHLIGHTS **Old Town** is a popular exploration spot. Look for the **Plaza de Bolívar** and the giant bronze statue of Simón Bolívar, who helped Colombia and other South American countries secure independence from Spain. Nearby are the **Museo del Oro y Arqueologia** and a 16th-century cathedral. The fortress **Castillo San Felipe de Barajas** presents a look into the area's past. The **Palacio de la Inquisición** exhibits artifacts from the Spanish Inquisition, including some very creative torture devices. For outdoor fun, Cartagena offers many beaches within a 10- to 20-minute taxi ride away from town. Divers will find scuba and snorkel equipment available for rent.

WHAT TO EAT Restaurants here serve food from most major cuisines. Traditional foods include grilled fish, meat, and rabbit; rice, cassava, and plantains are common side dishes. Street vendors sell *butifarras* (meatballs), *buñuelos* (cheese balls), and *arepas de huevo* (fried dough with an egg inside). Try the *mote de queso,* a local soup made from yams, eggplant, and cheese. Fruit juices are available in abundance, both in restaurants and in street shacks. The local beer is Club Colombia.

WHAT TO BUY You'll find plenty of jewelry, particularly emeralds, for sale here. Many vendors are open to bargaining. Ornate (and often obscene) woodcarvings are common finds. For local flavor, search out loose-fitting traditional dresses, baskets, or handmade musical instruments. Java junkies will naturally want to take home some Colombian coffee.

Cozumel, Mexico *(See page 252 for full profile.)*

Galveston, Texas *(See page 255 for full profile.)*

Grand Cayman, Cayman Islands *(See page 256 for full profile.)*

Miami, Florida *(See page 258 for full profile.)*

Panama Canal, Panama

HISTORY The Spanish government initially authorized construction of the Panama Canal in 1819. Progress was scattershot for several decades thereafter, with planning beginning in earnest in 1876 and construction starting in 1881. Engineering struggles plagued early efforts to dig the canal, eventually resulting in the plan for a system of raised locks. Continued disease and construction difficulties caused the bankruptcy of the original funders and a long stall in the work process. The project was revived following strategic interest from US President Theodore Roosevelt, with the United States taking formal control over the region in 1904. Several years were spent creating an infrastructure capable of supporting the materials and labor force required to complete the task. Lock building commenced in 1909 and was finished in 1913. In 1914 a French boat, the *Alexandre La Valley,* became the first to completely traverse the canal. The Panama Canal subsequently revolutionized world trade patterns, cutting nearly 8,000 miles off a sea journey from New York to San Francisco. In 1977, the United States began to reduce its role in the region, and today the Panama Canal Authority oversees the canal, which continues to be improved. Currently the locks cannot accommodate the size of the largest ships, and in 2007 a project began to create a new wider lane of locks.

WEATHER Warm. And wet. Because Panama is close to the equator, temperatures vary little, with lows throughout the year of around 75 and highs around 90. Disney ships generally visit in spring and early fall, which average 24–26 days of rain per month, with humidity above 90%. (On the upside, we hear big hair is back in style.)

THE PORT The ship moves through the canal without stopping to let off passengers.

TOURIST HIGHLIGHTS The highlight of the voyage is watching how the canal's locks fill and release water to move the ship up and down through the terrain. It takes 8–10 hours to get through all of the locks, so you have plenty of time to catch the action.

Port Canaveral, Florida *(See page 262 for full profile.)*

Puerto Vallarta, Mexico

LANGUAGE Spanish

HISTORY The native settlers were the ancient Aztlán peoples. European influence began in the early 1500s, when Spaniards, including Hernán Cortés, took control of the region. During the 17th and 18th centuries, the area was a known shelter for pirates and smugglers. Organized trade began to blossom in 1859, when the Union en Cuale mining company started operating in the region. In the early 1900s, the mining trade gave way to fruit farming, which then ceded influence to the growing tourism industry. Since the 1950s, Puerto Vallarta has been a resort and cruise destination.

WEATHER Disney cruises visit Puerto Vallarta in spring and fall. Average daytime highs during those months are in the mid-80s to low 90s, with average nighttime lows in the low to mid-70s. Precipitation is relatively low in May, averaging fewer than 2 inches of rainfall. October is slightly wetter, averaging about 3 inches for the month.

THE PORT From the **Marina Vallarta Terminal,** it's an easy walk to several restaurants, small shops, and hotels with bars. A full-size **Walmart** is about a 10- to 15-minute walk from the port, allowing you to pick up any basic necessity at a relatively reasonable price. Downtown Puerto Vallarta is about 3 miles from the port, accessible via taxi or bus.

TOURIST HIGHLIGHTS The beaches are the big draw here. Snooze by the waves or enjoy more-active pursuits such as snorkeling or biking. Animal lovers can enjoy dolphin excursions or watch whales and turtles. **El Centro,** Puerto Vallarta's downtown, features churches with charming colonial detail. Tequila manufacturing and tasting is a big draw to this area. Be sure to sample several varieties; you'll be amazed at the differences.

WHAT TO EAT Not surprisingly, you'll find tacos, taquitos, tostadas, and enchiladas on local menus, along with fresh seafood (try red snapper or marlin served with spices and lime). Those in the mood to imbibe will find no shortage of margaritas, daiquiris, and beer.

WHAT TO BUY Puerto Vallarta shopping caters to the tourist trade. You'll find silver, ceramics, leather, and woven goods in many forms, as well as the ubiquitous T-shirts and trinkets portside. Haggling is common with vendors by the beaches, so if you don't like the price you see, feel free to propose something lower. Several modern malls in the area sell brand-name cruise wear at typically reasonable prices. Foodies will want to bring home local chocolates or Mexican spices.

San Diego, California   *(See page 245 for full profile.)*

◼▮ TRANSATLANTIC

CRUISES SAIL FROM Barcelona, Port Canaveral

SHIP *Magic*

CRUISE LENGTHS 11 or 15 nights

PROS	CONS
■ This can be a cost-effective way to travel to Europe if you have the time to spare.	■ You may not have 2 weeks to dedicate to a transatlantic cruise.
■ A transatlantic crossing is on many cruisers' bucket lists.	■ This is one-way transportation, so you'll have to leave room in your budget for airfare.
■ You can sometimes find great last-minute deals on these cruises. (We all lead lives where we can drop everything and go to Europe, right?)	

DATES Spring and fall as the ship heads to Europe from Florida; eastward in the spring and westbound in the fall

WHAT TO PACK Your formalwear—you'll have plenty of opportunities to dress up—and a steamer trunk, if you have one.

SIGNATURE PORT ADVENTURE It's all about the journey rather than the destination.

CLASSIC DISNEY ADD-ON Disneyland Paris

COMMENTS Wanna travel to or from Europe without jet lag *and* pretend that you've gone back in time? Crossing the Atlantic by ship is the old-school way to do it, harking back to the era of the grand ocean liner.

ADDITIONAL PORTS Disney Cruise Line is not visiting the ports of **Boston, Massachusetts,** or **Gibraltar, United Kingdom,** in 2017, but we think they'll return to the schedule in the future. For more information on these ports, consult *The Unofficial Guide to Disney Cruise Line 2016* or visit touring plans.com/disney-cruise-line/ports (*note:* requires a TouringPlans.com subscription).

Amsterdam, The Netherlands   *(See page 293 for full profile.)*

Barcelona, Spain   *(See page 276 for full profile.)*

Halifax, Nova Scotia, Canada   *(See page 240 for full profile.)*

Lisbon, Portugal   *(See page 281 for full profile.)*

New York, New York

LANGUAGE English

HISTORY With a population of 8.4 million in the city proper and 23 million in the greater metro area, New York is the largest city in the United States and the eighth-largest urban agglomeration in the world. Many would also argue that it's the world's most important and most exciting city.

The first European exploration of the New York area began in the mid-1500s. Henry Hudson rediscovered the area in 1609, later claiming it for the Dutch East India Company. Permanent European presence in the area took root in the mid-1600s. New York was a center of conflict during the Revolutionary War, falling to British invaders in the late 1700s. By the early 1800s, the city had become one of the largest ports in North America, and its famed grid system of streets and avenues was developed. Immigrants from all over Europe arrived throughout the 1800s, creating unique ethnic enclaves. Along with immigration came the additional influx of commercial enterprise and cultural dominance in areas such as art, publishing, and fashion. New York's pivotal moment in recent history, of course, was the destruction of the World Trade Center in lower Manhattan on September 11, 2001.

WEATHER DCL cruises stop in New York in the autumn. The weather at this time of year can be lovely, with daytime highs in September averaging in the low to mid-70s, fading to daytime highs in the mid-50s during November. Expect nighttime lows to be about 10–15 degrees cooler. Precipitation is consistent most of the year, with an average of 4–5 inches of rain per month in the fall. The city's first snow generally falls in December, although it has arrived in October and November in years past.

THE PORT Cruise ships dock in midtown Manhattan, on the West Side. Within a 10-minute walk you'll find restaurants, shops, banks—you name it. The port itself is served by taxis and buses, and the subway is just a few blocks away, giving you access to the entire metropolitan area.

TOURIST HIGHLIGHTS We only have space to scratch the surface. Bustling **Times Square** and the **Theatre District** are just a few blocks from the port; keep an eye out for the **Naked Cowboy.** Museum lovers have their pick of the **Museum of Natural History,** the **Museum of Modern Art,** the **Metropolitan Museum of Art,** the **Guggenheim,** and scores more. **Central Park** and its zoo are a moderate walk or a short cab ride from Midtown. **Columbia** and **New York Universities** can be reached easily by subway. And of course, the **Statue of Liberty,** the **Empire State Building,** and the **World Trade Center Memorial** are must-dos for many visitors. For a bird's-eye view of Manhattan, visit **Top of the Rock** in **Rockefeller Center.**

If you have time to do more than just hit the high spots, we recommend Ellen Levitt's excellent *Walking Manhattan* (Wilderness Press).

WHAT TO EAT If you can eat it, someone in New York can cook it. You truly can find nearly every cuisine in the world represented in the kitchens of New York restaurants. Try dim sum in Chinatown, Greek specialties in Queens, soul food in Harlem, sushi on nearly every corner, and the only North American outposts of Paris's famed **Ladurée** macaron shop on the Upper East Side and in SoHo. For an "only in New York" experience, eat a "dirty-water dog" and a hot pretzel from a cart in Central Park, savor the pastrami-on-rye from **Zabar's,** grab some real coal-oven thin-crust pizza from **Patsy's,** and choose something to nosh on from the appetizing counter at **Zabar's** on the Upper West Side—for bagels, lox, knishes, blintzes, and sour pickles, this is THE place. And *shhhh,* don't tell anyone else, but our favorite cookies in the universe come from **Levain Bakery,** on 74th Street near Columbus Avenue. They're big enough to share . . . but why would you want to?

WHAT TO BUY As if we even needed to mention it, New York is home to major department stores, art galleries, designer-sample sales, luxury-goods purveyors, specialty shops of every stripe, and bodegas filled with endless trinkets. Whatever you want to buy, you can get it here. Shoppers who like to haggle should visit the **Diamond District** in Midtown. Classic New York gifts include memorabilia from Broadway shows, **Yankees** or **Mets** jerseys, and coffee-table books that describe the collections of the myriad local museums.

Ponta Delgada, Azores Islands, Portugal

LANGUAGE Portuguese

HISTORY The first known settlement in the Azores occurred during the mid-15th century, with most residents coming from mainland Portugal. Other early residents were Flemish sailors. English incursions onto the islands failed, but the Spanish were more successful and held control for a period in the early 1600s. The Portuguese later resumed rule of the area. During the 18th and 19th centuries, the Azores served as a stopping point for trade and travel voyages, and during WWII, the Azores were home to a British Naval station that provided aerial U-Boat surveillance. In 1976, the Azores became the Autonomous Region of the Azores (Região Autónoma dos Açores), which together with mainland Portugal and the Autonomous Region of Madeira comprises the Portuguese Republic.

WEATHER Disney Cruise Line visits Ponta Delgada in May and September. Daytime highs in May average in the mid-60s, with nighttime lows in the mid-50s. In September, daytime highs average in the mid-70s, with nighttime lows in the high 60s. Rainfall is similar in both months, with average precipitation of about 3 inches per month.

THE PORT There are few basic services at the port terminal itself; however, there are many shops and restaurants within a 5-minute walk of port. Taxis and car-rental desks are available at the port area. There is also a public bus line that serves much of the island.

TOURIST HIGHLIGHTS The town of Ponta Delgada is a picturesque place for a stroll, featuring lovely whitewashed buildings with red roofs. The **Convent of Esperança** and the **Church of Santo Cristo** are located near the city center. The convent features an ornate public chapel as well as a modest private chapel for the nuns' worship. Many guests of the Azores are interested in the islands' geological activity. **Fire Lake** has interesting craters and lush greenery. **Siete Cidades Crater Lake** is another nice option for hiking or photography. There are two tea plantations in the northern part of the island; both offer tours and tastings. The **Arruda Açores Pineapple Plantation** is another place to explore the agriculture of the region. Whale- and dolphin-watching excursions are also offered.

WHAT TO EAT Azorean cuisine is a hearty and peasant-based style of cooking. A typical family meal will include *caldo verde,* a kale soup studded with chunks of potato and *linguiça* sausage. Seafood figures heavily in traditional dishes, *bacalhau* (salt cod) being a staple. Also look for octopus, lamprey, and limpet, along with more-familiar fish. The Azores are also known for their rich dairy products—cows tend to be used for milk rather than as meat. Pork is the main meat used in cooking. Yogurt is typical breakfast food. Coffee is served with steamed milk, and the cheese selections are top-notch. Pineapples grown in the Azores are often exported to the Portuguese mainland, but you will find them as part of many dessert items on the islands. *Massa sovada,* or Portuguese sweet bread, originated in the Azores and is a ubiquitous part of all celebrations.

WHAT TO BUY The Azores are known for their embroidery and lace production. You can find intricate designs on tablecloths, bedspreads, and clothing. Other local crafts include wicker-work baskets and furniture and ceramic items such as dishes, vases, teapots, and mugs. The locally produced teas are another popular take-home item.

Port Canaveral, Florida   *(See page 262 for full profile.)*

Portland, England, United Kingdom

LANGUAGE English

HISTORY Portland is in the central part of England's so-called Jurassic Coast, known for its significant limestone deposits. The area was inhabited by humankind as early as the Middle Stone Age and, later, by the ancient Romans. Motivated by Viking raids, King Henry VIII erected Portland Castle in the 16th century to protect the land from foreign threats. Portland's man-made harbor—the second-largest such harbor in the world, built between 1848 and 1905—was originally a Royal Navy base and is now a popular recreation area.

Stonehenge—perhaps the world's most famous prehistoric monument—is Portland's biggest tourist draw and has been for at least 200 years. It was built in several stages: The first monument was an early henge monument, built about 5,000 years ago, and the unique stone circle was erected in the late Neolithic period, in about 2500 BC.

WEATHER Disney Cruise Line visits Portland in May. Daytime highs during May average in the low to mid 60s, with nighttime lows averaging in high 40s. Typical rainfall is about 2 inches per month during May.

THE PORT Ships dock directly quayside at **Portland Harbor;** expect to be greeted by a town crier in historical garb. Taxis and shuttle buses are available to take you to Portland Castle or to the nearby town of **Weymouth,** which has many quaint shops and cafés. The port area proper has few services and is primarily configured to meet the needs of the many freight ships docking nearby.

TOURIST HIGHLIGHTS About an hour away from Portland is **Stonehenge,** a UNESCO World Heritage site. Archaeologists believe that this ancient circle of standing stones was constructed from 3000 BC to 2000 BC. If you don't want to make the trek, the charming seaside town of **Weymouth** is nearby. Its attractions include **Nothe Fort, Abbotsbury Swannery and Gardens, Sandworld Sculptural Park,** and **Sea Life Adventure Park** (profiled in our *Unofficial Guide to Britain's Best Days Out*). Portland itself is home to **Portland Castle** (small as castles go), a quaint lighthouse, and several lovely stone churches.

WHAT TO EAT Expect to find the typical pub fare and seafood: haddock, mackerel, sea bream, and shellfish prepared fried or in stews or casseroles. Dorset sheep and lamb are renowned for their tender meat. Dorset sausage, similar to American meatloaf, is served as an appetizer or a main dish. Local blueberries and gooseberries find their way into pastries and ice creams. A favorite local cheese is Dorset Blue Vinny, a firm white cheese with veins of blue. And if at all possible, you should partake of a proper English tea, complete with scones topped with jam and clotted cream.

WHAT TO BUY You'll find all manner of Stonehenge-related souvenirs, from books of art and historical analysis to keychains, snow globes, and, yes, trilithon flash drives. Other area favorites include clothing and housewares decorated with emblems of the British monarchy, fine woolens, and scented soaps and bath products.

St. John's, Newfoundland and Labrador, Canada

LANGUAGE English

HISTORY St. John's takes pride in its status as one of the oldest settlements in North America. Sir Humphrey Gilbert claimed the area as England's first overseas colony in 1583, and the English maintained control for about the next hundred years. During the 1700s, the area saw attacks by Dutch and French forces. A period of growth followed, with St. John's serving as a trading port and naval base. Today, its chief employers are educational institutions and the oil-and-gas industry.

WEATHER Disney Cruise Line visits St. John's in September, when average daytime highs are in the low 60s and average nighttime lows in the high 40s. Precipitation is moderate, with about 5 inches of rainfall for the month.

THE PORT Services directly at the pier are minimal. The cruise dock is about 5 minutes from town by foot. Taxis are also available.

TOURIST HIGHLIGHTS **Signal Hill** is a rocky point offering expansive views of the harbor. Nearby **Johnson Geo Centre** includes an insightful exhibit on the sinking of the *Titanic*. **Cape Spear** is the easternmost point in North America. Whale-watching is a great activity for nature lovers. The **Railway Coastal Museum** showcases several vintage train cars.

WHAT TO EAT With Newfoundland being one of Canada's Maritime Provinces, fresh fish is a given. Find it baked, fried, or in stews and cakes. Moose meat is regularly eaten here as well, often served with boiled potatoes and carrots. The region's longstanding British influence has given St. John's a thriving pub community, where you'll find a multitude of beers and ales as well as pub grub such as meat pies and lamb stew. Afternoon tea is another English-influenced tradition.

WHAT TO BUY A native mineral is labradorite, used in jewelry and decorative items. Local potters and woodworkers offer unique handcrafted works. Foodies will want to take home a jar of local cloudberry jam.

Sydney, Nova Scotia, Canada   *(See page 242 for full profile.)*

PART TWELVE

PORT ADVENTURES

DISNEY CRUISE LINE OFFERS more than 600 shore excursions—"port adventures," in Disney-speak—for families to experience while their ship is docked. While it's impossible for us to have tried them all, we have embarked on quite a few. We've also interviewed scores of families and DCL employees to learn which are the most popular and which ones they'd recommend to friends.

Because most Disney cruises stop at **Castaway Cay** (see Part Ten), this section includes detailed reviews of its port adventures. These generally last 1–3.5 hours; others, such as snorkeling or biking, are self-guided. Disney staff leads most (but not all) of these excursions.

Beyond Castaway Cay, most port adventures last 3–6 hours, including transportation time, and all are designed to fit comfortably into the ship's schedule. Third-party companies based near the port run virtually all of the port adventures, except those on Castaway Cay. On the day of your activity, you'll be instructed to gather somewhere on the ship, such as a restaurant or lounge, at a predetermined time. Once you're there, a Disney cast member will ensure that you have the correct port-adventure tickets and identification to reboard the ship. You also may be asked to sign a liability waiver to participate in a particular activity.

When those tasks are complete, everyone signed up for the activity will be escorted by cast members off the ship to a meeting point on the port's docks. There, representatives of the third-party company running the port adventure will meet you. You'll be in their care until you're returned to the port after your activity.

FINDING PORT ADVENTURES

IF YOU'VE BOOKED A CRUISE, you can see your port-adventure options in the DCL **Planning Center** for your voyage (see page 35). But before you book, you can also see full lists of options that may help you choose a specific itinerary.

Your typical starting point for researching DCL port adventures online is disneycruise.disney.go.com/cruises-destinations. Click on the region where you'll be cruising—Alaska, for example—and then click "Ports of Call." Clicking the name of the port will bring you to a page with sections labeled "Destinations Details," "Things to See and Do," and "Port Adventures." Clicking "Port Adventures," "Show More," and then "Learn More" lets you drill down to the specifics about a particular port adventure: price, age requirements for participants, how long the excursion lasts, and how suitable the activity level is for given cruisers, along with a brief summary of the port adventure, a bulleted list of the excursion's highlights, and important "Know Before You Go" information. Some ports offer dozens of choices at a wide range of price points and activity levels.

Information about DCL port adventures, organized by region, is also available at disneycruise.disney.go.com/port-adventures.

Of course, you're not limited to Disney's offerings: You can explore on your own (see Part Eleven for general suggestions in the profile for each port), or you can book an alternative excursion through another vendor. If you don't see something that strikes your fancy on the DCL website, check the shore-excursion information for other cruise lines. There will likely be overlap, but Norwegian or Carnival, for example, may have identified a third-party vendor that better suits your style.

If you're headed to a sun-and-sand destination, you may want to explore the website resortforaday.com. This source for day passes to hotels and resorts allows guests to use amenities such as pools, beaches, spas, and the like while their ship is in port. Some packages include transfers and meal vouchers as well. If you're not up for an excursion but you don't want to hang out on the ship all day, this can be an easy/safe alternative to finding a beach on your own.

Still another option is to try our **custom walking tours.** See page 344 for details.

Finally, remember that you're under no obligation to participate in *any* organized adventures. Feel free to hang out on the ship or just amble aimlessly around the port city. Your vacation, your call.

EVALUATING A PORT ADVENTURE

THE PORT ADVENTURES OFFERED through Disney Cruise Line have all been vetted by DCL staff for quality and reliability. When you book your excursion through DCL, it's unlikely that you'll end up with an experience that's *completely* without merit. However, just because an excursion is right for one person doesn't mean it's right for you. If you ask yourself the questions in the chart on the next page, you should increase your odds of choosing the best option for your needs.

20 QUESTIONS TO ASK WHEN CHOOSING A PORT ADVENTURE
1. Have I looked at all the physical requirements of the excursion?
2. Does this excursion's price make sense to me?
3. Are there hidden fees that increase the cost of the excursion—for example, add-on photo packages or meals?
4. How does the price of this individual excursion fit into my overall excursion budget?
5. What percentage of the excursion will be spent in transportation?
6. What percentage of the excursion will be spent with a guide versus on my own?
7. Is there an adult-only or teen-only version of this excursion? Do those variations make more sense for me?
8. Does the excursion's mode of transportation make sense for me? (Guests who get motion sickness or are afraid of heights, for example, may want to avoid helicopter excursions.)
9. Is a meal or snack provided as part of the excursion? Do I want there to be?
10. Will adverse weather conditions drastically affect my enjoyment of the excursion?
11. Does the excursion take place in a port where guests tender to shore? (Tender excursions are more likely to be canceled.)

Our research shows that two of the largest factors affecting a guest's enjoyment of an excursion are the weather in port and the quality of the guide. Even with the best planning, you may find that a sudden storm or an inexperienced guide dims the quality of the adventure. Of course, if the excursion turns out to be a total wash or the guide behaves unprofessionally, you should speak to the tour provider and to Disney, but try not to let normal ups and downs derail your enjoyment.

BOOKING EXCURSIONS ON YOUR OWN VS. THROUGH DISNEY

AS WE'VE MENTIONED, YOU CAN BOOK port adventures on your own or through Disney. Some advantages to booking through Disney include the following:

- **CONVENIENCE OF SELECTION.** To book through Disney, just head over to the DCL website (see page 35). For each port, you'll see a menu of options; it's a one-stop spot for information, including activity descriptions, age/height/weight restrictions, costs, and related data. If you find an excursion appealing, you book it with just a few clicks.

- **CONVENIENCE OF BILLING.** When you book your excursion through Disney, the fee appears on your stateroom bill, which you can pay using any of the acceptable DCL methods, or in US dollars, British pounds, or euros. As an added bonus, you don't pay a deposit and you don't pay until you sail. If you're booking an excursion in another country on your own, you may have to pay a large deposit,

20 QUESTIONS TO ASK WHEN CHOOSING A PORT ADVENTURE

12. Are there similar excursions at other ports during my itinerary? (For example, numerous ports have dolphin encounters—is this particular port the best for such an excursion?)

13. Are there similar excursions at the same port? (For example, several dogsledding variations are available in Juneau—consider which one appeals to you the most.)

14. How long is the excursion? What percentage of my day will it encompass? Are there other things I'd rather do in port?

15. Is a similar experience available close to home or at another frequently visited vacation spot? (For example, zip-line and go-kart experiences are available in several ports—ask yourself whether you want to spend cruise time for these when you could easily do them elsewhere.)

16. What is the level of activity involved in this excursion?

17. Is this excursion too similar to something I'm doing in another port?

18. Will the timing of the excursion interfere with my child's dining or nap schedule?

19. Can I bring a stroller on the excursion?

20. Are there elements of the excursion specifically designed with children in mind?

you may have to pay in another currency, or you may be limited to use of a particular credit card or other form of payment. And remember that if you're using Disney Gift Cards as a payment method on the ship, you may get an effective 5% discount if you've purchased your gift cards through Target, or other discounts when purchasing through Sam's Club, Costco, or another retailer.

■ **SAFETY.** Of course, whenever you're on any port adventure, you'll want to exercise an abundance of caution, but if you book a Disney-vetted excursion, you know that they've done some of the work for you. Disney verifies that the excursions they offer are via legitimate businesses. They make sure that the transportation used is safe and that the guides are accountable for your whereabouts. If you book an excursion on your own, the onus is on you to do the research.

■ **COMMUNICATION WITH THE SHIP.** When you book an excursion through Disney, they know where you are. If something unforeseen happens, they have representatives who can contact your group and vice versa. If you book your excursion on your own, cast members on the ship will likely have no idea where you are. And they're not going to wait for you if you don't arrive back at the dock before sail-away time.

■ **LANGUAGE ISSUES.** Booking your excursion through Disney means that the transaction will take place in English. If you're booking an excursion on your own for a port in another country, the website or phone representative may use another language.

■ **CANCELLATION POLICIES.** DCL's port-adventure cancellation policy is clearly stated on its website (also see page 331). If you book on your own, you may be subject to an entirely different set of policies, which may or may not be clearly outlined—or fair.

On the other hand, some advantages to booking your port adventures through an outside vendor are as follows:

- **PRICE.** Many guests have found that similar excursions to Disney's can be booked independently at a lesser cost. Additionally, when booking on your own, you'll be able to construct an excursion at a budget or luxury level that specifically suits your needs.

- **MORE OPTIONS.** While Disney offers a range of excursions at each port, the list of options is certainly finite. If you book on your own, there's no limit to the number of choices you might have.

- **CUSTOMIZATION.** When booking on your own, you can often work with a vendor to put together an excursion custom-tailored to your interests or hobbies. You might be able to combine visits to two disparate sites in one excursion. You might be able to skip part of a standard tour that doesn't interest you. You might be able to linger longer at a favorite venue. Or you might be able to arrange

---

SCOTT SAYS   *by Scott Sanders*

PLANNING YOUR PORT ADVENTURE

I'M A BIG PROPONENT of putting together my own port adventures, either with just my family or a small group. It's easy to plan a walking tour with public transportation, and not much more difficult to book a private tour—also significantly cheaper than those offered by Disney. The only caveat is that it's your responsibility to get back to the ship on time.

No matter how you explore a port, it's a good idea to take water and snacks ashore. In a pinch, you can grab some boxed cereal from the breakfast buffet. If you're traveling with kids and the tour involves traveling on a bus or van for a considerable amount of time, consider bringing an activity for them to do during the trip. We've been on excursions where the total travel time was pushing 4 hours—and not all of it was scenic.

Finally, take some cash to tip your tour guides if appropriate for the excursion; US dollars are almost always welcome worldwide.

for transportation that accommodates a physical need, such as wheelchair use.

■ **BOOKING WINDOW.** On the DCL website, your ability to access excursion booking is based on your Castaway Club status (see page 49). First-time cruisers booking through Disney might be locked out of some popular activities because they've become fully booked before they had access. When booking excursions on your own, you're not subject to any waiting period.

CANCELING A PORT ADVENTURE

DEPENDING ON YOUR CASTAWAY CLUB LEVEL, you may make port-adventure reservations up to 120 days in advance. Once you make a reservation, you may cancel it with no penalty up to three days before you sail—no refunds after that. Of course, you're not charged if Disney or the tour provider cancels the excursion due to weather or other unforeseen circumstances.

The only other exception to the cancellation penalty occurs if you decide to upgrade your excursion. You may change a previously booked port adventure to one that's more expensive. You'll simply pay the difference in excursion fees without any penalty. You may upgrade on board at Guest Services or at the Port Adventures desk.

Port adventures booked on your own or through other vendors may have different cancellation policies, so always ask when booking.

PORT ADVENTURES *on* CASTAWAY CAY

WE CONSIDER CASTAWAY CAY'S SHORE EXCURSIONS among the best values of any that DCL has to offer. Here's a quick rundown of what's available.

BICYCLE RENTALS

THESE SINGLE-SPEED ROAD BIKES with plump tires are good for getting some exercise while exploring the island. Men's and women's models are available, and the seats are designed for comfort. The seats can be adjusted up and down to suit your leg length, although years spent on the island have rusted many of the metal cams used to loosen the seats. Ask a cast member to help (they have wrenches!) if yours won't budge.

Pick up your bicycles just past the Pelican Point tram stop, near the middle of the family

*un*official **TIP**
The **Castaway Cay Getaway** and **Extreme Getaway Packages** include activities listed here and are cheaper than purchasing à la carte, but we don't recommend them—trying to fit all that adventure into one or two days seriously cuts into your relaxation (and eating!) time.

CASTAWAY CAY 5K RUN FAQS

What should I pack? Don't forget your running shoes and clothes.

Can my kid join me? Sort of. Disney officially restricts participants to folks age 12 and older, so your child won't get a bib or medal. Because of the informal setup of the race, though, there's no way to stop kids under 12 from running along with you. Parents are given time during the walk to the race start to drop off kids at Scuttle's Cove.

Is it a race? This 5K brings out people of all abilities and seriousness about their running. Take it at your own pace and just enjoy it.

Is there a time limit? Not officially, but the cast members would probably appreciate it if you're done within 40–45 minutes. (There's also a Castaway Cay Power Walk if that's more your speed.)

Can I buy a souvenir? Yes. When RunDisney began sponsoring this event, we got "medals" (plastic) and the opportunity to purchase T-shirts at the end (in addition to the race bibs you receive). The T-shirts, while attractive, are cotton instead of tech material.

Can I shower after the race? There are no private showers on the island, just the ones by the restrooms for knocking off the sand. If you didn't bring a swimsuit with you and don't plan to get right into the water, you'll need to walk back to the ship to shower in your cabin.

How's the weather? Hot. Drink lots of water. Wear sunscreen. Eating at Remy or Palo the night before probably isn't the best idea. Did we mention that it's hot?

What about itineraries with two stops at Castaway Cay? You get two opportunities to run. Yay! You can do both or either.

Is water available? Yes. Not only does a cast member offer water on the course, but the 5K also begins and ends by a regular water stop for the island. Drink lots!

beaches. You can also rent bikes next to the Serenity Bay adult beach, just behind the Castaway Air Bar. Cost is $10.75 for a one-day rental or $14 for two days. The rental is theoretically for 1 hour, but in practice we've never seen anyone keep track of how long you use the bike.

BOAT RENTALS

VARIOUS WATERCRAFT, including one- and two-seat kayaks, sailboats, and paddleboats, are available for rent in half-hour increments. Costs range from $14 for a single-seat kayak to $27 for a Hobie Cat catamaran. The paddleboats require an extraordinary amount of leg power to get anywhere, and 30 minutes is going to be plenty for most people. Previous sailing experience is required to rent a sailboat.

CASTAWAY CAY 5K RUN

ONE OF THE BEST PORT ADVENTURES to start your day on Castaway Cay is fun, well organized, and totally free. Runners and walkers who wish to participate in the 5K meet around 8:15 on the morning the ship arrives at the island. The meeting location is almost always at one of the bars in the adult area of the ship because that's the way the best races begin; check your *Personal Navigator* the night before for details on when and where to meet.

Sign up for the 5K at the Port Adventures desk anytime; you also can just show up at the designated meeting place on the morning of the race. Two cast members will meet you there and make sure you have your Key to the World Card and ID. They'll give you a runner's bib (a nice touch for this unchipped race) and safety pins; then you'll walk off the ship with the rest of the runners toward the start of the race, by the Pelican Point tram stop. Parents who need to drop their kids off at Scuttle's Cove will be given time to do so on the way.

Once you arrive at the start, everyone is given a chance to hit the restroom and drop anything they don't want to run with in the storage area by the bike rentals. This is unsecured, so don't leave your gold doubloons, but other stuff is fine.

Once everyone is ready, you're off and running. The route includes a trip up and down the airstrip and two loops out to the viewpoint. You'll be sharing the road with the trams as well as folks on bicycles, so be aware of your surroundings. One cast member will be at the entrance to the loop with water—take advantage of it, because this run is hot.

The other cast member will be by the digital timer at the end of the race to congratulate you on your spectacular finish and give you a medal. Wear it proudly for the other folks who were still at the breakfast buffet while you were out running 3 miles in the heat.

The 5K and snorkeling are the two port adventures that we always do on the island. They're two fun and affordable ways to enjoy your day.

BOTTOM FISHING

A 3-HOUR CATCH-AND-RELEASE fishing excursion ($147 per person) takes place in the waters around Castaway Cay, with Disney-provided fishing rods and bait. Your boat's captain will take you into the waters around the island; the most commonly caught species are yellow jack, grouper, various porgies, and snapper. It's not unheard of to hook a barracuda or small shark, too. Most charters leave around 9 a.m. and are back in time for lunch. Cruisers who are prone to seasickness shouldn't take this excursion, and children must be age 6 or older to participate.

CASTAWAY RAY'S STINGRAY ADVENTURE

THIS IS YOUR CHANCE TO PET AND FEED small- and medium-size stingrays in a supervised, structured setting on the shore of the Stingray Lagoon. Disney keeps dozens of these stingrays in a sectioned-off part of Castaway Cay's lagoon, and the stingrays are trained to use a special feeding platform at mealtimes. The cost is $51 for guests age 10 and up, $40 for kids age 5–9.

Holding a specially formulated pellet of food between two fingers, you'll place your hand, palm down, on the platform. A stingray will swim up to the platform, glide over your hand, and grab the food in its mouth. You'll also have the chance to pet each ray as it swims by.

There's plenty of food and plenty of stingrays for everyone. Besides the feeding, you'll get a brief introduction to stingrays, skates, and sharks before you begin, when a cast member reviews rules and procedures.

Many children are worried about being bitten by the stingrays, and let's face it: The word *sting* in their name doesn't exactly make rays the poster children for cuddly animals. But rays don't have teeth, and the only thing that seems to get them excited is the prospect of feeding time. Calling them rays may help your kids find these animals more approachable. Kid fears might also be assuaged by a mention of the friendly Mr. Ray in *Finding Nemo*.

FLOAT AND TUBE RENTALS

INNER TUBES AND RECTANGULAR FLOATS are available for $10.75 for one day or $14 for two days. You can swap out one type for the other during the day.

GLASS-BOTTOM-BOAT EXCURSION

GUESTS BOARD A SMALL MOTORIZED WATERCRAFT that holds about 25 people and that ventures about 15 minutes out into the ocean. You can observe sea life below through several "windows" in the floor of the boat. During the trip, you're accompanied by a local guide who discusses the fish and other natural elements you'll encounter.

The highlight of the tour takes place at approximately the midpoint of the journey: Guests are given a cup filled with about 1 ounce of oatmeal, which they toss overboard to attract fish. During the feeding portion of the tour, several hundred tropical fish of various species surround the boat, and the guide points out the characteristics of as many fish as possible. The feeding lasts about five minutes, after which the fish will disappear quickly. Sightings of fish at other points of the tour are sporadic.

The trip takes about 45 minutes to an hour (about 15 minutes out, 15 minutes back, and around 15 minutes parked at viewing spots along the reef adjacent to Castaway Cay). Cost is $42 for adults and $29.50 for kids ages 9 and under, including infants and toddlers. Guests must be able to climb five steps to board and debark the boat to participate, and guests will stand aboard the boat for the duration of the excursion.

PARASAILING

GUESTS LOOKING FOR A BIRD'S-EYE VIEW OF PARADISE should check out this excursion. Floating hundreds of feet in the air, you're master of all you survey, or at least it seems that way for several minutes.

You board a speedboat and travel several hundred yards away from land. Then, in singles or pairs, you stand at the back of the boat and are harnessed to a line-bound parachute that is slowly let out until you and the parachute are 600–1,000 feet above the water. Enjoy panoramic views of your ship, Castaway Cay, and beyond.

Each excursion takes about 10 people onto the boat. There are no ride-alongs; every guest on the boat must pay. Your actual parasail event will last about 5–7 minutes. Depending on the number of other guests, the entire experience lasts 45 minutes–1 hour.

Open to guests age 8 and up, parasailing excursions cost $102.25 for both adults and kids. Guests must weigh between 90 and 375 pounds; those who weigh less than 90 pounds may be able to ride if they fly in tandem with another guest, but their combined weight may not exceed 375 pounds. Determination of single or tandem rides is fully at the discretion of the staff.

Kids under age 13 must be accompanied by a paying adult age 18 or older. Guests ages 13–17 may go on the excursion unaccompanied but must be escorted to the Marge's Barges excursion meeting site by an adult age 18 or older. All guests must sign a safety waiver.

You must leave your shoes on the dock and are strongly discouraged from wearing a hat or glasses during your sail; there is a storage area on the boat for your personal belongings. Wheelchairs and other wheeled mobility devices cannot be accommodated.

No photography service is provided during the excursion—you're welcome to bring cameras onto the boat, but you assume all liability for the loss of anything you bring up with you. Understandably, anything dropped into the ocean can't be retrieved.

SNORKELING

THIS IS ONE OF THE LEAST EXPENSIVE, most rewarding shore excursions offered on a Disney cruise. We recommend it for every family. Cost is $15.05 for kids ages 5-9 for one day, $19.35 for two days; $31.18 for age 10 and up for one day, $38.70 for two days.

First, find some chairs on the family beach, where you can store your stuff while you're in the water. If possible, choose something near a vertical landmark such as a tree; it will be easier to find when you come back to shore.

Next, pick up your snorkeling gear at Gil's Fins and Boats, a short walk from Scuttle's Cove, the island's first tram stop. You'll be given a mask, snorkel, fins, and an inflatable buoyancy vest to make swimming easier. Also pick up a blue-mesh gear bag, which makes it easier to haul your stuff back to your beach chairs.

Put on your vest before you get in the water, but don't inflate it just yet. Wait until you're in hip-high water to put on your flippers because it's impossible to walk in them on shore (and they'll get sandy). Keep your mask off until you get into the water.

If you're snorkeling with younger children, plan on spending 10–15 minutes adjusting the fit of masks and vests. Inflate their vests by blowing into the vertical tube on the left side of the vest, adding just enough air to keep the top of their heads above water. (If you overinflate the vests, they'll have trouble getting their masks below the surface.) Also, practice using the flippers, which work best with slow, deliberate leg movements.

Once everyone's gear is working, take one last look at the lagoon to get your bearings. Disney has placed orange-and-white buoys above the underwater sites, so head for those.

There usually aren't a lot of fish in the first 30–40 yards nearest the shore, though it's possible to see almost anything once you're in the water. Fish species in the lagoon include yellowtail snapper, sergeant major, banded butterfly fish, blue tang, and barracuda. Obviously, you shouldn't try to catch any of these fish with your hands.

If you've snorkeled before and you enjoy it, Castaway Cay offers another snorkeling excursion in the waters off the island. You board a 28-foot Zodiac rigid-hull inflatable boat and head 30 minutes off-shore for a 90-minute open-water snorkeling session. Cost is $113.50 for adults, $102 for kids ages 6–9.

WALKING AND KAYAK NATURE ADVENTURE

THIS PORT ADVENTURE BEGINS at Marge's Barges, where every-one boards a tram to the Serenity Bay adult beach. Next you walk behind the adult beach cabanas to a nature trail, which leads to the beach beyond. During the walk, your guide will point out interesting plants and animals and talk about the history of the Bahamas.

Upon reaching the beach, participants don their life jackets and head out in their kayaks. This is the part where you're at Mother Nature's whim. We took this tour after a friend raved about it. She headed out in the morning and was able to kayak to the interior of the island. Our own tour was later in the afternoon as the tide was going out. The inte-rior of the island was inaccessible by kayak, and the tides made piloting our single kayak very difficult. We wouldn't book this adventure in the afternoon again, even if it were the only time available.

Even if you're able to book this in the morning, however, the tour is 3–3½ hours long—time you could spend snorkeling, biking, or laz-ing on the beach. Ideally, you would book this on the morning of the second stop of a five-night Castaway Cay cruise.

Be sure to bring walking shoes, sunglasses, a hat, sunscreen, and an underwater or water-resistant camera; consider gloves for paddling to avoid blisters. Wear a swimsuit under your clothes for swimming. You must stow your belongings on the beach for the kayaking, so leave the doubloons in the cabin. Water is provided. Cost is $67 for guests age 10 and up.

WATERCRAFT SKI ADVENTURE

BOOKING THIS PORT ADVENTURE is the only way that guests can use WaveRunner watercraft on Castaway Cay, and that fact alone makes it worth your while if you're willing to spend the money.

Riders begin this port adventure at the Boat Beach (the beach closest to where the ship docks), where they're given life jackets and a safety briefing. While you must be at least 18 years old to drive the WaveRunner, kids as young as age 8 may ride along. Our advice for two adults is for each to ride as a single unless one is truly afraid of piloting a craft alone—a single rider will go much faster than two adults due to the weight difference.

If you've never piloted a WaveRunner before, don't worry; it's fairly easy. It's actually easier to maneuver once you get up to speed than when you're idling or going slowly at the beginning of the excursion. If you know how to drive a motorcycle or Vespa, then you've got this down. Most participants get the hang of things quickly.

As you head out, riders will start in single file with a guide leading and one more assistant bringing up the rear. Try to avoid hitting the wake of the craft in front of you because the bumpiness can be a little scary when you're up to speed, which tops out at a little more than 30 miles per hour at full throttle.

Unless you choose to swim or tip your craft, you won't get especially wet, though you will want to wear waterproof shoes or sandals or go barefoot. Flip-flops aren't allowed, because they're likely to come off in the water (along with hats). You may store anything that you don't want to take with you in an unlocked chest at the beginning of the tour. We recommend taking a waterproof camera for photos on the beach; just secure it around your neck for the trip out.

Disney says the hour-long tour may have two stops, but ours had just one—the same beach you visit on the Walking and Kayak Nature Adventure. The fact that you can visit this beach on the WaveRunner without having to kayak there is a plus, but perhaps we're still bitter about the blister we got kayaking. The other stop is an island opposite the beach.

When you arrive, your tour guide will give you a very brief history of the islands and point out any interesting flora and fauna, much like an abbreviated version of the Walking and Kayak tour. Then you can swim in the ocean for a bit before heading back to the Boat Beach to end your port adventure. The piloting of the WaveRunners, not the nature talk or the beach visit, is the real highlight.

Would we book this again? *Maybe*. This is one of the more expensive port adventures for its length. The WaveRunners are fun, but the Boat Beach is far enough away that just getting there and back will cut into your time on the island.

If you have the chance, you may want to book this for earlier in the day as you're just getting off the ship, or later as you're heading back. Price is $100.25 for a single rider, $168.75 for two riders.

NASSAU

A NOTE ABOUT NASSAU SAFETY

WE'VE NEVER HAD A BAD EXPERIENCE IN NASSAU. We'd be remiss, though, if we didn't tell you that crime is a problem here—more so than in other cruise ports.

The **US Embassy in Nassau** issued several security-awareness memos for tourists in 2014–16, and in 2015 the **US State Department**'s Overseas Security Advisory Council assessed the threat of violent crime in Nassau as "critical."

A recent security notice about the Bahamas from the **UK government** states, "There have been incidents of violent crime including robbery, which is often armed and sometimes fatal, in residential and tourist areas. . . . Be vigilant at all times, and don't walk alone away from the main hotels, tourist areas, beaches, and downtown Nassau."

The **Canadian government** advises, "You should exercise a high degree of caution due to high rates of crime, especially in Nassau."

Even DCL prints a safety advisory in the *Personal Navigator* for the Nassau port day on cruises that stop there—something it doesn't do for other ports. For our sailing on the *Dream* in May 2016, the *Navigator* didn't mince words:

> *While you will find many great experiences in Nassau, there have been reports of increased crime, including assaults and robberies involving tourists in the area. As in any large city, you'll want to take some basic precautions to make the most of your time ashore. . . . Avoid shortcuts, narrow alleys, or poorly lit streets. We recommend that guests visit only the downtown shopping areas and other tourist locations. Leave valuables in your room. . . . Cameras and handbags should be carried out of sight. . . . Use only licensed taxi operators.*

If you're participating in a port adventure at **Atlantis** (see next section), which has its own security staff, or another Disney-vetted excursion, your odds of trouble are quite low. If, however, you haven't signed up for any port adventures and relaxation is your number-one vacation priority, **we recommend that you stay on the ship if your cruise stops at Nassau.**

unofficial **TIP**
If you do want to explore Nassau on your own, **exercise the utmost vigilance about your surroundings,** and let family remaining on board (or DCL Guest Services staff) know about your on-shore plans.

Remaining on board lets you experience more amenities than you'd have time to otherwise during a brief sailing: visit the spa, stuff yourself at the buffet, or have your kids participate in club activities. Remember that many onboard activities are included in the cost of your sailing, so staying put can be an easy way to save some money you might otherwise spend on tacky souvenirs.

NASSAU PORT ADVENTURES

AFTER CASTAWAY CAY, the port most visited by DCL is Nassau. Virtually all *Disney Dream* sailings stop here, as do many sailings of the *Magic, Wonder,* and *Fantasy.*

The DCL website currently lists about 35 port adventures for Nassau, with 15 of them taking place at **Atlantis,** a Las Vegas–style resort about a 25-minute drive from the port (888-877-7525; atlantisbahamas .com). In addition to Disney cruisers, you'll encounter guests of other cruise lines, Atlantis guests, and guests of other area hotels during your time at Atlantis; it's a high-volume operation. The resort generally does things well, but due to the sheer numbers of people who cycle through every day, it can feel a bit like a factory for fun. We're Disney-theme-park fans, so we don't necessarily think that's a *bad* thing, but if you're in the market for privacy or quiet, you'll want to look elsewhere.

Crowd levels vary substantially at Atlantis depending on how many cruise ships are in port on a specific day. If your ship is the only one in port, you'll find plenty of open lounge chairs and short lines for the slides; if there are eight large ships in port, you'll be fighting for a place just to lay your towel on the sand.

Most of the Atlantis-based excursions are variations on a theme: Spend time with a dolphin, visit the beach, visit the waterpark-like **Aquaventure,** go shopping, or some combination thereof. The animal encounters receive uniformly moderate to high marks from guests. They're a commodity item, with almost all of the variation in opinion based on whether they thought their specific guide was funny, how the weather was, if they were aware in advance that just a small part of the excursion would be spent interacting with the animal, and if they were aware in advance that there would be a substantial upcharge for photos and video of their animal encounter. The weather and your rapport with your guide are the luck of the draw, so adjust your expectations accordingly and you're likely to have a positive experience.

Here's a rundown of the different port adventures at Atlantis:

- **Discover Atlantis Tour** Free for kids under age 3; $40.75 ages 3–9; $63 age 10 and up. Includes transportation, an aquarium tour, and access to the casino and shopping. Does not include access to the beach, pools, or Aquaventure.

- **Atlantis Beach Day and Discover Atlantis** Free for kids under age 3; $61.75 ages 3–9; $105 age 10 and up. Includes everything on the Discover Atlantis tour, plus beach access. Does not include access to the pools or Aquaventure.

- **Atlantis Aquaventure** Free for kids under age 3; $124.75 ages 3–9; $182 age 10 and up. Includes everything on the previous two tours, plus access to Aquaventure—a mini-waterpark with 11 pools, several waterslides, and a "lazy river"—as well as a voucher for a fast food–style lunch.

- **Atlantis Snorkel the Ruins and Aquaventure** $225 ages 8–9; $259 age 10 and up. Spend 30 minutes on a guided snorkel experience in the marine habitat (like a giant fish tank) with rays, sharks, and tropical fish. Includes transportation, access to the casino and shopping, a voucher for a fast food–style lunch, and access to Aquaventure.

- **Atlantis Dolphin Cay Shallow Water Interaction and Discover Atlantis** Kids age 2 and under admitted free but not permitted in the dolphin experience; $40.75 age 3; $169 ages 3–9; $190 age 10 and up. Includes transportation, a self-guided tour of the aquarium, and access to the casino and shopping; no access to pools (other than the dolphin pool) or Aquaventure. Includes an educational segment about dolphin life and a 30-minute wading-depth "meet and greet" with dolphins. *Note:* You *don't* get to swim with the dolphins.

- **Atlantis Dolphin Cay Shallow Water Interaction and Aquaventure** Kids age 2 and under admitted free but not permitted in the dolphin experience; $124.75 age 3; $242 ages 3–9; $275 age 10 and up. Includes everything in the Atlantis Dolphin Cay Shallow Water Interaction and Discover Atlantis, plus access to Aquaventure.

- **Atlantis Dolphin Cay Deep Water Interaction and Discover Atlantis** Kids age 5 and under not permitted; $219 ages 6–9; $232 age 10 and up. Includes transportation, a self-guided tour of the aquarium, and access to the casino and shopping; no access to pools (other than the dolphin pool) or Aquaventure. Includes an education segment about dolphin life and a 30-minute swim in a dolphin habitat, including one dolphin "push" across the lagoon.

- **Atlantis Dolphin Cay Deep Water Interaction and Aquaventure** Age 5 and under not permitted. $299 ages 6–9; $317 age 10 and up. Includes everything in the Atlantis Dolphin Cay Deep Water Swim and Discover Atlantis, plus access to Aquaventure.

- **Observer at Dolphin Cay and Discover Atlantis** Kids age 2 and under admitted free but not permitted in the dolphin experience; $40.75 age 3; $57.50 ages 4–9; $87 age 10 and up. Includes transportation, an aquarium tour, and access to the casino and shopping; does *not* include access to the beach, pools, or Aquaventure. This can be booked only if other members of your party are doing the Dolphin Cay Shallow Water or Deep Water Interaction. The observer is allowed to stand at the edge of the dolphin facility and take photos but may not interact with the animals. This is a good choice for parents who don't want to swim with the dolphins but whose kids do.

- **Observer at Dolphin Cay and Aquaventure** Kids age 2 and under admitted free but not permitted in the dolphin experience. $124.75 age 3; $140.50 ages 4–9; $205 age 10 and up. Includes transportation, an aquarium tour, and access to the casino and shopping, plus access to Aquaventure and a voucher for a fast food–style lunch. Again, the observer is allowed to stand at the edge of the dolphin facility and take photos but may not interact with the animals.
- **Ultimate Trainer for a Day** $519 age 10 and up. A behind-the-scenes tour of the veterinary hospital and lab for the dolphins and sea lions. Swim in deep water with the dolphins and have a double dorsal tow and "foot push." Feed predatory nurse sharks and cow nose stingrays, then snorkel with them and hundreds of other tropical fish. Includes lunch and photos.

If you just want to walk around the shops or eat at the restaurants at Atlantis on your own without using the pools, beach, or water park, you can do this at no charge. Taxis from the port to Atlantis typically run in the ballpark of $10 per person.

If you want to use the beach, pools, or Aquaventure without adding a dolphin experience, you may end up saving money, depending on the size of your party, if you actually book a room for the day at Atlantis (the **Beach Tower** is the least expensive part of the resort) or the nearby **Comfort Suites** (comfortsuitespi.com/atlantis-paradise-island.php), a 5-minute walk away.

At both locations, rates start at about $225 depending on the time of year. Neither hotel offers day rates, but renting a room for a few hours will give you a quiet space for the kiddos to nap, Wi-Fi access, safe storage for valuables, and a private shower, along with other resort privileges. On the downside, you'll have to spend a few minutes at the check-in desk, and you'll certainly spend valuable time walking from the pools to your room—Atlantis is huge, so this is a real consideration. However, given the high cost of Atlantis-based excursions, your savings could be substantial.

If you don't want to book a hotel room, consider an **Aquaventure Day Pass.** In 2016, passes were priced at $120–$150 (depending on the season) for guests age 13 and up; passes for kids ages 4–12 cost $80. Guests for whom kids' passes could be particularly appealing are those with 3-year-olds (Disney charges admission fees for 3-year-olds, but Atlantis doesn't charge until kids turn 4) and those with 10- to 12-year-olds (Disney charges them an adult rate, but Atlantis still allows them to pay a child's rate).

After Atlantis, the next largest block of Nassau excursions takes place at **Blue Lagoon,** a beach area about 40 minutes away from the

unofficial **TIP**
The Atlantis website misleadingly states in a few places that Aquaventure Day Passes must be purchased in person at the resort—however, advance booking is available at atlantisbahamas.com/daybooking.

port, via catamaran. You can spend your day at the beach, have a dolphin or sea lion experience, or enjoy some combination thereof. Prices are quite a bit less than the Atlantis equivalents. If you don't mind a longer transit time or the lack of a water park, then you'll probably be happier at Blue Lagoon than Atlantis. Again, the animal encounters are typically well rated, with most of the variation coming from rapport with a specific guide, the weather, and the guest's awareness that photos cost extra.

Other Nassau excursions that receive high marks include the following:

- **Catamaran Sail and Reef Snorkeling** A well-priced ocean-snorkeling experience.
- **Graycliff Escape** A relaxing pool area and a lovely place for a meal.
- **Nassau Forts and Junkanoo Discovery** A relatively painless history lesson for kids.

Nassau excursions that garner less-than-stellar reviews include these:

- **Ardastra Gardens and City Tour** A small, underwhelming "zoo." Avoid this tour if birds weird you out.
- **Seaworld Explorer Semi-Submarine** The windows of the sub are often so dirty that it's impossible to view the sealife.
- **Sunshine Glass Bottom Boat Tour** Guests must stand for the entire tour. There's not much viewing space, and you can see the fish for just a few minutes while they're being fed.

OUR SUGGESTIONS *Beyond* CASTAWAY CAY

DOLPHIN ENCOUNTERS

THESE ARE THE MOST POPULAR shore excursions for families. Every port in Mexico, along with Nassau, Falmouth, Grand Cayman, and St. Thomas, offers one. If your Caribbean or Bahamian cruise includes a port besides Castaway Cay, you'll almost certainly have a chance to book one.

Because of the dolphins' popularity, these port adventures aren't cheap, generally starting at around $180 for adults and $160 for children, or roughly $700 for a family of four.

Most dolphin-related port adventures last 4–7 hours, roughly 30 minutes of which are actually spent in the water with a dolphin and 10–20 other tourists. During our visits, we took turns with the rest of the group in petting, feeding, and taking photos with the dolphin.

In hindsight, the remarkable thing is that we spent perhaps 1 minute each in direct contact with the animal. The rest of your time is taken up by transportation to and from the port, a background class and instruction on how to interact with the dolphin, a short show during which the dolphins demonstrate their jumping skills and tricks, and some beach or pool time once your encounter is done.

MAYAN PYRAMIDS

DCL TOURS OF TULUM MAYA RUINS take place in **Cozumel, Mexico.** Be aware that the trip involves considerable transportation time: 4 of its 7½ hours are spent on ferries or buses. Prices are $129 ages 10 and up, $99 ages 5–9.

SKAGWAY, ALASKA

ANNOYINGLY LONG-WINDED NAME ASIDE, the **Liarsville Gold Rush Trail Camp and Salmon Bake Featuring Exclusive Disney Character Experience** is a fun port adventure for families (2½–3 hours; $99 ages 10 and up; $59 ages 3-9). Guests board a bright-yellow school bus and take a 15-minute drive through downtown Skagway to Liarsville, a re-created mining camp at the foot of White Pass. When you arrive, you're greeted by "locals" dressed in period attire and escorted to the Hippodrome, a covered pavilion where you'll see a puppet show that highlights the history of the Gold Rush in Alaska, including how Liarsville came to receive its name.

After the show, you'll receive instructions on how to pan for gold—*scoop, swirl, spill*—before you're released to your very own "handler" and set out to seek your fortune. The pans are prepared and handed out as you approach the mining troughs. Getting the hang of the technique isn't as easy at it looks, but your handler is there to help. While you're panning, Chip 'n' Dale stop by to steal some gold, and Donald, dressed in flannel and a hunting cap, pays a visit. Gold in every pan is guaranteed, but even the most successful panning won't make you rich, or even earn you enough to help pay off your stateroom balance.

The salmon bake is set up across the way, buffet-style. Guests trickle over to the food after they strike it not-so-rich, so crowds aren't a problem. Choose from rotisserie chicken, baked beans, rice pilaf, coleslaw, and salads, plus bread and blueberry cake. Wild-caught salmon is served from an open-air grill; the fish is tasty, but be aware that it contains small bones—we guess that's what makes it wild.

This reader liked (but didn't love) the experience:

The Liarsville gold panning was fun, and it was a huge hit with my stepson (age 8). I felt the price could have been a bit more affordable, the puppet show a bit shorter, and the gold panning a bit longer and more involved. For us it was a one-time experience, but an enjoyable one.

WALKING TOURS

FOR THOSE WHO WANT TO STEP OFF THE BEATEN PATH of organized excursions, we've created our own walking tours of DCL ports around the globe. Each tour includes not only things to see and do but also recommendations for places to eat. These tours are less expensive than almost any port adventure, offer a more flexible schedule, allow you to see a great deal of the port, and offer a wider choice of dining options.

Alaska

Juneau Walking Tour

Duration About 3 hours depending on your walking pace, how much you stop to shop, and how long it takes you to eat. Add another 1–2 hours if you decide to take the tram to Mt. Roberts. **Walking distance** About 2.5 miles. **Cost** Lunch varies. Mt. Roberts tramway: $33 adults, $16 kids ages 6–12, free kids age 5 and under. **Accessibility** This is a walk up paved roads with several large hills. Nothing is specifically inaccessible, but guests using wheelchairs might find the route somewhat strenuous. **Kid-friendliness** Best for adults—kids will probably get bored hiking past municipal buildings and museums; plus, we've included an optional detour into a bar. **Map** See tinyurl.com/downtownjuneaumap.

STEP 1 Depending on which dock the ship is using, you're about 0.75 mile down a nondescript service road from the port to town. You can walk the road or take the free shuttle bus that continuously ferries cruisers from the ship. Start touring at the **Downtown Public Library** (292 Marine Way); pop in and use their free Wi-Fi if you need a fix and didn't purchase Internet access on the ship. Nearby, look for the bronze sculpture of city founders **Joe Juneau, Richard Harris,** and **Chief Kowee.**

STEP 2 Proceed toward town up South Franklin Street. Depending on the time of day, you may need some fortification to start your tour. If that's the case, the **Red Dog Saloon** (278 S. Franklin St.) has so-so food, but the classy-sounding Duck Fart—a layered shot of Kahlúa, Bailey's, and Crown Royal—is one of those things that you just have to try in Juneau.

STEP 3 Continue up South Franklin, stopping in whatever shops strike your fancy along the way. We like the **Alaska Brew Company Depot** (219 S. Franklin St.) for T-shirts and to see the brewery information upstairs; the **Alaskan Fudge Company** (195 S. Franklin St.) to check out and sample the creatively named candies (puffin paws, sea otter paws, husky paws, and huckleberry jelly sticks); and the **Mt. Juneau Trading Post** (151 S. Franklin St.) for pelts and native artwork. If you have room in your luggage, you can buy a woolly-mammoth tusk. Pop your head in the **Alaskan Hotel** bar (167 S. Franklin St.) to check out the Victorian-era decor.

STEP 4 South Franklin becomes North Franklin after Front Street. Proceed up North Franklin to Fifth Street and make a right to see **St. Nicholas Russian Orthodox Church** (326 Fifth St.), built in 1894. Walk back down Franklin and take a left onto Fourth Street. The **Alaska State Capitol** will be a few steps up on your left, at 120 E. Fourth St. Cross Main Street and see the **Juneau-Douglas City Museum** (114 W. Fourth St). Note the large totem pole out front, and spend a bit checking out the exhibits. (Open Tuesday–Saturday, 10 a.m.–4 p.m.; free admission.)

STEP 5 Bear right at the end of Fourth Street as it turns into Calhoun Avenue. At Calhoun and Seventh Street, see the **Alaska Governor's Mansion** (716 Calhoun Ave.). (No, you can't see Russia from this house.)

STEP 6 Continue on Calhoun, making a left onto Capitol Avenue. Follow Capitol until it dead-ends at Willoughby Avenue. Take a left onto Willoughby and a quick right onto Whittier Street. The **Alaska State Museum** (395 Whittier St.) reopened in June 2016 after a major renovation. The newly redesigned museum joins the Alaska State Library and Alaska State Archives in one comprehensive research facility, with many exhibits open to the public.

STEP 7 Continue down Whittier Street to Egan Drive. The **Centennial Hall Convention Center** (101 Egan Drive) is a good source for maps and general information.

STEP 8 Egan Drive turns into Marine Way. Note **Juneau City Hall** at the corner of Marine and Seward. Continue on Marine Way to end up back at the Downtown Public Library. Continue down Marine and bear right as Marine turns into the lower part of South Franklin Street—you've walked a large circle.

STEP 9 If you want to eat light, grab something at one of the food carts near the port, but we highly recommend **Tracy's King Crab Shack** (406 S. Franklin St., behind the Trove boutique and gift shop), our favorite Alaskan cruise-stop restaurant. The Crab Shack Combo (about $32) will feed one hungry or two not-so-hungry people with a cup of crab chowder, a giant king crab leg, and four mini–crab cakes. Add a side of slaw and you can definitely feed two. Seating is at covered outdoor picnic tables. While you're waiting for your order, pop behind the order-prep station to watch the cooks tend to the 9- to 10-pound crabs. *Note:* We've heard that Tracy's may be moving in mid-2017, so check kingcrabshack.com for updates.

STEP 10 If you're tuckered out, grab the shuttle back to the ship. If not, head to the **Mt. Roberts Tramway** station (490 S. Franklin St.; open daily, 8 a.m.–9 p.m.). Buy tickets for the tramway and take the 5-minute ride to the top of Mt. Roberts. While you're at the top, check out the film in the visitor center, snap photos of the view, scout for bald eagles, or take a brief nature hike. Back at the tramway station, you'll see the ship; take the shuttle from there or walk back.

Ketchikan Walking Tour

Duration About 2–3 hours. **Walking distance** About 3 miles. **Cost** About $30 per person, including admission to the Tongass Historical Museum, admission to Dolly's, and a chowder or sandwich along the way. For the Great Alaskan Lumberjack Show, add $38 for each adult and $18.50 for kids ages 3–12. **Accessibility** Not technically wheelchair-inaccessible, but this is a walk of several miles, up several steep hills. Use your best judgment. **Kid-friendliness** Little kids may get antsy during Steps 6–8. **Map** See tinyurl.com/ketchikanmap.

STEP 1 Exit the ship and head to the end of the pedestrian-only dock area. Start at the corner of Mill and Front Streets, near the **Fish Pirate's Saloon.** Walk one block down Mill Street and turn right down Main Street to the **Southeast Alaska Discovery Center** (50 Main St.), operated by the US Forest

Service. Check out the exhibits on the Alaskan rainforest, native peoples, and natural resources; there also may be classes or lectures for kids. (Admission is $5 for adults, free for kids age 15 and younger; see tinyurl .com/seakdiscovery for hours.) While you're at the Discovery Center, note that you're adjacent to the **Great Alaskan Lumberjack Show** (420 Spruce Mill Way); if you're so inclined, stop in and buy tickets for a show later in the afternoon (see Step 10).

STEP 2 Go back to the corner of Mill and Front streets. If you need maps or information, stop at the **Ketchikan Visitors Bureau** (131 Front St.). Proceed up Front Street, away from the ships, to Mission Street. Turn left onto Mission and take a photo under the glamorous and exciting KETCHIKAN: THE SALMON CAPITAL OF THE WORLD sign.

STEP 3 Step back on Front Street and stop at **Alaska Fine Art** (224 Front St.) to see an incredible mammoth-tusk carving by sculptor Eddie Lee. Also look for eagles, bears, mountain goats, and other carved animals.

STEP 4 If you're hungry, grab a bite at **Annabelle's Famous Keg & Chowder House** (326 Front St.). The three-chowder sampler is a popular choice. When you're done, take a look farther down Front Street to see the **Ketchikan Tunnel.** Locals like to brag about the tunnel because it was once noted in the *Guinness Book of World Records* as the only tunnel in the world that you could go completely through, over, and around. To us, though, it looks like a minor traffic pass-through. Just on the other side of the tunnel is **Burger Queen** (518 Water St). Every local we've talked to raves about it, but we think the burgers are just so-so, and it has ambience only in an ironic sense—it's a shack with the Tasmanian Devil from the *Looney Tunes* cartoons painted on the front.

STEP 5 Go back down Front Street to Mission Street, and head down Mission away from the water. If you find yourself in need of some canned salmon, buy some at the **Salmon Market** on the corner of Mission and Main. At 503 Mission St., note **St. John's Episcopal Church,** which has stood in its current location since 1904. Turn around and enter the **Cape Fox Marketplace** at 500 Mission St. Inside this (very) mini-mall, where you'll find **Tall Tale Taxidermy,** a family-run furrier and taxidermist. We bought a beaver pelt.

STEP 6 Proceed back up Mission Street and bear left as it turns into Dock Street. Just ahead, at 629 Dock St., visit the **Tongass Historical Museum.** Pay the small admission fee ($3 for adults May–September, free October–April; free for kids age 12 and younger; see tinyurl.com/tongasshistoricalmuseum for hours). View artifacts and photos of Ketchikan's history as a fishing port and mining center. Check out the native totem pole out front.

STEP 7 Proceed up Dock Street and follow it as it turns into Bawden Street. Bawden soon forks—take the right fork onto Park Avenue. Continue on Park to see the **salmon-spawning river.** In season, see salmon struggle to get back to their native streambed; a concrete "fish ladder" aids their passage.

STEP 8 Continue on Park, past Venetia Avenue, Harris Street, and Freeman Street, then turn right at Woodland Avenue (Herring Way will be on the left). Continue on Woodland until it dead-ends at Deermount Street. Turn right onto Deermount. Along the way, you'll pass one of Ketchikan's Alaska Native–American Indian neighborhoods. Deermount dead-ends into

Stedman Street—turn right and proceed along Stedman. Pass the **Sun Raven Totem Pole,** just beyond Inman Street, and the **University of Alaska Southeast** campus.

STEP 9 Continue on Stedman Street until you get to Thomas Street. Turn left down Thomas to view the harbor from the wood-planked dock. Continue on Stedman until you get to the red trestle bridge, just past the New York Hotel. Instead of crossing the bridge, take the small path on the right that turns into board-walked **Creek Street,** the old red-light district, which once had more than 30 houses filled with "working girls." Stop in at **Dolly's House** (24 Creek St.), where local madam Dolly Arthur and her staff plied their trade, to see period artifacts and photos. (Open daily, 8 a.m.–4 p.m. when ships are in port; closed in winter. Admission is $10.)

STEP 10 Exit Creek Street onto Dock Street, back near the Tongass Historical Museum. Proceed down Dock toward the water. Make a left onto Bawden Street, then a right onto Mill Street. If you've had enough, head back to the ship. Or if you want some more Alaska fun, make a left onto Main Street and head back to the **Great Alaskan Lumberjack Show;** to see the schedule, go to alaskanlumberjackshow.com and click "Tickets." The lumberjacks impress with their feats of skill, and anyone who appreciates male eye candy will be delighted—one online reviewer sums them up as "hot guys with chainsaws." (*Update:* Two lovely "lumberjills" have joined the cast since the last edition of this guide.) If you're hungry, make a pit stop next door at the **Alaska Fish House** (5 Salmon Way) for a cod burger or some halibut tacos.

Skagway Walking Tour

Duration About 3 hours, depending on the timing of any shows/presentations you partake of. **Walking distance** About 2 miles. **Cost** About $45 per person; includes $20 fee for the *Days of '98* show, $10 fee for a Red Onion Saloon brothel tour, a burger lunch, and a beer at the end. **Accessibility** Most of Skagway is on level surfaces. Wheelchair users shouldn't find it a problem. **Kid-friendliness** The Red Onion allows kids on its brothel tours, but we don't recommend them for little ones. **Map** See tinyurl.com/skagwaymap. The entirety of Skagway is about 7 blocks long by 2 blocks wide—you can see the ship from anywhere in town, so it's virtually impossible to get lost. **Special comments** Be aware that while the ship will likely dock at about 7:30 a.m., most of the shops in town, including the restaurants, won't open until after 9 a.m., so unless you have an excursion, there's no reason to rush in the morning. If you want to go farther afield, stop by the **Chilkoot Trail Center,** on Broadway between First and Second Avenues. Run by the US National Park Service and Parks Canada; it offers maps and advice on day hikes in the surrounding area (open daily, 8 a.m.–5 p.m. June 1–Labor Day weekend).

STEP 1 Assume that you're exiting the ship from the Ore Dock (the most likely option). Directly ahead, you'll see the **White Pass & Yukon Route** train tracks.

STEP 2 Follow the tracks up Broadway until just before First Avenue. Take a photo at the WELCOME TO SKAGWAY, ALASKA sign. Walk forward about 30 feet to view the old **Yukon Engine #52** (1881) and **Rotary #1 Snowplow** (1899), which was capable of clearing up to 12 feet of snow off the tracks.

STEP 3 Proceed up Broadway and turn right onto Second Avenue. Stop into the **White Pass & Yukon Route headquarters,** at the corner of Second and

Spring, and see the exhibits about Alaskan train travel (open weekdays, 8 a.m.–5 p.m.). You'll find slightly less-tacky souvenirs here than elsewhere. If you haven't booked a train excursion on board the ship and would like to do one, purchase your tickets here.

STEP 4 Also on Second Avenue is the **Klondike Gold Rush National Historical Park Visitor Center.** Check out the exhibits discussing the Gold Rush experience in the Klondike Region. Stay for the free 30-minute movie, *Gold Fever: Race to the Klondike,* or a 45-minute ranger presentation. Rangers are also available to answer general questions about Alaska and mining. (Open daily, 8 a.m.–6 p.m. May–September; open weekdays, 8 a.m.–5 p.m. October–April.)

STEP 5 Head back out to Broadway and walk toward Sixth Avenue, browsing in the shops along the way. Poke your head into the **Mascot Saloon** (corner of Broadway and Third Avenue), a National Park Service reproduction of a Gold Rush–era watering hole. If you've forgotten any basics for your trip, stop in **Skagway Hardware,** on the corner of Fourth Avenue and Broadway. They have everything from mouthwash to suitcases and power strips.

STEP 6 On the corner of Broadway and Sixth Avenue, take in the hour-long *Days of '98* stage show. This campy musical tells the tale of Soapy Smith, a notorious con man who duped many prospectors during the late 1800s (see thedaysof98show.com for showtimes). If you have time to kill before the next show, grab a muffin at the best bakery in town, **Bites on Broadway,** directly across Sixth Avenue. Or cross to the other side of Broadway to snap a photo in front of the **Skagway Post Office,** which has one of the highest zip codes in the country: 99840.

STEP 7 After the show, turn right down Sixth Avenue (away from town) and take a look at the **William and Ben Moore Cabin & Homestead,** a National Park Service–restored Gold Rush–era home.

STEP 8 Back on Broadway, find the **Skagway Bazaar,** on the post-office side of the street between Fifth and Sixth Avenues. Scoot down the narrow passageway to find the **BBQ Shack,** which serves caribou, elk, buffalo, and venison burgers, as well as halibut or smoked-salmon chowder.

STEP 9 Return to Broadway, heading back toward the ship. Stop in the **Red Onion Saloon,** once Skagway's premier house of joy, at the corner on Second Avenue. Relax with an Alaska Brewing Company beer on tap, or try the Fire Dance, an Alaskan-moonshine shot sprinkled with real gold flakes. The curious—including, sort of surprisingly, kids accompanied by an adult 21 or older—can take one of the various **bordello tours,** which offer a look at the upstairs "cribs." Free garters with every tour! See redonion1898.com for more information.

STEP 10 Revisit any interesting shops, and then return to the ship via Broadway.

Bahamas and the Caribbean

Nassau Walking Tour

If you do this walking tour, use common sense: Walk with a partner or group, avoid deserted areas, don't carry large sums of cash, don't use ATMs by yourself or in out-of-the-way places, leave expensive jewelry and electronics on the ship, secure your passport and other documents, and don't interact with anyone who seems suspicious. See "A Note About Nassau Safety," page 338, for additional advice.

Nassau Walking Tour

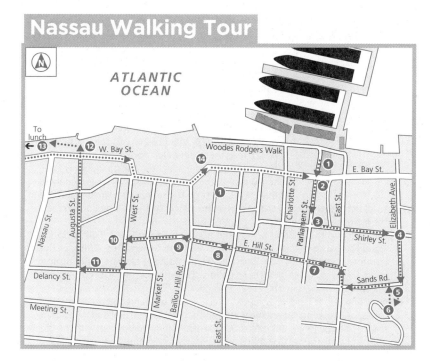

Duration About 3 hours. **Walking distance** 4.5 miles. **Cost** Around $20/person (including lunch and a cocktail at the distillery). **Accessibility** Good except for the Queen's Staircase, which is inaccessible. **Kid-friendliness** Best for adults—while children are allowed on the distillery tour, they'll probably be bored to tears there and at the various cultural sites. **Map** See above for a map coded to the steps below, or pick up a city map in Festival Place as you leave the port. **Special comments** Wear good walking shoes, bring swimwear if you intend to enjoy the beach, and **heed our previous advice.**

STEP 1 Exit the cruise ship through Festival Place. You can pick up a map of Nassau here.

STEP 2 Outside Festival Place, take Parliament Street across Bay Street to Parliament Square.

STEP 3 Continue on Parliament Street to Shirley Street, and take a left.

STEP 4 Continue on Shirley Street across East Street to Elizabeth Avenue.

STEP 5 Take a right onto Elizabeth Avenue to continue to the base of the **Queen's Staircase.** Named for Queen Victoria, this is perhaps the most tranquil spot on our tour. Enjoy the cool shade, the junglelike greenery, and the artificial waterfall cascading to the left of the stairway before ascending the 65 steps to the entrance of Fort Fincastle. The stairs, while steep, aren't overly challenging, but alternatively you can take East Street to Prison Lane to the top of the staircase. Be careful, though, because there's no sidewalk along this route.

STEP 6 Climb the Queen's Staircase to reach the **Water Tower** and **Fort Fincastle.** Pay a small admission fee ($1 per person) to enter the fort, built in 1793 by Lord Dunsmore, a.k.a. Viscount Fincastle, then-royal governor of the Bahamas. Intended to protect Nassau from invasion and constructed to resemble the bow of a paddlewheeler, the fort never actually saw battle. (Open every day except Monday, 8 a.m.-4 p.m.)

unofficial **TIP**

Note: Self-appointed "tour guides" at Fort Fincastle may try to hustle you for tips. Give only if you feel like it.

The Water Tower, built in 1928, no longer holds any water. For a few years now, it's been closed for repairs, with no reopening announced; before you go, try calling ☎ 242-322-2442 to see if it's open. At 126 feet, the observation deck, reached by elevator or 216 stairs, is the highest point in not only Nassau but also the entire island of New Providence. Even if you can't go to the top, it's a great landmark to let you know early on that you were headed in the right direction to reach the staircase and the fort.

STEP 7 Descend the staircase and take a left on Sands Road. Follow Sands Road to East Street, and make a right. Visit the **General Post Office,** at the corner of East Street and East Hill Street. Postage stamps make a nice, inexpensive souvenir whether you're a collector or not; US currency is accepted.

STEP 8 Continue on East Hill Street and take a right on Market Street. Take a left on Duke Street to **Government House**, the seat of the Bahamian government—you can't miss this pink-stucco, white-columned building with the big statue of Christopher Columbus out front. The Government House is mostly closed to the public but hosts a monthly English high tea for tourists and locals. If your cruise schedule coincides with the event, it's a charming way to spend an afternoon and make some new friends. Proper attire is required to enjoy the *veddy* proper repast of scones, clotted cream, cucumber sandwiches, and different types of tea. (Held the last Friday of the month, January–November, at the Government House Ballroom, 4-5 p.m.; reservations required. Go to tinyurl.com/governmenthousetea for booking information.)

STEP 9 Across Blue Hill Road from Government House is the **Graycliff Hotel** (8-12 W. Hill St.). Tour the grounds and check out the gardens and pools. There's a chocolate shop on-site.

STEP 10 Continue along West Hill Street to West Street. Here you'll find the **National Art Gallery of the Bahamas** and **St. Francis Xavier Cathedral.** The oldest Catholic church in the Bahamas, the cathedral is currently undergoing an extensive renovation but remains open to the public. Beautiful in its simplicity, the church is a nice stop along the way for rest and reflection. (Open to visitors weekdays, 9 a.m.-4:30 p.m.)

STEP 11 After touring the cathedral, head south (away from the water) on West Street to **John Watling's Distillery,** on your right at 17 Delancy St. The only distillery in the Bahamas, John Watling's makes rum on-site in a fantastically restored colonial estate. Tour the distillery and try a generous sample at no charge. The gift shop sells liquor and offers tastings; lunch is also served in the on-site pub. (Open daily, 10 a.m.-6 p.m., until 9 p.m. Friday.)

STEP 12 Return to West Bay Street and take a left, continuing west, away from the cruise terminal. Walk along the public beach. If you've packed a swimsuit, enjoy some time in the water.

STEP 13 (LUNCH) Instead of going to the Fish Fry, a cluster of tourist restaurants on Arawak Cay near the terminal, follow our advice and eat with the locals at the **food trucks** across the street—you'll know you're there when you see Bahamians buying food. Picnic tables are available. A large lunch plus drink runs about $10. The food is cooked to order, so relax and enjoy yourself. This is the freshest seafood we've ever eaten—don't be thrown off if your fish arrives with its head still attached.

STEP 14 Return to the ship via **Bay Street,** the center of duty-free shopping in Nassau. We don't find the goods worth haggling over, but you may enjoy browsing. Jewelry and accessories are the big draws here, as is liquor. Two shops we like are **The Linen Shop,** which sells a nice selection of kitchen linens and Christmas decor, and **Cole's of Nassau** (Bay and Parliament Streets), for women's fashions.

Stop at Bay Street's **Straw Market** only if you feel you must in order to say you've been. Once upon a time, Laurel lived in the Bahamas, and going to Nassau was a trip to the big city. The market sold high-quality straw goods that were tasteful and well made—Laurel has bowls that still look like new after 40 years—but, sadly, that's no longer the case. You may still find a few nice locally made pieces among the ones imported from China, but mostly it's the same old cheesy, overpriced T-shirts, beach towels, baseball caps, and fake designer bags you can get at any port.

Sint Maarten/Saint-Martin Walking Tour

Duration 4-7 hours. **Walking distance** About 1 mile not counting the time you'll spend in taxis. **Cost** About $35 per person for the Dutch side, plus an all-day taxi rental, which usually runs $120–$140 (plus tip) for 4-6 people. The French side of the island uses the euro as its currency, so you should also bring about €40 per person for lunch and drinks. **Accessibility** Most taxi drivers are happy to accommodate passengers who use wheelchairs. Fort Louis, however, can be accessed only by climbing stairs. Shops and restaurants in Marigot and Philipsburg are at ground level, but many require navigating a step or two out front. Many public restrooms have doorways that are too narrow to accommodate a wheelchair. **Club Orient** resort, which isn't on our tour, has beach wheelchairs—the catch is naked people. An excellent resource is the tour operator **Accessible Caribbean Vacations;** for their St. Maarten advice, along with accessible port adventures, see accessiblecaribbean vacations.com/st-maarten-disabled-access. **Kid-friendliness** Parents with young children should skip Maho Beach and start at Marigot. Also, the stairs at Fort Louis are too taxing for little ones. **Map** See tinyurl.com/stmaartenwalkingtour. **Special comments** Bring water, sunscreen, bathing suits, and a change of clothes.

Note: This is a walking tour only in the loosest sense—because you'll be visiting a large swath of the island, you'll need to hire a taxi driver for the day. Typical rates are $120–$140 for four people, plus gratuity, for a safe, relatively modern, air-conditioned ride. Drivers are generally very friendly and occasionally hilarious, as this reader found:

My partner was champing at the bit to check out the clothing-optional section of Orient Beach. (Myself, not so much.) When he told our taxi driver where we wanted to go, she laughed, "Ah, so ya wanna go to the NEKKID beach!"

Our friend Matt Hochberg of royalcaribbeanblog.com recommends **Leo Brown** (☎ 721-524-4290), whose rates are negotiable. We've also heard great things about **Gerard France** (☎ 721-553-4727 or ☎ 590 690 76 73 13; face book.com/gerard.taxi.1), who charges around $260 for the day.

STEP 1 It's a 25-minute cab ride from the port in Philipsburg to the Dutch side's **Maho Beach,** a tiny strip of sand maybe 600 feet long and 50 feet wide, on the west side of the island. What makes Maho Beach unique is that it sits on the other side of a small two-lane road from the main landing strip of **Princess Juliana International Airport.** Most planes landing on the island pass directly over the beach at no more than a couple hundred feet of altitude and land at the edge of the runway directly across. Watching the approach of small planes is a thrill; watching the big jets land is terrifying. You'll love it! Check flightaware.com/live/airport/sxm for the airport's arrival and departure schedule.

Because of the island's prevailing winds, planes taking off start at the end of the runway closest to the beach, too. The propeller and jet wash from the engines are enough to push adults back on their heels and knock over small children. That's lots of fun, too, but be careful.

Sunset Bar & Grill (2 Beacon Hill Road), a small outdoor restaurant at the far end of the beach, serves burgers, sandwiches, and drinks of all kinds. At the opposite end of the beach is the **Sonesta Maho Beach Resort** (Rhine Drive), and nearby are plenty of shopping and dining options.

STEP 2 When you're ready for lunch, hop in your cab for the 20-minute ride to the middle of **Marigot,** on the French side. The main drag, the **Boulevard de France,** has some of the island's best dining and shopping. It's also home to the marina and to **Fort Louis,** built in 1767.

If you're looking for island cuisine, try **Rosemary's,** on Boulevard de France near the marina and Fort Louis. Rosemary's is a *lolo*—a grill serving fresh seafood, stews, and other local favorites. The food is tasty, and service is very friendly. While the menu is priced in euros, they'll usually accept a one-for-one exchange of US dollars, giving Americans a 30% discount.

If you're in the mood for a quick bite of French food, grab a *croque monsieur* or other sandwich at **Sarafina's,** a *pâtisserie* about a block from Rosemary's on Boulevard de France. Usually crowded, Sarafina's serves a surprisingly large selection of fresh French pastries, sandwiches, and desserts. We suggest grabbing a baguette sandwich to go and eating it while you window-shop along the boulevard.

The hike up to Fort Louis, northeast of Boulevard de France, is strenuous, especially in the sun, but it does offer the best views of this side of the island. (Open daily, sunrise–sunset; free admission.) To keep up your energy levels, pick up a quick something from Sarafina's after you return.

STEP 3 Here's your chance to work in some beach time. Skip **Orient Beach,** which is overcrowded and not the best choice if you're uncomfortable with toplessness or nudity. (On the upside, **Club Orient,** a naturist resort, provides beach wheelchairs for visitors with disabilities.) We recommend one of the following beaches instead:

Baie de L'Embouchure is located off Rue du Coconut Grove, on the east side of the island, about 20 minutes from Marigot and a half-mile south of Orient Beach. A crescent-shaped bit of beach about half a mile long, the beach is protected by an offshore reef that dampens the incoming waves. This, along with its relatively small crowds, makes it great for families with young children.

Mullet Bay Beach, about a 15-minute taxi ride southwest of Marigot, has a wide, sandy shore. The south side of the beach sits across from the Mullet Bay Golf Course, so there's no string of high-rise hotels to hamper your view.

Baie Longue is on the northwest side of the island, about a 15-minute taxi ride from downtown Marigot. Again, it's much less crowded than Orient Beach; the one downside is that the shoreline is filled with coral, making it unsafe for small children to play in. But it is pretty.

St. Thomas Walking Tour

Duration 3–5 hours. **Walking distance** About 6 miles on foot, 3 miles if you take a taxi back to the port, or less than a mile if you take a taxi both ways. **Cost** $22–$27/ person, including lunch; add $4 each way if using a taxi. **Accessibility** The first two steps in the tour are out of the question for wheelchair users. **Kid-friendliness** Recommended for children age 6 and up; parents with small children should bring a stroller and use a taxi to get to Blackbeard's Castle and back to the ship. **Map** See tinyurl.com/stthomaswalkingtour. **Special comments** Bring water and sunscreen; swimsuits and towels are optional if you want to use the pools at Blackbeard's Castle.

STEP 1 It's a pleasant walk from the port to **Blackbeard's Castle,** on Blackbeard's Hill; if you take a taxi instead, the fare should be around $4 per person. Depart the ship at the West Indian Company Dock and walk northeast toward Edward Wilmot/Long Bay Road. Follow the road as it runs along the coast, and bear left toward the water when it becomes Veterans Drive. One block past the DeLugo Federal Building, turn right on Hospital Gade and walk north about four blocks; then turn left on Prindsens Gade. Turn right on Lille Taarne Gade and look for the signs.

There's no evidence that the British pirate whose real name was Edward Teach ever laid a boot upon "Blackbeard's Castle"—the reference is pure marketing. The "castle" is part of a hotel; what's more, it's a lookout tower, never meant for habitation—originally called Skystborg Tower, it was built far up on the hill by 17th-century Danish settlers for spotting incoming ships that wouldn't be seen from Fort Christian, farther down.

A climb to the top of the tower will get you a lovely panoramic view of the harbor and the town laid out in front of you, and of the mountains behind you. If you're a small group, the scenery alone is probably worth the $10 admission. If the view isn't enough, your admission also includes access to the adjacent hotel's pools and tours of two restored Colonial-era homes nearby, and you can return later for those. (Tour hours are usually 9 a.m.– 2 p.m. Tuesdays and Wednesdays, but check at blackbeardscastle.com before you go; you can also book your tour at the website.)

Before you climb the tower's narrow stairs, you're asked to watch an almost certainly apocryphal, extremely corny, but mercifully brief retelling of Blackbeard's death. A good way not to dwell on your secondhand embarrassment for the "actor" is to imagine he's wearing tights and holding a human skull, à la Hamlet.

STEP 2 Follow the signs from Blackbeard's Castle south, toward the harbor, to the **99 Steps.** These stone-and-concrete stairs built into the side of the mountain afford good views of the harbor and town. (For the fact-checkers among us, there are actually more than 100 steps.)

STEP 3 Turn left and walk one block east to the **Government House.** Built in the 1860s, it holds the offices of the island's governor (currently Kenneth Mapp), and tourists may visit the first two floors of the building. Besides Colonial architecture, on display are two small works by Camille Pissarro, a Danish-French Impressionist painter who was born on St. Thomas in 1830. (Open 8 a.m.–5 p.m. weekdays; closed holidays; free admission.)

STEP 4 From Government House, head south one block on Torvets State Road, then turn right on Norre Gade. About 100 feet ahead, on your right, is **Frederick Lutheran Church** (open daily, 9 a.m.–5 p.m.; free admission). Built in 1666, it's the oldest church in St. Thomas and one of the oldest Lutheran churches in the New World. The church's simple, elegant architecture features a vaulted ceiling. A narrow set of stairs leads to better views from the second floor's musician's area. Before you leave, donate a couple bucks and light a candle to commemorate making a pig of yourself at the ship's buffet.

STEP 5 From the church entrance, turn right and walk to the corner of Norre Gade and Fort Pladsen. Turn left on Fort Pladsen, toward the harbor; about 75 feet down the road, on your left, is **Emancipation Park,** which commemorates the emancipation of slaves in the Danish West Indies following the Danish revolution of 1848. Inside the park are a memorial to the emancipation; a memorial to King Christian IX of Denmark, who brought parliamentary rule to the island; and a copy of the United States's Liberty Bell, which commemorates the temporary landing on St. Thomas, in April 1607, of British settlers bound for Virginia. (*Bonus fact:* Every US state and territory has a copy of the Liberty Bell. Find yours at tinyurl.com/statelibertybells.)

Jen's Island Café is across the street from the northeast corner of the park, at the intersection of Tolbod Pladsen and Forte Strade. The food is fresh and tasty, with friendly service. A full meal takes about an hour, so we recommend a quicker stop at the bar for a fast sandwich and drink.

Adjacent to Emancipation Park and Jen's Island Café is **Fort Christian,** the oldest building on St. Thomas. Completed around 1680, it served as a government building, church, and prison before being converted to a museum in the 1970s. Unfortunately, it's been closed since 2005 due to an unfinished renovation project, with no reopening in sight. Even so, the fort, painted a bright red, is impressive to look at from the outside, and it makes for a striking photo op.

STEP 6 On the west side of the park, follow Fort Pladsen Street north, away from the harbor, to Tolbod Pladsen, which turns into Kongens Gade after about a block. Stay on Kongens Gade, which will change names to Main Street, then Dronningens Gade, then Curaçao Gade, then Kronprindsens Gade, all within the half-mile walk to **Saints Peter and Paul Cathedral.** You'll see the church's high school, on the corners of Kanal Gade and Kronprindsens, just before you get to the church. The church will be on your right. The oldest Catholic church on the island and the seat of the Diocese of St. Thomas, the present building was dedicated in 1848, although previous buildings on the site date back to 1802. Inside, columns support vaulted arches, giving the sanctuary a Gothic-inspired island feel; the stained-glass windows depict various scenes from the Old and New Testaments. (See cathedralvi.com for hours; call ☎ 340-774-0201 to schedule a guided tour.)

STEP 7 Upon exiting the church, walk down either Brond State Road or Stoners Alley one block toward the harbor. You'll end up on Veterans Drive; look for taxis heading east toward the port. Note that there are two ports in St. Thomas, so make sure that you're on the correct ship. The fare should be about $4 per person back to the port.

By foot, we recommend following Veterans Drive, which hugs the waterfront on your right, all the way back to the ship. You'll find plenty of spots for shopping, food, and drinks along the sidewalk on the left side of the street. With a bit of luck, you'll catch a seaplane landing or taking off at the nearby seaport. The walk is around 1.8 miles.

Europe

Copenhagen Walking Tour

Duration 4–6 hours, depending on how long you linger in the castle and museum. **Walking distance** About 2 miles. **Cost** About $30/person, plus food; about an extra $75/person if you dine at Geist. **Accessibility** The Round Tower does not allow wheelchairs; strollers are not allowed past the first ramp levels. Only the ground floor of Rosenborg Slot is wheelchair-accessible. **Kid-friendliness** There's nothing that's *not* kid-friendly on this tour, but honestly, if you have preteens or younger and you've got just one day in Copenhagen, you should bypass everything else and just head to **Tivoli Gardens** (tivoli.dk/en). Your kids will be over the moon if you spend the day at this center-city amusement park that provided Walt Disney himself with inspiration about how to structure an amusement park. With rides, toy soldier–style marching bands, clouds of cotton candy bigger than your head, and free-roaming peacocks, you really can't go wrong. **Map** tinyurl.com/dcl-copenhagenwalkingtour.

STEP 1 Start at the **Rundetarn (Round Tower),** at Købmagergade 52. Wind your way up a spiral ramp to the observation deck for a bird's-eye view of the city. Continue to the top of the tower for a look at Europe's oldest functioning astronomy observatory. If you're lucky, a docent will give you a peek at the view through the resident refracting telescope (Open 10 a.m.–8 p.m. during summer; admission is about $4 per adult and $1 per child.)

STEP 2 Your next stop is **Rosenborg Slot (Castle),** home of the Danish crown jewels and lovely manicured grounds and gardens. To get there, head northwest on Købmagergade toward Landemærket, then continue straight onto Kultorvet; continue onto Frederiksborggade, turn right onto Nørre Voldgade, and continue onto Øster Voldgade. This walk will take about 10 minutes and bring you past many shops and restaurants in the city's Latin Quarter area. If you haven't had breakfast, grab a Danish on the way. (We mean a pastry. Grabbing a Danish person will probably get you in a mess of trouble. Or perhaps not, this being Scandinavia. . . .) The castle is open from 10 a.m. to 5 p.m. during the summer. Admission to the grounds is free for all. If you want to see inside the castle, admission is about $16 for adults and free for children 17 and under. In addition to holding the royal bling, the interior of the castle displays original decor from the Renaissance reign of King Christian IV, as well as ornate stucco ceilings and some of the most eerie royal busts we've ever seen.

STEP 3 If the weather is good, continue on to the **University of Copenhagen Botanical Garden,** part of the Natural History Museum of Denmark. (If the weather is poor, skip to Step 4.) Exit the Rosenborg Slot at the Øster Voldgade gate. Turn left and walk about 3 minutes to the corner of Gothersgade and the Botanical Garden entrance. The gardens feature more than 12,000 plant species situated in lush outdoor spaces as well as inside the publicly accessible glass conservatory. There are beautiful areas to explore and get lost in, but we must confess that we spent most of our time watching the many Eurasian red squirrels on the grounds. These rust-colored squirrels have enchanting tufted ears and are friendlier than their gray North American cousins. During the summer, the Botanical Garden is open 8:30 a.m.–6 p.m.; admission is free.

STEP 4 Exit the Botanical Garden via the Øster Farimagsgade gate, behind the Conservatory. Turn right and walk half a block to the corner of Solvgade; turn right and continue one block to the Danish National Gallery, the **Statens Museum for Kunst.** The museum's collection showcases Danish art through the 20th century, as well as European art from 1300 to 1800, including many works by Titian, Rubens, and Rembrandt; a large collection of French art from the early 1900s includes pieces by Matisse, Picasso, and Braque. Interactive children's exhibits are common. The museum is open Tuesday and Thursday–Sunday, 10 a.m.–5 p.m.; Wednesday, 10 a.m.–8 p.m.; general admission is free, but fees are charged for selected special exhibits; check smk.dk/en for details.

STEP 5 Exit the museum grounds at Solvgade, turn left, and walk down Solvgade one long block to Kronprincessgade. Walk about 5 minutes to Gothersgade. Turn left and walk along Gothersgade (which will turn into Kongens Nytorv) until you reach **Nyhavn** (KNEE-hav-inn), Copenhagen's picturesque canal area, with brightly painted houses and shops. Hans Christian Andersen lived at #6 Vingardssteaede as a young man. Enter via the **Magasin du Nord.**

STEP 6 If you have an hour, take a **canal tour** by boat. It's well worth the $12-per-person price to see the waterways of Copenhagen. (Information at stromma.dk, but there's no need to buy tickets in advance.) Nearly all canal tours pass the *Little Mermaid* statue. As you'll see, the statue really is little. Wave at her from the boat and you can feel like you've crossed her off your to-do list.

STEP 7 After your canal tour, a great spot for dinner is **Geist** (8 Kongens Nytorv; restaurantgeist.dk/en), which you passed on the way to Nyhavn. Geist is a good example of contemporary Danish cuisine, which combines familiar foods with nontraditional ingredients and cooking techniques. It's kinda pricey—expect to pay about $75 per person, plus alcohol—and a little out there—we loved the grilled avocado with green almonds and curry, the heart of lamb with cherries and wood sorrel not so much—but it's neither as pricey nor as out there as Copenhagen's storied **Noma,** which is nearly impossible to get into. Consider this Noma-lite.

Two More Easy Options

BARCELONA WALKING TOUR: CHURCHES, MEATS, AND CHEESES Several of DCL's Mediterranean cruises begin or end in **Barcelona, Spain.** If you've got a few hours to spare, here's a quick side trip into the heart of Barcelona. (See tinyurl.com/barcelonawalkingtour for a map and bus/subway options.) Beginning at the Port of Barcelona, walk to the Paral-lel L2 subway stop on Avinguda del Paral-lel. Take the L2 to the Monumental station and walk four blocks northwest to the **Sagrada Família** church.

Construction on the church, designed by Spanish architect Antoni Gaudí as a blend of Gothic and Art Nouveau themes, was begun in 1882 and is scheduled to be finished around 2026. Along with Paris's Notre Dame and London's Westminster Abbey, this is one of Europe's great churches; it's also the most airy and colorful. The church is open daily, 9 a.m.–8 p.m. Admission is around $26 US per person, giving you access to one of the towers, which affords spectacular views of the city. For more information, see sagradafamilia.cat/sf-eng.

Next, pick up supplies for a picnic lunch by heading for **Croissantería Forn de Pa** (34 Carrer de Sant Antoni Maria Claret), a 13-minute walk from the church. You'll find delicious French-quality croissants, baguettes, and pastries here, which is exactly *not* what you'd expect in the middle of Barcelona. Next, make the 10-minute walk to **Charcutería Simón** (392 Carrer de València), a small neighborhood store stocked with delicious meats, cheeses, and olives. Pick up some drinks from any nearby grocer, head around the corner from Charcutería Simón to **Plaça de la Sagrada Família** park (12 Plaça de la Sagrada Família), find some shade, and enjoy your meal in the shadow of the church.

SAUNTER AROUND SAN JUAN In **San Juan, Puerto Rico,** DCL offers a popular guided tour of the **Castillo de San Cristóbal;** built in 1783, it's the largest Spanish-built military structure in the New World. Disney's tour costs around $54 per person, but the US National Park Service runs the fort, which is part of the **San Juan National Historic Site,** and admission through the NPS is only $5 per person. Free guided tours are also available—check nps.gov/saju/index.htm for details. A cab ride between the fort and the port shouldn't run more than $20, so a family of four can save a lot of money this way.

*un*official **TIP**
We don't recommend the $45-per-adult **Casa Bacardí** tour, which doesn't actually tour the rum distillery itself. It's little more than a marketing presentation with a couple of piddly drinks—nothing like, say, the excellent tour of **John Watling's Distillery** in Nassau (see page 350).

When you're done touring San Cristóbal, step out of the fort and into **Old San Juan.** Take a walk down Avenida Juan Ponce de León, heading west. Ponce de León becomes Calle Fortaleza, where you'll find lots of good restaurants for lunch, from all different cuisines. It's a nice walk, a little more than a mile one-way. Take a cab back to the port when you're done.

PART THIRTEEN

RIVER CRUISING

DISNEY HAS BEEN DIPPING ITS TOE IN the increasingly popular river-cruise market, with branded sailings beginning in 2016. Disney river cruises are offered through **Adventures by Disney** (**AbD**), the world-travel arm of Disney Destinations, not Disney Cruise Line. AbD (adventuresbydisney.com) is tasked with bringing Disney service and quality to world exploration, not having Mickey moments around the clock.

Rather than starting its river-cruise operation from scratch, AbD worked in conjunction with river-cruise line **AmaWaterways** to construct two new ships: the **AmaViola,** which debuted in 2016, and the **AmaKristina,** which goes into service in 2017. These new ships are similar to existing ships in AmaWaterways' fleet (notably the *AmaSerena*), but Disney requested many family-friendly touches in their construction, such as more cabins with connecting doors and cabins with pull-out sleeper chairs—rarities in the river-cruise market.

The deck plans of the ships are available at amawaterways.com/ships/amaviola and amawaterways.com/ships/amakristina. We also have a full photo tour of the *AmaViola* available at tinyurl.com/amaviola. The *AmaViola* has a spacious sundeck, a walking track, a bar, a plush lounge and sitting areas, a small gift shop, a fitness room, a soaking pool, and two restaurants. Most staterooms are configured so that the main sleep surface can be converted from one queen-size bed to two twin-size beds, according to guests' needs. We expect the *AmaKristina* to be configured essentially identically to the *AmaViola*.

Because Disney does not own these ships, there is no Disney theming in the decor or finishings, such as hidden Mickeys in the upholstery or ironwork. Further, there are no Disney

unofficial TIP

When AbD is running a river cruise, it charters the entire ship: All guests follow an AbD group itinerary, booked through and organized by AbD. At other times of year, AmaWaterways books its own guests on its ships, but at no point are Disney and non-Disney guests on board at the same time.

characters on board, nor are there dozens of Disney-owned channels on your stateroom TV or Disney-themed items sold in the gift shop. Rather than live-performance variations of Disney films, the onboard evening entertainment is provided by local performers—a light-opera concert in Vienna or a Hungarian dance lesson in Budapest, for example.

The initial series of AbD river cruises had five **Danube River** departure dates in July and December 2016. Demand was so high that AbD immediately added two more Danube sailings, in August and December 2016. Ports included Budapest, Hungary, and Vienna, Austria. In 2017, AbD continues on the Danube with eight sailings on the *AmaViola,* as well as seven **Rhine River** sailings on the *AmaKristina,* in April, June, July, October, and December. Pre- and postcruise tour supplements are available for **Prague, Czech Republic,** on the Danube cruises, and for **Amsterdam, The Netherlands,** on the Rhine cruises.

Unlike DCL cruises, for which your booking price includes just your stateroom and nonpremium meals, AbD river cruises are all-inclusive: excursions; gratuities; airport/hotel transfers; adult dining; Wi-Fi; and free-flowing beer and wine during lunch, dinner, and various receptions. It can be much easier to anticipate your total costs on an AbD river cruise versus a DCL sailing. On the other hand, if you want a bare-bones, budget-friendly trip, that's significantly easier to achieve with DCL (see page 22).

RIVER CRUISING *for* FAMILIES

THE STEREOTYPICAL RIVER-CRUISE GUEST IS A RETIREE. (We've had 60-year-old friends return from other river cruises saying they were the youngest people on board.) Adventures by Disney is one of the first river-cruise operators to cater to families and offer primarily family-friendly activities. Kids will be occupied and entertained throughout their vacation.

Also expect adults on board to be younger than those on other river cruises. On our 2016 AbD Danube River cruise, the 140 guests included about 20 kids ages 6–12, plus a dozen teens. Most of the adults were in their late 30s to late 50s, with just a handful of seniors on board. In the mix were a number of adults, most in their 40s and 50s, traveling without children.

While AbD river cruises welcomes children, there are two main differences between traveling with children on AbD rather than DCL:

AGE TO TRAVEL On most DCL voyages, children may be as young as 6 months old (see page 185). Nurseries and other facilities are available to accommodate their needs. On AbD river cruises, children must be at least 6 years old; age 8 is recommended. There are no cribs, high chairs, baby food, or the like.

DEDICATED CHILDREN'S SPACES For many families, the big draw of DCL is its kids' clubs (see page 187). In contrast, there are no corresponding space on the river-cruise ships—kids mix with adults virtually everywhere on the ship.

What's more, AbD river cruises offer no drop-off child care—you can't leave your child with a babysitter for 3 hours while you and your spouse head into town to see a movie. There are, however, plenty of opportunities for kids and parents to get a break from each other. Every night, AbD guides invite "Junior Adventurers" (kids ages 6–12) to the lounge while their parents eat dinner in the dining room. In the lounge, kids watch movies, make crafts, and play games. While they're welcome to dine with the grown-ups, the fun—and the piles of chicken nuggets and fries—makes this a rarity.

Additionally, child-specific activities are offered during the "boring" excursions. For example, at many museum stops, kids are invited to play outdoor games with guides in the garden or participate in hands-on activities like baking a regional dessert. That said, if your child doesn't like being separated from you, you have a particularly rambunctious youngster, or your child doesn't enjoy group activities, an AbD river cruise may not be for you.

EXCURSIONS *on an* ABD RIVER CRUISE

A NUMBER OF DIFFERENCES EXIST between DCL port adventures (see Part Twelve) and AbD river-cruise excursions. On DCL, there is typically a menu of at least a dozen, usually many more, port activities at a range of price points for an additional fee; a penalty fee may be charged if you make a last-minute change or cancellation. Plus, DCL contracts out its port adventures, which are run by outside companies once you're off the ship.

Many DCL cruisers elect to book excursions on their own or forgo them altogether. Guests have access to excursion booking at different points depending on their Castaway Club status (see page 49), and some port adventures may become fully booked many weeks prior to sailing.

In contrast, all AbD port excursions are included in your cruise fee. Every morning or afternoon, one to four excursions are offered. Nearly every guest on board participates. There is no prebooking—an AbD guide sits with each family on embarkation day to discuss their options. There is no danger of a particular excursion being oversold, and you may make changes to your selections during your cruise at no charge.

As with DCL, AbD contracts with local guides for some excursions; however, Disney guides, with access to Disney resources, accompany you at all times.

Also as with DCL, families on AbD river cruises are welcome to choose their port excursions together or separately according to their interests. If Dad wants to go on the *Sound of Music* tour (singing "Lonely Goatherd" all the way) and Mom wants to tour the Hallein Salt Mines, that's not a problem.

SAMPLE ABD RIVER-CRUISE EXCURSIONS

Danube Cruises

VILSHOFEN, GERMANY Oktoberfest party

PASSAU, GERMANY Walking tour of the town of Passau; hike through the countryside; marzipan-making lesson; visit to an aerial tree path and adventure playground

LINZ (SALZBURG), AUSTRIA Walking tour of Salzburg; visit to the **Basilica of Mondsee** (where Georg and Maria von Trapp's wedding was filmed for the movie version of *The Sound of Music*); meal at **Stiftskeller St. Peter,** the world's oldest restaurant; tour of the **Hallein Salt Mines and Underground Slides**

MELK (KREMS), AUSTRIA Tour of **Melk Benedictine Abbey;** lesson in preparing local foods; hike to **Dürnstein Castle;** bike trip along the Danube; visit to a family-run apricot farm

VIENNA, AUSTRIA Coach tour of Vienna; tour of **Schönbrunn Palace;** marionette show and strudel-making class; visit to the **Spanish Riding School;** bike trip to **Klosterneuburg Monastery;** visit to a traditional wine bar; concert featuring the music of Mozart and Strauss

BRATISLAVA, SLOVAKIA Walking tour of Bratislava; tours of **Devin Castle** and **Schloss Hof Palace**

BUDAPEST, HUNGARY Tour of **Lazar Equestrian Park;** lesson in making Hungarian goulash; nighttime tour of Budapest

Rhine Cruises

BASEL, SWITZERLAND Fondue party

STRASBOURG, FRANCE Tour of the **Black Forest,** with an alpine toboggan run and zip-line adventure; lesson in traditional woodcarving; guided horseback ride through the medieval town of **Riquewihr;** private organ concert of Mozart music; walking tour of Strasbourg; canoe trip in **Alsace;** riverboat trip to **Strasbourg Cathedral of Notre Dame;** bike trip through the Alsatian countryside; lesson in baking French macarons; tour of the wine cellars of the **Cave Historique des Hospices de Strasbourg;** visit to a beer hall

SPEYER, GERMANY Visits to the **Porsche** and **Mercedes-Benz Museums;** walking tour of **Heidelberg** and **Heidelberg Castle;** walking or biking tour of local villages

RÜDESHEIM, GERMANY Bike tour of wine country; gondola ride to **Niederwald Monument;** visit to **Siegfried's Mechanical Music Cabinet Museum;** coffee tasting at **Rüdesheim Schloss;** cruise through the **Rhine River Gorge**

KÖLN (COLOGNE), GERMANY Curling, zip-lining, and snow biking in an indoor winter park; walking tour of Köln; fragrance-making and chocolate-making classes; chocolate tasting; pub tour

AMSTERDAM, THE NETHERLANDS Tours of the **Anne Frank House, Rijksmuseum,** and **Van Gogh Museum;** tour of the **Delft Earthenware Factory;** visit to the fishing village of **Volendam;** wooden-clog painting. (See page 293 for more about Amsterdam.)

MORE DIFFERENCES BETWEEN ABD RIVER CRUISING *and* DCL OCEAN CRUISING

SIZE OF THE SHIPS The *Disney Magic* and *Disney Wonder* are 964 feet long; the *Disney Dream* and *Disney Fantasy* are 1,114 feet long. The DCL ships are also tall: 11 and 14 decks high, respectively, for the *Magic/Wonder* and the *Dream/Fantasy.* Because of size constraints related to rivers and river-lock systems, however, the river ships are necessarily much smaller—the *AmaViola* is just 443 long and three decks high. The river ships' petite footprint also allows them to maneuver quickly and dock in tight spaces.

PASSENGER CAPACITY While the *Magic* and *Wonder,* the smaller of the four DCL ships, have a maximum capacity of about 2,700 passengers, the *AmaViola* and *AmaKristina* river ships can carry a total of just 158 guests.

DISTANCES TRAVELED Some DCL voyages cover many thousands of miles. In contrast, the entire AbD Danube River cruise is just 650 miles. Some guests choose to bike between port stops. If you were to miss the all-aboard time on a DCL cruise, you might have to catch a plane to your next port; with an AbD river cruise, on the other hand, you could call an Uber. On our 2016 Danube sailing, the ship took just 10 minutes to pull over at a dock to drop off a local entertainer near his home in town.

PRICING VARIABILITY DCL cruise prices may vary hundreds or even thousands of dollars depending on when you book (see page 24 for price trends). AbD river-cruise pricing remains constant—other than a potential lack of availability, there is no pricing advantage or disadvantage to when you book your river cruise.

CABIN TYPES There are nearly 30 different stateroom configurations on the DCL ships. On the river-cruise ships, there are just 8, with only minor differences among them, making it easy to figure out which type of cabin is best for you.

RELATIONSHIPS The river ships' smaller scale means you'll see the same guests all the time, giving you an opportunity to really get to know them. The ship's officers and crew are also close at hand at all times. The AbD guides are extremely friendly and strive to foster personal relationships with all guests.

PRIVACY On DCL, how much you interact with other guests is largely up to you: You can request your own table in the dining rooms, skip group excursions, and just generally keep to yourself. On a river cruise, it's all but inevitable that you'll be interacting with other guests throughout the day. There are no private or assigned dining tables. Excursions are group affairs in which nearly everyone participates. And the AbD guides work to engage guests in conversation. A river cruise might not be the ideal way to spend a honeymoon.

FLEXIBILITY DCL is a huge operation that must enforce strict rules to maintain order. On the other hand, AbD river ships are smaller, making it easier to focus on guests' needs and wants. For example, a child who is nearly but not quite old enough for a particular kids' club on DCL will be denied admission, whereas kids on AbD cruises can participate in activities geared to them as they desire.

MOTION OF THE SHIPS During even the calmest of ocean voyages, you'll feel the ship in motion, and on open seas during turbulent weather, you may find yourself overcome by motion sickness (see page 45). On a river cruise, however, you may be entirely unaware that the ship is moving at all. Placid river waters and slower travel speeds make motion sickness extremely rare.

THE JOURNEY VS. THE DESTINATION Many DCL guests book a cruise without a particular destination in mind—they want someplace, anyplace warm on the right dates, at the right price. They care more about grazing at the buffet or getting pampered at the spa than experiencing whatever there is to experience in port. But on a river cruise, it's all about where you're going. Instead of playing bingo and watching shows on sea days, you'll be exploring historic sites, seeing magnificent artwork, and taking in lush landscapes. The draw is off the ship rather than on it.

WHERE THE SHIPS DOCK Depending on the DCL destination, your ship may dock at a forlorn industrial port several miles from town. This is rare with a river cruise, where much of the time the ship can dock right next to a city sidewalk. Hopping off for a walk around town can take less than a minute.

TIME IN PORT   On DCL, most sailings leave port by dinnertime. On AbD river cruises, early all-aboard times are often around 8 p.m.— and sometimes well after midnight.

FOOD AVAILABILITY   On DCL, there are two rotational dinner seatings, a full buffet that's open most of the day, a multitude of quick-bite windows, and 24-hour room service. While there's certainly plenty of food on board a river cruise, mealtimes are more condensed, with just one seating for the three main meals. Limited snacks are available at other times, but there's nothing comparable to full room service. On the other hand, you're likely to dock literally steps away from a quaint café with amazing food.

FOOD QUALITY   Daily port stops and smaller guest loads make it easy for a river ship to acquire fresh (versus frozen and prepackaged) produce, meats, and dairy. Overall, we find AbD's food quality superior to DCL's.

ALCOHOL   There is plenty of alcohol of all sorts available on both DCL and AbD cruises. The difference is that all alcohol costs extra on DCL, while beer and wine are included with both lunch and dinner on river cruises. Plus, many AbD river excursions offer wine, beer, and schnapps tastings—all included in the cost of your cruise.

INTERNET   Wi-Fi generally costs extra on DCL (see page 84), and the connection quality can be spotty, particularly when you're at sea. In contrast, AbD river ships have free, good-quality Wi-Fi—plus a full-size desktop computer in every stateroom.

GUESTS WITH DISABILITIES   Here, AbD lags behind DCL. For example, while a river ship has an elevator, it serves just part of the ship. This means that a guest who uses a wheelchair can't access the sundeck. Additionally, AbD river ships sometimes "double-park" at a dock— meaning that guests may have to walk through another ship, or possibly over its sundeck, to get to shore. Exiting the ship this way is all but impossible for someone with restricted mobility.

TRAVELING *with* ADVENTURES BY DISNEY

ADVENTURES BY DISNEY TRIPS, including river cruises, are overseen by **Disney Adventure Guides.** Part tour guide, part cheerleader, part therapist, part PhotoPass photographer, part medic, part waiter, and part teacher, they're the best camp counselors you've ever had. Many Adventure Guides work at Walt Disney World or Disneyland in the off-season, while others are Disney-trained experts in a particular region, fluent in the language and customs of the country you're visiting. One guest writes:

> *Of all the Disney cast members I've encountered, the Disney Adventure Guides are my favorites. Every one of them is fabulous, fun, and incredibly competent. Their energy level is off the charts—which is impressive because they never seem to sleep!*

Typical land-based AbD trips have 2 guides for 30–40 guests, yielding a guide-to-guest ratio of about 1–20 or better. AbD river cruises are staffed by 8 Adventure Guides who attend to 135–150 guests, which comes out to more or less the same guide-to-guest ratio above.

On a standard AbD trip, including AbD supplements to DCL sailings (see page 30), you'll have the same 40 or so guests and the same 2 guides for the entire trip. On river cruises, however, the 8 guides rotate among the 140 or so guests as needed. You won't be assigned your own pair of guides.

You'll also be touring with different subsets of the guest pool, depending on which excursions you and they choose. All eight guides will be on the ship in the morning and the evening, so you'll see them all then. But you may have a different pair of guides on different excursions. For example, Guides A and B might lead a farm visit in the morning, with Guides C and D leading a museum visit in the afternoon. The next day, you could have Guides A and E for a wine tasting and Guides C and F for a city walk. If a particular excursion is especially popular, there might be two or three guide pairs at that stop—the Pink Guides, the Blue Guides, and the Orange Guides, for example. You might have the same guides leading your excursions many times; on the other hand, there might be a guide or two whom you never have leading your excursions.

Guest groups are similarly fluid on river cruises. You and the Smith family might both go to the Hallein Salt Mine on Day Three and to an apricot farm on Day Four. But if on Day Three you're randomly assigned to the Blue Group and the Smiths are assigned to the Pink Group and on Day Four you're in the Orange Group and the Smiths are in the Purple Group, you might have minimal contact with the Smiths off the ship.

If you're a veteran of AbD land-based trips, it may take you a day or two to get the hang of things. While river cruises certainly have a strong AbD feel, the shifting groups and guides make for slightly less continuity than on a land-based trip. If, however, your only cruising experience is on DCL, a river cruise will feel significantly more welcoming and personal than your previous experiences. Novice cruisers will also feel right at home on the AbD river ships.

COST CONSIDERATIONS

DCL VS. ABD

WHILE IT'S A BIT OF AN APPLES-TO-ORANGES COMPARISON, here's a look at potential costs for a DCL European sailing and an AbD European river-cruise sailing. All pricing is for two adults. We found the stated pricing for the DCL trip in mid-August 2016; DCL prices vary and may change depending on your search date.

Let's examine two cruises in August 2017 with the closest comparable travel dates: the **August 12, 2017, DCL Mediterranean cruise on the *Magic,*** sailing from Barcelona, Spain, and the **August 2, 2017, AbD Danube River cruise on the *AmaViola,*** sailing from Vilshofen (Munich/Prague), Germany. Both trips include stops in major European cities with similar opportunities for sightseeing. We'll assume that flight prices to/from your home to Barcelona or Munich will be similar, as will the price for a precruise hotel night near your point of embarkation.

Staterooms on the DCL ships and the AbD river ships are not directly comparable. Going by square footage, the closest match would be a 214-square-foot Category 9A Oceanview stateroom for two adults on the *Magic* for $4,501, compared with a 210-square-foot Category BA stateroom for two adults on the *AmaViola* for $12,018.

At first glance, this looks like a shocking difference: The river cruise appears to be almost three times as expensive as the ocean cruise. But in terms of the feel of the room, it makes more sense to compare the river-cruise stateroom with a 268-foot Category 7A Verandah stateroom on DCL, priced at $6,111. While the river-cruise stateroom has a slightly smaller footprint than the DCL 7A, the wall of windows, plus the balcony, makes it feel much more like a DCL Verandah room than a standard Oceanview room. Still, the base DCL price is about half of the AbD price.

There are other considerations, however. **Gratuities** are included in the AbD price but not in the DCL price. The minimum suggested tip for two people for a seven-night DCL cruise is $168 (see page 89); we usually add a bit more, so we'll say $200. Let's also add $40 for a moderate-level DCL **Internet** package, versus free Wi-Fi on the river cruise. For DCL, you also have to add $120 per person for **transportation** from the airport to your Barcelona hotel and from the hotel to the port on the way there, plus $60 per person for transportation from the port to the airport on the way home ($360 total for your party of two); again, all transfers are included in the river-cruise price. These necessities raise the base cost of the DCL trip to $6,711, which is still a far cry from the price of the river cruise. If cost is your main concern and you're not going to book excursions or drink alcohol, DCL is the clear winner.

Adding **excursions** on DCL also adds expense. In this example, let's look at full-day excursions that cover the highlights of a particular destination. The selected excursions are similar to those included in an AbD supplement to a DCL cruise (see page 30). For the four Mediterranean ports, these might be **Best of Rome** ($360 per adult); **Pompeii, Sorrento, and Capri** ($250 per adult); **Florence and Pisa** ($159 per adult); and **Monaco and Èze** ($94 per adult)—for a total of $1,726 in excursion fees.

Adult dining at Palo on DCL costs $30 per person, but similar chef's-table dining is included on the river cruise. Add a $150 **bar tab** if two adults are going to have two beers each on the DCL cruise each evening; again, beer is free with meals on the river cruise. The real cost of the DCL trip has now risen to $8,647.

In 2016, previous AbD guests were given a free night at the upscale **Budapest Marriott,** plus associated transfers (promotions vary annually), adding perhaps $500 of value to the river-cruise package. Nevertheless, the DCL cruise is clearly far cheaper than the $12,000 AbD river cruise. Even adding excursions and booze, your total vacation outlay with DCL could be about $4,000 less than with AbD.

So what do you get for that $4,000? Some of the "plus" elements on AbD are intangibles like more flexibility, more personal attention, and more time in port. Others are perhaps quantifiable: additional port stops/excursions and higher-quality food. To get the same level of personal attention on DCL that you'd get on the river cruise, you'd have to upgrade to a Concierge-level stateroom, which would make the DCL and AbD cruise costs more comparable—with DCL's perhaps exceeding AbD's.

ABD VS. OTHER RIVER-CRUISE LINES

WHILE COMPARING ABD RIVER-CRUISE PRICES with DCL's is an apples-to-oranges proposition, you can compare apples to apples if you look at the cost of an AbD cruise versus one on a competing river-cruise line.

Because **AmaWaterways** uses its ships for non-Disney-branded river cruises, we can compare its regular pricing with its AbD pricing. Again, let's use the price for two adults for the seven-night August 2, 2017, Danube River cruise in an *AmaViola* Category BA stateroom booked through AbD: $12,018. Disney guests debark in the morning on August 9, and then the ship immediately picks up non-Disney AmaWaterways passengers that afternoon for the reverse trip, which stops at the exact same ports.

The price for two adults for the seven-night AmaWaterways cruise on *AmaViola* in the same stateroom category is $10,132—a difference of $1,886. The AmaWaterways price doesn't include transfers, whereas the AbD price includes transfer from the airport to a precruise hotel, from the hotel to the ship, from the ship to a postcruise hotel (if needed), *and* from the ship or postcruise hotel to the airport. Those transfer prices add up and could easily total $400. Let's say the real difference between the AmaWaterways Danube price and the AbD Danube price is $1,500.

But what else is different? When AbD charters the ship, it includes more excursions, along with excursions that are geared to families. For example, on the Bratislava, Slovakia, day, both the standard AmaWaterways and AbD trips include a walking tour of the city in the morning. However, AmaWaterways offers nothing in the afternoon, while AbD offers a tour of Devin Castle. At the castle, AbD conducts an assortment of activities for families, such as candlemaking, coin stamping, calligraphy, archery, and medieval fighting (with a humorous twist). AbD even arranges to have the castle's ancient cannons fire for guests. (Trust us—you don't know loud until you've heard an ancient cannon fire 10 yards away from you.)

Another key difference with the AbD version of the cruise is that there are children on board. Standard AmaWaterways river cruises have children on board only rarely—typically just during the odd Christmas cruise—and almost never during the summer. The presence of kids also brings down the average age of adult guests on board considerably. Even if you don't have kids, if you're a preretirement adult you're likely to find many more contemporaries on your ship when sailing with AbD versus AmaWaterways.

The biggest difference, of course, is that when AbD charters the ship, you enjoy the services of the eight Disney Adventure Guides. They run activities for the kids both on the ship and during excursions. They make sure every birthday and anniversary is acknowledged. They crack jokes on boring bus rides. They distribute special Disney collector pins acquirable only on the ship. One guide on our trip—an actor who's a veteran of several Broadway musicals—even sang show tunes on request. Generally, Adventure Guides make sure that everyone is engaged and having a good time.

Are extra excursions and extra attention worth about $750 more per person than an equivalent non-Disney river cruise? As with most things, that depends. If you're a retiree and you don't mind vacationing with your peers, then probably not. Many older adults won't need some of the Disney bells and whistles, and they'll likely appreciate the more serene atmosphere on board without kids around. On the other hand, if you have kids with you, or even if you don't and you're younger than 55–60, then the Disney version of the cruise will probably be more to your liking.

By way of additional comparison, **Tauck River Cruises** offers a nearly identical seven-night Danube cruise starting on August 5, 2017, on its *msSavor*. The price for two adults in a Ruby Deck Category 5 stateroom (similar to the *AmaViola*'s BA category) is $11,480. The price includes transfers and gratuities, as does Disney's. For two adults, AbD's price is only about $500 more than Tauck's.

Viking River Cruises also offers a Danube cruise departing on August 6, 2017, on its *Viking Longship Vilhjalm;* it has the same port stops as AbD's and Tauck's Danube cruises, but slightly fewer excursions. The "brochure price" for a Verandah Stateroom A (similar to the AmaWaterways and Tauck cabins we've mentioned) is $17,196, but Viking often runs two-for-one specials, making its price closer to $8,600 plus transfers and other incidentals, and giving you a real price in the low to mid–$9,000s.

While the price for an AbD river cruise is significantly higher than that of a comparable DCL European cruise, it's in the same ballpark as other river-cruise lines with the same itinerary. The extra service and children's activities may make the premium pricing worthwhile, particularly if you have kids who might not otherwise be interested in a river cruise vacation.

The Bottom Line

AbD river cruises are a luxury product with a luxury feel. Everything is included, all details are taken care of, and you get fantastic personal service and gourmet food. But unless you sail DCL at the Concierge level, you're almost certainly going to pay more for an AbD European river cruise than you would for a DCL Mediterranean cruise. Compared with the price of a budget DCL Mediterranean cruise with an inside stateroom, the river-cruise price could be nearly three times the price of the bare-bones trip.

Also, you'll have to stick with DCL if you have children younger than 6 years old or if you strongly prefer to be immersed in Disney-themed entertainment and decor. Choose the river cruise if you have older kids and want to introduce them to central Europe, if you have a particular interest in the AbD river ports, if you're accustomed to luxury travel, if you have severe motion-sickness issues, or if you're not big on all Disney all the time.

WHAT'S NEXT FOR DISNEY *and* RIVER CRUISING?

AS OF PRESS TIME, Disney hadn't announced any river-cruise offerings past its 2017 AmaWaterways sailings on the Rhine and Danube. But if we had to venture a guess, we'd say that Disney will be building on its river-cruise product in the near future. When we asked a Disney executive who happened to be on our 2016 *AmaViola* sailing about this, he simply smiled and said, "There are a lot of rivers out there."

Disney-history geeks will remember that the very first Disney cruises weren't offered through its own line but rather in partnership with **Premier Cruise Line.** Founded in 1983, Premier was an upstart company that introduced the idea of family cruising out of Port Canaveral. An initial agreement to become "The Official Cruise Line of Walt Disney World" later evolved into a paint job for Premier's *StarShip Oceanic* that was marketed throughout the late 1980s as "The Big Red Boat," with costumed Disney characters on board. Disney terminated its relationship with Premier in 1993 when it announced plans to launch its own cruise line; Premier disbanded in 2000.

While it's just speculation at this point, we wouldn't be surprised to see Disney follow a similar pattern with river cruising—testing the waters (literally) with a marketing partnership before launching its own branded fleet. Stay tuned.

GLOSSARY

A CRUISE VACATION means you'll encounter a great deal of specialized lingo unique to the industry. That goes double for a Disney cruise, which has its own subjargon as well. Here are some general and Disney Cruise Line–specific terms that you may encounter both in your planning and on the ship.

ADULT DISTRICT The area on each DCL ship that includes most of the bars and lounges. These areas are typically restricted to guests age 18 and up after 9 p.m.

ADULT DINING Describes the premium restaurants on the ship that require guests to be age 18 or older to attend and that carry an additional fee.

AFT The rear of the ship.

ALL ABOARD The time at which you're required to be back on board the ship following a day in port. Pay strict attention to this time. If you're not back at the ship by all-aboard time, you'll be left behind.

ALL ASHORE The time at which guests may disembark the ship for a day in port.

ASSISTANT SERVER This is the person on your serving team who is primarily responsible for your beverage orders and for making sure your plates are cleared between courses.

BACKSTAGE Behind the scenes. Refers to any area of the ship that is not normally accessible to guests. (*Backstage* has the same meaning at the Disney parks.)

BACK TO BACK (B2B) Booking two consecutive cruises. This is most common on the *Disney Dream,* where guests with a fondness for Castaway Cay can book a three-day and four-day cruise one after the other. You can sometimes keep the same stateroom for B2B sailings.

BLACKOUT DATES Specific sail dates for which OBB discounts (see page 374) are unavailable.

BOW The front of the ship.

BRIDGE The area at the front of the ship where the captain and his staff navigate the vessel.

CAPTAIN The leader of the entire vessel. Responsibilities include navigating, operating the ship's equipment, overseeing personnel, and tending to miscellaneous business. Many longer cruises include an opportunity to meet the captain, take a photo with him, or have an item signed by him.

CAST MEMBER Disney-speak for "employee." Everyone who works for Disney is a cast member.

CASTAWAY CAY Disney's private island in the Bahamas. (*Cay* is pronounced "key.")

CASTAWAY CLUB Disney Cruise Line's "frequent flyer" program. See page 49.

COSTUME Anything worn by a DCL cast member.

CREW MEMBER Generally, the employees of a ship. On DCL, **cruise staff** (see below) are distinct from crew members.

CRUISE DIRECTOR Holds responsibility for onboard hospitality, entertainment, and social events; serves as the public face of the cruise line on his or her ship. (A good reference for Gen Xers is Julie McCoy on *The Love Boat.*) On the DCL ships, you'll hear the cruise director make most onboard loudspeaker announcements. He or she also will appear in the theater on most evenings, giving opening remarks.

CRUISE STAFF You'd think this would mean everyone who works on the ship. On DCL, however, "cruise staff" refers to the dozen or so attractive, personable, and hyperenergetic cast members who run the onboard family and adult entertainment activities: bingo, karaoke, dance parties, and so on. If they're not dolled up for some themed event, you'll find them wearing a nautical look, white shoes, and shorts with a red-and-navy-striped top.

DECK Nautical verbiage for "story," "floor," or "level." For example, your stateroom isn't on Floor 6 but Deck 6.

DCL Disney Cruise Line. (*Duh!*)

DOUBLE DIP (DD) DCL parlance for cruises that make two stops at Castaway Cay (see page 223). These trips are prized by Disney-cruise aficionados. There are typically a handful of DD sailings each year.

DVC Disney Vacation Club, Disney's program for its time-share condominiums at Walt Disney World; Disneyland; Disneyland Paris; Aulani, A Disney Resort & Spa; Disney's Hilton Head Island Resort; and Disney's Vero Beach Resort. There will be several DVC presentations during your DCL sailing.

EXCURSION Known in Disney lingo as a **port adventure,** this is any organized land-based activity in the ship's port of call.

FISH EXTENDER (FE) A sort of "Secret Santa" gift exchange among Disney cruisers. Next to each stateroom door is a metal fish that serves as a hook/mail slot. Some guests hang fabric pockets from the fish (thus extending the fish), which they use to accept gifts from their Fish Extender group. To participate in an FE exchange, search Facebook for a group for your specific sailing. This is completely optional and not recommended during your first sailing.

FORWARD The front part of the ship.

GANGWAY The ramp or staircase that guests use to embark and disembark the ship. Depending on the specifics of a particular port, the location of the gangway may vary.

GTY Guarantee. Some guests book a stateroom without knowing the exact room number. Such bookings are known as guarantees because Disney guarantees that it will be in the category that the guest pays for or better. This is a nice way to book a room if you're not too picky about the location of the stateroom.

GUEST Customer or passenger.

HEAD SERVER The waiter in charge of the entire dining room in Disney's rotational restaurants. You may not see your head server much, but that's because he's extremely busy making sure the entire dining operation runs smoothly. If you're having any trouble with your primary serving team, speak with the head server.

IGT Inside Guarantee (see **GTY**). This is a nonrefundable fare for an inside stateroom, typically booked at the last minute. You won't get to choose your exact stateroom, but you will get the category of room you want.

KEY TO THE WORLD (KTTW) CARD The card you receive upon check-in at the ship that functions as your room key, identification during onboard photo opportunities, and a charge card for merchandise and additional-cost food and beverage items on the ship. You will need your KTTW Card many times throughout your day on board, as well as to get on or off the ship. *Always* keep it with you during your cruise.

KNOT A unit of speed equal to 1 nautical mile (1.852 kilometers) per hour, or approximately 1.151 miles per hour.

MDR Main dining room, also known as a rotational dining room. Each DCL ship has three MDRs.

MUSTER The required first-day safety drill.

NAUTICAL MILE See **Knot.**

NAVIGATOR See *Personal Navigator.*

OBB Onboard booking, or booking your next Disney cruise while you're on your current cruise. All DCL ships have a dedicated Onboard Booking desk. If you book your next cruise while on board, you usually receive an onboard credit, a reduction in the required deposit, and a discount on the OBB sailing (typically 10%).

OFFICER A member of the leadership team of the ship. On Disney Cruise Line, officers typically wear white uniforms.

OGT Oceanview Guarantee. This is a nonrefundable fare for an Oceanview stateroom, typically booked at the last minute. You won't get to choose your exact stateroom, but you will get the category of room you want.

ONBOARD CREDIT "Gift" money that you can apply to your onboard account. Guests are often given onboard credit when they book their cruise through a travel agent. Guests also get an onboard credit when they've booked their current cruise on a previous cruise. You also can win onboard credit at bingo games on the ship and at promotional Disney Vacation Club, spa, and shopping presentations. Onboard credit can be used to pay for shore excursions, adult dining, shipboard merchandise purchases, and so on.

PERSONAL NAVIGATOR The daily publication detailing each ship's onboard activities. Available as a hard-copy brochure and a mobile app.

PFD Personal flotation device, or life vest.

PORT (ADJ.) The left side of the ship, as you face the front of the ship.

PORT (N.) A town or city with a harbor. The ships makes stops in ports.

PORT ADVENTURE See **Excursion.**

ROTATIONAL DINING ROOM See **MDR.**

SERVER Your waiter. The server will guide you through the menu each night, take your order, and ensure that it's delivered to your table properly and promptly. If you have any dietary issues or food idiosyncrasies, your server will be the one who makes sure your needs are met.

SHIP A large oceangoing vessel—don't call it a boat. While there are exceptions, the general rule of thumb is that a ship can carry a boat but a boat can't carry a ship.

STARBOARD The right side of the ship, as you face the front of the ship.

STATEROOM Your room on the ship. Most other cruise lines call them cabins; DCL calls them staterooms regardless of the size or location of the room.

STATEROOM HOST The person who cleans your room. Your stateroom host will also turn down your bed at night, deliver messages, and generally assist with any aspect of your room's functionality. Don't forget to tip!

STERN The back of the ship.

TENDER A small boat that transfers guests from the cruise ship to land. Tenders are used when a port's waters are too shallow for a large ship to dock next to a pier.

TRANSFER The Disney-arranged method of getting you to the ship prior to sailing or to another form of transportation after sailing. For example, you can purchase transfers from a hotel at Walt Disney World to Port Canaveral or from Port Canaveral to Orlando International Airport. Transfers are available at all home ports.

VGT Verandah Guarantee (see **GTY**). This is a nonrefundable fare for a Verandah stateroom, typically booked at the last minute. You won't get to choose your exact stateroom, but you will get the type of room you want.

WAVE PHONE The mobile phone provided in your stateroom for communication with other guests while you're on board the ship.

ITINERARIES INDEX

DISNEY CRUISE LINE'S FOUR SHIPS serve seven main geographic areas: **Alaska, Atlantic Canada** (which DCL refers to more vaguely as the Canadian Coastline), the **Bahamas,** the **California Coast,** the **Caribbean,** the **Mediterranean,** and **Northern Europe.**

(The DCL website lists **Mexico** as an eighth region for 2017, but all but one of the ports are also visited on California Coast and Panama Canal cruises. This particular group of cruises sails during September and October and has a "Halloween on the High Seas" theme.)

DCL also offers **repositioning cruises** when it needs to move a ship between the United States and Europe, between the Atlantic and the Pacific, or from one base port to another within a geographic area (say, from San Juan to Port Canaveral). Any cruise that starts at one port and ends at another is a repositioning cruise, the most notable being DCL's **Transatlantic** and **Panama Canal** cruises.

To appeal to as wide an audience as possible, Disney cruises vary in length (and price) within each geographic area. Guests interested in visiting the Bahamas, for instance, can choose from cruises of three, four, or five nights.

There's even more variation, however, because Disney's ships visit the same ports as every other cruise line's ships and the destination ports can't dock every line's ship at the same time. (Disney's Castaway Cay is a good illustration—it can dock just one ship at a time.)

To help fit its ships into the ports' schedules, DCL offers multiple versions of most itineraries, each of which visits exactly the same ports, but in different order. As an example, consider a four-night Bahamian cruise out of Port Canaveral, which visits Nassau and Castaway Cay and usually includes a day at sea. Disney offers at least five separate itineraries:

SHIP AND ITINERARY VERSION				
	NIGHT 1	NIGHT 2	NIGHT 3	NIGHT 4
Dream A	Port Canaveral	Nassau	Castaway Cay	At Sea
Dream B	Port Canaveral	Nassau	At Sea	Castaway Cay
Dream F	Port Canaveral	Nassau	Castaway Cay	Castaway Cay
Dream I	Port Canaveral	At Sea	Nassau	Castaway Cay
Dream J	Port Canaveral	Castaway Cay	Nassau	Castaway Cay

Taking these variations into account, Disney's four ships sail more than 50 distinct itineraries, listed in the following section. We've also included maps of the ports for each geographic area. To keep things simple, the maps show only the ports visited along the ships' routes, not the order in which each port is visited.

See Part Eleven for detailed port information.

ONLINE FARE TRACKER

OUR WEBSITE HAS AN INTERACTIVE TOOL that demonstrates how Disney Cruise Line fares vary by date, stateroom type, and the size of your party. Access it here: touringplans.com/disney-cruise-line/tools /fare-tracker.

By viewing this data, you can get a sense of the best time(s) to book a cruise, and you can see which cruises are likely to have last-minute discounts. Full access to the Fare Tracker and other Disney Cruise Line content is available as an add-on to a TouringPlans.com subscription; the fees are nominal, and owners of the current edition of *The Unofficial Guide to Disney Cruise Line* get a substantial subscription discount. If you aren't satisfied for any reason, we offer a 45-day money-back guarantee.

NEW ITINERARIES

DISNEY USUALLY ANNOUNCES its ships' schedules in seasonal blocks (spring, summer, and so on) 13–15 months in advance of the first sailings of that season. For example, the summer 2017 sailings (beginning in mid–May 2017) were announced on April 12, 2016, and available to the general public for booking on April 14, 2016. Following this pattern, you should expect to hear about summer 2018 itineraries in spring 2017 and fall 2018 itineraries a few months later.

Knowing when new itineraries are released can be helpful if you're trying to get the lowest possible price for a specific cruise. (See "Saving Money," page 22.) It's also helpful if you want to book a specific type of stateroom for a typically popular sailing (such as a Christmas cruise) or if you want a low price or specific stateroom type for a new route. For example, when Disney started sailing to Northern Europe in 2015, several stateroom categories sold out almost immediately. Disney doesn't give advance notice about specific dates of itinerary releases, but savvy travel agents can usually suss this out a few days in advance.

Also, our friend Scott Sanders posts notices about new sailings at the **Disney Cruise Line Blog** (disneycruiselineblog.com).

ITINERARY CHANGES

BE AWARE THAT WHILE CHANGES to itineraries are infrequent, they're also not unheard of. We've seen port stops changed several months, or even just hours, in advance due to issues in a foreign country. We've seen itineraries change a few days ahead or even midtrip due to weather conditions. For example, on one of our trips on the *Fantasy*, ocean conditions became too rough for tender travel; therefore, a scheduled stop in Grand Cayman was canceled and became a sea day instead. And in 2015, the *Magic* made substantial modifications to its eastbound transatlantic crossing a few days before the sailing, skipping two major ports and substituting another, due to iceberg activity on the initially planned route. In situations like these, Disney will refund all fees for missed port excursions booked through them. DCL may also refund port docking fees and the like if an itinerary stop is omitted.

In late 2015, Disney announced a substantial itinerary change to a Mediterranean sailing originally scheduled to make stops in Greece and Turkey. Due to concerns about political unrest and guest safety, those port calls were replaced with visits to additional locations in Italy. Guests with prior reservations on this cruise were offered no-penalty cancellations or a $1,000 onboard credit if they elected to remain on the sailing with the altered itinerary.

Less common are cancellations or reschedulings of entire sailings. A few published sail dates for 2015 were canceled and rescheduled due to issues with a planned regular maintenance dry dock of the *Dream*. Notice of the cancellations came nearly a year in advance, but some guests who were booked on these voyages had their plans impacted by the change. Guests who had been booked on the canceled dates were offered assistance with rebooking and given a $250 onboard credit.

Cancellations can also happen much closer to the published sail date. In October 2016, one sailing of the *Dream* was cancelled just before departure due to the impact of Hurricane Matthew. The storm also necessitated a minor rerouting of other *Dream* and *Fantasy* sailings, as well as a complete overhaul of one *Magic* voyage, which was originally scheduled as a trip to the Bahamas but ended up visiting Atlantic Canada instead. Again, guests were offered financial remediation for the changes.

Nevertheless, you may want to consider whether this information affects the purchase of trip insurance or the timing of when you buy your airline tickets.

ALASKAN CRUISES *(see map on next page)*
Disney Wonder

5-NIGHT ALASKAN CRUISE

ITINERARY Day 1 Vancouver, British Columbia, Canada; Day 2 at sea; Day 3 Tracy Arm, Alaska; Day 4 Ketchikan, Alaska; Day 5 at sea; Day 6 Vancouver, British Columbia, Canada.

2017 SAIL DATES August 2-7.

7-NIGHT ALASKAN CRUISE: ITINERARY A

ITINERARY Day 1 Vancouver, British Columbia, Canada; Day 2 at sea; Day 3 Tracy Arm, Alaska; Day 4 Skagway, Alaska; Day 5 Juneau, Alaska; Day 6 Ketchikan, Alaska; Day 7 at sea; Day 8 Vancouver, British Columbia, Canada.

2017 SAIL DATES May 22-29, May 29-June 5, June 5-12, June 12-19, June 19-26, June 26-July 3, July 3-10, July 10-17, August 7-14, August 14-21, August 21-28, August 28-September 4, September 4-11.

7-NIGHT ALASKAN CRUISE: ITINERARY Z

ITINERARY Day 1 Vancouver, British Columbia, Canada; Day 2 at sea; Day 3 Icy Strait Point, Alaska; Day 4 Skagway, Alaska; Day 5 Juneau and Tracy Arm, Alaska; Day 6 Ketchikan, Alaska; Day 7 at sea; Day 8 Vancouver, British Columbia, Canada.

2017 SAIL DATES July 17-24.

9-NIGHT ALASKAN CRUISE

ITINERARY Day 1 Vancouver, British Columbia, Canada; Day 2 at sea; Day 3 Ketchikan, Alaska; Day 4 Icy Strait Point, Alaska; Day 5 Hubbard Glacier, Alaska; Day 6 Juneau, Alaska; Day 7 Skagway, Alaska; Day 8 Tracy Arm, Alaska; Day 9 at sea; Day 10 Vancouver, British Columbia, Canada.

2017 SAIL DATES July 24-August 2.

BAHAMIAN AND CARIBBEAN CRUISES
(see map on pages 382-383)
Disney Magic

3-NIGHT BAHAMIAN CRUISE: ITINERARY C

ITINERARY Day 1 Miami, Florida; Day 2 Nassau, Bahamas; Day 3 Castaway Cay, Bahamas; Day 4 Miami, Florida.

2017 SAIL DATES January 8-11.

3-NIGHT BAHAMIAN CRUISE: ITINERARY E

ITINERARY Day 1 Miami, Florida; Day 2 at sea; Day 3 Castaway Cay, Bahamas; Day 4 Miami, Florida.

2017 SAIL DATES January 5-8.

Alaskan Ports of Call (*Wonder*)

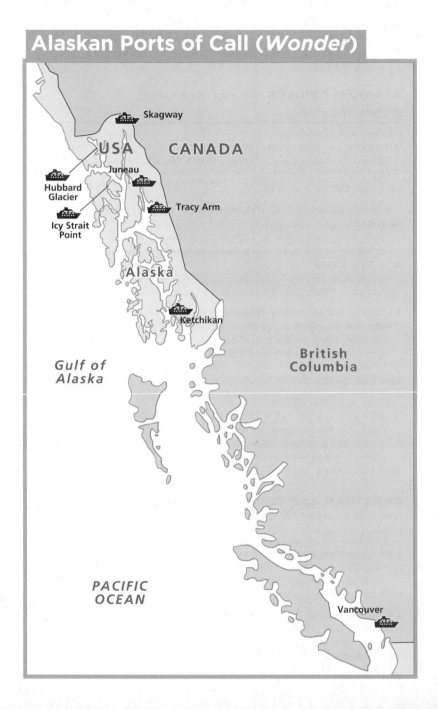

4-NIGHT BAHAMIAN CRUISE: ITINERARY E
ITINERARY Day 1 Miami, Florida; Day 2 Castaway Cay, Bahamas; Day 3 at sea; Day 4 Key West Cay, Florida; Day 5 Miami, Florida.
2017 SAIL DATES January 25–29, February 8–12.

4-NIGHT BAHAMIAN CRUISE: ITINERARY H
ITINERARY Day 1 Miami, Florida; Day 2 Key West, Florida; Day 3 Nassau, Bahamas; Day 4 Castaway Cay, Bahamas; Day 5 Miami, Florida.
2017 SAIL DATES January 11–15, December 6–10.

4-NIGHT BAHAMIAN CRUISE: ITINERARY I
ITINERARY Day 1 Miami, Florida; Day 2 Castaway Cay, Bahamas; Day 3 Key West, Florida; Day 4 at sea; Day 5 Miami, Florida.
2017 SAIL DATES February 22–26.

4-NIGHT BAHAMIAN CRUISE: ITINERARY J
ITINERARY Day 1 Miami, Florida; Day 2 Castaway Cay, Bahamas; Day 3 Nassau, Bahamas; Day 4 at sea; Day 5 Miami, Florida.
2017 SAIL DATES March 8–12, March 22–26, December 20–24.

4-NIGHT MIAMI–SAN JUAN CRUISE
ITINERARY Day 1 Miami, Florida; Day 2 Castaway Cay, Bahamas; Day 3 Nassau, Bahamas; Day 4 at sea; Day 5 San Juan, Puerto Rico.
2017 SAIL DATES April 5–9.

5-NIGHT BAHAMIAN CRUISE: ITINERARY E
ITINERARY Day 1 Miami, Florida; Day 2 Key West, Florida; Day 3 at sea; Day 4 Nassau, Bahamas; Day 5 Castaway Cay, Bahamas; Day 6 Miami, Florida.
2016 SAIL DATES December 18–23.
2017 SAIL DATES March 17–22.

5-NIGHT BAHAMIAN CRUISE: ITINERARY F
ITINERARY Day 1 Miami, Florida; Day 2 Key West, Florida; Day 3 Nassau, Bahamas; Day 4 Castaway Cay, Bahamas; Day 5 at sea; Day 6 Miami, Florida.
2017 SAIL DATES February 3–8, February 17–22, March 31–April 5, December 15–20.

5-NIGHT BAHAMIAN CRUISE: ITINERARY G
ITINERARY Day 1 Miami, Florida; Day 2 Key West, Florida; Day 3 at sea; Day 4 Castaway Cay, Bahamas; Day 5 Nassau, Bahamas; Day 6 Miami, Florida.
2017 SAIL DATES March 3–8.

5-NIGHT BAHAMIAN CRUISE: ITINERARY H
ITINERARY Day 1 Miami, Florida; Day 2 Key West, Florida; Day 3 Nassau, Bahamas; Day 4 at sea; Day 5 Castaway Cay, Bahamas; Day 6 Miami, Florida.
2017-18 SAIL DATES December 29, 2017–January 3, 2018.

5-NIGHT EASTERN CARIBBEAN CRUISE: ITINERARY B
ITINERARY Day 1 San Juan, Puerto Rico; Day 2 Basseterre, St. Kitts and Nevis; Day 3 Tortola, British Virgin Islands; Day 4 at sea; Day 5 Castaway Cay, Bahamas; Day 6 Miami, Florida.
2017 SAIL DATES December 1–6.

Continued on page 384

Bahamian and Caribbean Ports of Call

USA

Galveston

Port
Canaveral

Florida

Gulf of
Mexico

Key
West

Miami

Grand Cayman

Cozumel

Costa Maya

MEXICO

PACIFIC
OCEAN

Not shown: Fort-de-France, New York, Tortola

ATLANTIC
OCEAN

Castaway Cay

BAHAMAS

Nassau

San Juan   St John/
            St Thomas

                        St John's

Falmouth

                        Philipsburg

JAMAICA

                        Basseterre

Caribbean
Sea   Castries

Oranjestad, Willemstad   St George's

                        Bridgetown

Continued from page 381

5-NIGHT EASTERN CARIBBEAN CRUISE: ITINERARY C
ITINERARY Day 1 New York, New York; Day 2 at sea; Day 3 at sea; Day 4 at sea; Day 5 Tortola, British Virgin Islands; Day 6 San Juan, Puerto Rico.
2017 SAIL DATES November 26–December 1.

5-NIGHT WESTERN CARIBBEAN CRUISE: ITINERARY A
ITINERARY Day 1 Miami, Florida; Day 2 at sea; Day 3 Cozumel, Mexico; Day 4 at sea; Day 5 Castaway Cay, Bahamas; Day 6 Miami, Florida.
2017 SAIL DATES January 20–25, December 10–15, December 24–29.

5-NIGHT WESTERN CARIBBEAN CRUISE: ITINERARY B
ITINERARY Day 1 Miami, Florida; Day 2 at sea; Day 3 Grand Cayman, Cayman Islands; Day 4 at sea; Day 5 Castaway Cay, Bahamas; Day 6 Miami, Florida.
2017 SAIL DATES January 15–20, January 29–February 3, February 12–17, February 26–March 3, March 12–17, March 26–31.

6-NIGHT EASTERN CARIBBEAN CRUISE: ITINERARY B
ITINERARY Day 1 San Juan, Puerto Rico; Day 2 Basseterre, St. Kitts and Nevis; Day 3 St. John's, Antigua; Day 4 Tortola, British Virgin Islands; Day 5 at sea; Day 6 Castaway Cay, Bahamas; Day 7 Port Canaveral, Florida.
2017 SAIL DATES May 7–13.

6-NIGHT WESTERN CARIBBEAN CRUISE: ITINERARY B
ITINERARY Day 1 Miami, Florida; Day 2 at sea; Day 3 Cozumel, Mexico; Day 4 Grand Cayman, Cayman Islands; Day 5 at sea; Day 6 Castaway Cay, Bahamas; Day 7 Miami, Florida.
2016–17 SAIL DATES December 30, 2016–January 5, 2017.

7-NIGHT BAHAMIAN CRUISE
ITINERARY Day 1 New York, New York; Day 2 at sea; Day 3 at sea; Day 4 Castaway Cay, Bahamas; Day 5 Port Canaveral, Florida; Day 6 at sea; Day 7 at sea; Day 8 New York, New York.
2017 SAIL DATES October 14–21, October 28–November 4, November 4–11, November 11–18.

7-NIGHT EASTERN CARIBBEAN CRUISE: ITINERARY C
ITINERARY Day 1 Miami, Florida; Day 2 at sea; Day 3 at sea; Day 4 Tortola, British Virgin Islands; Day 5 St. Thomas/St. John, US Virgin Islands; Day 6 at sea; Day 7 Castaway Cay, Bahamas; Day 8 Miami, Florida.
2017 SAIL DATES November 27–December 4, December 11–18.

7-NIGHT EASTERN CARIBBEAN CRUISE: ITINERARY D
ITINERARY Day 1 Miami, Florida; Day 2 at sea; Day 3 at sea; Day 4 Tortola, British Virgin Islands; Day 5 San Juan, Puerto Rico; Day 6 at sea; Day 7 Castaway Cay, Bahamas; Day 8 Miami, Florida.
2017 SAIL DATES December 23–30.

7-NIGHT SOUTHERN CARIBBEAN CRUISE
ITINERARY Day 1 San Juan, Puerto Rico; Day 2 at sea; Day 3 Bridgetown, Barbados; Day 4 Castries, Saint Lucia; Day 5 Fort-de-France, Martinique; Day 6 St. John's, Antigua; Day 7 Basseterre, St. Kitts and Nevis; Day 8 San Juan, Puerto Rico.
2017 SAIL DATES April 9–16, April 16–23, April 23–30, April 30–May 7.

7-NIGHT WESTERN CARIBBEAN CRUISE

ITINERARY Day 1 Miami, Florida; Day 2 Key West, Florida; Day 3 at sea; Day 4 Grand Cayman, Cayman Islands; Day 5 Cozumel, Mexico; Day 6 at sea; Day 7 Castaway Cay, Bahamas; Day 8 Miami, Florida.

2016 SAIL DATES December 4–11.

8-NIGHT BAHAMIAN CRUISE

ITINERARY Day 1 New York, New York; Day 2 at sea; Day 3 at sea; Day 4 Nassau, Bahamas; Day 5 Castaway Cay, Bahamas; Day 6 Port Canaveral, Florida; Day 7 at sea; Day 8 at sea; Day 9 New York, New York.

2017 SAIL DATES October 6–14, November 18–26.

Disney Wonder

3-NIGHT BAHAMIAN CRUISE: ITINERARY A

ITINERARY Day 1 Port Canaveral, Florida; Day 2 at sea; Day 3 Castaway Cay, Bahamas; Day 4 Port Canaveral, Florida.

2017 SAIL DATES February 2–5, February 9–12, February 16–19, March 9–12, March 23–26, April 13–16, April 20–23.

3-NIGHT BAHAMIAN CRUISE: ITINERARY B

ITINERARY Day 1 Port Canaveral, Florida; Day 2 Nassau, Bahamas; Day 3 Castaway Cay, Bahamas; Day 4 Port Canaveral, Florida.

2017 SAIL DATES February 23–26, March 2–5, March 16–19, March 30–April 2, April 6–9.

3-NIGHT BAHAMIAN CRUISE: ITINERARY C

ITINERARY Day 1 San Juan, Puerto Rico; Day 2 at sea; Day 3 Castaway Cay, Bahamas; Day 4 Port Canaveral, Florida.

2017 SAIL DATES January 26–29.

4-NIGHT BAHAMIAN CRUISE: ITINERARY A

ITINERARY Day 1 Port Canaveral, Florida; Day 2 Nassau, Bahamas; Day 3 Castaway Cay, Bahamas; Day 4 at sea; Day 5 Port Canaveral, Florida.

2017 SAIL DATES January 29–February 2, February 5–9, February 19–23, February 26–March 2, March 5–9, March 12–16, March 26–30, April 2–6, April 9–13, April 16–20.

4-NIGHT BAHAMIAN CRUISE: ITINERARY F

ITINERARY Day 1 Port Canaveral, Florida; Day 2 at sea; Day 3 Castaway Cay, Bahamas; Day 4 Nassau, Bahamas; Day 5 Port Canaveral, Florida.

2017 SAIL DATES February 12–16.

4-NIGHT BAHAMIAN CRUISE: ITINERARY G

ITINERARY Day 1 Port Canaveral, Florida; Day 2 Castaway Cay, Bahamas; Day 3 at sea; Day 4 Nassau, Bahamas; Day 5 Port Canaveral, Florida.

2017 SAIL DATES March 19–23.

4-NIGHT WESTERN CARIBBEAN CRUISE

ITINERARY Day 1 Galveston, Texas; Day 2 at sea; Day 3 Cozumel, Mexico; Day 4 at sea; Day 5 Galveston, Texas.

2017 SAIL DATES November 10–14, November 14–18.

6-NIGHT GALVESTON–SAN JUAN CRUISE

ITINERARY Day 1 Galveston, Texas; Day 2 at sea; Day 3 Cozumel, Mexico; Day 4 Grand Cayman, Cayman Islands; Day 5 Falmouth, Jamaica; Day 6 at sea; Day 7 San Juan, Puerto Rico.

2017 SAIL DATES January 20–26.

7-NIGHT BAHAMIAN CRUISE: **ITINERARY A**

ITINERARY Day 1 Galveston, Texas; Day 2 at sea; Day 3 Key West, Florida; Day 4 Castaway Cay, Bahamas; Day 5 Nassau, Bahamas; Day 6 at sea; Day 7 at sea; Day 8 Galveston, Texas.

2017–18 SAIL DATES November 17–24, November 24–December 1, December 8–15, December 22–29, December 29, 2017–January 5, 2018.

7-NIGHT BAHAMIAN CRUISE: **ITINERARY B**

ITINERARY Day 1 Galveston, Texas; Day 2 at sea; Day 3 Key West, Florida; Day 4 Nassau, Bahamas; Day 5 Castaway Cay, Bahamas; Day 6 at sea; Day 7 at sea; Day 8 Galveston, Texas.

2016–17 SAIL DATES December 9–16, December 30, 2016–January 6, 2017.
2017 SAIL DATES January 6–13, January 13–20.

7-NIGHT BAHAMIAN CRUISE: **ITINERARY D**

ITINERARY Day 1 Galveston, Texas; Day 2 at sea; Day 3 at sea; Day 4 Nassau, Bahamas; DAY 5 Castaway Cay, Bahamas; Day 6 Key West, Florida; Day 7 at sea; Day 8 Galveston, Texas.

2016 SAIL DATES December 23–30.
2017 SAIL DATES December 15–22.

7-NIGHT WESTERN CARIBBEAN CRUISE: **ITINERARY D**

ITINERARY Day 1 Galveston, Texas; Day 2 at sea; Day 3 at sea; Day 4 Falmouth, Jamaica; Day 5 Grand Cayman, Cayman Islands; Day 6 Cozumel, Mexico; Day 7 at sea; Day 8 Galveston, Texas.

2016 SAIL DATES December 2–9.

7-NIGHT WESTERN CARIBBEAN CRUISE: **ITINERARY E**

ITINERARY Day 1 Galveston, Texas; Day 2 at sea; Day 3 Cozumel, Mexico; Day 4 Costa Maya, Mexico; Day 5 Grand Cayman, Cayman Islands; Day 6 at sea; Day 7 at sea; Day 8 Galveston, Texas.

2016 SAIL DATES December 16–23.

7-NIGHT WESTERN CARIBBEAN CRUISE: **ITINERARY F**

ITINERARY Day 1 Galveston, Texas; Day 2 at sea; Day 3 Cozumel, Mexico; Day 4 Grand Cayman, Cayman Islands; Day 5 Falmouth, Jamaica; Day 6 at sea; Day 7 at sea; Day 8 Galveston, Texas.

2017 SAIL DATES November 10–17, December 1–8.

Disney Dream

3-NIGHT BAHAMIAN CRUISE: **ITINERARY A**

ITINERARY Day 1 Port Canaveral, Florida; Day 2 Nassau, Bahamas; Day 3 Castaway Cay, Bahamas; Day 4 Port Canaveral, Florida.

2016 SAIL DATES December 2–5, December 9–12, December 16–19, December 19–22, December 30–January 2.

2017 SAIL DATES January 6–9, January 13–16, January 20–23, January 27–30, February 3–6, February 10–13, February 17–20, February 24–27, March 3–6, March 10–13, March 17–20, March 24–27, March 31–April 3, April 7–10, April 14–17, April 21–24, April 28–May 1, May 5–8, May 12–15, May 19–22, May 26–29, July 14–17, July 21–24, July 28–31, August 4–7, August 11–14, August 18–21, August 25–28, September 1–4, September 8–11, September 15–18, September 22–25, September 29–October 2, October 6–9, October 13–16, October 20–23, October 27–30, November 3–6, November 10–13, November 17–20, November 24–27, December 1–4, December 8–11, December 15–18.

3-NIGHT BAHAMIAN CRUISE: ITINERARY C

ITINERARY Day 1 Port Canaveral, Florida; Day 2 Castaway Cay, Bahamas; Day 3 at sea; Day 4 Port Canaveral, Florida.

2017 SAIL DATES December 26–29.

4-NIGHT BAHAMIAN CRUISE: ITINERARY A

ITINERARY Day 1 Port Canaveral, Florida; Day 2 Nassau, Bahamas; Day 3 Castaway Cay, Bahamas; Day 4 at sea; Day 5 Port Canaveral, Florida.

2016 SAIL DATES December 5–9, December 12–16, December 22–26, December 26–30.

2017–18 SAIL DATES January 23–27, January 30–February 3, February 6–10, February 13–17, February 20–24, February 27–March 3, March 13–17, March 20–24, March 27–31, April 3–7, April 10–14, April 17–21, April 24–28, May 1–5, May 8–12, May 15–19, May 22–26, May 29–June 2, July 17–21, July 24–28, July 31–August 4, August 7–11, August 14–18, August 21–25, August 28–September 1, September 4–8, September 11–15, September 18–22, September 25–29, October 2–6, October 9–13, October 16–20, October 23–27, October 30–November 3, November 6–10, November 27–December 1, December 4–8, December 11–15, December 18–22, December 29, 2017–January 2, 2018.

4-NIGHT BAHAMIAN CRUISE: ITINERARY B

ITINERARY Day 1 Port Canaveral, Florida; Day 2 Nassau, Bahamas; Day 3 at sea; Day 4 Castaway Cay, Bahamas; Day 5 Port Canaveral, Florida.

2017 SAIL DATES November 20–24.

4-NIGHT BAHAMIAN CRUISE: ITINERARY I

ITINERARY Day 1 Port Canaveral, Florida; Day 2 at sea; Day 3 Nassau, Bahamas; Day 4 Castaway Cay, Bahamas; Day 5 Port Canaveral, Florida.

2017 SAIL DATES January 2–6.

4-NIGHT BAHAMIAN CRUISE: ITINERARY J

ITINERARY Day 1 Port Canaveral, Florida; Day 2 Castaway Cay, Bahamas; Day 3 Nassau, Bahamas; Day 4 Castaway Cay, Bahamas; Day 5 Port Canaveral, Florida.

2017 SAIL DATES June 7–11, June 21–25, July 5–9.

4-NIGHT BAHAMIAN CRUISE: ITINERARY K

ITINERARY Day 1 Port Canaveral, Florida; Day 2 Nassau, Bahamas; Day 3 at sea; Day 4 Castaway Cay, Bahamas; Day 5 Port Canaveral, Florida.

2016 SAIL DATES November 14–18.

4-NIGHT BAHAMIAN CRUISE: ITINERARY L

ITINERARY Day 1 Port Canaveral, Florida; Day 2 Castaway Cay, Bahamas; Day 3 Nassau, Bahamas; Day 4 at sea; Day 5 Port Canaveral, Florida.

2017 SAIL DATES December 22–26.

4-NIGHT BAHAMIAN CRUISE: ITINERARY Z

ITINERARY Day 1 Port Canaveral, Florida; Day 2 at sea; Day 3 Castaway Cay, Bahamas; Day 4 Nassau, Bahamas; Day 5 Port Canaveral, Florida.

2017 SAIL DATES January 9–13, January 16–20, March 6–10.

5-NIGHT BAHAMIAN CRUISE

ITINERARY Day 1 Port Canaveral, Florida; Day 2 Castaway Cay, Bahamas; Day 3 Nassau, Bahamas; Day 4 Castaway Cay, Bahamas; Day 5 at sea; Day 6 Port Canaveral, Florida.

2017 SAIL DATES June 2–7, June 11–16, June 16–21, June 25–30, June 30–July 5, July 9–14.

Disney Fantasy

7-NIGHT EASTERN CARIBBEAN CRUISE

ITINERARY Day 1 Port Canaveral, Florida; Day 2 at sea; Day 3 at sea; Day 4 Tortola, British Virgin Islands; Day 5 St. John/St. Thomas, US Virgin Islands; Day 6 at sea; Day 7 Castaway Cay, Bahamas; Day 8 Port Canaveral, Florida.

2016–17 SAIL DATES December 3–10, December 17–24, December 31, 2016–January 7, 2017.

2017–18 SAIL DATES January 14–21, January 28–February 4, February 11–18, February 25–March 4, March 11–18, March 25–April 1, April 8–15, April 22–29, May 20–27, June 3–10, July 15–22, July 29–August 5, August 12–19, August 26–September 2 (*note:* exclusively for Disney Vacation Club members), September 9–16, September 23–30, October 7–14, October 21–28, November 4–11, November 18–25, December 2–9, December 16–23, December 30, 2017–January 6, 2018.

7-NIGHT WESTERN CARIBBEAN CRUISE: ITINERARY C

ITINERARY Day 1 Port Canaveral, Florida; Day 2 at sea; Day 3 Cozumel, Mexico; Day 4 Grand Cayman, Cayman Islands; Day 5 Falmouth, Jamaica; Day 6 at sea; Day 7 Castaway Cay, Bahamas; Day 8 Port Canaveral, Florida.

2016 SAIL DATES December 10–17, December 24–31.

2017 SAIL DATES January 7–14, January 21–28, February 4–11, February 18–25, March 4–11, March 18–25, April 1–8, April 15–22, May 27–June 3, June 10–17, July 8–15, July 22–29, August 5–12, August 19–26, September 2–9, Septermber 16–23, September 30–October 7, October 14–21, October 28–November 4, November 11–18, November 25–December 2, December 9–16.

7-NIGHT WESTERN CARIBBEAN CRUISE: ITINERARY E

ITINERARY Day 1 Port Canaveral, Florida; Day 2 Castaway Cay, Bahamas; Day 3 at sea; Day 4 Grand Cayman, Cayman Islands; Day 5 Cozumel, Mexico; Day 6 at sea; Day 7 Castaway Cay, Bahamas; Day 8 Port Canaveral, Florida.

2017 SAIL DATES December 23–30.

10-NIGHT SOUTHERN CARIBBEAN CRUISE

ITINERARY Day 1 Port Canaveral, Florida; Day 2 at sea; Day 3 at sea; Day 4 Oranjestad, Aruba; Day 5 Willemstad, Curaçao; Day 6 at sea; Day 7 Basseterre, St. Kitts and Nevis; Day 8 Tortola, British Virgin Islands; Day 9 at sea; Day 10 Castway Cay, Bahamas; Day 11 Port Canaveral, Florida.

2017 SAIL DATES June 28–July 8.

11-NIGHT SOUTHERN CARIBBEAN CRUISE

ITINERARY Day 1 Port Canaveral, Florida; Day 2 at sea; Day 3 at sea; Day 4 Oranjestad, Aruba; Day 5 at sea; Day 6 Bridgetown, Barbados; Day 7 Fort-de-France, Martinique; Day 8 Basseterre, St. Kitts and Nevis; Day 9 Tortola, British Virgin Islands; Day 10 at sea; Day 11 Castaway Cay, Bahamas Day 12 Port Canaveral, Florida.

2017 SAIL DATES June 17–28.

BRITISH ISLES CRUISES *(see map on pages 396–397)*
Disney Magic

12-NIGHT BRITISH ISLES CRUISE

ITINERARY Day 1 Dover, England, United Kingdom; Day 2 Le Havre, France; Day 3 St. Peter Port, Guernsey, United Kingdom; Day 4 at sea; Day 5 Dublin, Ireland; Day 6 Liverpool, England, United Kingdom; Day 7 Greenock, Scotland, United Kingdom; Day 8 Hebrides Islands, Scotland, United Kingdom; Day 9 Kirkwall, Orkney Islands, United Kingdom; Day 10 Invergordon, Scotland, United Kingdom; Day 11 Newcastle, England, United Kingdom; Day 12 at sea; Day 13 Dover, England, United Kingdom.

2017 SAIL DATES July 9–21.

CALIFORNIA COAST CRUISES *(see map on next page)*

At press time, DCL also listed these itineraries under Mexico. See page 394 for two additional itineraries that visit there.

Disney Wonder

2-NIGHT BAJA CRUISE

ITINERARY Day 1 San Diego, California; Day 2 Ensenada, Mexico; Day 3 San Diego, California.

2017 SAIL DATES May 12–14, September 15–17, September 22–24, October 13–15.

3-NIGHT BAJA CRUISE

ITINERARY Day 1 San Diego, California; Day 2 Ensenada, Mexico; Day 3 at sea; Day 4 San Diego, California.

2017 SAIL DATES May 14–17, October 5–8.

California Coast Ports of Call
(Wonder)

4-NIGHT VANCOUVER–SAN DIEGO CRUISE

ITINERARY Day 1 Vancouver, British Columbia, Canada; Day 2 Victoria, British Columbia, Canada; Day 3 at sea; Day 4 at sea; Day 5 San Diego, California.

2017 SAIL DATES September 11–15.

4-NIGHT BAJA CRUISE

ITINERARY Day 1 San Diego, California; Day 2 at sea; Day 3 Cabo San Lucas, Mexico; Day 4 at sea; Day 5 San Diego, California.

2017 SAIL DATES October 1–5.

5-NIGHT BAJA CRUISE: **ITINERARY A**

ITINERARY Day 1 San Diego, California; Day 2 Ensenada, Mexico; Day 3 at sea; Day 4 Cabo San Lucas, Mexico; Day 5 at sea; Day 6 San Diego, California.

2017 SAIL DATES May 7–12, September 17–22, October 8–13.

5-NIGHT BAJA CRUISE: **ITINERARY B**

ITINERARY Day 1 San Diego, California; Day 2 at sea; Day 3 Cabo San Lucas, Mexico; Day 4 at sea; Day 5 Ensenada, Mexico; Day 6 San Diego, California.

2017 SAIL DATES October 22–27.

5-NIGHT SAN DIEGO–VANCOUVER CRUISE

ITINERARY Day 1 San Diego, California; Day 2 at sea; Day 3 San Francisco, California; Day 4 at sea; Day 5 at sea; Day 6 Vancouver, British Columbia, Canada.

2017 SAIL DATES May 17–22.

CANADIAN COASTLINE CRUISES
(see map on pages 400–401)

Disney Magic

4-NIGHT CANADIAN COASTLINE CRUISE

ITINERARY Day 1 New York, New York; Day 2 at sea; Day 3 Saint John, New Brunswick, Canada; Day 4 at sea; Day 5 New York, New York.

2017 SAIL DATES October 2–6.

5-NIGHT CANADIAN COASTLINE CRUISE

ITINERARY Day 1 New York, New York; Day 2 at sea; Day 3 Bar Harbor, Maine; Day 4 Saint John, New Brunswick, Canada; Day 5 at sea; Day 6 New York, New York.

2017 SAIL DATES September 27–October 2.

7-NIGHT CANADIAN COASTLINE CRUISE

ITINERARY Day 1 New York, New York; Day 2 at sea; Day 3 at sea; Day 4 Charlottetown, Prince Edward Island, Canada; Day 5 Sydney, Nova Scotia, Canada; Day 6 Halifax, Nova Scotia, Canada; Day 7 at sea; Day 8 New York, New York.

2017 SAIL DATES October 21–28.

Continued on page 394

Mediterranean Ports of Call
(*Magic*)

Continued from page 391

MEDITERRANEAN CRUISES
(see map on pages 392–393)

Disney Magic

5-NIGHT MEDITERRANEAN CRUISE
ITINERARY Day 1 Barcelona, Spain; Day 2 Cannes, France; Day 3 Livorno, Italy; Day 4 Civitavecchia, Italy; Day 5 at sea; Day 6 Barcelona, Spain.
2017 SAIL DATES August 7–12.

7-NIGHT MEDITERRANEAN CRUISE: **ITINERARY B**
ITINERARY Day 1 Barcelona, Spain; Day 2 at sea; Day 3 Naples, Italy; Day 4 Civitavecchia, Italy; Day 5 Livorno, Italy; Day 6 Villefranche, France; Day 7 at sea; Day 8 Barcelona, Spain.
2017 SAIL DATES August 12–19, August 19–26, August 26–September 2, September 9–16.

7-NIGHT MEDITERRANEAN CRUISE: **ITINERARY C**
ITINERARY Day 1 Barcelona, Spain; Day 2 at sea; Day 3 Naples, Italy; Day 4 Civitavecchia, Italy; Day 5 Livorno, Italy; Day 6 Cannes, France; Day 7 at sea; Day 8 Barcelona, Spain.
2017 SAIL DATES September 2–9.

7-NIGHT WESTERN EUROPE CRUISE
ITINERARY Day 1 Dover, England, United Kingdom; Day 2 Le Havre, France; Day 3 at sea; Day 4 at sea; Day 5 Lisbon, Portugal; Day 6 Cádiz, Spain; Day 7 at sea; Day 8 Barcelona, Spain.
2017 SAIL DATES July 21–28.

10-NIGHT MEDITERRANEAN CRUISE
ITINERARY Day 1 Barcelona, Spain; Day 2 Villefranche, France; Day 3 Livorno, Italy; Day 4 Olbia, Italy; Day 5 at sea; Day 6 Civitavecchia, Italy; Day 7 Naples, Italy; Day 8 Palermo, Italy; Day 9 at sea; Day 10 Palma de Mallorca, Balearic Islands, Spain; Day 11 Barcelona, Spain.
2017 SAIL DATES July 28–August 7.

MEXICAN CRUISES
(see maps on pages 382–383, 390, and 398–399)

Several DCL cruises that visit Mexico are also grouped with Bahamian and Caribbean Cruises (page 379), California Coast Cruises (page 389), and Panama Canal Cruises (page 402). We've broken out the following two because they're the only ones that include **Mazatlán** *(see page 288 for port information).*

7-NIGHT MEXICAN RIVIERA CRUISE: **ITINERARY A**
ITINERARY Day 1 San Diego, California; Day 2 at sea; Day 3 at sea; Day 4 Puerto Vallarta, Mexico; Day 5 Mazatlán, Mexico; Day 6 Cabo San Lucas, Mexico; Day 7 at sea; Day 8 San Diego, California.
2017 SAIL DATES September 24–October 1.

7-NIGHT MEXICAN RIVIERA CRUISE: ITINERARY B

ITINERARY Day 1 San Diego, California; Day 2 at sea; Day 3 Cabo San Lucas, Mexico; Day 4 Mazatlán, Mexico; Day 5 Puerto Vallarta, Mexico; Day 6 at sea; Day 7 at sea; Day 8 San Diego, California.

2017 SAIL DATES October 15–22.

NORTHERN EUROPEAN CRUISES
(see map on next page)

Disney Magic

7-NIGHT NORTHERN EUROPE CRUISE: ITINERARY A

ITINERARY Day 1 Copenhagen, Denmark; Day 2 at sea; Day 3 Tallinn, Estonia; Day 4 St. Petersburg, Russian Federation; Day 5 Helsinki, Finland; Day 6 Stockholm, Sweden; Day 7 at sea; Day 8 Copenhagen, Denmark.

2017 SAIL DATES May 28–June 4.

7-NIGHT NORTHERN EUROPE CRUISE: ITINERARY B

ITINERARY Day 1 Copenhagen, Denmark; Day 2 at sea; Day 3 Stockholm, Sweden; Day 4 Helsinki, Finland; Day 5 St. Petersburg, Russian Federation; Day 6 Tallinn, Estonia; Day 7 at sea; Day 8 Copenhagen, Denmark.

2017 SAIL DATES June 11–18.

7-NIGHT NORWEGIAN FJORDS CRUISE

ITINERARY Day 1 Copenhagen, Denmark; Day 2 at sea; Day 3 Stavanger, Norway; Day 4 Ålesund, Norway; Day 5 Geiranger, Norway; Day 6 Bergen, Norway; Day 7 at sea; Day 8 Copenhagen, Denmark.

2017 SAIL DATES June 4–11.

10-NIGHT NORTHERN EUROPE CRUISE

ITINERARY Day 1 Copenhagen, Denmark; Day 2 Warnemünde, Germany; Day 3 at sea; Day 4 Stockholm, Sweden; Day 5 Helsinki, Finland; Day 6 St. Petersburg, Russian Federation; Day 7 Tallinn, Estonia; Day 8 at sea; Day 9 at sea; Day 10 Amsterdam, Netherlands; Day 11 Dover, England, United Kingdom.

2017 SAIL DATES June 18–28.

11-NIGHT NORWEGIAN FJORDS CRUISE

ITINERARY Day 1 Dover, England, United Kingdom; Day 2 at sea; Day 3 Stavanger, Norway; Day 4 Ålesund, Norway; Day 5 at sea; Day 6 Akureyri, Iceland; Day 7 Reykjavík, Iceland; Day 8 Reykjavík, Iceland; Day 9 at sea; Day 10 Invergordon, Scotland, United Kingdom; Day 11 at sea; Day 12 Dover, England, United Kingdom.

2017 SAIL DATES June 28–July 9.

Continued on page 402

British Isles and Northern European Ports of Call (*Magic*)

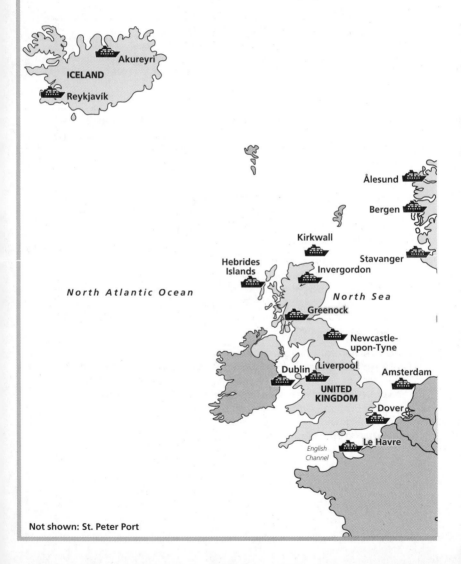

Norwegian Sea

ICELAND

Akureyri

Reykjavík

Ålesund

Bergen

Kirkwall

Hebrides Islands

Stavanger

Invergordon

North Atlantic Ocean

North Sea

Greenock

Newcastle-upon-Tyne

Dublin

Liverpool

Amsterdam

UNITED KINGDOM

Dover

Le Havre

English Channel

Not shown: St. Peter Port

Panama Canal and Mexican Ports of Call *(Wonder)*

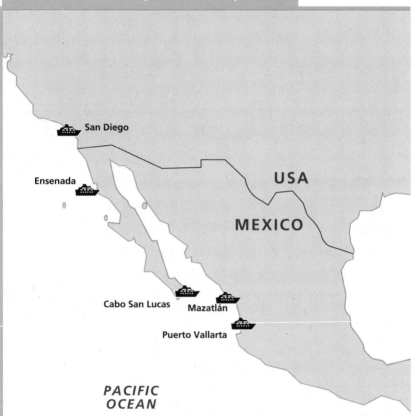

San Diego

Ensenada

USA

MEXICO

Cabo San Lucas   Mazatlán

Puerto Vallarta

PACIFIC OCEAN

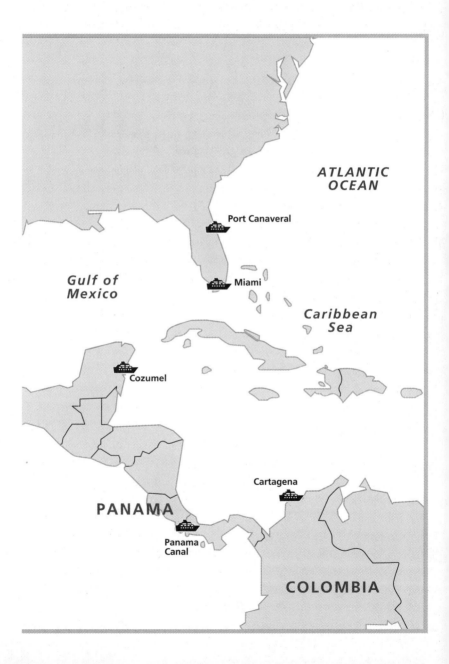

ATLANTIC
OCEAN

Port Canaveral

Gulf of
Mexico

Miami

Caribbean
Sea

Cozumel

Cartagena

PANAMA

Panama
Canal

COLOMBIA

Canadian Coastline and Transatlantic Ports of Call (*Magic*)

ohn's

SPAIN

PORTUGAL

Amsterdam

Dover

Portland

Barcelona

Ponta Delgada

Cádiz

ATLANTIC OCEAN

Not shown: Copenhagen

Continued from page 395

PANAMA CANAL CRUISES
(see map on pages 398–399)

Disney Wonder

14-NIGHT WESTBOUND PANAMA CANAL CRUISE

ITINERARY Day 1: Port Canaveral, Florida; Day 2 at sea; Day 3 Cozumel, Mexico; Day 4 at sea; Day 5 at sea; Day 6 Cartagena, Colombia; Day 7 Panama Canal, Panama; Day 8 Panama Canal, Panama; Day 9 at sea; Day 10 at sea; Day 11 at sea; Day 12 Puerto Vallarta, Mexico; Day 13 Cabo San Lucas, Mexico; Day 14 at sea; Day 15 San Diego, California.

2017 SAIL DATES April 23–May 7.

14-NIGHT EASTBOUND PANAMA CANAL CRUISE

ITINERARY Day 1 San Diego, California; Day 2 at sea; Day 3 Cabo San Lucas, Mexico; Day 4 Puerto Vallarta, Mexico; Day 5 at sea; Day 6 at sea; Day 7 at sea; Day 8 at sea; Day 9 Panama Canal, Panama; Day 10 Cartagena, Colombia; Day 11 at sea; Day 12 Grand Cayman, Cayman Islands; Day 13 Cozumel, Mexico; Day 14 at sea; Day 15 Galveston, Texas.

2017 SAIL DATES October 27–November 10.

TRANSATLANTIC CRUISES *(see map on pages 400–401)*

Disney Magic

11-NIGHT WESTBOUND TRANSATLANTIC CRUISE

ITINERARY Day 1 Barcelona, Spain; Day 2 at sea; Day 3 Cádiz, Spain; Day 4 Lisbon, Portugal; Day 5 at sea; Day 6 Ponta Delgada, Azores Islands, Portugal; Day 7 at sea; Day 8 at sea; Day 9 St. John's, Newfoundland and Labrador, Canada; Day 10 at sea; Day 11 at sea; Day 12 New York, New York.

2017 SAIL DATES September 16–27.

15-NIGHT EASTBOUND TRANSATLANTIC CRUISE

ITINERARY Day 1 Port Canaveral, Florida; Day 2 at sea; Day 3 at sea; Day 4 at sea; Day 5 at sea; Day 6 at sea; Day 7 at sea; Day 8 Ponta Delgada, Azores Islands, Portugal; Day 9 at sea; Day 10 at sea; Day 11 Portland, England, United Kingdom; Day 12 Dover, England, United Kingdom; Day 13 Amsterdam, Netherlands; Day 14 at sea; Day 15 Copenhagen, Denmark; Day 15 Copenhagen, Denmark.

2017 SAIL DATES May 13–28.

SUBJECT INDEX